Traffic Safety

Traffic Safety

Leonard Evans

SSS Science Serving Society
Bloomfield Hills, Michigan

Permission requests should be sent by email to:
    LE@ScienceServingSociety.com

For more information contact:

    Dr. Leonard Evans
    President, *Science Serving Society*
    973 Satterlee Road
    Bloomfield Hills, MI 48304-3153
    USA

    email: LE@ScienceServingSociety.com
    web: http://www.ScienceServingSociety.com

Printed in the United States of America.
Second printing (with minor corrections and changes) 2006
Jacket design by Anita Evans

Library of Congress Control Number: 2004095056
Traffic safety / Leonard Evans.
Bloomfield, Mich. : Science Serving Society, ©2004.
xiv, 444 p. : ill. ; 24 cm.

ISBN 0-9754871-0-8
HE5614.2 .E958 2004

To:

My family. In many ways this book was a family project. Our children, Anita, David, Edwin, and Edwin's wife Elaine, were all creatively helpful as software consultants, photographers, and critical reviewers. My wife Wendy was deeply involved in every aspect. This work owes much, and its author everything, to her.

Contents

Preface

More than a million people are killed in the world's traffic each year, more than 40,000 in the United States. A problem of such staggering magnitude cries out for increased systematic understanding and more effective countermeasures. *Traffic Safety* presents what science has taught us about harm in traffic. It spells out what countermeasures can more effectively reduce harm in traffic, and offers a blueprint for how to achieve a dramatic improvement in safety.

Traffic Safety is quite different from my 1991 book *Traffic Safety and the Driver*, although it does build upon strengths of the earlier work. The present work places more focus on safety policy. It goes to the heart of the problem, with unconstrained analyses of the inadequacies of government in one of its chief responsibilities – to protect life and enhance public safety. It is not just government policy that can increase or decrease traffic deaths. Actions of other organizations can also help or harm. These are identified and critically analyzed.

One of the most dramatic developments since the earlier book is the way the United States has fallen so far behind other countries in traffic safety. Prior to the mid 1960s, the US had the world's safest traffic, whether measured by deaths per registered vehicle, or deaths for the same distance of travel. By 2002, the US had dropped from first to sixteenth place in deaths per registered vehicle, and from first to tenth place in deaths for the same distance of travel. From 1979 to 2002, over 200,000 more Americans were killed in traffic than would have been killed if the US had matched the safety progress in such better performing countries as Britain, Canada, or Australia. This topic is treated in some detail, and explanations are offered for the ongoing US failure.

The better performing countries did not do anything all that remarkable – it is the US that is aberrant. All jurisdictions fall well short of what can reasonably be achieved in traffic safety. The last chapter offers a vision of a breakthrough in which all countries can achieve huge reductions in casualties. What is required is a number of coordinated changes which, as a complete package, can attract the public support necessary for success.

Whereas *Traffic Safety and the Driver* (1991) was devoted mainly to reviewing and synthesizing research that had already appeared in the research literature, about half of the technical material in *Traffic Safety* (2004) is presented here for the first time. The absence of a cited source indicates that the material is original to the book. The present book makes extensive use of graphical and tabular presentations of recent data. It is intrinsically more up-to-date than *Traffic Safety and the Driver* could ever have been because *Traffic Safety* includes just-completed research and avoids the additional one to two year delay that is normal for major publishing houses.

This work benefits from over three decades of interactions, in many cases lively interactions, with a vast number of professional colleagues from myriad disciplines in many countries. I have personally interacted with most of the authors whose work is cited, and received from them much more than the contents of their published work.   In addition, I have benefited from many discussions with professionals in policy, law, engineering, management, the media, and enforcement who are less likely to document their contributions in the technical literature. It is with some difficulty that I resisted the temptation to include a detailed acknowledgement list of some 200 names.   Let me instead acknowledge here my debt, and express my thanks, to all those from whom I have learned so much and received so much encouragement. A broader thanks is due from the world community to those same individuals who have contributed greatly to the core purpose of this work, reducing harm from traffic crashes.

Traffic Safety

1 Introduction

Traffic safety – a grossly underemphasized problem

More than a million people are killed on the world's roads each year.[1] The total is expected to increase steeply as the number of motor vehicles increases rapidly in many formerly less-motorized countries, and will likely exceed 2 million by the year 2020. Traffic crashes are one of the world's largest public health problems. The problem is all the more acute because the victims are overwhelmingly young and healthy prior to their crashes.

More than 40,000 people are killed on the roads of the United States each year.[2,3] In a typical month more Americans die in traffic than were killed by the 11 September 2001 terrorist attacks on New York and Washington. The families of the traffic-crash victims receive no particular consideration or compensation from the nation or its major charitable organizations. Since the coming of the automobile in the early days of the twentieth century, more than three million Americans have been killed in traffic crashes,[4] vastly more than the 650,000 American battle deaths in all wars, from the start of the revolutionary war in 1775 through the 2003 war in Iraq.[5]

When 14 teenagers died in the 1999 Columbine High School shootings,[6] much of the population of the US, led by President Clinton, grieved along with the bereaved families. Yet more teenagers are killed on a typical day in US traffic. In 2002, 5,933 people aged 13-19 were killed, which is an average of 16.3 teenagers killed per day.[7] These deaths barely touch the nation's consciousness. Families bereaved by a traffic death are no less devastated than the Columbine families. Indeed, their burden may be even more unbearable as they do not receive the support provided to the Columbine families.

Injuries due to traffic crashes vastly outnumber fatalities, with over 5 million occurring per year in the US, most of them minor.[8] The number of injuries reported depends strongly on the level of injury included. Applying the US ratio of 120 injuries for each fatality implies about 120 million annual traffic injuries worldwide. Dividing this by the world population of 6 billion,[9] implies that the average human being has a near two percent chance of being injured in traffic each year – more than a fifty percent chance in a lifetime.

Traffic crashes also damage property, especially vehicles. By converting all losses to monetary values, it is estimated that US traffic crashes in 2000 cost $231 billion,[8] an amount greater than the Gross Domestic Product of all but a few countries.

This book describes what has been learned by applying the methods of science to understand better the origin and nature of the enormous human and economic losses associated with traffic crashes. Particular attention is devoted to describing successful and unsuccessful interventions. Information from throughout the world is used, although more from the US than from any other country. This is mainly because, with 226 million vehicles in 2002,[3] the US provides more data than any other single nation. In addition, the US Department of Transportation maintains data files of unmatched magnitude, availability, and quality.[10]

In view of the enormity of the losses in traffic, it is not surprising that different facets of the problem are illuminated by many disciplines. Guidance is sought from basic physical principles, engineering, medicine, psychology, behavioral science, law, mathematics, logic, and philosophy. Phenomena that flow in a fairly direct way from the properties of mechanical systems and the human body are expected to apply in general and not just to the laboratory or jurisdiction in which they were measured. We assume this to be so, notwithstanding the closing remarks of an attorney to a New Jersey jury, "The laws of physics are obeyed in the laboratory, but not in rural New Jersey."[11] The jury, evidently moved by the force of this argument, found in favor of his client!

There is no reason why the effectiveness of occupant protection devices such as safety belts or airbags in preventing fatalities should vary all that much from jurisdiction to jurisdiction. For the same wearing rates, safety belts are expected to produce a similar percent reduction in fatalities in New Jersey as anywhere else. However, because no single state provides sufficient data to estimate belt effectiveness satisfactorily, such estimates are better based on data from the entire nation. On the other hand, many aspects of traffic safety are highly jurisdiction-specific due to variations in cultural or legal traditions. For example, alcohol plays different roles in traffic safety in Sweden, Saudi Arabia, the US, and Israel.

While safety is an important consideration in many human activities, it has a particularly prominent role in transportation. Every type of transportation system involves some risk of harm, as has been the case since antiquity, and seems likely to remain so in the future. The primary goal of transportation, the effective movement of people and goods, is better served by ever increasing speeds. A substantial proportion of technological innovation for the last few thousand years has focused on increasing transportation speeds, from human and animal muscle power to supersonic flight.

The subject of this book is crashes of vehicles running on wheels propelled by engines along public roads. The term *traffic* will refer to this system unless stated otherwise. Many concepts that pervade traffic safety and apply to vehicle crashes in general can be illustrated using the example of the most famous transportation crash of all time – one which did not occur on a road.

The sinking of the *Titanic*

On Sunday 14 April 1912, the 47,000-ton liner *Titanic* maintained its top speed of 22.5 knots (42 km/h) despite receiving nine ice warnings. At 11:40 pm the crew reported an iceberg directly ahead. Despite evasive action, a glancing impact ripped a 90 meter gash in the starboard side. The *Titanic* sank at 2:20 am on Monday 15 April, 2 hours and 40 minutes after the impact, with the loss of over 1,500 lives, including that of the 62-year-old captain, Edward J. Smith.[12]

Figure 1-1. Bow of the *Titanic*, 3.8 km under the Atlantic Ocean. Photographed 2 September 2000 by Leonard Evans.

What if?

Any incident leading to harm begs a series of agonizing "what if" questions. What if, by chance, the *Titanic* had been a few dozen meters north or south of its actual position? What if the lookout had spotted the iceberg a few seconds earlier? What if there had been more effective procedures for deploying the available lifeboats? What if there had been more lifeboats? If the available lifeboats had been safely filled well beyond their stated heavy-sea capacity, could everyone have been saved? It is generally concluded that if the ship had maintained its initial high speed, the resulting increase in rudder effectiveness would have prevented contact with the iceberg. It is also claimed that cutting the speed to half, rather than stopping completely after impact, forced additional water into the vessel. Another hour afloat could have had a substantial effect on casualties, as the liner *Carpathia* arrived less than two hours after the *Titanic* sank.

What if the captain had been younger? The *Titanic's* skipper, 62-year-old Captain Edward J. Smith, senior captain of the White Star Line, was on his last scheduled voyage.[12] In finest maritime tradition, he went down with his ship. Notwithstanding all the advances in gerontology, medicine, monitoring, and anti age-discrimination legislation, present US law prohibits anyone of Captain Smith's age from piloting a passenger-carrying aircraft. Captain Smith's behavior, before and after the crash (well portrayed in Cameron's movie *Titanic*), [13] was likely markedly different from what it would have been when he was in his 40s. This raises the question "Was the sinking of the *Titanic* an older driver problem?"

What if impact had been head-on? One "what if" given less attention than others is: What if no one had spotted the iceberg and the *Titanic* had crashed head-on into it at 42 km/h? When a car traveling at 42 km/h strikes an immovable barrier, about 8% of its total length (or about 0.4 m) is crushed.[14] The uncrushed portion of the car experiences an average deceleration of 170 m/s^2, equivalent to 17 times the acceleration due to gravity, or 17 G. The associated forces of the occupants against their safety belts are likely to produce some injuries (unbelted occupants would sustain greater levels of injury as they continue to travel at 42 km until abruptly stopped by striking the near-stationary interior of the vehicle). Assume, as a very rough approximation, that 8% of the *Titanic's* 269 m length would have been crushed by the head-on impact. This 21.5 m of crush would generate an average deceleration of 3 m/s^2, or about 0.3 G. The energy dissipated, equivalent to 30,000 cars crashing (in the 4 seconds required to complete the crushing), would have made an enormous noise. Those in the 92% of the liner that was not crushed by the impact would have experienced a mild deceleration, not too unlike that of a car or train coming to a gentle stop. Anyone in the portion that was crushed would likely have been killed or seriously injured. As few crewmembers, and even fewer passengers, would be close to the front of the ship at near midnight on a cold night, casualties would have been light. The ship would have been in no danger of sinking because of its watertight compartment structure. It would likely have returned to its maker in Belfast for repairs, and today almost nobody would have heard of it.

Crashworthiness and crash prevention

Neither builder nor owner ever used the term "unsinkable." However, the claim of a high level of design safety was well justified, notwithstanding many later questions about the quality of the steel sheeting, the absence of tops on the watertight compartments, and the number of lifeboats. The *Titanic* contained the best crashworthiness that had ever been engineered into a ship. However, engineering safety must be viewed in the context of the way it is used. Interactions between crashworthiness and crash avoidance are examples of more general behavior feedback effects (or technology/human interface effects) that are important in safety.[15-17] Changes in any factor tend to generate changes in all the others. Every piece of the safety puzzle tends to connect with many others. Less confidence in the *Titanic*'s crashworthiness would likely have led to more caution on the bridge. Shakespeare writes, "Best safety lies in fear." (*Hamlet*: Act I, Scene 3). Because of the unsafe ice conditions, many less safe vessels spent the night still in the water waiting for better sailing conditions after sunrise.

Number of fatalities – reliability of data

Immediately after the sinking, official inquiries were conducted by a special committee of the US Senate (because American lives were lost) and the British Board of Trade (under whose regulations the *Titanic* operated). The total numbers of deaths established by these hearings were:[18]

> US Senate committee: 1,517 lives lost
>
> British Board of Trade: 1,503 lives lost

Confusion over the number of fatalities was exacerbated by the official reports to the US Senate and the British Parliament that revised the numbers to 1,500 and 1,490, respectively. Press reports included numbers as high as 1,522. Additional revisions cement the conclusion that we will never how many people died on the *Titanic*. (We do know that there were 705 survivors).

The uncertainty regarding the number of deaths on the *Titanic* alerts us to the likelihood of uncertainties in even the most seemingly reliable data. At some intuitive level, one might expect the number of deaths to be generally determinable without mistake. For various reasons, this is rarely the case. While there is uncertainty associated with fatality data, such data constitute, by far, the most reliable safety data available. Hence, much of the scientific study of traffic safety focuses on fatalities.

Number of lives lost – influence on public interest and concern

Another general safety lesson from the *Titanic* – the total number of lives lost is not the primary influence on our thoughts. This is important because if people see a problem as important they are more willing to support the cost and possible inconvenience of countermeasures. After the sinking of the *Titanic* many safety measures were enacted which are still at the core of passenger safety at sea – yet it is not clear how many lives, if any, they have saved.

In January 1945, the German troop carrier *Wilhelm Gustloff* was sunk by a torpedo fired from a Russian submarine with the loss of about 10,000 mainly civilian lives.[19] (There is much uncertainty about the total, but certainly about six times as many perished as on the *Titanic*). Nor is the overriding criterion the nation of origin or the nationality of the victims. The largest number of deaths in an airship resulted from the crash of the US Navy helium-filled dirigible *Akron* in 1933[20] The 73 lives lost were more than twice as many as the 36 lost in the vastly more famous 1937 *Hindenburg* disaster. Four airship crashes (one

US, one French, and two British) each produced greater loss of life than the *Hindenburg* crash. All these losses are, of course, minor compared to losses in war and in traffic.

Terminology

The above discussion has introduced a number of terms, which we now discuss more formally.

Traffic safety

The term *traffic safety* is used widely by specialists and the public. Such use rarely generates serious misunderstanding even though there is no precise, let alone quantitative, definition of traffic safety. The general concept is the absence of unintended harm to living creatures or inanimate objects. Quantitative safety measures nearly always focus on the magnitudes of departures from a total absence of some type of harm, rather than directly on safety as such. Depending on the specific subject and on available data, many measures are used. As mentioned above, in this book the term *traffic* will be confined to vehicles with engines traveling on wheels along public roads.

Crash

A vehicle striking anything is referred to as a *crash*. The widely used term *accident* is considered unsuitable for technical use.[21-26] *Accident* conveys a sense that the losses are due exclusively to fate. Perhaps this is what gives *accident* its most potent appeal – the sense that it exonerates participants from responsibility. *Accident* also conveys a sense that losses are devoid of predictability. Yet the purpose of studying safety is to examine factors that influence the likelihood of occurrence and the resulting harm from crashes. Some crashes are purposeful acts for which the term *accident* would be inappropriate even in popular use. At least a few percent (perhaps as much as 5%) of driver fatalities are suicides.[27,28] There is a body of evidence that media reports of suicide generate copycat suicides,[29,30] including by motor vehicle,[31,32] which provides the most socially acceptable and readily available means. Although the use of vehicles for homicide may be less common than in the movies, such use is certainly not zero. Popular usage refers to *the crash of Pan Am flight 103*, now known to be a purposeful act and therefore no *accident* in any sense of the word. Even more so, the events of 11 September 2001 were known to be intentional acts immediately after the second plane crashed into the World Trade Center. There is ongoing discontinuance of the word *accident*. In 2001 the British Medical Journal prohibited the use of the term in its publications,[26] and in 1999 the NHTSA renamed various data files. For example, the former Fatal Accident Reporting System had its name changed to the present Fatality Analysis Reporting System, thus preserving the acronym FARS. The traffic engineering profession is proving a slower learner on this matter.

Factors rather than cause

The term *cause* is used cautiously because it can too easily invoke the inappropriate notion of a single cause, such as is common in the physical sciences. Crashes result from many factors operating together. To say that the loss of life on the *Titanic* was caused by the absence of a mandatory retirement age for captains, the owner being on board, the lookout being not alert enough (or too alert), by climate conditions, or by poor quality steel may generate more confusion than clarity. Instead of focusing on a single cause, we generally think in terms of a list of factors, which, if different, would have led to a different outcome. The goal in safety analysis is to examine factors associated with crashes with the aim of identifying those that can be changed by countermeasures (or interventions) to enhance future safety.

Passengers, drivers, occupants

Any person in (or in the case of a motorcycle, on) a vehicle is referred to as an *occupant*. For the vehicles that form the main subject of this book, occupants are either *drivers* or *passengers*. Using the term *passenger* to include passengers and drivers leads to needless confusion. For example, US Government data compilations apply the term *passenger miles* to different transportation modes.[33] While it is clear that drivers are included for personal automobiles and motorcycles, it is not clear who is included for taxis, busses, aircraft, rail, etc. Different vehicles can include various categories of occupants (passengers, drivers, flight crew, cabin crew, stowaways, hijackers, etc). Although the term *passenger car* rarely causes much confusion, it is particularly inappropriate because most *cars* (the preferred term) travel with zero passengers.

Data, airbag, age, GB, gender, consequences of crashes

Collections of observed numbers are referred to as *data* and not *statistics*. Since statistics is the name of a branch of mathematics dealing with hypothesis testing and confidence limits, using it to also mean data invites needless ambiguity. *Data* will always be treated as plural (singular is *datum*). Treating *airbag* as one word is a clear choice – it shortens, simplifies, and avoids ambiguities.

We follow common usage in referring to ages – *age 20* means people with ages equal to or greater than 20 years, but less than 21 years. This is plotted at 20.5 years, very close to the average age of 20-year-olds; 40-year-olds are not quite twice as old as 20-year-olds, which might come as good news to some!

British data and laws are sometimes for the entire United Kingdom, sometimes for Great Britain, sometimes for England and Wales, and sometimes for England. Accuracy is compromised in favor of simplicity by using *GB* in this book on many occasions when *UK* is correct. Likewise, this book uses only *gender*, even in cases in which *sex* would be more correct.

The consequences of crashes include fatalities, injuries and property damage. Useful terms encompassing all of these are *harm* and *losses*. *Casualties* means injured plus killed. Context determines whether *injured* excludes fatally injured.

Crashworthiness and crash prevention

Measures that reduce harm can be placed into two distinct categories.

- **Crashworthiness**, or *crash protection*, refers to engineering features aimed at reducing losses, given that a specific crash occurs. Examples include padding the vehicle interior, making structure that is not close to the occupant crumple during the crash while keeping the occupant compartment strong to prevent intrusion of struck objects, and devices such as airbags and collapsible steering columns. Reducing risks of post-crash fires (and in the case of ships, of sinking after crash impact) are crashworthiness features.

- **Crash prevention** refers to measures aimed at preventing the crash from occurring. Such measures may be either of an engineering nature (making vehicles easier to see, better braking, radar, etc.) or of a behavioral nature (driver selection, training, motivating and licensing, enforcing traffic laws, etc.).

Comparison of effectiveness of crashworthiness and crash prevention
A fundamental difference between crashworthiness and crash prevention is that when a crash is prevented all harm is reduced to zero. Improved crashworthiness rarely eliminates all harm, but instead reduces the level of harm (say, converting a fatality into quadriplegia, or quadriplegia into paraplegia, or an expensive vehicle repair into a less expensive repair). The finding that safety belts reduce car-driver fatality risk by 42% means that a population of unbelted drivers sustaining 100 driver fatalities would have sustained 42 fewer if all drivers had used belts. However, the 42 survivors would sustain injuries, in many cases very severe injuries. Crashworthiness is measured by the percent reduction in risk for some specific level of injury, such as fatality or minor injury. A crash prevention measure that reduces crash risk by some percent is necessarily a far more effective intervention than a crashworthiness measure with the same percent effectiveness.

Less-motorized countries

Countries containing few vehicles per million population are central to many studies. The term *less-motorized countries* is a straightforward way to refer to such countries. Yet all too often the designation *developing countries* is used without justification or explanation. A common indication of development is growth of Gross Domestic Product. By this measure, the countries of North America and Western Europe are developing, while many less-motorized countries are not. Technical writing should strive for simple value-free terms, resisting the currently fashionable intrusion of Orwellian language aimed at furthering political agendas at the expense of accuracy and clarity.

Units

Given the high level of uncertainty intrinsic in many traffic safety studies, it is important to avoid injecting extraneous confusion and ambiguity from other sources. Accordingly, when questions of units arise, I have tended to be explicit. The workings of nature are, of course, independent of units. An intelligent visitor from another galaxy could accurately predict when a dropped object would strike the ground using the same physical laws familiar to us. However, the numerical values used in the calculation would have nothing in common with values in a calculation performed by an earth inhabitant.

The core of science is quantification, which requires measuring values of quantities, or variables. Variables should, to the extent practicable, be considered without regard to their units of measurement. For example, *fatalities for the same distance of travel* is preferred over *fatalities per billion kilometers of travel*. The statement that fatalities for the same distance of travel tends to decline by about 5% per year is independent of the units in which distance is measured. Thinking about variables without regard to the units in which they are measured is universal in science, and common in general usage. For example, one asks for a person's height, an appropriate variable name; one does not ask for their inchage or meterage. The answer must contain units, but units need not appear in the question. Sometimes it is impractical to avoid using units in table column headings or in names of variables, such as fatalities per year; here the unit of time is so universal that little confusion can result.

The term *billion* will be used, as in the US, to mean one thousand million, or 10^9. The "British billion", still occasionally used in Britain and Continental Europe is 10^{12}, a thousand times as large. So it is not true that everything is bigger in the US!

Another reason why throughout the book I am particularly explicit about units is the hope that by doing so I might help encourage a more unified and rational practice. Such optimism probably merits the same dismissal as Dr. Samuel Johnson's description of a second marriage as "the triumph of hope over experience." I have tended to use the SI system, the internationally agreed-upon metric system of units which is accepted by most of the world's countries but rarely used correctly in any of them. For topics in which British or US data are particularly relevant I generally use the customary units of those countries. For some topics the awkwardness of mixed units was unavoidable.

Simple questions without simple answers

Such simple safety questions as "Is this type of vehicle safer than that type of vehicle?" or "Are women safer drivers than men?" often arise. The questioners are usually disappointed when informed that the question is a lot more complicated than it appears. We illustrate the problem with a different simple question to which most of us do know the answer. Is it safer to keep a pet crocodile or a pet dog?

Figure 1-2. Which are more dangerous – dogs or crocodiles? (Cartoon by Ray Vogler, reproduced from Reference 34).

Is it safer to keep a pet crocodile or a pet dog?

If one knew little about crocodiles or dogs, the first thing to do would be to consult data, where one would find that far more people are killed per year by dogs than by crocodiles. It would be unwise to conclude that such a clear difference justified favoring a pet crocodile over a pet dog on grounds of safety.[34] Even after recognizing that fatalities per year is not an appropriate measure, the way to proceed is far from obvious. Human fatalities per animal appears a better, yet still flawed, measure. People approach close to dogs, but keep far from crocodiles. Even if one normalized for proximity, the problem remains that even without the benefit of data-based studies, people exercise more care near crocodiles than near dogs. So, all in all, it would be very difficult to answer the question "Is it safer to keep a pet crocodile or a pet dog?" based on comparing fatalities from dog and crocodile attacks.

The problem of exposure

The example above illustrates that knowledge about the numbers of persons injured at some level is rarely sufficient to answer specific traffic safety questions without an appropriate measure of *exposure* – the numbers exposed to the risk of being injured. There is no all-purpose definition of exposure; it always depends on the question being addressed. If we want to know if more males or females are killed in traffic crashes in the US, the answer is simply the count of the number of deaths. The answer is unmistakably clear – more males are killed. We may want to know how the risk per capita depends on gender – then again, using population data, we find the equally clear answer that there are more male deaths per capita than female deaths per capita. This does not address how the risk of crashing for the same distance of travel depends on gender. To do this we compute the number of deaths for the same distance of travel, and find little difference depending on gender. This provides a measure of the rate for the same distance of driving, but not for the same distance of driving under identical driving conditions. As it is likely that males do more driving under more risky conditions (while intoxicated, at night, in bad weather, etc.), these additional factors might also be considered part of the measure of exposure.

Assume that it turned out that one gender did have a higher crash rate under identical driving conditions, but that it is suggested that this is due to faster driving under the same conditions, and that this should be incorporated into the measure of exposure. Suppose that when this is done, a difference in fatality rate is now thought to be due to one gender being more vulnerable to death from the same impact, and that this also should be normalized. It should be apparent that this process must ultimately end in the rates being identical, and the vacuous conclusion that when you correct for everything that is different, there cannot be any differences!

All measures are rates

Because of the above considerations, it is probably best to use the term *exposure* sparingly, and with caution. One should certainly not use the frequently occurring expression that some measure is "corrected for exposure."

The quantities that can be measured in traffic safety are nearly always rates. That is, some measure of harm (deaths, injuries, or property damage) divided by some indicator of exposure to the risk of this harm. Simple counts are almost never used. The annual count of fatalities is a rate, namely, the number of fatalities per year. Rates related to driver deaths include the number of driver deaths per head of population, per registered vehicle, per licensed driver, or per same distance of travel.

There is no one rate that is superior to others in any general sense. The rate to be selected depends on the question being asked – and often also on what data are available. What is important is to specify exactly what rate is measured and how it relates to the problem being addressed.

Poisson distribution

Much of this book deals with factors that affect crash risk. This implies that crashes are not just random events. However, crashes do have important random components. It is therefore instructive to examine what properties crashes would have if they were perfectly random events. Such an examination provides a reference and framework to better interpret what is observed in actual crashes.

Perfectly random process can be well described and analyzed using a simple mathematical formalism called a Poisson process,[35] named for its originator, the French mathematician Siméon Denis Poisson (1781-1840). This can be explained in an example in which we assume that all drivers have the same average crash rate, λ, per some unit of time. If λ were 0.1 crashes per year, then drivers have, on average, 1 crash in 10 years, or 2 crashes in 20 years, and so on. The underlying assumption for Poisson processes is that the observed risk of crashing is the result of a uniform risk of crashing at all times (a 0.1 probability of crashing per year means a 0.1/365 probability of crashing each day, and so on). If all drivers have the same probability of crashing each day, at the end of a year all will not have the same number of crashes because of randomness. The Poisson distribution enables us to compute the probability, $P(n)$, that a driver will have precisely n crashes during a period of N years as

$$P(n) = \frac{(\lambda N)^n e^{-\lambda N}}{n!}$$ 1-1

where $n!$ (n factorial) means $1 \times 2 \times 3... \times n$ and λ is the crash rate in crashes per year. Rather than thinking of $P(n)$ as the probability that an individual driver has n crashes, we can think of it as the fraction of drivers from a population of identical drivers who will have n crashes. Substituting $\lambda = 0.1$ into Eqn 1-1 gives that in one year (that is, $N = 1$) 90.48% of drivers are crash free, 9.05% have one crash, 0.45% have two crashes, and 0.02% have three or more crashes. This and other examples are presented in Table 1-1.

The actual number of crashes per year experienced by the 190,625,000 drivers[2] in the US is estimated[8(p 9)] to be 16,352,041, giving an average driver crash rate of 0.0858 crashes per year (equivalent to an average interval between crashes of 11.7 years). If crashes were a Poisson process, 91.78% of drivers would enjoy a crash-free year. Purely by chance, 0.01% of drivers (19,000 drivers) would experience three or more crashes. In the following year these 19,000 drivers would have the same crash risk as the overall population. Removing them from the driving population would not change the overall crash rate. It would reduce the number of crashes because there would be fewer drivers, but the reduction would be the same if 19,000 drivers chosen at random were removed, or for that matter, if 19,000 crash-free drivers were removed.

The example that a driver has only a 1.629% chance of being crash free after 48 years of driving ($N = 48$) at the average risk will be used later (p. 359).

Table 1-1. Probability (percent) of having exactly *n* crashes in *N* years if the average number of crashes per year is λ.
- **The last column shows observed California data with an average crash rate of 0.0625 crashes per year.**[36]
- **All the other values are calculated using Eqn 1-1.**

$\lambda =$	0.1	0.0858	0.0858	0.0858	0.0625	0.0625
$N =$	1	1	10	48	1	1
n						
0	90.484	91.780	42.409	1.629	93.923	94.135
1	9.048	7.873	36.379	6.705	5.880	5.500
2	0.452	0.338	15.603	13.805	0.184	0.341
3	0.015	0.010	4.462	18.947	0.004*	0.024*
4	0.000	0.000	0.957	19.504		
5			0.164	16.061	* 3 or more	
6			0.023	11.022		
7			0.003	6.483		
8			0.000	3.337		
9				1.527		
10				0.629		
11				0.235		

"Accident proneness"

The observation that some individuals experience a much larger than average number of industrial injuries or traffic crashes gave birth to the notion of *accident proneness* in the early decades of the twentieth century. Those with elevated numbers of crashes were designated *accident prone*, and it was claimed that prohibiting them from driving would substantially improve safety. The notion became thoroughly discredited in the face of greater appreciation of the statistical properties of crashes and when empirical studies failed to find that drivers with a large number of crashes in one period had an appreciably above average number in subsequent periods.

The dismissal of the notion of *accident proneness* has generated some confusion. What is discredited is the notion that an above average number of crashes in one period, by itself, can provide sufficient predictive power to be useful as an effective safety policy measure. However, dismissing the notion of *accident proneness* does not mean that individual drivers, or groups of drivers, cannot be reliably identified by other methods as posing greater than average driving risks. Indeed, that is a central theme of this book. For example, it can be predicted with confidence that an individual driver convicted of many traffic-law violations will have higher future crash risks if permitted to continue to drive, and it can be predicted with near certainty that a group of 20-year-old male drivers will have higher than average crash rates.

Comparison with observed data

The last two columns in Table 1-1 show predicted crash frequencies assuming a Poisson process and observed frequencies, based on a data set in which the average crash rate for all drivers was 0.0625 crashes per year.[36] The Poisson prediction reproduces the general pattern, but with important departures. The observed data have a greater percent of crash-free drivers than predicted, and six times as many drivers with three or more crashes as predicted. Such departures indicate major departures from the assumption that all drivers have the same crash risk. One might suggest that 1/6 of the drivers with three or more crashes were average drivers who were unlucky, while the other 5/6 arose from a population with above average crash risk. However, it is not possible to determine, based on crash-frequency alone, whether any individual driver is in the three or more crashes category due to bad luck or risky driving. The very same randomness keeps many of the high-risk drivers crash free. Assuming that different subsets of the total driving population have different values of λ can reproduce the observed distribution.

Computing errors from Poisson processes

Many safety analyses rely on counts of items, such as the number of single-vehicle crashes or number of driver fatalities. By assuming that observed numbers originated from a Poisson process we can estimate errors. Suppose there is, on average, one crash per day, so that after n days we would expect n crashes. However, a rate of one crash per day may produce more or fewer than n crashes in n days because of randomness. Many replications will produce an average value of n. For a Poisson process, the standard deviation of this distribution is equal to $\sqrt{n}$, and when n is reasonably large (say, more than about 6), the distribution is close to the normal distribution, which has convenient properties. An observed n fatalities in a month is interpreted to arise from a process generating fatalities at a rate of $(n \pm \sqrt{n})$ fatalities per month, where the error is one standard error. In this book all quoted errors are standard errors, a common practice in science. There is a 68% probability that the true value is within one standard error, and a 16% probability that it is either higher or lower. Errors in the literature are often given as two standard errors – there is a 95% probability that the true value is within two standard errors.

If we observe that a particular vehicle model, say car_1, has $n_1 = 100$ crashes in a year, then there is a 68% probability that the process generating these crashes is doing so at a rate of between 90 per year and 110 per year, or (100 ± 10). If we observe that car_2 has $n_2 = 110$ crashes, the car_2 rate is (110 ± 10.49). The rates for the two models overlap when the errors are included, suggesting an absence of strong evidence that car_1 is safer than car_2. More informatively, we can compute the car_2 risk, R_2, relative to the car_1 risk, R_1, as

$$\frac{R_2}{R_1} = \left(\frac{n_2}{n_1} \pm \frac{n_2}{n_1} \sqrt{\frac{1}{n_1} + \frac{1}{n_2}} \right) = 1.100 \pm 0.152 \qquad 1\text{-}2$$

which may be expressed by saying that the car_2 risk is $(10 \pm 15)\%$ higher than the car_1 risk. This is the type of quantitative answer that is informative and useful, and should be sought. Statements to the effect that there is no statistically significant difference between the risks for the two cars are of no value, yet they pervade safety and other literature. Based on principles of reason and logic, it is essentially certain that one of the models is safer than the other. The fact that the result failed to show any difference is a comment on the study, not on the relative safety of the two models. From the quantitative result we can be very confident that the risk in one model is not 50% higher than in the other, whereas the statement that there is no statistically significant difference justifies no such conclusion.

If four later studies reported quantitative results $(-3 \pm 13)\%$, $(11 \pm 7)\%$, $(16 \pm 20)\%$, and $(12 \pm 8)\%$, combining all values gives[37] that car_2 risk is $(9.8 \pm 4.5)\%$ higher than car_1 risk, a result providing evidence that car_2 risk exceeds car_1 risk by an important amount. If all of the studies had reported merely no statistically significant difference, then, collectively, the value of the studies would be, at best, worthless. The value of the studies would be less than zero if someone were to conclude that many studies reporting no statistically significant effect provides strong evidence that there is really no effect! The goal of science, namely quantification, cannot be achieved by results presented only in terms of non-quantitative hypotheses that meet some standard, no matter how stringent, of statistical significance.

Three levels of knowledge

Because the goal of quantification with specified error limits is not always attainable, it is helpful to distinguish three levels of knowledge:

1. Not based on observational data.

2. Hinted at by observational data.

3. Quantified by observational data.

It might seem surprising that the first level should appear at all in any effort focused on technical understanding. Yet there are many cases in traffic safety and in other aspects of life in which we have confident knowledge not supported by a shred of observational data. The policy that is at the very core of pedestrian safety is such a case. Pedestrians are advised to look before crossing the road.

There are no observational data showing that it is safer to look than not to look, nor is it likely that the question will ever be addressed experimentally. Even in the absence of empirical evidence, I nonetheless look myself, and consider it good public policy to vigorously encourage everyone to do likewise.

Such a conclusion is based on reason and judgment. Most people agree that it would be foolish to suspend judgment until a study satisfying strict standards of rigor is published in the scientific literature. There are many important traffic safety problems where reason and judgment are our only guides. When this is all that is available, there is nothing shameful about using it, provided that the basis for the belief is apparent.

Differences in traffic are immediately apparent between different countries, but are not quantified, and would in fact be difficult to quantify in a way that would capture well what the eye immediately perceives. Traffic in Cairo, Egypt looks much different from traffic in Adelaide, Australia in ways that must surely contribute to the much greater safety in Adelaide (Fig. 13-2, p. 335).

The second level of knowledge occurs when there are data, but for various reasons the data do not support clear-cut quantitative findings. The problem is generally that using the data to make inferences requires assumptions of such uncertainty that more than one interpretation is possible. Another problem could be that there are too few data to support statistically confident conclusions. This is less common, but cited more often. Experience with research methods, knowledge of the literature, and long-term immersion in the field are the best tools to arrive at appropriate conclusions when information is loosely structured and questionable.

The firmest knowledge flows from the third level, the one to which we always aspire. That goal is captured in the often-quoted words of physicist Lord Kelvin (1824-1907), for whom the absolute temperature unit, degrees K, one of the seven basic units in the SI system, is named:

I often say that when you can measure what you are speaking about, and express it in numbers, you know something about it; but when you cannot express it in numbers, your knowledge is a meager and unsatisfactory kind. It may be the beginning of knowledge, but you have scarcely in your thoughts advanced to the stage of science, whatever the matter may be.

Summary and conclusions

Traffic crashes are a major world public health problem. More than a million people are killed on the world's roads annually, more than 40,000 in the US. Injuries vastly outnumber deaths. The problem is all the more acute because the victims are overwhelmingly young and healthy prior to their crashes. The magnitude of the problem is grossly underemphasized, in part because large numbers of deaths occur every day and are accordingly not newsworthy in the way that an unusual harmful event killing far fewer people is.

Interventions adopted to reduce harm from crashes are of two types. Crash prevention reduces harm by preventing the crash from occurring, while crashworthiness interventions reduce the harm produced when a crash does occur. Traffic law aims at preventing crashes, while softer interior surfaces and airbags aim at reducing harm when crashes occur. Preventing 10% of crashes provides more benefit than a crashworthiness measure that reduces fatality risk by 10%. This is because crashworthiness measures typically convert fatalities prevented into serious injuries, whereas when the crash is prevented, all harm from it is prevented.

Traffic safety is measured using rates – one quantity divided by another. Common examples are fatalities per year, fatalities per thousand registered vehicles, and fatalities per billion km of vehicle travel. Different rates address different questions – no one rate is superior to others in any general sense. Some simple questions are difficult to answer because of the problem of exposure. The number of people hurt is known, but the extent to which they are exposed to the risk of being hurt is not known.

Properties of a hypothetical population of identical drivers all having the same risk of crashing every day can be computed using the Poisson distribution. Due to randomness alone, some drivers will have two, three or even more crashes at the end of a year, while other "identical" drivers will be crash free. Removing the high-crash drivers from such a hypothetical population has no effect on average crash risk the next year. All drivers do not have equal crash risks, but the expected random variation in numbers of crashes if they did makes license revocation based solely on above-average crash experience a relatively ineffective countermeasure.

References for Chapter 1

1 World Health Organization. Burden of disease project. Global burden of disease estimates for 2001. http://www3.who.int/whosis/menu.cfm?path=burden

2 National Highway Traffic Safety Administration. Traffic Safety Facts 2000 – A compilation of motor vehicle crash data from the Fatality Analysis Reporting System and the General Estimates System. Report No. DOT HS 809 337. December 2001. http://www-fars.nhtsa.dot.gov/pubs/1.pdf

3 Fatality Analysis Reporting System (FARS) Web-Based Encyclopedia. Data files and procedures to analyze them at http://www-fars.nhtsa.dot.gov

4 National Safety Council. *Injury Facts* (prior to 1999 called *Accident Facts*). Itasca, IL: published annually.

5 America's wars: US casualties and veterans. http://www.infoplease.com/ipa/A0004615.html

6 A time line of recent worldwide school shootings. http://www.infoplease.com/ipa/A0777958.html

7 Fatality Analysis Reporting System. http://www-fars.nhtsa.dot.gov

8 Blincoe LJ, Seay AG, Zaloshnja E, Miller TR, Romano EO, Luchter S, Spicer RS. The economic impact of motor vehicle crashes, 2000. Report DOT HS 809 446. Washington, DC: National Highway Traffic Safety Administration, US Department of Transportation; May 2002. http://lhsc.lsu.edu/OutsideLinks/EconomicImpact-1.pdf

9   US Census Bureau. World POPClock Projection – gives estimate of world population at time consulted. http://www.census.gov/cgi-bin/ipc/popclockw

10 National Center for Statistics and Analysis (NCSA), National Highway Traffic Safety Administration, US Department of Transportation, Washington, DC. http://www-nrd.nhtsa.dot.gov/departments/nrd-30/ncsa

11 Damask AC. Forensic physics of vehicle accidents. *Physics Today.* 1987; 40: 36-44.

12 Captain Edward John Smith R.N.R. http://www.titanic-titanic.com/captain%20edward%20smith.shtml

13 Titanic – the movie. http://www.titanicmovie.com

14 Wood DP. Safety and the car size effect: A fundamental explanation. *Accid Anal Prev.* 1997; 29: 139-151.

15 Evans L. *Traffic Safety and the Driver.* New York, NY: Van Nostrand Reinhold; 1991.

16 Evans L. Traffic safety measures, driver behavior responses, and surprising outcomes. *J Traf Med.* 1996; 24: 5-15.

17 Evans L. Transportation Safety. In: Hall RW, editor. *Handbook of Transportation Science,* Second Edition. Norwell, MA: Kluwer Academic Publishers; p. 67-112, 2002.

18 Titanic: A special exhibit from Encyclopedia Britannica. http://search.eb.com/titanic/researchersnote.html

19 Wilhelm Gustloff, 1945. http://ycaol.com/wilhelm_gustloff.htm

20 US Navy. USS Akron airship http://www.arlingtoncemetery.net/uss-akron.htm

21 Haddon W Jr. The changing approach to the epidemiology, prevention, and amelioration of trauma: The transition to approaches etiologically rather than descriptively based. *Am J Public Health.* 1968; 58: 1431-1438.

22 Doege TC. Sounding board – an injury is no accident. *New Engl J Med.* 1978; 298: 509-510.

23 Langley JD. The need to discontinue the use of the term "accident" when referring to unintentional injury events. *Accid Anal Prev.* 1988; 20: 1-8.

24 Evans L. Medical accidents: No such thing? (editorial). *Brit Med J.* 1993; 307: 1438-1439.

25 Evans L. What's in a word? (Letter to the editor). *J Traff Med.* 1999; 27: 3-4.

26 Pless B, Davis RM. BMJ bans "accidents": Accidents are not unpredictable. *Brit Med J.* 2001; 322: 1321-1322.

27 Ohberg A, Penttila A, Lonnqvist J. Driver suicides. *Brit J Psychiatry.* 1997; 171: 468-72.

28 Hernetkoski K, Keskinen E. Self-destruction in Finnish Motor Traffic accidents in 1974-1992. *Accid Anal Prev.* 1998; 30: 697-704.

29 Stack S. Media coverage as a risk factor in suicide. *Inj Prev.* 2002; 8: 30-2.

30 Jamieson KH. Can suicide coverage lead to copycats? *Am Editor.* 2002; 824: 22-3.

31 Philipps DP. Suicide, motor vehicle fatalities, and the mass media: Evidence towards a theory of suggestion. *Am J Sociology.* 1979; 84: 1150-1174.

32 Bollen KA, Philipps DP. Suicidal motor vehicle fatalities in Detroit: A replication. *Am J Sociology.* 1981; 87: 404-412.

33 Table 1-34: US Passenger-Miles, National Transportation Statistics 2002. Washington, DC: US Department of Transportation. http://www.bts.gov/publications/national_transportation_statistics/2002/html/table_01_34.html

34 Evans L. The science of traffic safety. *Physics Teacher.* 1988; 26: 426-431.

35 Haight FA. *Handbook of the Poisson Distribution.* New York, NY: John Wiley; 1967.

36 Peck RC, McBride RS, Coppin RS. The distribution and prediction of driver accident frequencies. *Accid Anal Prev.* 1971; 2: 243-299.

37 Young HD. *Statistical Treatment of Experimental Data.* New York, NY: McGraw Hill; 1962.

2 Data sources

Introduction

Quantification is at the core of scientific understanding, and quantification requires data. Few subjects provide more data than traffic crashes. Nearly all the world's countries record and classify crashes. Since the beginning of motorization, this has resulted in the collection of information on about a billion traffic crashes. Despite so much data, many questions remain unanswered because factors of interest have not been recorded or the data are not sufficiently reliable, complete, or conveniently accessible.

A characteristic common to all data sets is that they include only crashes that meet specified criteria. The data set therefore is only a subset of the total reality. It follows that even reliable inferences from data sets do not necessarily provide useful information about real-world phenomena. For example, it is straightforward to estimate the most common crash severity in any data set which records crash severity. However, it is incorrect to conclude that this is also the most common crash severity. The most common crash severity for real crashes is just marginally above zero, but such low severity crashes do not get recorded in data sets.

In general, the more serious the outcome of a traffic crash, the more likely the crash is well documented in data sets. Below we discuss different sources of data, starting with data on the most severe crashes.

Fatalities

Most of the literature on traffic safety, including this book, has a strong emphasis on fatalities. Not only are fatalities the most serious and permanent consequence of traffic crashes, but fatality data are vastly more reliable and readily interpretable than data for any other level of harm. However, fatality data are still subject to uncertainties. As was noted in discussing the *Titanic*, even a simple count may contain mistakes of both omission and incorrect inclusion.

What is a traffic fatality?

The definition of a traffic fatality is far from simple. The problems are readily illustrated by the definition used in the Fatality Analysis Reporting System (FARS).[1] This data set defines a traffic fatality as a person who dies within 30 days of a crash on a US public road involving a vehicle with an engine, the death being the result of the crash. If a driver has a non-fatal heart attack that leads to a crash that causes death, this is a traffic fatality. However, if the heart attack causes death prior to the crash, then this is not a traffic fatality. If a victim dies many days after a crash, a difficult judgment may be required to decide whether it is a traffic fatality. For example, a frail person may die from pneumonia during hospitalization to treat crash trauma. As we all have some chance of dying at any moment, some people die within 30 days of even the most minor crash.

The 30-day inclusion criterion is by no means universal. The National Safety Council uses one year.[2] Their estimate of total US traffic fatalities typically exceeds the FARS total by about 4%, suggesting that a similar percent of crash victims die between one and 12 months after their crashes. As a victim may die from crash injuries decades after a crash, no feasible selection criterion can guarantee complete inclusion. The choice must be a compromise between completeness and timeliness. With a 30-day criterion, the complete data for (say) 2000 includes events through 30 January 2001. The administrative tasks required to produce the data set prevent it from being available until much later. Thus results derived by analyzing data cannot provide direct information about what is currently happening, only what happened in the past.

Fatality Analysis Reporting System (FARS)

The FARS[1] data set that provides many of the results in this book is maintained by the National Highway Traffic Safety Administration (NHTSA), part of the US Department of Transportation. It is a census of all US fatal crashes occurring since 1 January 1975. The FARS system now provides information on more than a million Americans killed in traffic, another reminder of the enormous harm from traffic crashes. The information is based mainly on police completing forms providing details in three categories:

1. **Crash**   (date, time, roadway category, etc.)

2. **Vehicles** (number involved, types, model year, etc.)

3. **People** (age, gender, alcohol use of involved persons including pedestrians and all occupants of all vehicles, belt use by vehicle occupants, etc.)

Each crash has more than 100 data elements coded by FARS analysts who may make some judgments based on the information available.[3] For most fatally injured drivers, Blood Alcohol Concentration (BAC) is measured in an autopsy. In seeking mainly objective data elements, FARS lacks information on many factors of interest. The speed limit on the road on which the crash occurred is noted, but the police officer has no way to know what speed vehicles were traveling prior to the crash, or the impact speed. Likewise, fault is not indicated. Some variables are of uncertain reliability, including belt use of surviving occupants, which is based largely on what they tell police.

A strange and needless deficiency in FARS is that cases in which deliberate intent, such as suicide, can be definitively identified are excluded. Thus FARS abandons, for no good reason, the goal of being a census of those killed in traffic. By excluding some small but unknown percent of traffic suicides it makes the file less useful for investigating traffic suicides. All traffic deaths should have been coded, and if deliberate intent was suspected or confirmed, this should have been noted in an additional data element. Hopefully FARS can correct this deficiency. Indirect methods applied to Finnish data indicate that as many as 5.9% of traffic deaths may be suicides (p. 225).

Some characteristics of fatal crashes

Table 2-1 shows basic information from FARS for 2002. Logically, the number of fatal crashes cannot be larger than the number of fatalities or the number of involved vehicles. A crash in which anyone is killed is a rare event among crashes, just as a crash is a rare event among trips. A crash in which more than one person is killed is a rare event among fatal crashes. 9% of the fatal crashes killed more than one person. 13% of the two-vehicle fatal crashes killed more than one person. 22,086 of the fatal crashes, or 57.7%, were single-vehicle crashes. 23,639 of those killed, or 55.4%, were killed in single-vehicle crashes.

Table 2-1. US fatal crashes in 2002.[1]

quantity	number	ratio
fatal crashes	38,309	
fatalities	42,815	
fatalities per fatal crash		1.12
involved vehicles	58,113	
vehicles per fatal crash		1.52
total involved people	101,195	
survivors of fatal crashes	58,380	
survivors per fatal crash		1.52

Note that the majority of people involved in fatal crashes are not themselves killed. For example, consider a car with four occupants crashing into two pedestrians, killing one and injuring the other. Assuming no car occupants are killed, this crash will have six involved people, one being killed. On the other hand, 13,339 of the fatal crashes (35.0%) involved only one person – the unaccompanied driver of a vehicle striking a fixed object, overturning, etc. without impacting any other person or vehicle. These crashes account for 13,339/42,815 = 31.3% of all fatalities.

Although not part of the FARS data set, it is estimated by other methods that about 65 fetuses are killed annually in traffic crashes.[4]

Non-fatal injuries

While fatal injuries conceptually involve only a yes or no determination, non-fatal injuries lie along a severity continuum, from minor scratches to near death, and apply to different regions of the body. The question "How many injuries?" has little meaning in the absence of some defined level of injury. Generally, the less severe the injury, the more frequently it occurs, so the total number of injuries increases steeply as the threshold for inclusion is lowered.

The Abbreviated Injury Scale (AIS)

Because categorizing injuries is so complex, no single classification coding scheme has achieved universal acceptance. The Abbreviated Injury Scale (AIS),[5] developed by the Association for the Advancement of Automotive Medicine, is the most widely used and accepted scale. The AIS classifies injuries by body part, specific lesion, and severity on a 6-point scale in terms of the threat to life of a single injury. The scale is ordinal, meaning that an AIS 2 injury is greater than an AIS 1 injury, but is in no sense twice as great. It is therefore formally incorrect to apply arithmetical operations to sets of AIS values. The AIS level is determined by comparing injuries diagnosed by a physician to those listed in the detailed documentation that defines the scale. Other scales are also used, such as the International Classification of Diseases,[6] which includes injuries as a subset of all illnesses. There is ongoing research to compare results from different scales in order to expand and improve them.

The AIS level is determined soon after the crash, and not by final outcome. As a consequence, it is possible for injuries at any AIS level to prove fatal later, although the observed risk of death increases steeply with increasing AIS level, as illustrated in Table 2-2. The values given for probability of death are not part of the AIS level definitions, nor are they expected to be closely replicated in general. They are the observed values in one study[7] and are presented to indicate more clearly how the potential for injuries to be life-threatening increases with increasing AIS. If an examination uncovers no injury at a level matching any on the scale, this is recorded as AIS = 0. The scale is based exclusively on medical criteria – it does not reflect how the same injury can generate vastly different degrees of impairment for different individuals. An AIS 3 injury to a finger may have little effect on the life of a singer, but may end the career of a violinist.

Injury victims often sustain injuries to more than one body region. For many analyses it is convenient to use only one measure of injury severity, which is the maximum AIS, or MAIS. A victim with three injured regions of the body, all at AIS 1, would have a MAIS of 1; a victim with one region injured at AIS 1 and one at AIS 2 would have a MAIS of 2.

KABCO classification

The AIS is known for very few cases, because it requires a physician to examine the victim and then input the findings into the appropriate data file. A simple

Table 2-2. The Abbreviated Injury Scale and observed probability of fatality reported in one study.[7]

AIS level	injury description	fraction of those injured who died
0	no injury	—
1	minor (may not require professional treatment)	0.0%
2	moderate (nearly always requires professional treatment, but is not ordinarily life-threatening or permanently disabling)	0.1%
3	serious (potential for major hospitalization and long-term disability, but not normally life-threatening)	0.8%
4	severe (life threatening and often permanently disabling, but survival is probable)	7.9%
5	critical (usually require intensive medical care; survival uncertain)	58.4%
6	maximum (untreatable; virtually unsurvivable)	100.0%

classification that has proved useful for many studies is the "KABCO" scheme, where K = killed, A = incapacitating injury, B = non-incapacitating injury, C = possible injury, and O = no injury. These classifications can be made at the crash scene by police officers, leading to their inclusion in large data files. KABCO values are coded for 99% of the 100,968 people included in FARS for 2001. A comparison of KABCO and AIS coding for the same crashes found that 49% of those coded as A (= incapacitating injury) had no more than minor injuries (AIS = 0 or 1).[8]

Disability-adjusted and quality-adjusted life year (DALY and QALY)

The *disability-adjusted life year* (DALY) is a measure that reflects the total amount of healthy life lost to all causes, whether from premature mortality or from some degree of disability during a period of time.[9] One DALY is defined as one lost year of healthy life due to premature death or disability. While the World Health Organization estimates that traffic fatalities will be the sixth leading cause of death in the world in 2020, they are expected to be the third leading cause of DALYs lost.[10]

Another metric often used in benefit-cost studies is the *quality-adjusted life year* (QALY).[11] A year in perfect health is considered equal to 1.0 QALY. The value of a year in ill health would be discounted. For example, a year bedridden might have a value equal to 0.5 QALY.

Number of US injuries at different injury severities

Deciding how to code injuries is only one step along the way to answering such questions as how many injuries of a specified severity occur. There are too many injuries for all of them to be documented in detail, as is done for fatalities.

Instead, a number of data sets have adopted sampling schemes. In most cases, the more severe the crash and the injuries it produces, the more likely it is to be selected for the expensive scrutiny necessary to determine injury levels and vehicle damage. Data sets including useful estimates of injuries include the Crashworthiness Data System (CDS), the General Estimates System, and the National Automotive Sampling System (NASS),[12] and others.[13]

The National Automotive Sampling System Crashworthiness Data System (NASS CDS) is a stratified probability sample of all US crashes involving a passenger vehicle that required towing due to damage. The probability that a crash is included depends strongly on crash characteristics. For example, the more severe the crash the more likely it is to be included (otherwise the system would be swamped with minor crashes). This makes the raw data unsuitable for most studies. Instead, the sampled crashes are scaled up to national estimates based on the structure of the sampling protocol. Such a process necessarily injects substantial additional uncertainty.

The estimates in Table 2-3 showing the numbers of people injured at different levels in the US in 2000 were obtained by synthesizing information from different data sets.[14] Fatalities are included as a separate category to avoid double counting. Totals for all MAIS levels, especially the higher levels, would be larger if those who subsequently died were kept with the MAIS totals. Over 5 million injuries are estimated, with the vast majority being minor (MAIS = 1).

Table 2-3. The number of people suffering different levels of injury from traffic crashes in the US in 2000.[14]

injury level	number of injured people (thousands)	percent of all injured
MAIS 1	4,660	88.48
MAIS 2	436	8.28
MAIS 3	126	2.39
MAIS 4	37	0.70
MAIS 5	9	0.17
total injured	**5,267**	**100.00**
fatal	42	
MAIS 0	2,548	

The monetary cost of US traffic crashes

The estimates of total monetary cost in Table 2-4 include cost of lost productivity, medical costs, legal and court costs, emergency service costs, insurance adminis-tration costs, travel delay, property damage, and workplace losses.[14] Converting all costs into the one metric of dollars has important advantages, but can be done only by invoking many assumptions. The authors of the report stress that economic costs represent only one aspect of the consequences of motor vehicle crashes, and do not reflect the pain, loss of function, disfiguration, emotional stress, and other suffering to the victims and immediate families.[14] The lifetime economic cost to society for each fatality is estimated at just under a million dollars, over 80 percent of which is attributable to lost workplace and household productivity. The difficulties in estimating the cost of a fatality is succinctly captured in an essay titled: *And how much for your grandmother?*[15(p 245)] The fact that most victims are young crucially affects the estimated cost of a fatality, which must necessarily be based on many assumptions.

Table 2-4. Monetary cost of motor-vehicle crashes in the US in 2000 (in billions of 2000 US dollars).[14]

	dollar cost	*percent of all costs*
property damage only	60 billion dollars	26.9%
MAIS 0	5	2.2
MAIS 1	49	21.3
MAIS 2	29	12.6
MAIS 3	23	10.2
MAIS 4	13	5.5
MAIS 5	10	4.5
fatal	41	17.7
	231* billion dollars	100.0%

* Not identical to sum of entries in column due to rounding. This comment applies to many later tables, but will not be stated again.

The largest dollar cost is property damage. This includes property damage from all crashes, including those also involving injury. The largest contribution is from the 13.5 million non-injury crashes. The $231 billion cost of motor vehicle crashes represents $820 for each person in the US, and is 2.3 percent of the US gross domestic product.

Crash severity – damage to vehicles

FARS contains a variable *extent of deformation* in four categories; none, minor, moderate and severe, based on visual inspection of the vehicle by police. Even though it is coded for 98% of the vehicles in FARS, it tends to be of limited use because more than 90% of the vehicles in which the driver is killed are, as one would expect, coded as having severe deformation.

Ideally, one would like to know in detail how the forces on occupants varied in time during crashes to better understand how crash and vehicle characteristics influence injuries.   Such information is available only for anthropometric dummies in instrumented laboratory crash tests.   An overall measure that relates to forces during a crash is the change in vehicle speed due to the crash (delta-v or Δv).   A vehicle traveling at, say 60 km/h, crashing head-on into an immovable barrier would have $\Delta v = 60$ km/h.   If it crashed into a stationary car of similar mass, each vehicle would have $\Delta v = 30$ km/h.   It is found that injury outcomes in real crashes are related to delta-v.   Such relationships arise only because the time during which the crash occurs is relatively similar for different crashes.   Arguably, a safely landing airliner has $\Delta v = 800$ km/h.   However, this change from cruising speed to stationary takes place over 20 minutes, imparting minimal forces on occupants.   A delta-v of 60 km/h occurring in 70 ms generates an average deceleration of 238 m/s^2, or 24 times that due gravity (often written 24 G's) with associated potentially lethal forces.   Falling from the same height onto a cushion or onto concrete produces the same delta-v. The cushion causes the delta-v to occur over a longer time, thereby reducing injury forces.

The data plotted in Fig. 2-1 are for crashed vehicles with unbelted drivers, derived from weighted NASS data.[16]   The number of crashed vehicles increases very steeply with decreasing delta-v, reaching a peak at Δv just under 20 km/h. There have been many comments to the effect that the most common crash delta-v is some value, say about 20 km/h.   This is not so.   The peak in the top graph in Fig. 2-1 is a characteristic of the data set, not a characteristic of crashes. There are compelling reasons to believe that more crashes occur with Δv in the range 0-1 km/h than occur in the range 1-2 km/h, and so on, with the number of crashes increasing systematically with decreasing severity.   At below about 20 km/h, the probability that a crash is recorded in the data set declines reaching essentially zero for $\Delta v = 1$ km/h, thus producing the observed pattern in the recorded data.   The straight line fitted to the main body of the data in the top plot in Fig. 2-1 estimates about 9 times as many crashes in the range 0-1 km/h as in the range 19-20 km/h.

The middle plot shows how the risk of death and severe injury increases with delta-v.   At high values of delta-v there are few cases, which leads to the noisy pattern.

The bottom plot is the number of crashes times the probability that the crash causes a severe injury or death.   The peak values here are real and have important implications for occupant protection, because when different occupant protection devices are adjusted to protect best at a particular severity, their effectiveness will be less at other severities.   The goal is not to provide the greatest protection for the greatest number of crashes (low Δv), nor is it to provide the greatest protection where risk is highest (high Δv), but to provide the greatest protection at the value of Δv at which the most harm occurs.   This value depends on balancing large numbers of minor injuries against small numbers of more severe injuries and fatalities.

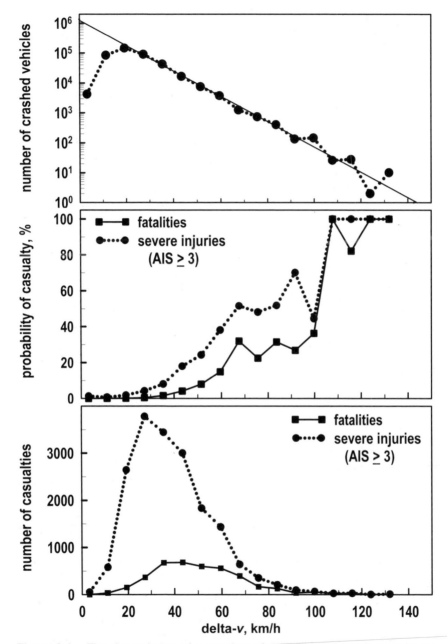

Figure 2-1. The dependence of a number of quantities on crash severity as measured by delta-*v*.

How reliable are injury reports?

The omission of large numbers of low-severity crashes from the data used to produce the top plot of Fig. 2-1 is a feature built into the data set – only crashes above a specified level of severity were supposed to be included (indeed, they were all tow-away crashes). The *missing* cases were not supposed to be included. Because almost no injuries are expected in even very large numbers of sub-threshold crashes, their omission is of no material importance. Real problems do arise when cases that should be included are omitted, and when cases are included when they should not be.

It is unlikely that examining the content of a data set can reveal missing values, or plausible entries that should not have been included. However, a number of different types of investigations shed light on the reported numbers of injuries.

Fatalities compared to reported injuries from Irish data

Fig. 2-2 shows the number of traffic fatalities per million population versus road user age for Northern Ireland and for the Republic of Ireland for 1990-1992. Northern Ireland, which is a province of the much larger United Kingdom, and the Republic of Ireland, an independent nation, share the same small island of Ireland, not always amicably. As physical environment, climate, vehicles, and general human behavior are similar in the two jurisdictions, it is not surprising that fatalities show similar characteristics. However, reported injuries do not, as indicated by 1991 data for each jurisdiction:[17]

Northern Ireland: 6.9 reported injuries per thousand population.

Republic of Ireland: 2.7 reported injuries per thousand population.

The authors of the report providing the data comment on the dramatic difference in reported injury rates compared to the lack of difference in fatality rates as follows:

> The most likely solution to this conundrum is that reporting practices are very different in the two jurisdictions, with "minor" injuries likely to go unrecorded in the Republic but to be "over-reported" in the North.[17]

The more generous British social welfare benefits available in Northern Ireland provided monetary compensation for genuine injuries. However, the same benefits were available for reporting injuries even if none occurred. Such benefits being less available in the Republic at the time covered by the study may have led some real injuries to go unreported, because those injured did not feel it worth the time and trouble to report them.

Another finding was that even at the height of the political violence in Northern Ireland in the early 1990s, traffic fatalities still remained the major cause of sudden violent death.[17]

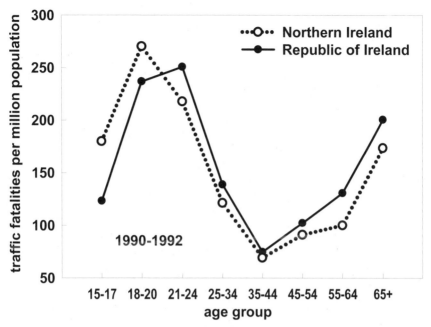

Figure 2-2. Traffic fatalities per million population in Northern Ireland and the Republic of Ireland. Data from Reference 17.

Whiplash

The term "whiplash" refers to injuries associated with occupants' heads moving rearward relative to their bodies when vehicles in which they are traveling are struck in the rear by other vehicles. Late whiplash syndrome refers to symptoms that persist, or arise, long after the crash. Unquestionably many injuries occur in rear-impact crashes, many of which cause major pain and disability. Such injuries can be difficult to diagnose by objective medical tests, so patients' reports of neck pain are often the only basis of diagnosis.

There are innumerable published estimates of more than a million whiplash injuries in the US each year, with some estimates being as high as 4 million.[18] The total monetary cost is estimated to be 29 billion dollars per year.[19] For Western Europe over a million whiplash injuries are reported, and estimated to cost 8 billion euros a year.[20]

It is common knowledge in the US and Western Europe that a reported whiplash injury can lead to monetary compensation. It is likewise well known that a rear-impact crash has a very high probability of being followed by claims of whiplash injury. The expectation that such injuries are a near inevitable consequence of a rear-impact crash may generate genuine symptoms that, absent such expectation, might not occur.

How widespread would reports of whiplash injuries be if people did not expect to suffer them after rear-impact crashes, or could not receive payment for claiming symptoms? This question was addressed by two studies using similar methodology conducted in Lithuania. In Lithuania, few car drivers and passengers were covered by insurance, and there was little awareness among the general public about the potentially disabling consequences of a whiplash injury.

In the first study, 202 occupants of cars that had been struck in the rear were interviewed 1-3 years after their crashes.[21] A control group of 202 individuals matched in age and gender who had not been involved in any type of traffic crash completed the same questionnaire. Members of the study and control groups were asked to report symptoms associated with whiplash, with the results summarized in Table 2-5. The authors report that no one in the study group claimed disabling or persistent symptoms as a result of the crash.

Table 2-5. Comparison of reported whiplash symptoms by occupants of cars struck in the rear 1-3 years earlier topeople not involved in traffic crashes. Data from Lithuania, where few car drivers and passengers are covered by insurance. From Ref. 21.

self-reported complaint	202 occupants of cars struck in rear	202 random people
neck pain	71	67
headache	107	100
chronic neck pain	17	14
daily headache	19	12
disabling or persistent symptoms as a result of the crash	0	not applicable

The second study used 210 subjects in cars struck in the rear, and 210 crash-free subjects matched in age and gender.[22] Unlike the earlier investigation, study subjects were mailed questionnaires soon after the crash to obtain information about short-term effects. Follow up questionnaires were sent to the study subjects two months after their crashes, and one year after their crashes. A follow up questionnaire was sent to the control subjects a year after they were first identified. The results are summarized in Table 2-6. The authors conclude:

> In a country were there is no preconceived notion of chronic pain arising from rear end collisions, and thus no fear of long term disability, and usually no involvement of the therapeutic community, insurance companies, or litigation, symptoms after an acute whiplash injury are self limiting, brief, and do not seem to evolve to the so-called late whiplash syndrome.[22]

Table 2-6. Comparison of reported whiplash symptoms by occupants of cars struck in the rear and respondents not involved in traffic crashes. Data from Lithuania, where few car drivers and passengers are covered by insurance. From Ref. 22.

frequency of neck pain	crash victims before crash n=210	controls at identi- fication n=210	crash victims after 2 months n=198	crash victims after 1 year n=200	controls after 1 year n=193
no neck pain	148 (70%)	146 (70%)	132 (67%)	140 (70%)	114 (59%)
neck pain					
< 1 day per month	37 (18%)	38 (18%)	36 (18%)	27 (14%)	39 (20%)
1-7 days per month	18 (8.6%)	16 (7.6%)	18 (9.1%)	25 (13%)	28 (15%)
8-15 days per month	2 (1.0%)	4 (1.9%)	3 (1.5%)	3 (1.5%)	4 (2.1%)
> 15 days per month	1 (0.5%)	3 (1.4%)	2 (1.0%)	0 (0.0%)	1 (0.5%)
every day	4 (1.9%)	3 (1.4%)	7 (3.5%)	5 (2.5%)	7 (3.6%)

NHTSA estimates that about 1.5 million vehicles are struck in the rear annually in the US.[23] The more than a million reported cases of whiplash injury implies that a rear-end crash has about a 67% chance of generating a reported whiplash injury, so that samples of over 200 occupants struck in the rear would be expected to produce about 130 cases of whiplash. The data in Tables 2-5 and 2-6 convincingly reject any possibility that whiplash injuries are nearly that common. In fact, there are no more than minor differences between the self-reported symptoms of occupants of vehicles struck in the rear and people not involved in any type of traffic crash. The conclusion is inescapably clear. It is insurance compensation and litigation that is responsible for most of the whiplash injuries reported in the US and Western Europe, not crash forces.

Injuries per fatality

In Canada from 1970 to 2001 the number of traffic fatalities decreased by 45%, but the number of injuries increased by 24%. A number of explanations have been offered to explain this dramatic contrast. These include the suggestion that occupant protection has made enormous strides in preventing fatalities, but not in preventing injuries. This is unconvincing. There is no reason to suppose that measures that reduce the forces on the human body in a crash will particularly alter the distribution of injuries by severity. All injury levels are expected to decline by comparable proportions. Such evidence as there is suggests occupant protection improvements will reduce injury risk more than fatality risk. For example, safety belts are probably more effective at preventing injuries than fatalities (p 283). Another suggestion is that improved trauma care reduces fatalities, but an injury remains an injury even if given better medical treatment. This is qualitatively correct. But, as more than half of fatalities in FARS 2002 died within an hour of their crashes, the quantitative effect of improved trauma care, while an important contributor, cannot explain more than a small portion of the enormous divergence between the fatality and injury trends.

There are general reasons why the ratio of injuries to fatalities is expected to be fairly robust, and to not depend much on country, safety policy (for example, belt wearing laws) or vehicle design, and to change only gradually in time. Even if vehicle factors did somehow influence the ratio, the effect from year to year could be no more than a percent or so, because 90% of the vehicles on the road in a given year are the same vehicles that were on the road in the previous year.

The data in Fig. 2-3 defy any plausible interpretation in terms of engineering or medical factors. The number of injuries per fatality should be similar in Canada and Britain, and change only slowly, and similarly, in each country. What Fig. 2-3 appears to be reflecting is not changes in the risk of injury, but changes in the probability that an injury is reported. The reporting probability depends on politics, medical policy, insurance policy, and law, all factors that can change quickly, and differ from country to country, and from era to era.

In Britain in the Second World War years 1942-1944 there were 20 reported injuries per fatality, compared to 34 in the pre-war years 1935-1938. After the war the number of reported injuries per fatality increased, but stabilized at close to 50 during the prolonged period from 1950 and 1970. This period was just after the introduction of the National Health Service in 1948. Everyone requesting health care received it free of cost, but opportunities for additional compensation for injuries were generally unavailable. Beyond the 1970s, opportunities for monetary compensation expanded. Fig. 2-3 shows a marked increasing trend in the number of reported injuries per fatality after 1970.

In Canada in the 1960s, when medical care was largely paid directly out of patients' pockets, the number of reported injuries per fatality was substantially lower than in Britain. However, it later increased rapidly as Canadian provinces moved more in the direction of public payment for medical care, and later opportunities expanded for compensation in addition to medical care.

There are two effects that can make the number of reported injuries increase even if the actual number of injuries remains constant. First, in the past injuries occurred but were not reported. Direct out-of-pocket expenditures discourage reporting. Because of increased emphasis on health care, someone suffering a

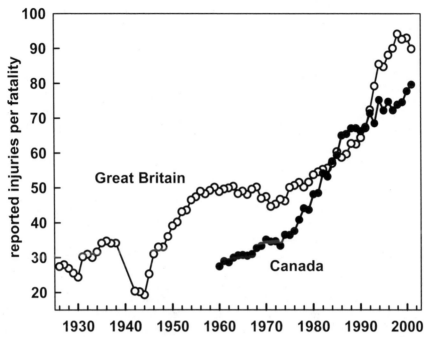

Figure 2-3. The number of reported injuries divided by the number of reported fatalities in Canada and Great Britain. Data from Refs. 25 and 24.

cut, scratch, or bump today is more likely to seek medical care than in the past even if cost is not a consideration.

The second way that reported injuries might depart from actual injuries is through injuries being reported when none is present. Providing rewards for reporting injuries encourages such behavior. Transport Canada defines *injuries* to "include all those who suffered any visible injury or **complained of pain**" (bold added).[25]

A broader message

Data from a number of countries and sources show consistently that reported injuries can depart from actual injuries by large systematic amounts. This finding teaches two principles important to traffic safety. First, clear effects observed in data sets do not necessarily imply real phenomena, but may instead be due to data selection and definition. The second principle is more universal, and is well understood by economists, but often ignored, or even hotly denied, by others. The principle is that as the cost of an activity increases, less of it occurs, while as the reward for an activity increases, more of it occurs. The empirical data show that this principle explains variations in reported injuries per fatality. The same principle applies to many traffic safety topics. If the cost of crashing increases, fewer crashes occur. If the cost decreases, say, because of insurance, more crashes occur. Any policy that increases the cost of drunk driving, such as increased alcohol taxes, reduces drunk driving.

Summary and conclusions

Data sets are essential to derive the quantitative results that are at the core of scientific understanding. The most complete and reliable traffic safety data sets document fatal crashes. The definition of a fatality is conceptually simpler than that of an injury, though less simple than might at first appear. The Fatality Analysis Reporting System, or FARS, defines a traffic fatality as a person who dies within 30 days of a crash on a US public road involving a vehicle with an engine, the death being the result of the crash. FARS is a census of all fatal crashes on US public roads since 1 January 1975, and provides information on more than one million fatalities.

The injury classification system most used in traffic crashes is the Abbreviated Injury Scale, or AIS. The AIS classifies injuries by body part, specific lesion, and severity on a 6-point scale in terms of the threat to life of a single injury. The AIS level is determined by medical examination shortly after the crash, and not by final outcome. Therefore, there is a possibility of death at any AIS level, but it is observed to increase from essentially zero at AIS 1 or AIS 2 to essentially 100% at AIS 6. When victims sustain injuries to more than one body region it is convenient to use only one measure, which is the maximum AIS, or MAIS.

Data from a number of countries, and spanning many decades, imply that the number of reported injuries may differ by large amounts in either direction from the number of actual injuries. If injury victims must pay for medical treatment themselves, it is likely that injuries go unreported. If reporting an injury can result in compensation, injury reports may be filed even in the absence of injuries.

References for Chapter 2

1 Fatality Analysis Reporting System (FARS) Web-Based Encyclopedia. Data files and procedures to analyze them at http://www-fars.nhtsa.dot.gov

2 National Safety Council. *Injury Facts* (prior to 1999 called *Accident Facts*). Itasca, IL: published annually.

3 Tessmer JM. FARS analytic reference guide 1975 to 2002. Washington, DC: National Highway Traffic Safety Administration, Department of Transportation.

4 Weiss HB, Songer TJ, Fabio A. Fetal deaths related to maternal injury. *J Am Medical Assoc.* 2001; 286: 1863-1868.

5 Association for the Advancement of Automotive Medicine. The abbreviated injury scale. AAAM; 1990.

6 National Center for Health Statistics. *International Classification of Diseases*, Ninth Revision, Clinical Modification, Sixth Edition.
http://www.cdc.gov/nchs/datawh/ftpserv/ftpicd9/ftpicd9.htm#guidelines

7   Malliaris AC, Hitchcock R, Hedlund J. A search for priorities in crash protection. SAE paper 820242. Warrendale, PA: Society of Automotive Engineers; 1982.

8   Farmer CM. Reliability of police-reported information for determining crash and injury severity. *Traf Inj Prev.* 2003; 4: 38-44.

9   Homedes N. The disability-adjusted life year (DALY) definition, measurement and potential use. Worldbank Human Capital Development and Operations Policy working paper. http://www.worldbank.org/html/extdr/hnp/hddflash/workp/wp_00068.html

10 World Heath Organization. *The Injury Chartbook.* Geneva; 2002.

11 Graham JD, Thompson KM, Goldie SJ, Segui-Gomez M, Weinstein MC. The cost-effectiveness of airbags by seating position. *J Am Medical Assoc.* 1997; 278: 1418–1425.

12 National Center for Statistics and Analysis (NCSA), National Highway Traffic Safety Administration, US Department of Transportation, Washington DC. http://www-nrd.nhtsa.dot.gov/departments/nrd-30/ncsa//

13 Blincoe LJ, Faigin BM. The Economic Cost of Motor Vehicle Crashes. Report DOT HS 807 876. Washington, DC: National Highway Traffic Safety Administration, US Department of Transportation; 1990.

14 Blincoe LJ, Seay AG, Zaloshnja E, Miller TR, Romano EO, Luchter S, Spicer RS. The economic impact of motor vehicle crashes, 2000. Report DOT HS 809 446. Washington, DC: National Highway Traffic Safety Administration, US Department of Transportation; May 2002. http://www.nhtsa.dot.gov/people/economic/EconImpact2000

15 Adams J. *Transportation Planning – Vision And Practice.* London, UK: Routledge and Kegan Paul, 1981.

16 Evans L. Safety-belt effectiveness: The influence of crash severity and selective recruitment. *Accid Anal Prev.* 1996; 28: 423-433.

17 Leslie JC, Rooney F. Psychological factors in road traffic accidents: Statistical evidence and a study of the effects of viewing an anti-speeding film. *Irish J Psychol.* 1996; 17: 35-47.

18 Whiplash and temporomandibular disorders: Medico-legal issues. http://www.whiplashandtmj.com/index26.html

19 Schmid P. Whiplash-associated disorders. Notfallzentrum, Chirurgie, Inselspital Bern. http://www.smw.ch/pdf/1999_38/1999-38-101.pdf

20 Whiplash prevention: A major car safety issue. http://europa.eu.int/comm/research/growth/gcc/projects/in-action-whiplash.html

21 Schrader H, Obelieniene D, Bovim G, Surkiene D, Mickeviciene D, Miseviciene I, Sand T. Natural evolution of late whiplash syndrome outside the medicolegal context. *Lancet* 1996; 347: 1207-1211.

22 Obelieniene D, Schrader H, Bovim G, Miseviciene I, Sand T. Pain after whiplash: A prospective controlled inception cohort study. *J Neurol Neurosurg Psychiatry.* 1999; 66: 279-83. http://jnnp.bmjjournals.com/cgi/content/full/66/3/279

23 NHTSA Performance Specifications: IVHS countermeasures for rear-end collisions. http://www-nrd.nhtsa.dot.gov/departments/nrd-01/summaries/its_06.html

24 Department for Transport. Transport Statistics, Table 9.10 Road accidents and casualties: 1950-2002. http://www.dft.gov.uk/stellent/groups/dft_transstats/documents/page/dft_transstats_506740.xls

25 Transport Canada. Canadian motor vehicle traffic collision statistics: 2001, footnote 4. http://www.tc.gc.ca/roadsafety/tp/tp3322/2001/en/page1_e.htm

3 Overview of traffic fatalities

The beginnings

The first automobile propelled by an internal combustion engine is generally considered to be a three-wheeled vehicle introduced in 1886 by Germany's Karl Benz. Vehicle development thereafter proceeded rapidly in Europe and in the US. A revolutionary development occurred in 1913 near Detroit, Michigan, when Henry Ford introduced the moving assembly line to mass produce the Ford Model T. The assembly line so reduced production costs that vehicles could be offered at prices that a substantial portion of the US public could afford, leading to rapid growth in vehicle ownership. As the number of vehicles increased, so did the number of crashes and the number of fatalities.

The first known fatal traffic crash killed a 44-year-old female pedestrian on 17 August 1896 in London.[1] The first fatal crash to be well documented and photographed occurred on 25 February in 1899 in Harrow, near London. A detailed account of it appears in the 4 March 1899 issue of the *The Autocar,* a British weekly started in 1895 and still being published. Six men were traveling in the vehicle shown in Fig. 3-1 when the driver applied maximum braking as the vehicle gained speed on a down hill. This caused the tires to separate from the wheels, with subsequent wheel failure. The vehicle dropped to the ground, coming to an abrupt stop. In accord with well-known physical laws, all six occupants continued to move forward until stopped when their bodies struck the ground or other objects in the roadway environment.

The driver died instantly from head injuries, and one passenger died after spending more than three days unconscious in the hospital. The inquest into the two deaths focused on factors remarkably similar to those that would arise today. Many questions were asked about driver alcohol consumption prior to the crash (no more than modest quantities were consumed, and well prior to the crash). Witnesses attested to the skill of the driver, one stating "he is a splendid driver." However, based on testimony by many witnesses, the coroner advised the jury, "the car appeared to be going at too rapid a pace to be safe, either for the occupants themselves or the public." The quality of the tires and the spokes of the wheel were criticized as contributory factors to the deaths.

In the investigation of this early crash, important themes at the core of traffic safety were already being recognized, including:

- Tension between technology and how it is used

- Tension between driver skill and how it is used

Figure 3-1. The first well documented fatal crash, Harrow, GB, 25 February 1899.

Long term trends

Figure 3-2 illustrates the rapid growth in fatalities as motorization increased in the US. The general pattern applies to other countries that began to motorize later than the US, and seems likely to occur in the future in countries now in the early stages of motorization. As US vehicle ownership increased rapidly, so did traffic deaths, peaking at 54,589 in 1972, and declining later to a fairly stable rate of just over 40,000 per year.

Annual traffic fatalities are increasing rapidly in China in the same way as happened in the US in the 1920s. There is no way to reliably estimate what the maximum number of fatalities per year will be in China, or when that maximum will occur. However, current trends indicate ongoing increases. Other countries in the midst of rapid motorization are experiencing corresponding increases in traffic deaths.

Deaths for the same distance of travel (distance rate)

The number of traffic deaths per year shows little in the way of an interpretable pattern. However, if we instead examine the number of traffic deaths in the US for the same distance of vehicle travel (the distance rate), the clear trend in Fig. 3-3 emerges. A straight line on the log-linear scale corresponds to a constant percent change each year. Ever since 1921, when data on the total

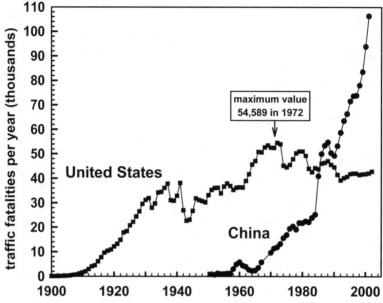

Figure 3-2. Traffic fatalities per year in the US and in China.

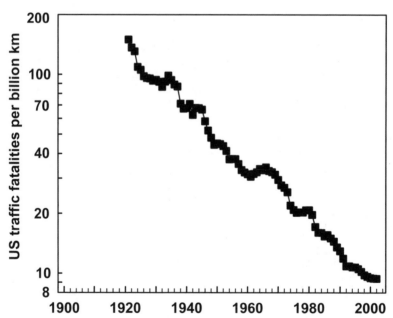

Figure 3-3. Traffic fatalities for the same distance of travel in the US since travel distance was first estimated in 1921.

distance traveled by all vehicles were first collected, the distance rate has trended downwards at an average decrease of about 3.5% per year.

Figure 3-4 shows the percent change in the distance rate in a given year compared to the previous year (that is, the percent difference between each of the 82 pairs of consecutive points plotted in Fig. 3-3). Of the 81 resulting differences, 64 are negative, indicating a reduction in the rate from that of the previous year, with an average reduction over all 81 values of 3.5% per year. There is no obvious trend in the data in Fig. 3-4, so that if such a trend-free pattern persists, the number of fatalities for the same distance of travel will continue to decline at about 3.5% per year.

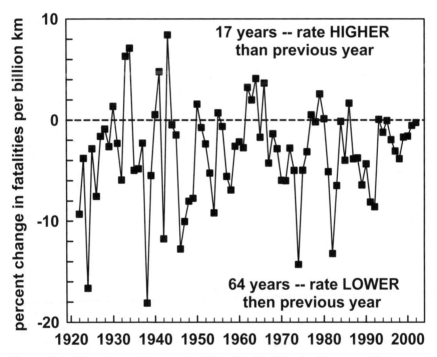

Figure 3-4. The percent change in US traffic fatalities for the same distance of travel from one year to the next (equivalent to the slope of the data in Fig. 3-3).

The 2002 rate of 9.4 US traffic deaths per billion km of travel is 94% below the 1921 rate of 150. If the 1921 rate had applied in 2002, the number of US traffic fatalities in 2002 would have exceeded half a million. The downward trend in the distance rate is also observed in other countries.[2,3(p 155)]

The variable that is the basis of Figs 3-3 and 3-4 is available only after a nation establishes a procedure to estimate the distance traveled by all of its vehicles. Even when available, estimates of distance of travel differ widely in reliability from country to country. The distance traveled by all US vehicles is estimated by summing estimates obtained in different ways from each of the states. While this process may provide a fairly accurate measure of year-to-year percent changes, the value (estimated at 4.60 billion km for 2002)[4] is of uncertain absolute accuracy. The best estimates are for Great Britain, based on observations at 50 sites supported by the Department of Transport.

Deaths per registered vehicle (the vehicle rate)

The registration, and thereby counting, of vehicles is routinely performed by nearly all jurisdictions for taxation purposes, and is considered fairly reliable even from the earliest days of motorization. Figure 3-5 compares the vehicle and distance rates for the US. Fatalities per vehicle have been declining at an average rate of 3.3% per year since the early 1920s, compared to 3.5% for fatalities for the same distance of travel.

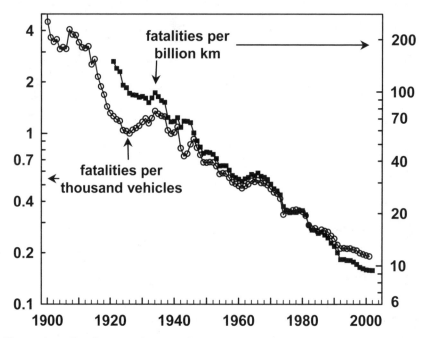

Figure 3-5. Fatality rates for the US based on distance of travel and on number of registered vehicles.

If the average distance traveled per vehicle remained constant from one year to the next, then the two plots in Fig. 3-5 would be identical (apart from a scaling factor). They differ to the extent that they do because the average distance traveled per year per vehicle has been increasing since the early days of motorization (Fig. 4-13, p. 91).

Figure 3-6 shows that not only does the vehicle rate vary by large amounts from country to country, but it also changes at different rates. The fatality rate has been declining in China at 10 percent per year, or halving in 7 years. The US decline of 3.3% per year corresponds to halving in 21 years. One might conclude that the explanation is simply that it is easier to achieve a high rate decline when the absolute value is higher. However, this is not the complete explanation, as the data for Sweden show. Even after achieving a lower absolute value than that for the US, the Swedish rate continued to decline faster than the US rate. We compare changes in rates in different countries in detail in Chapter 15.

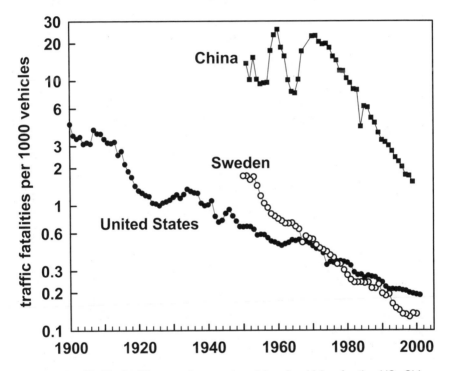

Figure 3-6. Traffic fatalities per thousand registered vehicles for the US, China, and Sweden.

Fatality rates versus degree of motorization. The US vehicle-rate values in Fig. 3-6 are shown again in Fig. 3-7, but plotted versus the number of vehicles per thousand population. The number of vehicles per capita can be regarded as a measure of degree of motorization, and may therefore offer insight into why fatality rates decline. In the US and GB, vehicle registrations per capita in any year have nearly always exceeded the rate in the previous year. Exceptions are related to periods of economic depression or war.

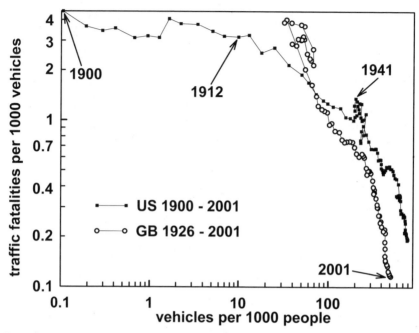

Figure 3-7. The evolution of safety as motorization in the US and GB increased. Adjacent points are for consecutive years. Year increases from left to right except for the few years in which vehicle ownership per capita was less than in the previous year (generally years of economic depression or war).

Extended time series as in Fig. 3-7 are not available for many countries. However, nearly all countries have available counts of fatalities, registered vehicles, and human population for some recent years. The number of deaths per thousand vehicles varies greatly between countries – from under 0.13 for Japan, Norway, Sweden, Great Britain, and the Netherlands to 65 for Mozambique, a factor of over 400 (Table 3-1 and Fig. 3-8). The data are mainly from Refs 5 and 6, but augmented by personal communications from colleagues in a number of countries. There is a general tendency for the number of traffic fatalities per vehicle to be lower the higher the degree of motorization, although departures of 50% from the trend occur. The relationship between different countries observed at similar times (Fig. 3-8) has features in common with the relationship for the data for one country observed at different times (Fig. 3-7).

Note that the US, with over three motorized vehicles for every four people, is the most motorized country in the world but has far from the lowest fatality rate, a theme to which we return in Chapter 15.

Table 3-1. Some rates for 35 countries. Data are mainly from Refs 5 and 6, augmented by personal communications from a number of countries.

country	vehicles per 1000 people	fatalities per 1000 vehicles	fatalities per million people	fatalities per year	data year
USA	777	0.190	148	42,116	2001
New Zealand	684	0.173	118	455	2001
Germany	638	0.133	85	6,977	2001
Japan	625	0.126	79	10,060	2001
Australia	625	0.143	89	1,737	2001
Spain	604	0.228	138	5,517	2001
Norway	599	0.102	61	275	2001
France	589	0.235	138	8,160	2001
Canada	582	0.153	89	2,778	2001
Sweden	549	0.114	62	554	2001
Slovenia	526	0.265	139	278	2001
Great Britain	517	0.118	61	3,598	2001
Netherlands	514	0.121	62	993	2001
Ireland	461	0.232	107	411	2001
Czech Rep.	418	0.311	130	1,334	2001
Poland	381	0.376	143	5,534	2001
Korea	293	0.583	171	8,097	2001
Slovak Rep.	293	0.390	114	614	2001
Hungary	278	0.436	121	1,239	2001
Israel	254	0.290	74	469	1999
Russia	215	0.952	214	29,600	2000
Turkey	143	0.391	56	3,840	2001
South Africa	121	1.600	193	9,068	1998
Brazil	119	1.500	179	30,000	1998
Egypt	50	1.875	95	6,000	2000
China	45	1.546	70	83,529	1999
Zimbabwe	31	3.394	106	1,205	1996
Nigeria	21	4.485	94	6,185	1995
Argentina	17	1.260	210	7,545	2000
Kenya	14	7.290	103	2,617	1995
Ghana	7	12.193	86	1,646	1998
Malawi	5	24.491	119	1,382	1996
Tanzania	5	11.389	53	1,583	1998
Ethiopia	2	19.907	29	1,693	1998
Mozambique	1	65.182	43	805	1997

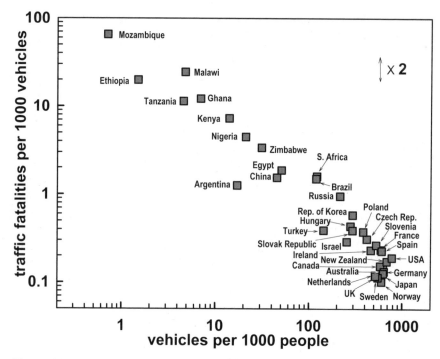

Figure 3.8. Fatality rate versus motorization for the 35 countries in Table 3.1. The largest fatality rate is more than 400 times the smallest. The size of a factor of two difference on the logarithmic scale is indicated in the top right corner.

Who is killed?

All the discussion above has focused on the total numbers killed per year, without regard to category of road user. Although essentially every traffic crash involves at least one driver, Table 3-2 (based on FARS 2001)[4] shows that 38% of those killed are not drivers. (Rare crashes with no drivers occur, such as when a child alone in a vehicle sitting in a passenger seat, sets it in motion). The patterns in Table 3-2 change only moderately from year to year (compare with data for 1988[3(p 45)]). However, this pattern should be interpreted to apply specifically to the US. The percent of fatalities that are drivers is much lower in earlier stages of motorization.

Male fatalities in the US in 2001 totaled 28,878, compared to 13,168 female fatalities, giving a male-to-female ratio of 2.19 to 1 The World Health Organization[7] estimates that of 1,194,115 people killed in 2001 in traffic worldwide, 848,234 were male compared to 345,881 female, giving a male-to-female ratio of 2.34 to 1. The predominance of male fatalities in all types of injury deaths is a universal phenomenon, applying to essentially all types of non-disease deaths,

Table 3-2. US traffic fatalities according to the person killed. FARS 2001.[4]

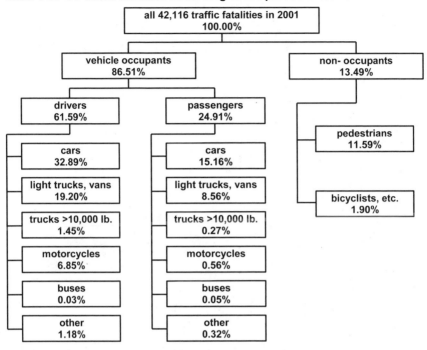

including firearm and other homicides, suicide, drowning, and falling. The preponderance of male over female traffic fatalities persists at all ages (Fig. 3-9). This is not exclusively a driver phenomenon. Figure 3-10 shows that 60% of non-driver (passenger, pedestrian, etc.) road user fatalities in the US were male. (Relationships focusing on ages of drivers are given in Chapter 7).

Trends in pedestrian fatalities

The percent of all traffic fatalities that are pedestrians declines as nations motorize (Fig. 3-11). Note how similar the curves are between the US and Canada on the one hand, and GB and Ireland on the other, reflecting readily observable differences in urban landscape and walking patterns in everyday life. The percent of all fatalities that are pedestrians is much higher in less motorized countries (for example, 80% in Kenya).[8]

Missing values in data sets

Of the 42,116 fatalities coded in FARS 2001, 25,840, or 61.35%, were coded as drivers. The reason why this percent is not identical to the 61.59% in Table 3-2 illustrates features common to all large traffic data sets – nearly all variables have missing (or unknown) values. There were 105 fatalities classified as

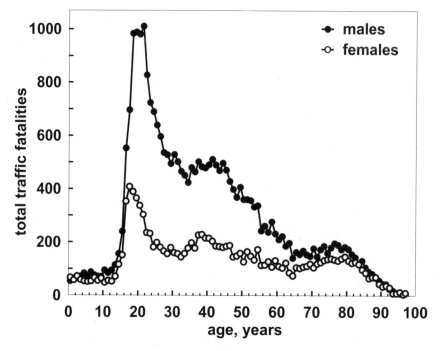

Figure 3-9. The distribution by age and gender of the more than 42,000 fatalities documented in FARS 2001. The maximum value corresponds to 1,010 deaths to 21-year-old males.

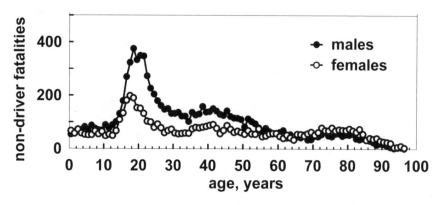

Figure 3-10. The distribution by age and gender of the more than 16,000 people killed who were <u>not</u> driving in the crash in which they were killed (passengers, pedestrians, etc.) as documented in FARS 2001. The maximum value corresponds to 375 deaths to 18-year-old males.

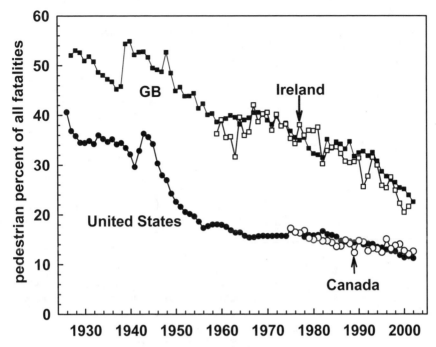

Figure 3-11. Percent of all fatalities that are pedestrians.

vehicle occupants, but no information was available identifying whether they were drivers or passengers. Such lack of identification can arise in the case of vehicle fires, or if multiple occupants are ejected from vehicles, and so on. In Table 3-2 these unidentified occupants were distributed among drivers and passengers in the same proportion as identified drivers and passengers so that the distribution would reflect all those killed. This provides a better estimate of the number of driver fatalities than the alternative of assuming that none of the occupants of unknown type was a driver. Likewise, the total numbers of fatalities used to produce Fig. 3-9 is slightly less than the total in Table 3-2 because there are cases for which gender or age is not coded.

Missing values make it impossible to achieve identical totals from one tabulation to another. For variables like age, gender, and vehicle model year, this is no more than an irritating untidiness that has no material effect on results. However, it becomes a major hurdle for analyses using variables, such as alcohol level or belt use, which have a large fraction of missing values.

Drivers rates are usually best measure

In addressing how factors, especially vehicle factors, affect safety, driver rates rather than occupant rates should be used in most cases. Focusing on drivers avoids the confounding influence of occupancy. If vehicle A experienced 50% more occupant fatalities than vehicle B, this does not mean that an occupant of A is at greater risk than an occupant of B. If the average occupancy of A was 1.9, and that of B was 1.1, then the risk to each traveler in A is 13% lower than the risk to each traveler in B. The aim should usually be to determine driver risk. The assumption that passenger risk is proportional to driver risk is generally appropriate.

Number of vehicles

More drivers (and occupants) are killed in single-vehicle crashes than in two-vehicle crashes. Much coverage of traffic safety in the media presumes that the major risk is from two-vehicle crashes, with the characteristics of the other vehicle exercising a more central role in overall risk than is consistent with the pattern in Table 3-3.

Table 3-3. Distribution of number of drivers killed according to the number of vehicles (any type) involved in the crash. For single-vehicle crashes the object struck, or event, associated with most harm is indicated. FARS 2001.

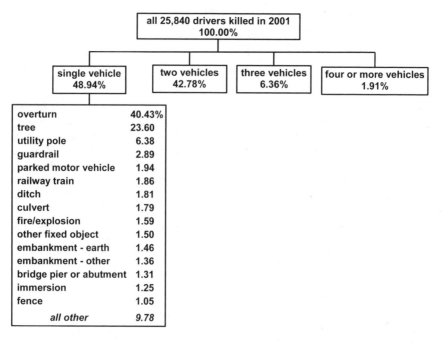

Although under two percent of occupants killed are killed in crashes involving more than 4 vehicles, fatal crashes involving large numbers of vehicles do occur. In 2001, one crash involving 56 vehicles killed three drivers and three passengers. There were also fatal crashes involving 15, 16, 31, and 57 vehicles, each crash killing one driver (one passenger was also killed in the 15-vehicle crash).

The most harmful event is indicated in Table 3-3 for single-vehicle crashes. If, say, a vehicle strikes a curb, and subsequently overturns leading to occupant ejection, then overturn is likely to be coded in FARS as the most harmful event for that vehicle. This variable is not listed in Table 3-3 for multiple-vehicle crashes because it is associated with vehicles, not crashes. Another variable, the first harmful event, is associated with the crash. The first harmful event might be two vehicles striking each other, leading to one of them subsequently overturning. For this vehicle the most harmful event might be the overturn, and for the other, striking another vehicle.

The most harmful event associated with 40% of the drivers killed in single-vehicle crashes is overturn (or rollover). Most of the other most harmful events involve striking objects that are part of the extended roadway environment. The most commonly struck object leading to death is a tree, reflecting the large number of trees adjacent to roadways. The *all other* category includes more than 30 additional most harmful events listed in FARS. For vehicles involved in multiple-vehicle crashes, striking another vehicle is the most harmful event for 90% of the fatalities.

Fraction of deaths due to rollover and ejection

Figure 3-12 shows the percent of fatalities in light trucks and cars in which overturn was the most harmful event. Given a driver death, rollover is much more likely to be the most harmful event for a driver of a light truck than for the driver of a car. While this likely reflects the typically higher center of gravity of light trucks compared to cars, care must always be exercised in interpreting ratios such as those in Fig. 3-12. Reductions in risk in non-rollover crashes lead to higher values for the percent of all deaths that are from rollover crashes even if the risk of a rollover fatality were to remain unchanged. The age and gender dependence shows how much the probability that a driver death is from rollover depends on driver as well as vehicle characteristics, being about twice as great for 20-year-old drivers as for 70-year-old drivers, and about twice as great for light trucks as for cars. Given a driver death, rollover is as likely to be involved when a 20-year-old is driving a car as when a 70-year-old is driving a light truck.

Alcohol is a large factor in overturn crashes, with 55% of car drivers and 53% of light-truck drivers killed in rollover crashes having blood alcohol concentration levels exceeding 0.8%, the legal limit in most US states. For non-rollovers the corresponding figures are 35% and 35%. All these values are based only on data for which the blood alcohol level was known.

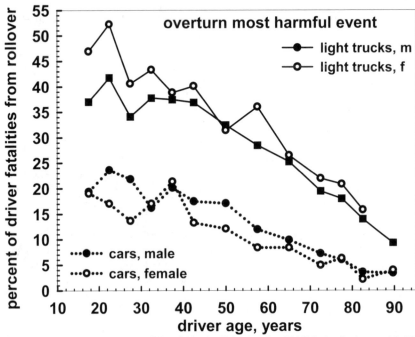

Figure 3-12. The percent of fatalities in light trucks (FARS *body types* 11-49) and in cars (*body types* 1-10) in which overturn was the most harmful event. Belt use by the drivers of light trucks was 17% for males and 24% for females (for cars, 22% and 26%). FARS 2001.

Also, it should be kept in mind how total fatality risk depends on gender and age (Fig. 3-9), so the apparent lack of a major gender dependence in Fig. 3-12 means only that the absolute gender dependence is not materially different from that in Fig. 3-9. Far more male than female drivers are killed in rollover crashes, but given a driver death, the probability it is a rollover is not strongly gender dependent.

For the fatalities represented in Fig. 3-12, 17% of the male drivers of light trucks wore belts (24% of females did). For car drivers the rates were 22% for males and 26% for females. These rates are well below the approximately 50% rates for fatal crashes overall, which are in turn well below rates observed in traffic (p. 52 and Chapter 11).

Many occupants are ejected and killed in non-rollover crashes, so ejection and rollover are separate, although related, factors. Of those killed in rollover crashes, 54% were fully ejected from their vehicles; 59% of fatalities with total ejection resulted from rollover crashes. Fig. 3-13 shows the percent of all drivers killed who were totally ejected from their vehicles.

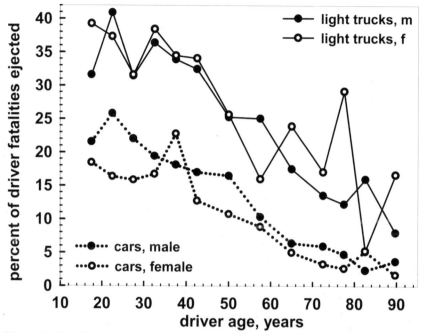

Figure 3-13. The percent of fatally injured drivers of light trucks and cars who were fully ejected from their vehicles. Belt use by the drivers of light trucks was 1.6% for males and 4.2% for females (for cars, 6.2% and 8.2%). FARS 2001.

Belt use by ejected drivers of light trucks was 1.6% for males and 4.2% for females. For drivers of cars, it was 6.2% for males and 8.2% for females. Overall, 96% of the drivers included in Fig. 3-13 were not wearing belts. Properly worn lap/shoulder belts make ejection exceedingly improbable. Being ejected increases fatality risk three to four times compared to remaining in the vehicle in a same severity crash[9]. The effectiveness of safety belts in reducing fatality risk when rollover is the first crash event is 82% (p. 281-282).

Fatalities according to seating position

Figure 3-14 shows the percent of occupants killed according to the seat they occupied. The data are for car occupants only as the six seats represented do not apply to vehicles in general. Indeed, many of the cars included have only four seats, and those with six seats tend to be older model year cars. This figure reflects the mix of cars on the roads in 2001 by type and model year. All the occupants in Fig. 3-14 are fatalities – so the pattern does not represent

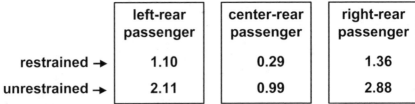

	driver	center-front passenger	right-front passenger
restrained →	33.73%	0.05	10.70
unrestrained →	35.66	0.17	10.97

	left-rear passenger	center-rear passenger	right-rear passenger
restrained →	1.10	0.29	1.36
unrestrained →	2.11	0.99	2.88

Figure 3-14. The percent of all fatally injured occupants of cars (FARS *body types* 1-10 according to seating position). FARS 2001.

occupancy patterns for vehicles on the road that do not crash, for which reliable data do not seem to be available.

The restrained category includes the use of lap and shoulder belt, shoulder belt only, lap belt only, child safety seat or unknown type of restraint. Those coded as not using the devices properly are excluded. Ninety percent of restrained drivers and right-front passengers were using the familiar integrated lap/shoulder belt combination that became standard for all 1974 and later model year cars. The restraint use variable is, in general, not all that reliable because many occupants who survive tell police officers that they were belted when they were not. However, as all occupants included in Fig. 3-14 are fatalities, the coded restraint use is considered reliable. The cells show the percent relative to the 18,216 occupants with known restraint use killed as occupants of cars – all 12 values sum to 100%.

Belt use by fatalities compared to observed belt rates

The data in Fig. 3-14 show 49% of driver and right-front passengers killed in cars were belted. The corresponding value for light trucks is 31%. For all fatalities in cars and light trucks, 43% were unbelted. In 2001, the observed belt use for drivers and passengers was 73%.[10]

The difference between the wearing rates of those killed and those observed in traffic has been incorrectly attributed exclusively to the reduction in fatality risk produced by belts, and the reduction incorrectly used to estimate the effectiveness of safety belts in reducing fatality risk in crashes. The erroneous calculation proceeds along the following lines. If one had a population of identical drivers experiencing random crashes, with 73% using a protective device, then a finding of 43% of fatalities using the device would imply that the device reduced fatality risk by $1 - (27 \times 43)/(73 \times 57) = 72\%$. This is not even an approximate estimate of safety-belt effectiveness, but rather a value that is necessarily substantially higher than the true value because three effects bias the estimate upwards:

1. The belt wearing estimates are based on daytime observations.[11] It is difficult to see if people are wearing their belts in the dark! Also, nighttime traffic is too sparse to collect observational data efficiently, yet this is when many fatal crashes occur (Fig. 3-19, p. 58). Nighttime wearing rates are expected to be lower than daytime rates.

2. Drivers who wear belts have lower crash rates than non-wearers, so some of the reduction in deaths attributed to the belt's effectiveness is due instead to the avoidance of crashes.

3. When belt wearers do crash, they have lower severity crashes than wearers.

The effects listed above are treated in detail in Chapter 11.

Relative fatality risk in different seats

The data in Fig. 3-14 do not address the relative risk of sitting in different seats, because the number of fatalities in a seat is determined mainly by the occupancy of that seat. Even if we could correct for different occupancy rates, other factors that affect fatality risk would still make it difficult to isolate the influence of the seating position. Cars with only one occupant are involved in crashes of different types and severity than those with more than one occupant. Occupants in different seats have different distributions by gender and age, factors that influence fatality risk in a crash (Chapter 6). We thus encounter another example of the problem of exposure referred to in Chapter 1.

The risk associated with different seating positions was addressed by selecting, from 1975-1985 FARS data, cars containing drivers and passengers in specified seats.[12] In order to avoid confounding gender and age effects, only cases in which the driver and passenger were of the same gender, and had ages the same to within three years, were included. Also, occupants coded as using any restraint system, or who were less than 16 years old, were excluded from the analysis. Data restricted in this way were used to compute the ratio

$$R = \frac{\text{Number of passenger fatalities in specified seat}}{\text{Number of driver fatalities}} . \qquad \text{3-1}$$

R provides a largely assumption-free estimate of the difference in risk due to differences in the physical environment of the different seating positions. It is essentially free from the confounding effects that arise from occupant characteristics being correlated with different seating positions because all occupants for Eqn 3-1 were killed in crashes in which the other occupant was also present in the same car involved in the same crash, and both occupants were of the same gender and similar age.

Raw data and computed values of R are shown in Fig. 3-15. Because all values are relative to the driver, there is no computed relative risk for the driver, for whom, by definition, $R = 1$.

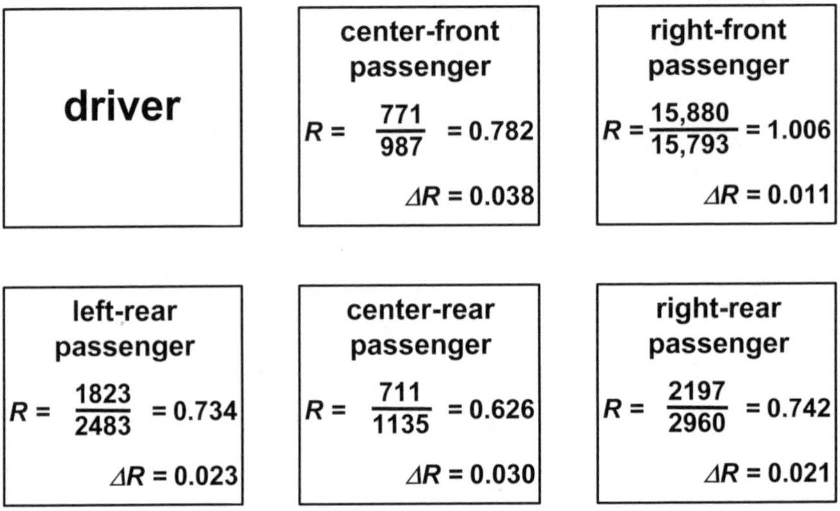

driver	center-front passenger $R = \dfrac{771}{987} = 0.782$ $\Delta R = 0.038$	right-front passenger $R = \dfrac{15{,}880}{15{,}793} = 1.006$ $\Delta R = 0.011$
left-rear passenger $R = \dfrac{1823}{2483} = 0.734$ $\Delta R = 0.023$	center-rear passenger $R = \dfrac{711}{1135} = 0.626$ $\Delta R = 0.030$	right-rear passenger $R = \dfrac{2197}{2960} = 0.742$ $\Delta R = 0.021$

Figure 3-15. The risk, R, of death for passengers in various seats relative to the risk in the driver seat. ΔR is the standard error in R. FARS 1975-1985.

For cars containing a driver and a right-front passenger, there were 15,880 right-front passenger fatalities compared to 15,793 driver fatalities, for a right-front passenger relative fatality risk of $R = 1.006 \pm 0.011$. The error is computed assuming that the fatalities arise from a Poisson process (p. 14). Thus, to high precision, no difference is found in fatality risk to drivers and right-front passengers. The center-front seat $R = 0.78 \pm 0.04$ indicates that this position is associated with a $(22 \pm 4)\%$ lower fatality risk than the outboard (driver or right-front passenger) front positions. The outboard-rear seats have a composite $R = 0.739 \pm 0.015$. That is, for unrestrained occupants in outboard seating positions, rear seats are associated with a fatality risk $(26.1 \pm 1.5)\%$ lower than for front seats. The safest seat of all is the center rear, where risk is $(37 \pm 3)\%$ lower than in the driver seat. The earlier FARS data used in this study documented a fleet of larger cars with larger numbers of center seats than the 2001 data used for Fig. 3-14.[12] Another study using more recent vehicles reports a 39% lower risk of fatality and 33% lower risk of injury in rear compared to front seats.[13]

Seating position and direction of impact

FARS data contain a principal impact point variable, defined as the impact that is judged to have produced the greatest personal injury or property damage for a particular vehicle. The impact refers to the location on the vehicle sustaining damage, so that principal impact point at 12 o'clock means that the damage is in the center-front of the vehicle (Fig. 3-16). The region damaged does not necessarily indicate the direction of impact, because the center front could be damaged by, say, an oblique impact into a tree. A detailed post-crash investigation is necessary to determine the actual direction of impact. However, principal impact point 12 o'clock may be approximately interpreted as indicating, on average at least, head-on impacts.

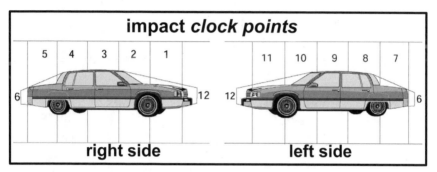

Figure 3-16. Regions corresponding to impact clock points.

Figure 3-17 shows relative risk for the five passenger seating positions versus principal impact point displayed in the same bird's eye view of the vehicle traveling up the page used in Figs 3-14 and 3-15. All values are relative to a value one for drivers.

Focusing on the right-front passenger data (top-right circle) shows that when the impact is from the right, the right-front passenger is 2.74 times as likely to die as is the driver (as before, both occupants are of the same gender, and ages not different by more than three years). When the impact is from the left, the right-front passenger is 0.38 times as likely to die as the driver. This can be expressed equivalently by saying that the driver is $1/0.38 = 2.63$ times as likely to die as is the right-front passenger. The essential symmetry (reflected in the closeness of the ratios 2.74 and 2.63) is to be expected on physical grounds, and increases confidence in the estimates. For principal impact point 12 o'clock the value of R for right-front passengers is $R = 0.988 \pm 0.019$. Thus the similarity of fatality risk to drivers and right-front passengers applies also to the frontal case. Drivers and right-front passengers are at similar fatality risks from rear impacts ($R = 1.00 \pm 0.10$).

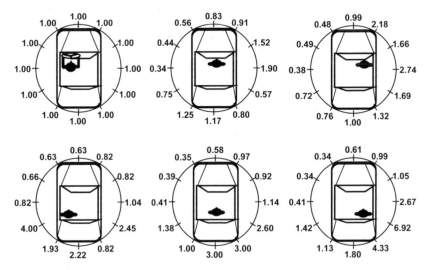

Figure 3-17. Fatality risk, relative to that of a driver, for passengers in different seats as a function of principal impact point. 1975-1985 FARS.[12]

The safety advantage of sitting in a rear seat compared to the corresponding front seat is larger for frontal crashes than for all crashes without regard to direction of impact (Fig. 3-16). The general pattern in Fig. 3-17 shows that occupants near the point of impact are at greater fatality risk than those far from the point of impact. Although rear occupants are at much greater risk than front occupants in rear impact crashes, such crashes account for less than 5% of all fatalities. The overall 26% lower fatality risk in rear than in front seats reflects that frontal crashes account for most fatalities. The lower risk in center seats is likely reflecting greater distance from the highest risk points of impact, as well as protective cushioning from other passengers.

A corresponding phenomenon occurs for motorcyclists, where it is found that fatality risk in the driver seat is $(26 \pm 2)\%$ greater than that in the passenger seat; for frontal crashes the difference is $(40\% \pm 6)\%$, again demonstrating the greater risk associated with being nearer the impact.[14] Also, the motorcycle driver probably helps cushion the impact for the passenger. For non-frontal motorcycle crashes, drivers and passengers are at similar risk ($R = 1.01 \pm 0.04$).

An additional finding in the car occupant risk study is that there are 38% more impacts of high severity from the right than from the left, a result possibly reflecting asymmetries resulting from driving on the right.[12] It would be informative to know if countries that drive on the left experience more severe impacts from the left than from the right.

Variation throughout year and day

Fatalities occur at a far from uniform rate, varying systematically throughout the year, as shown in Fig. 3-18. In each of the 8 years plotted, the lowest number of fatalities was recorded for February, and by an amount larger than due to the fewer number of days in February. In all cases, the highest number of fatalities was recorded for July or August, a pattern similarly stable in 1983-1988 data.[3(p 86)] The pattern occurs largely because more difficult driving conditions in winter months reduce speeds (see also Chapter 5).

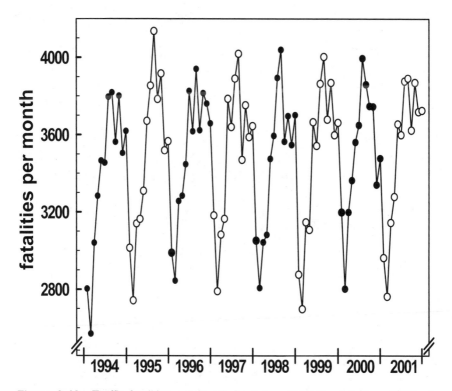

Figure 3-18. Traffic fatalities per month from Jan. 1994 through Dec. 2001. A symbol change indicates the first month of the next year. FARS data.

Fatalities follow the regular daily pattern shown in Fig. 3-19. The hour with the fewest number of fatalities is from 4 am to 5 am on the normal workdays Monday through Friday. The hour with the largest number of fatalities – about four times the lowest – is from 2 am to 3 am on Saturday and Sunday mornings, with weekend drinking playing a key role.

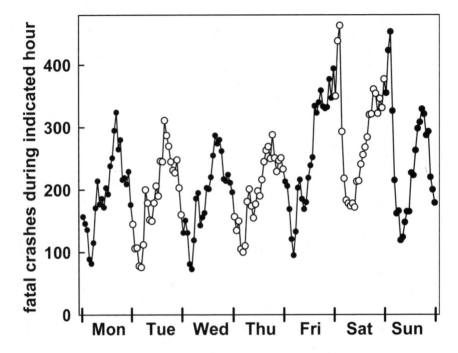

Figure 3-19. Number of fatal traffic crashes in each hour of the day (average of all values in FARS 2001). The first point shows the average number occurring between midnight and 0:59 am on Monday morning, the second point between 1:00 am and 1:59 am on Monday morning, and so on. A symbol change indicates the first hour of the next day.

Someone does NOT get killed every 13 minutes

If the 42,116 US fatalities in 2001 are divided by the number of minutes in the year the result is an average rate of one per 12.5 minutes. This has led to many statements like, "There is a death caused by a motor vehicle crash every 13 minutes and a disabling injury every 14 seconds."[15] This is far from being strictly correct. No fatal crash occurred between 3:30 am and 7:00 am on Tuesday 6 March 2001, or between 3:00 am and 6:30 am on Tuesday 27 November 2001. In both these cases, three and a half hours elapsed without anyone being killed. Note how these extreme values relate to the hourly and monthly dependencies in Figs 3-18 and 3-19. On the other hand, there are many occurrences of three, four, and five crashes being coded as occurring at the same time. Indeed, if crashes were a perfectly random Poisson process, more would be coded as occurring at the same time than separated by any other time interval.

The distribution of the times between crashes coded in FARS 2001 is plotted in Fig. 3-20. All crash times are converted to Eastern time, so a crash occurring at 1:00 pm California time is converted to 4:00 pm Eastern time, and is therefore correctly interpreted as occurring at the same time as a 4:00 pm crash in New York.

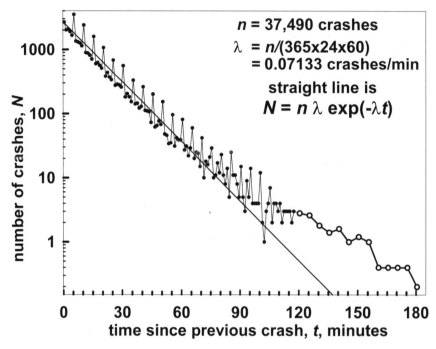

Figure 3-18. The distribution of the times between consecutive fatal crashes in the US in 2001.

The first seven values plotted in Fig. 3-20 are:

Indicated time between crashes, minutes	*Number of occurrences*
0	2,660
1	2,013
2	2,063
3	1,899
4	1,661
5	3,496
6	1,347
7	1,309

If the data were a perfect representation of reality, the largest number of occurrences listed above would be for time zero between crashes. As the smallest time unit in the data is one minute, a recording of no time difference between a pair of crashes implies that they occurred within a minute of each other. The probability that two crashes in fact occur at exactly the same time (or are separated by any specified time) is, of course, zero. Compelling statistical reasoning implies that the number of occurrences should decline systematically with increasing time since the previous crash. Thus fewer crashes are expected to occur 5 minutes after the previous crash than to occur 4 minutes after the previous crash. The prominent peak at 5 minutes results from the tendency to record times in multiples of 5 minutes, a tendency reinforced by traditional mechanical analogue devices which display time using circular dials marked in five-minute intervals. This tendency (it may disappear when the digital revolution is complete) also leads to the prominent cyclical pattern of peaks at multiples of five minutes evident in Fig. 3-20. If one assumes that about 20% of readings are rounded to the nearest five minutes, a smoother pattern results.

The straight line in Fig. 3-20 is the theoretical prediction based on assuming that crashes are a Poisson process with an average risk of crashing per minute, $\lambda = 0.07133$ (calculated as 37,490 crashes divided by the number of minutes in 2001). This corresponds to fatal crashes occurring at an <u>average</u> rate of one every 14.02 minutes. The number of crashes reflects the exclusion of 372 for which the time of crash was not adequately coded (see p. 45 on missing values).

The open symbols in Fig. 3-20 represent averaging over five minutes rather than one minute as data become sparse due to few occurrences of crash-free periods of more than a couple of hours. The greater number of crash-free periods of more than an hour or so observed compared to the Poisson process prediction reflects major departures from the assumption of a constant rate of crashing, as is clearly apparent in the monthly and hourly variations in Fig. 3-18 and Fig. 3-19. However, even if the crashes were perfectly random, the relationship in Fig. 3-20 still predicts that in a year we should expect one period of 110 minutes to elapse with no crashes anywhere in the US.

Caution in interpreting averages

Much of the material in this and other chapters relates to averages. Averages do not apply to individuals. As shown for the case of the claim that someone gets killed every 13 minutes, averages can convey a misleading impression. Averages should be interpreted with a caution well captured in the quip: *An average is like a bikini swimsuit – what it reveals is interesting, but what it conceals is crucial.* It has also been remarked that the average human has approximately one breast and one testicle.

Summary and conclusions

As countries motorize, traffic fatalities per year initially increase steeply to a maximum and then decline. In the US the maximum of just under 55,000 occurred in 1972. From 1993 to 2002 the rate has been between 40,100 and 42,815 fatalities per year. The distance rate (fatalities for the same distance of vehicle travel) has trended downwards systematically by about 3.5% per year since the 1920s. If the 1921 rate were to apply in 2002, US fatalities in 2002 would have exceeded half a million.

The vehicle rate (fatalities per registered vehicle) is available for nearly all counties, whereas the distance rate is available for only the few that estimate the distance traveled by all of their vehicles. The vehicle rate varies by more than a factor of 400 between countries, from under 0.13 fatalities per thousand vehicles in some countries to over 60 in others. The vehicle rate (a measure of safety) is related to the number of vehicles per inhabitant (a measure of degree of motorization). The higher the motorization, the lower the fatality rate.

Male fatalities outnumber female fatalities by more than a factor of two in the US, and worldwide. Even for non-drivers, such as pedestrians and passengers, male fatalities outnumber female (by a ratio of 1.5 for the US).

More vehicle occupants are killed in single-vehicle crashes than in two-vehicle crashes. Rollover is the most harmful event for 40% of single-vehicle crash fatalities. The probability that a driver death is due to a rollover crash depends on the type of vehicle and the age of the driver, being about twice as great for light trucks as for cars, and about twice as great for 20-year-old drivers as for 70-year-old drivers. Similar relationships apply when the victim was fully ejected from the vehicle in any type of crash.

Safety belt use by occupants killed after ejection and in rollover crashes is substantially lower than for fatal crashes overall, which in turn is much lower than use rates observed in traffic. Of the male light-truck drivers who were ejected and killed, only 1.6% were wearing belts. Remaining in the vehicle reduces risk by about 80%, and a properly worn safety belt makes ejection exceedingly improbable.

Fatality risk is substantially lower in rear seats than in front seats. This is because the most common severe crash impact is at the front of the vehicle. In rear-impact crashes (under 5% of fatal crashes) the rear seat is less safe. A driver is 2.6 times as likely to be killed by an impact on the left side of the vehicle compared to one on the right side. Risk is lower in the center than in outboard seats, likely reflecting greater distance from the highest risk point of impact and cushioning effects from other passengers.

Even if fatal crashes were a perfectly random Poisson process, they would not flow at an approximately constant rate corresponding to the yearly average of one per 14 minutes. An assumption of Poisson randomness indicates one annual crash-free period of more than an hour and a half, but thousands of crashes occurring within a minute of the preceding crash. Crashes are far from random throughout the year and week, leading to crash-free periods in excess of three hours. There are consistently fewer fatal crashes in February, and more in July and August than in other months. There are more than four times as many crashes per hour from 1:00 am to 3:00 am on Saturday and Sunday than from 2:00 am to 6:00 am on weekdays.

References for Chapter 3

1   RoadPeace. World's first road death.
    http://www.roadpeace.org/articles/WorldFirstDeath.html

2   Evans L. A crash course in traffic safety. *Encyclopædia Britannica Medical and Health Annual*, 1997, p.126-139.

3   Evans L. *Traffic Safety and the Driver*. New York, NY: Van Nostrand Reinhold; 1991.

4   Fatality Analysis Reporting System (FARS) Web-Based Encyclopedia.   Data files and procedures to analyze them.   http://www-fars.nhtsa.dot.gov/

5   International Road Traffic and Accident Database (OECD) (2002), March 2004. http://www.bast.de/htdocs/fachthemen/irtad/english/englisch.html

6   Jacobs G, Aeron-Thomas A. Africa road safety review final report. Report PR/INT/659/2000 prepared by TRL (UK) for US Department of Transportation, Federal Highway Administration, December 2000.   http://www.hsph.harvard.edu/traffic/papers/AfricaRoadSafetyReview2000.pdf

7   World Health Organization. *Burden of Disease Project*. Global burden of disease estimates for 2001. http://www3.who.int/whosis/menu.cfm?path=burden

8   Odero W, Khayesi M, Heda PM. Road traffic injuries in Kenya: Magnitude, causes and status of intervention. *Inj Control Saf Promot*. 2003; 10: 53-61.

9   Evans L, Frick MC. Potential fatality reductions through eliminating occupant ejection from cars. *Accid Anal Prev*. 1989; 21: 169-182.

10 The Transportation Link, October 2001.   NHTSA Reports: Seat belt use by drivers and passengers reaches 73%. http://osdbuweb.dot.gov/translink/oct2001/index8.htm

11 Glassbrenner D. Safety belt use in 2002 – Demographic characteristics. Research note DOT HS 809.557. Washington, DC: US Department of Transportation, National Highway Traffic Safety Administration; March 2003.
    http://www.nhtsa.dot.gov/people/injury/airbags/demographic03-03/demographic.htm

12 Evans L, Frick MC. Seating position in cars and fatality risk. *Am J Pub Health*. 1988: 78; 1456-1458.

13 Smith KM, Cummings P. Passenger seating position and the risk of passenger death or injury in traffic crashes. *Accid Anal Prev*. 2004; 36; 257-260.

14 Evans L, Frick MC. Helmet effectiveness in preventing motorcycle driver and passenger fatalities. *Accid Anal Prev*. 1988; 20: 447-458.

15 National Safety Council. Report on injuries in America, 6 June 2000.
    http://www.nsc.org/lrs/statinfo/99report.htm

4 Vehicle mass and size

Introduction

Since the early 1970s, research established that drivers of larger, heavier cars have lower risks in crashes than drivers of smaller, lighter cars.[1-5] The effects are large and have been examined in detail in many studies. Examining effects in increasing detail has added to knowledge on a number of broad safety questions. This is why we devote this complete chapter to how vehicle mass and size affect safety. Although mathematical details are given for some topics, it is not necessary to follow the mathematics to grasp the main ideas and their applicability to other safety matters.

Vehicle factors

The term *vehicle factors* refers to physical attributes of a vehicle that affect risks. The term is most often applied to factors that influence risk to occupants when crashes occur, but may also refer to factors that affect the risk of crashing, such as the presence of antilock brakes or the height of the vehicle's center of gravity. The overriding concept is a difference in outcomes related to vehicle attributes if all other factors, especially driver behavior, are the same. This chapter focuses mainly on how driver risk is affected by the mass and size of vehicles, given that a crash occurs.

It is difficult to determine how any individual factor influences traffic safety because nearly all factors occur in the presence of other factors that have important effects on outcomes. This is particularly so in the case of vehicle factors, because the crash experience of a particular set of vehicles is so intertwined with use and driver behavior factors. Any particular vehicle factor is likely to attract purchasers with driver characteristics different from those who purchase other vehicles. Sporty vehicles attract different drivers than more narrowly utilitarian vehicles. In real-world crashes, all other things are never equal, and indeed are often far from equal. Effects that might seem due to vehicle factors are often enormously confounded by driver characteristics and use patterns.

Deaths per million registered cars does not measure vehicle factors

Figure 4-1 shows that the number of driver deaths per million registered cars trends lower with increasing mass. Much clearer than the dependence on mass is the dependence on the number of doors. There is no reason why adding doors to a car should substantially affect occupant protection. This effect is due not to the addition of the doors, but because the life-style and risk-taking characteristics of drivers who choose two-door cars differ in so many ways from those choosing four-door cars. These effects are far larger than explainable in terms of differences in the distributions of age and gender associated with drivers of the different car types.

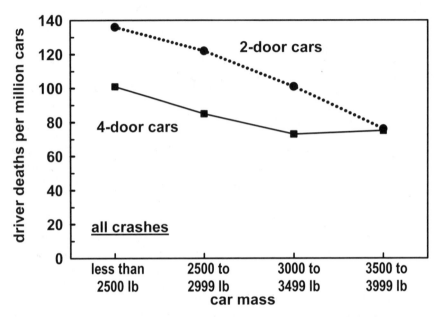

Figure 4-1. Car-driver deaths in all crashes per million registered cars for 1994-97 models during 1995-98. Insurance Institute for Highway Safety (IIHS) data.[6]

Examining only rollover crashes (Fig. 4-2) reveals even larger differences dependent on number of doors. Rollover risk depends particularly steeply on driver behavior, particularly speed choice.

Figure 4-3 shows data for single-car crashes. The effect of mass is less systematic, but there is still a general average increase in risk as mass decreases. Nominally, Fig. 4-3 indicates that 2,500-2,999 pound cars have higher risks than cars that are either lighter or heavier. Yet there are clear theoretical reasons, backed up by much empirical evidence, that vehicle mass affects the risk when a crash occurs in a systematic continuous manner. The non-systematic features of the relations provide additional evidence of the large role of non-vehicle factors.

Figure 4-4 shows that deaths in smaller cars do not result exclusively from crashes with heavier vehicles. Indeed, over a third of the deaths in cars of all the mass categories are in single-car crashes.

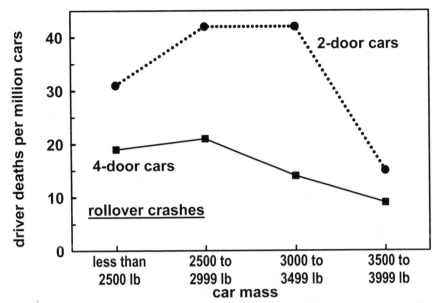

Figure 4-2. Car-driver deaths in rollover crashes per million registered cars for 1994-97 models during 1995-98. IIHS data.[6]

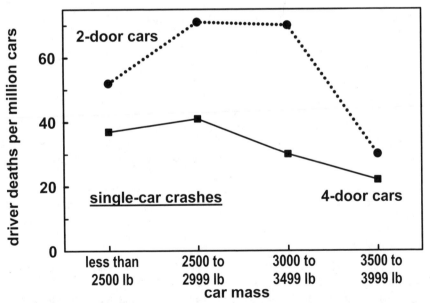

Figure 4-3. Car-driver deaths in single-car crashes per million registered cars for 1994-97 models during 1995-98. IIHS data.[6]

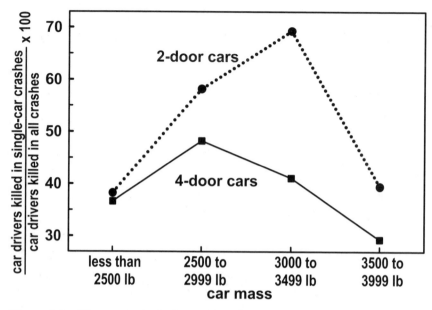

Figure 4-4. The percent of all car-driver fatalities that result from single-car crashes. IIHS data.[6]

An examination of fatal crash involvements for the same travel distance found corresponding effects. The rate for two-door cars was 44% higher than the rate for four-door cars, and the rate for two-door sports utility vehicles was 50% higher than the rate for four-door sports utility vehicles.[7(p 179)]

Rates are for drivers

All the rates in Figs 4-1 to 4-4 are for drivers. This is the appropriate measure because occupancy systematically increases with vehicle size. So, even if all vehicles had identical occupant protection and crash experience, larger vehicles would have more fatalities per vehicle because more occupants would, on average, be at risk in each crash (p. 47). While risks are different in different car seats (Fig. 3-15, p. 54), the risks closely scale. So it seems likely that, although rear-seat passengers have lower absolute fatality risks than front seat occupants, the relative risks to rear seat occupants would follow patterns similar to those in Figs 4-1 through 4-4.

Mass or weight?

An object's *weight* is the force of gravity upon it, while its *mass* is the amount of substance it contains, as indicated, for example, by how much force is required to accelerate it. In most circumstances there is little practical difference, even though, conceptually, weight and mass are distinct. The mass of a body is typically determined by weighing it (determining the force necessary to prevent it from falling). When moving at constant speed a vehicle's weight generates the rolling resistance that primarily determines fuel use. In outer space the car would need no fuel to continue to move at constant speed, while on the moon propulsion energy to maintain a constant speed on a flat hard road would be substantially less than on earth. When a vehicle accelerates, fuel is used primarily to overcome inertia, which is proportional to mass. When in motion, the vehicle has kinetic energy determined by its mass and speed. When its speed is reduced due to breaking or crashing, this kinetic energy is converted into other energy forms, mainly heat. So, when vehicles crash, mass is the relevant characteristic. If a heavy and a light vehicle collided in space, each vehicle would undergo a speed change governed by Newton's laws of motion. The speed changes would not be all that different from those on a road because the earth's gravity is not a major factor.

There are over 20 definitions of vehicle mass. The one coded in FARS data is derived from the Vehicle Identification Number (VIN) and is generally the curb mass,[7(p 17)] defined as the mass of the vehicle with standard equipment and a full complement of fuel and other fluids, but with no occupants or cargo. This mass is determined by the design of the vehicle. We do not know how much cargo or fuel (filling the fuel tank typically adds about 50 kg) was on board a vehicle when it crashes. We know the numbers, ages, and genders of occupants, but we do not know their masses. The mass of four large occupants can exceed the mass of four small occupants by over 250 kg. Such uncertainties are unlikely to generate important systematic biases in most analyses, but will add substantial random noise.

In most of what follows, vehicle size is characterized by curb mass. When any relationship is plotted versus curb mass, this does not mean that mass is the causal factor. It might be size, or some combination of size and mass. In a typical set of vehicles, heavier vehicles are larger; smaller vehicles are lighter. (We use *heavier/lighter* to denote larger/smaller mass).

Two-vehicle crashes

Of the 25,840 drivers killed in US traffic in 2001, 43% died in two-vehicle crashes compared to 49% in single-vehicle crashes (Table 3-3, p. 48). Two-vehicle fatal crashes tend to be studied more than single-vehicle crashes because more important information is available. For single-car crashes, little information is generally available on damage suffered by struck objects. For a two-vehicle crash, the injuries sustained in one vehicle provide information relating to the crash forces on the other.

Definitions for two-vehicle crashes

From a formal perspective, each of the vehicles involved in a two-vehicle crash can be considered to have a symmetrical role – they crash into each other.

However, for expository clarity it is convenient to make an arbitrary distinction between them, using such terminology as:

vehicle$_1$ = *first, striking, bullet, subject, driven, or your vehicle*

vehicle$_2$ = *second, struck, target, partner, or other vehicle.*

Vehicle masses are designated by m_1 and m_2. It is convenient for the heavier of the two vehicles to be vehicle$_2$, so we can define a mass ratio, μ, for every crash between two vehicles of known mass as

$$\mu = \frac{m_2}{m_1} = \left(\frac{\text{mass of heavier vehicle}}{\text{mass of lighter vehicle}} \right) . \qquad \text{4-1}$$

Choosing vehicle$_2$ to be the heavier insures that μ is greater than one.

Consider a set of crashes with the same value of μ, or with values of μ confined to a narrow range. Assume that the total number of drivers killed in the lighter vehicles is N_1 and that N_2 drivers are killed in the heavier vehicles. A driver fatality ratio, R, can be defined as

$$R = \frac{N_1}{N_2} = \frac{\text{Number of driver fatalities in the lighter vehicles}}{\text{Number of driver fatalities in the heavier vehicles}} . \qquad \text{4-2}$$

The interpretation of R is remarkably assumption free – a simple count of driver fatalities in two clearly defined sets of vehicles. It is a measure of relative fatality risk in pairs of crashing vehicles, essentially regardless of driver behavior or vehicle use patterns. Higher risk driving by, say, drivers of heavier vehicles will increase the number of driver fatalities in heavier vehicles, but also in lighter vehicles into which they crash by a similar proportion. Higher risk driving affects the total number of fatalities, which affects the precision with which R can be determined, but not its expected value. R is affected by factors that affect survivability in crashes, such as systematically different belt-wearing rates or systematically different driver ages in vehicles of different mass.

Effect of mass in two-car crashes

The above definitions and equations apply to crashes between vehicles of any type that differ in mass. We now focus on one class of vehicle, namely cars (*body type* 1-10 in FARS). This is because curb masses are coded in FARS for cars, but not for other types of vehicles. Cars constitute less than half of the vehicles on US roads. About one fifth of two-vehicle crashes involve two cars. There were 3,288 fatalities in two-car crashes in 2001, 7.8% of all fatalities. Even though two-car crashes are not responsible for a major portion of fatalities, they are studied intensively because they lead to findings that increase understanding of general effects that apply to any type of vehicle involved in any type of crash.

Empirical findings

Many analyses using FARS data[8-11] have found that R and μ for cars are related according to

$$R = \mu^\lambda. \qquad 4\text{-}3$$

The example in Fig. 4-5 is for crashes between pairs of cars with unbelted drivers crashing into each other head-on (principal impact points 11, 12 or 1 o'clock – Fig. 3-16, p. 55). Placing any restriction on both vehicles involved in two-vehicle crashes greatly reduces sample sizes. If, say, half of all crashed vehicles suffer frontal damage, filtering out all vehicles not sustaining frontal damage reduces sample sizes by 75%. The relationship in Fig. 4-5, based on 15,356 unbelted drivers killed in 13,162 crashes, gives $\lambda = 3.58 \pm 0.05.$[12]

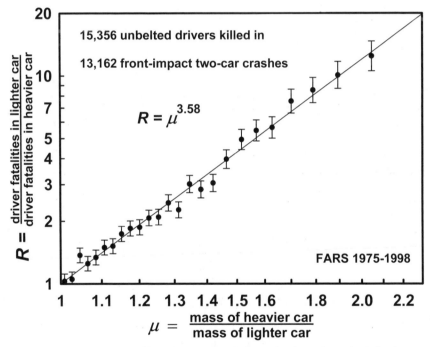

Figure 4-5. Fatality ratio, R, versus mass ratio, μ, for frontal crashes (both cars with principal impact point at 11, 12 or 1 o'clock).[12] The relationship $R = \mu^\lambda$ is the *first law of two-car crashes* (with $\lambda = 3.58$ for the data shown). FARS 1975-1998.

Some examples from the 30 values of λ reported in one study[9] are included in Table 4-1. Requiring that each driver be of the same gender and similar age does not appreciably affect λ, justifying including drivers of both genders and all ages in the other analyses.

Table 4-1. Illustrative values of the parameter λ in Eqn 4-3. The first row uses FARS 1975-1998.[12] All the other rows use FARS 1975-1989.[9]

Description	$\lambda \pm \Delta\lambda$
unbelted drivers, frontal crashes (Fig. 4-5)	3.58 ± 0.05
all drivers and crash directions	3.53 ± 0.03
unbelted drivers	3.58 ± 0.04
belted drivers	3.60 ± 0.13
frontal crashes	3.74 ± 0.05
drivers same gender, age within 5 years	3.80 ± 0.09
rural crashes	3.45 ± 0.03
urban crashes	3.63 ± 0.05

Explanation based on Newtonian mechanics

Simple Newtonian mechanics of two objects crashing into each other can offer insight into Eqn 4-3. Consider two cars, car$_1$ and car$_2$ with masses m_1 and m_2 traveling at speeds v_1 and v_2 towards each other with their centers of gravity moving along the same straight line (Fig. 4-6). Assume that after they collide they remain locked together (this is equivalent to the collision being non-elastic) in one clump of mass $M = m_1 + m_2$ traveling at speed V along the same straight line. Applying the law of conservation of linear momentum gives

$$V = (m_2 v_2 - m_1 v_1)/M .$$

4-4

When $m_2 v_2 > m_1 v_1$ the clump will move in the same direction as the initial direction of car$_2$, as represented in Fig. 4-6, so that the crash will impose on car$_2$ a speed change (delta-v, as described in Chapter 2) given by

$$\Delta v_2 = v_2 - V = m_1 (v_1 + v_2)/M .$$

4-5

Because the crash reverses the direction of travel of car$_1$, its speed change is given by

$$\Delta v_1 = v_1 + V = m_2 (v_1 + v_2)/M .$$

4-6

Dividing Eqn 4-6 by Eqn 4-5 gives

$$\Delta v_1 / \Delta v_2 = m_2 / m_1 = \mu ,$$

4-7

showing that the ratio of the delta-v values is simply the inverse of the mass ratio. Equations 4-4 through 4-7 apply to any vehicles, or for that matter, to any objects crashing into each other.

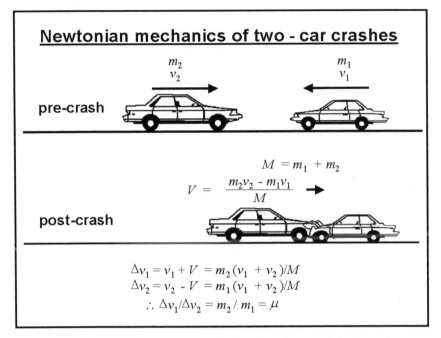

Figure 4-6. Newtonian mechanics of idealized head-on crash between two cars.

If the masses and initial speeds of both cars were identical, both would stop at their point of contact immediately after the crash ($V = 0$). Indeed, an observer might find it difficult to distinguish between one car crashing into an unbreakable mirror in front of a barrier (vertical, unmovable, etc.) and two identical cars crashing into each other. (In the mirror case, the "identical" vehicles would have steering wheels on opposite sides).

Relationship between delta-v and fatality risk. Figure 4-7 shows the fraction, P, of unbelted drivers involved in all types of crashes coded in the National Accident Sampling System who were killed versus an estimate of the vehicle's Δv.[13] The data for $\Delta v < 114$ km/h fit well the function

$$P = \left(\Delta v / 114\right)^{3.54}, \qquad (\Delta v < 114 \text{ km/h}) . \qquad \text{4-8}$$

This simple *rule of thumb*[14] provides an effective fit to the data but has the undesirable formal property of an unrealistic discontinuity at $\Delta v = 114$ km/h. Consider a two-vehicle crash in which the vehicles experience delta-v values of Δv_1 and Δv_2 (both values less than 114 km/h). The ratio of the risks of death, R, to the drivers in the two vehicles is immediately computed from Eqn 4-8 as

$$R = P_1 / P_2 = \left(\Delta v_1 / \Delta v_2\right)^{3.54} = \left(m_2 / m_1\right)^{3.54} = \mu^{3.54}. \qquad \text{4-9}$$

So, combining the relationship between fatality risk and Δ*v* in Eqn 4-8 with fundamental Newtonian mechanics reproduces the firmly established functional form of Eqn 4-3. The closeness of the power 3.54 to the values of *λ* in Table 4-1 (ranging from 3.45 to 3.80) is fortuitous as there is no reason to expect a calculation that ignores so many details to agree this closely with the empirical data.

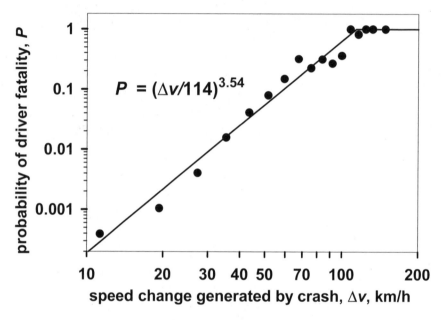

Figure 4-7. Probability of death versus delta-*v* for unbelted drivers. Data from Ref. 13, fit based on *rule of thumb* in Ref. 14.

First law of two-car crashes

Explaining a major portion of empirical relationships in terms of Newtonian mechanics unambiguously identifies mass, as such, as the major causal factor in the difference in driver risk when vehicles of dissimilar mass crash into each other. The robustness of the relationship Eqn 4-3 together with its explanation from basic physical principles and a relationship between fatality risk and delta-*v* suggests that $R = \mu^{\lambda}$ is a *law*, the first of two *laws of two-car crashes*.

The relationship in Fig. 4-5 indicates that if two cars differ in mass by a factor of two, the driver in the lighter car is 12 times as likely to be killed as the driver in the heavier car ($2^{3.58} = 12.0$). Only about 1% of US two-car crashes involve a mass disparity as great as a factor of two.[15] Half of two-car crashes in the US involve cars with masses differing by more than 20%. For a 20% mass disparity, the driver in the lighter car is almost twice as likely to be killed as the driver in the heavier car ($1.20^{3.58} = 1.92$).

The above risk comparisons are essentially unaltered if the relationship derived by considering how fatality risk depends on delta-v, Eqn 4-9, is used instead of the empirical relationship between fatality risk and mass ratio. The Eqn 4-9 relationship can be used to infer results for cases for which direct empirical information is unavailable.

Application to crashes between cars and large trucks. It might seem intuitively reasonable to assume that if a car and a large truck crash head on, the mass of the car is so much less than the mass of the truck that the car's mass would have little influence on the car-driver's risk. However, risk increases so steeply with delta-v that this is not so.

Consider a large 1,800 kg car traveling at 50 km/h crashing head-on into a 12,000 kg truck traveling at 50 km/h in the opposite direction. The equations in Fig. 4-6 show that after the (assumed inelastic) crash, the clump comprising both vehicles travels at 37.0 km/h in the direction in which the truck was traveling. The unaided eye would likely perceive the truck continuing at its prior speed undiminished by the impact. However, the truck does have a delta-v of 13.0 km/h, which poses little risk to its driver. The large car has a delta-v of 87.0 km/h. Now repeat this scenario with a small 900 kg car replacing the 1,800 kg car. The lighter car has a delta-v of 93.0 km/h, which is 7% larger than the delta-v of the heavier car. Since fatality risk depends so steeply on delta-v this translates into a substantial 27% higher risk in the lighter car. Note that this calculation considers only how the mass of the car affects its delta-v. Even if the truck were of infinite mass, so that both cars had identical delta-v values of 100 km/h, risk would be lower in the heavier car because it would also be larger. Empirical evidence does indeed indicate that in car-truck crashes, risk to car drivers increases more steeply than due to delta-v effects alone.[7(p 103),16]

Application to crashes between cars and pedestrians. Even when cars strike pedestrians, the mass of the car influences the pedestrian's speed change. A 75 kg stationery pedestrian struck by an 1,800 kg car traveling at 50 km/h will experience a delta-v of 48.0 km/h. If the striking car is 900 kg, the delta-v becomes 46.2 km/h. Thus the pedestrian struck by the heavier car has a delta-v that is 4% larger. While Eqn 4-8 was derived from vehicle crashes, it seems plausible that it would give an order of magnitude estimate for pedestrian impacts also, thus implying that the pedestrian struck by the heavier car is, solely from considerations of Newtonian mechanics, about 15% more likely to die.

Effect of other crash and driver characteristics

The relative risk to each of the drivers involved in a right-side impact crash is plotted in Fig. 4-8. The car struck on the side has damage at principal impact points 2, 3 or 4 o'clock, the other has frontal damage at impact points 11, 12 or 1 o'clock. The fitted line,

$$R = \alpha \mu^{\lambda} ,$$ 4-10

is Eqn 4-3 with the parameter α added to reflect how the risk depends on an attribute in addition to mass ratio. When $\mu =1$, the parameter α measures how that attribute influences risk. The data in Fig. 4-8 imply that the driver in the right-side-impacted car is 4.53 times as likely to be killed as the driver in the front-impacted car when the masses of each are the same. For the risk to be equal in each car, $\mu = (1/4.53)^{(1/3.47)} = 0.647$. Thus, if the car struck on the side is 55% heavier than the other car, both drivers are at equal risk.

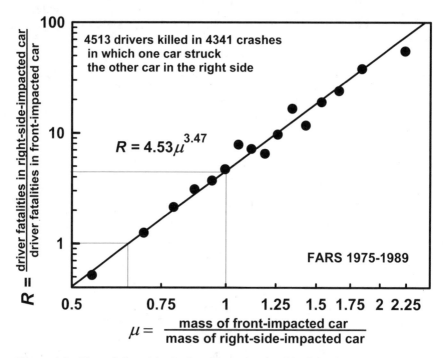

Figure 4-8. The relative risks to the drivers involved in right-side impact two-car crashes. The right-side-impacted car has principal impact damage at clock points 2, 3 or 4; the other car at 11, 12 or 1. FARS 1975-1989.[9]

This same approach was also applied to determine how driver characteristics affect driver fatality risk, thus providing approximate indications of a number of effects that will be determined more precisely by other methods in later chapters. The results are summarized in Table 4-2.

The first two rows show that a driver in a left-impacted car is 10.08 times as likely to be killed as the driver in the car with frontal damage, compared to the 4.53 times ratio for the impact on the right side. If we make the plausible

Table 4-2. Effect of various factors on fatality risk inferred using two-car crashes. The parameter α (Eqn 4-10) measures the risk in one car compared to that in the other when the masses of both cars are identical. The last row uses FARS 1975-1998.[12] All the others use FARS 1975-1989.[9]

	$\alpha \pm \Delta\alpha$	$\lambda \pm \Delta\lambda$	comment
right vs front impact	4.53 ± 0.18	3.47 ± 0.12	plotted in Fig. 4-8
left vs front impact	10.08 ± 0.51	3.24 ± 0.15	$10.08/4.53 = 2.2$
rear vs front impact	1.09 ± 0.09	3.71 ± 0.25	–
unbelted vs belted	2.40 ± 0.06	3.50 ± 0.08	compare with Chapter 11
BAC>0 vs untested or 0	1.94 ± 0.11	3.42 ± 0.07	compare with Chapter 6
female vs male	1.16 ± 0.02	3.57 ± 0.06	compare with Chapter 6
age > 40 vs ≤ 25	3.15 ± 0.07	4.01 ± 0.07	compare with Chapter 6
passenger present vs not	0.855 ± 0.023	3.36 ± 0.10	plotted in Fig. 4-11

assumption that risk in the frontally-impacted car does not depend on whether it strikes the left or right side of the other car, these results imply the risk to the driver in a side-impacted car is $10.08/4.53 = 2.2$ times as great when the impact is on the left compared to on the right. A study based on simple counts of fatalities finds the side-impacted driver to be 3.5 times as likely to die as the front-impacted driver in a right-side impact and 6.6 times as likely in a left-side impact for a 1.9 risk ratio.[17] These values, together with the 2.6 and 2.7 ratios on page 55, support the interpretation that risk increases steeply the closer the occupant is to the point of contact.

The other values in Table 4-2 show that not wearing a belt, consuming alcohol, being female, or being older are all risk-increasing factors. The simple comparison for belt wearing overestimates the risk-reducing effectiveness of belts because of biases discussed in Chapter 11. Otherwise the effects corroborate those determined with higher precision in later chapters. All the results refer to the risk of death <u>given</u> that the crash occurs – the drivers compared were each involved in the same two-car crash.

Other vehicles

Table 4-3 shows relative risks when vehicles of different types crash into each other, with all types of crashes included. Quantitative mass estimates are available in FARS only for cars. When light cars and large trucks crash into each other, the driver in the light car is 44 times as likely to die as the truck driver. When heavy cars and large trucks crash into each other, the driver in the heavy car is 22 times as likely to die as the truck driver. If one assumes that the car-size has little influence on the truck driver's risk, this implies that the driver of the light car is about twice as likely to die as a driver of the heavy car, in agreement with other findings.[16] When small cars and mopeds crash into each other, the moped driver is 139 times as likely to die as the car driver.

Table 4-3. Risk to driver in vehicle$_1$ relative to the risk in vehicle$_2$ when these two vehicles crash into each other. Based on Ref. 9 using FARS 1975-1989.

vehicle$_2$	*vehicle$_1$*		
	light car	*medium car*	*heavy car*
moped	1/139	1/202	1/205
motorcycle	1/42	1/85	1/153
light car	$\boxed{1}$	1/3.1	1/7.7
medium car	3.1	$\boxed{1}$	1/2.4
heavy car	7.7	2.4	$\boxed{1}$
pick-up	7.1	2.7	1.3
van	9.3	3.3	1.7
medium truck	34	18	12
heavy truck	44	29	22

definitions:	light car:	mass from 655 kg to 1,227 kg, mean 1,014 kg
	medium car:	mass from 1,227 kg to 1,599 kg, mean 1,428 kg
	heavy car:	mass from 1,599 kg to 2,606 kg, mean 1,833 kg
	medium truck:	Gross Vehicle Weight (GVW) > 10,000 pounds (4,536 kg), but not a heavy truck
	heavy truck:	GVW > 26,000 pounds (11,794 kg), or tractor-trailer combination, or with cargo trailer(s), or truck tractor pulling no trailer.

Interpreting risk ratios

The comparisons above are based on risk ratios – the risk to one driver divided by the risk to the other. While large risk ratios have been recognized for many decades, it is only more recently that the term *vehicle aggressivity* has been used. This term has been most commonly applied to crashes between cars and light trucks, especially sport utility vehicles (SUVs).[17,18] For frontal crashes a ratio of 5 car-driver fatalities for each SUV-driver fatality is reported.[17] The major portion of this difference arises because of a difference in average mass between the vehicles. When the mass factor is controlled, the car driver is about twice as likely to die as the SUV driver.[19]

The following hypothetical example illustrates that larger risk ratios do not necessarily indicate lower safety. Suppose we start with two identical *original* vehicles. If they crash head-on into each other, each driver has identical risk, say equal to 1 in arbitrary units. Now suppose that one vehicle is replaced by a *new* vehicle that reduces risk to its occupants by 15%, but also reduces risk to occupants of any vehicle into which it crashes by 5%. The redesigned vehicle thus reduces risk to all occupants in any two-vehicle crash in which it is involved.

If new and old vehicles crash into each other, the risk ratio is 0.95/0.85 = 1.12, compared to a former value of 1.0. The driver of the old vehicle is now 12% more likely to die than the driver of the new vehicle, whereas formerly they had equal risks. Although the risk ratio to the driver of the older vehicle increased by 12%, it clearly does not imply the new vehicle is "more aggressive."

Available data could not uncover the properties hypothesized for this new vehicle. All that would be observed is that drivers of vehicles into which it crashed were at higher relative risks than before the design change. The literature is replete with inappropriate interpretations of risk ratios as meaning more than changes in relative risk, which in this case, would suggest that the new vehicle is reducing net safety when it is in fact increasing it.

Separating causal roles of mass and size

While robust relationships have been shown between various factors and vehicle mass, this does not mean that mass is the causal factor. Vehicle size also affects safety, and heavier vehicles tend to be larger. Size and mass both affect safety. One wants to separate the causal roles, especially as this could suggest vehicle design changes to improve safety.

The relationship between car size and car mass

Imagine a hypothetical world in which all cars are made from material of the same density. If cars were of identical shape, differing only by a scale factor, then mass would be proportional to any linear dimension to the power three. However, regardless of their size, cars must be of sufficient height to accommodate seated humans. If all cars had the same height, so that only length and breadth varied, then mass would be proportional to length (or breadth) to the power two.   Real cars are likely to be intermediate between these two hypothetical cases, suggesting a relationship between mass and a linear dimension of the form

$$m = (\alpha w)^{\beta} \qquad\qquad 4\text{-}11$$

where m is the mass of the car and w is a linear dimension (other than height) and α and β are constants, with β expected to be between 2 and 3.

Figure 4-9 shows mass versus wheelbase (the distance between the front and rear wheels) for each of the 4,081 unique pairs of wheelbase and mass combinations for cars of all model years coded in 2001 FARS. Cars associated with more than one mass (because they are sold with choices of different engines, etc.) contribute more than one data point. However, the number of unique wheelbase-mass pairs reflects mainly the enormous variety of cars. Because mass is available only for cars of model year 1966 and later, 115 earlier models going back to model year 1930 are not included in Fig. 4-9. The fit to Eqn 4-11 gives

$$m = (7.10w)^{2.45} \qquad\qquad 4\text{-}12$$

thus validating our intuitive understanding that β should be between 2 and 3.

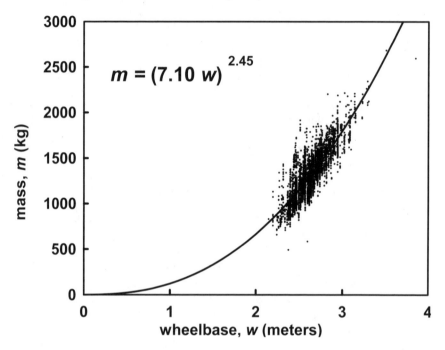

Figure 4-9. Relationship between car size (as measured by wheelbase) and car mass, based on 4,081 unique wheelbase-mass pairs coded in FARS 2001.

The value of β was investigated as a function of model year, with little indication of any obvious dependency. A lower value, $\beta = 1.9 \pm 0.2$, is reported for the relationship between total car length and mass for 12 European car models.[20] A value of $\beta=2$ is consistent with constant density and car height not increasing with increasing length. The larger value in Fig. 4-5 is consistent with height or density increasing with car mass.

Additional data on the close relationship between measures of size and weight are indicated by correlation coefficients between curb weight and wheelbase, curb weight and trackwidth (the distance between the left and right wheels), and wheelbase and trackwidth of 0.93, 0.92 and 0.91.[21] Any observed empirical relationship between any safety measure and one of these quantities is going to provide a similarly good relationship with any of the others. In multivariate analyses, simply as a result of Eqn 4-12, coefficients associated with length will be about 2.45 times as large as those associated with mass. Early suggestions that size is a more important causal factor than mass might have arisen simply because of larger regression coefficients being found for size than for mass.[3]

Second law of two-car crashes – crashes between cars of same mass

When cars of the same mass crash into each other, Eqn 4-3 provides no useful information. However, Fig. 4-10 shows that five sets of data[22,23] and a calculated relationship[24] support that the relative driver risk, R_{MM}, when two cars of the same mass, M, crash into each other is given by

$$R_{MM} = \frac{k}{M} \qquad\qquad 4\text{-}13$$

where k is a constant.[12] Although the relationship is in terms of mass, it is size that is the causal factor. Mass is irrelevant to the Newtonian mechanics of two cars of the same mass crashing into each other. Further evidence that, when cars of similar mass crash into each other, driver fatality risk is proportional to the common mass is provided by regression relationships for 1991-1999 model-year cars.[7(p 103)] Reducing the masses of cars weighing less that 2,950 pounds (average 2,612 pounds) by 100 pounds, or a 3.8% decrease, was associated with a 4.9% increase in fatality risk. The corresponding result for cars weighing 2,950 pounds or more (average 3,402 pounds), or a 2.9% decrease, was associated with a 3.2% increase in fatality risk. The Eqn 4-13 relationship can be considered a *second law of two-car crashes*.

Mass as a separate causal factor

Relationships so far introduced do not address how adding mass to an existing car affects risk. Nor do they answer the question, "Am I safer if I put bricks in my trunk?" Data sets rarely contain information on cargo, or on actual mass during crashes. All that is generally coded is a curb mass that is identical for all cars of the same make, model, and engine.

However, although FARS has no information on cargo, it does have information on the presence of passengers. By assuming that cars carrying a passenger were heavier by the mass of the passenger, the causal role of mass was estimated using head-on crashes between pairs of cars coded in 1975-1998 FARS.[12] One car contained only a driver, while the other contained a driver and a right-front passenger. The effect of the passenger on driver fatality risk is shown in Fig. 4-11 (and listed also as the last entry in Table 4-2). The result is that when the curb masses of their cars are equal, then

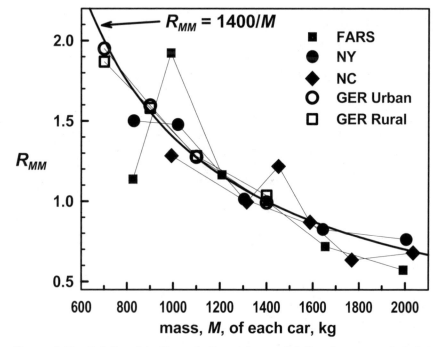

Figure 4-10. Relative risk, R_{MM}, of driver injury or fatality when cars of similar mass crash head-on into each other versus M, the mass of each car.[12]   In all cases the data are scaled so that $R_{MM} = 1$ for $M=1,400$ kg. The relationship $R_{MM} = k/M$ is the second of the two *laws for two-car crashes*.

FARS	fatalities in US[22]
NC	injuries in North Carolina[22]
NY	injuries in New York State[22]
GER Urban	injuries on roads in built-up areas in Germany[23]
GER Rural	injuries on rural roads in Germany[23]
Analytical curve	computed from structural considerations, etc.[24]

$$R = \frac{\text{risk to driver accompanied by passenger}}{\text{risk to driver traveling alone}} = 0.855 \pm 0.023 . \quad 4\text{-}14$$

That is, the accompanied driver is $(14.5 \pm 2.3)\%$ less likely to die than the lone driver solely due to mass difference resulting from the passenger's presence. This result is a risk ratio. It therefore does not indicate the extent to which it reflects reduced risk to the accompanied driver and increased risk to the lone driver. To answer this requires a model.

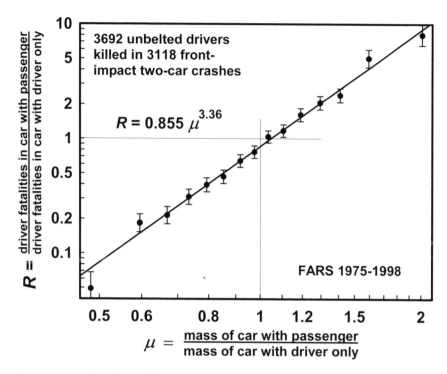

Figure 4-11. How the additional mass of a passenger affects the probability that a driver is killed.[12] FARS 1975-1998.

Model separating causal roles of mass and size

The previous two *laws of two-car crashes*, Eqns 4-3 and 4-13, can be combined to give

$$r_{1,2} = k \times \frac{1}{m_1 + m_2} \times \left(\frac{m_2}{m_1}\right)^t \qquad 4\text{-}15$$

$$\left[\begin{array}{c}\text{net}\\\text{effect}\end{array}\right] = \left[\begin{array}{c}\text{intrinsic}\\\text{size}\end{array}\right] \times \left[\begin{array}{c}\text{intrinsic}\\\text{mass}\end{array}\right]$$

where $r_{1,2}$ is the risk to the driver of car$_1$ when it crashes into car$_2$, assuming car$_1$ and car$_2$ have masses m_1 and m_2 and sizes equal to those of average cars of masses m_1 and m_2, respectively.[12] The parameter t has the value = $\lambda/2 = 1.79$ (where λ is from Eqn 4-3). The masses in the intrinsic size term should be interpreted to mean sizes corresponding to cars with the indicated masses.

   If cars of unequal mass crash into each other, the ratio of the risks to the drivers, $r_{1,2}/r_{2,1}$, is computed from Eqn 4-15 as

$$\frac{r_{1,2}}{r_{2,1}} = \frac{m_2 + m_1}{m_1 + m_2} \times \left(\frac{m_2}{m_1}\right)^t \times \left(\frac{m_1}{m_2}\right)^{1/t} = \mu^{2t} = \mu^\lambda \qquad 4\text{-}16$$

thus showing that Eqn 4-15 contains the *first law*, Eqn 4-3.

If the cars are of the same mass M, Eqn 4-15 computes the risk in each as k/M, the same as the *second law* relationship in Eqn 4-13. Thus Eqn 4-15 contains both *laws of two-car crashes.*

Computed versus observed effect of adding a passenger. If two 1,400 kg cars crash into each other, Eqn 4-15 shows each driver has identical risk $r_{1,2} = r_{2,1} = 1$ (taking $k = 2,800$ kg). This is the base case in Table 4-4, in which the mass of car$_2$ remains fixed at 1,400 kg. If the mass of car$_1$ is increased to 1,475 kg by adding 75 kg cargo, the risk to its driver is reduced to $(1,400/1,475) = 0.911$ but the risk to the driver in car$_2$ is increased to $(1,475/1,400) = 1.098$. Thus Eqn 4-15, which was derived only from the two laws, predicts that adding 75 kg leads to a value of $R = 0.911/1.098 = 0.830$. The closeness of this to the empirically observed $R = 0.855$ (Fig. 4-11) supports the validity of Eqn 4-15.

Table 4-4. Estimates from Eqn 4-15 of changes in risk when changes are made to an initial 1,400 kg car crashing head-on into another 1,400 kg car.

($m_2 = 1,400$ kg) car$_1$ description	driver fatality risks and % change from base case			$R = r_{1,2}/r_{2,1}$
	$r_{1,2}$	$r_{2,1}$	r_T	
add cargo to 1,400 kg car				
1,400 kg car (base case)	1 –	1 –	2 –	1 –
1,400 kg car with 75 kg cargo added	0.911 -8.9%	1.098 9.8%	2.009 0.4%	0.830 -17.0%
1,400 kg car with passenger (empirical result)	na	na	na	0.855 -14.5%
adjust 75 kg cargo case to make $R = 0.855$	0.925 -7.5%	1.081 8.1%	2.006 0.3%	0.855 -14.5%
replace by a different car				
1,475 kg car	0.887 -11.3%	1.069 6.9%	1.956 -2.2%	0.830 -17.0%
1,670 kg car (largest reduction in total risk)	0.665 -33.5%	1.251 25.1%	1.916 -4.2%	0.532 -46.8%
2,015 kg car (crossover case – $m_1 > 2,015$ kg increases total risk)	0.427 -57.3%	1.573 57.3%	2.000 0.0%	0.272 -72.8%

If the risks to the individual drivers are rescaled so that the risk ratio matches the empirically determined value, we conclude that the addition of a passenger reduces the risk to the accompanied driver by 7.5%, but increases the lone driver's risk by 8.1%. A small net risk increase of 0.3% averaged over both drivers results.

The risk reduction due to the presence of a passenger or other cargo is expected to apply also to single-car frontal crashes into objects that deform in ways not too differently from cars. The addition of cargo increases damage to the struck object, but with no corresponding increase in human harm. When the larger risk reduction from some single-car crashes is combined with the small net increase in two-car crashes, adding mass in the form of passengers reduces total driver deaths.

Different effect of replacing a car by a heavier one. If, instead of adding 75 kg of cargo, car_1 is replaced by a different car that is 75 kg heavier and correspondingly larger, the driver of the 1,475 kg car will enjoy an 11.3% reduction in risk, but will increase the risk to the other driver by 6.9%. The net effect is a 2.2% net risk reduction averaged over both drivers. The maximum net reduction of 4.2% is produced when car_1 has $m_1 = 1,670$ kg. As m_1 exceeds this value, the reduction in net risk declines.

When $m_1 = 2,015$ kg there is no change in net risk. Replacing an $m_1 = 2,015$ kg car by one even heavier leads to a net increase in risk in crashes with 1,400 kg cars. This can be understood in terms of the risk in the heavier car becoming so small that further proportionate reductions are of little consequence, while even small proportionate increases in the large risk in the smaller car add to total risk. Various crossover effects of this type have been observed – safety increases as vehicle mass increases, but not indefinitely.[7]

Replacing a 1,400 kg car with a heavier one will reduce total risk in crashes with 1,400 kg cars unless the replacement is more than 2,015 kg. Since only about 3% of cars in FARS are heavier than 2,015 kg, this hypothetical replacement would almost always reduce total risk. In general, replacing a car of any weight with a heavier car will in the vast majority of cases reduce total population risk. Eqn 4-15 always computes a net risk reduction when the mass of the lighter car is increased to become closer to the mass of the heavier car.

Equation expressing risks as functions of size and mass of both cars

As the first term in Eqn 4-15 relates to the car size, it is desirable that it should be expressed directly in terms of a linear dimension of the cars of indicated mass. While Eqn 4-12 relates mass to wheelbase, the same relationship will apply, to within a scaling constant, if we assume that vehicle length is proportional to wheelbase. It is convenient to define a risk of unity for a driver in a *typical* 1,400 kg car of length 4.8 m crashing into an identical *typical* car. This leads to

$$r_{1,2} = c \times \frac{1}{L_1^{2.45} + L_2^{2.45}} \times \left(\frac{m_2}{m_1}\right)^t \qquad \text{4-17}$$

$$\begin{bmatrix} \text{net} \\ \text{effect} \end{bmatrix} = \begin{bmatrix} \text{intrinsic} \\ \text{size} \end{bmatrix} \times \begin{bmatrix} \text{intrinsic} \\ \text{mass} \end{bmatrix}$$

where L_1 and L_2 are the lengths of car$_1$ and car$_2$ (meters)

m_1 and m_2 are the masses of car$_1$ and car$_2$ (kilograms)

$t = 1.79$

$c = 2 \times 4.8^{2.45}$ so that $r_{1,2} = r_{2,1} = 1$ when $L_1 = L_2 = 4.8$ meters and $m_1 = m_2 = 1{,}400$ kg.

With the constant c specified, the equation measures **absolute risks**.

Making a car lighter and safer

The generality of Eqn 4-17 enables us to explore what happens to safety as characteristics of a car are changed.[25] For case 1 in Table 4-5, car$_1$ and car$_2$ are both *typical* cars with length 4.8 m and mass 1,400 kg. This is the case that defines the unit of risk – so each driver has an absolute risk of one unit. In the other cases car$_2$ remains unchanged but the properties of car$_1$ vary. For case 2, m_1 is increased to 1,475 kg without changing its size, thereby reproducing the same result as in Table 4-4. In case 3, the mass is unchanged but the length is increased by 20 cm. This reduces the risk to both drivers by 5%.

Table 4-5. Results for two-car crashes derived from Eqn 4-17. In case 1 the first car has the characteristics of a *typical* car, defined as m_1 = 1,400 kilograms and L_1 = 4.8 meters. In the other cases the characteristics of the first car are varied, but the second car is always a *typical* car.

case number	car$_1$ characteristics		driver fatality risks and % change from case #1		
	L_1, meters	m_1, kilograms	$r_{1,2}$	$r_{2,1}$	r_T
1	4.8	1,400	1 —	1 —	2 —
2	4.8	1,475	0.911 -8.9%	1.098 +9.8%	2.009 +0.4%
3	5.0	1,400	0.950 -5.0%	0.950 -5.0%	1.900 -5.0%
4	4.8	1,362	1.050 +5.0%	0.952 -4.8%	2.002 +0.1
5	5.0	1,362	0.998 -0.2%	0.904 -9.6%	1.902 -4.9%

In case 4 the mass of the first car has been reduced, thus increasing risk to its driver, and increasing overall risk. However, if this is accompanied by a 20 cm length increase (case 5), the driver in the lighter, larger car is now at reduced risk, while the other involved driver is at substantially reduced risk, for an overall net risk reduction. This is just one example of a combination of mass reductions and length increases that reduce risks to all. Through Eqn 4-17 different combinations of weight reductions and size increases that lead to safety improvements for all can be estimated. Additional examples are given in Ref. 25. Making vehicles lighter and larger requires use of more expensive lightweight materials. However, note that airbags cost US consumers $6.35 billion in 2003 (Table 12-6, p. 320), and making vehicles larger provides passive protection, while airbags do not (Chapters 12, 15).

Single-vehicle crashes

Single-vehicle crashes, which account for half of occupant fatalities, are conceptually simpler than multiple-vehicle crashes because outcome depends on the properties of only one vehicle. Other vehicles in the fleet are irrelevant. This same simplicity makes unavailable many of the methods used to study two-vehicle crashes, resulting in far less substantial knowledge about single-vehicle crashes.

Information is available from FARS on occupants killed in different types of vehicles in single-vehicle crashes. However, the same source provides no information for crashes in which no one is killed. In order to determine the crashworthiness in single-vehicle crashes of a set of vehicles, we need to know the number of people killed in the vehicles divided by the number of crashes in which the vehicles were involved. It turns out to be very difficult to discover how many vehicles are involved in single-vehicle crashes that do not produce serious injury or death.

There is a legal requirement to report a crash only when damage exceeds a specified monetary amount. Yet the cost of damage, and whether the vehicle can be driven after the crash, are all related to vehicle properties. For example, a heavier vehicle may uproot a tree and suffer little damage, whereas a lighter vehicle might be more damaged if the tree remains standing. If a vehicle can still be driven after a single-vehicle crash, the driver may not wish to inform the police, even if legally obliged to do so. Thus whether or not identical crashes are reported depends on vehicle factors, but in ways that elude empirical examination.

Measures such as fatalities per police-reported crash, fatalities per injury, severe injuries per minor injury, injuries per police-reported crash are all ratios of crash outcomes. They are therefore subject to the same pitfalls mentioned in *Interpreting risk ratios* (p. 76). The absence of a dependence on mass in any such ratio does not mean that mass does not affect risk, but rather that mass has the same proportionate effect on the risks in the numerator and denominator.

The much-used measure, fatalities per million registered vehicles has the problems that different vehicles attract drivers with different use patterns and crash risks (Figs 4-1 through 4-4).

Pedestrian fatality exposure approach

Ideally, we would like to know the number of driver deaths from, say, impacts with trees divided by the number of impacts with trees. The FARS data provide information on drivers killed in vehicles striking trees, but little information on non-fatal tree impacts. However, if the vehicle strikes a pedestrian, this event is coded in FARS if the pedestrian is killed. Therefore, the ratio of the number of driver deaths to the number of pedestrian deaths for a set of vehicles is a surrogate for the number of driver deaths per tree impact, and accordingly measures how driver risk depends on the physical properties of the vehicle. This ratio plotted versus vehicle mass will therefore estimate how driver fatality risk depends on vehicle mass, subject to the additional assumption that the probability of pedestrian death is independent of vehicle mass. This is approximately so because even the lightest vehicle is so much heavier than the heaviest pedestrian (but see p. 73).

The finding that the ratio of driver deaths to pedestrian deaths is relatively independent of driver age supports the interpretation that the ratio reflects mainly the physical properties of vehicles.[16,26(p 73)] Suppose two types of vehicles with equal crashworthiness are driven so that they differ by a factor of two in the number of crashes per year. The vehicles with the higher number of crashes would have twice as many driver fatalities from impacts with trees, but would also kill twice as many pedestrians, so that both vehicle types would have equal values of the ratio of driver to pedestrian fatalities.

Figure 4-12, derived from 1975-1983 FARS data,[26(p 74)] shows the number of driver deaths per pedestrian death versus car mass, which is interpreted to measure how driver fatality risk depends on mass. Fig. 4-12 shows a relatively noise-free relationship, with the data fitting well

$$R = \alpha \times \exp(\beta m) \qquad\qquad 4\text{-}18$$

where α is a scaling factor and β indicates the fractional change in risk per linear change in mass.

Systematic relationships between risk and vehicle mass are expected on physical grounds. Nearly all crashes are into objects that will to some extent move, bend, uproot, break, or distort, so that increased mass of the vehicle will systematically reduce the deceleration forces experienced within the vehicle. More damage being sustained by the struck object lowers risk to the vehicle occupants. While mass should not have a direct influence on rollover risk, vehicle size, which is correlated strongly with mass (Fig. 4-9, p. 78), does (as does, of course, the height of the center of gravity). Wider vehicles offer more resistance to rollover, and longer vehicles have higher lateral stability. Thus

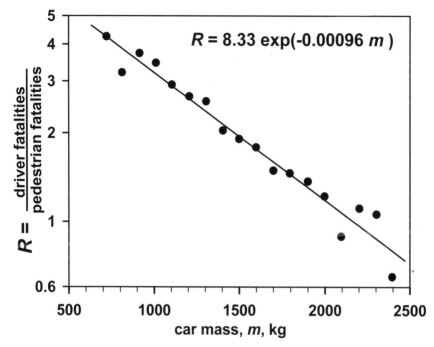

$$R = 8.33 \exp(-0.00096\ m)$$

Figure 4-12. The number of driver deaths in single-car crashes in cars with masses in a narrow range divided by the number of pedestrians killed in crashes involving cars in the same mass range. 1975-1983 FARS.[26(p 74)]

physical reasoning and the empirical data in Fig. 4-12 show that single-car fatality risk decreases systematically with increasing mass. Non-systematic behavior of measures based on driver fatalities per million vehicles likely reflects driver use and behavior effects.

It seems that the best way to estimate how single-vehicle (and rollover) fatality risk depend on mass is to assume that risk is a simple continuous function of mass, such as the functional form in Eqn 4-18. The slope parameter, β, is determined by the best fit to whatever data are available. While measures such as driver deaths per million registered vehicles have inadequacies, they are the best available data to determine the parameter. The value $\beta = -0.00096$ in Fig. 4-12 indicates a 9.6% decrease in single-vehicle fatality risk for an additional 100 kg of vehicle mass. This is equivalent to a 4.5% increase in fatality risk for a 100 pound reduction in vehicle mass, a measure we use because it has appeared in the literature.[7] This is the first case in Table 4-6.

The results from Fig. 4-2 and Fig. 4-3 are from least-squares fits (poor fits) to the four points for each case. The estimate from Fig. 4-12 is expected to be high because it is based on assuming that pedestrian fatality risk does not increase with increasing mass of the striking vehicle, when in fact Newtonian mechanics

Table 4-6.   The percent, P, increase in fatality risk for a 100 pound reduction in vehicle mass in single-vehicle crashes.   The cases without figure references are from Ref. 7 (p. 107 for cars, p. 159 for light trucks).

vehicles	crash type	measure	P
all cars (Fig. 4-12)	all single vehicle	driver per pedestrian deaths	4.5%
4-dr cars (Fig. 4-3)	"	driver deaths per million cars	3.7%
2-dr cars (Fig. 4-3)	"	"	3.1%
4-dr cars (Fig. 4-2)	rollover	"	5.2%
2-dr cars (Fig. 4-2)	"	"	4.1%
cars <2,950 lb	fixed object	fatal crashes per billion miles	3.2%
"	rollover	"	5.1%
cars >2,950 lb	fixed object	"	1.7%
"	rollover	"	4.7%
lt trucks < 3,870 lb	fixed object	"	4.0%
"	rollover	"	3.2%
lt trucks ≥ 3,870 lb	fixed object	"	3.1%
"	rollover	"	2.6%

indicates it does slightly (p. 74). Further indication that the risk of death to pedestrians increases somewhat with vehicle mass is provided by various results in Ref. 7. While there is substantial quantitative variation among the results in Table 4-6, all values of P are positive. This leaves little doubt that as the mass of cars or light trucks is reduced, fatality rates increase for single-vehicle crashes overall, and for the single-vehicle crash subcategories of rollover and crashes into fixed objects.

Corporate Average Fuel Economy (CAFE)

In response to the 1973 oil crisis, the US Congress passed the Energy Policy and Conservation Act of 1975, with the goal of reducing fuel use as a means of lessening US dependence on imported oil. The act established the Corporate Average Fuel Economy (CAFE) program, which required each vehicle manufacturer to meet a sales-weighted average fuel use standard for its passenger car and light-duty truck fleets sold in the US. Since 1996 the standards have been 27.5 miles per gallon for passenger cars and 20.7 mpg for light trucks (minivans, pickups, and sport utility vehicles).

A vehicle's fuel use is intrinsically related to its mass. The energy required to accelerate a vehicle from rest to a given speed is proportional to the mass of the vehicle. When in motion, rolling resistance forces are proportional to vehicle weight, which is proportional to mass. Thus the energy required to move a vehicle is linked to its mass through fundamental physical laws. Other factors being equal, making a vehicle lighter reduces its fuel use and increases injury risk to its occupants.

The influence of CAFE was more complex than merely leading to lighter cars and trucks. Indeed, the unintended consequences eclipse the intended. In order to meet CAFE requirements manufacturers had to sell a mix of vehicles different from the mix their customers wanted. This was achieved by, in effect, subsidizing small cars to increase their sales while adding a premium to the cost of large cars to discourage their purchase. Consumers who wanted larger vehicles but were reluctant to pay this premium found attractive alternatives in personal transportation vehicles classified as light trucks, which were subject to less stringent CAFE standards. Thus CAFE contributed to a major change in the types of vehicles on US roads.

Effect of CAFE on safety

From the time it was introduced, the effect of CAFE on safety was controversial. CAFE proponents seemed unwilling to accept that a policy they believed to be good for energy conservation and the environment could possibly cause additional deaths. They claimed that all cars becoming lighter would not increase fatalities because the driver in a two-car crash would benefit by being struck by a similarly lighter car. Such a claim flies in the face of two clear effects. First, when cars of the same mass crash into each other, risk increases as the common mass decreases (Fig. 4-10, p. 80), so that a fleet of identical lighter cars produces more two-car crash fatalities than a fleet of identical heavier cars. Second, about half of the car occupants killed are killed in single-car crashes in which risk increases with decreasing car mass. Drivers of lighter cars crashing into large trucks are at higher risk than drivers of heavier cars crashing into large trucks (p. 73 and Table 4-3, p. 76). Large trucks cannot be made much lighter as cargo is a major portion of their mass. There can be no doubt that policies that lead to a fleet of cars being replaced by a fleet of lighter cars must necessarily increase fatalities, because all resulting safety changes are in the same direction.

The widespread replacement of cars by light trucks complicates the safety computation. However, there is no evidence that this made the fleet safer by an amount that could negate the safety decreases from the lighter cars. Indeed, there is much opinion that these substitutions further reduced safety because of the higher rollover rates for SUVs, and suggestions that two-vehicle risks were increased by the presence of SUVs. The conclusion is inescapable that CAFE increased fatalities. A National Academies of Sciences report concluded "the downweighting and downsizing that occurred in the late 1970s and early 1980s, some of which was due to CAFE standards, probably resulted in an additional 1,300 to 2,600 traffic fatalities in 1993."[27(p ES-4)]

The government body responsible for the CAFE program is the National Highway Traffic Safety Administration. Thus, the agency charged with reducing traffic deaths administers and supports policies that increase traffic deaths.

Effect of CAFE on fuel use

While there is no doubt that CAFE increased fatalities, its effect on fuel use is far less clear. CAFE unquestionably led to vehicles with higher fuel economy, meaning that a vehicle could travel further using the same amount of fuel. However, national fuel use depends on the numbers and types of vehicles in use and on how far they are driven, and not just on fuel economy.

When a vehicle buyer chooses a light truck rather than a large car, this choice increases the average fuel economy of the car fleet, and also increases the average fuel economy of the truck fleet. Although the choice increases the fuel economy of both fleets, it nonetheless reduces the average fuel economy of all vehicles. Another effect of CAFE is that it reduces travel costs per mile for most drivers. Reducing the cost of travel increases the amount of travel, with consequent increases in fatalities, and fuel use increases that partially offset any reductions from higher fuel economy.

Figure 4-13 shows the average distance traveled per vehicle per year since data were available.[28,29] The rate remained remarkably constant between 1947 and 1977, never varying outside the range 9,315 to 10,906 miles per vehicle per year. In the period after CAFE went into effect in 1978, the average increased substantially. As with all regulations that affect new vehicles, it takes about a decade before the vast majority of vehicles on the roads include the changes. This does not, of course, suggest that CAFE caused the increase in travel per vehicle that coincided with it. But it does show clearly the failure of a national policy aimed at reducing fuel for transportation, which had as its centerpiece CAFE regulations.[27]

Traveling 12,670 miles (the average for 2000) in a car meeting the CAFE standard of 27.5 miles per gallon requires 461 gallons of gasoline costing $691 at the typical cost in 2000 of $1.50 per gallon. The average annual cost of auto insurance in 2000 was $786.[30] American families spend about three times as much on eating out as on transportation fuel. One of the effects of CAFE was to render fuel cost so inconsequential that it played no more than a minor role in vehicle or travel choices. Forcing consumers to drive higher fuel economy vehicles than they would have chosen reduced their incentives to carpool, use public transportation, more carefully plan shopping trips, live closer to work, etc.

While there may be some disagreement on the effect of CAFE on fuel use, there is no disagreement among economists that increasing the cost of a commodity reduces its consumption. Figure 4-13 shows clear drops in the distance traveled per vehicle related to increases in the cost and availability of fuel following the first and second oil embargoes of 1973 and 1979. An increase in the tax on fuel is guaranteed to reduce fuel use. This could be applied in ways that would avoid economic disruption,[31] and, depending on the freely made spending choices of individuals, might increase or decrease safety.

The main reason one sees far more SUVs (and other large personal transportation vehicles) in the US than in Europe is not because Europeans do

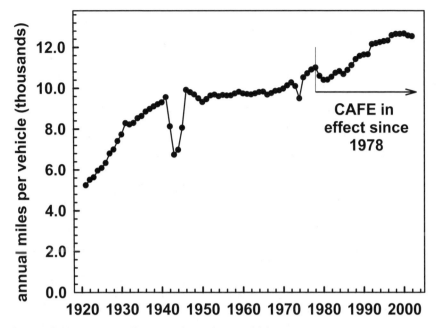

Figure 4-13. Average distance of travel per vehicle per year.

not like SUVs, but because European fuel costs discourage the selection of such vehicles. US consumers make rational choices based on US fuel costs. The US government used CAFE regulations as an excuse to avoid addressing policies that could really reduce oil imports. The absence of an effective policy precipitated momentous consequences for the nation and the world.

There is a taboo in US politics against even mentioning increases in the federal tax on fuel. The US approach to reducing foreign oil consumption is like a 300-pound patient asking a doctor how to lose weight, but insisting that the answer must not mention eating or exercise. If the one and only policy that can really affect energy consumption is off limits, then it would be preferable to formalize the decision to do nothing rather than enact policies which have only one clear effect – to increase fatalities.

Total safety, vehicle type, vehicle mass

The shift from cars to light trucks was not due entirely to CAFE – many consumers like such vehicles, especially SUVs. Quantifying how changes in the types and sizes of vehicles affect net safety is a problem of high complexity. Even if the fleet consisted only of cars, all driven identical distances in identical ways by identical drivers, the task of estimating overall effects from knowledge of outcomes for single- and multiple-vehicle crashes would not be trivial. The mix of single- and multiple-vehicle crashes is affected by rollover risk, which is related to car mass, thus making the mix of single-vehicle to multiple-vehicle crashes dependent on car mass. Cars of different masses are used in different ways, are driven differently, and attract different types of drivers. Even the same driver pursuing the same strategy may unknowingly drive cars of different mass in different ways (Fig. 8-1, p. 180).

When other vehicles are included, complexity and uncertainty increase. There is no analytical model of SUVs crashing into SUVs comparable to Eqn 4-17. What is more critical, there is no model of outcomes when cars and light trucks crash into each other. Simple risk ratios indicate that the car driver is 5 times as likely to die as the SUV driver when an SUV and a car crash into each other.[17] When the comparison is restricted to vehicles of equal mass, the car driver is about twice as likely to die as the SUV driver.[19] However, these are risk ratios and accordingly do not, by themselves, prove that a car-SUV crash poses more risk than a car-car crash. There are structural considerations that indicate that this is likely, but no quantification from field data.

The SUV, with a higher center of gravity than a car, offers less resistance to rollover (Fig. 3-12, p. 50). However, belt wearing in fatal rollover crashes is even lower for drivers of light trucks than for drivers of cars. This indicates higher risk-taking and law-violation by drivers of light-trucks, which would increase the overall fatality rates for these vehicles without regard to the properties of the vehicles.

Whether widespread replacement of cars by SUVs has increased or decreased the total number of US fatalities is difficult to answer. Cars and light trucks are driven different distances in different places by drivers with different characteristics. By far the most thorough study on this subject incorporated a host of confounding factors, including the age and gender of drivers of the different vehicle types, urban versus rural use, different speed limits, and night versus day.[7] The distances driven by different vehicles were estimated from odometer readings in the NASS file (light trucks travel further than cars), and also by additional methods. The report, with over 300 pages, contains a wealth of information and insights relevant to many aspects of traffic safety. To compliment such completeness the author comments:

> *The analysis is not a "controlled experiment" but a cross-sectional look at the actual fatality rates of MY 1991-99 vehicles, from the heaviest to the lightest. Since most people are free to pick whatever car or light truck or van they wish (limited only by their budget constraints), owner characteristics and vehicle use patterns can and do vary by vehicle weight and type. This study tries, when possible, to quantify and adjust for characteristics such as age/gender or urban/rural, and at least to give an assessment of uncertainty associated with the less tangible characteristics such as "driver quality." But, ultimately, we can never be sure that a 30-year-old*

male operating a large LTV on an urban road at 2:00 p.m. in a Western State drives the same way as a 30-year-old male operating a smaller LTV/light car/heavy car on an urban road at 2:00 p.m. in a Western State. We can gauge the uncertainty in the results, but unlike some controlled experiments, there is not necessarily a single, "correct" way to estimate it.[7(p 13)]

The main findings were that decreasing the masses of cars or masses of the lighter categories of light trucks led to net increases in fatalities (fatalities to occupants of the vehicle plus fatalities to other road users). No clear difference in net fatalities resulted from decreasing the masses of the heaviest light trucks. Pick-up trucks and SUVs, had, on the average, higher fatality rates than MY 1996-99 passenger cars or minivans of comparable weight.

The finding that pick-up trucks and SUVs had higher fatality rates than cars of the same weight does not necessarily mean that a person switching from a car to an SUV would increase net fatality risk. A car would typically be replaced by an SUV of greater weight.

Another study including considerable detail confirms that driver factors, vehicle mass, and whether the vehicle is a car or a light truck have a clear influence on risk.[32] Various studies have made claims that SUVs have produced dramatic increases in total deaths. Such studies have not taken into account, as is done in Ref. 7, the many factors that can influence results by large amounts. For example, the simple measure of deaths per million registered vehicles is elevated for light trucks because they are driven further, and in higher speed rural driving, than cars.

Does increase in number of SUVs increase risks to car drivers?

One common claim is that SUVs sharply increase total fatalities by increasing fatalities in the cars into which they crash. Such a possibility is inconsistent with Fig. 4-14. The number of car drivers killed in single-car crashes does not depend on other vehicles. From 1994 to 2002 the number of cars on US roads remained relatively constant while the total light truck population increased by more than 30%.[33,34] If the increase in SUVs led to large increases in fatality risk to car drivers from car-SUV crashes, the number of car drivers killed in two-vehicle crashes would increase relative to the number killed in single-car crashes, leading to an increasing trend in the percent of all fatally injured car drivers who were killed in two-vehicle crashes. No such trend occurred. Indeed, if there is a trend, it is in the opposite direction. The most plausible interpretation of the data in Fig. 4-14 is that SUVs posed about as high a risk to car drivers as did the generally large cars they replaced. In any event, the data are inconsistent with a large national fatality increase from SUVs killing large numbers of car drivers who would not have been killed if the SUV's had been cars.

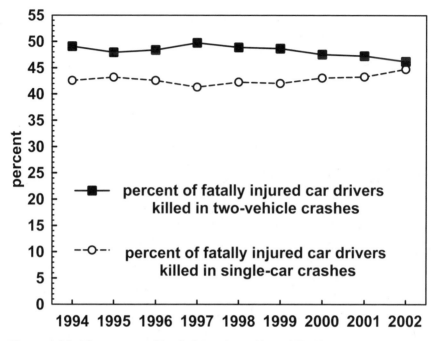

Figure 4-14. The percent of fatally injured car drivers killed in single-car crashes and in two-vehicle crashes in which the other vehicle is of any type. The percents do not total to 100% because about 9% of car drivers were killed in crashes involving three or more vehicles. FARS.

What is effect of changing composition of fleet?

Unfortunately, complexity precludes a definitive conclusion. Overall, the evidence suggests that the widespread substitution of cars by SUVs may have increased net fatalities, but not by much. However, the uncertainties are so great that the effect could be in the opposite direction. For example, the SUV's may have siphoned off riskier drivers, thus increasing SUVs fatality rates and lowering car fatality rates.

The question of how the composition of the fleet affects safety is almost exclusively a question of changes in risk, given that crashes occur. In the aggregate, it is difficult to conclude even the direction of the effect. However, one can be confident that it is not one of the largest factors influencing safety. We noted previously that CAFE increased US fatalities by 1,300 to 2,600 in 1993, say about 2,000 per year. While of great importance, eliminating such an effect would reduce 2002 fatalities from 42,815 to 40,815. Important though this is, we show in Chapters 13 and 15 much larger and more clearly established effects due to non-vehicle factors.

Summary and conclusions

Rates such as driver deaths per million vehicles do not measure how vehicle factors affect safety because different types of vehicles have different uses and attract different types of drivers.   Data show that two-door cars have systematically higher rates than four-door cars. This reflects different use and driving behavior by drivers who choose two-door and four-door cars, not the effect of doors on crashworthiness.

For two-vehicle crashes, the relative risk to each driver does not depend on driver behavior, because each driver is involved in the <u>same</u> crash. Data and physical theory consistently show that for two-car crashes, driver fatality risk in the lighter car divided by risk in the heavier car depends strongly on the ratio of the masses of the cars. If one car is twice as heavy as the other, the driver in the lighter car is 12 times as likely to die as the driver in the heavier car. If the cars have the same mass, the greater that mass, the lower the risk. This is not caused by the mass, as such, but by size, because heavier cars are also larger.

Analyses of two-car crashes led to an equation expressing a driver's fatality risk in terms of four quantities, namely, the mass and length of the driver's car and the mass and length of the other car. The equation separates causal effects of mass and size, and so can estimate the effect of adding cargo to a given car. The estimate it provides for adding cargo with mass equal to that of a passenger agrees with an empirical estimate of the effect on driver risk of having a passenger on board. A car can be made lighter while at the same time safer to its occupants and to the occupants of other vehicles into which it crashes by increasing its length by an amount that can be computed by the equation.

A number of analyses show consistently that in single-vehicle crashes, decreased mass increases driver fatality risk. Fatality risk increases are observed for all crashes, and also for rollover crashes and crashes into fixed objects.

Corporate Average Fuel Economy (CAFE) standards enacted to reduce US dependence on imported oil led to lighter cars.   CAFE also encouraged the purchase of light trucks, especially sports utility vehicles (SUVs), because they were subject to less stringent standards than cars. While making vehicles lighter increases fatalities, the net safety effect of replacing a car by an SUV is uncertain. On the one hand, the SUV is likely heavier than the car it replaces, which tends to increase safety. On the other hand, SUVs, with higher centers of gravity, have higher rollover fatality rates.   As the number of light trucks increased, data show no corresponding increase in the percent of all car driver fatalities that are due to two-vehicle crashes, thus refuting any possibility that the move to light trucks appreciably increased risks to car occupants.   The switch to SUV's could not have generated a safety benefit (if it was a benefit) nearly as great as the safety reduction from reducing the weight of cars. It is clear that CAFE generated many thousands of additional deaths.   However, whether it decreased or increased the nation's dependence on imported oil is far from clear.

References for Chapter 4

1 Severy DM, Harrison MB, Blaisdell DM. Smaller vehicle versus larger vehicle collisions. Paper number 710861. *SAE Transactions*. 1971; 80: 2929-58.

2 Campbell BJ, Reinfurt DW. The relationship between driver crash injury and passenger car weight. Chapel Hill, NC: Highway Safety Research Center, University of North Carolina; 1973.

3 ONeill B, Joksch H, Haddon W Jr. Empirical relationships between car size, car weight and crash injuries in car-to-car crashes. Proceedings of the Fifth International Technical Conference on Experimental Safety Vehicles, London, UK, p 362-368. Washington, DC: National Highway Traffic Safety Administration, 4-7 June 1974.

4 Joksch HC. Analysis of the future effects of the fuel shortage and increased small car usage upon traffic deaths and injuries. Report DOT-TSC-OST-75-21. Washington, DC: US Department of Transportation; January 1976.

5 Grime G, Hutchinson TP. Vehicle mass and driver injury. *Ergonomics*. 1979; 22: 93-104.

6 Insurance Institute for Highway Safety. Special issue: Driver death rates. Status Report, Vol. 35, No. 7, August 19, 2000. http://www.hwysafety.org/sr_ddr/sr3507_t1.htm

7 Kahane CJ. Vehicle weight, fatality risk and crash compatibility of model year 1991-99 passenger cars and light trucks. Report DOT HS 809 662. Washington, DC: US Department of Transportation, National Highway Traffic Safety Administration; October 2003.

8 Evans L, Frick MC. Car size or car mass — which has greater influence on fatality risk? *Am J Public Health*. 1992; 82: 1009-1112.

9 Evans L, Frick MC. Mass ratio and relative driver fatality risk in two-vehicle crashes. *Accid Anal Prev*. 1993; 25: 213-224.

10 Evans L. Driver injury and fatality risk in two-car crashes versus mass ratio inferred using Newtonian Mechanics. *Accid Anal Prev*. 1994; 26: 609-616.

11 Evans L, Frick MC. Car mass and fatality risk — has the relationship changed? *Am J Public Health*. 1994; 84: 33-36.

12 Evans L. Causal influence of car mass and size on driver fatality risk. *Am J Pub Health*. 2001; 91: 1076-81.

13 Evans L. Safety-belt effectiveness: The influence of crash severity and selective recruitment. *Accid Anal Prev*. 1996; 28: 423-433.

14 Joksch HC. Velocity change and fatality risk in a crash — a rule of thumb. *Accid Anal Prev*. 1993; 25: 103-104.

15 Toy EL. The distribution of vehicle mass in the on-road fleet of passenger vehicles. SAE paper 2004-01-1161. Warrendale, PA: Society of Automotive Engineers; 2004.

16 Evans L. Driver fatalities versus car mass using a new exposure approach. *Accid Anal Prev*. 1984; 16: 19-36.

17 Joksch H, Massie D, Pichier R. Vehicle aggressivity: Fleet characterization using traffic collision data. Report DOT HS 808 679. Washington, DC: US Department of Transportation, National Highway Traffic Safety Administration; February 1998.

18 Gabler HC, Hollowell WT. The aggressivity of light trucks and vans in traffic crashes, SAE paper 980908. Warrendale, PA: Society of Automotive Engineers; 1998. http://www-nrd.nhtsa.dot.gov/departments/nrd-11/aggressivity/980908/980908.html

19 Joksch H. Vehicle design versus aggressivity. Report DOT HS 809 194. Washington, DC: US Department of Transportation, National Highway Traffic Safety Administration; April 2000.

20 Wood DP, Ydenius A, Adamson D. Velocity changes, mean accelerations and displacements of some car types in frontal collisions. *Int J Crashworthiness*. 2003; 8: 591-603.

21 Kahane CJ. Effect of car size on the frequency and severity of rollover crashes. Proceedings of the 13th International Technical Conference on Experimental Safety Vehicles, Paris, France; 4-7 November 1991. Document DOT HS 807 990, Washington DC, Vol. 2, p. 765-770, July 1993.

22 Evans L, Wasielewski P. Serious or fatal driver injury rate versus car mass in head-on crashes between cars of similar mass. *Accid Anal Prev.* 1987; 19: 119-131.

23 Ernst E, Bruhning E, Glaeser KP, Schmidt M. Compatibility problems of small and large passenger cars in head on collisions. Paper presented to the 13th International Technical Conference on Experimental Safety Vehicles, Paris, France; 4-7 November 1991.

24 Wood DP. Safety and the car size effect: A fundamental explanation. *Accid Anal Prev.* 1997; 29: 139-151.

25 Evans L. How to make a car lighter and safer. SAE paper 2004-01-1172. Warrendale, PA: Society of Automotive Engineers; 2004.

26 Evans L. *Traffic Safety and the Driver.* New York, NY: Van Nostrand Reinhold; 1991.

27 National Research Council. *Effectiveness and Impact of Corporate Average Fuel Economy (CAFE) Standards.* Washington, DC: National Academy Press; 2001. http://www.nap.edu/catalog/10172.html

28 National Highway Traffic Safety Administration. *Traffic Safety Facts 2001.* Report DOT HS 809 484. Washington, DC: US Department of Transportation; December 2002. http://www-nrd.nhtsa.dot.gov/pdf/nrd-30/NCSA/TSFAnn/TSF2001.pdf

29 Complete details of this and other calculations available at http://www.ScienceServingSociety.com/data.htm

30 Auto Insurance Rates Results. http://info.insure.com/auto/autorates/dsp_AvgResults.cfm

31 Evans L. The foreign policy of SUVs. Letter to the Editor, New York Times, 22 October 2002. http://www.ScienceServingSociety.com/p/144b.htm

32 Padmanaban J. Influences of vehicle size and mass and selected driver factors on odds of driver fatality. Proceedings of the 47th Annual Meeting of the Association for the Advancement of Automotive Medicine, p. 507-524, Lisbon, Portugal; September 22-24, 2003.

33 US vehicle population. http://www.autonews.com/files/00regvehiclepop.pdf

34 Davis SC. *Transportation Energy Data Book: Edition 21*, ORNL-6966. Table 4.9: Light vehicle market shares by size class, sales periods, 1976-2002. Oak Ridge, TN: Oak Ridge National Laboratory, US Department of Energy; 2001. http://www-cta.ornl.gov/data/tedb23/Spreadsheets/Table4_09.xls

5 Environment, roadway, and vehicle

Introduction

A new car with antilock brakes, a clear blue sky, dry roadway, no traffic – close to most drivers' notion of ideal driving conditions. It is commonly assumed that the most desirable driving conditions are also the safest. In this chapter we will find that this is often not the case.

Weather

The vast majority (84%) of fatal crashes occur on dry roads (Table 5-1). Roadway surface condition and atmospheric conditions are highly related, but not identical. The roadway surface is wet after rain has stopped. It is, in principle, possible to drive in the rain while the roadway surface is dry – but not for long. The data in Table 5-2 compliment those in Table 5-1, showing that an even larger proportion (88%) of fatal crashes occurs under no adverse atmospheric conditions than occurs on dry roads.

Table 5-1. Percent of fatal crashes occurring under different roadway surface conditions. FARS 2001.

roadway surface condition	percent of fatal crashes
dry	83.6%
wet	12.7
ice	1.4
snow or slush	1.2
sand, dirt, oil	0.1
other, unknown	1.0
total	100.0

Effect of snow

Figure 3-18 (p. 57) showed that February consistently had fewer fatal crashes than any other month, while the largest monthly totals were in summer. As weather seems a likely contributor to this, we seek to examine how the variation in fatal crashes differs between states that experience a lot of snow and states that have no snow.

Table 5-2. Percent of fatal crashes occurring under different atmospheric conditions. FARS 2001

atmospheric condition	percent of fatal crashes
no adverse atmospheric conditions	88.1%
rain	7.5
snow	1.5
fog	1.4
sleet or hail	0.3
other, unknown	1.1
total	100.0

The monthly snowfall in different states is an unsatisfactory measure to investigate how snow affects crash risk because weather conditions averaged over a state may not, even approximately, reflect weather while driving. For example, isolated mountains may receive much snow while little falls on roads.

The following approach was used to investigate the influence of weather. All 50 US states were rank-ordered according to the percent of all their fatal crashes that took place when the roadway surface condition was coded as snow, slush, or ice. Four states (Florida, Georgia, Hawaii, and South Carolina) had no fatal crashes under such roadway conditions in 2001. Seven states (Alaska, Maine, Minnesota, Montana, North Dakota, Vermont, and Wyoming) had more than 10% of their fatal crashes under such roadway conditions. We designate the two groups of states as *snow-free states* and *snow states*.

Effect of snow on fatal crashes per day. The variation in the number of fatal crashes per day in each month is plotted in Fig. 5-1 for the snow-free and snow states. The values are relative to the number of fatal crashes averaged over the entire year. If crashes were a Poisson process with a daily rate that was constant throughout the year, the data would distribute randomly around the value one, indicated by the broken line. For the snow-free states this is approximately what is observed. The average rate of crashes per day in any month does not depart from the yearly average by more than 9%.

The pattern is markedly different for the snow states, in which lower rates are observed in the winter (which requires higher rates in the summer so that the overall average is close to one). The February rate is 43% below the yearly average, while the July and August rates are 38% above the yearly average. The February rate is well under half of the July and August rates.

Effect of snow on crashes for same travel distance. Complete data giving the distance of vehicle travel by month in each of the states are not available. What is available are estimates of vehicle travel on rural arterials. This shows

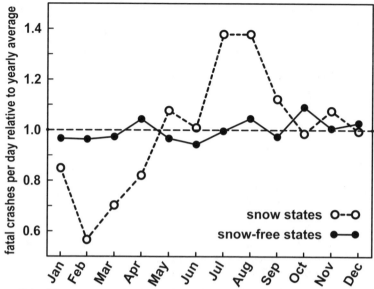

Figure 5-1. The average number of crashes per day by month for seven US states with the highest percent of crashes on snow-covered roads (Alaska, Maine, Minnesota, Montana, North Dakota, Vermont, and Wyoming) compared to four snow-free states (Florida, Georgia, Hawaii, and South Carolina). FARS 2001.

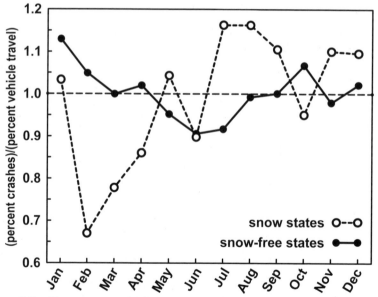

Figure 5-2. The percent of all fatal crashes divided by the percent of rural distance of vehicle travel for snow and snow-free states. FARS 2001.

substantially larger reductions in travel in the winter months in the snow states than in the snow-free states, so that a portion of the difference in Fig. 5-1 is because of reduced travel due in part to actual or expected unfavorable traveling conditions.

There are insufficient fatal crashes to provide reliable estimates of the distance rate for rural, so we assume that the vehicle distance of travel on all roads is proportional to the travel on rural arterials. This enables us to examine how the distance rate varies by month for states with and without snow (lower plot in Fig. 5-2).

The pattern is noisier, perhaps due to uncertainties in the estimates of travel distance. However, the indication is clear – the risk of a fatal crash for the same distance of travel is lower when the road is snow-covered than when it is not.

Number of vehicles per fatal crash. Table 5-3 shows that the average number of vehicles involved in a fatal crash on snow-covered roads is substantially higher than on dry roads. On snow-covered roads, 55% of fatal crashes are multiple-vehicle compared to 43% on dry roads. As the overall fatality risks are lower in snow, the risk of fatality in a single-vehicle crash will be additionally lower. This provides supporting indirect evidence that fatality risks are lower in snow, due presumably to lower speeds. Such an interpretation finds further support in the finding that when a pedestrian injury crash occurs, the probability that the pedestrian is killed is greatest when the road surface is dry, and least when it is ice covered.[1] When it is snowing pedestrian fatality risk when a crash occurs is half what it is when visibility is clear.

Table 5-3. Average number of vehicles per crash for all fatal crashes. FARS 2001.

roadway surface condition	average number of vehicles per crash
dry	1.52
wet	1.58
ice	1.58
snow or slush	1.76

Data from Ontario, Canada. The variation in the number of fatalities through-out the year in Ontario, Canada is similar to that observed for the US snow states, with fatalities in January, February and March being about half those in July, August and September.[2(p. 204,205)] The climate in Ontario is somewhat similar to that in the US states with most snow. The finding in Fig. 5-3 that the number of deaths per injury is lowest in the winter is consistent with the interpretation that snow covered roads lead to lower speeds and consequent lower fatality risks.

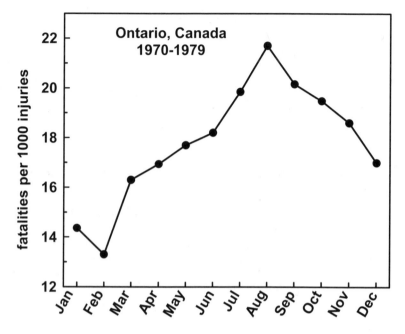

Figure 5-3. Seasonal variation of the number of fatalities per 1,000 injuries in Ontario, Canada.[2]

Lighting conditions

Table 5-4 shows that more than half of fatal crashes occur in daylight, while 29% occur in darkness (no daylight or artificial light). Thus the most common weather and lighting conditions in which fatal crashes occur are daylight, no precipitation or other environmental factors degrading visibility, and on a dry pavement. For every person killed while traveling in the dark while it is snowing, 87 are killed traveling in daylight under no adverse atmospheric conditions. For every person killed while traveling in the dark while it is raining, 19 are killed traveling in daylight under no adverse atmospheric conditions.

Roadway

The 6.35 million kilometers of roads in the US (Table 5-5) exceeds 150 times the earth's circumference, or 15 times the distance between the earth and the moon; the overview presented in Table 5-5 is based on various US Department of Transportation data sources.[3-5] These roads vary greatly in characteristics, quality, and use; 35% of the total length is unpaved. Local roads are supported mainly by local taxes (city, township, state), whereas Interstate system roads are supported mainly by Federal taxes (in some cases augmented by user tolls). The

Table 5-4.   Percent of fatal crashes occurring under different light conditions. FARS 2001.

light condition	percent of fatal crashes
daylight	50.7%
dark	29.0
dark but lighted	15.6
dawn	1.9
dusk	2.2
unknown	0.7
total	100.0

Table 5-5. Overview of US road system and the fatalities that occur on it. 2001 data from various US Department of Transportation data sources.[3-5]

roadway classification	length[3] (km)	travel[4] (billions of vehicle-km)	traffic fatalities[5]	traffic volume (veh/day)	fatalities per billion km
RURAL					
Interstate	**53,206**	**441**	**3,105**	**22,708**	**7.0**
arterial	381,045	687	8,692	4,940	12.7
collector	1,134,035	436	7,305	1,054	16.8
local	3,374,511	214	4,296	174	20.0
URBAN					
Interstate	**21,575**	**644**	**2,371**	**81,724**	**3.7**
arterial	244,851	1,470	8,838	16,454	6.0
collector	142,769	222	1,007	4,259	4.5
local	1,002,198	362	3,001	989	8.3
ALL RURAL	4,942,797	1,778	23,398	986	13.2
ALL URBAN	1,411,392	2,698	15,217	5,237	5.6
			(3,501)*		
ALL US	**6,354,190**	**4,476**	**42,116**	**1,930**	**9.4**

* fatalities in crashes for which complete roadway classification information is not coded in FARS

Interstate system originated in the 1950s to achieve the national defense goals of connecting the nation with efficient road transportation and facilitating speedy exit from cities. It is built to the highest design standards, with traffic in opposite directions separated by wide medians, or when space is restricted, as in urban areas, by physical barriers. Arterials include many state freeways supported mainly by state taxes that are similar in physical characteristics to the Interstate system, but are not part of it. While Interstates represent only 1.2% of all roads (by length), they carry 24% of the traffic and account for 13% of the traffic fatalities. The distance fatality rate on the Interstate system is less than half that on the non-Interstate system (5.0 fatalities per billion km compared to 10.8 fatalities per billion km).

On average, fatal crashes occur at a rate of one per 168 km of roadway per year, making them rare events on any particular section of roadway notwithstanding the 2001 total of 37,795 fatal crashes. The annual total of 16.35 million crashes of all types[6(p 9)] gives an average of 2.6 crashes per km of roadway per year. Crashes are of course not distributed even approximately randomly over the length of the road system.

Rural compared to urban

Rural roads account for 78% of all roads (by length), and for 60% of traffic fatalities. Yet only 40% of travel is on rural roads. The distance fatality rate on urban roads is 57% lower than the rural rate. Differences in physical characteristics contribute to this difference. A much larger contribution is due to differences in travel speed. Speed limits and congestion reduce travel speeds.

The average daily traffic (the number of vehicles traveling in either direction passing the same location on a road) on urban roads is more than five times the rural rate. During the morning and late afternoon peak travel periods, urban traffic is normally constrained to travel slower than the speeds drivers would choose, and often slower than posted speed limits (which are generally lower on urban than on rural roads).

For the Interstate system, physical characteristics are similar on rural and urban roads. Such physical differences as do exist between the urban and rural Interstates tend to generate a safety disadvantage for the urban roads (more lanes, more exits generating more merging, overtaking, and lane changing). Yet the rural Interstate fatality rate is 89% higher than the urban rate. As physical features of the roadway cannot explain this, it is most plausibly attributed to speed. Speed limits are, on average, higher on the rural system than on the urban system. However, from 1974 to 1987 speed limits were identical on rural and urban Interstates, as required by the nationwide maximum speed limit of 55 mph. Yet fatality rates were still lower on the urban sections. For example, for 1985 the urban Interstate fatality rate was 32% lower than the rural rate, a substantial difference, but less than the 48% difference in 2001. This lower rate in 1985 is due to the safety benefits of congestion.

Fatality rates for different roadway classifications

For rural roads, the fatality rate on the Interstate is 65% lower than on local roads. Local roads include many that are two-lane on which vehicles may approach each other at legal closing speeds in excess of 200 km/h and pass separated by only a few meters. A head-on crash at such relative speeds will likely be fatal. Improper overtaking or loss of control on curves can produce such crashes. When multiple-vehicle crashes do occur on freeways they usually involve vehicles traveling in the same direction, for which relative speeds are much less. Freeways also largely eliminate some of the most hazardous types of crashes that occur on local roads, including striking trees near the roadway, intersection crashes, and impacts with pedestrians.

Speeds are, on average, lower on non-Interstate roads than on the Interstates, yet fatality rates are more than twice as high on the lower-speed non-Interstates. This could be interpreted to mean that replacing all roads by Interstates would reduce the nation's traffic deaths by more than half. While this is neither feasible nor desirable for a host of reasons, it does underline the important role of the physical characteristics of the roadway in safety.

Many safety interventions, such as speed limits, reduce mobility. However, replacing higher fatality rate roads by lower fatality rate freeways increases both mobility and safety. There are, however, interactive effects that reduce the safety benefits. Enhanced mobility generates more travel. Providing additional roadway capacity to alleviate congestion leads not only to higher speeds, but also to additional traffic.

Keeping roadways in good condition increases mobility, but not necessarily safety. If a speed bump enhances safety, why would a pothole not enhance safety?

Traffic engineering

The central impetus for much of traffic engineering is the efficient operation of the traffic system, with safety an important consideration. The decision to, say, replace a stop sign with a more expensive traffic light is based mainly on traffic volume and other operational considerations. It is surprisingly difficult to determine how such changes influence safety. An intrinsic problem is that, despite the more than 16 million crashes per year in the US,[6] crashes are rare events at any particular site. This makes it difficult to get enough *before* and *after* data to support reliable conclusions.[7] Other relevant factors also change between the before and after periods.

Selecting sites for treatment because they have unusually high crash experience encounters another technical problem – *regression to the mean*.[7] To illustrate the concept, assume that all intersections have identical crash risks. Then, as discussed in Chapter 1, all will not have the same number of crashes in some *before* period because of randomness. The intersections with the largest number of *before* crashes are not expected to have a number different from the average in any *after* period. If some treatment that has no influence on crash risk is applied to the high-crash risk intersections, a reduction will still likely be observed due purely to randomness. It would be incorrect to attribute it to the treatment.

All intersections do not have equal risk, but it is difficult to infer from counting crashes how much of an above average number is due to random fluctuations, and how much is due to the risk at the intersection really being higher. Techniques have been developed to address these problems, and the influence of many traffic engineering and roadway features has been reliably estimated.[7] As this is an extensive subject with an extensive literature venturing beyond the scope of this book, we limit the present discussion to one item that is in a state of flux in the US.

Roundabouts. Roundabouts are a form of intersection control in widespread use throughout the world, being particularly common in Britain. They are relatively uncommon in North America. As roundabouts require more land than traffic lights, one might have expected them to be more common in North America than in much higher population density Britain. The higher use of roundabouts in Britain is, like the choice of left or right-side driving, a manifestation of independent evolution of traffic practice in different continents. This may perhaps be like the evolution of polar bears in the Arctic and penguins in Antarctica – either creature would likely find the opposite polar region just as congenial.

Some of the early roundabouts in the United States were of poor design, which discouraged expanded deployment. The term *modern roundabouts* refers to more recent US roundabouts of improved design.[8,9] As the schematic in Fig. 5-4 indicates, even the simplest roundabout controlling the right-angle intersection of two roads, each with only one lane in either direction, requires many design decisions. The goals of mobility and safety are often in conflict, so that trade-offs are required. For example, a smaller angle between the approach lane and the circulatory roadway will enable vehicles to maintain higher speeds, but an angle approaching closer to 90 degrees will reduce speeds and lead to greater safety, especially for any pedestrians present. The complexity increases as the number of intersecting roads, and the number of lanes per road, increases. Efforts are underway in the US to further refine design guidelines for improved operation and safety with the possibility of more extensive use of roundabouts in the US.

Roundabouts essentially eliminate the most severe type of intersection crash – one vehicle striking another on the side. One study found that existing modern roundabouts in the US compared to traffic signals reduced crashes by 38%, injury crashes by 76%, and fatal and incapacitating injury crashes by about 90%.[10] These findings, which are in line with experience in other countries, imply that increased use of roundabouts in North America will substantially reduce intersection casualties.

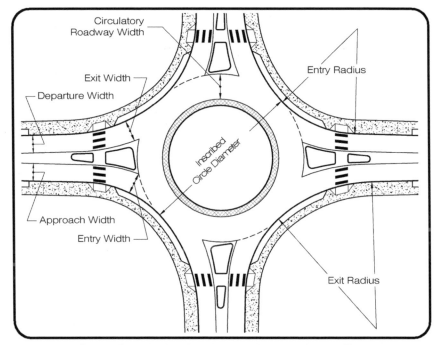

Figure 5-4. Some of the design decisions required to achieve effective operation for even a simple roundabout.[8,9]

Vehicle factors

Vehicle factors fall into two broad categories – those aimed at reducing harm when crashes occur, and those aimed at reducing the risk of crashing. Chapter 4 was devoted to the vehicle factor that has the greatest influence on the risk of death when a crash occurs, namely, the mass (and size) of the vehicle. Another set of vehicle factors, occupant protection devices such as safety belts and airbags, will be dealt with in Chapters 11 and 12. Here we consider just one device aimed at reducing the risk of crashing, especially in adverse weather conditions, and then discuss a number of safety standards.

Antilock braking systems (ABS)

Antilock braking systems (ABS) use electronic controls to maintain wheel rotation under hard braking that would otherwise lock a vehicle's wheels. Keeping the wheels rotating increases vehicle stability, especially when tire/roadway friction is reduced or varying, as when the roadway is wet. Anyone who informally investigates the emergency-braking performance of ABS on a snow-covered deserted parking lot will soon be impressed by the effectiveness of the technology.   Systematic test-track evaluations have convincingly demonstrated the technical advantages of ABS under a wide variety of conditions.[11-13] However, the influence of ABS on crash risk cannot be investigated on test tracks (or in parking lots) – this requires data from real crashes.

A number of studies used the crash experience of seven General Motors cars (Chevrolet Cavalier, Chevrolet Beretta, Chevrolet Corsica, Chevrolet Lumina APV, Pontiac Sunbird, Pontiac Trans Sport, and Oldsmobile Silhouette). These were relatively unchanged between model year 1991 and model year 1992, except that none of the 1991 models had ABS while all the 1992 models did. Thus, comparing the crash experience of the 1992 and 1991 models is equivalent to comparing the experience of vehicles with and without ABS.

Two-car crashes were examined using data from five states (Indiana, Missouri, North Carolina, Pennsylvania and Texas).[14] It was found that on wet roads ABS reduced the risk of crashing into a lead vehicle by $(32 \pm 8)\%$, but increased the risk of being struck in the rear by $(30 \pm 14)\%$. These results provide unmistakable evidence that ABS led to large differences in braking in traffic.

Another study using the same data compared crash risks under one condition to risks under another condition, as summarized in Table 5-6. [15] The first entry shows that ABS vehicles have $(10 \pm 3)\%$ fewer crashes on wet roads relative to their experience on dry roads compared to the corresponding ratio for non-ABS vehicles. If one makes the plausible assumption that ABS does not affect crash risk on dry roads, the result implies that ABS reduced crash risk on wet roads by $(10 \pm 3)\%$. Likewise, assuming that ABS does not affect crash risk when it is not raining leads to the result that ABS reduced crash risk when it is raining by $(12 \pm 2)\%$. These important crash-risk reductions appear to be the result of ABS preventing skidding on slippery surfaces, what the system was designed to do. If ABS has no effect on the dry roads on which 80% of crashes occur, then the net effect on all crashes would be a reduction of about 2%. This is consistent with the findings of the many studies cited in Refs 15 and 16 that find no net ·reduction in crashes to be associated with ABS. It is extremely unlikely that an effect as small as 2% can be detected in an overall crash rate. Early plans by insurance companies to give premium reductions for ABS were soon abandoned in the face of no demonstrable benefits.

The last entry in Table 5-6 shows that ABS is associated with a $(39 \pm 16)\%$ increase in rollover risk. After the first report[17] that ABS substantially increased rollover risk, a number of studies[18-20] found similarly large risk increases, as summarized in Table 5-7. While the results are in some cases based on multiple analyses of the same or overlapping data, they nonetheless paint a picture that leaves little doubt that equipping cars with ABS increases rollover risk. As rollover crashes pose a high fatality risk, it is not surprising that there is no evidence that ABS reduces fatality risk overall.[20,21] Indeed, the data suggest an increase is more likely than a decrease.

Table 5-6. Effects of ABS on some relative crash risks.[15]

condition investigated	comparison condition	risk change associated with ABS
wet roadway	dry roadway	$-(10 \pm 3)\%$
raining	clear or cloudy weather	$-(12 \pm 2)\%$
crashes involving rollover	all crashes not involving rollover	$+(39 \pm 16)\%$

Table 5-7.   Rollover risk increase associated with ABS estimated in a number of studies.

author	crash severity	surface condition	rollover risk increase associated with ABS
Evans[17]	all	all	44%
Evans[15]	all	all	39%
Kahane[18]	all	dry	54%
Hertz et al.[19]	all	dry	27%
Kahane[18]	all	wet	34%
Hertz et al.[19]	all	wet	94%
Hertz et al.[19]	fatal	dry	54%
Farmer et al.[20]	fatal	dry	65%
Hertz et al.[19]	fatal	wet	14%
Farmer et al.[20]	fatal	wet	53%

Why does ABS increase rollover risk? The finding that ABS increased rollover risk generated much concern by government officials and auto executives, who urgently sought explanations. Surveys showed that many drivers did not know that their vehicles had ABS, and those who did know were often unaware what ABS did, or how they were supposed to use it.[16]   There seems to be no convincing reason why a lack of knowledge about ABS should increase rollover risk. It is, of course, possible that wheels rotating rather than locking, or other engineering effect could, could promote rollover, but evidence is lacking.

The finding of higher rollover risk for ABS cars is not all that surprising given that one of the earliest technical papers on driving, published in the *American Journal of Psychology* in 1938, discussed why better breaking does not enhance safety.[22] (We discuss this in detail in Chapter 13). Here we address specifically why ABS does not enhance safety even though it provides demonstrably superior braking.

Evidence the ABS-equipped vehicles are driven at higher average speeds.
I believe that the reason behind these effects is that ABS leads to marginally
higher average travel speeds. While there are no rigorous studies showing that
ABS vehicles travel at higher speeds than non-ABS vehicles, I am nonetheless
confident that this is the explanation because of the combined weight of the
following evidence:

1. Data from Oregon for the same previously mentioned seven GM cars
   showed that the fraction of all traffic violations that were for speeding was
   greater for the ABS cars.[15]

2. ABS-equipped taxis in Norway were observed to follow at shorter headways
   than non-ABS taxis.[23]   Other research indicates that tailgaters drive
   faster.[24,25]

3. The previously mentioned result that on wet roads ABS cars were
   $(30 \pm 14)\%$ more likely to be struck in the rear than non-ABS cars is consistent with the interpretation that ABS was facilitating closer following, which
   led to braking levels that following cars without ABS could not match.

4. A 10% increase in average severity was associated with ABS in Canadian
   insurance claims, consistent with higher speeds.[26]

5. A test-track experiment suggested that drivers of ABS vehicles choose
   higher travel speeds.[27]

6. I have asked the following question to many audiences. "Have any of you,
   under any circumstances, on any occasion, ever driven faster because your
   vehicle was equipped with ABS"? Generally a few hands are raised. I then
   ask the parallel question with "slower" replacing "faster". It is rare for
   anyone to indicate that they ever drove slower because they had ABS. Any
   instance of faster driving not balanced by one of slower driving implies that
   average speed is higher with ABS. The accumulated responses provide
   overwhelming statistical evidence that drivers self-report that, on average,
   they drive faster when they have ABS.

7. Respondents to a formal written questionnaire indicated they would drive
   faster if driving an ABS-equipped vehicle.[28]

8. My own average speed is unquestionably higher with ABS. Before I had
   ABS and snow covered the two-lane road on which I commuted, I chose a
   speed sufficiently low to preclude much risk of moderate braking. I did not
   relish the possibility of skidding into oncoming traffic or into the deep
   drainage ditch on my right. When ABS eliminated these risks, I naturally
   drove faster. (As stated on p. 359, I have never been in a crash).

The risk of rollover is expected to depend very steeply on speed, so that even
small speed increases generate large increases in rollover risk. While injury risk

from, say, hitting a tree depends strongly on speed, it does so as a continuous function of speed. Rollover is more of a trigger, or threshold, phenomenon. A small increment of speed can make the difference between no incident of any type and a fatal rollover crash. Fatality risk, averaged over all crashes, increases as the fourth power of travel speed, so rollover fatality risk is expected to increase even more steeply than this. It is plausible that an undetectable small increase in travel speed associated with ABS would lead to the observed increases in rollover risk.

Is ABS a desirable technology? It is hard to imagine reasons why a driver would not prefer a vehicle with ABS over one without ABS, other factors being equal. Better braking is a desirable vehicle feature. However, it can be used to increase mobility or safety. Mobility may be increased by traveling at higher speeds, maintaining cruising speeds longer before beginning to stop, or by completing severe-weather journeys that would be abandoned if ABS were unavailable. We have treated this subject in some detail because it illustrates many themes that are central to traffic safety. It particularly provides guidance regarding the likely performance of proposed new technologies.

Major public efforts to incorporate advanced technologies

ABS is an example of applying advanced technology in an effort to enhance vehicle safety. It is the example that has had by far the most thorough evaluation. Many ABS effects in traffic are well established in multiple studies. The motivation and funding for ABS technology came from the auto industry, and led to a product that found widespread customer demand, notwithstanding its lack of any demonstrated overall safety benefit.

Major public funds have been spent in attempts to increase the use of modern technology to improve the performance of vehicles and the systems in which they operate. In the US, part of the Intermodal Surface Transportation Efficiency Act of 1991 authorized substantial expenditures to support *Intelligent Vehicle Highway Systems (IVHS)*.[29] The goal was to use a range of smart car and smart highway technologies to improve the safety, efficiency, and environmental friendliness of the highway system. This concept later evolved into *Intelligent Transportation Systems (ITS)*, with stated aims of applying electronic, computer, and communication technology to vehicles and roadways to increase safety, reduce congestion, enhance mobility, minimize environmental impact, increase energy efficiency, and promote economic productivity for a healthier economy.[30] In Europe *Programme for European Traffic with Highest Efficiency and Unprecedented Safety (PROMETHEUS)* was generously funded.

These programs generated massive activity, committees, bureaucracy, and extensive documentation on process, coordination, goals, needs, problem statements, definitions, and so on. Claims were made that reducing congestion would enhance safety, whereas the opposite is to be expected. It was likewise claimed that improved driver information would reduce congestion, without realizing that such a claim implied rejecting Wardrop's celebrated 1952 principle, "journey times on all routes actually used are equal."[31] This principle is at the core of traffic assignment modeling and has been accepted for decades as a good approximation when traffic is in a normal, or equilibrium, state. If the equilibrium is disturbed by, for example, a crash, then information can be helpful in selecting an alternate route. However, a few drivers receiving such information by traditional radio broadcasting will soon establish a new equilibrium, restoring a new parity between routes. Under the umbrella of these government-supported programs some technologies, such as on-board vehicle navigation, in-vehicle telephones, Internet, and on-board television reception, advanced. However, the advances were underway and would have occurred through the same competitive forces that produced earlier automotive innovation. I have been unable to discover in the mountain of literature any understandable summary of what was accomplished at such vast public expense. An approximate estimate of the expense is also unavailable because each item is a not too clearly identified portion of some larger transporting allocation.

The situation brings to mind comments of Ezra Hauer, the distinguished Professor Emeritus of Transportation at Toronto University.

> *Those amongst you who have attempted a critical review of the literature will attest that many of the research reports found will be quickly discarded. They will be found deficient in method, too small to draw conclusions from, inconclusive, obsolete, of obscure message, biased, or otherwise fatally flawed. In the end one is left with very few studies that are not obviously unreliable and the results of which do not contradict each other. That this is not an exaggeration but the actual state of affairs I know from rich personal experience and from noting the experience of many others. The obvious question is why so much effort, by so many, on so many subjects has produced so little light? Why so much that has been published is unsound, inconclusive and generally of little practical use. The answer becomes obvious if one recognizes how much is produced and published by one-day wonders, by itinerant and untrained researchers without experience, here today – gone tomorrow. How much research has been ill conceived by those who set the question to be answered, who provided the money, who approved the research method, who accepted the product and who published the results.*[32]

US Federal Motor Vehicle Safety Standards (FMVSS)

Since the beginning of motorization auto manufacturers developed and marketed vehicle features aimed at increasing safety, including automatic windshield wipers (1921), four-wheel brake systems (1924), interior sun visors (1931), electric turn signals (1938), door safety latches (1955), etc. The National Motor

Vehicle Safety Act of 1966 empowered NHTSA to develop Federal Motor Vehicle Safety Standards (FMVSS). All vehicles manufactured in 1968 or later had to meet a number of these in order to be offered for sale. New standards continue to be promulgated and those in place continue to be refined. In some cases standards required all vehicles to include features already available on some, while in other cases completely new performance standards were specified.

There are three main categories of standards for cars. Those numbered in the 100's apply to crash avoidance, those numbered in the 200's apply to occupant protection, given that a crash occurs, and those in the 300's apply to the post-crash period. The standard generating by far the most comment and controversy is FMVSS 208, which deals with occupant protection (safety belts, airbags). This is treated in Chapters 11 and 12.

Here we mention only standards (other than FMVSS 208) that have led to a measured change in fatality risk. The effectiveness of a standard can be estimated by comparing the fatality rate of a vehicle satisfying the standard with the rate of pre-standard model year versions of the same vehicle. The estimates discussed below are all from NHTSA. The largest effects are associated with the earliest standards introduced. As evaluation must use data from periods close to the introduction of the standard, the estimates are necessarily from earlier periods. The calculations below use the mix of vehicles, crashes, etc. applying at the times of the studies.

The largest fatality reductions are from the combined effects of FMVSS 203 and FMVSS 204. FMVSS 203 required energy-absorbing steering columns designed to cushion the driver's chest in a frontal crash. FMVSS 204 limited the rearward displacement of the steering wheel towards the driver. The energy-absorbing, or collapsible, steering column which meets these standards was first introduced by General Motors in 1966. It involves dividing the steering column into two separate sections, and joining them with a sleeve made from relatively thin sheet metal. When a driver's chest impacts the steering wheel, the sleeve crumbles thereby reducing the forces on the driver's chest.

The collapsible steering column was designed to reduce driver fatality risk in frontal crashes, but should not affect passenger risk or driver risk in non-frontal crashes. Hence, effectiveness could be estimated by comparing right-front passenger to driver fatality risk, or by comparing driver risk in frontal crashes to driver risk in non-frontal crashes. Applying each method to 1975-1979 FARS data produced estimates of 13% and 11%.[33,34] Although these estimates are not independent in that each uses the same driver fatalities, the agreement nonetheless suggests a fairly robust effect. The average, $(12.1 \pm 1.8)\%$, applies to frontal crashes which accounted for 54% of driver fatalities. Thus the device provides a net 6.6% reduction in driver fatality risk or, when averaged over all car occupants, a 4.4% reduction (Table 5-8).

The 6.6% reduction in driver fatality risk from this very simple, reliable, and inexpensive device that hurts no one is two thirds that of the 10% reduction from

Table 5-8.   Effect on fatality risk of US Federal Motor Vehicle Safety Standards (FMVSS).

description	FMVSS number	occupants protected	fatalities prevented protected occupants	fatalities prevented average over all occupants
energy absorbing column column displacement[33,34]	203 204	driver	6.6%	4.4%
instrument panels[35]	201	front passengers	7.0	1.7
side structure[36]	214	all	1.7	1.7
door locks[37]	206	all	1.5	1.5
roof crush resistance[37]	216	all	0.43	0.43
windshield glazing[38]	212	all	0.39	0.39
head restraints[39]	202	driver and right-front passenger	0.36	0.33
hydraulic brake systems[40]	105	all	0.9	0.9

airbags (Chapters 11 and 12). The collapsible steering column, unlike the airbag, is a passive device in that the user does not have to know anything or take steps, such as avoiding being close to it. Indeed, few users even know it is there.

Improvements in instrument panels from 1965 to 1975 are estimated to reduce fatality risk by about 13% for unrestrained front passengers in frontal crashes, or by 7% for all crashes.[35]   As right-front plus center-front passengers constituted 24% of car-occupant fatalities, this reduces unrestrained car-occupant fatalities by about 1.7%.

Side door beams (FMVSS 214) are estimated to have reduced risk by about 1.7%.[36] Improved door locks and door retention components (FMVSS 206) and improved roof crush resistance (FMVSS 216) are estimated to reduce fatality risk by 1.5% and 0.43%.[37] Adhesive bonding is estimated to halve windshield bond separation and occupant ejection through the windshield, thereby preventing 105 fatalities annually.[38] As an approximation, we express this as an average risk reduction of 0.39% for all occupants.

Head restraints for drivers and right-front passengers are estimated to reduce overall injury risk in rear impacts by 12%.[39] Let us make the very approximate assumption that this applies also to fatalities, about 3% of which result from rear impact (principal impact point 6 o'clock), so we obtain a net reduction in outboard-front occupant fatalities of 0.36%, or 0.33% of all occupant fatalities.

One measure aimed at crash prevention rather than occupant protection, namely dual master brake cylinders, is estimated to prevent 260 fatalities, or 0.9%.[40]

Combined effect of all standards. Although summing contributions in Table 5-8 gives an approximate estimate of the total reduction in risk from the combined effects of all the individual reductions, this is an incorrect calculation. The application of two measures that reduce risk by 50% does not eliminate risk, but reduces it by 75%. There are no logical problems with three measures that each reduce risk by 50%. If better brakes prevent a crash, then the contribution of the energy absorbing steering column must not be included for the crash that did not occur.

Seven of the eight items in Table 5-8 apply to drivers. Their combined effect is a reduction in driver fatality risk computed as

$$1 - (1-0.066)(1-0.017)(1-0.015)(1-0.0043)(1-0.0039)(1-0.0036)(1-0.009)$$

$$= 11.43\%. \qquad\qquad 5\text{-}1$$

Applying similar reasoning gives that the combined effects of all the standards reduce fatalities to right-front, center-front and all rear passengers by 11.8%, 11.5%, and 4.8%. These passengers are 23%, 1%, and 8%, respectively, of all occupant fatalities, drivers being the remaining 68%. By weighting each reduction by the corresponding occupancy, the combined effect of the six measures in Table 5-8 is estimated to reduce car occupant fatalities by 10.9%.

Table 5-8 does not include all changes that may have reduced car-occupant fatalities, but only those for which fatality reductions have been quantitatively estimated. Other FMVSS standards may be associated with fatality reductions too small to have been measured, yet important in terms of total numbers. If a change prevents, say, 20 fatalities per year, it is exceedingly unlikely that it will be detected in field data. If the 10.9% estimate is increased by half of its estimated value to capture the missed effects, this implies that vehicle changes have reduced occupant fatality risk by about 16%. Many automotive engineers consider that the cumulative effect of vehicle changes have reduced car-occupant risk somewhere in the range 10% to 25%, a range consistent with the above discussion.

It is to be expected that the largest fatality reductions are associated with the earliest standards, as the most fruitful opportunities are naturally addressed first. While it is in principle possible to always keep generating some increment of increased safety in vehicles, the law of diminishing returns soon sets in.

The discussion has attributed the risk reductions to the standards. As many of the changes would (and in fact did) occur without the standards, and vehicle safety improved prior to the standards, only some unknown fraction of the reductions can be attributed directly to the standards.

Attempts to estimate aggregate effects of FMVSS standards directly. Rather than estimating the aggregate effect of the standards by combining contributions from specific standards, it would be desirable to examine the overall effect by a more general change in fatalities from pre-regulation to post-regulation vehicles.

Such a task is rendered difficult because the earliest calendar year for FARS data is 1975, by which time the newest cars unaffected by FMVSS standards, namely 1967 model-year (MY) cars, were already eight years old. Thus any study using FARS data must necessarily focus on very old cars, which have use and ownership patterns that differ from those for newer cars by larger amounts than are expected to be associated with vehicle design standards.

One much cited study estimated the combined effects from all changes by comparing fatalities per unit distance of travel for pre-1964 MY cars, 1964-1967 MY cars, and 1968-1977 MY cars, as estimated by applying multivariate analysis to 1975-1978 FARS data.[41] The study concluded, "The numbers of deaths avoided by the federal safety standards amount to 26,500 occupants, 7,600 pedestrians, 1,000 pedalcyclists and 2,000 motorcyclists – for a total of about 37,000 people who would have died without the standards in those years" (the four years 1975-1978). Another much cited study applying multivariate analysis to similar data finds no net reduction associated with the standards.[42] I have previously discussed these studies in greater detail.[43(p 81-83)]

Such disparate conclusions from the same data illustrate what seems to be an intrinsic problem with complicated multivariate analyses. There are so many choices of variables and of transformations at the discretion of the analyst that the detached reader rarely has any way of knowing whether the analysis is performed to discover new information or to buttress prior beliefs. The reader cannot generally check the calculation, nor get a clear sense of the origin of the claimed effects. Differences in interpretation often do not flow from, say, different assumptions that can be discussed in terms of plausibility, but from such arcane issues as whether to use the logarithm or the reciprocal of the dependent variable in specifying the model. Often effects are reported that exceed reasonable physical explanations, or are inconsistent with straightforward observations. Claims of large benefits based on multivariate analyses seem so often to represent the triumph of zeal over science, or even over common sense.

A simple examination of the trends in Figs 3-3 through 3-5 (p. 38-40) is sufficient to refute any claim that a dramatic reduction in fatalities followed the introduction of vehicles satisfying safety standards in the late 1960s. Extravagant claims of benefits from US vehicle regulation continue to be made[44] – and refuted by data.[45] In Chapter 15 we discuss the role that inflated claims of benefits from vehicle factors played in the dramatic failure of US safety policy.

Summary and conclusions

The vast majority of fatal crashes occur on dry roads in daylight. For every person killed while traveling in the dark while it is snowing, 87 are killed traveling in daylight under no adverse atmospheric conditions. In states with no snow, the number of fatal crashes per day shows little change throughout the year. However, for the states with the most snow, fatalities per day are substantially lower in winter months than in summer months – the average daily rate for February being under half that for July and August. Part of the effect is that unfavorable driving conditions reduce travel. However, the number of fatal crashes for the <u>same</u> distance of travel is still less in the winter than in the summer for the states with the most snow. A likely interpretation is that snow reduces travel speed leading to greater safety. Such an interpretation finds additional support in the finding that the probability that a fatal crash is a single-vehicle crash is less when there is snow on the road. Further support is provided by data from Ontario, Canada showing that the probability that a crash injury is fatal is lowest in winter, highest in summer.

Fatality rates for the same distance of travel are substantially lower on Interstate System roads than on any other category of US road. This illustrates the large safety benefits from measures such as separating traffic moving in opposite directions and protecting vehicles from impacting roadside objects. Although the general physical structure of the rural and urban sections of the Interstate System is similar, the fatality rate on rural Interstates is 89% higher than the urban rate. This large difference is due to lower speed limits and lower urban speeds produced by congestion. In the period 1974 to 1987 when a uniform speed limit of 55 mph applied for all Interstate System roads, fatality rates on the rural sections were still substantially higher than on the urban sections, illustrating the safety benefits produced by traffic congestion.

Antilock braking systems (ABS) provide easily observed improvements in braking capabilities on wet roadways. Yet this impressive technology has not been shown to enhance safety. On the contrary, it is associated with a large increase in rollover fatality risk. The likely explanation is that the superior braking performance encourages small increases in speed.

Many engineering innovations have enhanced automotive safety since the beginning of motorization. In the late 1960s Federal Motor Vehicle Safety Standards (FMVSS) were adopted to insure that all vehicles offered for sale included specified safety technology. Some mandated items, such as the collapsible steering column, which reduces driver fatality risk by 6.4%, were available in some vehicles before the standard requiring them in all vehicles. The combined effect of all the standards is to reduce occupant fatality risk by, perhaps, about 15-20%. It is not possible to know how many of the items required by the standards would have been in vehicles if the standards had not existed. However, one can be very confident that the standards have made important contributions to improving vehicle safety.

References for Chapter 5

1 Mueller BA, Rivara FP, Bergman AB. Factors associated with pedestrian-vehicle collision injuries and fatalities. *Western J Med.* 1987; 146: 243-245.

2 Adams JGU. Smeed's law, seat belts and the emperor's new clothes. In: Evans L; Schwing RC, editors. *Human Behavior and Traffic Safety.* New York, NY: Plenum Press, p. 193-238; 1985.

3 US Department of Transportation, Bureau of Statistics. Table 1-5 - U.S. Public Road and Street Mileage by Functional System.
http://www.bts.gov/publications/national_transportation_statistics/2002/excel/table_01_05.xls

4 US Department of Transportation, Bureau of Statistics. Table 1-33 - Roadway Vehicle-Miles Traveled (VMT) and VMT per Lane-Mile by Functional Class.
http://www.bts.gov/publications/national_transportation_statistics/2002/excel/table_01_33.xls

5 Fatality Analysis Reporting System (FARS) Web-Based Encyclopedia. Data files and procedures to analyze them.   http://www-fars.nhtsa.dot.gov

6 Blincoe LJ, Seay AG, Zaloshnja E, Miller TR, Romano EO, Luchter S, Spicer RS. *The Economic Impact of Motor Vehicle Crashes, 2000.* Report DOT HS 809 446. Washington DC: National Highway Traffic Safety Administration, US Department of Transportation; May 2002.

7 Hauer E. *Observational Before-After Studies in Road Safety.* Oxford, UK: Pergamon; 1997.

8 Robinson BW, et al. *Roundabouts – An Informational Guide.* Publication FHWA-RD-00-067. Washington DC: US Department of Transportation, Federal Highway Administration; June 2000.

9 Eisenman S, Josselyn J, List G, Persaud B, Lyon C, Robinson B, Blogg M, Waltman E, Troutbeck R. Operational and safety performance of modern roundabouts and other intersection types. New York State Department of Transportation, NYSDOT SPR Project C-01-47, Final Report, 7 April 2004.   http://www.dot.state.ny.us/roundabouts/rac0147.html

10 Retting RA, Persaud BN, Garder PE, Lord D. Crash and injury reduction following installation of roundabouts in the United States. *Am J Public Health.* 2001; 91: 628-31.

11 Eddie R. Ice, ABS, and temperature. SAE paper 940724. Warrendale, PA: Society of Automotive Engineers; 1994. (Also included in: *Accident Reconstruction: Technology and Animation IV,* AE Special Publication SP-1030, p. 163-8).

12 Lambourn RF. Braking and cornering effects with and without anti-lock brakes. SAE paper 940723. Warrendale, PA. Society of Automotive Engineers; 1994. (Also included in: *Accident Reconstruction: Technology And Animation IV,* SAE Special Publication SP-1030, p. 155-61).

13 Rompe K, Schindler A, Wallrich M. Advantages of an anti-wheel lock system (ABS) for the average driver in difficult driving situations. Proceedings of the Eleventh International Technical Conference on Experimental Safety Vehicles, p. 442-448. Report DOT HS 807 223. Washington, DC: National Highway Traffic Safety Administration; 1988.

14 Evans L, Gerrish PH. Antilock brakes and risk of front and rear impact in two-vehicle crashes. *Accid Anal Prev.* 1966; 28: 315-323.

15 Evans L. Antilock brake systems and risk of different types of crashes in traffic. *Crash Prev Inj Control.* 1999; 1: 5-23.

16 Broughton J, Baughan C. The effectiveness of antilock braking systems in reducing accidents in Great Britain. *Accid Anal Prev.* 2002; 34: 347-355.

17 Evans L. ABS and relative crash risk under different roadway, weather, and other conditions. SAE paper 950353. Warrendale, PA. Society of Automotive Engineers; 1995. (Also included in: *Accident Reconstruction: Technology and Animation V,* SAE Special Publication SP-1083, p. 177-186).

18 Kahane CJ. Preliminary evaluation of the effectiveness of antilock brake systems for passenger cars.   Report DOT HS 808 206.   Washington, DC: National Highway Traffic Safety Administration; December 1994

19 Hertz E, Hilton J, Johnson DM. An analysis of the crash experience of passenger cars equipped with antilock braking systems. Report DOT HS 808 279. Washington, DC: National Highway Traffic Safety Administration; May 1995.

20 Farmer CM, Lund AK, Trempel RE, Braver ER. Fatal crashes of passenger vehicles before and after adding antilock braking systems. *Accid Anal Prev.* 1997; 29: 745-757.

21 Farmer CM. New evidence concerning fatal crashes of passenger vehicles before and after adding antilock braking systems. *Accid Anal Prev.* 2001; 33: 361-369.

22 Gibson JJ, Crooks LE. A theoretical field-analysis of automobile driving. *Am J Psych* 1938; 51: 453-471.

23 Sagberg F, Fosser S, Saetermo I-A F. An investigation of behavioural adaptation to airbags and antilock brakes among taxi drivers. *Accid Anal Prev.* 1997; 29: 293-302.

24 Wasielewski, P. Speed as a measure of driver risk: Observed speeds versus driver and vehicle characteristics. *Accid Anal Prev.* 1984; 16: 89-103.

25 Evans L, Wasielewski PF. Do accident-involved drivers exhibit riskier everyday driving behavior? *Accid Anal Prev.* 1982; 14: 57-64.

26 Barr A, Norup H. Anti-lock braking systems study. Markham, Ontario, Canada: Vehicle Information Center of Canada; 1994.

27 Smiley A, Rochford S. Behavioural adaptation and anti-lock brake systems. Report for Transport Canada; 3 October 1991.

28 Jonah BA, Thiessen R, Au-Yeung E. Sensation seeking, risky driving and behavioral adaptation. *Accid Anal Prev.* 2001; 33: 679-684.

29 IVHS   http://www.bergen.org/AAST/Projects/ES/TA/ivhs2.html

30 ITS   http://www.its.dot.gov/welcome.htm

31 Wardrop JP. Some theoretical aspects of road traffic research. *Proc. Inst. Civil Engineers, Part II.* 1952; 1: 325-378.

32 Hauer E. An (Old) Researcher's Tale. Toronto; 1 August 2002. http://members.rogers.com/hauer/Pubs/old%20researcher.pdf

33 Kahane CJ. An evaluation of Federal Motor Vehicle Safety Standards for passenger car steering assemblies: Standard 203 - impact protection for the driver; Standard 204 - rearward column displacement. Report DOT HS-805 705. Washington, DC: National Highway Traffic Safety Administration; January 1981.

34 Kahane CJ. Evaluation of current energy-absorbing steering assemblies. SAE paper 820473. Warrendale, PA: Society of Automotive Engineers. 1982. (Also included in: *Occupant Crash Interaction with the Steering System*, SAE special publication SP-507, p. 45-49).

35 Kahane CJ. An evaluation of occupant protection in frontal interior impact for unrestrained front seat occupants of cars and light trucks. Report DOT HS 807 203. Washington, DC: National Highway Traffic Safety Administration; January 1988.

36 Kahane CJ. An evaluation of side structure improvements in response to Federal Motor Vehicle Safety Standard 212. Report DOT HS 806 314. Washington, DC: National Highway Traffic Safety Administration; November 1982.

37 Kahane CJ. An evaluation of door locks and roof crush resistance of passenger cars -- Federal Motor Vehicle Safety Standards 206 and 216. Report DOT HS 807 489. Washington, DC: National Highway Traffic Safety Administration; November 1989.

38 Kahane CJ. An evaluation of windshield glazing and installation methods for passenger cars. Report DOT HS-806 693. Washington, DC: National Highway Traffic Safety Administration; February 1985.

39 Kahane CJ. An evaluation of head restraints -- Federal Motor Vehicle Safety Standard 202. Report DOT HS-806 108. Washington, DC: National Highway Traffic Safety Administration; February 1982.

40 Kahane CJ. A preliminary evaluation of two braking improvements for passenger cars -- dual master cylinders and front disc brakes. Report DOT HS-806 359. Washington, DC: National Highway Traffic Safety Administration; February 1983.

41 Robertson LS. Automobile safety regulations and death reductions in the United States. *Am J Pub Health.* 1981; 71: 818-822.

42 Peltzman S. The effects of automobile safety regulation. *J Political Economy* 1975; 83: 677-725.

43 Evans L. *Traffic Safety and the Driver.* New York, NY: Van Nostrand Reinhold; 1991.

44 Vernick JS, Teret SP. Making vehicles safer. *Am J Public Health.* 2004; 94: 170.

45 Evans L. Evans responds (to previous reference). *Am J Public Health.* 2004; 94: 171-172.

6 Gender, age, and alcohol effects on survival

Introduction

This chapter has nothing to do with the risk of being involved in a crash. Instead, it deals with the risk of surviving, given that a crash has occurred. Drivers involved in identical crashes can have different risks of dying due to factors that affect the human body's ability to survive a given impact. The chapter is therefore devoted to examining the fragility of the human body when subject to blunt trauma from physical impacts, also called physical insults.

We investigate how the risk of death from the same impact depends on gender, age, and alcohol consumption. Although such fragility effects originate in fundamental human physiology, and apply to blunt trauma insults from sources other than traffic crashes, it is only traffic crash data sets that provide sufficient numbers of fatalities to determine quantitative relationships.

Gender and survivability

If a female and a male suffer similar potentially lethal physical impacts, which of them (other factors being equal) is more likely to die? This question cannot be answered by standard epidemiological methods because adequate samples of sufficiently similar cases are unavailable, and likely to remain unavailable. Even though the FARS data set (Chapter 2) codes hundreds of thousands of female and male fatalities, such data do not immediately answer the question. To illustrate the problem, consider that the most common type of US fatal crash involves one vehicle (Table 3-3, p. 49) containing one person, the driver. Examining such crashes when the driver is female reveals that 100% of them are killed. If they were not killed, the case would not be in FARS. The corresponding male case similarly shows 100% of male drivers killed. The FARS data do show about three times as many male deaths as female deaths in single-vehicle, single-occupancy crashes. This provides no information on how gender affects outcome, given that a crash occurs. The question was answered[1] using a technique that extracts the required information from FARS data.

Double pair comparison method

The double pair comparison method was devised specifically to make inferences from FARS data.[2] The method effectively isolates the influence of a particular factor of interest (in the present case, gender) from the multitude of other influences that affect fatality risk in a crash. The method focuses on vehicles containing two specific occupants, at least one being killed. We refer to one as the *subject* occupant, and aim to discover how some characteristic of the subject occupant affects that person's fatality risk. The other, the *control* occupant, serves to standardize conditions in order to estimate risk to the subject occupant.

The method is described below for the specific case in which the subject occupant is a car driver and the control occupant is a male passenger seated in the right-front seat. The aim is to determine how the driver's gender influences the driver's fatality risk in a crash.

Two sets of crashes are selected. The first contains cars with a female driver and a male passenger, at least one being killed. This first set of crashes provides

$$r_1 = A/B \qquad\qquad\qquad 6\text{-}1$$

where

A = number of female drivers killed in cars with male passengers,   6-2

and

B = number of male passengers killed in cars with female drivers.   6-3

It might seem that r_1 immediately measures how risk depends on gender. As driver and passenger are involved in the same crash, factors like impact speed, or type and properties of object struck (tree, vehicle, etc.), apply equally to both occupants. Factors that influence the risk of crashing, such as driver behavior, change sample sizes but should not systematically affect r_1. However, a factor that could contribute to differences in risk between drivers and passengers is the different risk associated with different vehicle seats (p. 53-57).

To correct for this, a second set of crashes uses male driver subjects accompanied by male control passengers, at least one being killed. That is, the subject gender is different from the first set of crashes, but the control characteristics are the same. These crashes provide

$$r_2 = C/D. \qquad\qquad\qquad 6\text{-}4$$

where

C = number of male drivers killed in cars with male passengers   6-5

and

D = number of male passengers killed in cars with male drivers,   6-6

Dividing the two ratios gives

$$R = r_1/r_2 = AD/(BC). \qquad\qquad\qquad 6\text{-}7$$

Subject to assumptions that are likely to be more than adequately satisfied, the quantity R measures the risk of death to a female driver compared to the risk of death to a male driver, other factors being essentially the same.[2] The crash conditions are effectively standardized because the female and male drivers experienced their injuries in a mix of crashes that posed similar risks to accompanying male passengers.

The control occupant does not enter directly into the result. Because of this, many separate estimates can be calculated using various control occupants. Combining estimates based on many controls helps diminish potential confounding due to differences that may exist between subject and control occupant with regard to such factors as age and safety belt use. The basic assumptions of the method require that the probability of a passenger death should not depend (in the present example) on the gender of the driver. This assumption would be violated if, for example, the same physical impact was less likely to kill a passenger traveling with a male driver than one traveling with a female driver. Departures from this assumption could arise if, for example, passengers traveling with male drivers tended to be younger than those traveling with female drivers. The biasing influences of such potential confounding can be reduced by dividing control subjects into gender and age categories, thus insuring that passengers of similar age and gender accompany the female and male drivers being compared. As the use of such occupant-protection devices as safety belts or helmets affects fatality risk, the control occupant should have the same use in the first and second set of crashes.

Numerical example

The calculations are described below using the example of comparing unbelted car-driver fatality risk for females aged 38-42 to that for males in the same age interval (call them 40-year-old drivers). For the control occupant we first choose unbelted male right-front passengers aged 16-24, hereafter referred to as 20-year-old male passengers. The 1975-1998 FARS data give $A = 90$ female drivers aged 40 were killed while traveling with 20-year-old male passengers, while $B = 36$ male passengers aged 20 were killed while traveling with female drivers aged 40. These give a 40-year-old female driver to 20-year-old male passenger fatality risk ratio $r_1 = 2.500$. This departs substantially from unity because, as we quantify later, fatality risk from the same impact depends strongly on age. For the second set of crashes, $C = 244$ and $D = 133$, giving $r_2 = 1.835$. The ratio of r_1 to r_2 gives $R = 1.363$, so this combination of subject and control estimates that females are 36% more likely to die than males from the same physical impact.

Deriving relationship from large numbers of data

The above example provides the first of the eight estimates for 40-year-old subject drivers shown in Table 6-1. Summing the appropriate columns in Table 6-1 shows 3,038 driver fatalities (930 female and 2,108 male) and 2,870 right-front passenger fatalities. The conclusion from Table 6-1 is that 40-year-old female car drivers are (19.9 ± 7.8)% more likely to be killed than 40-year-old male drivers in similar severity crashes. This value provides the point for age 40 (plotted at age = 40.5) in the top left graph in Fig. 6-1.

Table 6-1. Female to male fatality risk, R, for 40-year-old[a] unbelted car drivers.[1] FARS 1975-1998.

control- occupant gender: age	fatalities				ratios			
	A	B	C	D	$r_1 =$ A/B	$r_2 =$ C/D	$R =$ r_1/r_2	ΔR^b
m: 16-24	90	36	244	133	2.500	1.835	1.363	0.314
m: 25-34	93	49	359	230	1.898	1.561	1.216	0.246
m: 35-54	243	206	439	448	1.180	0.980	1.204	0.152
m: 55+	33	76	76	158	0.434	0.481	0.903	0.231
f: 16-24	169	77	116	61	2.195	1.902	1.154	0.249
f: 25-34	73	51	303	297	1.431	1.020	1.403	0.289
f: 35-54	144	133	532	597	1.083	0.891	1.215	0.174
f: 55+	85	214	39	104	0.397	0.375	1.059	0.247
					weighted average		1.199[c]	0.078[d]

A = number of 40-year-old female drivers killed traveling with control passengers (with characteristics indicated in column 1)

B = no. of control passengers killed traveling with 40-year-old female drivers

C = no. of 40-year-old male drivers killed traveling with control passengers

D = no. of control passengers killed traveling with 40-year-old male drivers

[a] drivers aged 38, 39, 40, 41, or 42 years.

[b] computed as $\Delta R = R\sqrt{1/A+1/B+1/C+1/D+0.05^2}$

[c] weighted average, $\bar{R}$, computed as

$$\bar{R} = \exp\left[\sum[\log(R_i)\times(R_i/\Delta R_i)^2]/\sum(R_i/\Delta R_i)^2\right] = 1.199$$

[d] standard error in $\bar{R}$ computed as $\bar{R}/\sqrt{\sum(R_i/\Delta R_i)^2} = 0.078$

where the summation is over the eight values

[c,d] the result indicates that 40-year-old female unbelted drivers are (19.9 ± 7.8)% more likely to be killed than 40-year-old males from the same impact.

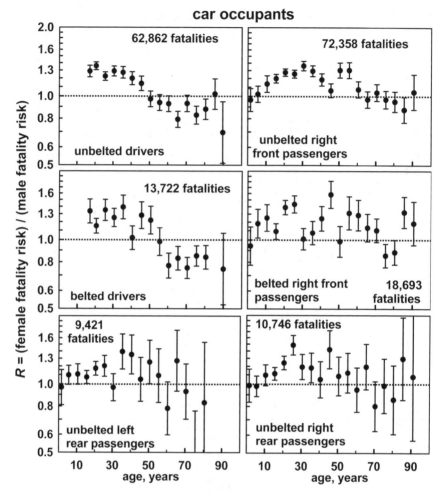

Figure 6-1. Female to male fatality risk, *R*, from similar physical impacts estimated using car occupants.[1]   Based on 75,066 female and 112,736 male subject fatalities. The sixth point from the left in the top left graph is the value *R* = 1.199 ± 0.078 calculated for age 40 in Table 6-1. This and Figs 6-2 through 6-12 all use FARS 1975-1988.

The other points plotted in the top-left graph in Fig. 6-1 are based on extracting data in the same form as Table 6-1 for other driver ages, using a total of 14,873 female and 47,989 male driver fatalities. The total number of subject fatalities is given on this and subsequent graphs. All errors are standard errors.[3-6]   For driver subjects, there are no estimates at ages below the age of licensure due to too few cases (but far from zero cases, see Table 9-5, p. 228). When passengers are subjects and drivers serve as controls, estimates at younger ages are available, as shown in the other five graphs in Fig. 6-1. *Belted* includes the use of any restraint system, such as a baby or infant seat.

A parallel process produces corresponding results for occupants of light trucks (Fig. 6-2) and for motorcycle passengers (Fig. 6-3). There were insufficient female motorcycle-driver fatalities to perform the analysis for motorcycle drivers.

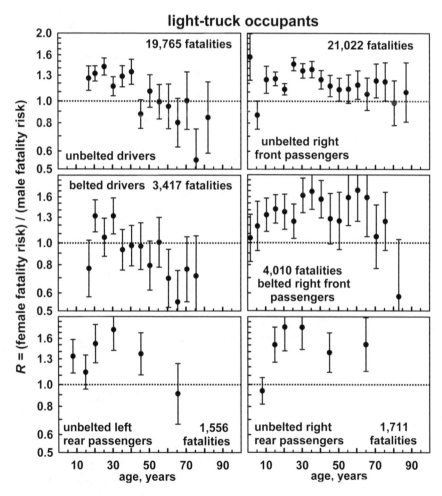

Figure 6-2. Female to male fatality risk, R, from similar physical impacts, estimated using occupants of light trucks.[1] Based on 14,444 female and 37,037 male subject fatalities.

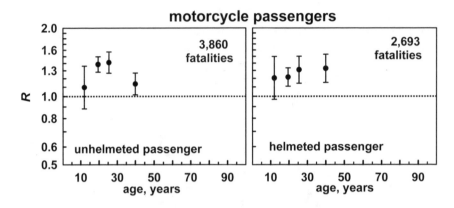

Figure 6-3. Female to male fatality risk, *R*, from similar physical impacts, estimated using 3,879 female and 2,674 male subject fatalities.[1] There are no estimates for motorcycle drivers because the 139 female motorcycle driver fatalities were insufficient to provide reliable results.

If there were no systematic differences between male and female risk, then all of the data in the 14 graphs in Figs 6-1 through 6-3 would distribute randomly around the value $R = 1.0$ (marked by a dashed line). Instead, clear systematic departures are apparent in every graph, with the departures being similar from graph to graph.

None of the six individual graphs in Fig. 6-1 departs systematically from their collective trend. It is therefore appropriate to combine all these data to obtain a best estimate for car occupants (top graph in Fig. 6-4). The values plotted are the weighted averages of the values plotted at the indicated ages in Fig. 6-1. The other two graphs in Fig. 6-4 show corresponding information for light trucks and motorcycles. Weighted average values of *R* at age 20 are 1.285 ± 0.027 for cars, 1.241 ± 0.052 for light trucks, and 1.312 ± 0.078 for motorcycle passengers. Female risk exceeds male risk by amounts that are not systematically different depending on which of the three vehicles provides the data. The *R* values for occupants of each of the three vehicle types are, to within their error limits, consistent with the weighted average of 1.279 ± 0.023

As results for individual vehicle categories do not depart systematically from their collective trend, it is appropriate to combine the data in Fig. 6-4 to produce Fig. 6-5. Each point plotted can be considered the weighted average of the (up to 14) values from the 14 occupant categories, or the mathematically identical weighted average of the values from each of the three vehicle categories. The relationship in Fig. 6-5 is the best estimate of how the risk of death from the same impact depends on gender.

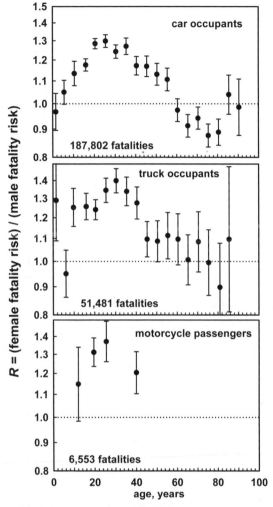

Figure 6-4. Female to male fatality risk, R, from similar physical impacts derived using data for specific vehicle categories.[1] The weighted average of the values for the three vehicle categories produces Fig. 6-5.

The values in Fig. 6-5 at ages 20, 25, 30, and 35 are 1.279 ± 0.023, 1.301 ± 0.028, 1.291 ± 0.033, and 1.287 ± 0.038. These values show consistently that, between ages 20 and 35, female risk exceeds male risk by $(28 \pm 3)\%$. From about age 10 to the late 50s, female risk exceeds male risk by amounts that depend on age. For ages below 10 or above 60, the data provide no indication of clear differences, although there is a weak suggestion that older men might be more vulnerable than older women.

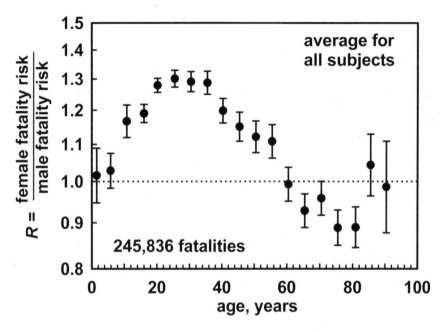

Figure 6-5. Female to male fatality risk, *R*, from similar physical impacts.[1] The points plotted are the weighted averages for the three vehicle categories (Fig. 6-4) or, the mathematically identical weighted average over data for all 14 occupant categories (Figs 6-1 through 6-3).

A physiological gender-dependent difference

Subjects in the 14 categories are killed by a wide variety of impact mechanisms. For example, fatalities to belted vehicle occupants usually result from impacts with the vehicle interior, while motorcyclist fatalities result from impacts into objects external to the motorcycle. The absence or presence of steering wheels, safety belts, helmets, cushioning effects of occupants in front, car interiors compared to truck interiors, etc. all affect injury mechanisms. Yet the results obtained for the 14 occupant categories are similar. In particular, for ages 20-35 female risk exceeds male risk by the same $(28 \pm 3)\%$ for occupants of cars, trucks, and motorcycles.

Further evidence supporting how robust these findings are is provided by a study[7] focused on examining if the relationships found in an earlier study,[8] which used FARS 1975 to 1983 data, were similarly revealed in FARS

1984-1996 data. No distinguishable differences were found dependent on which of the independent data sets was used. This supports that the effects remain unchanged in time, and apply for different vintage vehicles.

The finding that female risk exceeds male risk by amounts that do not appear different for different time periods, different types or vintages of vehicles, seating positions, or use of occupant restraints, supports the interpretation that females are intrinsically more likely to die from physical impacts in general. This is a finding somewhat parallel to other findings of gender-dependent physiological differences. For example, females live longer than males and are more likely to survive infancy. In each case the findings are phenomenological in nature – they are unambiguous inferences from large data sets. Explanations of why such phenomena occur await different types of investigations than the investigations that established that they do occur. However, greater risk of blunt trauma fatality, greater longevity, and higher survivability in infancy all likely reflect basic physiological differences between females and males.

Although traffic-crash data and the method used provided a *laboratory* to discover and quantify gender-dependent differences, these differences are interpreted to apply beyond the laboratory in which they were investigated. Thus Fig. 6-5 is interpreted to apply not just to risks from traffic crashes, but from other sources such as falling from a roof or down stairs. This interpretation is consistent with cadaver tests using fixed impacts, which find that females have a 20% greater risk of injury to the thorax than males.[9]

The age range in which female risk from blunt trauma exceeds male risk (pre-teens to late fifties) is similar to the child-bearing years, thus inviting speculation that biological factors associated with the potential to have children could increase risk from physical impacts.

Males and females involved in identical crashes are subject to similar decelerations rather than similar forces. As force is the product of body mass times deceleration, heavier subjects experience proportionally higher forces, just as they do when they fall or walk into a fixed object. The results have been derived for forces that generally increase with body mass. For an impact with a fixed amount of energy, say being struck by a falling object or an inflating airbag, even larger gender-dependent effects are expected. This is because the gender effects found are based on risks in identical crashes in which females are subject to smaller forces on account of their smaller masses.

Inferring involvement rates from fatality data

FARS data for 2001 show 3.4 times as many 20-year-old male driver deaths as 20-year-old female driver deaths. Such ratios are often interpreted to mean that males are 3.4 times as likely as females to be involved in lethal crashes. The results here show that this interpretation should be modified. If 20-year-old males and females had equal involvement rates, females would experience 28%

more deaths. The driver fatality ratio should be multiplied by 1.28 to take account of the different risk from the same impact, so a 20-year-old male is 4.4 times, not 3.4 times, as likely to be involved in a potentially lethal crash.

Male deaths far exceed female deaths from all types of injuries, including interpersonal violence, suicide, drowning, fire, falls and poisoning.[10]   Male road-user deaths far exceed female road-user deaths – and not just drivers (Fig. 3-10, p. 46). The results here show that male involvement risk exceeds female involvement risk by even larger amounts than captured by the numbers of casualties for cases in which death is due to blunt trauma.

Possible biases

The estimates of differences between male and female fatality risk from the same physical impact use the double pair comparison method. It is therefore appropriate to examine if the findings could be due to biases in the method or data, or if the results could have an explanation based on the method rather than intrinsic gender differences.

The fact that male drivers have higher crash involvement rates does not systematically affect R for drivers. Higher crash rates generate additional crashes which increase subject and control fatalities by similar proportions, but do not change ratios systematically. The data show no systematic differences in estimates of R for passengers dependent on whether the driver is male or female (male controls provide about three times as many data).

Let us assume that males not only have more crashes than females, but when they do crash they also have crashes of higher severity. Formal mathematical reasoning shows that plausibly different distributions by severity can have, at most, only small influences on R.[2] This result is more immediately apparent from the following data-based examples.

Safety belts reduce fatality risk for drivers by 42% (Chapter 11) and by a similar percent for right-front passengers. Yet values of R are not systematically different for belted and unbelted occupants (compare rows 1 and 2 in Figs 6-1 and 6-2). Could incorrect coding of belt use bias results? Perhaps about 10% of surviving occupants coded as belted were unbelted. This is a major problem in estimating belt effectiveness, but will influence the gender effect only if miscoding rates are highly gender dependent. If R does not much depend on belt use, which appears to be the case in Figs 6-1 and 6-2, then males and females being miscoded in similar proportions will not systematically affect R. Plausible departures from these assumptions could lead to no more than small changes in R. It is widely accepted that when occupants are coded as unbelted they are very likely unbelted. Cases with unknown belt use were excluded.

Rear-seat unbelted occupants have fatality risks 26% lower than unbelted front-seat occupants, yet R values for rear-seat occupants do not differ systematically from those for front-seat occupants (compare rows 1 and 3 in

Figs 6-1 and 6-2). Motorcycle helmets reduce passenger fatality risk by 28%, yet values of R do not systematically depend on helmet use (Fig. 6-3). Fatality risk differs between cars, trucks and, particularly, motorcycles, yet values of R do not systematically differ (compare the 3 graphs in Fig. 6-4).

The study was replicated using only rural, and then using only urban, crashes.[1] A typical rural crash is about four times as likely to be fatal as a typical urban crash. Despite such a large difference in severity, the rural and urban replications produced values of R that are in good agreement with each other and with Fig. 6-5.

Possible alternate explanations

Could the results reflect merely differences in stature? One could certainly speculate that risk might be greater for smaller drivers because of differences in the details of their interaction with the steering wheel during a crash (cases with airbag deployment were excluded). However, it seems implausible that the same explanation could apply to occupants whether or not they were belted, as belts alter the mix of injury mechanisms. Rear-seat occupants strike different parts of the vehicle from those struck by front-seat occupants. There does not seem to be any plausible mechanism that would favor taller individuals in all seats by amounts approaching the 28% found here. As motorcyclists are typically killed by striking objects external to the motorcycle, characteristics of the interaction between occupant and vehicle can have little bearing on outcome.

An additional reason why the effects cannot plausibly be attributed to differences in stature is because at older ages female risk is, if anything, less than male risk (Fig. 6-5), yet at all ages females remain about the same percent shorter than males. International anthropometric data show consistently that at age 20, females are 7.5% shorter than males compared to 7.4% shorter at age 70.[11,12]

The discussion above showed that factors known to have large influences on traffic fatality risk do not substantially affect R. The results, in common with results from any study using real-world data, may still be influenced by an essentially unlimited list of possible biases. However, it seems difficult to posit any plausible bias in the data that could change R values by amounts that would materially change the values shown in Fig. 6-5.

Helps explain observed fatality risk differences

The finding that females are more likely than males to die from the same severity impact helps explain two much-reported traffic safety topics.

Increased female risk from airbags. When injuries result from airbag deployments, they are of a different nature from other crash injuries in that the device provides its own source of energy. Unlike crash forces which are proportional to body mass, the impact delivered to an occupant in the deployment envelope of an airbag is independent of the occupant's body mass. Thus the increased risk airbags pose to females is expected to be greater than the 28% found (for ages 20-35) for crash forces. This may be an important part of the explanation why it is found that, while airbags reduce net risk to males, they increase net risk to females.[13] The females, being shorter, are more likely to be in the deployment envelope thereby increasing the risk of being struck by the airbag, and if they are struck, the blow is more likely to be fatal.

Suicide seat. In the 1960s the right-front seat was commonly referred to as the *suicide seat* because police officers observed that its occupants were more likely to be killed than drivers, or occupants of rear seats. At that time a male driver and a female right-front passenger was an even more common combination than today. The 28% higher risk to females would generate a sufficient disparity to be noticed and attributed to the risk in the seat. When both occupants are of the same gender and age, the risk in driver and right-front passenger seats are not distinguishably different (Fig. 3-15, p. 54).

Age and survivability

It is common knowledge that, as people age, their injury risk from the same physical impact, as might occur in falling, increases. A study comparing fatality rates to crash rates for the same distance of travel showed an increase in the risk of death per crash as drivers age.[14] Detailed quantification of the relationship between the risk of death from the same severity impact and age proves elusive because it can rarely be concluded that subjects received similar physical insults. An approach parallel to that used to investigate gender effects was adopted to compare risk for either gender at any age to the risk for a 20-year-old male.[15] An important difference in method from the gender investigation was required because of the age and gender mix of passengers who accompany drivers.

Most commonly, the right-front passenger accompanying a driver is of similar age and opposite gender. This facilitated the investigation of gender effects, but is a difficulty for the age analysis because there are few cases in which, say, a 70-year-old driver will be accompanied by a passenger of similar age to a passenger accompanying a 20-year-old driver. This makes it infeasible to compare risks to 70-year-old and 20-year-old drivers directly. Instead, the risk at 70 was compared to the risk at 65, the risk at 65 compared to the risk at 60, and so on through comparing the risk at 25 to the risk at 20. The risk at age 70 was compared to the risk at age 20 by multiplying the series of risk factors for each of the 5-year steps. Because each step has an associated error, the error in the risk at any age increases the further this age is from the reference age 20.

For ages below 20, comparisons are direct between the younger age categories and 20-year-old males.

Male age effect

Figure 6-6 shows results for male car occupants, based on 112,736 fatalities (all male). Values, plotted on a logarithmic scale, are relative to the risk to 20-year-old males, marked by diamond symbol on each graph. The parameter β is the slope of a least squared fit to the data constrained to pass through the point (age = 20, $R = 1$). The interpretation is (using the top-left graph for unbelted

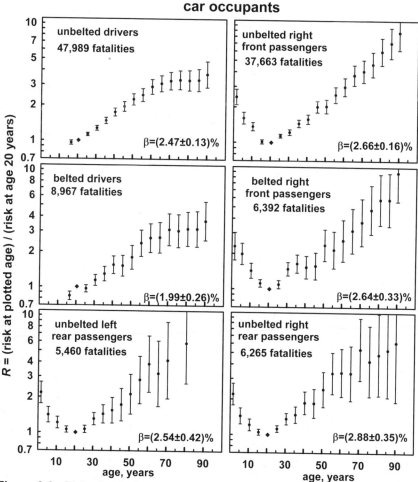

Figure 6-6. Risk of male fatality at specific ages compared to risk at age 20 for male occupants of cars. The solid diamond indicates $R = 1$ at age 20. The value $\beta = 2.47\%$ (in the top left graph) means that each additional year of aging increases risk by 2.47%.[15]

drivers) that after age 20, the risk of death from the same physical impact increases at a compound rate of 2.47% per year.

Corresponding graphs are given in the source paper for light-truck occupants and motorcyclists (drivers and passengers), leading to 16 graphs (6 for cars, 6 for light trucks and 4 for motorcyclists).[15] There are no indications of systematic differences between the 16 graphs, thus supporting the same interpretation as in the gender case that the effects are of a basic physiological nature and apply in general, not just to crashes.

The composite graphs for the data from each vehicle in Fig. 6-7 additionally support that the effect is relatively independent of vehicle type. The slopes are all consistent with a 2.5% annual compound increase in risk after age 20.

The summary result for males is given in Fig. 6-8. This can be viewed as either the weighted average of the values for the individual vehicles in Fig. 6-7, or the mathematically identical weighted average of the (up to) 16 values from each of the 16 graphs.

Before age 20, risk increases with decreasing age. After age 20, risk increases at $(2.52 \pm 0.08)\%$ per year. The risk at a given age is computed as

$$R_{\text{male}}(age) = \exp\left[0.0252 \times (age - 20)\right] \quad (\text{for } 20 \le age < \sim 80) . \qquad 6\text{-}8$$

Female age effect

The analysis proceeds in parallel with the male case. All risk values are relative to the same reference value used in the male analysis, namely a 20-year-old male. Hence the fit to the female data is not constrained to pass through any point, but rather, the value at age 20 provides a separate estimate of the risk to 20-year-old females compared to the risk to 20-year-old males.

The summary graph in Fig. 6-9 is the average for the three vehicles, or, equivalently, the weighted average for 14 individual graphs (two less than the male analysis because there were insufficient female motorcycle driver fatalities). The parameter α is the value of the fit with $age = 20$. The interpretation is that this analysis gives that female risk at age 20 is $(31.1 \pm 2.2)\%$ higher than male risk at age 20, an estimate in good agreement with the $(27.9 \pm 2.3)\%$ value obtained for age 20 in the gender comparison.

As for the male case, risk increases with decreasing age for ages younger than 20. This is not due simply to increased risk to infants seated on the laps of adults being at increased risk due to loading from the adult. Increasing risk with decreasing age is similarly present for belted occupants (*belted* here means that some type of restraint, including a baby or infant seat, was used). It is also present for rear-seat occupants. It thus appears that effects due to infants on the laps of adults can make no more than a small contribution to the observed risk increase. The risk for one-year-old babies of either gender is about twice the risk at age 20.

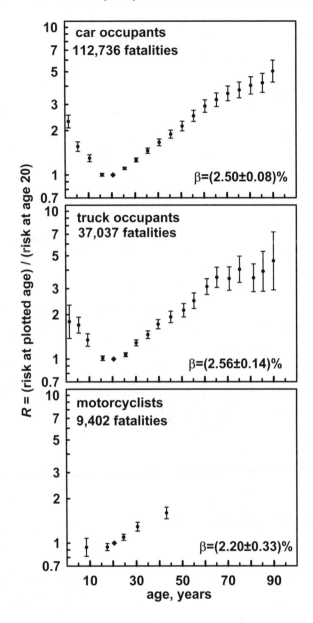

Figure 6-7. Risk of male fatality at specific ages compared to risk at age 20 for male occupants of cars, trucks, and motorcycles. The solid diamond indicates $R = 1$ at age 20. The value $\beta = 2.50\%$ (in the top graph) means that each additional year of aging increases risk by 2.50%.[15]

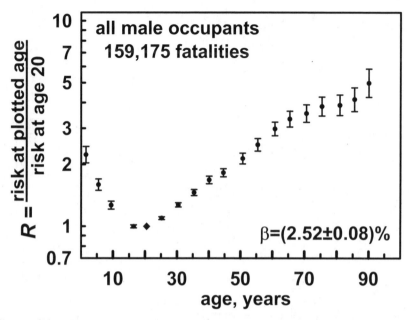

Figure 6-8. Average over all male occupants. Each point is the weighted average of the three values, one for each vehicle from Fig. 6-7.[15]

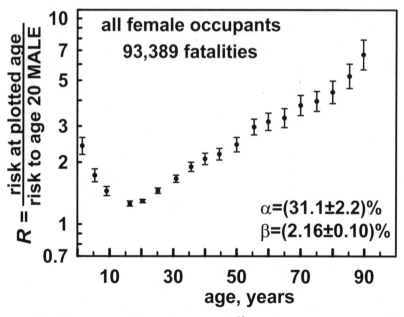

Figure 6-9. Average over all female occupants.[15]

After age 20, female risk increases at a compound rate of (2.16 ± 0.10)% per year, somewhat lower than the (2.52 ± 0.08)% yearly increase for males. The risk at a given age is computed as

$$R_{\text{female}}(age) = 1.311 \times \exp[0.0216 \times (age - 20)] \quad (\text{for } 20 \le age < \sim 80) . \qquad 6\text{-}9$$

Following the same reasoning applied to the gender examination, the age dependence of the risk of death from similar physical impacts is interpreted to reflect fundamental physiological processes. The relationships in Eqn 6-8 and Eqn 6-9 apply to physical impacts in general, and not just to those resulting from crashes.

After age 20 risk increases at compound rates of more than 2% per year for males and females. So anyone who believed that life was straight downhill after age 20 was being far too optimistic – it is downhill at an exponentially increasing rate!

Gender and age effects determined using two-car crashes

All the inferences above relating to gender and age were derived using the double pair comparison method. All vehicles used contained at least one passenger. Results were interpreted to apply to blunt trauma in general. Such a universal interpretation would receive additional support if similar effects were revealed in studies using different methods and data.

This was pursued using outcomes of two-car crashes in which at least one driver was killed.[16] The analysis was confined to cars containing only one occupant, the driver, thereby assuring that no crash used in double pair comparison analyses contributed to the two-car crash analyses. Each method therefore used independent data.

The two-car crash method is conceptually very simple. Measure the ratio, R, of female to male fatalities when cars with female drivers and cars with male drivers of similar age crash into each other. It is, however, not quite that simple because of the presence of another large confounding factor, namely, car mass. This effect of mass was removed by analyzing R versus the ratio of the car masses, and inferring the value of R if the cars had equal mass using the same method that produced Fig. 4-8, p. 74 and Fig. 4-11, p. 81.

Gender effect estimated using two-car crashes

Results are plotted using the bold symbols in Fig. 6-10. The R values measure female fatality risk divided by male fatality risk when drivers of similar age traveling in cars of the same mass crash into each other. The double pair comparison method results in Fig. 6-5 are shown again in Fig. 6-10 using smaller symbols. As the two-car crash method provides far fewer data, the data were divided into just four broad age categories centered at ages 20, 30, 45, and 70 years. The risk ratios for ages 20, 30, and 45 (which together included ages in the range 16-56 years) are $(22 \pm 14)\%$, $(23 \pm 19)\%$, and $(21 \pm 14)\%$. The weighted average of these indicates that females older than about 20 but not older than the mid fifties are $(22 \pm 9)\%$ more likely to die than males of the same age when their cars crash into each other, a result in good agreement with the $(28 \pm 3)\%$ value expected based on the double pair comparison method.

The finding for age 70 (which included ages in the range 56-97) that females are $(15\% \pm 12)$ less likely to die than males corroborates the trend towards values of R less than one found in the double pair comparison study. The consistency of the findings supports the interpretation that both methods are measuring the same fundamental difference between female and male risk of death from the same impact.

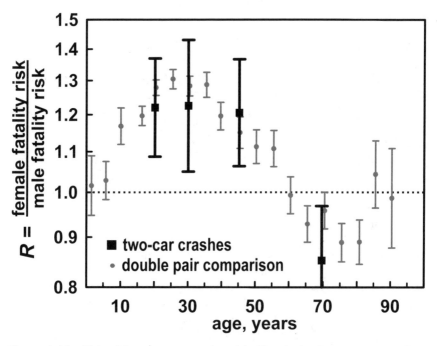

Figure 6-10. Risk of female compared to risk of male fatality versus age. The bold symbols are results from two crashes in which one driver is female and the other male, using 1,484 female and 1,078 male driver fatalities in FARS 1975-1998.[16] The smaller symbols reproduce the data in Fig. 6-5.

Age effects estimated using two-car crashes

For the age investigation, one car is always driven by a 20-year-old male driver (age 16-24), and the other by a male driver (for the male analysis) or a female driver (for the female analysis). Thus risks for both genders are relative to risks to 20-year-old males, as before.

Age effect for males. The data in Fig. 6-11 for males show good agreement between the two-car method and the double pair comparison method except at older ages. The line is a least square fit to an equation of the same form as Eqn 6-8 constrained to pass through the point $R = 1$ at $age = 20$ (and ignoring the outlier point at age 80). The fit gives $\beta = (2.86 \pm 0.32)$, meaning that risk increases at a compound rate of 2.86% per year. This may be compared to $\beta = (2.52 \pm 0.08)\%$ obtained using the double pair comparison method.

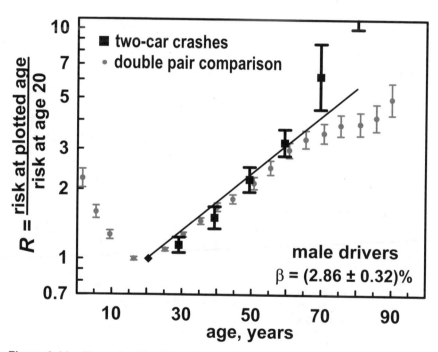

Figure 6-11. The ratio, R, of the risk of death at the indicated age to the risk of death at age 20 for males. The bold symbols are results from two-car crashes in which one driver differs in age from the other using 3623 male driver fatalities in FARS 1975-1998.[16] The smaller symbols reproduce the data in Fig. 6-8.

Age effect for females. In Fig. 6-12 the straight line is a fit to the data (excluding the outlier point at age 80) yielding two parameters (Eqn 6-9). The first, $\alpha = (20.6 \pm 11.3)\%$ estimates that at age 20 female risk exceeds male risk by 20.6%. The second, $\beta = (2.66 \pm 0.37)\%$, indicates that female risk increases at a compound rate of 2.66% per year. These values may be compared to the double pair comparison values $\alpha = (31.1 \pm 2.2)\%$ and $\beta = (2.16 \pm 0.10)\%$. Both methods show higher rates of increase per year for males than for females.

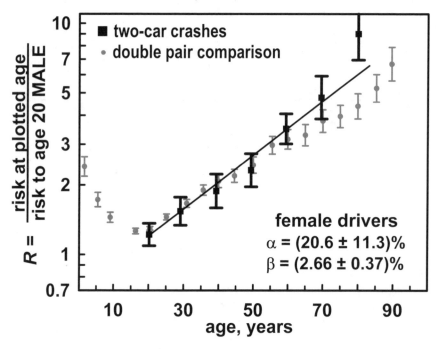

Figure 6-12. The ratio, R, of the risk of death for a female of the indicated age to the risk of death to a 20-year-old <u>male</u>. The bold symbols are results from two-car crashes in which one driver is a 20-year-old male and the other is a female of the indicated age. Based on 1768 female and 877 male fatalities in FARS 1975-1998.[16] The smaller symbols reproduce the data in Fig. 6-9.

Comments on results from the two methods

In the age analyses, the higher than trend values of R at the oldest ages likely reflects that when older drivers are involved in two-car crashes, their vehicles are more likely to be struck on the side (Fig. 7-20, p. 165). A driver in a car struck on the side is at much higher risk than a driver of a frontally-impacted car (Fig. 4-8, p. 74). Thus, the data at the oldest ages reflect that average impact severity is greater for older drivers than for the 20-year-old comparison drivers. There are insufficient data to restrict this study to frontal crashes only, which would avoid this problem.

The relatively close quantitative agreement between the two-car and double-pair-comparison estimates for the gender and for the age analyses increases confidence in the validity of both methods, in the results derived from them, and in the interpretation given to these results.

Alcohol consumption and survivability

Background

There is a common impression that the presence of alcohol reduces the likelihood of injury, given an impact of specific severity. This fits a common notion that, by being more relaxed, drunks are more likely to "roll with the punches." More importantly, some clinical studies seemed to support this notion. In general, these studies monitored the progress of sets of *drunk* and *sober* patients admitted to hospitals with injuries of similar severity. It was generally observed that the drunks exhibited higher rates of recovery or survivability. These studies were methodologically flawed in that the agent being studied, namely alcohol, played a crucial role in subject selection.[17] If alcohol increases the probability of dying at the scene of a crash, then subjects whose injuries proved fatal because of alcohol use were excluded from the comparison in the hospital tests. Similarly, if being sober compared to being drunk were to reduce injury to below that requiring hospitalization, this would similarly negate any conclusions based exclusively on those admitted to hospital. Indeed, instead of examining how alcohol influences injury risk, such studies examine secondary and unimportant details of the non-normalized distributions of injury versus recovery curves for drunk and sober drivers.

The first study to really address how alcohol affected survivability in a crash compared injuries to drunk and sober drivers involved in crashes matched in a sufficient number of important characteristics that they could be judged to be of similar severity.[18] It concluded, based on data on 1,126,507 drivers involved in 1979-1983 North Carolina crashes, that alcohol-impaired drivers were 3.85 times as likely to die as alcohol-free drivers in crashes of comparable severity. Being overweight was found to increase an occupant's risk of death and serious injury in traffic crashes.[19] The authors comment that co-morbid factors could have contributed to the effect. Interactive effects between alcohol consumption and being overweight could be one of those.

Additional evidence that alcohol increases injury risk is provided by findings that an intoxicated person might be at greater risk of immediate death due to increased vulnerability to shock and therefore decreased time available for emergency medical intervention.[20,21] Alcohol was found to increase the severity of traumatic brain injury in motor vehicle crash victims controlling for crash severity characteristics.[22]

Addressing alcohol effect using FARS data

FARS contains a variable *Alcohol Test Result* presenting measured levels of Blood Alcohol Concentration (BAC) (Chapter 10). It might therefore appear that survivability could be addressed using the double pair comparison method or the two-car crash method. Three problems preclude using either method:

1. BAC is not measured for all drivers. In FARS 2002, 35% of fatally injured drivers had no BAC level coded (Table 10-3, p. 249).

2. The probability that BAC is measured is substantially lower for surviving than for fatally-injured drivers. In FARS 2002, 75% of the drivers who were not killed had no BAC level coded.

3. The probability that BAC is measured increases with BAC for surviving and for fatally-injured drivers.

FARS advises "Alcohol Test Results from this database should be interpreted with caution."[23] Because of the need to estimate the role of alcohol in the nation's fatal crashes, procedures to impute the missing BAC values based on relationships between such factors as nighttime driving and single-vehicle crashes that are known to correlate with alcohol use have been developed and refined over the years.[24]

Any attempt to use the double pair comparison method runs into yet another problem. Only 12% of passengers involved in fatal crashes have BAC values coded in FARS. There is rarely a reason to measure the BAC of a surviving passenger, so that most values are from autopsies. If used to investigate how alcohol affected risk of survival, control occupants in the first and second comparisons must have similar alcohol use. If driver and passenger BAC were identical (and they tend to be similar), then no effect would be measured regardless of its magnitude.

In view of these problems, an approach was adopted that used only fatally injured drivers with measured BAC.[25] Although the approach used two-car crashes, it was described in terms of the following non-traffic analogy. Assume that elevators are dramatically less safe than they are, and that they are prone to come crashing freely to the ground. Assume that a sober person has a 1% probability of being killed in a low severity crash in which the elevator falls from the second floor. Assume that being drunk doubles that probability to 2%.

From many such crashes a *treatment* data set is formed consisting exclusively of fatally-injured elevator riders with known BAC. In order to extract from such data the assumed doubling of risk associated with alcohol, we need to know the mix of drunk and sober people who ride elevators. This is obtained from an *exposure* data set consisting of fatalities in elevators that fell from, say, the 40th or higher floors. Essentially everyone in such a crash will be killed, so the mix of drunk and sober fatalities provides the required exposure.

If two cars crash head on into each other and one car is more than 25% heavier than the other, the driver of the heavier car is far less likely to die than the driver of the lighter car (Fig. 4-5, p. 69). A *treatment* set can therefore be formed from drivers who died in heavier cars, given that drivers in lighter cars survived. All these *treatment* drivers died in crashes in which the probability of death was low, so that any factor that increased risk of death would increase their numbers. The *exposure* set is formed from drivers in lighter cars in two-car crashes in which the driver of the heavier (by $\geq$ 25%) car was killed. The probability that sober drivers are killed in the lighter car is so high that any additional risk-increasing factor has little opportunity to influence the outcome.

Additional two-car crash configurations were included, including side impact compared to frontal impact (Fig. 4-8, p. 74) to augment the small sample sizes resulting from the strict criteria for data inclusion. The probability of death in the treatment sample was 9.2% (higher than ideal), and in the exposure set 76.2% (substantially lower than ideal). Correction factors were applied to extrapolate these to the more extreme values of near zero and 100% assumed by the method.[25]

This same method was applied to investigate how age affected risk of death from the same physical impact. The results, based on much larger samples than available for the alcohol analysis, agreed with those reported above, providing additional validation for the age effects, and more importantly for the present method.[25]

A comparison of the distributions of BAC in the treatment and exposure sets led to the result plotted in Fig. 6-13. The straight line

$$R = 1 + k \times BAC \qquad\qquad 6\text{-}10$$

is a least-squares fit to the data reflecting the definition that $R = 1$ at $BAC = 0$. Thus R gives the risk at a given BAC relative to a value of unity for a driver with BAC = 0. The value derived for the parameter from the fit is

$$k = (9.1 \pm 2.0) . \qquad\qquad 6\text{-}11$$

Equation 6-10 with k = 9.1 estimates that, given involvement in a crash, the risk of death is increased by 73% by a BAC of 0.08%, the legal limit for driving in most US states. The average BAC in the bodies of fatally injured drivers who have a non-zero BAC in 2001 FARS is 0.17%, at which level the risk of death in a crash is 2.5 times that for a zero BAC driver.

While the effect of alcohol on increasing risk of death in a given crash is substantial, it is much smaller that the effect of alcohol on increasing a driver's risk of crashing. However, the increasing effect on fatality risk in a crash is present whether the person drives or travels as a passenger. Thus, a taxi passenger with BAC = 0.17% is 2.5 times as likely to die as a taxi passenger with BAC = 0 if the taxi crashes.

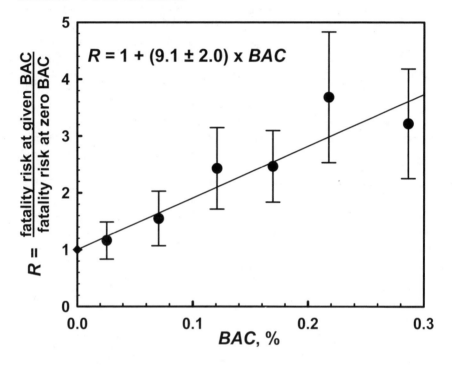

Fig. 6-13. The influence of alcohol on the risk of death from the same physical impact estimated using FARS 1975-1988 data.[25]

Summary and conclusions

Various analyses of traffic fatality data show that being female, being older, and being drunk are factors that increase the risk of death from the same physical impact. Although traffic crash data provided the "laboratory" for determining these fragility effects, they are interpreted to apply to physical impacts in general, not just to those from traffic crashes. The effects arise from differences at the basic human physiological level.

Gender effects on the risk of death from the same impact include:
- For ages 20-35 female risk exceeds male risk by $(28 \pm 3)\%$
- From mid teens to late 50s, female risk exceeds male risk
- For age <10 and age > 60, no gender-dependent difference is measured

Age effects on risk of death from the same impact include:
- For age <20, risk increases with decreasing age for males and females
  - 1-year-old baby risk is about twice that of 20-year-olds
- For age >20, risk increases with aging, at compound annual rates of
  - $(2.52 \pm 0.08)\%$ for males
  - $(2.16 \pm 0.10)\%$ for females
- A 70-year-old man is 3.5 times as likely to die as a 20-year-old man
- A 70-year-old woman is 2.9 times as likely to die as a 20-year-old woman and 3.9 times as likely to die as a 20-year-old man

Quantitatively similar gender and age effects were found in studies using different methods and data. Such agreement supports the validity of the different methods, the results derived from them, and the interpretation that the effects are basic human attributes that apply to situations beyond traffic.

Alcohol effects on the risk of death from same impact include:
- Having a BAC of 0.08% (legal driving limit in most US states) compared to zero BAC increases the risk of dying in a given crash by 73%
- Drivers with BAC = 0.17% (the average for fatally injured drivers with non-zero BAC) are 2.5 times as likely to die as zero-BAC drivers
- Passengers with BAC = 0.17% are likewise 2.5 times as likely to die as zero-BAC passengers if the vehicle in which they are riding crashes

----

There is old adage that God protects drunks and babies. The detailed analyses in this chapter show it is false on both counts – from the same severity impact babies and drunks are more likely to die.

References for Chapter 6

1 Evans L. Female compared to male fatality risk from similar physical insults. *J Trauma*. 2001; 50: 281-288.

2 Evans L. Double pair comparison – a new method to determine how occupant characteristics affect fatality risk in traffic crashes. *Accid Anal Prev*. 1986; 18: 217-27.

3 Fleiss JL. *Statistical Methods for Rates and Proportions*. New York, NY: Wiley; 1973.

4 Schlesselman JJ. *Case-Control Studies: Design, Conduct, Analysis*. New York, NY: Oxford University Press; 1982.

5 Young HH. *Statistical Treatment of Experimental Data*. New York, NY: McGraw-Hill; 1962.

6   Evans L. Rear seat restraint system effectiveness in preventing fatalities. *Accid Anal Prev.* 1988; 20: 129-36.

7   Evans L. Age dependence of female to male fatality risk in the same crash: An independent reexamination. *Crash Prev Inj Control.* 2000; 2: 111-21.

8   Evans L. Risk of fatality from physical trauma versus sex and age. *J. Trauma.* 1988; 28: 368-78.

9   Foret-Bruno JY, Faverjon G, Brun-Cassan F, et al. Females more vulnerable than males in road accidents. Paper no. 905122, Proceedings of the XXIII FISITA Congress, Torino, Italy; 7-11 May 1990. Volume 1, p. 941-950.

10 World Health Organization. *The Injury Chartbook*, p. 14. Geneva; 2002.

11 Pheasant S. *Body Space: Anthropometry, Ergonomics and Design.* London: Taylor & Francis; 1986.

12 Najjar MF, Rowland M. *Anthropometric reference data and prevalence of overweight, United States, 1976-1980.* Hyattsville, MD: US Department of Health and Human Services, Public Health Service, National Center for Health Statistics; 1987.

13 Dalmotas DJ, Hurley J, German A, Digges K. Air bag deployment crashes in Canada. Paper 96-S1O-05. 15th Enhanced Safety of Vehicles Conference, Melbourne, Australia; 13-17 May 1996.

14 Li G, Braver ER, Chen LH. Fragility versus excessive crash involvement as determinants of high death rates per vehicle-mile of travel among older drivers. *Accid Anal Prev.* 2003; 35: 227-235.

15 Evans L. Age and fatality risk from similar severity impacts. *J Traf Med.* 2001; 29: 10-19.

16 Evans L, Gerrish PH. Gender and age influence on fatality risk from the same physical impact determined using two-car crashes. SAE paper 011174. Warrendale, PA: Society of Automotive Engineers; March 2001. (Also included in: *Vehicle Aggressivity and Compatibility in Automotive Crashes.* SAE special publication SP-1601, 2001).

17 Waller JA. Methodologic issues in hospital based injury research. American Association for Automotive Medicine, 31st Annual Proceedings, New Orleans, LA, p. 95-108; 1987.

18 Waller PF, Stewart JR, Hansen AR, Stutts JC, Popkin CL, Rodgman EA. The potentiating effects of alcohol on driver injury. *J Am Med Assoc.* 1986; 256: 1461-1466.

19 Mock CN, Grossman DC, Kaufman RP, Mack CD, Rivara FP. The relationship between body weight and risk of death and serious injury in motor vehicle crashes. *Accid Anal Prev.* 2002; 34: 221-228.

20 Anderson TE, Viano DC. Effect of acute alcohol intoxication on injury tolerance and outcome. In: Noordzij P, Roszbach R, editors. *Alcohol, drugs and traffic safety – T86*, p. 251-254. Amsterdam, Netherlands: Excerpta Medical Elsevier Science Publisher; 1987.

21 Dischinger PC, Soderstrom CA, Shankar BS, Cowley RA, Smialek JE. The relationship between use of alcohol and place of death in vehicular fatalities. Association for the Advancement of Automotive Medicine, 32nd Annual Proceedings, Seattle, WA, p. 299-311; 12-14 September 1988.

22 Cunningham RM, Maio RF, Hill EM, Zink BJ. The effects of alcohol on head injury in the motor vehicle crash victim. *Alcohol Alcoholism.* 2002; 37: 236-240.

23 Fatality Analysis Reporting System (FARS) Web-Based Encyclopedia. Create a query, and choose "Alcohol Test Result" as a variable to obtain caution regarding use of BAC values in site. http://www-fars.nhtsa.dot.gov

24 Subramanian R. *Transitioning to Multiple Imputation – A New Method to Estimate Missing Blood Alcohol Concentration (BAC) Values in FARS.* Report DOT HS 809 403. Washington, DC: US Dept of Transportation; January 2002 (Revised October 2002). http://www-nrd.nhtsa.dot.gov/pdf/nrd-30/NCSA/Rpts/2002/809-403.pdf

25 Evans L, Frick MC. Alcohol's effect on fatality risk from a physical insult . *J Stud Alcohol.* 1993; 54: 441-449.

7 Older drivers

Introduction

Older drivers have been the focus of an extensive and expanding literature, reflecting concerns that projected increases in the number of older drivers will increase societal harm from traffic crashes.[1,2] A 1998 review focusing on just one aspect of older-driver research lists 428 references.[3] Much additional literature has appeared since then documenting relationships between advancing driver age and medical conditions relevant to driving,[4,5] including vision[6] and cognition.[7] Specific driver performance skills have been shown to decline with increasing age.[8]

In the United States, influential organizations, including the National Highway Traffic Administration, the American Medical Association, the American Association for Retired Persons, and the American Automobile Association, have ongoing activities and policies relating to older drivers. Other motorized countries have similarly high interest in older drivers.

This chapter provides a broad epidemiological overview of how various risk measures change as drivers age. The approach is to display graphically many different rates as a function of gender and age. As discussed in Chapter 1, measures in traffic safety are nearly always rates. Different rates provide answers to different questions. The question, "Does risk in traffic increase as drivers grow older?" is insufficiently specific to have an answer. If the risk is specified as say, the risk that a driver will be killed in same distance of driving, then the question does have a quantitative answer, which will be provided below.

Although the main emphasis here is on older drivers, age is treated as a variable. While all quantitative results are presented in terms of this variable, the terms *young* and *old* are used in the text for expository convenience, just as one would use *cold* and *hot* if the variable were temperature. In neither case would quantitative definitions of these terms be necessary or helpful. Risks to older drivers are measured relative to risks to drivers of other ages, particularly risks to younger drivers. Hence risks to older and younger drivers are intrinsically components of the same broad technical question of how risk depends on age.

Two distinct types of risks

Two conceptually distinct types of risks change as drivers become older:

1. Risks to the drivers themselves.

2. Threats the drivers pose to other road users.

These risks are of a different nature. There is near universal agreement that there should be more, and stronger, laws to prevent people from harming others than to prevent them from harming themselves. Indeed, the view that there should be no laws aimed at preventing people from harming only themselves always finds some support. Public safety makes a stronger claim on public resources than does personal safety, some aspects of which are generally supported using personal resources. Differences between the risks we assume ourselves and threats we pose to others have important impacts on legislation, licensing policy, and police enforcement.

Changing risks drivers face as they age

The risks that drivers face as they age are examined in terms of the numbers of them killed per year while driving (Fig. 7-1) as recorded in FARS data.[9] *Drivers* includes drivers of any motorized vehicle. The values plotted are the sums of values for the three years 2000, 2001 and 2002 divided by three. The resulting average number of deaths per year provides a more reliable estimate than data for a single year, especially at ages for which there are few fatalities in any one year. The peak numbers occur at age 19 years (plotted at 19.5) for both genders. The general pattern for drivers is similar to that for all fatalities shown previously in Fig. 3-9, p. 46. This is to be expected, as the majority of fatalities in US traffic are drivers. However, note how similar the patterns also are for non-drivers (Fig. 3-10, p. 46).

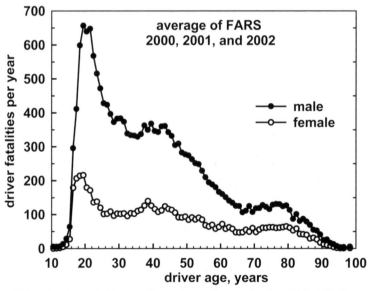

Figure 7-1. Number of drivers of any type of motorized vehicle killed per year versus driver gender and age. Average values for FARS 2000-2002.[9]

One of the reasons why the number of driver deaths declines with increasing age is that there are fewer people of older age in the population. It is therefore appropriate to examine the *population* rate, the number of deaths per million people (Fig. 7-2). This was derived using Bureau of the Census estimates for 2001,[10] so this and other plots may be interpreted to apply to the central year, 2001. The population rate shows a U-shaped pattern between ages 20 and 80 that recurs for many rates. The rate begins to increase with age in the early 60s for men and women, peaking in the mid 80s at values close to the maximum values for younger drivers.

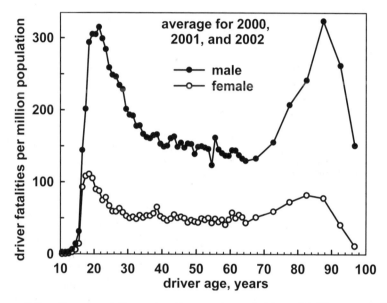

Figure 7-2.   The *population* rate, the number of driver fatalities per million population versus gender and age.   FARS 2000-2002[9] and US Bureau of the Census data for 2001.[10]

Drivers and licensed drivers

The population rate is based on dividing the number of drivers killed by the number of people in the population without regard to whether or not they are licensed drivers.   Many people in the US do not have driver licenses, as is illustrated by the Federal Highway Administration data shown in Fig. 7-3.[11]   For ages prior to the mid 20s, males and females have remarkably similar probabilities of being licensed to drive.   With increasing age women have increasingly lower rates of licensure than men.   This reflects earlier social norms.   A woman aged 85 in 2001 was born in 1916 and entered the years of license eligibility in the 1930s, a period when it was not so common for women to drive.

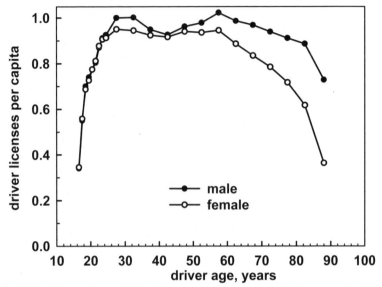

Figure 7-3. The number of driver licenses per capita, which is approximately the same as the probability that a person has a driving license. (A commercial truck driver, for example, may have multiple licenses). FHWA data for 2001.[11]

Some of the drivers included in Figs 7-1 and 7-2 were killed while driving without licenses. There are many reasons for not having a license, including being too young to be eligible, not applying, failing license tests, not renewing through forgetfulness or fear of failing tests, or having a license suspended or revoked for traffic law violation. The mix of reasons will be different for younger and older drivers. Figure 7-4 shows that the probability that a fatally injured driver did not have a valid driver license at the time of his or her fatal crash depends strongly on gender and age. Unlicensed drivers killed are overwhelmingly male, with FARS data for 2002 recording 3,524 males and 595 females – a male-to-female ratio of 5.9 to 1. The increases in Fig. 7-4 at older age may reflect that some older drivers whose licenses are revoked on medical or competency grounds still continue to drive, sometimes with fatal consequences. The increases at younger ages relate more to driving before applying for or obtaining a license.

The plot in Fig. 7-4 does not include data for 336 boy and 75 girl drivers aged 13 and younger, for a male-to-female ratio of 4.5 to 1 (more on this topic on p. 227-228). As all these drivers are below the age of licensure in all US states, their data would correspond to points at 100 percent. The first point plotted is for 14-year-old fatally injured drivers, where the percents without valid licenses are 93% for boys and 88% for girls. Seven US states issue learner-driver permits to drivers under age 15 (Table 8-1, p. 200), although the most common US practice is to issue learner permits at age 15.[12]

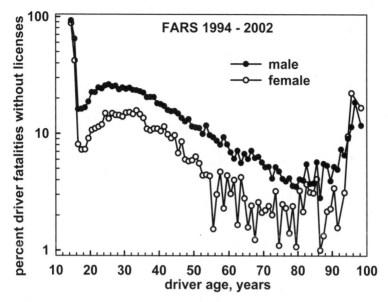

Figure 7-4. The percent of fatally injured drivers without valid driver licenses at the time of their fatal crash. FARS 1994-2002.[9]

The data plotted in Fig. 7-5, unlike in the earlier figures, include only those fatally-injured drivers who had valid driver licenses at the time of their fatal crashes. The *license* rate, the number of licensed drivers killed per million licensed drivers, shows a much clearer increasing trend with increasing age, the effect being similarly prominent for men and women. The downward trend in the population rate at the oldest ages (Fig. 7-2) was largely reflecting a lower rate of licensure.

Distance of travel

The 2001 National Household Travel Survey (NHTS)[13] was a survey of travel for all members of about 66,000 households contacted by telephone between April 2001 and May 2002. This provided the estimates of the average distance of travel per driver in 2001 shown in Fig. 7-6.

The number of licensed drivers killed per billion kilometers of licensed driving, the *distance* rate, is estimated by multiplying the estimates in Fig. 7-6 by the numbers of licensed drivers. The *distance* rate (Fig. 7-7) varies so much more than the *population* or *license* rates that it is plotted on a logarithmic scale. Relationships similar to Fig. 7-7 are found for cars and light trucks separately using estimated travel distance derived from odometer readings of vehicles in NASS data.[14(p 68-74)] Drivers older than 80 suffer more driver deaths for the same distance of travel than the highest values for drivers in the late teens and early twenties.

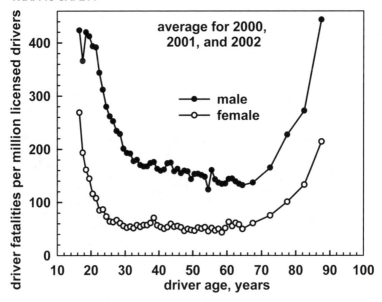

Figure 7-5. The *license* rate, the number of driver fatalities per million licensed drivers. FARS data for 2000-2002,[9] driver license data for 2001.[11]

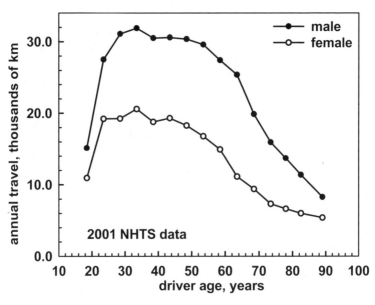

Figure 7-6. Annual distance of travel based on telephone survey data. NHTS 2001.[13]

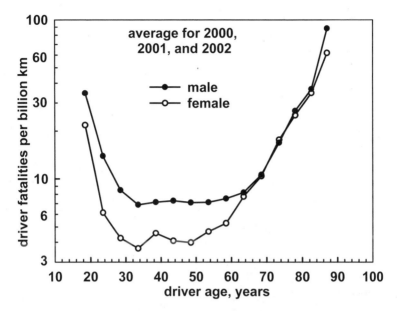

Figure 7-7. The *distance* rate (licensed driver fatalities per billion km of travel by licensed drivers) versus gender and age.   Based on FARS 2000-2002[9] and NHTS 2001.[13]

The reason why the *distance* rate increases at young and old ages so much more than the other rates is because of the variation in travel as a function of driver age.   One of the largest changes to occur as drivers age is that they drive less.   A major contribution to this is reduced commuting trips to places of employment.   Such trips account for about half of personal travel. Another contribution comes from decisions to drive less because of concerns about driving competency in general, and more particularly at night, on freeways, or in inclement weather.   In general, aging is accompanied by reductions in activities requiring travel.   The data in Fig. 7-7 are for licensed drivers.   As people become older it is increasingly likely that they will not have a license and cease driving entirely (Fig. 7-3).   While safety is one component of what has been referred to as *the older driver problem*, another major factor is reduced mobility.[15,16]

Fragility – increased risk of death in given crash as drivers age

Increases in the *population, license,* and *distance* rates with increasing age should not be interpreted to reflect increases in the driver's risk of crashing with aging.   Such an interpretation misses the crucial point that the number of drivers of given gender and age killed is the product of two factors:

1. The number of involvements in severe crashes.

2. The probability that involvement proves fatal.

The first factor reflects influences due to use and behavioral factors, such as amount of driving, environmental conditions, roadway classification, intoxication, driver capabilities, and, most importantly, driver risk taking. Chapter 6 showed that when a crash occurs, the risk of death depends on the gender and age of the occupant. Alcohol consumption was also shown to affect survival as a factor separate from its much larger influence on the risk of crashing. One behavioral factor that has a large influence on survival is the use of a safety belt. This does not depend too strongly on gender and age, the variables of interest in this chapter. We therefore assume that when a crash occurs the dependence on survival is represented by the previously derived Eqn 6-8, p. 134, for male drivers and Eqn 6-9, p. 137, for female drivers. We use these relationships to estimate involvement rates in crashes of similar severity by considering crashes in a severity range greater than sufficient to likely kill 80-year-old male drivers, for which case Eqn 6-8 gives $R_{male}(80) = 4.54$.

Consider the mix of crashes in which N fatalities occur to 80-year-old males. If these crashes were repeated keeping all factors except the drivers the same, then we would expect $N/(4.54)$ fatalities for 20-year-old male drivers and, by using Eqn 6-9, $1.311 \times N/(4.54) = N/(3.46)$ fatalities for 20-year-old female drivers. In order to obtain the same number of fatalities, 4.54 times as many crashes by 20-year-old male drivers, and 3.46 times as many crashes by 20-year-old female drivers are required. In this way we can use the observed numbers of fatalities to infer involvement rates in crashes in a severity range sufficient to likely kill 80-year-old male drivers.

Figure 7-8 shows the number of involvements in similar severity crashes per licensed driver versus gender and age. This is obtained from the licensed driver deaths in Fig. 7-5 by the calculation described above. The point for 80-year-old males has the same value in Fig. 7-8 as in Fig. 7-5, but the value of the point for 20-year-old males in Fig. 7.8 is 4.54 times that in Fig. 7-5. In contrast to the earlier figures, there is only a modest increase in involvements in severe crashes per licensed driver with increasing age, showing that a major component of increasing fatality risk with increasing age is greater risk of being killed in the same crash. Also note that the number of severe crashes per licensed driver for older drivers never approaches even close to the high values for younger drivers.

Severe crash involvements for the same distance of travel (Fig. 7-9) increase with increasing driver age for ages above about 60. However, the increase is modest compared to that for the distance fatality rate (Fig. 7-7). Even for the oldest age category (85 and older) severe crash involvements for the same distance of travel are less than that for the youngest age category (16-20 years).

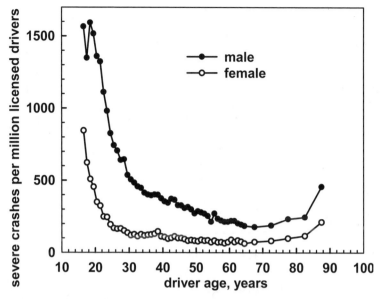

Figure 7-8. Estimated involvements per million licensed drivers in crashes of sufficient severity to likely kill 80-year-old male drivers.

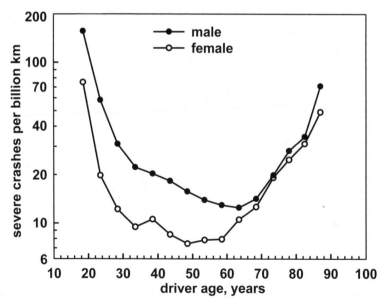

Figure 7-9. Estimated involvements per billion km of driving in crashes of sufficient severity to likely kill 80-year-old male drivers.

Threat to other road users

The threat drivers impose on other road users is estimated by examining the number of pedestrians killed as a function of the gender and age of the involved driver. Only single-vehicle crashes are included, so a typical case will be a vehicle striking and killing a pedestrian but without injuring the driver. No assumption is made regarding legal responsibility in pedestrian fatality crashes. FARS data show about one third of fatally injured pedestrians have blood alcohol concentrations that would be illegal for drivers (there are no laws relating to blood alcohol concentration for pedestrians or passengers, only laws against behavior in public resulting from intoxication). I suggest in Chapter 16 that regardless of the behavior of the pedestrian, there should be a default legal presumption of driver responsibility.

The number of pedestrians killed versus the gender and age of the involved driver shows that the main threat to other road users is overwhelmingly from young drivers (Fig. 7-10). Even after adjusting for the fewer numbers of older people in the population, it is still the young who pose the greatest threat to other road users (Fig. 7-11). Another way of interpreting Fig. 7-11 is that it represents the threat to other road users of the average individual of given gender and age, and that the greatest threat comes from 20-year-old males.

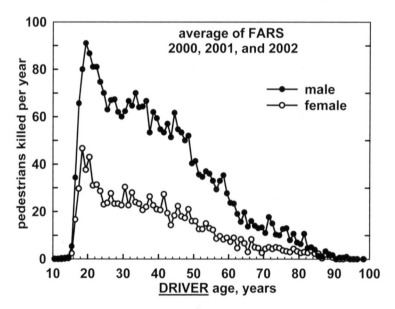

Figure 7-10. Number of pedestrians killed per year in single-vehicle crashes according to the gender and age of the driver of the involved vehicle. FARS 2000-2002.

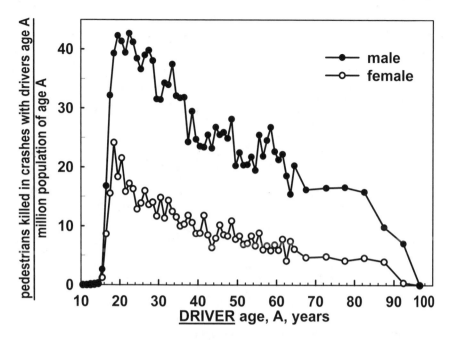

Figure 7-11. Number of pedestrians killed per year in single-vehicle crashes divided by the number (millions) of people in the population of the same gender and age as the involved <u>driver</u> versus the gender and age of the involved <u>driver</u>. FARS 2000-2002, Bureau of the Census, 2001.

The number of pedestrians killed per licensed driver (Fig. 7-12) shows no more than a modest increase with increasing age at the oldest age interval (85 years and older) for women drivers. In general, a license holder of almost any younger age poses a greater threat to other road users than even the oldest license holder for whom data are available.

For the same distance of travel, drivers pose increasing risks to other road users as they age past about 60 (Fig. 7-13). However, even at ages past 80 they still pose lower risks than do 20-year-old drivers.

Pedestrian involvements in fatal and severe crashes

Above we noted that as people become older they drive less. Some driving may convert into more walking. In this section we examine how pedestrian risks depend on pedestrian age.

Figure 7-14 shows the distribution of pedestrian fatalities by pedestrian gender and age. The same data normalized by population are shown in Fig. 7-15. After age 60 the risk of pedestrian death per person increases steeply to a peak, and then declines (likely reflecting reduced walking).

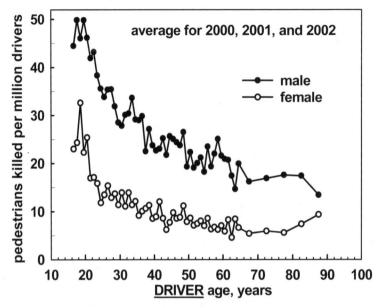

Figure 7-12. Number of pedestrians killed per year in single-vehicle crashes per licensed driver. FARS 2000-2002, FHWA data for 2001.[11]

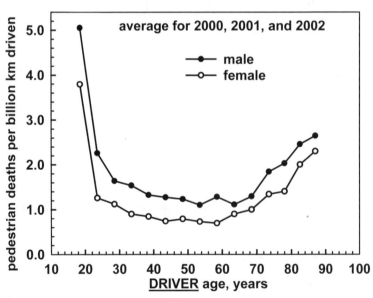

Figure 7-13. Number of pedestrians killed per year in single-vehicle crashes per billion kilometers of travel by licensed drivers of given gender and age. FARS 2000-2002, NHTS 2001.[13]

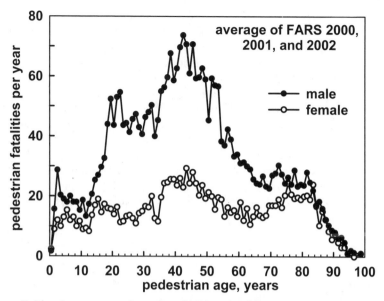

Figure 7-14. Average number of pedestrian fatalities per year versus gender and age. FARS 2000-2002.

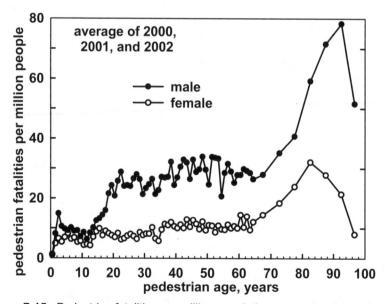

Figure 7-15. Pedestrian fatalities per million population versus gender and age. FARS 2000-2002, FHWA data for 2001.[11]

Part of the large increase in pedestrian fatalities per capita at older ages in Fig. 7-15 is due to the greater likelihood that the older person is killed by an impact that would not kill a younger person. In order to estimate the risk that a pedestrian is struck by a vehicle, as distinct from the consequences of being struck, we again use the relationships between risk of death from the same impact and gender given in Eqns 6-8 and 6-9 (p. 134 and 137). Figure 7-16 shows the number of pedestrian involvements in crashes in the severity range equal to or greater than would likely kill an 80-year-old male pedestrian. Like the driver fatality data, the pedestrian fatality data show peaks at the late teens or early 20s. The increasing involvement in severe pedestrian crashes with increasing age at ages above about 65 probably reflects decreasing perceptual skills and agility, and also perhaps increased pedestrian exposure related to driving less. The declines after age 80 likely reflect reduced activity.

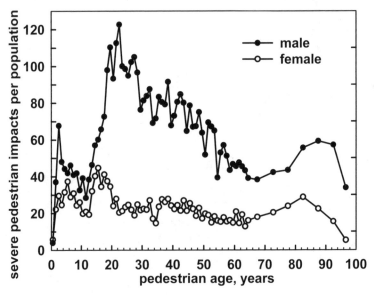

Figure 7-16. Estimated pedestrian involvements per million population in crashes of sufficient severity to likely kill 80-year-old male pedestrians versus gender and age.

Cross sectional compared to longitudinal analyses

All the above analyses, in keeping with nearly all analyses of age effects in traffic, have been *cross sectional*. That is, rates for people of different ages are compared in a specific year. While results have been discussed in terms of drivers aging, strictly speaking cross sectional analysis cannot address what happens as individuals age. Apparent aging effects would be generated even if every driver were assigned a risk at birth that remained unchanged throughout his or her life, but drivers born a long time ago were given higher rates than those born recently. The overall declines in fatality rates over time presented in Chapter 3 indeed suggest that today's drivers of a given age have lower risks than drivers of the same age in earlier decades.

Studies that trace the characteristics of a given group, or *cohort*, of people as they age are referred to as *longitudinal*. There is a convention in epidemiology to connect data points only for longitudinal data, but not for cross sectional data, as we have done in all the figures. The non-adherence to this convention in the interests of clarity is unlikely to generate ambiguity. In order to explore how the risks of a group of 20-year-old drivers changed as they aged into 85-year-old drivers, data from 1935 through 2001 would be required, but the earliest FARS data are for 1975. Even if the data were available, many other factors that influence safety have changed dramatically since 1935, so that there does not seem any way, even in principle, to estimate how a driver's risk changes with aging that is free from substantial uncertainty. It is cross sectional data, such as presented here, that provide information relevant to policy decisions for today's population. Decisions rarely require information about how safe today's 80-year-olds were 60 years ago, or how safe today's 20-year-olds will be in 60 years. It is today's drivers who are licensed, or have their licenses revoked.

While not so central to policy decisions, longitudinal analyses add to understanding of how aging impacts driving, and can add insights into long-term future trends. One longitudinal study tracing a group of drivers over 16 years of FARS data (1975-1990) found that risks increased later and less steeply than in cross sectional comparisons. Another longitudinal study examined how crash types varied for drivers over age 60 in 1987-1995 Finnish data, and found that the proportion of older-driver crashes that were at intersections depended on cohort and age.[17] A longitudinal analyses using the much longer series of FARS data now available would provide useful new information.

Traffic deaths relative to all deaths

2,403,351 people died from all causes in 2000 in the US.[18] Of these, 41,945, or 1.75%, died in traffic crashes. The vast majority of deaths are from diseases, for which risk generally increases steeply with increasing age, whereas traffic deaths peak at young ages. The age dependencies for disease and traffic combine to make the probability that a given death is a traffic fatality depend very steeply on age, as shown in the logarithmic plot in Fig. 7-17. An exponential decline (straight line in the graph) fits the data well ($r^2 = 0.99$) for both genders between ages 20 and 80, leading to, *probability male death is traffic fatality* $= 188\,e^{-0.079\,a}\ (20 < a < 80)$ 7-1

and

probability female death is traffic fatality $= 145\,e^{-0.078\,a}\ (20 < a < 80)$ 7-2

where *a* is age in years. Thus the probability that a death is a traffic fatality declines at just under 8% per year for both genders during most of their lives.

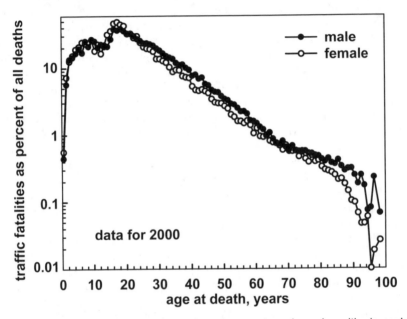

Figure 7-17. Traffic deaths expressed as a percentage (on a logarithmic scale) of total deaths from all causes (including traffic). FARS 2000 and NCHS(CDC) data for 2000.[18]

Given the much higher numbers of young males than young females killed in traffic, the absence of a clear difference between the genders in Fig. 7-17 might seem surprising. The explanation is that most deaths of younger people are from injuries, not diseases. The gender-dependence for non-traffic injuries, in the US mainly firearm deaths, follows a pattern similar to the dependence for traffic crashes, so the ratio of traffic deaths to all deaths ends up relatively gender independent.

Table 7-1 shows illustrative ages selected from the plotted data. Given that a death occurs to a 20-year-old, the probability that it is a traffic fatality is over 30%. Given that a 17-year-old girl dies, it is about as likely to be due to a traffic crash as from all other (injury plus disease) causes combined. As people age, the risks from other causes of death increase much more rapidly than any increase of risk in traffic. Given that a 65-year-old dies, the probability that death is due to a traffic crash is less than one percent. For an 80-year-old it is less than half a percent, and less than a quarter of a percent for ages above 90.

Table 7-1. Given that a death occurs, the percent probability that it is a traffic fatality of any kind. Based on data from FARS 2000 and NCHS(CDC) 2000.[18]

| age | *probability that death is traffic fatality (%)* | |
	male	*female*
0	0.45	0.56
3	14.34	15.24
5	19.30	20.70
10	25.13	18.11
16	37.98	46.65
17	36.58	48.85
20	32.97	32.60
25	23.37	20.69
30	18.23	13.65
40	7.61	5.32
50	3.44	2.69
60	1.48	1.25
65	0.86	0.77
70	0.59	0.57
80	0.43	0.33
90	0.25	0.10
97+	0.07	0.03

Types of crashes

Not only do the numbers of crashes vary by gender and age, but the types of fatal crashes in which older drivers are involved differ from the mix for the overall population.

Rollover and driver age

Fig. 7-18 shows that as drivers age, when a driver is killed, the probability that it occurs in a crash in which rollover is the most harmful event declines, reaching very low values at the oldest ages. For age 90 and older, FARS 2000-2002 documents 299 male driver fatalities – eight of them in rollover crashes. For female drivers, 118 fatalities, three in rollovers. For both genders, given a driver death at age 90 or older, there is a less than 3% chance that it is a rollover, compared to a 25% chance for drivers in their mid-twenties. The higher rates for males and for younger drivers supports that rollover is related more to driver risk-taking than vehicle characteristics. Ninety percent of rollover crashes are single vehicle.

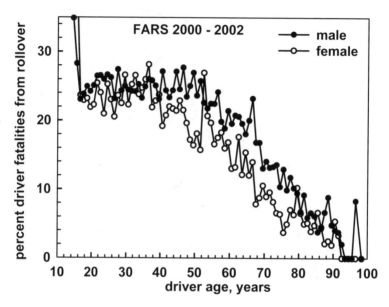

Figure 7-18. Probability that, when a driver is killed, rollover is the most harmful event. FARS 2000-2002.

Two-vehicle crashes and side impact

Given that a driver is killed the probability that it is in a rollover crash, or more generally a single-vehicle crash, decreases steeply with age. As a consequence, the probability that the death results from a two-vehicle crash must increase with age (Fig. 7-19). The type of two-vehicle crash also depends on driver gender and age. Figure 7-20 shows the percent of all drivers killed in two-vehicle crashes who were killed in vehicles struck on the side.

The three figures (Figs 7-18 to 7-20) show patterns consistently interpretable in terms of risk taking. Consider a hypothetical extremely risky male driver who crashes into the first available object. This is unlikely to be a vehicle – there are far more trees than vehicles. His crashes will be overwhelmingly single vehicle, likely involving rollover. Although a small percent of his crashes will be two-vehicle crashes, he will still be involved in more two-vehicle crashes than an average driver. If he is involved in a two-vehicle crash, his vehicle is more likely to have a frontal than a side impact. Now consider a hypothetical very safe female driver. She is going to avoid single-vehicle, and therefore also rollover crashes, or crashing head-on into other vehicles. Her main risk in

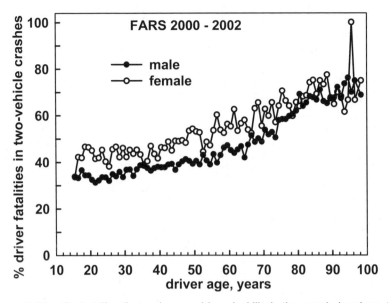

Figure 7-19. Probability that, when a driver is killed, the crash involves two vehicles. FARS 2001-2002.

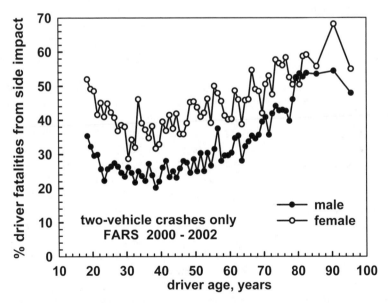

Figure 7-20. Probability that, when a driver is killed in a two-vehicle crash, the impact is from the side (initial impact points 8, 9, or 10 for left side and 2, 3, or 4 for right side). FARS 2000-2002.

traffic is being side impacted by other vehicles, so that a high percent of her low crash risk is from side impact crashes.

The high proportion of older drivers who are killed in side impacts, and the high risks faced by older pedestrians (Fig. 7-15) suggests that the most productive way to protect older road users is to address the behavior of younger road users.

All the above relationships are based on relative risks, so the comments in the section *Interpreting risk ratios* (p. 76-77) should be kept in mind. Fig. 7-20 does not imply that an elderly woman driver is more likely to be killed on her next trip by side impact than is a young male driver. It implies that if she is killed, the probability that it is from a side impact is higher than the probability that the young male driver, if he is killed, will be killed by a side impact.

Risk comparisons using specific examples

The material above shows many measures, each addressing how some specific risk changes as drivers age. Below, specific examples are presented in tabular form to summarize and simplify the main features of the different measures. The values quoted are in many cases obtained by interpolating between values plotted, and in a few cases are based on relatively small sample sizes.

Threats to other road users

Table 7-2 compares the risks imposed on other road users by drivers aged 20, 45, and 70 years, as indicated by the number of single-vehicle pedestrian fatality crashes in which the divers were of those ages. For fatalities to others per licensed driver (the first row), all the relative risks shown are substantially less than one. This means renewing the license of a 70-year-old for another year imposes far less risk on other road users than renewing the license of a 45- or 20-year-old. The effects are so large and clear as to leave little doubt that, from a public safety perspective, there should be less concern over renewing the license of an average 70-year-old applicant than of applicants of any younger age. For example renewing the license of a 70-year-old female imposes 41% less risk than renewing for a 45-year-old female, and 77% less risk than for a 20-year-old female. If the rate is for the same distance of travel rather than per year, then 70-year-olds impose more risk than 45-year-olds, but about half the risk of 20-year-olds.

Table 7-3 shows parallel information for 80-year-old drivers. Renewing the license of an 80-year-old for another year imposes substantially less risk on other road users than renewing the licenses of younger drivers, but by lesser amounts than noted above for 70-year-old drivers.

While data become sparse at ages beyond 80, the indications are clear that renewing for another year the license of drivers at any age up to the maximum for which data are available (near 90) poses less risk to others than renewing licenses of substantially younger drivers (Fig. 7-12).

Table 7-2. Threats 70-year-old drivers pose to other road users compared to the threats posed by 45- and 20-year-old drivers, as measured by pedestrians killed in single-vehicle crashes. The first entry indicates that, on average, licensing a 70-year-old male poses 34% less threat than licensing a 45-year-old male, and 64% less threat than licensing a 20-year-old male.

rate	male		female	
	age 70 / age 45	age 70 / age 20	age 70 / age 45	age 70 / age 20
pedestrians killed per licensed driver (Fig. 7-12)	0.66	0.36	0.59	0.23
pedestrians killed for same distance of driving (Fig. 7-13)	1.19	0.41	1.48	0.46

Table 7-3. Threats 80-year-old drivers pose to other road users compared to the threats posed by 45- and 20-year-old drivers, as measured by pedestrians killed in single-vehicle crashes.

rate	male		female	
	age 80 / age 45	age 80 / age 20	age 80 / age 45	age 80 / age 20
pedestrians killed per licensed driver (Fig. 7-12)	0.70	0.38	0.68	0.26
pedestrians killed for same distance of driving (Fig. 7-13)	1.79	0.62	2.24	0.70

Risks older drivers themselves face

As drivers age, some measures indicate increases in risk (Tables 7-4 and 7-5). A major contributor to this is that the same severity crash is more likely to lead to the death of an older person. In terms of the measures which best reflect the behavioral aspects of driving, namely, driver involvements in severe crashes for the same distance of travel (Table 7-4), and crashes in which pedestrians are killed for the same distance of travel (Table 7-2), the values for 70-year-old male drivers are within 19% of those for 45-year-old male drivers. (Many factors could contribute to the lack of a larger difference, such as the older drivers confining driving to safer periods, less alcohol use, etc.). The involvement rates for 80-year-old drivers are 80% above those for 45-year-old drivers (Tables 7-3 and 7-5).

Table 7-4. Risks faced by 70-year-olds compared to risks faced by 45- and 20-year-olds. The last two entries in the first row indicate that a random 70-year-old woman in the population is 7% more likely to become a driver fatality in the next year than is a 45-year-old woman, but 38% less likely than is a 20-year-old woman.

rate	male		female	
	age 70 / age 45	age 70 / age 20	age 70 / age 45	age 70 / age 20
driver fatalities per head of population (Fig. 7-2)	0.94	0.48	1.07	0.62
driver fatalities per licensed driver (Fig. 7-5)	0.94	0.39	1.25	0.60
driver fatalities for the same travel distance (Fig. 7-7)	1.77	0.53	3.19	0.98
severe crashes per licensed driver (Fig. 7-8)	0.56	0.13	0.78	0.22
severe crashes for same travel distance (Fig. 7-9)	0.94	0.15	1.85	0.34

Table 7-5. Risks faced by 80-year-olds compared to risks faced by 45- and 20-year-olds.

rate	male		female	
	age 80 / age 45	age 80 / age 20	age 80 / age 45	age 80 / age 20
driver fatalities per head of population (Fig. 7-2)	1.47	0.74	1.51	0.87
driver fatalities per licensed driver (Fig. 7-5)	1.55	0.64	2.14	1.03
driver fatalities for the same travel distance (Fig. 7-7)	4.42	1.33	7.44	2.29
severe crashes per licensed driver (Fig. 7-8)	0.73	0.18	1.08	0.31
severe crashes for same travel distance (Fig. 7-9)	1.83	0.30	3.50	0.64

Examples using hypothetical families

The illustrations above can be simplified further by comparing risks to members of hypothetical families. Let us consider a family with the following three members:

son   age 20

dad   age 45

granddad age 70

We focus on male members because males comprise 70% of driver fatalities. Assume all have driving licenses, and crash rates equal to the averages reported above. Based on the results in Figs 5, 7, 8, 9, 12, and 13, the risk associated with each of the family members can be ranked from the highest risk (rank 1 in Table 7-6) to the safest (rank 3). The first row indicates that the son is most likely to die in the forthcoming year as a driver, the granddad least likely. The second row indicates that in a trip of fixed distance, say to the drugstore, the son is most likely to die, the dad the least likely to die.

Table 7-6. Comparison of risks associated with 3 family members. The first row indicates that the son is most likely (rank 1) to die in the forthcoming year as a driver, the granddad least likely (rank 3).

family member → *age* →	*son* *20*	*dad* *45*	*granddad* *70*
Who is most likely to die as a driver?			
In the next year	1 son	2 dad*	3 granddad*
On a trip, say, to the drugstore	1 son	2 granddad	3 dad
Who is most likely to crash?			
In the next year	1 son	2 dad	3 granddad
On a trip to the drugstore	1 son	2 dad*	3 granddad*
Who is most likely to kill another road user?			
In the next year	1 son	2 dad	3 granddad
On a trip to the drugstore	1 son	2 granddad*	3 dad*

* Little difference in values – ranks not clearly differentiated.

For all the measures listed, the son has the highest risk, in all cases by large amounts. In a few of the comparisons, indicated by asterisks, the risks for the dad and granddad were quite close, but the ranks listed reflect the nominal values read from the plots.

For the case when the granddad is 80, the rankings are all unambiguous (Table 7-7). In a trip to the drugstore, the 80-year-old granddad is more likely to be killed than the 20-year-old son. For all the other cases listed, the son has the highest risk.

Table 7-7. Comparison of risks associated with 3 family members. The first row indicates that the son is most likely (rank 1) to die in the forthcoming year as a driver, the dad least likely (rank 3). Granddad is 80, compared to 70 in previous table.

family member → age →	son 20	dad 45	granddad 80
Who is most likely to die as a driver?			
In the next year	1 son	2 granddad	3 dad
On a trip, say, to the drugstore	1 granddad	2 son	3 dad
Who is most likely to crash?			
In the next year	1 son	2 dad	3 granddad
On a trip to the drugstore	1 son	2 granddad	3 dad
Who is most likely to kill another road user?			
In the next year	1 son	2 dad	3 granddad
On a trip to the drugstore	1 son	2 granddad	3 dad

The older driver problem – how is it changing?

The findings here are based on data centered in 2001. Analyses with features in common with the present have been applied previously to data for the mid-1990s[19] and the early 1980s.[20,21] The more recent the study, the more data were available at older ages. Indeed, the studies using early 1980s data selected 65 as the main older driver age category because of the paucity of data at ages older than this.[20,21] The plots presented here have many data at ages above 90.

The decision of those setting up the FARS system to allow only two digits for age, although well justified by early 1970s experience, turns out to be unfortunate. The oldest specific age that can be coded is 96 (not 99, because fields are needed for such categories as *age unknown*). FARS 2002 codes 12 people aged 96. The next age category, which includes everyone 97 and older, has 17. It would be valuable to know the specific ages of those in this open-ended category, especially as the numbers at very old ages are expected to increase in the future. Also, accumulating small values over many FARS years often provides useful information.

The studies from the three periods indicate fairly robust relationships, with no more than minor differences in detail. The stability of the rates means that even as the number of older drivers increases, the present rates can be applied to larger numbers of drivers. The threat that older drivers pose to other road users was similarly small in all the studies.

The above discussion has focused on how various measures depend on average age. Not only do various measures of driver performance decline with age, but variability among individuals also increases, underlying the importance of not judging an individual's fitness to drive on the basis of chronological age. Licensing decisions should be based on tests that apply to all without regard to age. The admonitions about the uses and pitfalls of average values at the end of Chapter 3 (p. 60) apply here also.

The younger driver problem

The graphs and tables presented here consistently show that young male drivers have the highest fatality and crash rates, and pose the greatest threats to other road users. The same finding emerges from the prior studies discussed, and from many additional sources. While some measures for older drivers indicate above average risk, the amount that they are above average appears to be trending downwards in time. Such a tendency will elevate the already dominant contribution of young, especially young male, drivers to even greater prominence. One of the grand themes at the center of traffic safety in every country in the world is that traffic crashes are overwhelmingly a problem of young male drivers.

Summary and conclusions

Two conceptually distinct types of risks change as drivers become older:

1. Risks to the drivers themselves
2. Threats the drivers impose on other road users

Using single-vehicle crashes in which pedestrians were killed to measure the risks drivers impose on other road users shows:

- Renewing for another year the license of an <u>80-year-old man</u> imposes
  - 30% less risk on others than renewing license of a 45-year-old man
  - 62% less risk on others than renewing license of a 20-year-old man

- Renewing for another year the license of an <u>80-year-old woman</u> imposes
  - 32% less risk on others than renewing license of a 45-year-old woman
  - 74% less risk on others than renewing license of a 20-year-old woman

- Renewing for another year the license of a driver up to ages for which there are useful data (about 90 years old) imposes less risk on others than renewing the license of an average driver.

As the main public policy concern in licensing drivers is harm they may cause others, age alone is not a reason to deny licenses.

A major contributor to the reduced risk that older drivers impose on others in a year is that drivers travel less with advancing age. Reduced mobility is just as much part of what has been called the *older driver problem* as are changes in safety. In terms of traveling the same distance, older drivers do impose greater risks on others than 45-year-old drivers, but still much lower risks than the risks imposed by 20-year-old drivers.

As drivers age, various risks they face in traffic increase. For example an 80-year-old woman driver is 7 times as likely to be killed as a 45-year-old woman in trips of the same distance. A large portion of this difference arises because of increased fragility with increasing age – the same severity crash is more likely to kill the 80-year-old. However, the risk of crashing also increases steeply with increasing age at the oldest ages.

As drivers age, the types of crashes in which they are killed change, with rollover being less likely, and being side impacted more likely. The risk of being a pedestrian fatality increases to high levels at ages in the 80s. The most productive way to protect older road users from being killed in side impact and as pedestrians is to focus on the behavior of the younger drivers who are involved in a large portion of these – and all types of – crashes.

All results are averages. Characteristics at any age vary widely. Decisions about fitness to drive should be based on specific tests applied without regard to age. Chronological age is not associated with any risks that would justify using it alone as a basis for denying a license.

Given that someone dies, the probability that the death is a traffic fatality declines steeply with age, from over 30% at age 20, to under one percent at age 65, under half a percent at age 80.

Young male drivers have the highest fatality and crash rates, and pose the greatest threats to other road users. A central finding of traffic safety in every country in the world is that traffic crashes are overwhelmingly a problem of young male drivers.

References for Chapter 7

1 Lyman S, Ferguson SA, Braver ER, Williams AF. Older driver involvements in police reported crashes and fatal crashes: Trends and projections. *Inj Prev.* 2002; 8: 116-120.

2 Bedard M, Stones MJ, Guyatt GH, Hirdes JP. Traffic-related fatalities among older drivers and passengers: Past and future trends. *Gerontologist.* 2001; 41: 751-756.

3 Eby DW, Trombley DA, Moinar LJ, Shope TJ. The assessment of older drivers' capabilities: A review of the literature. Report UMTRI-98-24, University of Michigan Transportation Research Institute, Ann Arbor, Michigan; August 1998.

4 Owsley C, McGwin G Jr, Sloane M, Wells J, Stalvey BT, Gauthreaux S. Impact of cataract surgery on motor vehicle crash involvement by older adults. *J Am Medical Assoc.* 2002; 288: 841-849.

5 Lyman JM, McGwin GJ, Simms RV. Factors related to driving difficulty and habits in older drivers. *Accid Anal Prev.* 2001; 33: 413-421.

6 McGwin G Jr, Chapman V, Owsley C. Visual risk factors for driving difficulty in older drivers. *Accid Anal Prev.* 2000; 32: 735-744.

7 Lundberg C, Hakamies-Blomqvist L. Driving tests with older patients: Effect of unfamiliar versus familiar vehicle. *Trans Res, Part F.* 2003; 6: 163-173.

8 Warshawsky-Livne L, Shinar D. Effects of uncertainty, transmission type, driver age and gender on brake reaction and movement time. *J Safety Res.* 2002; 33: 117-128.

9 Fatality Analysis Reporting System (FARS) Web-Based Encyclopedia.   Data files and procedures to analyze them.   http://www-fars.nhtsa.dot.gov

10 Population Projections Program, Population Division, US Census Bureau, Department of Commerce Washington, DC (http://www.census.gov).   Specific data used was "(NP-D1-A) Projections of the Resident Population by Age, Sex, Race, and Hispanic Origin: 1999 to 2100." http://www.census.gov/population/projections/nation/detail/d2001_10.pdf

11 Federal Highway Administration, Office of Highway Policy Information. *Highway Statistics 2001.* http://www.fhwa.dot.gov/ohim/hs01/xls/dl20.xls

12 State-by-state driving rules for teenage drivers.   http://golocalnet.com/drivingage

13 2001 National Household Travel Survey (NHTS). http://nhts.ornl.gov/2001/html_files/introduction.shtml

14 Kahane CJ. Vehicle weight, fatality risk and crash compatibility of model year 1991-99 passenger cars and light trucks. Report DOT HS 809 662 2. Washington, DC: US Department of Transportation, National Highway Traffic Safety Administration; October 2003.

15 Stalvey BT, Owsley C. The development and efficacy of a theory-based educational curriculum to promote self-regulation among high risk older drivers. *Health Promot Pract.* 2003; 4: 109-119.

16 Keeffe JE, Jin CF, Weih LM, McCarty CA, Taylor HR. Vision impairment and older drivers: Who's driving? *Br J Ophthalmol.* 2002; 86: 1118-1121.

17 Hakamies-Blomqvist L, Henriksson P. Cohort effects in older drivers' accident type distribution: Are older drivers as old as they used to be? *Trans Res Part F.* 1999; 2: 131-138.

18 National Center for Health Statistics, Center for Disease Control. Table 310. Deaths by single years of age, race, and sex. http://www.cdc.gov/nchs/data/statab/wktbl310.pdf

19 Evans L. Risks older drivers face themselves and threats they pose to other road users. *Int J Epidemiology.* 2000; 29: 315-322.

20 Evans L. Older driver involvement in fatal and severe traffic crashes. *J Gerontology: Soc Sciences.* 1988; 43: S186-S193.

21 Evans L. *Traffic Safety and the Driver.* New York, NY: Van Nostrand Reinhold; 1991. Chapter 2. Effects of sex and age, p. 19-43.

8 Driver performance

Introduction

In this chapter we explore the elements that constitute the driving task and their relationship to safety. We use the term *driver performance* to refer to the driver's knowledge, skill, and perceptual and cognitive abilities. This is distinct from how the driver actually uses these attributes, for which we use the term *driver behavior*, the subject of the next chapter.

Components of the driving task

The driving task is a closed-loop compensatory feedback control process, meaning that the driver makes control inputs (to the steering wheel, brakes, and accelerator pedal), receives feedback by monitoring the consequences of the inputs, and in response to these consequences, makes additional inputs. An open-loop process is one in which additional inputs cannot be applied after initiating the process, such as throwing a ball. The ball's trajectory cannot be changed once it has left the hand.

When decomposed into fine detail, the driving task has much complexity, involving as it does the simultaneous control of lateral and longitudinal position through the use of steering wheel, accelerator, and brakes, together with many pattern recognition and other higher level cognitive skills, such as estimating future situations from present information. While the basic skills required to propel a vehicle are usually learned quickly and with ease, some of the higher-level skills that affect safety can be acquired only after many years of experience.

Predominance of visual feedback

The feedback used to monitor driving is overwhelmingly visual. I see no reason to dissent from a 1972 statement that vision provides over 90% of information used to drive.[1(p 150)] Drivers tend to ignore information on signs, or even be unaware of a sign's existence, if the relevant information can be derived directly from the driving environment. The driver's preferred mode of operation is to pursue a visual search, and resort to other information sources only when problems arise, perhaps somewhat like the way most people consult owners' manuals only after preferred methods of trying to solve problems have failed.

The preponderance of visual information over that from all other senses probably increases yet further with increasing skill levels. For example, proprioceptive cues (those from the force and position of hands and arms in supplying control inputs) are of minor importance, and, surprisingly, are even less likely to be noticed by more experienced than less experienced drivers. A skilled driver is relatively unaware of the gain in the steering system (the amount the steering wheel must be turned to alter the vehicle's direction by a given angle). When transferring to vehicles with different steering system gains, experienced drivers do not travel more, or less, sharply around corners, or have difficulty maintaining lane position. Instead, they react to the visual information by making the steering input necessary to achieve the desired visual result without being much aware how much they moved the wheel and in such a manner that there are no observable changes in the trajectory of the vehicle. Similar comments apply to different force characteristics, or, in the extreme, to power versus manual steering. Less experienced drivers are more aware of steering system gain and force-feel characteristics, and their driving can be noticeably influenced by changing them.

The dominance of visual feedback in driving is similar to dominance of aural feedback in the playing a stringed musical instrument. Intonation (playing in tune) is not controlled by the proprioceptive sense of remembering where to place the fingers, but by listening to the sounds produced. A learner trained on an instrument of one size will play one of a different size (on which all the finger placements are different) more out of tune, whereas a skilled player will be less aware that there is even a difference, just as in the steering gain case.

Visual performance

Given the predominance of the visual sense in driving, one might expect that visual performance and crash risks would be intimately related. Innumerable studies over many decades have failed to show any clear relationship between the most basic measure of visual performance, visual acuity, and crash risk. Crash rates decline to a minimum at about age 45, by which time visual acuity and contrast sensitivity have already begun to decline, as have other visual capabilities relevant to driving, such as the ability to withstand glare.[2]

Even so dramatic a visual impairment as the non-use of one eye does not have an overwhelming effect on safety, although it has been shown to have some influence.[3,4] However, the magnitude is sufficiently modest, and indeed uncertain, that a strong case is made that monocular drivers should not be excluded as racing drivers.[5] Although US inter-state truck drivers are subject to stringent license requirements, the agency responsible for licensing them approves licensing monocular drivers.[6]

Changes in higher-level visual characteristics, in particular the *useful field of view,* the area from which useful visual information can be extracted in a single glance, has been shown related to crash involvement risk.[7] Pattern recognition skills are central to driving task. From a loosely-structured, but stimuli-rich, visual environment the driver must select information that is relevant from much that is not.

Judgment of speed

Of the various quantities a driver is called upon to judge, speed is the only one for which instrumented quantitative feedback must, by law, be available. Each time a driver consults a speedometer, perceived speed can be compared to actual speed. Such consultations are additionally motivated by the need to obey speed limits. The repetitive practice, with feedback, of this task might suggest that drivers would become very good at estimating their speed. Many studies have examined the extent to which this is so.

In an experiment on a British test track, drivers of cars with obscured speedometers were instructed to double or halve an initial speed, the magnitude of which was known only to the experimenter.[8] The subjects' attempts to halve or double the initial speeds were biased by large amounts in the direction of the initial speed. For example, the goal of doubling an initial speed of 30 mph produced an average speed of 44 mph, while the goal of halving 60 mph produced 38 mph. In a study in Japan, drivers instructed to travel at their chosen speeds on closed roads drove, on average, 3 km/h faster when the speedometer was concealed.[9]

Subjects in other speed-estimation experiments traveled as passengers in vehicles with speedometers visible only to the drivers who conducted the experiments. This allowed greater task flexibility. Subjects instructed to keep their eyes straight ahead consistently underestimated the speed at which they were traveling.[9] The instructions more specifically asked subjects to fixate on the focus of expansion, the geometrical point from which a straight road appears to emerge as one travels forward. Two studies asked subjects to estimate speed without telling them where to look. Speeds were estimated without large average systematic errors; the errors averaged over all subjects tested was typically less than 5 km/h.[10,11] When hearing was restricted, both studies found systematic speed underestimation, typically by about 8 km/h.[10,11] Further evidence that hearing can play a role in estimating speed is provided by the ability of blindfolded passengers to judge speed without systematic error,[11] and by decreased ability of subjects in a driving simulator to maintain set speeds when auditory cues were removed.[12]

While the above experiments indicate that hearing can play a contributory role in estimating speed, it is the changing size and position of objects in the visual field that provide the main cues to speed, and variations in these can generate different sensations of motion. For example, a geometric pattern of bars with decreasing spacing on a roadway produced a sensation of increasing speed, which in turn led drivers to reduce speed.[13] This concept has been applied, for example, to slow traffic in work zones.[14] The main cue for speed comes from peripheral vision. When peripheral vision is eliminated leaving only the central field of view to determine speed, estimates become inaccurate because the vehicle's forward movement produces little change at the focus of expansion.[15]

Speed adaptation

A sensation familiar to nearly all drivers is that after prolonged driving at high speeds, slower speeds seem even slower than they really are. This phenomenon, referred to as *speed adaptation*, has been examined in a number of studies. In one, subjects were instructed to drive at 70 mph for specified distances, and then, without guidance from a speedometer, slow down to 40 mph. It was found that the longer the exposure to 70 mph, the higher is the speed later produced to represent 40 mph. After 40 miles driving at 70 mph, the average driver slowed to 53 mph in response to the request to produce 40 mph.[16] A simulator study found that a subject's selection of a target speed is highly influenced by the subject's previous speed. After simulated driving at about 70 mph for three minutes, subjects underestimated a simulated 30 mph by between 5 to 15 mph; the perception that the speed was lower than actual persisted for at least 4 minutes.[17]

Another approach to examining speed adaptation is to observe, in traffic, groups of vehicles that previously have been traveling at different speeds. Speeds of vehicles traveling in opposite directions on a four-lane divided highway were compared.[18] One direction of traffic had been exposed previously to expressway speeds of about 60 mph, while vehicles in the other direction had been exposed to about 40 mph. For each of seven categories of vehicles examined, higher speeds were observed for those exposed to the higher prior speed. The magnitude of the effect is that those previously exposed to 60 mph traveled about 7% faster than those exposed to 40 mph. It is not possible to determine to what extent this difference is due to speeds being perceived differently, or to drivers merely tending to continue driving close to their prior speeds because of behavioral inertia. This distinction was addressed in another study using sites that required drivers to slow down or stop prior to entering the section of roadway on which their speeds were measured.[19] The observed effects were about half of the 7% observed without the slow-down or stop. It is, however, worth noting that the act of slowing down after prolonged freeway driving may itself influence the speed adaptation phenomenon, in that the prior speed becomes not the freeway speed, but the briefly experienced low or zero speed.

The tendency to drive faster on a given road because of prior high speeds on a different road, regardless of the extent to which it is due to perceptual biases in speed estimation or to speed perpetuation, has important safety implications. Through this phenomenon, speed limits, and changes in speed limits, may have spillover effects that influence safety on roads other than the ones directly affected. There are many indications that the 1974 reduction in the speed limit on US Interstate highways from 70 mph to 55 mph led to reductions in speeds on other roads with unaltered speed limits, and that this *spillover* effect is responsible for some of the reduction in fatalities from 54,052 in 1973 to 45,196 in 1974. The 16% drop is the largest yearly decline ever recorded in peacetime in the US. After 1987, when the US Congress relaxed, and in 1995 removed, the 55 mph limit, increased speed limits on rural sections were associated with higher speeds on urban sections with unchanged limits.[20]

Speed adaptation appears to be largely a perceptual illusion not unlike many optical illusions in which how part of a simple drawing is perceived is greatly influenced by adjacent parts of the drawing. As visual training and experience do not make optical illusions disappear, it seems unlikely that experience or training would make speed adaptation disappear. This underlines the importance of speedometer use, especially when exiting freeways after prolonged travel, or when traveling on streets with low speed limits after traveling at higher speeds. The speedometer provides important information that drivers are unable to obtain using only their unaided senses.

Judgment of relative speed

Much driving is spent following vehicles that are following other vehicles. The field of *traffic science* originated in elegant mathematical descriptions of vehicle following.[21] Each vehicle (except the lead) in a platoon of vehicles is assumed to react, after a time delay, to a stimulus arising from its relationship with the vehicle it is following. A typical time delay for test track experiments is 1.6 s. The reaction is an acceleration or deceleration. Various forms of the stimulus have been explored, but the one most successful at explaining a great deal of experimental data is the relative speed divided by the spacing.

Drivers' abilities to judge relative speeds have been measured in a number of experiments.[22] In keeping with the results from the vehicle-following experiments, it is found that the ability to judge relative speed is approximately inversely proportional to inter-vehicle spacing. This is consistent with drivers reacting to changes in the perceived area of the followed vehicle rather than to changes in a linear dimension.

The ability to judge the sign of relative motion in a car-following situation was investigated by occluding the vision of subjects who rode in the right-front passenger seat of an instrumented car that followed another instrumented car on a freeway.[23] When the experimenter in the following car judged that the relative speed between the vehicles to be sufficiently close to zero to make judging its sign difficult, the subject was permitted to see the lead car for four seconds. The subject's task was to indicate whether the vehicles moved closer together or further apart. Instructions called for a *forced choice* – one or other response was required for each stimulus. As is common in forced choice experiments, even for stimuli so small that subjects indicated that they were only guessing, correct responses were in fact well above the chance level.

One surprising result of this experiment was a highly consistent bias in favor of judging that the cars were approaching when they were not. This bias, in the direction of increased safety, is likely induced by peripheral vision cues related to the forward motion of the vehicle in which the subject is traveling. Because of the bias, which increased in magnitude with inter-vehicle spacing, it is not possible to express the results in terms of one threshold value because different values for positive and negative relative speed pertained at each spacing. However, the experiment showed high capabilities at judging the sign of relative motion. For example, if a lead car 60 m away is approaching the following car at 5 km/h, the following driver's probability of correctly judging that the vehicles are closing rather than pulling further apart was 0.99. The results show that it is unlikely that a factor in rear-end crashes is attentive drivers being unable to judge that they are approaching a lead car.

Judgment of spacing

People tend to be able to judge distance reliably over a wide distance range.[24] The short distance cues of accommodation (the focusing of the eye's lens) and binocular disparity (the eyes having to aim more towards each other as viewed objects become nearer) are of little consequence in judging distances of objects outside a vehicle. Most distances that require judgment are in the range 5 m to 500 m. Many factors have been shown to influence spacing judgments. For example, size constancy, the built-in knowledge we have about the size of familiar objects. Vehicles that are larger are judged to be further away. The finding that approaching motorcycles appear further away than trucks provides a likely explanation for why drivers give smaller safety margins to the motorcycles.[25]

Judgment of factors influencing spacing in car following was investigated by projecting static views of the rear of a lead car photographed from the driver's eye position of a following car.[26] Subjects judged whether a particular view represented a greater or lesser inter-vehicle spacing than a standard view. It was found that the same distance was perceived to be greater when viewed from a vehicle with hood geometry that exposed more roadway between the vehicles. This was additionally confirmed by viewing from the same vehicle with its rear raised in order to make more roadway visible. The lead car is actually the same distance from the camera in both photographs in Fig. 8-1.

The finding that the same spacing is perceived to be different from different vehicles has safety implications. Say a driver familiar with a vehicle with a long hood transfers to one with a less obstructed view. If the driver follows at his or her normal perceived spacing, then the vehicle with the less obstructed view will be driven closer to the one followed. Such an effect was observed directly in test-track experiments in which small cars (with short hoods) were observed to follow at closer headways than large cars driven by the same drivers.[27] The perceptual effect would cause drivers of sport-utility vehicles (SUVs) to follow closer than car drivers without knowing they were doing so. This could explain why one hears so many complaints that SUV drivers tailgate.

Overtaking

On a two-lane roadway the task of overtaking a lead vehicle in the face of an oncoming vehicle involves judging the distance of the oncoming vehicle, and the relative speed between the oncoming vehicle and the driven vehicle, which may be in excess of 200 km/h. Drivers' judgments and decisions in overtaking were investigated in extensive experiments conducted on one side of a completed but unopened four-lane section of Interstate freeway.[28] Subjects in

Figure 8-1. The perception of inter-vehicular spacing. Which picture shows a closer following distance?

one car followed another, while a third car approached in an adjacent lane. It was found that while drivers make reliable estimates of the distance to the oncoming car, they are insensitive to its speed. Basically, at distances required for this task, cues to relative speed (mainly the angle subtended at the driver's eyes by the oncoming car) provide minimal information. When the subjects were informed of the speed of the oncoming car, passing occurred at smaller, and less varying, spacing. These results parallel findings that pedestrians base road-crossing decisions on how far away approaching vehicles are, rather than on their speed.[29]

A follow-up overtaking study found that unsuspecting drivers on two-lane rural roads overtook slower moving cars with greater likelihood the greater the available passing distance, and the lower the speed of the lead car.[30] At night, drivers were more conservative and more variable in the passing distances they were willing to accept than in daytime driving. The inability of drivers to estimate oncoming speed leads them to decline safe passing opportunities when the oncoming car is traveling slower than expected, and to initiate unsafe passing maneuvers when the oncoming car is traveling faster than expected.

Reaction times

Reaction times are influenced by many factors, but, for driving, the two most important are, first, the number of stimuli and possible responses, and second, expectancy.[31] If a subject is instructed to fixate on an unlit lamp, and press a switch as soon as possible after it lights, then simple reaction times on the order of 0.15 s are generally recorded. If the number of stimuli and responses increase (say a number of lights, each with its own switch), then choice reaction times become progressively longer. If the lamp lights every few seconds, reaction times will be far shorter than if the lamp lights every few hours. Expectancy is crucial -- reaction times to expected events are short, to unexpected events much longer.[32]

Reaction times in driving involve identifying a variety of events in a complex environment, so it is not surprising that reaction times bear little resemblance to the minimum possible in laboratory tests. Indeed, it is convenient, conceptually, to divide the time from stimulus to driver response into two phases, decision or perception reaction time (time to decide to brake, for example), and response or movement reaction time (time to place foot on brake pedal), even though they are generally observed as one composite reaction time. While there is fairly extensive literature on reaction times relating to driving,[33] the most difficult factor to investigate, especially as it relates to crashes, is that of expectancy.

The reaction time that produced the best fit to the previously discussed car-following data is 1.6 s. It should be noted that this is for drivers specifically focusing on the car ahead in a test-track experiment. To address expectancy, an experiment was conducted in which young and old drivers of an instrumented vehicle suddenly encountered an object after traveling over a crest-vertical curve (a straight road traveling over a hill).[34] On the first trial, the drivers had been driving for about 10 to 15 minutes, and the object was unexpected. In subsequent trials subjects knew the goal of the experiment, but the location of the object changed. Perception and response times were considerably longer for the trial in which the drivers were not alerted than for the subsequent ones. The older subjects had longer perception and reaction times than the younger, in keeping with much research that shows that reaction times increase with age. For all the subjects combined, the 95th percentile total reaction time for the trials in which drivers were not alerted was 1.6 s. However, the authors point out that while driving an instrumented vehicle with an experimenter present, a driver may be more alert than an average driver. They recommend the use of a reaction time of 2.5 s for surprised drivers, a value that is the common choice in US traffic engineering practice for such purposes as computing sight distances in freeway design.

Reaction times in normal driving were measured by presenting an unexpected stimulus to actual drivers in Finland through the use of a parked instrumented vehicle.[35] When it was safe to do so, the door of this vehicle was opened presenting oncoming motorists with a view of the door close to, but not encroaching upon, the lane on which they were traveling. By means of eight pairs of infrared photocells, the moment at which the oncoming vehicle's trajectory first changed in response to the stimulus of the opened door was measured for 1,326 oncoming drivers. It was found that the average response time was about 2.5 s, with most response times being between 1.5 s and 4.0 s. Thus the 2.5 s value mentioned above finds additional support in this study, and is used in the following example constructed to bring out the importance of reaction time and stopping time.

An example illustrating reaction time and braking

Suppose a car traveling at speed v_1 drives over the crest of a crest-vertical curve, and is suddenly confronted by a large obstruction completely blocking the roadway (say, an overturned truck blocking all lanes). Let distances from the crest of the hill be represented by x. The car will travel to $d_1 = v_1 T$ before braking commences, where T is reaction time. Assume that applying maximum braking imparts a constant deceleration, α. The speed, $V_1(d)$, is given by

$$V_1(d) = \sqrt{v_1^2 - 2\alpha d} \qquad\qquad 8\text{-}1$$

where d is the distance traveled since braking commenced.

Let us proceed by assuming specific values. We take $\alpha = 5$ ms^{-2}, a reasonable value for good tires on dry level pavement (we ignore the hill which was for expository convenience only). This value is just over half the 9.8 ms^{-2} acceleration due to gravity. For reaction time we take $T = 2.5$ s, and for initial speed, $v_1 = 55$ mph (89 km/h, or 24.6 m/s). The driver will begin to brake at

$x = d_1 = 61.5$ m, and the car will come to a complete stop (if it does not crash) at $x = D_1$ where

$$D_1 = v_1 T + v_1^2/(2\alpha) = 121.9 \text{ m} . \qquad 8\text{-}2$$

The trajectory of this car is shown as the dashed line in Fig. 8-2. Also shown, as the solid line, is the trajectory of a second car that differs only in that its initial speed is $v_2 = 70$ mph (113 km/h, or 31.3 m/s), the value used to compute $d_2 = 78.2$ and $D_2 = 176.2$.

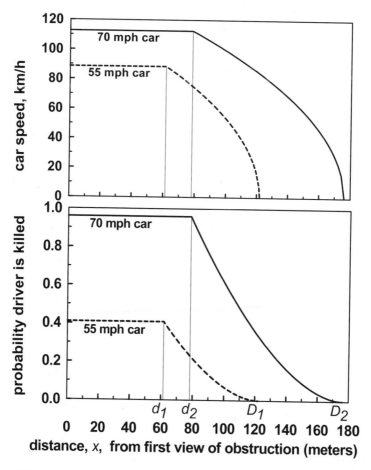

Figure 8-2. Schematic representation of how the speed of a vehicle varies along a roadway from the location $x = 0$ at which a large obstruction inviting maximum braking first appears (top) and how the probability of driver fatality depends on the location of the obstruction (bottom).

If the obstruction is located at $x > D_2$ neither car will crash into it. If it is located between D_1 and D_2 then the faster car will crash into it but the slower car will not. If it is located at $x < D_1$ then both cars will crash into it, but the faster car at a higher impact speed. If it is located at $x < d_1$ both cars will crash into it at their unaltered initial speeds v_1 and v_2.

If we assume that the obstruction on the highway does not move or crush when impacted by a car, then the striking car will experience a change in speed, or Δv, equal to its traveling speed on impact. Figure 4-7 (p. 72) shows that the probability, P, that an unbelted driver is killed is given approximately by $P = (\Delta v/114)^{3.54}$ provided $\Delta v < 114$ km/h. This is used to compute the probability of death as a function of where the obstruction is located along the roadway, as shown in the bottom graph in Fig. 8-2.

If the impact occurs prior to any braking ($x < d_1$) the driver of the faster car is $(70/55)^{3.54} = 2.3$ times as likely to be killed as is the driver of the slower car. If the impact occurs just as the faster car begins to brake ($x = d_2$), the driver of the faster car is 4.2 times as likely to be killed as the driver of the slower car, which has slowed from 89 km/h to 75 km/h when it reaches d_2. As x becomes greater than d_2 the ratio of the risk to the faster driver to that to the slower driver becomes larger and larger until the risk to the lower-speed driver becomes zero at $x = D_1$, while the faster driver still has some probability of death for $D_1 < x < D_2$.

The values of d_1 and d_2 are proportional to the reaction time, which was assumed to be 2.5 s. Outcomes are sensitive to this choice. If we chose a reaction time 10% shorter than this ($T = 2.25$ s) then, if the obstruction was at $x = 90$ m, the probability that the slower driver is killed decreases from its initial 13% to a lower 9%, and the probability that the faster driver is killed decreases from an initial value of 75% to a lower value of 65%. For $x = 100$ m the corresponding changes are from 7% to 4%, and from 61% to 51%.

This simple example illustrates three themes of central importance:

1. Small reductions in reaction time can produce large reductions in the probability and severity of crashes.

2. The probability of crashing increases with speed.

3. Given that a crash occurs, fatality risk increases steeply with speed.

In the next chapter relationships are provided suggesting that fatality crash risk is proportional to the fourth power of speed, so that traveling at 70 mph has a fatality risk $(70/55)^4 = 2.6$ times the risk traveling at 55 mph, a ratio that is plausible in terms of the illustrative values presented above.

Rear impact crashes

As rear-impact crashes generally involve vehicles traveling in the same direction, with perhaps one of them stationary, they tend to be of below-average severity, accounting for 5% of US fatal crashes. However, a total of 1.9 million rear-end crashes occurred in 2000, accounting for 30% of all crashes.[36] They also accounted for 30% of the crashes for which injuries were reported, even though some of these may be due more to litigation than impact, as discussed in Chapter 2.

Technology to reduce the risk of rear impact appeared as early as 1916 in the form of a rudimentary stop lamp.[37] Because small reductions in reaction time promise large reductions in crash rates, there has been much research on refining the details of stop lamps.   Such factors as light configuration, color, and brightness have been examined, as well as methods of indicating the magnitude of deceleration of the lead car.[38,39]

Center high mounted stop lamps

A major change in alerting following drivers that a lead vehicle was braking occurred with the introduction of the *center high mounted stop lamp*, a red stop lamp mounted on the centerline of the rear of vehicles. It is generally higher then the other two side-mounted stop lamps, leading to a triangular configuration. Federal Motor Vehicle Safety Standard FMVSS-108 required that the system be installed on all new cars sold in the US after 1 September 1985. The required features of the system were determined based on a number of large-scale experiments in actual traffic. In the first, the experience of a fleet of Washington, DC taxicabs fitted with this type of device or other innovative stop lamps was compared to that of a control group of the same makes, models and driver characteristics, but with the conventional stop lamps of the time.[40] Drivers reported details of all crash involvements. The study analyzed changes in the number of impacts on the rear during braking -- the only type of crash subject to potential influence from changing stop lights. In the field tests, 67% of the taxis struck in the rear were struck while braking. The key finding in the experiment is that the Washington taxicabs with center high mounted stop lamps were struck in the rear while braking 54% less often for the same distance of driving as the taxis in the control group.

A follow-up study used 5,400 telephone company passenger vehicles driven 55 million miles during a 12-month period in locations scattered widely throughout the US. For the same distance of driving, the 2,500 vehicles equipped with center high mounted stop lamps were struck in the rear while braking 53% less than those not so equipped.[41] Another study found a 51% reduction.[42]

The three studies find close agreement that center high mounted stop lamps reduce the risk of being rear-impacted while braking by about 50%. Since about two-thirds of all rear impact crashes involve pre-impact braking by the lead vehicle, these results are equivalent to a 35 percent reduction of rear-impact crashes of all types.

Based on such large risk reductions, the devices were mandated for all cars, and effectiveness in actual use estimated in many studies. All found reductions in rear impacts, but by amounts well short of the 35% reduction suggested so consistently in the experiments. Indeed, after trends became apparent in the first few years of evaluation there was speculation that effectiveness of the device was trending to zero.

In 1998 an evaluation was performed to examine the effectiveness over a long period by estimating the effect on rear impacts for each year in the same manner.[43] This involved using police-reported crash data from eight states to compare the ratio of rear impacts to non-rear impacts for model year 1986-89 cars (all equipped) to the corresponding ratio for 1982-85 cars (mostly not equipped). The same calculation was performed for data for each calendar year from 1986 onwards. The ratios were adjusted for vehicle age because when newer cars are involved in crashes, they are more likely to be struck in the rear than are older cars (possibly because they use higher levels of braking).[44]

Figure 8-3 shows the findings of the study[43] together with the 35% reductions reported in the pre-introduction fleet experiments. Although the effectiveness declines in time, it appears to have reached a stable level of about 4%. The benefits from such a risk reduction far exceed the modest cost of the device.

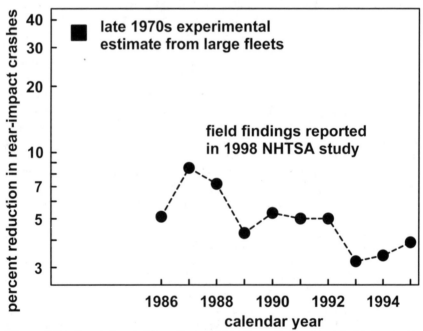

Figure 8-3. Percent reductions in rear-impact crashes associated with center high mounted stop lamps estimated in experiments using large fleets of vehicles equipped with prototypes, and in police-reported rear-impact crash rates in eight states.[43]

The reason for the lower effectiveness in use than in the trials as well as for the subsequent further declines may be related to what might be called the *novelty effect*. Anything unusual on the rear of a vehicle might invite a following driver to fixate on that vehicle and increase caution, thereby reducing the chances of crashing into it. The finding of positive effectiveness in 1995, when the vast majority of vehicles on the roads were equipped, supports the interpretation that the device is providing superior cues than the earlier lighting systems that the vehicle in front is braking. As time goes forward and there are fewer vehicles without the device, evaluation becomes more and more difficult, so there does not appear to be any possibility of an empirical evaluation of the effect when all vehicles are equipped. Even in the unlikely event that it did become zero, all the accumulated crashes prevented in the meantime would pay for decades of future installation.

There are additional approaches to further reducing reaction times. The lights in a traditional or center mounted stop light are incandescent. That is, when a switch completes a circuit, electricity flows through a tungsten filament, heating it to a high enough temperature to glow brightly. This process takes about 200 ms to reach near full intensity. Accordingly, there are proposals to replace incandescent bulbs with other types of light sources with shorter rise times, including light emitting diodes.[45]

A vehicle lighting feature addressing frontal impacts is daytime running lamps. These are reduced-intensity lights on the front of vehicles that automatically illuminate when a vehicle is started, making the vehicle easier to see by other drivers and pedestrians. Although first introduced in Sweden, Norway, and Finland where the greatest benefit from increased conspicuity might be expected, since they have long periods of dusk due to their northerly latitudes, daylight running lamps have also been shown effective in the US, especially at reducing pedestrian risk.[46]

Driving simulators

The difficulty, lack of control and reproducibility, and danger of conducting various types of driving research in actual traffic provided the impetus to develop driver simulators, devices which replicate driving with varying degrees of fidelity within the confines of the laboratory. Driving simulators are of two types, fixed base and moving base.

The most rudimentary fixed base simulator consists of little more than a screen presenting pictures to which subjects react, or a mock-up of a vehicle to familiarize students with control devices. Such equipment has proved useful in research and training. It is relatively inexpensive to build, maintain, and use. Valuable research information has come from such simulators, including selecting the road signs that offer superior visibility and earlier detection.

Moving base simulators provide acceleration cues by moving a cab containing a mock-up of a vehicle in all directions within a large interior space. The sensation of accelerating, for example, may be simulated by tilting the cab upwards as well as accelerating it forward. Moving base simulators cost vastly more than fixed base simulators and, because of set-up time, can generally accommodate fewer subjects in a day at vastly greater running cost.

It was the success of sophisticated moving base aircraft simulators that led to the application of similar technology to the driving case. Yet there is little in common between the two situations. The aircraft simulator is a device costing tens of millions of dollars representing an aircraft costing hundreds of millions of dollars. For the automobile case, it seems harder to justify a device costing tens of millions of dollars, when the real article can be purchased for under 20 thousand dollars. High realism simulators appear to offer nothing for training regular drivers. An accompanied learner driver can practice starting and stopping a real car every 15 s or so; a simulator offers little difference in training rate or safety. In contrast, it would be difficult to fit in more than a few real aircraft take-offs and landings in an hour, not to mention the risks and the cost of the aircraft and fuel. The aircraft simulator allows take-offs, followed by take-offs without intervening landings, to be repeated under varying conditions. While the performance skills learned in simulators can be critical in emergencies in the air, car driving emergency situations usually arise because of violations of expectancy which allow little time for corrective actions.

Enthusiasm for driving simulators ignores some of the most basic understanding about the nature of traffic crashes. The discussion above on reaction time showed the primacy of expectancy. Even in experiments using actual instrumented vehicles, reaction times are substantially shorter than in normal driving. Any reliance by traffic engineers on reaction times determined on a simulator, no matter how realistic, could produce unfortunate results. However, the reason that simulators are unlikely to produce knowledge relevant to traffic safety is more fundamental than this. Simulators measure *driver performance*, what the driver *can do*. However, safety is determined primarily by *driver behavior*, what the driver in fact *chooses to do*. It is exceedingly unlikely that a driver simulator can provide useful information on a driver's tendency to speed, drive while intoxicated, run red lights, pay attention to non-driving distractions, or not fasten a safety belt. Twenty-year-olds perform nearly all tasks on simulators better than the 50-year-olds, but it is the 50-year-olds who have sharply lower crash risks.

Driving simulators are far from new. A 1972 article[47] refers to an earlier 1970 article[48] listing 28 devices then in use, 17 of them in the US. Since the 1960s, driver simulators have incorporated moving bases and multiple movie projectors to provide visual information, including to the rear view mirror. Figure 8-4 is a reproduction of a list of research topics alleged to be suitable for research using driving simulators. The list was published in 1972.[47] The research literature provides scant evidence that research agenda was advanced by simulators, neither by those in existence in 1970, nor by the much larger number of far more expensive and sophisticated simulators that have since been built. More than a decade ago I wrote:

RESEARCH ACTIVITY

The relatively few existing research simulators have been and are be-ing actively used in studies of the following important categories of driving behavior:

  I. Traffic Control Devices
     a Wrong way driving warnings
       1. Signs and pavement markings at off-ramps and on ramps
       2. Red-colored raised pavement markers on the highway
     b. Tangent off-ramp exit signs placed in the gore
     c. Passing zone markings and signs
     d. Automatic passing control system for rural highways
     e Route guidance system
 II. Drug Effect
     a. Alcohol
     b. Tranquilizers used for mental patients
     c. Marihuana
     d. Cold remedies (antihistamines)
     e. Alcohol plus mild tranquilizers
     f. Alcohol plus mild stimulants
     g. Alcohol plus carbon monoxide
III. Driver as Control Element
     a. Car-following behavior
     b. Random path following
     c. Overtaking and passing
     d. Speed estimation
     e. Vigilance
     f. Fatigue effects
     g. Age effects
     h. "Bad" versus "good" driving record groups
IV. Vehicle Characteristics
     a. Steering system response
     b. Vibration and large-amplitude vertical displacement
     c. Visibility
     d. Rear lighting systems
 V. Highway Design
     a. Left-hand off-ramps
     b. Tangent off-ramps
     c. Freeway interchange design
VI. Driving Conditions
     a. Reduced visibility in fog
     b. Against glare of oncoming headlights

Figure 8-4. List of candidate projects suitable for simulator investigation reproduced from a 1972 publication.[47]

Can the lack of progress be traced specifically to insufficient realism in the simulator, thus justifying a more sophisticated simulator?   Any decisions regarding major investments in additional driver simulators should identify what specific problems they can be used to solve, and why they can solve them when only slightly less sophisticated simulators could not.

The following thought experiment helps address such questions. Consider a make-believe simulator consisting of an actual car, but with the remarkable property that after it crashes a reset button instantly cancels all damage to people and equipment. What experiments could be performed on such make-believe equipment which would increase our basic knowledge about driving? The answers provide an upper limit on what might be done using improved simulators. Defining subject areas, such as alcohol and driving, should not be confused with defining specific questions; there are already over 500 technical papers on how alcohol affects performance. Increased knowledge about driving is most likely to be discovered using the normal processes of science. In these, problems are first defined, and if they can be solved using existing equipment, they are. If they cannot be solved using existing equipment, new equipment is developed only if it is considered likely to contribute to the solution, and not for its own sake.[49(p 127)]

Alas, the remarks fell upon deaf ears. The US supports a *National Advanced Driving Simulator* with a project cost of $50 million, claiming it to be the most sophisticated simulator available.[50] Although the research literature documents 1,733 papers on alcohol and skill, the first sentence of justification for the $50 million expenditure is *The effects of alcohol, drugs, visual impairments and aging on driving will all be safely studied using the new research tool.* How like the 1972 list this justification sounds, and I fear that in the decades to come there will be just as little research progress to report.

Acquisition of driving skill

A remarkable feature of vehicle driving is that almost everyone can do it. Not only can most people learn to drive, but they acquire in a matter of weeks the necessary skills to start, stop, and propel a vehicle down a road and around corners. This is achieved without intensive study or extended practice. In 1901 Karl Benz thought that the global market for the automobile was limited because *There were going to be no more than one million people capable of being trained as chauffeurs.*[51] Given the state of knowledge at the time, his conclusion was not unreasonable.

If automobiles and stringed musical instruments did not exist, but were suddenly invented, even today there are no known general principles of how people learn that would predict which would be easier to master. Given that music is about as old as humanity, it might seem natural to expect people to realize quickly that you just slide your finger up and down the string until you hear the desired note. A common-sense guess might therefore be that within an hour of first encountering a stringed instrument just about everyone could rattle off any tune they knew, but only the gifted few, after years of dedicated training, could reliably keep a 1,500 kg vehicle traveling round a curve at 100 km/h within a 4 m freeway lane surrounded on all four sides by other vehicles.

Although there are no effective models to predict the rate of learning and proficiency at one task compared to another, some patterns have been observed common to the acquisition of complex skills in general. These have been considered to occur in three phases:[32]

1. Early, or cognitive phase

2. Intermediate, or associative phase

3. Final, or autonomous phase

This categorization fits well the acquisition of driving skill. In the early, or cognitive phase, the learner tries to understand the components. For driving, the location of the controls and what vehicle responses they produce must be learned. In the intermediate phase, different strategies are explored, and the learner is acutely attentive to feedback. The learner-driver devotes full attention to the task, and increases skill by responding to feedback either from observed consequences of inputs, or from directions from an instructor. The skill of knowing what output is required in specific traffic situations develops together with the skill of knowing what input produces the desired output. In the third, or autonomous phase, the task is performed at a high level with minimal effort, in part because behavior becomes rather fixed and inflexible. In this autonomous phase, the task can be performed using a small fraction of the driver's attention. Other tasks, such as navigation, conversation, admiring the scenery, listening to the radio, talking on a cell phone, or thinking about other matters can be performed. Although the mental capacity devoted to driving is small in this autonomous phase, it is still such that, if a threat occurs and is recognized, all attention is quickly switched to the driving task. Most drivers have personally experienced this many times in, say, driving along waiting for specific information from a radio broadcast. An incident occurs in traffic, the driver reacts to the incident, and later realizes that the sought-after radio information, although broadcast, has not been perceived. Of course, if the threatening incident is not recognized because the driver's attention is elsewhere, such as talking on a cell phone, the result can be a crash.[52]

The beginning driver

As people learn to drive, the direction in which they look changes in ways that relate to the three learning stages mentioned above. Experimental studies reveal that in the first hours of driving experience, drivers scan over a wide area, including well above the horizon.[49(p 102)] After about a month's experience, fixations are more confined in the vertical direction, but still vary horizontally.

After three months' experience, fixations are more concentrated at the focus of expansion, with a much greater reliance on peripheral vision for cues to control the vehicle's position in the lane. As drivers gain experience they concentrate their eye fixations in smaller areas. Novice drivers look closer in front of the vehicle and more to the right of the vehicle's direction than experienced drivers, and are more likely to glance at the curb to estimate the vehicle's lane position. Novice drivers sample the rear-view mirrors much less frequently than experienced drivers.

These findings indicate that during the first few times behind the wheel almost all information processing capacity is absorbed in simply maintaining the vehicle's position in the lane. As experience is gained, peripheral vision is used more to locate the vehicle in the lane, with fixations focused further down the road to allow more time to process information that becomes increasingly relevant with increasing vehicle speed. When specifically instructed to pay attention to road signs, novice drivers are more likely to miss them than are experienced drivers, another indication that the task of controlling the vehicle is placing more mental workload on novice drivers.[53]

In an experiment in which novice and experienced drivers watched video-recordings taken from a car traveling along a variety of roads, the experienced drivers showed more extensive scanning in attempting to recognize hazards.[54] The authors interpreted the result to mean that the inspection of the roadway by novices is limited not because they have limited mental resources residual from the task of vehicle control, but that they have an impoverished mental model of what is likely to happen in freeway driving. Another study concludes that, compared to experienced drivers, novice drivers detect hazards less quickly and efficiently and perceive them less holistically.[55]

The early stages of learning to drive are generally accompanied by anxiety, tension and fear. Training courses aimed at producing relaxed and confident drivers may reduce the very fear that in some situations could be protective. Although driving remains one of the riskiest activities, it soon becomes relatively unconnected with fear. Evolution has implanted in us much greater fears of less dangerous activities. Experiments have shown that babies refuse to crawl in the direction of a simulated sharp drop even in response to their mothers' voices.[56] This fear of heights is so ingrained, perhaps even instinctive, that we retain it in the absence of reinforcing experiences to ourselves or acquaintances. We do not lean far out of a window on the fourth floor, from which height a freely falling object would strike the ground at 50 km/h. Yet we travel at much higher vehicle speeds without anxiety. As smooth locomotion through the environment is not part of our evolutionary heritage, we have no instinctive fear of it. Once facility is acquired at basic driving skills, driving becomes relaxed and unassociated with danger. We largely lose that protection described by Shakespeare, "Best safety lies in fear." (*Hamlet*: Act I, Scene 3).

The material introduced in this chapter shows that, beyond the elementary control skills that are quickly learned, there are many higher level skills involved in driving that cannot be learned quickly. The only way to gain high level performance at these skills, like so many others, is practice, and a learning curve extending over many years is to be expected. However, unlike improving your golf game, practicing to improve driving skill comes with the risk of crashing.

Early stages of driving and crash rates

Many of the fatal-crash relationships in Chapter 7 show sharply higher risks at the earliest ages of driving compared to rates just a year or so later. Younger drivers pose the greatest fatality threats to themselves and to other road users. For involvement in crashes of all types, 16-year-old drivers have crash rates for the same distance of travel about 10 times those of 40- to 50-year-old drivers.[57] Among teenagers, crash rates decline consistently and steeply with each yearly increase in age.

Specific evidence that lack of skill and knowledge is a factor in crashes of beginning drivers is provided by an examination of narrative descriptions of more than 2,000 crashes involving 16- to 19-year-old drivers.[57] The results indicated that the great majority of non-fatal crashes resulted from errors in attention, visual search, speed relative to conditions, hazard recognition, and emergency maneuvers.[57] High speeds and patently risky behavior accounted for only a small minority of crashes. Differences in the types of errors by first year novices and more experienced youth were relatively few in number and small in magnitude, indicating that the benefits of experience apply rather generally across all aspects of driving. Another study[58] found that crash rates drop most precipitously during the first 6 months of driving. Involvement in certain types of crashes, such as run-off-the-road, single vehicle, night, and weekend crashes had the largest declines. The findings suggest that novices improve their driving in a relatively short period of time.

Lack of skill likely has a large effect on rollover risk. A beginning driver is more likely than an experienced driver to run off the right side of the road because of less skill in maintaining the vehicle's lateral position, and perhaps through increased fear and poorer judgment of oncoming traffic. A beginning driver will have less experience in handling a vehicle that has left its lane, and is more likely to overcompensate, thereby either crashing or, as is more common, receiving a valuable lesson in what not to do. As is common in skilled tasks, the inexperienced make more errors than the experienced.

Another contribution is overall higher levels of risk-taking by drivers less than 30, particularly male drivers. If skill were the sole factor, then the observed lower crash rates for 45-year-old drivers than for 30-year-old drivers would imply major additional skill acquisition even after more than a decade since first learning to drive. While additional experience might reduce crash risk, it is not a plausible explanation of effects of the magnitude observed. It is not possible to separate the roles of skill and youthful risk-taking in a completely satisfactory way. In motorized societies almost all the inexperienced drivers are also young.

However, one can examine data from drivers with little experience who are not young, based on their possession of a learner's permit rather than a full driver license. The plot in Fig. 8-5 uses all 877 fatally injured drivers coded in FARS 1994-2002 as driving with a learner's permit. More than half were teenagers. It is plausible to interpret that driving with a learner permit indicates a comparable lack of driving experience. Given that a driver is killed, the probability that it is in a rollover crash is much higher for younger inexperienced drivers than for older inexperienced drivers, showing that age, as such, is exercising a large influence. For all drivers, Fig. 7-18 (p. 164) shows that, when a driver is killed, the probability that rollover is the most harmful event is higher for male and for younger drivers, thus associating rollover crash fatalities with increasing risk taking. The data in Fig. 8-5 therefore indicate that an important component of the higher risks for younger drivers is due to their youth, and not just to their inexperience.

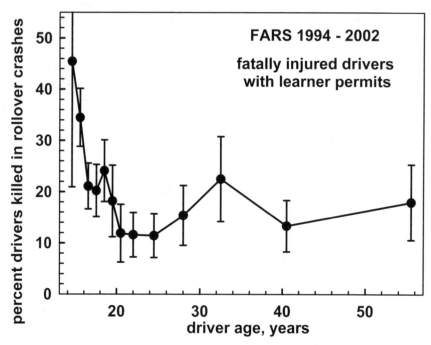

Figure 8-5. The percent of fatally-injured drivers with learner permits who were killed in crashes in which rollover was the most harmful event. FARS 1994-2002.

The relationship between driver skill/performance and safety

The evidence above shows that lack of skill contributes to higher crash risk. However, it does not follow that higher and higher levels of skill lead to lower and lower crash risk. Once the basics of driving are mastered and the task has become autonomous, its main characteristic is that it becomes what has been called a *self-paced* or *self-controlled* task.[31]   The driver chooses the level of difficulty that feels appropriate and comfortable, so that increased skill may translate into, for example, higher speeds. In Chapter 4 we found that although antilock braking produces superior braking, it was associated with higher fatality risk.   Through similar processes, increased skill may translate into increased crash risk.

Peak performance in tests of reaction time relevant to driving[59] and of visual acuity are achieved in the late teens/early twenties. Compared to females, males tend to be more interested and knowledgeable about driving and vehicles. The group with the fastest reaction time, best visual acuity, and most knowledge about vehicles and driving, namely young males, is the group with the highest crash risks.

The clearest indications of performance affecting safety are the increases in crash risks as drivers age.   Here deterioration in such performance-related attributes as visual capabilities, reaction times, and information-processing speeds and other cognitive skills leads to increasing crash rates. Eventually such performance degradation produces crash-rate increases even in the presence of likely reductions in risk taking.

One can consider each end of the U-shaped relationships (Chapter 7) to originate from different sources. The elevated rates for the young flow from a combination of lack of skill and higher risk taking, and the higher rates for the old from driver performance limitations.

Distraction

With increasing experience drivers acquire the impression, reinforced by vast numbers of safe trips, that driving is a safe and effortless task requiring only a small fraction of their total attention. Such an impression encourages drivers to perform a variety of other tasks while driving. A study in which subjects drove vehicles equipped with a video camera provided the following results.[60] During three hours of driving, nearly all subjects manipulated vehicle controls (such as air conditioning or window controls) and reached for objects inside their moving vehicle. Nearly as many were observed manipulating music/audio controls, or had their attention drawn to something outside the vehicle unrelated to driving. Approximately three-fourths ate or drank something while driving or conversed with a passenger. Reading, writing, and grooming activities were also relatively common, but declined to less than half of the participants when observations were restricted to moving vehicles only. About a third of the subjects used a cell phone while driving, and nearly as many were distracted by passengers riding in their vehicle. Taking into account the shorter amount of time that children and especially babies were present in vehicles, children were about four times and infants almost eight times more likely than adults to be a source of distraction to the driver, based on the number of distracting events per hour of driving.

While it is reasonable on intuitive grounds to surmise that, for example, distractions from an infant (especially one in a rear seat) might increase crash risk, it would be extremely difficult to examine this empirically, let alone measure the magnitude of the effect. The effect on safety of one source of distraction in the above list has however been quantified.

The influence on crash risk from the use of a cellular telephone while driving was investigated in a case-crossover analysis, a technique for assessing a temporary change in risk associated with a transient exposure.[52]   A major strength of the method is that each person serves as his or her own control. This eliminates confounding due to age, gender, personality, and other fixed characteristics. The study used 699 drivers, all of them involved in crashes and all having cell phones available in their vehicles. Comparing the time of their crashes to telephone company records showed that 170 of the drivers were using their telephones just prior to the crash. The telephone records further showed that in a control period, chosen for each driver to be 24 hours before their crashes, only 37 drivers were using cell phones. If telephone use had no influence on crash risk, one would expect similar numbers of drivers to be using the telephone during their crashes and during the control period. Because some drivers were on the telephone during their crashes and also during the control period, the simple relative risk associated with phone use is larger than 170/37 = 4.6. Taking into account the probability that the crash-involved driver may not have been driving 24 hours prior to his or her crash, and other details, led to a conclusion that the relative risk of crashing while using (compared to not using) a cell phone was 4.3 (95 percent confidence interval, 3.0 to 6.5).

This reliable indication of a large effect stimulated many studies to address various issues, such as the extent to which the effect was from the manipulative demands of dialing compared to the cognitive demands of the content of the telephone. The consensus seems to be favoring an interpretation in terms of cognitive demands, so that hands-free telephones may not make all that much difference. Many jurisdictions have passed legislation prohibiting the use of cell phones while driving. While such legislation certainly enhances safety, it still raises benefit-cost questions, because using a cell phone while driving does offer benefits.[61]

Unfamiliarity with vehicle

There is convincing evidence that unfamiliarity with a vehicle increases crash risk. One review examined incidental evidence in a number of previously published studies and concluded that driving an unfamiliar car increased crash risk by about a factor of two.[62] A more specific examination found that 8.9% of all drivers in NASS-reported crashes in 1981 had less than 150 miles driving experience with the crashed vehicle, compared to an approximately estimated 1.5% of all driving in such vehicles.[63] Older drivers with cognitive deterioration experience additional difficulties which pose potential risks in unfamiliar vehicles.[64]

Driver education and training

The evidence above shows that lack of skill can contribute to young drivers' higher crash risks. Education and training have the goal of imparting knowledge and skill. It therefore seems compelling to think that driver education and training must necessarily lead to enhanced safety. Such an intuitively appealing belief has helped spawn a massive worldwide driver education and training industry. There has been a correspondingly vast amount written on the subject, starting particularly in the 1970s.

One review of this literature by Canadian researchers concludes: *The international literature provides little support for the hypothesis that formal driver instruction is an effective safety measure.*[65]   Another review by an Australian researcher similarly concludes: *The research evidence suggests that driver training of a traditional and conventional nature contributes little to reductions in accident involvement or risk among drivers of all age and experience groups.*[66]

The Cochrane Library in the UK surveyed 19 reference data bases (MEDLINE, TRIS, etc.), the Internet, and other sources.[67] Their search was not restricted by language or publication status. They searched for randomized controlled trials comparing post-license driver education versus no education, or one form of post-license driver education versus another. They concluded: *This systematic review provides no evidence that post-license driver education is effective in preventing road traffic injuries or crashes.*

Despite these findings, the British Government still included driver education as a key element in an effort to reduce traffic crashes. The intuitive belief that it must be effective was reinforced by a driver education industry sponsored study that did not address crashes, but instead examined knowledge and stated intended behavior before and after a safety presentation. In disagreeing with the British Government's decision to include driver education, the authors of the comprehensive review of the world's literature comment on the need for evidence-based policy.[68]

One effect of driver education is that it enables students to qualify for licensure at earlier ages. Having acquired the licenses, the drivers then experience crash rates typical for their age, and as a consequence end up with more crashes than if they had not received driver education.

Because the evaluations of driver education have been conducted in motorized countries, the results should not be assumed to apply equally to countries in the early stages of motorization. The vastly higher crash rates in less motorized countries (Chapter 3) may have a component resulting from lack of basic skill and knowledge. Children in motorized countries have a large body of information about the rules of the road and how to behave in traffic long before they have driving licenses. They have been riding in, and getting out of the way of, motorized vehicles since infancy. The few weeks of driver education makes but a modest increment to this large pool of knowledge, and therefore renders it unlikely to reduce crash risk. People who start with a lesser pool of knowledge may gain more through driver education, so conclusions for less motorized countries must await specific evaluation studies.

The absence of proven safety benefits from driver education does not prove that training cannot increase safety, but merely that none of the methods so far applied have been demonstrated to do so. There is no theoretical principal stating that some type of education cannot reduce crash risk. The importance of traffic safety justifies supporting research to discover if there are training techniques that do reduce crash risk, but detached objective evaluation is crucial.

Longer term experience

While skill at the components of driving increases rapidly in early learning, the ability to identify and extract relevant information from a complex cluttered traffic environment appears to come more slowly. Perhaps a distinction should be drawn between perceptual-motor skills and total performance that additionally incorporates higher level skills. These additional abilities, which might be described as road sense, or good traffic judgment, develop over many years.

Although such effects may be of the utmost importance, there is limited empirical information. I share the view of most observers that higher-level driving skills continue to increase with driving experience over time frames of the order of decades. The ability to extract and appropriately process relevant information from a complex visual field appears to increase, and there appear to be ongoing increases in driver abilities to project further in time. We saw above that the novice driver is grimly focused on the present location of the vehicle, whereas as skills increase, visual attention focuses more on the vanishing point ahead - where the vehicle will be in the future. As each task becomes more thoroughly learned, the driver acquires more spare mental capacity that, through learning by feedback, focuses further ahead.

Driving seems to abound with examples in which events more and more in the future can beneficially influence present decisions. For example, a driver with a few years experience will likely approach a car stopped at a red light on a straight road in a manner that is independent of how many vehicles are stopped, or when the light turned red; all attention being focused on the rear of the vehicle ahead. A more experienced driver may slow down gently a long way from the light if it has just turned red or if there is a long line of stopped vehicles, but maintain a higher speed if the light has been red for some time and there are only a few vehicles waiting. The more experienced driver is more likely to have learned that in the first case stopping is nearly inevitable, whereas in the second case stopping, or even slowing down, may not be required. Which of these cases applies depends on perceiving, monitoring, processing and projecting into the future much information well beyond judging that the lead vehicle is slowing down or is stationary.

It should be emphasized that some less experienced drivers exhibit more advanced behavior, while some experienced drivers less advanced -- there are large variations among drivers at all stages of experience.

Even drivers with high crash rates complete the vast majority of trips without crashing. A driver with a crash rate ten times the average would still drive approximately 10 months (Table 1-1) between crashes. For such a driver, even the frequency of near-misses would still be insufficient to teach which actions are likely to lead to crashes. Drivers learn to negotiate corners skillfully by practicing such maneuvers thousands of times. Each time it is done badly, corrections can be planned for the next time. Thus driving skills are learned and polished largely by experimentation and frequent direct feedback. Learning by Shakespeare's recipe, "The injuries that they themselves procure must be their schoolmasters", (*King Lear*, Act III, Scene 1) is not effective for crash avoidance. Safety must be based on the knowledge of the whole society, as expressed in traffic law, rather than each driver learning from individual experience.

Graduated driver licenses

While young beginning drivers have highly elevated crash risks, seven US states issue learner-driver permits to drivers under age 15. The most common US practice is to issue learner permits at 15 and full driver licenses at 16. In the simplified list in Table 8-1 the full license for younger drivers may still differ from the license for other drivers, for example, by being differently colored to indicate that the holder is under 25. In all US states licenses are issued to drivers at younger ages than in most other countries. Additional details for each state are available in the source providing the information in Table 8-1.[69]

A major contributor to the elevated rates of younger drivers is lack of driving experience, yet the only way to get experience is by driving. But when they drive, they crash. This has been called the *young driver paradox*.[70] What is needed is a way to gain experience while minimizing risk. This is the goal of graduated licensing.

Graduated licensing is a way to phase in on-road driving by allowing beginners to get their initial experience under conditions that involve lower risk. Three stages are typically involved. The first is a supervised learner period of typically 6 months, then an intermediate licensing phase that permits unsupervised driving in less risky situations, and finally a full license becomes available when conditions of the first two stages have been met.

The concept originated in 1970s research identifying the high crash risks of younger drivers, and was first applied in New Zealand in 1984, with Michigan being the first US state to adopt a graduated licensing program in 1997.[71] Early evaluations were so positive that, by 2003 one or more elements of graduated licensing have been adopted in 58 North American jurisdictions (District of Columbia, 47 US states, 9 Canadian provinces, and 1 Canadian

Table 8-1. The minimum age for a learner's permit and full driver license in all 50 US states and the District of Columbia.[69]

states	minimum license age	
	learners	full
South Dakota	14	14
Alaska, Arkansas, Iowa, Kansas, North Dakota	14	16
Montana	14, 6 mo.*	15
Hawaii, Idaho, New Mexico, South Carolina	15	15
Alabama, California, Florida, Louisiana, Maine, Michigan, Minnesota, Mississippi, Nebraska, North Carolina, Oregon, Tennessee, Texas, Vermont, Virginia, Washington, West Virginia, Wyoming	15	16
Indiana	15	16, 1 mo.
Georgia	15	18
Colorado	15, 3 mo.	16
Illinois, Missouri, Nevada, Ohio, Oklahoma, Wisconsin	15, 6 mo.	16
Arizona	15, 7 mo.	16
Maryland	15, 9 mo.	16
Delaware	15, 10 mo.	16
New York, Pennsylvania, Rhode Island, Utah, District of Columbia,	16	16
New Jersey	16	17
New Hampshire	16	16, 3 mo.
Connecticut, Kentucky, Massachusetts	16	16, 6 mo.

* 14 years and 6 months

territory).[72] Although most North American programs are too new for formal evaluation, impressive crash and injury reductions have been reported in California, Florida, Kentucky, Michigan, North Carolina, Nova Scotia, Ontario, and Quebec.

Although the basic goals of all graduated licensing programs is the same, specific implementation details differ widely among different jurisdictions.[72] In a few cases graduated licenses do not apply to teenagers only, but to all newly licensed drivers. In a typical case an adult (usually a parent) must certify that the beginning driver has driven under supervision for 50 hours. After this first six-month phase is completed the beginning driver may drive alone, but not at night, and not with teenage passengers. At the completion of the second phase, or in some US states, when reaching the legal adult age of 18, a full license permitting unrestricted driving is granted.   While such variation makes it impossible to associate a single effectiveness with the concept, reductions in crash rates to the affected populations in excess 10%, and in some cases far in excess, have been observed.[73] Declines as large as 50% have been associated with the first six months.[74]

Graduated licenses constitute an effective approach to providing drivers with the experience that is crucial in acquiring the skills necessary for safe driving while at the same time lowering the risk intrinsic in acquiring these skills. Ongoing refinement and expansions of graduated licensing programs[72] will prevent large numbers of crashes by beginning drivers. This will not only reduce injuries and deaths to beginning drivers, but also to passengers and other road users at all levels of experience.

Summary and conclusions

The basic skills required to start, stop, and steer vehicles are acquired remarkably easily and quickly. Complex higher level skills that are acquired only after many years of experience can contribute to reducing crash risk.

Even experienced drives do not estimate vehicle speed without systematic errors. Recent exposure to a prior speed influences the estimate of present speed, so that changes in speed limits can affect speeds even on roads unaffected by the speed limit change. Other factors, such as geometric patterns painted on the roadway, can also influence speed estimates. These findings underline the importance of speedometers.

Drivers can estimate with high reliability whether they are approaching closer to or moving further away from a vehicle they are following.   There is a perceptual bias in favor of judging closing when it is not occurring, but as this bias is in the direction of increased safety, it has no adverse safety consequences.

The same distance between a driver's eyes and a lead vehicle appears greater if the length of roadway visible is greater. Such effects could cause vehicles with short hoods, like SUVs, to tailgate without their drivers realizing.

Expensive high-technology moving-base driving simulators have not contributed much of relevance to driver safety, and have little potential to do so. They represent a massive misallocation of a large portion of scarce resources.

Teenagers beginning to drive have crash risks about 10 times those of 40- to 50-year-old drivers. Risk-taking behaviors associated with youth and lack of higher level driving skills both contribute to overinvolvement.   Yet driver education has not been demonstrated to have any effect on crash rates of beginning drivers.

Graduated driver licenses have been effective in reducing crash risks to beginning drivers, especially in the first months of driving. Graduated licensing is a system for phasing in on-road driving to allow beginners to get their initial experience under low risk conditions, typically achieved by requiring a parent to be present for the first months of driving, and, in a second phase, restricting driving to lower risk conditions, such as daytime. Extending and refining graduated licensing has the potential to make a major contribution to traffic safety.

References for Chapter 8

1   Rockwell TH. Skills, judgment and information acquisition in driving. In: Forbes TW, editor. *Human Factors in Highway Traffic Safety Research.* New York, NY: Wiley-Interscience; 1972, p. 133-164.

2   Peli E, Peli D. *Driving with Confidence: A Practical Guide to Driving with Low Vision.* River Edge, NJ: World Scientific; 2002.

3   Johnson C, Keltner J. Incidence of field loss in 20 000 eyes and its relationship to driving performance. *Arch Ophthalmol.* 1983; 101: 371-375.

4   Wood JM, Troutbeck R. Effect of visual impairment on driving. *Human Factors.* 1994; 36: 476-487.

5   Westlake W. Is a one eyed racing driver safe to compete? Formula one (eye) or two? *Br J Ophthalmol* 2001; 85: 619-624.

6   Federal Motor Carrier Safety Administration, US Department of Transportation. *Qualification of Drivers; Exemption Applications; Vision.* Notice of final disposition. Federal Register, Vol. 68, No. 158, 48989-91; August 15, 2003.

7   Owsley C, Ball K, McGwin G Jr, Sloane M, Roenker DL, White MF, Overly ET. Visual processing impairment and risk of motor vehicle crash among older adults. *JAMA.* 1998; 279: 1083-1088.

8   Denton GG. A subjective scale of speed when driving a motor vehicle. *Ergonomics.* 1966; 9: 203-210.

9   Noguchi K. In search of optimum speed: From the users' viewpoint. *J Intl Assoc Safety Sciences.* 1990; 14: 66-75.

10 Milosevic S. Perception of vehicle speed. *Revija za psihologijy* (Yugoslavia). 1986; 16: 11-19.

11 Evans L. Speed estimation from a moving automobile. *Ergonomics* 1970; 13: 219-230.

12 McLane RC, Wierwille WW. The influence of motion and audio cues on driver performance in an automobile simulator. *Human Factors* 1975; 17: 488-501.

13 Denton GG. The influence of visual pattern on perceived speed at Newbridge M8 Midlothian. Transport and Road Research Laboratory, Crowthorne, Berkshire, UK; 1973.

14 Meyer E. Evaluation of data from test application of optical speed bars to highway work zones. Project No K-TRAN KU-00-4, Final Report. Kansas Department of Transportation; July 2000.

15 Smiley A. Driver speed estimation: What road designers should know. Paper presented at: Transportation Research Board 78th Annual Meeting, Workshop on Role of Geometric Design & Human Factors in Setting Speed; January 1999.   http://www.hfn.ca/driver.htm

16 Schmidt F, Tiffin J. Distortion of drivers' estimates of automobile speed as a function of speed adaptation. *J of App Psychology.* 1969; 53: 536-539.

17 Denton GG. The influence of adaptation on subjective velocity for an observer in simulated rectilinear motion. *Ergonomics.* 1976; 19: 409-430.

18 Matthews ML. A field study of the effects of drivers' adaptation to automobile velocity. *Human Factors.* 1978; 20: 709-716.

19 Casey SM, Lund AK. Three field studies on driver speed adaptation. *Human Factors.* 1987; 29: 541-550.

20 Insurance Institute for Highway Safety. *Status Report, Special Issue: Speeding.* Vol 38 (10); 22 November 2003. http://www.iihs.org/srpdfs/sr3810.pdf

21 Herman R, Potts RB. Single-lane traffic theory and experiment. In: Herman R., editor. *Theory of Traffic Flow.* Amsterdam, Netherlands: Elsevier; 1961, p. 120-146.

22 Evans L, Rothery R. Perceptual thresholds in car-following -- a comparison of recent measurements with earlier results. *Trans Science.* 1977; 11: 60-72.

23 Evans L, Rothery R. Detection of the sign of relative motion when following a vehicle. *Human Factors.* 1974; 16: 161-173.

24 Sedgwick HA. Space perception. Chapter 21 in Boff KR, Kaufman L, Thomas JP. editors. *Handbook of Perception and Human Performance, Volume 1, Sensory Processes And Perception.* New York: John Wiley, 1986.

25 Caird JK, Hancock PA. Perception of oncoming vehicle time-to-arrival. Proceedings of the Human Factors Society Annual Meeting, p. 1378-1382; 1992.

26 Evans L, Rothery R. The influence of forward vision and target size on apparent inter-vehicular spacing. *Trans. Science.* 1976; 10: 85-101.

27 Herman R, Lam T, Rothery R. An experiment on car size effects in traffic. *Traf Eng & Control.* 1973; 15: 90-93,99.

28 Farber EI, Silver CA. Knowledge of oncoming car speed as a determiner of driver's passing behavior. *Highway Research Record.* 1967; 195: 52-65.

29 Simpson G, Johnston L, Richardson M. An investigation of road crossing in a virtual environment. *Accid Anal Prev.* 2003; 35: 787-796.

30 Farber EI. Passing behavior on public highways under daytime and nighttime conditions. *Highway Research Record.* 1969; 292; 11-23.

31 Näätänen R, Summala H. *Road-User Behavior and Traffic Accidents.* Amsterdam, Netherlands: North Holland; 1976.

32 Fitts PM, Posner, MI. *Human Performance.* Belmont, CA: Brooks/Cole; 1967.

33 Shinar D. *Psychology on the Road -- The Human Factor in Traffic Safety.* New York, NY: John Wiley; 1978.

34 Olson PL, Sivak M. Perception-response time to unexpected roadway hazards. *Human Factors.* 1986; 28: 91-96.

35 Summala H. Driver/vehicle steering response latencies. *Human Factors.* 1981; 23: 683-692.

36 National Highway Traffic Safety Administration. *Traffic Safety Facts 2000 – A Compilation of Motor Vehicle Crash Data from the Fatality Analysis Reporting System and the General Estimates System.* Report No. DOT HS 809 337. Washington DC: US Department of Transportation; December 2001. (Table 32, p. 54). http://www-fars.nhtsa.dot.gov/pubs

37 Motor City Dream Cars, Auto history time line. http://www.motorcitydreamcars.com/memory_lane/timeline/timeline.html

38 Mortimer RG. A decade of research in vehicle rear lighting. What have we learned? American Association for Automotive Medicine, 21st Annual Proceedings, p. 101-112; September 1977.

39 Mortimer RG, Kupec JD. Scaling of flash rate for a deceleration signal. *Human Factors.* 1983; 25: 313-318.

40 Kohl JS, Baker C. Field test evaluation of rear lighting systems. Report DOT HS 803 467. Washington, DC: National Highway Traffic Safety Administration; 1978.

41 Reilly RE, Kurke DS, Buckenmaier CC. Validation of the reduction of rear-end collisions by a high-mounted auxiliary stoplamp. SAE paper 810189. Warrendale, PA: Society of Automotive Engineers; 1981.

42 Rausch A, Wong J, Kirkpatrick M. A field test of two single, center high mounted brake light systems. *Accid Anal Prev.* 1982; 14: 287-291.

43 Kahane CJ, Hertz E. The long-term effectiveness of center high mounted stop lamps in passenger cars and light trucks. Report DOT HS 808 696. Washington, DC: Department of Transportation; March 1998.

44 Evans L, Rothery R. Comments on effects of vehicle type and age on driver behaviour at signalized intersections. *Ergonomics.* 1976; 19: 559-570.

45 Sivak M, Flannagan MJ, Sato T, Traube EC, Aok M. Reaction times to neon, LED, and fast incandescent brake lamps. *Ergonomics.* 1994; 37: 989-994.

46 National Highway Traffic Safety Administration. A preliminary assessment of the crash-reducing effectiveness of passenger car daytime running lamps (DRLs). Technical Report DOT HS 808 645. Washington, DC: NHTSA; June 2000.

47 Hulbert S, Wojcik C. Driving task simulation. In: Forbes TW, editor. *Human Factors in Highway Traffic Safety Research.* New York, NY: Wiley-Interscience; 1972, p. 44-73.

48 Kuratorium für Verkehrssicherheit. Verkerspsychologie IV, Vienna, Austria, p. 149-184; May 1970.

49 Evans L. *Traffic Safety and the Driver.* New York, NY: Van Nostrand Reinhold; 1991.

50 NHTSA. The National Advanced Driving Simulator (NADS) is the most sophisticated. http://www-nrd.nhtsa.dot.gov/departments/nrd-12/NationalAdvancedDriverSimulator.html

51 Mackay M. Towards grand unification of traffic science. *J Intl Assoc Safety Sciences.* 1990; 14: 19. Also quoted in slightly different form by Macrae N. The next ages of man. London, UK: *The Economist*, p. 5-20; 24 December 1988.

52 Redelmeier DA, Tibshirani RJ. Association between cellular-telephone calls and motor vehicle collisions. *New Eng J. Med.* 1997; 336: 453-458.

53 Summala H, Näätänen, R. Perception of highway traffic signs and motivation. *J Safety Res.* 1974; 6: 150-153.

54 Underwood G, Chapman P, Bowden K, Crundall D. Visual search while driving: Skill and awareness during inspection of the scene. *Transp Res Traffic Psychol Behav.* 2002; 5: 87-97.

55 Deery HA. Hazard and risk perception among young novice drivers. *J Safety Res.* 1999; 30: 225-236.

56 Gibson EJ, Walk RD. The "visual cliff". *Scientific American.* 1960; 202: 64-71.

57 McKnight AJ, McKnight AS. Young novice drivers: Careless or clueless? *Accid Anal Prev.* 2003; 35: 921-925.

58 Mayhew DR, Simpson HM, Pak A. Changes in collision rates among novice drivers during the first months of driving. *Accid Anal Prev.* 2003; 35: 683-691.

59 Warshawsky-Livne L, Shinar D. Effects of uncertainty, transmission type, driver age and gender on brake reaction and movement time. *J Safety Res.* 2002; 33: 117-128.

60 Stutts J, Feaganes J, Rogman E, Hamlett C, Meadows T, Reinfurt D, Gish K, Mercadante M, Staplin L. The role of driver distraction in traffic crashes: Distractions in everyday driving. *AAA Foundation for Traffic Safety.* Washington, DC; July 2003. http://www.aaafoundation.org/pdf/DistractionsInEverydayDriving.pdf

61 Cohen JT, Graham JD. A revised economic analysis of restrictions on the use of cell phones while driving. *Risk Analysis.* 2003; 23: 5-17.

62 Perel M. Vehicle familiarity and safety. Report DOT HS 806 509. Washington, DC: US Department of Transportation, National Highway Traffic Safety Administration; July 1983.

63 Hoxie P. Assessment of driver inexperience with an automobile as a factor which contributes to highway accidents. Report DOT HS 806 593. Washington, DC: US Department of Transportation, National Highway Traffic Safety Administration; December 1984.

64 Lundberg C, Hakamies-Blomqvist L. Driving tests with older patients: Effect of unfamiliar versus familiar vehicle. *Trans Res, Part F.* 2003; 6: 163-173.

65 Mayhew DR, Simpson HM. The safety value of driver education and training. *Inj Prev.* 2002; 8: 3-8.

66 Christie R. The effectiveness of driver training as a road safety measure: A review of the literature. Report No. 01/03, Royal Automobile Club of Victoria, Australia. ISBN 1 875963 26 X; November 2001. http://www.racv.com.au/images/pdf/driver_training_report-nov_2001.pdf

67 Ker K, Roberts I, Collier T, Renton F, Bunn F. Post-licence driver education for the prevention of road traffic crashes (Cochrane Review). *The Cochrane Library,* 2003, Issue 4. Chichester, UK: John Wiley & Sons, Ltd; 2003. http://www.update-software.com/abstracts/AB003734.htm

68 Achara S, Adeyemi B, Dosekun E, Kelleher S, Landley M, Male I, Muhialdin N, Reynolds L, Roberts I, Smailbegovic M, van der Spek N. The Cochrane injuries group driver education reviewers: Evidence-based road safety: The Driving Standards Agency's schools programme (editorial). *Lancet* 2001; 358: 230-232.

69 State-by-state driving rules for teenage drivers. http://golocalnet.com/drivingage/

70 Warren RA, Simpson HM. The young driver paradox. Ottawa, Ontario, Canada: Traffic Injury Research Foundation; 1976.

71 Waller PF. The genesis of GDL. *J Safety Res.* 2003; 34: 17-23.

72 Insurance Institute for Highway Safety/Traffic Injury Research Foundation. *Graduated Licensing: A blueprint for North America.* Arlington VA/Ottawa Canada; July 2003. http://www.hwysafety.org/safety_facts/teens/blueprint.pdf

73 Branche C, Williams AF, Feldman D. Graduated licensing for teens: Why everybody's doing it. *J Law Med Ethics.* 2002; 30: 146-149.

74 Mayhew DR, Simpson HM, Desmond K, Williams AF. Specific and long-term effects of Nova Scotia's graduated licensing program. *Traf Inj Prev.* 2003; 4: 91-97.

9 Driver behavior

Introduction

It is crucial to distinguish between *driver performance* and *driver behavior*. Not differentiating between them has caused, and continues to cause, confusion. The two concepts are:

> *Driver performance* – what the driver CAN do.
>
> *Driver behavior*   – what the driver DOES do.

Driver performance relates to the driver's knowledge, skill, perceptual and cognitive abilities, as discussed in Chapter 8. Driver behavior is what the driver chooses to do with these attributes. The example in Fig. 8-2 (p. 183) showed that the probability and severity of a crash depends on driver reaction time, a driver performance attribute. However, the outcome also depends on the speed of the vehicle. The reason why drivers choose different speeds is not conveyed by Fig. 8-2. The ability to judge speed, and the capability to control the vehicle at that speed, are aspects of driver performance. The speed chosen is at the core of driver behavior.

As driver performance focuses on capabilities and skills, it can be investigated by many methods, including experiments using laboratory equipment, driving simulators, and instrumented vehicles traveling on test tracks. As driver behavior is what drivers actually do, it cannot be investigated by such methods. As a consequence, we have less solid quantitative information about driver behavior than about driver performance. Particularly important, but difficult to quantify, are relationships between driver behavior and crash risk.

Normal driving is a self-paced task

The distinction between performance and behavior is central to traffic safety because normal driving is a *self-paced* task.[1] That is, drivers choose their own desired level of task difficulty. Increased skill can be used for many purposes. A likely use is to choose a different level of task difficulty. In Chapter 5 we found that a technology that improved vehicle braking, antilock braking systems (ABS), was associated with a large increase in rollover risk, and did not enhance safety in the way that a naïve interpretation of impressive test track results indicated. In the same way, an increase in driving skill may not increase safety because it can be used for such purposes as increasing speed, overtaking in tighter situations, or performing more secondary tasks, like talking on cell phones. While crash rates of older drivers have been shown to increase with declining performance, there is a conspicuous absence of convincing evidence of any relationship between crash risks and performance measures for drivers who are not old.

A distinguished sea captain commented:

> *A superior seaman uses his superior judgment to keep out of situations requiring his superior skills.*[2]

Drivers behaving in such a way would enhance safety. However, a *superior driver* who has learned skid control or advanced braking techniques may well seek opportunities in traffic to exhibit these skills.

When task difficulty is maintained constant, higher skill has been shown to increase safety. Crash rates of Helsinki bus and streetcar drivers were found to be strongly correlated with a series of performance-measuring tests.[3]   In addition, crash rates were stable over long periods when monitored from 1947-1973. The basic distinction between these drivers, who were employed to perform specific tasks, and drivers in general, is that their schedules, and other aspects of driving behavior, were specified. Higher skill could not be used to increase speed – indeed, keeping closely on schedule would relate to skill. More recent research has developed screening procedures that identify commercial fleet drivers with higher than average probability of crashing.[4] Such procedures are not available for normal driving.

Driving in a regulated structured environment has features in common with piloting a commercial airliner, so that increased skill, knowledge and performance are expected to increase safety in both situations. However, what is crucial is that this does not apply to normal self-paced driving. Misguided policy has often resulted from a mistaken belief that safe driving is primarily a perceptual-motor skill, and that measures that increase driving skill will improve safety.

Racing drivers compared to average drivers

The belief that increasing skill would reduce crash rates has seemed to many too obvious to be worth investigating. Such a belief reinforces the view that driver education must increase safety, even in the face of so much evidence that it does not (Chapter 8). It is widely held by driving aficionados that high-skill drivers are inherently safe drivers.

This was examined directly by comparing the on-the-road driving records of unusually skilled drivers to the records of average drivers.[5] The investigators obtained the names and addresses of national competition license holders from the Sports Car Club of America. They compared the on-the-road driving records of these license holders (referred to in their paper as *racing drivers*) in Florida, New York, and Texas, to comparison groups of drivers in the same states matched in such characteristics as gender and age.

The results of the study are summarized in Fig. 9-1, which displays the violation and crash rates for the racing drivers divided by the corresponding rates for the comparison drivers. If there were no differences between the groups of drivers, these ratios would all be close to one, whereas if the racing drivers had lower rates, the ratios would be less than one. What is found is that in all 12 combinations examined, the rates for the racing drivers exceeded those for the comparison drivers, in most cases by considerable amounts. Thus, on a per year basis, the racing drivers not only had substantially more violations, especially speeding violations, but also more crashes.

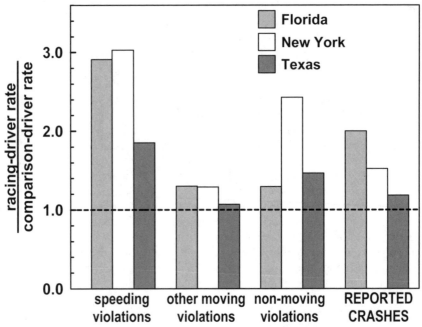

Figure 9-1. The number of incidents per year for racing drivers compared to the values of the same quantities for comparison average drivers matched in gender and age.[5]

It could be claimed that higher speeds by more skillful drivers do not cause harm if the person driving faster is more able to avoid crashes. What is most telling in this study is not the higher violation rates, but the higher crash rates. Self-reported estimates of distance of travel indicated that the racing drivers traveled more than the comparison drivers. However, additional analyses found that this does not explain all of the observed differences.

In interpreting the difference between the driving records of the racing drivers and the comparison drivers, it is not possible to determine whether the effect flows from the use of the additional skill acquired by the drivers to drive more aggressively, or whether it is simply high risk drivers who are attracted to racing. It is possible that without the additional skills acquired in pursuit of their advanced license they might have had yet higher crash rates, although I find this improbable. The study does show that higher skill levels are not associated with lower crash rates.

Effect of speed on risk

Quantitative relationships between crash risk and pre-crash travel speed are difficult to obtain because the speed that a vehicle was traveling prior to its crash is not generally known. Pre-crash speeds are rarely recorded, and it is an involved and uncertain process to infer speeds from such physical evidence as might be produced by the crash. Skid marks provide some information, but anti-lock brakes eliminate these by maintaining wheel rotation under maximum braking. When skid marks are present they still provide no information about how much speed reduction occurred when the vehicle was not skidding. The detailed post-crash examination required to estimate speed precludes its inclusion in large data files like FARS.

Urban speeds and injury crashes – case-control method

The effect of travel speed on crash risk was investigated by applying a case-control study design to data collected on urban streets in the Adelaide (Australia) metropolitan area.[6] The case-control method involves comparing the speeds of cars involved in crashes, or *case* cars, to the speeds of *control* cars not involved in crashes. The case sample included only cars involved in casualty crashes in which someone was transported to a hospital. All case drivers had zero blood alcohol concentration. Pre-crash speeds of case cars were determined using crash reconstruction techniques involving detailed investigations of the crash scenes. Features of the crash, such as skid marks, impact points, final positions of cars, damage to cars, and participant and witness statements contributed to the reconstruction process. The control cars matched the case cars in direction of travel, roadway location, time of day, day of week, and time of year. Control-car speeds were measured by a laser speed meter. All data were for roads with 60 km/h speed limits.

The data led to the risk ratios plotted in Fig. 9-2. All values are relative to the base case risk of traveling at the 60 km/h speed limit. The error limits are one standard error, as determined by the number of case and control cars at each speed interval and at 60 km/h.

Risk of involvement in a casualty crash increases steeply as speeds exceed the 60 km/h speed limit, approximately doubling for each additional 5 km/h. The increase is so steep that a logarithmic scale is used in Fig. 9-2. The risk at 80 km/h is 30 times the risk when driving at the speed limit.

There is no clear indication that risk decreases for travel speeds below the speed limit. There are other data associating speeds lower than the average with increased risk.[7] However, such findings underline some of the most difficult problems encountered in traffic safety research. Observing that slow drivers have higher crash risk does not imply that driving slower increases risk. The

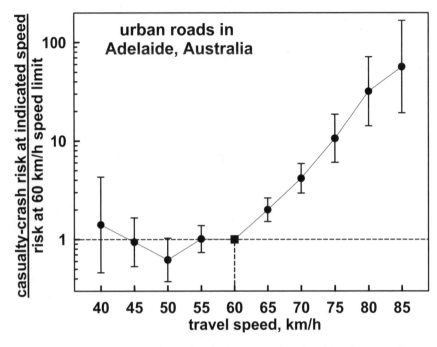

Figure 9-2. Crash risk at indicated speed compared to the risk when traveling at the 60 km/h speed limit on urban roads in Adelaide, Australia.[6]

reason they are driving slower could be in response to some other risk-increasing condition (fatigue, poor vision, major distraction, vehicle problems). Similarly, the higher speed drivers might have higher risks even when they drive slower. There is little opportunity for traffic safety studies to provide results that can be interpreted without some element of judgment regarding plausible and implausible explanations. Notwithstanding the uncertainties that are always present, the data in Fig. 9-2 provide clear evidence that risk of involvement in a casualty crash increases steeply as a function of how much a driver exceeds the speed limit.

Rural speeds and injury crashes – case-control method

The approach above was applied to rural roads in South Australia with speed limits of 80 km/h or higher.[8] Because of smaller sample sizes, different speed limits, and more varying driving conditions, the results were expressed in terms of deviations from average speeds of control cars rather than departures from speed limits. As with the urban study, all cars contributing to the study were traveling at free speeds, meaning that they were not overtaking, following, accelerating, slowing, etc.

The authors summarized the results as

$$R = e^{0.07039\delta v \, + \, 0.0008617\delta v^2} \qquad \text{(for -10 km/h} < \delta v < 20 \text{ km/h)} \qquad \text{9-1}$$

where δv = speed above the average speed (km/h), and

R = risk at speed δv above average compared to risk at average speed.

Eqn 9-1 estimates that a car traveling 10 km/h faster than the average speed in a rural area will be 2.2 times as likely to be involved in a casualty crash as a car traveling at the average speed.

Speed limit changes and casualty risk

Another approach to examining how speed affects risk is to relate changes in aggregate casualties on selected roads to changes in the average speed of the traffic on these roads. This approach provides relationships without the need to know how fast specific crash-involved vehicles were traveling prior to their crashes, which, as in the case-control studies described above, is difficult and expensive to obtain.

Claims in the literature that speed limits have had no effect on safety have led to some confusion. What is written in a legal statute or on a road sign does not, by itself, influence safety. If all 40 mph signs were replaced by 35 mph signs in the middle of the night, it is unlikely that many commuters would notice the change the next morning. It is travel speed, not speed limits, that affects safety. For speed limits to affect travel speed they must be known to motorists, and, for many motorists, they must also be perceived to be enforced.

Relationships between crash risk and travel speed were determined by examining casualty rates before and after changes in speed limits on many (mainly higher speed limit) roads in Sweden.[9] In many cases, speeds on roads with changed speed limits were compared to speeds on similar roads that did not have their limits changed. The results were found to fit the power function

$$\frac{rate\,after\,speed\,change}{rate\,before\,speed\,change} = \left(\frac{median\,speed\,after\,speed\,change}{median\,speed\,before\,speed\,change} \right)^P , \qquad \text{9-2}$$

which, for small percent changes in speed, can be approximated by

$$percent\ change\ in\ rate\ =\ (percent\ change\ in\ median\ speed)^P . \qquad \text{9-3}$$

P is a power that depends on the severity of the crash:

$$\text{for any crash} \qquad P = 2$$
$$\text{for serious-injury crash} \quad P = 3$$
$$\text{for fatal crash} \qquad P = 4$$

These results and the increasing value of P with increasing severity supports the pattern that speed increases lead to increases in the:

- Risk of crashing

- Risk of serious injury, if a crash occurs

- Risk of death, if a serious injury occurs

While these relationships estimate substantial increases in risk with increasing speed, the increases are not as large as found in the case-control studies. For example, Eqn 9-2 estimates traveling at 90 km/h compared to 80 km/h increases serious injury risk by a factor $(90/80)^3 = 1.42$. This 42% increase, while substantial, falls short of the 120% increase estimated by Eqn 9-1 for a vehicle traveling 10 km/h faster than the average speed. Fitting Eqn 9-2 to values computed using Eqn 9-1 gives $P = 6.6$, and the fit to the urban data in Fig. 9-2 gives $P = 12$. The differences could reflect that in the case-control studies, the speeding case drivers might be less safe than average drivers even when they were not speeding, because other risk-increasing behaviors are related to speeding.

A British study reports a value of $P = 2.5$ for all crashes involving injury, based on comparing rates on different roads with similar features but different observed average speeds.[10] Another British study reports that for every 1 mph rise in the mean traffic speed, crashes rise by about five percent, equivalent to $P = 5$ for all crashes.[11]

A study in Israel found that increasing speed limits from 90 km/h to 100 km/h on three inter-urban highways led to speed increases of about 7%.[12] Traffic deaths increased by 15%, but the authors claim that this observed increase would have been larger had it not been for other concurrent countermeasures. They found that the number of deaths per serious injury increased by 38%. If the P value for fatalities in Eqn 9-2 is P_F, and that for injuries is P_I, then the ratio of these gives approximately the increase in the risk of death in an injury crash as $P_F/P_I \approx (38\%)/(7\%) \approx 5$. This is consistent with high P values. This study finds increased casualties on roads with unchanged speed limits, providing further evidence of spillover effects.

The studies measuring mean speed cannot identify which individual vehicles contribute most to overall risk. However, the results from the case-control studies, which did measure speeds of individual vehicles, support that the major contribution to aggregate risk is from the few fastest vehicles. If we assume that the variance to mean ratio remains constant when a change in average speed occurs, then the fastest vehicles will increase their speeds by more than the increase in average speed. It is the fastest drivers who make the main contribution to risk before the speed increase, and it is their larger than average speed increase after the change that makes the major contribution to the aggregate risk increases observed after increases in average speed.

Lowering of speed limits on US rural Interstates and fatality rates. A national maximum speed limit of 55 mph became law throughout the US on 1 January 1974. It was introduced in response to the October 1973 Arab oil embargo in order to reduce fuel use – safety was not a consideration. However, the speed limit change provided a unique opportunity to evaluate how travel speed affects fatality risk.

Prior to the change, the speed limits on rural Interstates were nearly all 70 mph, with a few being higher. Average travel speed was observed to be 63.4 mph. After imposition of the 55 mph limit, the observed speed declined to 57.6 mph, a seemingly modest 5.8 mph drop compared to the 15 mph decrease in the speed limit. However, a sharp drop in the fatality rate occurred (Fig. 9-3). The change in the speed limit was one of many changes from 1973 and 1974 related to the oil embargo. Reduced travel was another. This and other changes should not directly affect the number of deaths for the same distance of travel, the rate plotted.

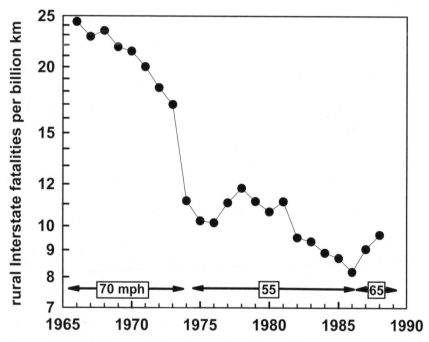

Figure 9-3. Fatalities per billion km on the US rural Interstate system. Until 1973 maximum speed limits were 70 mph (in some cases greater). From 1974 to 1987 there was a nationwide 55 mph speed limit. In 1987 some states increased limits on some portions to 65 mph. Based on Ref. 13, p. 340.

Substituting the after and before speeds into Eqn 9-2, with $P = 4$ for fatality crash risk, gives $(57.6/63.4)^4 = 0.68$, thus estimating a 32% decrease in fatality rate. The change in the fatality rates plotted between 1973 and 1974 is a 34% decrease. A small part of the decline is likely due to an ongoing trend (as expected, see Chapter 3), but even after taking this into account, the observed decline supports that $P = 4$ is an appropriate choice in Eqn 9-2 for fatalities.

Raising of speed limits on US rural Interstates and fatality rates. On 28 November 1995 the Federal Government terminated its involvement in speed limits, returning the responsibility entirely to the individual states. Before that, in April 1987, Congress had passed legislation allowing states to increase speed limits to 65 mph on some sections of rural Interstates. The introduction of the national maximum speed limit occurred at one time, and applied nationwide, which led to the large easily observed change in Fig. 9-3. When the limit was made more flexible, and later ended, states were not required to make any changes. Some did, some did not, and the states that made changes did not make identical changes, or change at the same time. As a result, estimating how increases in the speed limits affected fatalities cannot be performed by a simple calculation at the national level. Many evaluations were performed, including those by individual states, giving a consistent pattern that the states that increased their limits from 55 mph to 65 mph experience about a 10% increase in fatality rates.

Within a year after the Federal Government ended any role in setting speed limits, 23 states raised their rural Interstate speed limits to 70 or 75 mph. Many studies showed that this increased fatalities.[14] One study compared changes in the number of fatalities for the same distance of travel for states that increased their limits to states that kept their limits at the then prior limit of 65 mph.[15] The states that increased speed limits to 70 mph experienced a 35% increase in fatality rate, and the states that increased speed limits to 75 mph a 38% increase. Data are unavailable for actual changes in speed in response to the speed limit changes.

Speed and speed change – v and Δv

It is not travel speed, v, that plays the direct role in injuries, but the change in speed, Δv, the vehicle undergoes as a result of the crash (Chapter 2). Analysis of data for crashed cars showed that, when a crash occurs:[16,17]

$$\text{probability of fatality} = \left(\Delta v / 114\right)^{3.54}, \quad (\Delta v < 114 \text{ km/h}), \text{ and} \qquad 9\text{-}4$$

$$\text{probability of AIS} \geq 3 \text{ injury} = \left(\Delta v / 106\right)^{2.22}, \quad (\Delta v < 106 \text{ km/h}). \qquad 9\text{-}5$$

The fatality relationship, Eqn 9-4, was introduced earlier and used to produce Fig. 8-2, p. 183. In general Δv is smaller, usually much smaller, than v. However, the simple (but rare) case of a vehicle striking an immovable object without braking gives $\Delta v = v$ (assuming no bounce-back). If the risk of striking the object increases as v^2 ($P = 2$ for crash risk), then fatality crash risk will increase as $v^{(2 + 3.54)} = v^{5.54}$ giving, in terms of Eqn 9-2, the values $P = 5.54$ for fatalities and, similarly, $P = 4.22$ for injuries. When there is braking, Δv will increase more steeply than proportional to v (Fig. 8-2), so the values $P = 5.54$

and $P = 4.22$ may be low. This very approximate calculation supports the higher P values reported from the case-control studies.

German Autobahns

Opponents of speed limits often claim that German Autobahns have no speed limits yet low casualties. The claim of no speed limits is countered by temporary speed limits on most of Germany's highways.[18] Signs suggesting a recommended speed limit of 130 km/h (80 mph) are posted along most Autobahns, while urban sections and a few dangerous stretches sometimes have posted speed limits of 100 km/h. Congestion, which reduces fatality risk by reducing speeds (Chapter 5), is common.

Surprisingly, there does not appear to be any technical study comparing safety on Autobahns to safety on freeways in other countries. Data in a column listed *killed per 1 billion km – motorways*[19] shows that the German rate, while 27% lower than the US rate, is 48% higher than the Swedish rate and 76% higher than the British rate (see Chapter 15 on failure of US safety policy).

Speed variance

Variability around average speeds, or speed variance, has been discussed as a safety factor, especially since observations associated higher risks with speeds below as well as above the average.[7,20] An analysis interpreting crash risk as proportional to the number of times a vehicle is overtaken or overtakes concludes similarly that traveling below or above the average speed increases crash risk.[21] The common policy of setting lower speed limits for trucks than for other vehicles would seem to imply rejecting the notion that driving slower than the average speed increases risk.

From time to time there are claims that speed variance is as important as speed. The most extreme view claims that speed, as such, does not affect safety and that the safety goal should be to require all traffic to move at the same (presumably high) speed. After all, vehicles traveling at identical speeds in the same direction cannot crash into each other, and will never overtake. While there are indications (not supported in Fig. 9-2) that vehicles traveling slower than average have above-average crash rates, the reason they are traveling slower is because the driver chooses to do so, likely in response to known driver (or vehicle) inadequacies. If such drivers were encouraged or compelled to speed up to the average speed, an increase in crash risk seems more likely than a decrease. Even if slower-than-average drivers have crash rates similar to faster-than-average drivers, their injury and fatality rates will still be substantially less.

Higher speed variance would appear to increase the risk of rear-end crashes. However, only 5.0% of occupant fatalities in FARS 2002 occurred in rear-impacted vehicles (initial impact point 5, 6 or 7 o'clock). Single-vehicle crashes, for which the concept of speed variance is hardly relevant, account for 49% of driver fatalities (Table 3-3, p. 48). Thus speed variance can make no more than a modest contribution to fatalities, especially when one additionally considers how steeply the risk of death increases with speed. Traffic in which all vehicles traveled at 40 mph would, according to some definitions, have zero speed variance. Yet a head-on crash between two vehicles traveling at 40 mph is far more lethal to both drivers than one between a 40 mph and a 20 mph vehicle. The speed variance concept has been applied to vehicles traveling on different roads, not merely in opposite directions on the same road! Multivariate analyses that find speed variance a prime factor in determining fatalities simply provide another example of how such methods can be coaxed to support any conclusion. Even if speed variance were all that important, the way to reduce it is to reduce the speed of the fastest vehicles, which is already the current focus of enforcement.

Comments on relationship between speed and risk

An enormous body of evidence consistently supports that the risk of crashing, being injured, or being killed, increases with increasing speed. There is no doubt that the dose-response curve is very steep – a little extra speed generates a lot more harm. How much more harm per increment of speed increase is not known to much precision. One source of uncertainty is variability in results due in part to methodological differences. However, it is also likely that different relationships apply to different roads, circumstances, and driver populations.

For fatalities, a one percent increase in speed appears to increase fatality risk somewhere in the range 4% to 12%, with stronger support for a value towards the low end of the range. The lower value indicates that a 3% speed reduction reduces risk by 13%. This is larger than the reduction from frontal airbags. A 1% to 2% nationwide reduction in speed provides a nationwide reduction in traffic deaths similar to that provided by airbags. Property damage, a major cost of traffic crashes (Chapter 2), is reduced by speed reductions, but increased by airbags, which must be replaced after deployment (more on airbags in Chapter 12).

Lower speed limits reduce the efficiency of travel. The safest traffic system consists of gargantuan vehicles all of which are nearly stationary. Setting speed limits involves trade-offs. Studies taking into account delay, injury, fuel use, emissions, and other costs have estimated socially optimum speeds of about 50 km/h for urban streets,[22] and 85 to 105 km/h for rural roads.[23] Actual speed limits (which drivers routinely violate) are found to be generally higher than the estimated social optimum.[24]

Reducing speed limits is almost certain to increase the number of law violators. Opponents of lower speed limits often make a big issue out of the fact that more drivers violated the US national maximum speed limit of 55 mph speed limit than the prior 70 mph limit. A 150 mph speed limit would produce many deaths, but few speeding tickets (although there are 27 car models available in the US claiming top speeds in the range 150 to 240 mph).[25]

Demographic factors related to risk taking in traffic

The empirical studies showing that speed choice (a driver characteristic) has a large influence on crash risk were not based on measuring a characteristic of the driver, but a characteristic of the vehicle (its speed). In most of the studies, information about the driver traveling at the measured speed was not available. Obtaining driver information would require major increases in experimental difficulty and cost. Various methods have been used to relate aggregate driver characteristics to speeding, and, more generally, risk taking in traffic. No method is without some weaknesses, but as different methods have different weaknesses, they collectively generate a fairly consistent picture that provides insight into why so many crash rates have the clear gender and age dependencies reported in Chapter 7.

Traffic tickets

Table 9-1 shows the percent of residents of North Carolina with driver licenses who received a traffic-law violation citation (*ticket*) in 1998.[26] Violations related to crashes are excluded.

Table 9-1. The percent of North Carolina residents with driver licenses who received traffic citations (those involving traffic crashes excluded) in 1998.[26]

race→	white			African American		
age→	16-22	23-49	≥50	16-22	23-49	≥50
male	24.3%	11.1%	3.1%	18.7 %	14.6%	5.6%
female	12.3%	5.6%	1.1%	9.2%	7.1%	1.7%
male-to-female ratio	2.0	2.0	2.8	2.0	2.1	3.3

For each race and age comparison, the male rate far exceeds the female rate (by factors between 2.0 and 3.3). For each race and gender comparison, drivers aged 16-22 have rates far higher than those for drivers aged 50 or older (by factors between 3.3 and 11.2).

The number of traffic tickets a driver gets in a year reflects more than just the propensity to violate traffic law. Drivers in each of the 12 cells in Table 9-1 travel different distances at different times, and therefore necessarily have different probabilities of being observed by police. What is a more controversial and difficult issue is that all individuals may not have identical probabilities of receiving tickets even for identical behavior in identical circumstances. The probability that a police officer issues a ticket might be prejudicially affected by the gender, age, or race of the driver. The data alone cannot provide information on the extent to which sexism, ageism, or racism are present. The agreement of the gender and age dependence of ticket rates with casualty rates supports that a major reason why drivers receive tickets is that their behavior in traffic increases the risk that they will be in a fatal crash. However, contributions from other factors cannot be ruled out. Among young (aged 16-22) drivers, African Americans of both genders have lower citation rates than white drivers of the same gender and age. This may reflect less availability of vehicles, less driving, or perhaps young African Americans are driving more carefully because they believe that police are prejudicially targeting them. Such a belief, whether true or not, would save lives of those who believed it. The higher rates for African Americans in the other age groups may reflect a largely universal socioeconomic effect in which risk taking in a host of activities declines with increasing affluence.

Large data files

The only demographic factors recorded in US traffic crash files, such as FARS, are gender and age. Many results based on these variables have been presented in earlier chapters. Mortality from the National Center for Health Statistics contains more detailed information on those dying from any cause. By linking this data set with FARS, together with information on distance of travel from the 1990 Nationwide Personal Transportation Survey, fatality rates for the same distance of travel were estimated for factors in addition to those included in FARS.[27] The study examined occupant fatality risks for children (aged 5-12) and teenagers (aged 13-19 years), and compared the risks for Hispanics, non-Hispanic blacks, and non-Hispanic whites. For each billion vehicle miles of travel, 14 non-Hispanic black children were killed, compared to 8 Hispanics, and 5 non-Hispanic whites. For teenagers the rates were 45 for Hispanics, 34 for non-Hispanic blacks, and 30 for non-Hispanic whites. Unquestionably, socioeconomic status makes a large contribution to any such differences, as well as to the differences in Table 9-1. However, a later study of adult risk that does incorporate a measure of socioeconomic status concludes that this variable cannot account for all of the differences.[28]

Self-reported behavior in questionnaires

Questionnaire, or survey, studies have the advantage of producing information on many factors for large numbers of respondents. A disadvantage is that self-reports of behavior may depart substantially from actual behavior, particularly if the behavior is considered to be socially undesirable or is illegal. Even in the unlikely event that drivers knew how often they speeded, they might not respond truthfully. Comparing self-reports to observed behavior shows that speeders tend to underreport their speeding.[29] Still, responses reflect some mix of true speeds, the responder's ability to estimate true speeds, and the self-image the responder wishes to convey. These are all factors relevant to safety.

Responses were obtained from 1,095 licensed drivers in Scotland in a 20-minute in-home interview.[30] Table 9-2 shows the percent characterized as *speeders*, defined as reporting that they had been stopped by the police for

Table 9-2. The percent of respondents to a survey in Scotland classified as *speeders,* **defined as reporting that they had been stopped by the police for speeding during their driving career or had been flashed by a speed camera in the previous three years.**[30]

age→	17-24	25-34	35-44	45-54	55-64	≥65	total
male	29%	54%	59%	66 %	49%	41%	48.9%
female	15%	33%	29%	28%	26%	21%	26.0%
male-to-female ratio	1.9	1.6	2.0	2.4	1.9	2.0	1.9

speeding during their driving career, or had been flashed by a speed camera in the previous three years (the driver is aware when a flash photograph, indicating speeding, is taken). At all ages, male rates exceed female rates by factors between 1.6 and 2.4. The data do not provide information on speeding versus age because, as drivers age, their life-long exposure to the risk of a speeding offense can only increase.

The same survey asked drivers how they would adjust their speed under various driving conditions. Differences reported to be statistically significant are listed in Table 9-3, again demonstrating that males are associated with riskier behavior. The greater tendency of males to slow down in light rain could possibly reflect greater appreciation of the relationship between braking and wet roadways, or (more likely) driving closer to the margin on dry roads.

Table 9-3. How Scottish drivers of different genders indicated they would respond to changed conditions.[30]

percent of respondents who would:	male	female
drive faster if traffic was faster than they normally drove	32	24
drive slower if traffic was slower than they normally drove	69	76
drive slower if driving in the dark	56	70
drive slower if driving on unfamiliar roads	84	94
drive slower if driving in light rain	42	35

Observational studies

Driver propensity to take risk, as indicated by chosen speed or by following headway (gap between a driver's vehicle and the one in front), was measured in a series of observational studies in which oncoming cars were photographed from freeway overpasses.[31,32] The license-plate number, read from the photograph, was used to extract from state files the driving record, gender, and age of the registered owner of the vehicle. A photographed driver judged not to differ in age or sex from the registered owner was assumed to be the owner.

The studies found that speed on a rural two-lane road decreased with increasing driver age. The proportion of vehicles observed following the vehicle in front at dangerously short headways (*tailgating*) declined with increasing driver age. The risk taking behaviors of speeding and tailgating were more prevalent among male drivers. These results are summarized in more detail elsewhere.[13(p 137-138)]

Personality factors and crash rates

The above relationships between risk-taking in traffic and gender and age apply to averages of large groups. The behavior of individuals within a given demographic category vary more than differences between demographic categories – there are many young males who drive at lower risk than many older females. There has been much effort to attempt to explain such variation in terms of personality.

The first study indicating "we drive as we live"

One of the earliest studies to examine the relationship between crash involvement and personality was published in 1949.[33]   Characteristics of 96 Toronto taxi drivers who had four or more crashes were compared to those of 100 taxi drivers with no crashes. The two groups, matched in age and driving experience, provided the results in Table 9-4.

Table 9-4. Frequency of contact with social agencies by 96 Toronto taxi drivers with four or more crashes compared to 100 with no crashes.[33]

	adult court	juvenile court	public health	social service	credit bureau	at least one agency
four or more crashes	34%	17%	14%	18%	34%	66%
crash-free drivers	1%	1%	0%	1%	6%	9%

The authors conclude:

> *It would appear that the driving hazards and the high accident record are simply one manifestation of a method of living that has been demonstrated in their personal lives. Truly it may be said that a man drives as he lives. If his personal life is marked by caution, tolerance, foresight, and consideration for others, then he would drive in the same manner.   If his personal life is devoid of these desirable characteristics then his driving will be characterized by aggressiveness, and over a long period of time he will have a much higher accident rate than his stable companion.*[33(p 329)]

Although the methodology of the 1949 study can be criticized on many counts, it was the first study to provide specific evidence of a strong link between broad personality characteristics and crash involvement, and introduced the concept *a man drives as he lives*. A major deficiency of the study is that much of the interpretation is based on psychiatric-type interviews conducted while riding in the taxis. This procedure is subjective in nature, and given the extreme differences between the groups of drivers, it was not possible for the interviewer to remain unaware of the group to which the driver most likely belonged, thus raising the possibility of bias. The comparison is between extremes (some of the drivers with high crash rates verged on the psychopathic), so it could be argued that the results may not necessarily be applicable to a more moderate degree of crash over involvement.

Psychiatric profiles of fatally injured drivers

An imaginative technique was applied to obtain psychiatric profiles of 25 deceased drivers judged to be at fault in the crashes in which whey were killed in Houston, Texas, from 1967-1968.[34] The profiles were produced by conducting in-depth interviews with family members and associates of the deceased. These were compared to profiles of 25 control subjects selected from the same voter precincts in which the deceased had lived, and matched in such characteristics as age (all were males). Many criticisms of this study are possible. The information gathering processes were necessarily quite different for the deceased and control subjects, and the sample sizes were small. However, the differences found are much larger than any that appear likely to be due to possible biases in the technique. Personality disorders were associated with 75% of the fatally injured drivers, compared to 8% for the control sample. Even the few abnormal personalities among the control population were found to be less deviant, and to have more adequate coping mechanisms that helped compensate for their psychiatric liability.

Difficulties in researching the role of driver personality in crashes

Although personality factors play a central role, they are difficult to investigate. One problem is that crash rates depend strongly on factors, such as gender, age and alcohol use, so that any study of personality factors must control for these. This may require large sample sizes. Yet measures of personality are not available in large data sets, but must instead be determined by the investigators by, for example, administering one of many available personality instruments as components of questionnaire studies.

Large compared to normal departures from the norm. The large effects of personality discussed above were measured by comparing extreme cases, such as taxi drivers with four or more crashes to those with zero, or fatally injured drivers to typical drivers. Since the comparison is between such extremes, it could be argued that the results may not be valid when interpolated to the more moderate degrees of over involvement that are of such importance in traffic safety. This problem is parallel to the dose-response problem in toxicology. Does a large, easily measured, deleterious effect associated with a massive dose of some substance support the inference that one tenth of the dose would still produce some deleterious effect, perhaps about one tenth the effect of the large dose? Or is there some threshold below which the substance produces no deleterious effect? Given that most crashes involve drivers not as far from the average as those in the studies discussed, it is important to know whether moderate variations within the normal ranges of behavior can explain variations in crash rates. As in the toxicology case, the smaller the dose, the more difficult it is to measure the response, but the more people are involved.

Above-average crash risks are still small. There are methodological problems inherent in comparing those with moderately above-average crash rates to those with below-average crash rates. To illustrate, assume a hypothetical population of identical drivers each with the same average crash rate of 0.086 crashes per year used in Table 1-1. Column 4 of Table 1-1 (p. 15) shows that in a ten-year period 42% of the drivers have zero crashes, 36% one crash, and 21% two or more crashes. Suppose one compared driver characteristics of groups of *safe* (zero-crash) and *risky* (two or more crashes) drivers. Because membership of either group is determined by the pure randomness of a Poisson process, driver characteristics in each group are identical. Such a finding could be misinterpreted to conclude falsely that drivers who crash do not differ from those who do not crash.

Now suppose there is a group of genuine *risky* drivers who are twice as likely as average drivers to crash (that is, their crash rate is 0.172 crashes per year) and a group of *low risk* drivers who are half as likely as average driver to crash (that is, their crash risk 0.043 crashes per year). In a ten-year, period 18% of the risky drivers will still be crash free, whereas 7% of the low risk drivers will have two or more crashes. Likewise, any group of subjects selected on the basis of having no observed crashes will contain many high risk drivers, and any group selected on the basis of having two or more observed crashes will contain some low risk drivers. The high and low risk groups of subjects will indeed contain drivers with higher and lower average propensities to crash, but the difference will be but a fraction of the real factor of four difference. This makes it more difficult to detect relationships based on comparing high and low risk drivers, and the effects measured in any relationships that are found will systematically underestimate the magnitude of the true effects by substantial amounts.

There does not appear to be a way out of this dilemma. Statistical theory, together with various assumptions, can be used to estimate the most likely real effect from an observed difference, but as the observed difference is small even when the real difference is large, the estimate will lack precision. One cannot use very long periods to accumulate larger numbers of crashes because crash risk, which depends so strongly on age, is not stable over long periods.

Other studies on the relationship between personality and crash risk

Despite the difficulties, a large number of studies on personality factors, mainly using interview methods, have been performed. Reviews[13,35] mention studies that report that higher risk drivers are less mature, less intellectually oriented, less academically successful, less interested in aesthetic matters, lower in aspiration, poorer in attitudes toward the law, and generally less well adjusted socially. They are more emotionally unstable, unhappy, asocial, anti-social, impulsive, and under stress. They are more likely to smoke and to have personality disorders and paranoid tendencies. They have less happy childhoods, a tendency to express open feelings of hostility, increased sensation seeking, low tension-tolerance, increased aggressiveness, and are more likely to seek prestige and social roles oriented towards authority and/or competition. They are more likely to have family histories, and current family relationships, reflecting higher degrees of disruption and conflict.

More recent studies augment and extend these findings. Higher crash rates are related to high hostility in combination with poor self-esteem, high job stress, and self-reported tendencies to speed and to disregard traffic rules.[36] Type-A personality drivers self-reported being involved in more crashes and displaying more aggression on the road than average drivers.[37] Survey respondents reacting to behavior of other drivers in different scenarios were more likely to attribute hostility to male drivers.[38] Given all the correlates that have been identified with over involvement in crashes, it is not surprising that over involvement in crashes relates to a whole host of other unhealthy behaviors, such as smoking.[39] Credit histories have been shown to be good predictors of crash involvement. The auto-insurance industry is using the credit ratings available in large data files to set premiums.

Emotional stress. Personality denotes stable character traits that do not change over short time periods. Emotional stress may produce short or medium term departures from an individual's long-term average driving behavior. The risk of a driver being involved in a crash or violation is found to increase just prior to divorce proceedings.[40] Drivers killed in crashes are more likely than control drivers to be undergoing periods of personal stress.[34] A clustering of child pedestrian deaths around the time of the child's birthday is reported and attributed to the birthday excitement overriding the child's normal caution.[41] It is not possible to investigate this further using FARS data because date of birth is not recorded in FARS, just age to the nearest year.

Non-transport motives

Transportation is not the only goal of driving. In an extreme example, racing drivers are not going anywhere, but are driving for a mix of pleasure, excitement, glory, and prize money. While regular driving has little in common with racing, it still includes motives in addition to utilitarian transportation.

Most drivers find pleasure in driving fast and accelerating rapidly. We are all aware of the use of vehicles to show off, and to display competitive prowess in order to impress peers and attract members of the opposite sex. While the behavior of nearly all drivers is influenced at some times by non-transportation motives, this is particularly prevalent in young drivers, especially young male drivers. Such behavior is enshrined in our culture, and figures in many classic youth cult movies, such as *Rebel Without a Cause* and *American Graffiti*. Cars are used as an outlet for the independence, rebelliousness, and peer acceptance needs of newly licensed adolescents, a manifestation of a broader *adolescent problem behavior syndrome*.[42] These non-transportation motives seem to be at the very core of the problem of traffic crashes, because it is risky behavior, especially speeding, that is the major determinant of the number of casualties. It is unlikely that adolescents and young men do much of their speeding in order to keep appointments with strict deadlines. They are motivated much more by the enjoyment and thrill of traveling fast, breaking the law, and defying society. The importance of these non-transportation motives in safety underlines that the problem is not lack of skill or knowledge, and countermeasures ignoring such effects are unlikely to be successful.

Suicide

The US recorded 23,458 male and 5,741 female suicides in 1999,[43] giving an overall male-to-female ratio of 4.1 to 1. For ages 20-24 the ratio is 6.4, and declines systematically with age, reaching 3.1 for ages 45-54.

Given the large number of suicides, it would be remarkable if traffic crashes were not used for some of them, especially as use of a vehicle provides a convenient, undiscoverable, and honorable method of self-destruction. It minimizes guilt in those left behind, and avoids insurance and religious complications. Not only can crashes be used for premeditated suicides, but they may just happen to be available at the instant of a momentary, and perhaps otherwise temporary, impulse towards self-destruction. It is a near-perfect instrument with which to indulge the *death instinct* postulated by Freud.

The possibility that some traffic crashes are suicides has been discussed for decades. A 1973 book, *Accident or Suicide? Destruction by Automobile,* offers a plausible narrative supporting a strong connection, but provides no convincing evidence that any specific traffic fatality was really a suicide.[44] It is, of course, intrinsically difficult in most cases to determine definitively if a fatality is a suicide, so more indirect approaches are required.

A novel method examined time-series of suicides and crashes to see if traffic crashes increased after widespread reports of suicides of famous people.[45,46] An increase was observed, and attributed to suicides, based on research showing that media coverage of suicides leads to copycat increases in suicides in general.[47,48] Another empirical indication that some traffic fatalities are suicides was based on observed similarities in the day-to-day variations of suicides and traffic fatalities in the US.[49]

A more direct approach was possible using in-depth information available for all fatal traffic crashes in Finland. Based on preliminary identification by crash investigation teams, and further selection by two forensic pathologists, 84 drivers killed in Finland were classified as suicides.[50] This led to the conclusion that suicide accounted for 5.9% of driver fatalities. Head-on crashes with heavier vehicles were more common than single-car crashes. In 4% of cases, the crash led to the death of another person. This study found traffic suicides to be strongly related to alcohol abuse, a factor that plays a major role in suicides in general. Further analyses of additional years of data from the same sources indicated that the percent of all traffic deaths that were suicides was increasing in time.[51]

It is particularly difficult to use FARS data to analyze suicide because known suicide cases are excluded (p. 21).

Knowing the fraction of traffic fatalities attributable to suicide is important because most countermeasures are unlikely to have much influence on this component of traffic fatalities. The presence of suicides in data used to evaluate countermeasures will result in systematic underestimation of effectiveness for non-suicidal road users.

Family influence

It is well established that one of the largest factors determining whether young people smoke is if their parents smoke.[52] The corresponding question of whether parents who crash have children who crash is more difficult to address empirically. Propensity to crash is estimated by a small number of crashes in a necessarily long time period, and the estimate departs from the true propensity because of randomness. People can be adequately characterized as smokers or non-smokers by simply asking them. The solid relationships for smoking suggest possible, but more difficult to determine, relationships for crashes. Two studies do indeed consistently find large effects for traffic crashes.

Driving records of young drivers (age 18-21) were compared to the records of their parents using the driver history file for North Carolina.[53] It was found that children's driving records in the first few years of licensure are indeed related to the driving records of their parents. Children whose parents had three or more crashes on their record were 22% more likely to have had at least one crash compared with children whose parents had no crashes. Likewise, children whose parents had three or more violations were 38% more likely to have had a violation compared with children whose parents had none.

A 1970 study found that sons of fathers with one or more traffic convictions (in a six-year period) were 58% more likely to have one or more traffic convictions than sons of fathers with no traffic convictions.[54]

Earlier we showed that studies comparing drivers with many crashes to drivers with zero crashes systematically underestimate real effects because randomness will lead to some low risk drivers being included in the high risk category, and vice versa. This effect will be present also for violations, but because of the higher numbers of violations, it will have less influence. This interpretation is consistent with the 22% effect found for crashes compared to 38% for violations.[53]

The magnitudes of the effects found, even in the face of processes that inherently lead to their underestimation, suggest that parental influence has a large influence on a person's propensity to crash. Pursuing the smoking analogy suggests that the general social environment in which someone is embedded will strongly influence their tendency to crash. The main determinant of adult smoking is smoking as a teenager – once acquired, the behavior tends to persist. Once behaviors such as speeding, drunk driving, non-wearing of belts, or general risk-taking in traffic are acquired in youth, they will tend to persist. It seems likely that drivers who are more risky than average for their age when they are young will remain more risky than average for their age as they grow older, even though their absolute risks will decline as they age. I believe that the analogy with smoking is helpful for cases in which research on drivers is infeasible. Major progress has been achieved in smoking cessation, which further offers guidance for reducing crashes, as discussed in Chapter 13.

Crime rates and crash rates

There is much evidence that individuals who are involved in traffic crashes are more likely to commit crimes. A study conducted in the Netherlands obtained information on a random sample of 903 traffic crashes.[55] From a separate file of criminal involvement, the researchers obtained the crime histories of the 1,181 male and 350 female drivers involved in the crashes (a male-to-female ratio of 3.4 to 1). The aggregate data showed that the drivers involved in crashes were more likely to have criminal records than the general public, by 31.0% compared to 15.2% for males and 11.4% compared to 3.5% for females. The traffic-crash file was examined to distinguish between drivers who displayed risky behavior prior to their crashes and those who did not. This was important since most of the crashes involved two vehicles. The drivers displaying risky behavior were more involved in various types of crimes than the other drivers – by factors of 2.6 for having a police record for violent crime, 2.5 for vandalism, 1.5 for property crime, and 5.3 for having been involved in a traffic crime.

An examination of the driving records of 114 jailed criminals found that, compared to the general public, the criminals had 3.25 times as many citations for traffic violations, 5.5 times as many property damage and injury producing crashes, and 19.5 times as many involvements in fatal crashes.[56] Some of the criminals in the sample may have been in jail for traffic offenses, which would lead to an overestimation of effects. A large sample of respondents to a survey in the Netherlands showed relatively strong relationships between crime and involvement in traffic crashes as non-drivers, including while walking and riding a bicycle.[57]

The age dependence of involvement in crime has been described as follows:

The propensity to commit criminal acts reaches a peak in the middle to late teens and then declines rapidly throughout life. Further, this distribution is characteristic of the age-crime relation regardless of sex, race, country, time, or offense. Indeed, the persistence of this relation across time and culture is phenomenal.[58]

Speeding, running red lights, tailgating, drunk driving, and not wearing safety belts are themselves criminal activities, and all correlate with crash-involvement rates. So it is perhaps not all that surprising that crash involvement relates to crime in a more general way. Research further suggests that more serious traffic offenses correlate with more serious non-traffic crimes.[55-57]

Gender differences in risk taking by babies and children*

Some extremely rare events offer insights into how risk depends on gender from the earliest ages. Despite the rarity of the events, the 1.28 million traffic fatalities documented in FARS 1975-2003* provide usable samples.

Child "driver" fatalities

Table 9-5 shows the number of children in FARS 1975-2003* satisfying the following criteria:

- Child was the only occupant of a vehicle
- Vehicle was moving when it crashed
- Child was coded as the driver
- Child was killed

One baby boy less than one year old was killed as such a *driver*. One boy age 1 and another age 3 were killed. At age 5 or younger, 17 children were killed. The gender mix is 17 boys, no girls. The youngest girl killed was age 6, at which age there were 2 girl fatalities compared to 14 boy fatalities. For every age before eligibility for a driver license (15 in most states), the cumulative male total exceeds the cumulative female total by at least a factor of 10.

FARS data do not provide information about the circumstances of crashes. However, it seems plausible that babies, infants, and children were left alone in passenger seats of vehicles with engines running, or with ignition keys left inserted. It appears that in circumstances like these, boys were dramatically more likely than girls to venture into the driver seat and set the vehicle in motion. With increasing age it seems plausible that they were attempting to drive by copying observed adult behavior.

---

*Section updated in this *second printing* to include 2003 data.

Table 9-5.   The number of baby, infant, and child *driver* fatalities versus gender and age.   In all cases FARS coded the case as driver killed, single occupant, vehicle in transport.   Age zero is first year of life.   FARS 1975-2003.

age	"driver" fatalities		cumulative		boy-to-girl ratio
	boy	girl	boy	girl	
0	1	0	1	0	–
1	1	0	2	0	–
2	0	0	2	0	–
3	1	0	3	0	–
4	5	0	8	0	–
5	9	0	17	0	–
6	14	2	31	2	15.5
7	25	3	56	5	11.2
8	55	4	111	9	12.3
9	82	10	193	19	10.2
10	127	11	320	30	10.7
11	183	8	503	38	13.2
12	285	31	788	69	11.4
13	420	38	1208	107	11.3
14	809	92	2017	199	10.1
15	1552	247	3569	446	8.0
16	5318	1934	8887	2380	3.7

Gender and pedestrian fatalities

Figure 9-4 shows the number of male pedestrian fatalities per capita divided by the number of female pedestrian fatalities per capita in FARS 1975-2003. For ages less than 50 this ratio differs only slightly from the simple ratio of male pedestrian fatalities to female pedestrian fatalities. It is only after about age 50 that the number of females in the population begins to diverge appreciably from the number of males of the same age; by age 90 there are more than twice as many women as men.

If the probability of becoming a pedestrian fatality were independent of gender, the data would distribute randomly around the dashed line indicating equal risk. The data depart dramatically from such a pattern. At every age, in one-year increments, the male rate exceeds the female rate.

The raw fatality data shown in Table 9-6 for the youngest ages show that the differences are clear and reliable from the earliest ages. In the first year of life, 110 baby boys died as pedestrians, compared to 77 girls, for a gender ratio of 1.43 ± 0.21. By age one, sample sizes increase substantially, leading to

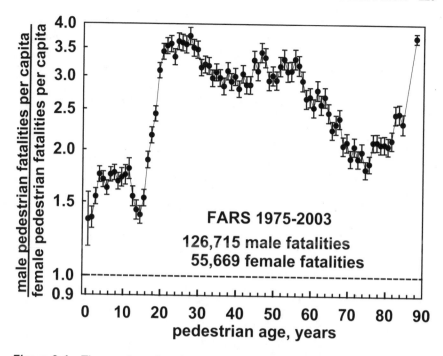

Figure 9-4. The number of male pedestrian fatalities per capita divided by the number of female pedestrian fatalities per capita. If there were no gender difference, the data points would distribute randomly about the dashed line indicating equal risk of being a pedestrian fatality. FARS 1975-2003*.

Table 9-6. Young boy and girl pedestrian fatalities. Age 0 is the first year of life. The ratios differ slightly from those plotted in Fig. 9-4 because the plotted values are normalized by population. FARS 1975-2003*.

age	pedestrian fatalities		boy-to-girl ratio
	boy	girl	
0	110	77	1.43 ± 0.21
1	715	496	1.44 ± 0.08
2	1336	826	1.62 ± 0.07
3	1513	829	1.83 ± 0.08
4	1458	821	1.78 ± 0.08
5	1708	1007	1.70 ± 0.07

*Updated in this *second printing* to include 2003 data.

increasingly precise estimates that show pedestrian risk is unmistakably greater for male infants than for female infants. The ratios in Table 9-6 are similar to, but not identical to, the values plotted in Fig. 9-4 because the raw fatality numbers in the table do not include the normalization by population.

While the male risk is about 40% above female risk in the early years, the difference begins to soar to more than 200% at an age that looks suspiciously like the onset of puberty.

Crashes, crimes, and testosterone

The three graphs (Figs 9-5 to 9-7) show similar dependence on gender and age. Yet they plot quantities that are seemingly unrelated.

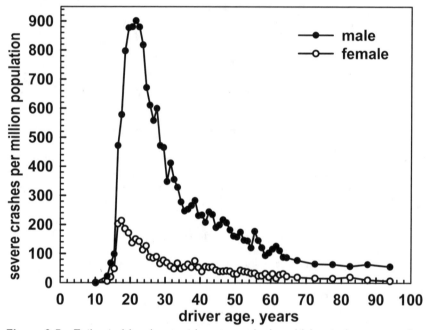

Figure 9-5. Estimated involvement in severe single-vehicle crashes per capita. Inferred from FARS 2002 data by same process that produced Fig. 7-8, p 155.

Figure 9-5 shows involvements in single-vehicle severe crashes per million population, calculated by applying Eqns 6-8 and 6-9 to FARS 2002 data in the same way as was done in Chapter 7. Single-vehicle crashes are selected because they depend on the actions of only one driver. Thus Fig. 9-5 reflects mainly the contribution of driver behavior, with the roles of other drivers and the dependence of survivability on gender and age removed.

Figure 9-6 has nothing to do with traffic. It shows the number of arrests per thousand population derived from FBI Uniform Crime Reports.[59] Only arrests

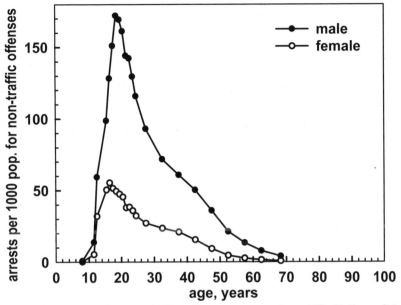

Figure 9-6. Arrests for non-traffic offenses per capita. FBI *Uniform Crime Reports* for 2002.[59]

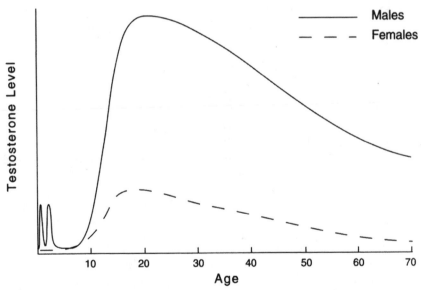

Figure 9-7. Testosterone levels measured in saliva of large numbers of subjects. Reproduced, with permission, from Dabbs & Dabbs, ***Heroes, Rogues, and Lovers***: ***Testosterone and Behavior***. McGraw-Hill Professional, 2000.[60]

for crimes unrelated to driving are included. Figs 9-6 and 9-5 both show incidents per capita per year.

Figure 9-7 shows chemical measurements of testosterone in a large sample of people, as measured in a simple saliva analysis.[60]

Safety and behavior as influenced by gender and age

The similarities between the graphs for crashes and crime suggest that they each share a common origin. The similarities between both these graphs and the one for the hormone testosterone suggest that the common origin is testosterone. Testosterone at the individual level also relates to the same pattern of personality characteristics found associated with high crash rates.[60] Sensation-seeking individuals have high crash risks and high testosterone levels. The two small peaks for males in Fig. 9-7 occur around the midtrimester of pregnancy and a few months after birth. This may help explain the higher number of boy than girl pedestrian deaths in the first year of life, and the one boy driver compared to no girl drivers killed in the first year of life.

The three graphs add emphasis to a central theme in traffic safety, the dominant role of behavior rather than knowledge or skill. No one would suggest that the lower arrest rate for 40-year-olds compared to 20-year-olds occurs because the 40-year-olds have at long last learned how to not commit crimes. Similarly, lower crash rates for 40-year-old compared to 20-year-old drivers does not mean that 40-year-old drivers have simply learned how to not crash.

Criminality is not produced by insufficient knowledge about ethics or the law. Lack of knowledge about correct driving procedures is not the primary source of traffic crashes by young male drivers, which is why driver education has little effect on safety.

Gender differences and socialization. Large gender-dependent differences pervade traffic safety findings. Recall from Chapter 3 that among the 1.2 million worldwide annual traffic fatalities, 2.3 males are killed for every female killed.

It is sometimes claimed that these effects are the result of socialization processes that constrain the genders to fulfill assigned roles prescribed for them by society. It is unquestionably true that in every society males and females experience different socialization. In some societies the differences are sanctioned in religion, law, and custom, and accordingly exercise an overwhelming influence that is bound to generate large gender-dependent differences in all types of behavior. For example, a society that effectively prohibits women from driving is going to observe a vastly larger gender ratio for driver fatalities than any reported here. Even when gender equality is official policy, there can still be many subtle, unconscious, or unobserved ways in which females are treated differently from males, or are expected to behave differently.

The findings for baby drivers and baby pedestrians consistently imply that gender-dependent behavior differences appear at the earliest ages – right from birth. It seems to me implausible that the large gender differences in baby-driver and baby-pedestrian fatalities could be due to socialization. It is difficult to imagine that baby boys would be left alone in vehicles or placed near traffic at rates different from girls to a degree that would explain the differences in fatality risks observed. The conclusion seems inescapable that at some fundamental level, right from birth, males and females behave differently in relation to risks in traffic. The testosterone measurements, which have nothing to do with socialization, leave little doubt that the differences in risk taking are in part innate rather than learned behavior. The magnitude of the male-to-female risk ratio is influenced by many social factors, but that it is greater than one appears to be an immutable fixture of the human condition.

Implications for interventions. In Chapter 7 we found that, when subject to the same physical impact, women were 28% more likely to die than men, a difference attributed to basic physiological differences between the genders. Here we find that the gender and age dependence of behavior central to traffic safety appears to originate, in large part, in basic hormonal differences. To realize the origins of these effects is to also realize that policy cannot make males as safe as females, or females as likely to survive crashes as males. Women live longer than men, but the goal of medicine is not to strive for equal longevity, but to increase everyone's lifespan. The goal of traffic safety is not the unattainable one of making risks equal for everyone, but the achievable one of reducing risks for everyone.

Summary and conclusions

Driver behavior is what drivers choose to do with the driver performance attributes they possess. Driving is a self-paced task in which drivers choose their own levels of difficulty. Additional knowledge and skill do not generally lower crash risk because they are likely to be used for such purposes as driving faster. Misguided policy has often resulted from a mistaken belief that safe driving is primarily a perceptual-motor skill, and that measures which increase driving skill will improve safety. Skilled racing drivers have higher crash rates in their normal driving than average drivers.

A central element of driver behavior is choosing travel speed. Increasing speed increases the risk of crashing, of being injured, and of being killed. The relationship is very steep – a small increase in speed leads to a large increase in risk. A one percent increase in speed increases fatality risk by between 4% and 12%.

Male drivers are more likely than female drivers to speed and exhibit other risky behavior in traffic. Males are more likely to indulge in violence, crime, suicide, and anti-social behavior. There is much evidence supporting the contention that people drive as they live. Involvement in traffic crashes is correlated with being emotionally unstable, unhappy, anti-social, impulsive, aggressive, and under stress. Among babies and infants, boys are more likely than girls to be killed sitting in the driver seat of an otherwise unoccupied moving vehicle, and boys are more likely than girls to be killed as pedestrians. Relationships with gender and age are similar for:

1. Involvement in crashes
2. Commission of crimes
3. Chemically measured testosterone levels

For all three relationships, male rates are higher than female rates, and peaks occur for both genders in late teens and early twenties. It appears that higher crash rates for male drivers, and young drivers, reflect inherent immutable life-long characteristics of humans. The goal of traffic safety is not the unattainable one of making risks equal for everyone, but the achievable one of reducing risks for everyone.

References for Chapter 9

1 Näätänen R, Summala H. *Road-User Behavior and Traffic Accidents*. Amsterdam, Netherlands: North Holland; 1976.

2 Cahill RA. *Collisions and their Causes*. London, UK: Nautical Institute; 1997.

3 Häkkinen S. Traffic accidents and professional driver characteristics: A follow-up study. *Accid Anal Prev*. 1979; 11: 7-18.

4 Murray W, Dubens E, Darby P. Virtual fleet risk manager. Napier University, Edinburgh, Scotland; 19 January 2004.

5 Williams AF, O'Neill B. On-the-road driving records of licensed race drivers. *Accid Anal Prev.* 1974; 6: 263-270.

6 Kloeden CN, McLean AJ, Moore VM, Ponte G. Travelling speed and the risk of crash involvement. Volume 1– Findings. CR 172. Canberra, Australia: Federal Office of Road Safety; November 1997.

7 Solomon D. Accidents on main rural highways related to speed, driver and vehicle. Washington, DC: Department of Commerce & Bureau of Public Roads; July 1964.

8 Kloeden CN, Ponte G, McLean AJ. Travelling speed and the risk of crash involvement on rural roads. Report No. CR 204 Department of Transport and Regional Services. Australian Transport Safety Bureau; July 2001.

9 Nilsson G. Reduction in the speed limit from 100 km/h to 90 km/h during summer 1989: Effects on personal injury accidents, injured and speeds. Report No. 358A. Linkoping, Sweden: Swedish Road and Traffic Research Institute; 1990.

10 Taylor MC, Baruya A, Kennedy JV. The relationship between speed and accidents on rural single-carriageway roads. TRL Report TRL511. Prepared for Road Safety Division, Department for Transport, Local Government and the Regions; 2002. http://www.trl.co.uk/static/dtlr/pdfs/TRL511.pdf

11 Finch DL, Kompfner P, Lockwood CR, Maycock G. Speed, speed limits and accidents. Project Report 58. Berkshire, UK: Transport Research Laboratory; 1994.

12 Richter ED, Barach P, Friedman L, Krikler S, Israeli A. Raised speed limits, speed spillover, case fatality and road deaths in Israel: A five-year follow-up. *Am J Public Health*. 2004; 94: 568-74.

13 Evans L. *Traffic Safety and the Driver*. New York, NY: Van Nostrand Reinhold; 1991.

14 Insurance Institute for Highway Safety. Status Report, Special Issue: Speeding. Vol 38 (10); 22 Nov. 2003.   http://www.iihs.org/srpdfs/sr3810.pdf

15 Patterson TL, Frith WJ, Povey LJ, Keall MD. The effect of increasing rural Interstate speed limits in the United States. *Traf Inj Prev.* 2002; 3: 316-320. http://www.ipenz.org.nz/test/ipenztg_cd/cd/2002_pdf/11_Patterson.pdf

16 Joksch HC. Velocity change and fatality risk in a crash – a rule of thumb. *Accid Anal Prev.* 1993; 25: 103-104.

17 Evans L. Safety-belt effectiveness: The influence of crash severity and selective recruitment. *Accid Anal Prev.* 1996; 28: 423-433.

18 Hyde F. *The German Way.* New York, NY: Passport Books (division of NTC/McGraw-Hill); 1997.

19 International Road Traffic and Accident Database (OECD). Selected risk values for the year 2001. http://www.bast.de/htdocs/fachthemen/irtad/english/we2.html

20 Cirillo JA. Interstate system accident research study II, interim report II. *Public Roads.* 1968; 35: 71-75.

21 Hauer E. Accidents, overtaking and speed control. *Accid Anal Prev.* 1971; 3: 1-12.

22 Cameron M. Estimation of the optimum speed on urban residential streets. Monash University Accident Research Centre. Report available from Australian Transport Safety Bureau, GPO Box 967, Canberra, ACT 2608, Australia; October 2000. http://www.general.monash.edu.au/muarc/rptsum/optspeed.pdf

23 Cameron M. Potential benefits and costs of speed changes on rural roads. Monash University Accident Research Centre. Report CR 216, available from Australian Transport Safety Bureau, GPO Box 967, Canberra, ACT 2608, Australia; October 2003. http://www.atsb.gov.au/road/pdf/cr216.pdf

24 Carlsson G. Cost-effectiveness of information campaigns and enforcement and the costs and benefits of speed changes. Paper presented to European Seminar in Luxembourg, Cost-effectiveness of road safety work and measures; 26 November 1997.

25 All cars – cars are our life. http://www.allcars.org/top_lists_topspeed.html

26 Zingraff MT, Mason HM, Smith WR, Tomaskovic-Devey D, Warren P, McMurray HL, Fenlon RC. Evaluating North Carolina State Highway Patrol data: Citations, warnings, and searches in 1998. Report submitted to North Carolina Department of Crime Control & Public Safety and North Carolina State Highway Patrol; Nov. 2000. http://www.nccrimecontrol.org/shp/ncshpreport.htm

27 Baker SP, Braver ER, Chen LH, Pantula JF, Massie D. Motor vehicle occupant deaths among Hispanic and black children and teenagers. *Arch Pediatr Adolesc Med.* 1998; 152: 1209-12.

28 Braver ER. Race, Hispanic origin, and socioeconomic status in relation to motor vehicle occupant death rates and risk factors among adults. *Accid Anal Prev.* 2003; 35: 295-309.

29 Corbett C. Explanations for 'understating' in self-reported speeding behaviour. *Trans Res Part F: Psych Behav.* 2001; 4(2): 133-150.

30 Campbell M, Stradling SG. Factors influencing driver speed choices. Transport Research Institute, Napier University, Edinburgh, Scotland; 14 October 2003. http://www.dft.gov.uk/stellent/groups/dft_rdsafety/documents/source/dft_rdsafety_source_024721.doc

31 Evans L, Wasielewski P. Risky driving related to driver and vehicle characteristics. *Accid Anal Prev.* 1983; 15: 121-136.

32 Wasielewski P. Speed as a measure of driver risk: Observed speeds versus driver and vehicle characteristics. *Accid Anal Prev.* 1984; 16: 89-103.

33 Tillmann WA, Hobbs GE. The accident-prone automobile driver. *Am J Psychiatry* 1949; 106: 321-331.

34 Finch, JR, Smith JP. *Psychiatric and legal aspects of automobile fatalities.* Springfield, IL: Charles C. Thomas; 1970.

35 Shinar D. *Psychology on the Road -- the Human Factor in Traffic Safety.* New York, NY: John Wiley; 1978.

36 Norris FH, Matthews BA, Riad JK. Characterological, situational, and behavioral risk factors for motor vehicle accidents: A prospective examination. *Accid Anal Prev.* 2000; 32: 505-15.

37 Perry AR, Baldwin DA.   Further evidence of associations of type A personality scores and driving-related attitudes and behaviors. *Percept Mot Skills.* 2000; 91: 147-54.

38 Yagel D.   Interpersonal antecedents of drivers' aggression.   *Trans Res Part F: Psych Behav.* 2001; 4: 119-131.

39 DiFranza JR, Winters TH, Goldberg RJ, Cirillo L, Biliouris T.   The relationship of smoking to motor vehicle accidents and traffic violations. *NY J Med.* 1986; 86: 464-466.

40 McMurray L.   Emotional stress and driving performance: The effects of divorce.   *Behavioral Research in Highway Safety.* 1970; 1: 100-114.

41 Keeling JW, Golding J, Millier HKGR.   Non-natural deaths in two health districts.   *Archives of Disease in Childhood.* 1985; 60: 525-529.

42 Jessor R.   Risky driving and adolescent problem behavior: An extension of problem-behavior theory.   *Alcohol, Drugs, and Driving.* 1987; 3: 1- 11.

43 Anderson N.   National vital statistics reports.   Deaths: Leading Causes for 1999, Volume 49, Number 11, Center for Disease Control, October 2001.   Table E. Deaths and percent of total deaths for leading causes of death by sex: United States.
http://www.cdc.gov/nchs/data/nvsr/nvsr49/nvsr49_11.pdf

44 Tabachnick N.   *Accident or suicide? Destruction by Automobile.*   Springfield, IL: Charles C. Thomas; 1973.

45 Philipps DP.   Suicide, motor vehicle fatalities, and the mass media: Evidence towards a theory of suggestion. *Am J Sociology.* 1979; 84: 1150-74.

46 Bollen KA, Phillips DP.   Suicidal motor vehicle fatalities in Detroit: A replication.   *Am J Sociology* 1981; 87: 404-412.

47 Bollen KA, Phillips DP.   Imitative suicides: A national study of the effects of television news stories. *Am Sociological Review.* 1982; 47: 802-808.

48 Jamieson KH.   Can suicide coverage lead to copycats?   *Am Editor.* 2002; 824: 22-3.

49 Bollen KA.   Temporal variations in mortality: A comparison of U.S. suicides and motor vehicle fatalities, 1972-1976. *Demography* 1983; 20: 45-59.

50 Ohberg A, Penttila A, Lonnqvist J.   Driver suicides.   *Brit J Psychiatry.* 1997; 171: 468-72.

51 Hernetkoski K; Keskinen E.   Self-destruction in Finnish Motor Traffic accidents in 1974-1992. *Accid Anal Prev.* 1998; 30: 697-704.

52 Soteriades ES, DiFranza, JR.   Parent's socioeconomic status, adolescents' disposable income, and adolescents' smoking status in Massachusetts. *Am J Pub Health.* 2003; 93: 1155-1160.

53 Ferguson SA, Williams AF, Chapline JF, Reinfurt DW, De Leonardis DM. Relationship of parent driving records to the driving records of their children. *Accid Anal Prev.* 2001; 33: 229-34.

54 Carlson WL, Klein D.   Familial vs. institutional socialization of the young traffic offender.   *J Safety Res.* 1970; 2: 13-25.

55 Junger M, West R, Timman R.   The relation between crime and risky behavior in traffic.   *J Res Crime and Delinquency.* 2001; 38: 439-459.

56 Haviland CV, Wiseman HAB.   Criminals who drive.   American Association for Automotive Medicine, 18th Annual Proceedings, Toronto, Ontario; 12-14 September 1974, p. 432-439.

57 Junger M, Terlouw G-J, van der Heijden PGM.   Crime, accidents and social control.   *Criminal Behaviour and Mental Health.* 1995; 5: 386-410.

58 Gottfredson M, Hirschi T.   The true value of lambda would appear to be zero: An essay on career criminals, criminal careers, selective incapacitation, cohort studies and related topics. *Criminology.* 1986;24:213-234.

59 US Department of Justice, Federal Bureau of Investigation, Uniform Crime Reports.   Arrests for males and females at:
http://www.fbi.gov/ucr/cius_02/html/web/arrested/04-table39.html
http://www.fbi.gov/ucr/cius_02/html/web/arrested/04-table40.html

60 Dabbs JM, Dabbs MG.   *Heroes, Rogues, and Lovers: Testosterone and Behavior.*   New York, NY: McGraw-Hill Professional; 2000.

10 Alcohol

Introduction

Alcohol has figured in human affairs since the beginning of recorded history. Beer making is described in Egyptian hieroglyphics. The use of wine is mentioned early in the Old Testament when Isaac's son "brought him wine, and he drank" (Genesis 27:25). The ancient Greeks had a god of wine, Dionysus, and the Romans had Bacchus. While alcoholic beverages are mainly associated with mood and behavior changes, health benefits have also been recognized. From antiquity alcoholic drinks were known to be free from disease risks posed by other beverages. The Qur'an (2:219) acknowledges positive effects, stating "They question thee about strong drink and games of chance. Say: In both is great harm and utility for men; but the harm of them is greater than their usefulness." Islamic tradition came to forbid alcohol consumption to such an extent that the devout are admonished to avoid medicines and toothpastes containing even a trace of it. Thomas Jefferson's doctor advised him to consume a glass and a half of wine daily for health reasons. He so favored the advice that he doubled the dose and lived to age 83. More recently, sixty studies collectively provide solid evidence that drinking one to two glasses of wine a day reduces the risk of heart attack.[1]

The problems resulting from consuming large quantities of alcohol far exceed the benefits of moderate consumption. The Old Testament includes "For the drunkard and the glutton shall come to poverty" (Proverbs 23:21). Alcohol plays a major role in a host of social ills in essentially all countries, the only exceptions being a few that have managed to effectively prohibit its availability through strong laws supported by tradition and religion. Foremost among the ills produced by alcohol is its role in traffic crashes.

Alcohol and traffic

The recognition that drunk driving posed a major danger to the public is as old as motorized traffic. A law passed in 1872 in England specified prison as a possible punishment for being drunk while in charge of a vehicle powered by a steam engine.[2(p 7)] The acronyms DUI (driving under the influence) and DWI (driving while intoxicated) are widely understood by the US public.

The role of alcohol in traffic safety has produced more activity, literature, passion, and controversy than any other safety topic. In many countries there are advocacy organizations, professional societies, and journals devoted exclusively to the effects of alcohol on traffic safety. A review of literature on just one aspect, namely, how alcohol affects skills related to driving, identified 1,733 titles.[3] A NHTSA review cites 738 recent papers on alcohol as particularly relevant.[4] Scores of additional papers appear each year.

Measurement of alcohol

Ethyl alcohol, or ethanol, is the active ingredient in beer, wine, and liquor (*liquor* means distilled spirits of any strength). With chemical composition C_2H_5OH, ethanol is the second simplest member of a family of compounds chemically classified as alcohols, the simplest being methanol, CH_3OH. Ethanol and methanol burn not all that differently from gasoline, and indeed both are used as automotive fuels. In the present context we use *alcohol* to denote only ethyl alcohol, which is a colorless liquid that generates a homogenous liquid when mixed with water in any proportion. Its specific gravity is 0.79, meaning that the mass (or weight) of a given volume of alcohol is 21% less than the mass of the same volume of water. Thus a solution made by combining equal volumes of alcohol and water will contain 44% alcohol and 56% water by mass, but 50% of each by volume. When indicating the proportion of alcohol in blood or alcoholic beverages it is therefore crucial to specify whether the proportion is of volume or mass.

Measurement of amount consumed

Although alcoholic beverages come in a wide variety of forms, colors, flavors and bouquets, their chief constituents are water and alcohol. Other ingredients appear to have only minor pharmacological significance, although mold may trigger allergic reactions in some individuals, while other ingredients may add to the severity of hangovers.[5(p 512)] Most US beers contain about 5% alcohol by volume. Light beers tend to be just under 5%, but some can be as low as 3%. *Alcohol-free* beers still contain about 0.4% alcohol. Alcohol content is not indicated on US beer containers and advertisements in order to preclude marketing based on escalating alcohol content. Alcohol content is printed on beer containers of other countries. Many beers, referred to in the trade as *super strong*, have over 12% alcohol. One has 17.5% alcohol.

The percent alcohol by volume in wine is normally printed on the label. In the US the designation *table wine* without a specified value implies between 8% and 14%. Specified values tend to range from 11.5% to 13.8%, with red wines generally having somewhat higher alcoholic content than white wines. Fortified wines, like sherry and port, tend to be close to 20% alcohol by volume.

In Europe the alcohol content of all alcoholic beverages is indicated in terms of the percent alcohol by volume. In the US, alcohol content for liquor is given in terms of *proof*, which, in a strange sort of logic, is simply twice the percent alcohol by volume. Proof originated in ignition tests to confirm alcohol content. Britain formally abandoned the proof measure in 1980 in favor of the simple percent alcohol by volume measure, sometimes referred to in Europe as the Gay-Lussac system, after the French chemist who introduced it. However, proof measures still persist in Britain, with UK proof $= 7/8 \times$ US proof $= 1.75 \times$ percent alcohol by volume. Scotch whisky has a minimum 40% alcohol by volume (US 80 proof, UK 70 proof). Gins, whiskeys, and vodkas are typically about 40% alcohol by volume, while liqueurs are less, in some cases much less.

In the units system used by most of the world, the volume of alcohol and the volume of the drink are understood by the public in the same units (mL), so the volume of alcohol in a drink is readily understood as the volume of the drink times the percent alcohol by volume. In the US and UK small volumes of fluid are usually measured in fluidounces. However, the US and UK fluidounce are defined in entirely different ways. Quantitatively, the difference is inconsequential, with the US fluidounce = 29.6 mL and the UK fluidounce = 28.4 mL. Approximately equal amounts of alcohol, namely 15 mL, are contained in 12 fluidounces of 4.3% beer, 4 fluidounces of 12.5% wine, 2.5 fluidounces of 20% fortified wine, and 1.27 fluidounces of 40% liquor. These are typical sizes for drinks, except that the most common liquor serving in the US is somewhat larger at 1.5 fluidounces. The same amount of alcohol drunk within similar time periods produces fairly similar pharmacological effects, regardless of which alcoholic beverage contained it.

Content in human body -- Blood Alcohol Concentration (BAC)

The amount of alcohol in the body can be determined by analysis of samples of blood or breath. The alcohol content of blood is commonly measured in terms of the mass of alcohol in a given volume of blood. In the US, laws pertaining to alcohol are commonly based on grams of alcohol per milliliter of blood. If a milliliter of blood had a mass of exactly one gram, this measure would be identical to mass of alcohol per mass of blood. In fact, a milliliter of blood has a mass of 1.05 g. If the small departure from 1.00 g is ignored as inconsequential, then the measure grams of alcohol per milliliter of blood is the same as grams of alcohol per gram of blood. This convenient dimensionless ratio (multiplied by 100) defines the Blood Alcohol Concentration, or BAC, as the percent, by mass, of alcohol in the blood. One part alcohol per 1,000 parts blood (by mass, or weight) gives BAC = 0.1%.

Various other measures appear in the literature. One that has the advantage of providing convenient numbers is milligrams of alcohol per deciliter of blood. A value 80 mg/dL is the same as BAC = 0.08% if the 1.05 factor is ignored. Other units can likewise be converted to BAC by moving the decimal point, and in some cases also ignoring the 1.05 factor.

The term Blood Alcohol Level (BAL) is sometimes used instead of Blood Alcohol Concentration.

Closely related to the amount of alcohol in blood is the amount of alcohol in breath. This has the advantage that it can be measured by less intrusive means.

The earliest practical breath-alcohol measuring instrument, the *Drunkometer*, was developed in 1938 by Rolla N. Harger. The best known breath-alcohol instrument, the *Breathalyzer*, was invented in 1954 by Robert Borkenstein.[6] Breath alcohol is closely related to BAC, with BAC = 0.1% being approximately equivalent to 1 gram of alcohol per 2,100 liters of breath.[7]

Continuous variables and ranges

Science is based on measurement, and BAC provides the foundation of the scientific study of the influence of alcohol. In science there is rarely a need to define ranges of values of a variable even though names such as those listed below are convenient in scientific writing and indispensable in everyday life.

scientific variable	non-quantitative useful terms in common use		
temperature	cold	warm	hot
age	young	middle-aged	old
BAC	sober	impaired	drunk

In Chapter 7 technical results on older drivers were presented in terms of the continuous variable *age*. The terms old, older, etc. were used for descriptive purposes. We found that at ages above 70, various crash risks increased with increasing age. In principle we expect a driver aged 80 years and 25 days to be at greater risk than one aged 80 years and 24 days, even though there is no possibility of measuring such differences empirically.

The needs of criminal law are quite different from those of science. Laws must be written in terms of thresholds, not continuous variables. US law prohibits people from purchasing alcoholic beverages the day before their 21st birthday. No such restrictions apply one day later. The law makes sense, even though no measurable change in maturity or responsibility can be detected from one day to the next.

While the above comments might seem too obvious to mention, they seem to be all too often ignored, or even denied, when the subject is alcohol. The law must define offenses such as impaired driving or drunk driving in terms of thresholds. Scientific research can determine how risk depends on BAC, but research cannot reasonably define impairment any more than it can define old or hot.

The term *sober* is commonly used to indicate no large observable effects from alcohol. It does not indicate zero alcoholic consumption. In what follows we will tend to use BAC = 0 when common usage might suggest *sober*. This does not necessarily imply no alcohol. The strict interpretation of BAC = 0 is that it means BAC < 0.005% if measurement precision is two decimal places.

Absorption and elimination of alcohol

After consumption, alcohol is readily and rapidly absorbed from the stomach, especially from the small intestine, and does not have to be digested before entering the blood. It distributes throughout tissues and fluids of the body in a manner similar to that of water. The bloodstream carries it to the brain, which is where it produces its well-known effects. Alcohol is eliminated from the body mostly through metabolism (enzymatic breakdown). A very small percent of alcohol is excreted unchanged in breath, urine, and sweat. The amount present at a given time in body fluids, organs, and other tissues is determined by rates of absorption, distribution, and elimination. The rate of absorption depends on the quantity drunk, its concentration, and the other contents of the gastrointestinal tract. Food in the tract delays absorption, so that the conventional wisdom that drinking on an empty stomach increases the rate of onset of intoxication is well founded.

The greater the concentration of alcohol in a drink, the more rapidly it is absorbed. Thus, alcohol in straight (undiluted) liquor enters the blood stream more rapidly than does the same amount of alcohol contained in a larger volume of wine, or an even larger volume of beer. Such differences have led to an erroneous impression that beer is substantially less likely to cause impairment than liquor, an impression that has in many cases supported less stringent controls on the sale and advertisement of beer (and wine) than on liquor. However, the differences in peak levels of intoxication associated with different levels of concentration when the same amount of alcohol is consumed are minor compared to the main influence, which depends on the amount of alcohol consumed, regardless of concentration.

Fig. 10-1 shows representative patterns of absorption and elimination of alcohol for a man of average mass, generated from published data.[8] Relationships of this type were first observed in pioneering studies conducted by Erik Widmark in Sweden in the 1920s and 1930s.[9] The approximately constant rate at which alcohol disappears from the blood, referred to as Widmark's Beta, is typically about 0.015% BAC units per hour, say from 0.050% to 0.020% in two hours.

It is found that the peak BAC is approximately proportional to the amount consumed, and inversely proportional to the mass of the person consuming it. For the same consumption and body mass, females reach peak BAC levels about 20% higher than those for men. The reason for this is due mainly to a smaller gastric metabolism in females that leads to more of the alcohol reaching the bloodstream.[10]

The pattern in Fig. 10-1 is for consuming all the drinks in a short time. If an appreciable period of time elapses between the consumption of drinks, metabolism of the first will be in progress before the absorption of the second is complete. By the time the alcohol from the second drink is producing its peak level in the

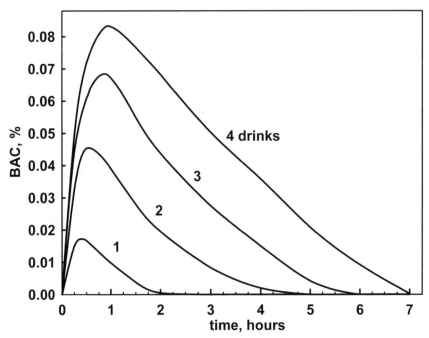

Figure 10-1.   Illustrative rates of absorption and elimination after consuming different numbers of alcoholic drinks. Based on data in Ref. 8 for fasting men of average weight .

blood, the effect of the first drink will have diminished, causing the peak from both to be (unlike Fig 10-1) less than twice the peak level due to one drink.

Peak alcohol levels reported in the literature can be approximated by the following formulae, which do not take into account many details, nor do they reflect variability between individuals:

$$Peak\ BAC,\% = C_m \times N/W - 0.015T \qquad \text{(males), and} \qquad 10\text{-}1$$

$$Peak\ BAC,\% = C_f \times N/W - 0.015T \qquad \text{(females),} \qquad 10\text{-}2$$

where

N = the number of drinks (each containing 15 mL alcohol)
T = the time, in hours, over which consumption was evenly spread
W = the weight of the person
C_m = 1.70 if weight is in kg; C_m = 3.75 if weight is in pounds
C_f = 2.06 if weight is in kg; C_f = 4.54 if weight is in pounds

These formulae provided the illustrative values in Table 10-1, which are for all drinks consumed in a short period ($T = 0$). The numbers in bold type are violations of the 0.08% BAC legal limit in most US States. The table shows that a 165 pound (75 kg) man consuming 4 drinks in a short time will achieve a peak BAC of 0.091%, but if consumption takes 2 hours, Eqn 10-1 calculates that the peak BAC drops to 0.061%. The equations are available on an Internet link which calculates peak BAC for any body weight and any number of drinks consumed over any time period.[11] Many tables with information presented in a format like Table 10-1 are widely available. Types and details of presentation vary, but the BAC values given are similar, but usually not identical. Devices to measure BAC by chemical means are also available, though there may be disadvantages in intoxicated drivers measuring their own BAC levels.[12]

Table 10-1. BAC, %, according to body weight, number of drinks consumed in a short time, and gender. Computed from Eqns 10-1 and 10-2 with $T = 0$. Bold indicates BAC above the 0.08% legal limit for most US states.

no. of drinks	120 pound male	120 pound female	165 pound male	165 pound female	220 pound male	220 pound female
1	0.031	0.038	0.023	0.028	0.017	0.021
2	0.062	0.076	0.045	0.055	0.034	0.041
3	**0.094**	**0.114**	0.068	**0.083**	0.051	0.062
4	**0.125**	**0.151**	**0.091**	**0.110**	0.068	**0.083**
6	**0.187**	**0.227**	**0.136**	**0.165**	**0.102**	**0.124**
8	**0.250**	**0.303**	**0.182**	**0.220**	**0.136**	**0.165**
10	**0.312**	**0.378**	**0.227**	**0.275**	**0.170**	**0.206**

How alcohol affects humans

Three earlier chapters (Chapters 6 on survivability, Chapter 8 on performance, and Chapter 9 on behavior) were devoted to human characteristics central to traffic safety. Alcohol is important in all three, through its effect on:

1. Survivability.

2. Performance.

3. Behavior.

The effect of alcohol on survivability from the same physical impact was unknown until a few decades ago. As shown in Chapter 6, a driver or passenger with BAC = 0.08% is 73% more likely to die from the same crash experience than one with BAC = 0.

Performance and behavior changes related to alcohol were likely observed shortly after alcohol first appeared. The Bible and other ancient writings mention people feeling happy, staggering, and falling asleep under the influence of alcohol. Shakespeare notes that, in respect to lechery, "it provokes the desire, but it takes away the performance." (*Macbeth*: Act 2, Scene 3). A large number of effects have been associated with increasing BAC, some examples of which are shown in Table 10-2. Responses vary greatly between individuals, and for each individual, changes are gradual. Many changes following alcohol consumption have performance and behavior aspects. Increased reaction time is purely performance, while increased aggressiveness is behavior. The earlier finding of that far more research was conducted on performance than on behavior applies particularly to the effects of alcohol.

Table 10-2. Performance and behavior characteristics that have been associated with increasing BAC levels. Bold type indicates behavior (but not performance) changes likely to have greatest impact on traffic safety.

BAC	performance and behavior changes
0.01%	Normal actions, hardly influenced.
0.02%	Changes in social behavior, mild euphoria, relaxation, increased gregariousness.
0.05%	Feeling good, **less inhibited, altered judgment**, lowered alertness.
0.07%	Judgment impaired, **likely to take risks and actions not taken when sober, release of inhibitions, impulsive behavior**, slight decrease in fine motor skills. **More bravado**, and less restraint for other behaviors such as eating, smoking, gambling, and drugs. Mood tends to shift from positive to negative.
0.10%	Slower reaction times and impaired motor function, **less caution**, slightly slurred speech, **increased aggressiveness**.
0.15%	Large, consistent increases in reaction time, balance impaired, slurring of speech
0.20%	Major memory impairment – "blackout" a possibility.
0.27%	Confusion, staggering, slurred speech.
0.30%	Double vision may occur; most drinkers become unconscious or fall asleep at this level and are difficult to awaken.
0.40%	Barely conscious.
0.45%	Death very likely.

Alcohol and performance

From the previously mentioned literature review[3] of 1,733 studies on the effects of alcohol on driving skills, 285 articles satisfying strict criteria were selected to examine the influence of measured levels of BAC on a host of performance measures. These included cognitive tasks, critical flicker fusion, divided attention, driving on simulators, drowsiness, perception, psychomotor skills, reaction time, tracking, vigilance, and various visual functions. Strong evidence showed performance declines for some driving-related skills at any measured BAC > 0. Performance declines were reported by the majority of studies for BAC ≥ 0.05%, and for 95% of studies for BAC ≥ 0.08%.

It is unfortunate that the legal term *impairment* is used outside legal contexts. All the reviewed experiments explore a dose (the amount of alcohol) versus response (the performance measure) relationship. Such relationships are nearly always one of two types. Either there is a threshold dose below which there is no response, or else the response is a continuous monotonically increasing function of the dose. None of the studies reviewed suggested a threshold. Thus a plausible assumption is that performance always declines as dose increases. Whether the performance reduction can be measured depends only on the precision of measurement.

Impairment has been defined as a statistically significant decrease in performance under alcohol treatment from the performance level exhibited under placebo treatment. This definition unambiguously identifies *impairment* as a property of the measuring technique, not of the phenomenon being measured. It is unhelpful to say that a certain level of alcohol does not lead to impairment today, but will when a study with sufficient precision is performed. Believing that human performance degrades with increasing alcohol consumption does not directly lead to policy conclusions any more than believing that human performance degrades with increasing fatigue, illness, sleep deprivation, aging, etc. has policy implications.

As discussed on p. 190, NHTSA is providing $5.1 million to the National Advanced Driving Simulator. A main goal is to "determine the degree of impairment associated with a particular blood alcohol concentration."[13] What could possibly be found that would add useful safety-relevant knowledge to what was already documented in the 1,733 studies available in 2000?[3] Or for that matter, to the 557 studies reviewed in 1987.[14] There are many important questions relating to alcohol and safety that cry out for serious investigation, yet so much of the scarce resources available are squandered on activity of so little value.

Alcohol and behavior

Alcohol has major effects on behavior, including reducing inhibitions and caution, and increasing aggressiveness and risk taking. While it seems plausible that such behavior changes would have a large impact on traffic safety, research is lacking. There is little literature on even so central a question as the influence of alcohol on speed choice. Drivers with illegal BAC ≥ 0.05% were observed in Adelaide, Australia, to drive about 3 km/h faster than BAC = 0 drivers. Small sample sizes precluded more definitive findings, such as a relationship between BAC and chosen speed. The main barrier to larger sample sizes is limited resources.

Many obvious studies seem not to have been performed. I have not encountered any paper reporting speeds and BAC levels of drivers stopped for speeding who were additionally administered BAC tests. I believe useful information might be extracted from large data files, even though there are problems to be overcome. Chapters 8 and 9 show that driver behavior has a larger influence on crash risk than driver performance. It therefore seems likely that it is alcohol's influence on behavior that is even more important for traffic safety than its already very well documented effect on performance. By about 1970 the effect of alcohol on performance was sufficiently well known for traffic safety policy purposes, but its much more important effect on behavior remains largely unquantified.

Crash risk and alcohol

It is not the direct effect of alcohol on driver performance or driver behavior that makes it so important in traffic safety, but the changes in crash risk that flow from these changes in performance and behavior. From the earliest days of the automobile it was well recognized that alcohol consumption sharply increased crash risk. An editorial in 1904 *Quarterly Journal of Inebriety* mentions 25 fatal crashes in which 19 of the drivers had consumed alcohol within an hour of their crashes. The first case-control study to quantify effects was conducted from 1935 to 1938 in Illinois.[15] In case-control studies, the BAC of a case driver who crashes is compared to the BAC of a matched control driver traveling on a similar road at a similar time. The control driver must be stopped by police, without cause, and then provide an alcohol test result.

The "Grand Rapids" study

While a number of case-control studies have been performed, the most important is that conducted by breathalyzer inventor Robert Borkenstein and his colleagues in 1962-1963 in Grand Rapids, Michigan.[16,17] This study is important for reasons that go beyond even its large sample sizes of 5,985 case drivers and 7,590 controls. In the early 1960s a larger proportion of drivers had BAC > 0 than after the later introduction of additional drunk driving countermeasures. Also, later changes in US law prevented police from stopping drivers at will in the way that the control drivers were stopped and requested to provide a breathalyzer reading voluntarily for research purposes only.

The question of responsibility for crashing is most easily addressed in single-vehicle crashes, yet even in the large Grand Rapids total samples, only 622 case drivers were involved in single-vehicle crashes. This provided insufficient data for effective analysis. In order to focus on how alcohol affects the risk of crashing, the drivers judged to be responsible in multiple-vehicle crashes were combined with drivers in single-vehicle crashes to produce a sample 3,305 case drivers responsible for their crashes. Of these 21% had BAC > 0, compared to 11% of the 7,590 control drivers.

The effect of alcohol on the risk of being responsible for a crash is plotted in Fig. 10-2. Crash risk increases so steeply with BAC that a logarithmic scale is used. A driver with BAC = 0.17% is 32 times as likely to crash as a BAC = 0 driver. The case-control method does not compare a driver's risk at a given BAC to that <u>same</u> driver's risk at BAC = 0, but to the risk of another BAC = 0 driver. It is logically possible that the high BAC driver would be just as risky when sober. The steeply increasing risk with increasing BAC in Fig. 10-2 is corroborated by other case-control studies.[15,18-20] Additional evidence is provided by a study[21] that combined fatalities recorded in FARS with exposure estimates obtained in the *1996 National Roadside Survey of Drivers*[22] to estimate risks for different age and gender groups.

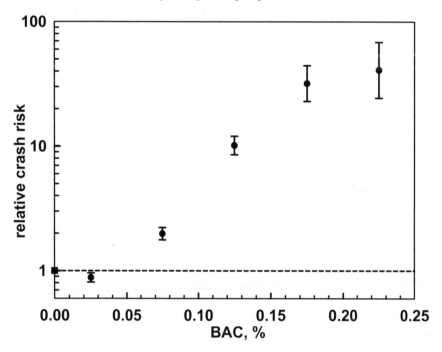

Figure 10-2. The risk of being responsible for a traffic crash as a function of BAC determined in the case-control study conducted in Grand Rapids, Michigan in 1962-1963.[16,17]

Many substances, legal and illegal, affect driver performance, behavior, and crash risk. Often a mix of other substances is detected in conjunction with alcohol in post-crash autopsies. While there is much literature on drugs and safety, it is only for alcohol that pharmacological effects relate closely to the amount measured at the time of measurement. There are no known quantitative relationships like that in Fig. 10-2 for substances other than alcohol.

The Grand Rapids dip. At BAC = 0.025% the nominal indication in Fig. 10-2 is a (12 ± 7)% risk reduction. This so-called *Grand Rapids dip,* has been, and continues to be, the source of much speculation and controversy.[23] It may be an artifact resulting from a weakness common to all case-control experiments. The case and control subjects may have different risks for unknown reasons. The BAC = 0 group contains many people who never drink. It is implausible to believe that drinkers at BAC = 0 would be identical in any attribute, including crash risk, to those who never drink. While a 17% greater risk by controls would convert a real 3% increase into an apparent 12% decrease, the same bias would convert a real 38 times increase into an observed 32 times increase (the value plotted in Fig. 10-2 for BAC = 0.175%), an important difference but hardly the stuff of controversy. Based on much smaller sample sizes, another case-control study likewise associated small quantities of alcohol with reduced risk.[18] A study using a different method also found lower risk at low BAC for one of a number of cases studied.[21] However, three studies report an increase in risk for low alcohol levels.[15,19,20]

The effects of alcohol on behavior, as distinct from performance, are so complex that the possibility that small quantities of alcohol might reduce risk cannot be dismissed as implausible. Behavior changes at low doses are not simply smaller amounts of the behavior changes at high does, but can be in the opposite direction (more pleasant social behavior at small doses, less pleasant at high). Also, anecdotally one hears of drinkers claiming that they drive more carefully after drinking to reduce the risk of being stopped by the police. If so, this could generate lower crash risk after low levels of alcohol consumption.

Alcohol in fatally injured road users

Figure 10-3 shows the distribution of BAC for fatally injured drivers with measured BAC > 0 in FARS 2002. A BAC reading (including BAC = 0) was recorded for 64.9% of fatally injured drivers. The probability that BAC is recorded in FARS varies widely over the US, from over 85% in the twelve highest reporting states to under 33% in the five lowest reporting states. As Table 10-3 shows, the probability that BAC is recorded depends also on many factors important in traffic safety, so the recorded cases should not be interpreted as a random samples of all cases. FARS advises "Alcohol Test Results from this database should be interpreted with caution."[24]

The majority of drivers whose BAC was recorded had BAC = 0. These are not included in Fig. 10-3. The average BAC for fatally injured drivers with any alcohol in their blood was 0.173%.

The distribution for fatally injured pedestrians whose BAC was recorded shows even higher levels than for drivers, the average being 0.202%. BAC > 0.3% was measured for 14% of the pedestrians, but under 5% of the drivers. This alcohol level is likely to induce unconsciousness or deep sleep (Table 10-2), making vehicle driving unlikely. Many of the pedestrians killed at such alcohol levels may have been asleep on the road. Irish data indicate almost one in ten

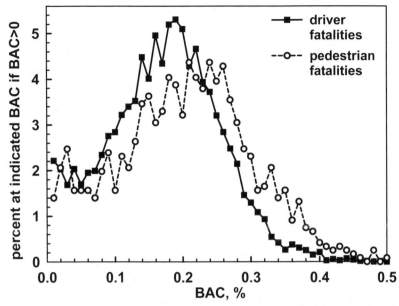

Figure 10-3. The percent of fatally injured drivers and fatally injured pedestrians with indicated BAC levels. The majority of those whose BAC was measured had BAC = 0, and are not included. FARS 2002.

Table 10-3. BAC for selected road users in FARS 2002.

road user	total number	BAC measured	BAC > 0	average BAC [a]
<u>fatally injured drivers</u>	26,549	17,241 *(64.9%)*	7,183 *(41.7%)*[b]	0.173%
single-vehicle crashes	13,399	9,026 *(67.4%)*	5,128 *(56.8%)*	0.178%
multiple-vehicle crashes	13,150	8,215 *(62.5%)*	2,055 *(25.0%)*	0.159%
male	19,773	13,090 *(66.2%)*	6,154 *(47.0%)*	0.173%
female	6,774	4,150 *(61.3%)*	1,028 *(24.8%)*	0.168%
fatally injured pedestrians	4,808	2,722 *(56.6%)*	1,214 *(44.6%)*	0.202%
fatally injured passengers	10,571	3,794 *(35.9%)*	1,313 *(34.6%)*	0.138%
uninjured drivers	13,138	2,934 *(22.3%)*	581 *(19.8%)*	0.118%
drivers killing pedestrians	4,372	1,048 *(24.0%)*	261 *(24.9%)*	0.126%
all fatalities	42,815	24,182 *(56.5%)*	9,842 *(40.7%)*	0.172%

[a] average BAC of those whose BAC was > 0
[b] percent of those with measured BAC whose BAC > 0

fatally injured drunk pedestrians appeared to have been lying on the roadway prior to being struck,[25] perhaps attracted to a dry crown of the road in a wet climate.

Two points are apparent from Table 10-3. First, when any amount of alcohol is present in the body of a road fatality, it is likely to be a large amount, much more than would be attained by a typical alcohol user. Second, the BAC levels of fatally injured drivers are not dramatically different from those of other fatally injured road users, or even drivers who are involved in fatal crashes in which they are not killed. In all cases, average BAC levels of those with any alcohol are higher than the highest legal driving limit in effect anywhere. This supports that the major contribution is from problem drinkers and alcoholics rather than social drinkers.[26,5(p 518)]

The number of US fatalities involving alcohol

BAC is not known for 18,633 of the 42,815 people killed on US roads in 2002 (Table 10-3). Because of the need to estimate the role of alcohol in the nation's fatalities, NHTSA developed procedures to impute the missing BAC values based on relationships between factors known to correlate with alcohol use, such as nighttime driving and single-vehicle crashes.[27] Using such procedures NHTSA estimates the percent of all fatalities in crashes in which alcohol was involved, some examples of which are shown in Table 10-4. Their estimates do not indicate the causal role of alcohol, nor how many fatalities would have been prevented if alcohol did not exist. Coffee is involved in most fatalities, yet eliminating coffee would have little effect on safety beyond preventing some drowsy driving crashes. Alcohol increases fatalities only because it increases crash risk. Sober drivers do not have zero risk, and drunk drivers do not have infinite risk. In order to estimate how much alcohol increases fatalities one must relate crash risk to BAC, using relationships such as in Fig. 10-2.

The causal role of alcohol. Suppose 100 drivers with BAC = 0.17% were killed in single-vehicle crashes. The risk of crashing at this alcohol level is 32 times the risk of crashing with BAC = 0, so even if alcohol had been absent, about 3 drivers would still be killed. One can therefore conclude that alcohol caused the death of the other 97. By applying similar calculations to the BAC distributions of drivers and pedestrians involved in different types of crashes, the fraction of traffic fatalities causally attributable to alcohol was estimated for 1987 to be 47%.[28] This estimated value is in bold type in Table 10-4. It is 0.9 times the 52% estimate of the fraction of fatalities in which alcohol was involved. That is, it was found that 90% of crashes in which alcohol was involved were caused by the alcohol. The fraction of fatalities caused by alcohol for the other years (for which the detailed calculation is not available) are obtained by multiplying the percent of all fatalities that involved alcohol by this same 0.9 factor, producing the estimates in Table 10-4.

The calculation indicates that alcohol was causally responsible for 54% of 1982 traffic deaths, and 38% of 2002 traffic deaths. For every fatality not attributable to alcohol in 1982, there were 1.17 fatalities attributable to alcohol.

Table 10-4. Percent of fatalities involving alcohol estimated by NHTSA, and percent caused by alcohol, estimated as explained in text.

year	percent of all traffic fatalities			alcohol caused per not alcohol caused
	involving alcohol	caused by alcohol	not caused by alcohol	
1982	60%[27]	54%	46%	1.17
1985	53[27]	48	52	0.91
1987	52[27]	**47[28]**	53	0.88
1990	51[27]	46	54	0.85
1995	42[27]	38	62	0.61
2000	41[27]	37	63	0.58
2001	41[29]	37	63	0.58
2002	42[30]	38	62	0.61

47% of fatalities caused by alcohol in 1987 estimated from detailed calculation.[28]
Values for other years are 47/52 = 0.9 times percent involving alcohol.

If in 2002 there had been 1.17 fatalities attributable to alcohol for every fatality not attributable to alcohol (instead of my estimate of 0.61), then fatalities in 2002 would have been larger by a factor $(1 + 1.17)/(1 + 0.61) = 1.35$. Thus, if alcohol had played the same role in 2002 that it did in 1982, about 15,000 additional fatalities would have occurred in 2002. By 1982 many anti-drunk driving measures were in place. While no quantitative estimate is available, it seems plausible to assume that perhaps another 15,000 annual deaths were being prevented, leading to a very crude approximation that all the measures in place in 2002 were preventing about 30,000 annual deaths. While this substantial reduction reflects the combined influence of many countermeasures, alcohol still killed more than 16,000 US road users in 2002.

Alcohol use by drivers in FARS. FARS 2002 includes 57,803 drivers involved in fatal crashes. 7,654 have measured BAC > 0.08%. Thus, FARS provides no evidence that 87% of the drivers involved in fatal crashes were in violation of a 0.08% limit. Test results are available for less than half of all drivers. Even though the probability of being tested increases with increasing BAC, 70% of those tested did not exceed 0.08%. For those drivers whose BAC was measured after involvement in a single-vehicle crash in which a pedestrian was killed, 83% had BAC ≤ 0.08%. Enormous though the problem of drunk driving is, one must keep in mind that sober drivers cause far more harm than drunk drivers.

If all the drivers with illegal BAC > 0.08 became marginally legal drivers with BAC = 0.08, this would reduce US traffic fatalities by 34%, rather than the 38% from eliminating alcohol entirely given in Table 10-4 (based on the calculation in Ref. 28). So, if all violations of drunk-driving laws were eliminated, 66% of US fatalities in 2002, or over 28,000 deaths per year, would remain. Even if alcohol were to disappear entirely, over 26,000 deaths per year would remain.

Alcohol's role in crashes of all severities

Table 10-5 shows estimates of the monetary costs of crashes in which alcohol was involved using data from the study previously described in Chapter 2.[31] The important feature to note is that the more severe the crash, the more likely it involves alcohol. Under 10% of the cost of minor crashes (mainly property damage, with at most a MAIS = 1 injury) is for crashes involving alcohol, whereas 45.5% of the cost of fatal crashes is for crashes involving alcohol. The increasing role of alcohol with increasing crash severity suggests that alcohol's main influence is changing driver behavior towards accepting higher risks and choosing higher speeds. If the only effect was impaired performance leading to increased driver error, then similar increases in crash risk at all severities might be a more likely outcome. It appears that drivers do things when they are drunk that they would not attempt when sober, rather than merely executing poorly the same things they would do more skillfully when sober.

Table 10-5.   Cost of crashes involving alcohol compared to cost to all crashes. Data for 2000.[31]

	cost (in 2000 dollars)		percent for alcohol-involved
	alcohol-involved crashes	all crashes	
no more than MAIS = 1	$10,511 million	$114,052 million	9.2%
MAIS = 2	$6,905 million	$29,134 million	23.7%
non fatal, but MAIS ≥ 3	$15,047 million	$46,513 million	32.4%
fatal	$18,600 million	$40,868 million	45.5%
total	$51,063 million	$230,567 million	22.1%

Drunk driving countermeasures involving criminal sanctions

The enormous harm that alcohol causes in traffic has spawned a long history of countermeasures. While much progress has been made, alcohol remains a major contributor to traffic deaths in every society in which alcohol is consumed. The earliest countermeasures focused exclusively on using criminal law to punish offenders. Evidence of intoxication was usually provided by a police officer reporting that the accused was unable walk a straight line or speak clearly. Such subjective judgments of performance measures were easily challenged in courts.

Per se laws

The pioneering work of Widmark[9] in the 1930s led to development of instruments to measure alcohol content in the body. This made possible *per se* laws making it a crime to drive with a BAC exceeding a statutory limit. This probably represents the largest single advance in controlling drunk driving, because the offence could be defined by objective chemical analysis rather than subjectively judged behavior. *Per se* laws were usually accompanied by *implied consent* laws. These required the driver to consent to be tested as a condition to hold a license, and agree that a later refusal to be tested would create a presumption of intoxication. Another measure that sometimes accompanies *per se* laws is *administrative license revocation*, the immediate removal of the license if the BAC exceeds the proscribed limit.

The first *per se* law was enacted in Norway in 1936. It criminalized driving with BAC > 0.05%.[32] The other Scandinavian countries, Sweden and Denmark, adopted similar laws. The term *Scandinavian approach* indicates *per se* laws enforced by severe punishments. This approach was generally considered successful in reducing drunk driving,[33] although the evidence did not convince all researchers.[34,35]

The first *per se* law outside the Nordic countries (the three countries of Scandinavia plus Finland) was included in the British Road Safety Act of 1967, which made it an offense to drive with BAC > 0.08%. Immediately after implementation, fatalities and serious injuries occurring on weekend nights, a surrogate for drunk driving, dropped by 66%.[36(p 30)] Further evidence of the success of the law is provided by a time series analysis that found that total traffic fatalities per unit distance of travel for 1968 dropped 11% below the long-term trend, but returned later to the trend.[37]

The apparent success of the British law led Canada in 1969 to make it illegal to drive with BAC > 0.08%. Most of the world followed by making *per se* laws the kingpin of their drunk-driving policies. By 1978 all US states had laws making it illegal to drive with BAC > 0.10%. (BAC > 0.08% in Utah and Idaho). In 2000 the US Congress passed legislation providing financial incentives for states to have BAC > 0.08% laws in effect by 2004. All but a few states did.

BAC limits (like speed limits) are usually specified amounts that must not be exceeded. It is generally not an offense to be tested at the limit, but only at a higher value. One encounters comments like "a pedestrian was above the legal alcohol limit". I am not aware of any jurisdiction that has a legal alcohol limit. The limits specified in *per se* laws apply only to vehicle drivers.

It was straightforward to examine the immediate effect of the British *per se* law by comparing casualties just prior and just after it went into effect. As time passes it becomes more difficult to estimate the effect of a law, because even if it were not passed, casualties would still increase or decrease for a whole host of reasons. Despite the difficulties, it is clear that the initial casualty reductions from the British law quickly declined. A major reason why crash rates tend to drift back towards prior levels after the introduction of interventions is that the objective risk of detection is small. The intervention is introduced with much publicity, convincing motorists that if they transgress, they will be subject to well-advertised penalties. Later, drivers become aware by observing or exchanging experiences with others that there is not a police officer at every corner or outside every drinking establishment. The key to sustaining casualty reductions is to maintain the belief that the probability of detection is high. An effective way to do this is to actually make the probability of detection high.

Random breath testing

Random breath testing was introduced in the Australian state of New South Wales on 17 December 1982; as in the US, traffic law in Australia is largely a matter for the individual states. The program in New South Wales, with its legal limit of 0.05% BAC, gave rise to the slogan "under .05 or under arrest."[38] (This is not strictly correct, as the offense was exceeding 0.05%). About 1.3 million tests were conducted annually on a driving population of 3.2 million; in other words, about a third of all drivers were tested each year, many being tested more than once. Figure 10-4 shows a time series of the number of fatalities per month. A drop of about 19% followed the introduction of random breath testing. This is one of the clearest and largest changes in traffic safety associated with a specific intervention.

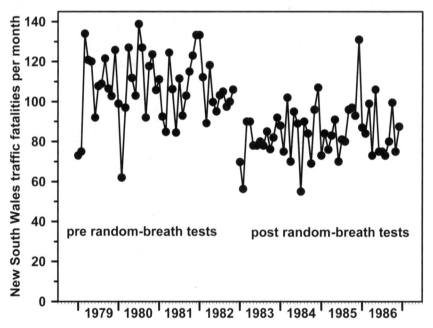

Fig. 10-4. Traffic fatalities per month in New South Wales, Australia, three years before and after the introduction of mandatory breath testing on 17 December 1982.[39(p 7)] The value (84 deaths) for December 1982 is not plotted.

An examination of the fraction of fatal crashes that involved alcohol shows a corresponding drop downwards, from about 28% to 22%.[39 (p 21)] Such a change implies that in the pre-testing period, there were 28 fatal crashes involving alcohol for every 72 not involving alcohol. In the post-testing period there were 22 involving alcohol for every 78 not involving alcohol, or alternatively, 20.3 crashes involving alcohol for every 72 not involving alcohol, so that due to reductions in the alcohol contribution, fatalities declined by a factor (72+28)/(72+20.3), or 8%. Although this is an approximate calculation resting on uncertain assumptions, the difference between the 8% effect estimated and the 19% decline apparent in Fig. 10-4 suggests strongly that part of the reduction in fatalities is due to factors other than reductions in driving while intoxicated.

A likely explanation is that the increased fear of interacting with police administering the testing program exercised a controlling influence on other types of driving behavior also likely to lead to fatal traffic crashes, or that driving, especially by high risk groups, was reduced. The primary goal of random breath testing is not to apprehend drunk drivers, but to make the probability of detection sufficiently high to deter drunk driving. Regardless of specific mechanisms, major casualty reductions resulted from the random breath-testing program. The benefits of the program were estimated to exceed its costs by over a factor of 30.[40]

Random breath testing has been widely adopted in other Australian states with comparable results.[41] It had in fact been first introduced in Victoria in 1976, but in a less abrupt manner making evaluation more difficult. The program there was found to be effective, especially after major changes were introduced in 1989.[42]

Sobriety checkpoints. The Australian approach could not be transferred directly to the US for legal reasons. However, in 1990, the US Supreme Court decided that *sobriety checkpoints* did not constitute illegal search and seizure if conducted strictly in accord with specified guidelines. At sobriety checkpoints, law enforcement officials evaluate drivers for signs of alcohol or drug impairment at certain points on the roadway. Vehicles are stopped in a specific sequence, such as every other vehicle or every fourth, fifth or sixth vehicle. The frequency with which vehicles are stopped depends on the personnel available to staff the checkpoint and on the traffic conditions.[43] Alcohol is measured only if there is judgmental evidence suggesting impairment. Sobriety checkpoints have been used in most US states and are effective in deterring alcohol-impaired drivers and in reducing crashes.[44]

Without sobriety checkpoints or similar programs, the probability that a driver with an illegal BAC will be detected on an individual trip is very low. Detection requires other clearly illegal driving to be observed by a police officer before an alcohol test can be administered. The probability that a trip by a drunk driver will lead to an arrest has been estimated at 1 in 2,000,[45] with a higher rate of 1 in 300 reported for high enforcement zones.[46] I suggest in Chapter 16 that one of the most effective drunk-driving countermeasures is to automatically detect illegal speeding and red-light running.

What is an appropriate legal BAC level?

Different jurisdictions choose different BAC limits for *per se* laws. In Sweden in the late 1980's there was support to make it an offense to drive with any detectable alcohol in the body. For various practical reasons, a zero BAC law was not accepted, but instead a 0.02% BAC law was passed by the Swedish Parliament, and took effect in July 1990. An average person will exceed this limit after one drink (Table 10-1).

The trend to lower legal BAC limits is in part propelled by the increasing body of research discussed earlier showing skill reductions at BAC values even lower than 0.02%. Yet the data in Table 10-3 show that the average BAC for any fatally injured driver with any alcohol in the body is 0.173%, far in excess of the level specified in any *per se* law. The average values in Table 10-3 are typical of those found in Sweden and other countries,[47] and do not appear to be depend much on the BAC limit defining drunk driving.

The percents of the fatally injured drivers plotted in Fig. 10-3 with BAC exceeding various levels are as follows:

BAC range	percent of drivers
BAC > 0.00%	100% (criterion for inclusion in Fig. 10-3)
BAC > 0.02%.	96%
BAC > 0.05%	90%
BAC > 0.08%.	84%
BAC > 0.10%	78%

The vast majority of fatally injured drivers with any alcohol have BAC levels above even the highest of the legal limits. Unless other factors were at work, it would appear to not make all that much difference which level is chosen. For example, if all the drivers formerly obeying a 0.08% law were to obey a stricter new 0.05%, law, this would affect only 6% of the drivers with some alcohol in their bodies. The change in risk from a BAC of 0.08% to 0.05% is modest compared to the large risks associated with the average BAC's of fatally injured drivers.

While the casualty change associated with drivers who remain just under the legal limit after it changes may be small, reducing limits may have a more general deterrent influence on drunk driving. The public discussion stimulated by introducing lower limits may in itself contribute to reductions in drunk driving. The move to ever-lower legal limits is also partly inspired by a view that increased risk from alcohol use is more morally reprehensible than increased risk from other sources, such as speeding, driving while fatigued, sleep-deprived, upset, distracted, medicated, or slightly ill. Driving 65 mph when the speed limit is 55 mph increases risk of involvement in a fatal crash by a factor of 2.0, similar to the risk increase associated with driving with BAC = 0.08% compared to driving at BAC = 0.

Alcohol ignition interlock systems

On-board devices to evaluate fitness to drive before the vehicle's engine can be started have been developed since the late 1960.[48] Early attempts to use tasks in which performance deteriorated with increasing alcoholic consumption were unsuccessful. Even after customizing the task for a particular driver, this driver would still sometimes fail the test when sober and pass it when drunk.[49(p 198-202)]

Technology that measures alcohol in breath after the driver blows into a tube has led to effective interlock devices. The vehicle cannot be started unless a BAC below a set limit is recorded. Although such devices work reliably, and in questionnaires seem to evoke positive reactions from the public, there has never been a consumer market for them, nor is there likely to be. People think they are great devices to install in other people's vehicles! It is difficult to imagine any set of circumstances that would lead people to want them in their own vehicles, or to vote to have them installed on all vehicles.

Where alcohol ignition interlock systems have proved successful is in reducing recidivism. A repeat offender may be offered a choice between driving only a vehicle with such a device installed and prison or license revocation. Reductions in recidivism of up to 90% have been found among interlock participants compared to those with suspended licenses.[50,51] Five Canadian jurisdictions, 43 US states, and many countries in Europe have legislation that allows the installation of interlock devices in offenders' vehicles.[52]

Alcohol ignition interlock programs are highly successful, but address only repeat offenders, who are a small minority of all offenders. For example, 2002 data for Connecticut show that 84% of those subject to administrative license revocation were first time offenders of drunk driving laws, 14% were committing their second offense, and 2% had previously committed three or more offenses.[53] An earlier analysis found that preventing all drivers arrested for drunk driving from ever driving drunk again would reduce fatalities by 4.7%, injuries by 3.5%, and property damage by 2.4%.[49(p 202)]

Above, and in common usage, *offender* means someone arrested and convicted. It is likely that as many as 2,000 offenses occur before an offender is arrested.[45]

Mothers Against Drunk Driving (MADD)

The criminal law's approach to drunk driving in the US prior to the early 1980s was somewhat ambiguous. Even when laws were stringent, enforcement tended to be lax. A major change occurred in the 1980s, largely stimulated by citizen activist groups representing the families of victims killed by drunk drivers. Mothers Against Drunk Driving (MADD) is the best known of a number of such groups. MADD was founded by Candy Lightner after one of her 13-year-old twin daughters was struck and killed by a drunk driver. The crash occurred in the middle of the day on 3 May 1980 as her daughter was walking on a bicycle path. The driver had prior convictions, and only two days before the fatal crash had been released from jail on bail for another hit-and-run drunk driving crash.

The release of this driver by the court focused attention on the judicial system's failure to protect the public from tragedies like this.

MADD has grown to over 600 chapters. Its central thrust has been to advocate more severe punishments, such as more and longer prison sentences. MADD furthered these goals by *court monitoring*, in which members observe the court proceedings and encourage the judicial process to take the rights of victims, and potential victims, into account at sentencing. Since its start, more than 2,300 anti-drunk driving laws have been passed.

Citizen activist groups deserve credit for a major portion of the 15,000 traffic deaths per year reduction from the early 1980s to 2002. I believe that their influence was not so much through the specifics of having new laws passed, but rather in using the media to inform the public and change public attitudes. Widespread media coverage, including a full-length television movie on the tragedy that devastated Candy Lightner's family, stimulated many people to reflect more on negative factors associated with drinking. Although the coverage was modest compared to that of television advertisements associating beer with positive characteristics, I believe that the impact was profound. The testimony of bereaved parents makes it harder for society to continue to look upon the drunk as an endearing figure of amusement. Such changing attitudes made drunk driving less acceptable. The 1981 comedy movie *Arthur*, named for its alcoholic hero, was a box-office hit, grossing over $95 million. A 1988 sequel *Arthur 2: On the Rocks* flopped, grossing under $15 million. One of the many factors that contributed to the difference was a change in public attitudes, so drunkenness was seen less as a source of humor and more as a likely precursor to killing a child. The social norm regarding what is acceptable behavior has a large influence on how people behave, and MADD made drunk driving more unacceptable.

In its early history, MADD accepted large donations from the beer industry. While it no longer accepts such donations, it still focuses mainly on the individual drunk driver, while ignoring the crucial role of the rich powerful institutions that encourage and profit by his and, less often, her abusive consumption of alcohol.

Availability of alcohol

Any decline in the overall consumption of alcohol is expected to lead to reductions in drunk driving. Many factors are known to affect how much alcohol is consumed, including the difficulty of obtaining it. The experience of *prohibition* in the US is sometimes invoked to support the claim that making alcohol more difficult to obtain does not reduce consumption. Prohibition was the period from 1920 to 1933 when the manufacture, sale, or possession of any drink with more than 0.5% alcohol was prohibited. The effects of this unfortunate attempt at social engineering were catastrophic, giving birth to many problems that persist to this day. However, the failure of prohibition does not mean that it did not reduce alcohol consumption. Data on how it affected alcohol consumption are not available, because all consumption was illegal and therefore not formally documented. However, time trend data for cirrhosis, admissions for alcoholic psychosis, and arrests for drunk and disorderly conduct suggest that alcohol consumption declined by more than half during prohibition.[54(p 195)] Traffic fatalities were changing too rapidly to allow any inferences about the effect of alcohol, which in any event could not yet be quantitatively measured.

While much less dramatic than prohibition, unmistakable links between abrupt interruptions in the availability of alcohol and alcohol-related harm have been shown in a number of studies from the Nordic countries.[55] In September 1978 workers at Norway's state operated Wine and Spirits Monopoly went on strike for nine weeks. The occurrence of various events during this period was compared to their occurrence in the same period in 1977. Drunkenness was down 40%, domestic disturbances down 22%, and acts of violence against the person down 15%. Comparisons between the same two years for non-strike affected periods showed increases of between 3% and 6%. Closing Norway's Wine and Spirits Monopoly outlets on Saturdays in some towns but not in others led to differences in drunkenness. Small sample sizes precluded detecting changes in crash risk.

Minimum drinking age laws

Perhaps the clearest indication of reductions in traffic deaths following reduced alcohol availability occurred when the US *National Minimum Drinking Age Act* of 1984 encouraged all states to raise their minimum age for purchase and possession of alcohol to 21.[56] All states complied, replacing prior laws that had generally specified ages 18, 19 or 20. NHTSA reported a 13% reduction in fatal-crash involvements by affected drivers.[57] A review of 241 studies of the effect of minimum drinking age laws provided overwhelming evidence of reduced alcohol consumption and traffic crashes in the affected age group.[58] These laws are estimated to prevent close to 1,000 traffic deaths per year.[56] All states have a *zero-tolerance* policy prohibiting driving with BAC > 0 at age under 21, as any alcohol in the blood implies violation of the law prohibiting the use of alcohol.

Minimum drinking age laws reduce traffic deaths without depending on police monitoring of drivers. Instead, the laws reduce the probability of intoxication by those under 21 by prohibiting them from purchasing alcohol in bars, restaurants, and retail outlets. The employees of such businesses are trained to *card* any patron who looks even remotely likely to be under the minimum age, meaning that proof of age must be provided, in almost all cases by showing a driver license. Very strict adherence to this procedure is widespread throughout the US, because the benefit to the business of an easily detected illegal sale is so small compared to the penalties for violating the law.

Under-age drinkers use many ways to circumvent the minimum drinking age law, including forged documents, and having older associates buy for them. Among some groups of young males the law is more honored in the breach than the observance, and underage drinking remains a major problem. It is unlikely that any law will meet with complete compliance, but what a law does do is increase the *cost* of alcohol, interpreting cost to mean all the ways that the user pays for it. Illegal under-age drinkers pay more for alcohol in terms of trouble, inconvenience, and obligations to those who assist them in violating the law, as well as risk of prosecution. Increasing the cost of anything reduces its consumption, but almost never to zero. One countermeasure to drunk driving is to increase any of the costs of consuming alcohol, the most obvious way to do so being to increase the purchase cost.

Cost of alcohol

Economists describe the relationship between price and consumption in terms of *price elasticity*. An elasticity of -1 means that a (say) 5% increase in price leads to an equal 5% decrease in consumption, whereas an elasticity of -0.4 means a 5% price increase leads to a 2% decrease in consumption.

Price elasticity for different alcoholic beverages has been determined in different studies in many countries. One source summarizes 73 estimates.[59] Simple averages of these, without regard to reliability or country, give the following elasticities: for beer -0.41, for wine -0.76, and for liquor -0.78. The authors of another study report values of -0.3, -1.0, and -1.5, respectively, but emphasize that these represent "best guesses" because of the wide range of estimates in the studies reviewed.[60]

While precise quantification is unavailable, there is little doubt that increases in price produce reductions in consumption. Given the difficulty of obtaining overall elasticities, there is scant information on elasticities for population subgroups. However, there is no basis for thinking that heavy drinkers are exempt from basic economic laws. While alcohol is more intensively desired by heavy drinkers, it consumes a larger portion of their disposable income, so that resource constraints are more relevant than for moderate drinkers. Most alcohol is consumed by heavy drinkers,[61,62] so the elasticity values measured reflect mainly consumption changes by heavy drinkers.

US Federal Excise Tax

The US Federal Government provided the leadership that led to minimum age drinking laws, thereby acknowledging its responsibility to address the national problem of drunk driving. The same Federal Government already exercises a statutory role in influencing the price of alcohol through the Federal Excise Tax, and therefore has at its disposal a potent weapon to reduce drunk driving. Not only has this weapon not been used, but the Federal Excise Tax has actually declined steeply in real terms from initially small amounts to even smaller amounts. Currently, the tax on the standard drinks defined earlier is 5¢ on beer, 4¢ on wine, and 13¢ on liquor. Adjusted for inflation, these amounts represent an 86% reduction from 1951 to 2003. (There are also state taxes on alcohol).

It is the consumption of beer, the beverage of choice of young males, which causes most drunk driving. Even if the Federal Excise Tax had kept step with inflation since 1951 and risen to 19¢ compared to its present 5¢, it would still add a small percent to the cost of a beer. While non-alcoholic beverages have increased in price relative to the consumer price index, alcoholic beverages have decreased in price.[61(p 8)]

A strange irony of US alcohol policy is that the beverage that is responsible for the most harm is treated is if it were the least harmful. A substantial increase in the tax on beer would have an important impact on drunk driving. At an absolute minimum, the tax on beer should not be less than that on liquor.

Seemingly, the death of 16,000 people from alcohol in traffic is not a political problem, but increasing the Federal Excise Tax on beer is. Such a tax increase could be politically acceptable if it was made clear that the purpose was to save lives. Its political acceptability would be assured if it were rendered revenue neutral by reducing another tax that did not save lives. The small minority who consume most of the alcohol would pay far more in taxes each year, notwithstanding their reduced consumption. The total tax paid by moderate drinkers would be less if a revenue-neutral change were enacted. Drunk driving and other social ills can be substantially reduced by increasing the excise tax on alcohol, particularly on beer.

Alcohol sales

Beer accounts for more than half of alcoholic beverage retail sales in the US (Table 10-6).[63] The heaviest 5% of drinkers, who, on average, consume more than four drinks per day, consume 42% of the alcohol sold, while the heaviest 2.5% of drinkers, who consume more than six drinks per day, account for more than a quarter of alcohol sales.[62] 29% of the population is teetotal (consume no alcohol).[64,] Young people (not necessarily underage) who consume hazardous quantities of beer are the alcohol industry's most important customers. Hazardous drinking, defined as 5 drinks or more per day, accounts for more than half the alcohol industry's market and 76 percent of the beer market.[65] Underage and adult excessive drinking account for half of the alcohol industry's sales.[66]

Alcohol advertising

The facts of alcohol consumption are in stark contrast to the belief that the alcohol industry has skillfully fostered, through massive advertising, that drinking is universal, glamorous, and largely devoid of negative consequences. In 2002, $1.9 billion was spent on alcohol advertising in measured media

Table 10-6. Retail sales of alcoholic beverages in the US in 2001.[63]

beverage	retail sales	percent
beer	$69.9 billion	55%
wine	$19.0 billion	15%
liquor	$38.4 billion	30%
total	$127.3 billion	100%

(television, radio, print, outdoor, major newspapers, and Sunday supplements).[67] The largest portion of this was on television advertisements for beer, most of which are placed in sports programs. Budweiser and Bud Light spent more than 87% of their combined television advertising expenditures on sports programming in 2001 and 2002.[68] Working from alcohol company documents, the Federal Trade Commission estimated that, in 1999, the alcohol industry's total expenditure to promote sales (including through sponsorship, Internet advertising, point-of-sale materials, product placement, items with brand logos, and other means) was three or more times its expenditure for measured media advertising.[69] This would mean that the alcohol industry spent a total of $5.7 billion or more on advertising and promotion in 2002. About 65% of the expenditure was for marketing beer. The American Medical Association estimates that young people are bombarded with $4 billion of alcohol marketing each year.[61(p 6)]

Beer is most advertised, causes most harm

Beer, which is 55% of alcoholic consumption, but a larger proportion of problem consumption, is advertised so widely on television as to constitute an important portion of television advertising revenues. In contrast, there is a voluntary ban on television advertising of liquor, the alcoholic beverage that accounts for 30% of alcohol consumption, and a yet smaller proportion of problem alcoholic consumption. Two percent of television advertising revenue in 2002 was from alcohol advertisements, largely for beer. The combination of massive advertising expenditures, and a television industry too timid to allow mention of obvious truths that would adversely affect business with a major customer, has led to uncritical acceptance of patently false claims.

The alcohol industry claims that advertising does not increase consumption. They allege that its sole purpose is to persuade customers to choose one brand over another without changing the total number of customers. The industry's actions show that they do not believe anything so foolish. If the industry believed that advertising did not increase consumption, then they would be expected to support (perhaps quietly) a universal ban on all advertising so that they could pocket the billions they pay in order to play what they are alleging is a zero-sum game with each other. Two companies, Anheuser-Busch and Philip Morris (owner of Miller Brewing Company), account for two-thirds of all beer sales. It is hard to believe that each symmetrically believes that the other would enjoy a sharp increase in market share at their expense if television advertising were discontinued. Their opposition to voluntary or statutory limits on advertising makes sense only if they believe that advertising increases beer consumption.

It is difficult to take seriously any claim that the large alcohol-advertising billboards that dominate the American urban landscape are there solely to persuade the generally poor inhabitants to switch brands. The advertising of just about any product increases consumption of it, as well as encouraging switching to the advertised brand. Even if the only effect of the advertising were to persuade some to switch brands from less advertised non-alcoholic drinks to alcoholic drinks, this would still increase alcohol consumption.

Advertising to under-age drinkers. The alcohol industry claims that it does not advertise to under-age drinkers. It would be unusual for any industry to not want to acquire new customers, and to acquire them at as early an age as possible. The industry behaves in accord with this economic law while denying it does so. The beer industry is a major sponsor of television sports with mainly young male viewers, a large portion known to be under 21.

Problem drinkers – core customers of alcohol industry

The alcohol industry claims that it wants to eliminate problem drinking and sell only to responsible drinkers. Successful businesses owe their success to their best customers, not to those who do not buy their products, or buy them sparingly. The highest consuming 5% of the population, those who consume four or more drinks per day, account for 42% of alcohol sales.[62] If all these individuals were to suddenly become responsible drinkers, drunk driving would largely disappear. The nearly 42% reduction in sales would transform profits into deep losses, forcing the alcohol industry to undergo major restructuring.

Tax and advertising policies that would save lives

Two simple "laws" apply to alcohol's role in traffic deaths.

Law 1. Decreasing national alcohol consumption leads to fewer traffic deaths.

As is usual with any law, we assume other things remain unchanged. Decreased consumption might not reduce traffic deaths if the lower consumption was more concentrated among fewer people, or more peaked by time of day, or if other successful anti-drunk-driving policies were discontinued. *Law 1* is so compellingly obvious that the onus is on anyone who does not accept it to provide specific evidence or convincing reasons why it is not so. This law does not have any immediate policy implications, nor does the similarly valid law that lower speeds reduce fatalities. There are benefits in higher speed and in consuming alcohol. Such laws illuminate policy decisions, but do not define policy. One profound difference between speed and alcohol is that there is no large politically powerful industry whose earnings depend directly and primarily on higher speeds.

Law 2. Alcohol consumption is decreased by:

- Decreased Advertising.
- Increased Price.
- Decreased Availability.

It is hard to imagine any set of circumstances, even of a hypothetical nature, in which any component of *Law 2* would not apply. Claims by the alcohol industry that aspects of *Law 2* do not apply are about as convincing as their claims that the only purpose of advertising is to move customers from one brand to another.

Reasonable approaches to harmful substances

While the ways to reduce drunk driving are clear, they involve a clash of interests and a US political tradition of foolish policy when it comes to substances that cause harm. Alcohol was banned entirely from 1920 to 1933 with catastrophic consequences. Efforts to reduce the 16,000 traffic deaths caused by alcohol are often countered by charges of *prohibition*. Prohibiting television and billboard advertising, and increasing the Federal Excise Tax are no more *prohibition* than are present prohibitions of beer vending machines in public places, selling to under-age drinkers, or the existence of the Federal Excise Tax. The alcohol industry opposes new restraints by invoking grand principles that apply just as strongly to previously passed well-accepted regulations that they also often opposed before implementation.

The US seems intent on not learning from the experience of prohibition in its present *war on drugs*. The political process has classified a number of harmful substances as illegal, just as alcohol was classified as illegal between 1920 to 1933. Because alcohol is now legal, the alcohol industry claims that it should be no more constrained than the manufacturer of any other legal product. At the same time, mere possession of another substance can lead to a prison life sentence. The distinction between legal and illegal substances is determined by the political process, not by how much harm is caused. It is a distinction that has served the US poorly. Legalizing any illegal substance will inevitably increase its use (legalizing alcohol in 1933 approximately doubled its use), but the increased harm must be balanced against the seemingly unbounded costs of making any widely demanded product illegal.

The distinction should be between products that cause large amounts of harm, particularly harm to people who do not use them, and the vast majority of products that do not cause appreciable harm. Products that cause major harm should be subject to regulation aimed at reducing the harm they cause, with regulation being more forceful if substantial harm is caused to non-users. Many teetotalers and light drinkers are killed by drunk drivers. The consumption of alcohol causes more harm in the US than the consumption of any other legal or illegal substance, with the possible exception of tobacco. Unlike alcohol, the victims of tobacco are overwhelmingly those who use it.

Each harmful substance should be evaluated in a similar manner. A reasonable analysis would rarely conclude that an absolute ban supported by severe penalties was the best policy. Nor would a reasonable analysis conclude that manufacturers should be permitted to increase consumption by using such potent means of persuasion as television advertising.

Summary and conclusions

The amount of alcohol (ethyl alcohol, or ethanol) in the body can be measured from samples of blood or breath, and expressed as Blood Alcohol Concentration (BAC). BAC is defined as the percent of alcohol (by weight) in the blood. The same amount of alcohol produces approximately the same peak BAC, whether consumed in beer, wine or liquor, although the time to reach the peak increases as the total liquid volume increases.

Three effects important in traffic safety occur with increasing BAC:

1.   Probability of death from the same physical impact increases.

2.   Performance at skilled tasks deteriorates.

3.   Behavior changes.

Crash risk increases steeply with increasing BAC. At a BAC of 0.17% (the average for all fatally injured drivers with any alcohol in their blood), risk is 32 times what it is at BAC = 0. Alcohol is involved in under 10% of minor crashes, but over 40% of fatal crashes. The increasing role of alcohol with increasing crash severity suggests that behavior change may be more important than impaired performance. It appears that drivers do things when they are drunk that they would not attempt when sober, rather than merely executing poorly the same things they do more skillfully when sober.

The effect of large doses of alcohol on fatality risk can be summarized as follows. The drunk driver is more likely to be killed in traffic because he (and less often, she) attempts riskier maneuvers, executes them with impaired skill, and if a crash does occur, is more likely to die.

Alcohol causes about 16,000 traffic deaths per year in the US. Without the many countermeasures already in place, the total would be more than twice this. One of the largest advances in reducing drunk driving was the advent of *per se* laws. These make it a criminal offense to drive with a BAC in excess of a specified limit, such as 0.08%, the current limit in most US states.

Drunk driving overwhelmingly involves males who consume very large quantities of alcohol, usually beer. Over half of all alcohol sales are beer. About half of all alcohol sold is sold to underage and problem drinkers. This puts the interests of traffic safety and the interests of the alcohol industry in sharp conflict.

Large reductions in US traffic deaths can be achieved by:

1. Expanding the use of sobriety check lanes.

2. Increasing Federal Excise Taxes on alcohol, especially beer.

3. Prohibiting beer advertising on television.

References for Chapter 10

1 Goldberg IJ, Mosca L, Piano MR, Fisher EA. Wine and your heart. *Circulation*. 2001; 103: 472.

2 Beirness DJ, Simpson HM. The safety impact of lowering the BAC limit for drivers in Canada. Ottawa, Ontario, Canada: Traffic Injury Research Foundation; May 2002. http://www. trafficinjuryresearch.com/publications/PDF_publications/BAC_Limits.pdf

3 Moskowitz H, Fiorentino D. A review of the literature on the effects of low doses of alcohol on driving-related skills. Report DOT HS 809 028. Washington, DC: US Department of Transportation, National Highway Traffic Safety Administration; April 2000. http://www. nhtsa.dot.gov/people/injury/research/pub/Hs809028/DocPage.htm

4 Jones RK, Lacey JH. Alcohol and highway safety 2001: A review of the state of knowledge. Report DOT HS 809 383. Washington, DC: US Department of Transportation, National Highway Traffic Safety Administration; November 2001.

5 Waller JA. *Injury Control -- A Guide to the Causes and Prevention of Trauma*. Lexington, MA: Lexington Books; 1985.

6 Borkenstein RF. Historical perspective: North American traditional and experimental response. *J Studies Alcohol*, Supplement. 1985; 10: 3-12.

7 Jones AW. Enforcement of drink-driving laws by use of 'per se' legal alcohol limits: Blood and/or breath concentration as evidence of impairment. *Alcohol, Drugs, and Driving* 1988; 4: 99-112.

8 Wilkinson PK, Sedman AJ, Sakmar E, Erhart RH, Weidler DJ, Wagner JG. Pharmacokinetics of alcohol after oral administration in the fasting state. *J Pharmacokinet Biopharm*. 1977; 5: 207-224.

9 Andréasson R. *Widmark's Micromethod and Swedish Legislation on Alcohol and Traffic*. Stockholm, Sweden: The Information Center for Traffic Safety; 1986.

10 Baraona E, Abittan CS, Dohmen K, Moretti M, Pozzato G, Chayes ZW, Schaefer C, Lieber CS. Gender differences in pharmacokinetics of alcohol. *Alcohol Clin Exp Res*. 2001; 4: 502-507.

11 BAC after quickly consuming a number of drinks as a function of gender and age. Calculator at: http://www.ScienceServingSociety.com/AlcoholCalculator.htm

12 Johnson MB, Voas RB. Potential risks of providing drinking drivers with BAC information. *Traf Inj Prev*. 2004; 5: 42-49.

13 NADS awarded $2.9 million for alcohol and driver performance research. University of Iowa press release, 31 December 2002. http://www.uiowa.edu/~ournews/2002/december/1231nads.html

14 Moskowitz H, Robinson C. Driving-related skills impairment at low blood alcohol levels. In: Noordzij P, Roszbach R, editors. *Alcohol, Drugs and Traffic Safety - T86*. Amsterdam, Netherlands: Excerpta Medical Elsevier Science Publisher; 1987, p. 79-86.

15 Holcomb RL. Alcohol in relation to traffic accidents. *J Am Medical Assoc.* 1938; 111: 1076-1085.

16 Borkenstein RF, Crowther RF, Shumate RP, Ziel WB, Zylman, R. The role of the drinking driver in traffic accidents. Department of Police Administration, Indiana University; 1964.

17 Borkenstein RF, Crowther RF, Shumate RP, Ziel WB, Zylman, R. The role of the drinking driver in traffic accidents. Blutalkohol 11 (supplement 1); 1974.

18 McCarroll JR, Haddon W Jr. A controlled study of fatal automobile accidents in New York City. *J Chronic Diseases.* 1962; 15: 811-826.

19 Perrine MW, Waller JA, Harris LS. Alcohol and highway safety: Behavioral and medical aspects. Report DOT HS 800 599. Washington, DC: US Department of Transportation, National Highway Traffic Safety Administration; 1971.

20 Farris R, Malone TB, Lilliefors H. A comparison of alcohol involvement in exposed and injured drivers. Phases I and II. Report DOT HS 801 826. Washington, DC: US Department of Transportation, National Highway Traffic Safety Administration; 1976.

21 Zador PL, Krawchuk SA, Voas RB. Relative risk of fatal crash involvement by BAC, age, and gender. Report DOT HS 809 050. Washington, DC: National Highway Traffic Safety Administration; April 2000.

22 National Commission Against Drunk Driving. Drinking and driving in the United States: The 1996 National Roadside Survey. http://www.ncadd.com/112.cfm

23 Corfitsen MT. Tiredness! A natural explanation to The Grand Rapid "DIP". *Accid Anal Prev.* 2003; 35: 401-406.

24 Fatality Analysis Reporting System (FARS) Web-Based Encyclopedia. Create a query, and choose "Alcohol Test Result" as a variable – caution regarding use of BAC appears: http://www-fars.nhtsa.dot.gov

25 An Foras Forbartha. *Road Accident Facts Ireland, 1984*. Dublin, Ireland: National Institute for Physical Planning and Construction Research; 1985.

26 Vingilis, E. Drinking drivers and alcoholics -- are they from the same population? In: Smart RG, Glasser FB, Israel Y, Kalant H., Popham R, Schmidt W, editors. *Research Advances in Alcohol and Drug Problems*, Vol. 7. New York, NY: Plenum Press; 1983, p. 299-342.

27 Subramanian R. Transitioning to multiple imputation – a new method to estimate missing blood alcohol concentration (BAC) values in FARS. Report DOT HS 809 403. Washington, DC: US Department of Transportation, National Highway Traffic Safety Administration; January 2002 (Revised October 2002). http://www-nrd.nhtsa.dot.gov/pdf/nrd-30/NCSA/Rpts/2002/809-403.pdf

28 Evans L. The fraction of traffic fatalities attributable to alcohol. *Accid Anal Prev.* 1990; 22: 587-602.

29 Subramanian R. Alcohol involvement in fatal crashes 2001. Report DOT HS 809 579. Washington, DC: US Department of Transportation, National Highway Traffic Safety Administration; April 2003. http://www-nrd.nhtsa.dot.gov/pdf/nrd-30/NCSA/Rpts/2003/809-579.pdf

30 US Department of Transportation. DOT releases preliminary estimates of 2002 highway fatalities. Press release, NHTSA 13-03; 23 April 2003 http://www.emcommunityconnection.com/nhtsa_13.htm

31 Blincoe LJ, Seay AG, Zaloshnja E, Miller TR, Romano EO, Luchter S, Spicer RS. The economic impact of motor vehicle crashes, 2000. Report DOT HS 809 446. Washington DC: US

Department of Transportation, National Highway Traffic Safety Administration; May 2002. http://www.nhtsa.dot.gov/people/economic/EconImpact2000

32 Glad A. After 50 years with a *per se* law -- the drinking and driving problem in Norway. In: Noordzij P, Roszbach R, editors. *Alcohol, Drugs and Traffic Safety - T86.* Amsterdam, Netherlands: Excerpta Medical Elsevier Science Publisher; 1987, p. 241-244.

33 Snortum JR. Deterrence of alcohol-impaired drivers. In: Laurence MD, Snortum JR, Zimring FE, editors. *Social Control of the Drinking Driver.* Chicago, IL: University of Chicago Press; 1988, p. 189-226.

34 Ross HL. The Scandinavian myth: The effectiveness of drinking-and-driving legislation in Sweden and Norway. *J Legal Studies.* 1975; 2: 1-78.

35 Ross HL. Deterrence-based policies in Britain, Canada, and Australia. In: Laurence MD, Snortum JR, Zimring FE, editors. *Social Control of the Drinking Driver.* Chicago, IL: University of Chicago Press; 1988, p. 64-78.

36 Ross HL. *Deterring the Drinking Driver.* Lexington, MA: Lexington Books; 1984.

37 Broughton J. Predictive models of road accident fatalities. *Traf Eng Control.* 1988; 29: 296-300.

38 Job RFS. The application of learning theory to driving confidence: The effect of age and the impact of random breath testing. *Accid Anal Prev.* 1990; 22: 97-107.

39 Roads and Traffic Authority. Road traffic accidents in New South Wales 1988. Rosebury, NSW, Australia: Road Safety Bureau; May 1989.

40 Arthurson RM. Evaluation of random breath testing. Research note RN 10/85. Rosebury, NSW, Australia: Roads and Traffic Authority, Road Safety Bureau; 1985.

41 Henstridge J, Homel R, Mackay P. The long-term effects of random breath testing in four Australian states: A time series analysis. Report CR162. Canberra, Australia: Federal Office of Road Safety; 1997.

42 Cameron M, Cavallo A, Sullivan G. Evaluation of the random breath testing initiative in Victoria 1989-1991. Multivariate time series approach. Report #38. Victoria, Australia: Monash University Accident Research Centre; 1992.

43 National Highway Traffic Safety Administration. Saturation patrols & sobriety checkpoints: A how-to guide for planning and publicizing impaired driving enforcement efforts. Report DOT HS 809 063. Washington, DC: US Department of Transportation, National Highway Traffic Safety Administration; Revised October 2002. http://www.nhtsa.dot.gov/people/injury/alcohol/saturation_patrols/SatPats2002.pdf

44 Insurance Institute for Highway Safety. Sobriety checkpoints work but they aren't used often. *Status Report.* Volume 36 (6); 30 June 2001.   http://www.hwysafety.org/srpdfs/sr3606.pdf

45 Borkenstein RF. Problems of enforcement, adjudication and sanctioning. In: Israelstam S, Lambert S, editors. *Proceedings of the 6th International Conference on Alcohol, Drugs And Traffic Safety,* p. 655–662. Toronto, Ontario; 8-13 September 1974.

46 Voas RB, Hause JM. Deterring the drinking driver: The Stockton experience. *Accid Anal Prev.* 1987; 19: 81-90.

47 Sjögren H, Björnstig U, Eriksson A, Öhman U, Solarz A. Drug and alcohol use among injured motor vehicle drivers in Sweden: Prevalence, driver, crash, and injury characteristics. *Alcohol Clin Exp Res.* 1997: 21: 968-73.

48 Voas, R.B. Emerging technologies for controlling the drunk driver. In: Laurence MD, Snortum JR, Zimring FE, editors. *Social Control of the Drinking Driver.* Chicago, IL: University of Chicago Press; 1988, p. 321-370.

49 Evans L. *Traffic Safety and the Driver.* New York, NY: Van Nostrand Reinhold; 1991.

50 Cobden JH, Larkin GL. Effectiveness of ignition interlock devices in reducing drunk driving recidivism. *Am. J. Prev. Med.* 1999; 16: 81–87.

51 Voas RB, Marques PR, Tippetts AS, Beirness DJ.   The Alberta interlock program: The evaluation of a province-wide program on DUI recidivism. *Addiction*. 1999; 94: 1849–1859.

52 Beirness DJ, Simpson HM, Robertson RD.   Commentary: International symposium on enhancing the effectiveness of alcohol ignition interlock programs. *Traf Inj Prev*. 2003, 4: 179–182.

53 Fazzalaro JJ.   Miscellaneous questions regarding drunk driving offenders.   OLR Research Report 2003-R-0729.   October 2003.   http://www.cga.state.ct.us/2003/olrdata/tra/rpt/2003-R-0729.htm

54 Gerstein DR.   Alcohol use and consequences.   In: Moore MH, Gerstein DR, editors.   *Alcohol and Public Policy -- Beyond the Shadow of Prohibition*.   Washington, DC: National Academy Press; 1981, p. 182-224.

55 Hauge R.   The effects of changes in availability of alcoholic beverages.   In: Laurence MD, Snortum JR, Zimring FE, editors.   *Social Control of the Drinking Driver*.   Chicago, IL: University of Chicago Press; 1988, p. 169-187.

56 National Highway Traffic Safety Administration.   Fact sheet: Minimum drinking age laws. Community *how to* guide on public policy, appendix 7.   http://www. nhtsa.dot.gov/people/injury/alcohol/Community%20Guides%20HTML/PDFs/Public_App7.pdf

57 National Highway Traffic Safety Administration.   The impact of minimum drinking age laws on fatal crash involvements: An update of the NHTSA analysis.   Report DOT HS-807-349. Washington; DC; January 1989.

58 Wagenaar AC, Toomey TL.   Effects of minimum drinking age laws: Review and analyses of the literature from 1960 to 2000. *J. Stud. Alcohol*. 2002: Supplement No. 14; 206-225.

59 Raistrick D, Hodgson R, Ritson, B.   *Tackling Alcohol Together: The Evidence Base for UK Alcohol Policy*.   London, UK: Free Association Books; 1999. http://www.scotland.gov.uk/health/alcoholproblems/docs/lire-05.asp

60 Leung SF, Phelps, CE.   "My kingdom for a drink?" A review of estimates of the price sensitivity of demand for alcoholic beverages.   In: Hilton ME, Bloss G, editors.   *Economics and the Prevention of Alcohol-Related Problems*, p. 1-32.   Bethesda, MD: National Institute on Alcohol Abuse and Alcoholism, NIAAA Research Monograph No. 25, NIH Pub. No. 93–3513; 1993.

61 American Medical Association.   Policy briefing paper: Partner or foe? The alcohol industry, youth alcohol problems, and alcohol policy strategies.   Chicago, IL; 2002. http://www.ama-assn.org/ama1/pub/upload/mm/388/partner_foe_brief.pdf

62 Greenfield T, Rogers J.   Who drinks most of the alcohol in the US? The policy implications. *J Studies Alcohol*. 1999; 60: 78-89.

63 Brandes R.   Beverage dynamics identifies the fastest-growing brands of wine, beer and spirits in the beverage alcohol industry. *Beverage Dynamics*; March/April 2002. http://www.beveragenet.net/bd/2002/0204/0204gb.asp

64 Global Alcohol Policy Alliance.   Partner or foe? (Paper produced by the American Medical Association), p. 18.   http://www.ias.org.uk/publications/theglobe/02issue2/globe02issue2.pdf

65 Rogers J, Greenfield T.   Beer drinking accounts for most of the hazardous alcohol consumption reported in the United States. *J Studies Alcohol*. 1999; 60: 732-39.

66 Foster SE, Vaughan RD, Foster WH, Califano JA Jr.   Alcohol consumption and expenditures for underage drinking and adult excessive drinking. *J Am Medical Assoc*. 2003; 289: 989-95.

67 The Center for Alcohol Marketing and Youth.   Alcohol advertising and youth.   2 January 2004. http://camy.org/factsheets/index.php?FactsheetID=1

68 The Center for Alcohol Marketing and Youth.   Alcohol advertising on sports television 2001 and 2002.   http://camy.org /factsheets/pdf/AlcoholAdvertisingSportsTelevision2001-2002.pdf

69 Federal Trade Commission.   Self-regulation in the alcohol industry: A review of industry efforts to avoid promoting alcohol to underage consumers.   Appendix B: Alcohol advertising expenditures, page iii; September 1999.   http://www.ftc.gov/reports/alcohol/appendixb.htm

11 Occupant protection

Why people get hurt in crashes – basic biomechanics

Biomechanics is the science that provides a bridge between medicine and engineering. It examines relationships between injuries and the mechanical forces that produce them in traffic crashes.[1,2] Trauma surgeons use the terms *penetrating trauma* and *blunt trauma* to distinguish between injuries produced by different types of impacts. Penetrating trauma occurs when small objects exert sufficient localized force to penetrate the human body, obvious examples being knife or bullet wounds. Blunt trauma occurs when a force applied over a large area of the body is sufficiently great to damage the body's structure, such as occurs when someone falls from a height. Nearly all injuries to vehicle occupants or pedestrians are from blunt trauma.

Consider a hypothetical situation in which a completely rigid vehicle traveling at 50 km/h crashes head-on into a perfectly rigid immovable horizontal barrier. Assume that the vehicle stops on impact, and does not bounce back from the barrier. After the vehicle strikes the barrier, its occupants would, in accord with Newtonian mechanics, continue to travel at 50 km/h until impacted upon by a force. Occupants, if not otherwise restrained, would move forward out of their seats until they struck the interior of the now stationary vehicle at a speed of 50 km/h. This impact provides the force that changes their speed from 50 km/h to zero. The magnitude of the force depends on the degree to which the body compresses on impact. If the body compressed, say, 10 cm, the average force on it would be about 100 times that due to gravity (represented by 100 *G*). This is equivalent to the person being compressed under a weight of about 100 times his or her own weight for a brief period, and is likely to prove fatal.[3] It is the collision of the occupant with the vehicle interior, the so-called *second collision,* that causes injuries, not the earlier first collision of the vehicle striking the barrier. A third collision has also been defined as the impact of internal organs with the structure of the body.

A person falling from a fourth floor window would strike the ground at a speed similar to that in the example above, and experience injury forces similar to those of the vehicle occupants if the ground were of a substance like concrete that did not compress much on impact. While evolution has provided humans with a protective fear of heights, no corresponding fear exists for the relatively new experience of traveling at speeds faster than can be produced by muscle power (page 192).

Goal of occupant protection

The reduction in speed divided by the time over which it takes place defines deceleration.   Injury-producing forces are proportional to the deceleration experienced by the occupant.   Occupant protection aims at reducing these forces by spreading the occupant's changes in speed over longer times.   The theoretical best protection would be for the occupant to slow down from the initial vehicle speed to zero speed at a constant deceleration using the entire distance between the occupant's body and the vehicle's point of impact.   In the previous example of an initial speed of 50 km/h, and assuming the driver is seated 2.5 m behind the front bumper, the resulting average deceleration would be $4\,G$, uncomfortable but unlikely to produce even a minor injury.   The engine and other rigid components make it impossible to get close to this ideal.   However, two approaches have led to major advances in occupant protection.   These are vehicle engineering changes and occupant protection devices.

Vehicle design and occupant protection

In the hypothetical example the vehicle was completely rigid, the worst case for occupant protection.   In fact, even without occupant protection considerations, it is not feasible to make a completely rigid vehicle – the structure is always going to crumple to some extent under severe impact.   However, how it crushes is important for occupant protection.   Consider two extreme possibilities.   First, the completely rigid case in the example.   The occupant's seat stops instantly and the unrestrained occupant continues forward at a speed of 50 km/h until striking the vehicle interior.   Now assume the other extreme in which all structure in front of the occupant offers no resistance and compresses offering less resistance than cotton candy.   The occupant will continue moving forward in the normal seating position, unhindered until arriving at the barrier.   The occupant will then be slowed from 50 km/h to stationery on impact with, in effect, the barrier.   So, although the sequence of events is different, the outcome is the same – the occupant, traveling at the vehicle's prior speed, strikes a solid stationery object.

Vehicle crush characteristics between these two extremes substantially enhance occupant protection.   For unconstrained occupants (those without airbags or safety belts) the goal is that impact with the vehicle interior should occur while the vehicle is still moving forward, thereby reducing the impact speed between occupant and vehicle interior.   The remainder of the vehicle's slow down until stopped should be over as long a time as possible, which is achieved by designing the vehicle to be not too stiff (resisting crushing) or too soft (easily crushed).

Intensive research, including models taxing even the largest computers, has been devoted to designing vehicle structures that crush in ways that improve occupant protection.   There is no single best design, not even in principle. Instead, there is a different best design for each impact speed.   A design that provides the best protection at very high impact speeds will be stiffer than one that provides the best protection at lower impact speeds. Thus difficult trade-offs are unavoidable, especially between reducing severities of major injuries or severities of moderate injuries, which are far more numerous (Chapter 2) and therefore cause more societal harm.

While the structure in front of occupants should crush as much as possible in a severe crash, it is also important that occupants be protected in a strong compartment, referred to as a *safety cage*. The goal here is provide a survival space that helps prevent intrusion of other objects, such as the front of another vehicle in a side impact. A direct impact on the human body from an external object presents a particularly high risk. While the safety cage is designed to crush as little as is feasible, the remainder of the vehicle should contain crumple zones designed to crush in controlled ways.

One specific vehicle design change that reduces driver fatality risk by 6% is the collapsible steering column.[4] In a frontal crash the chest of an unrestrained driver strikes the steering wheel, which, when sufficient force is applied, is designed to move forward because of a collapsible section included in the steering column. The driver's chest continues to move forward in contact with the steering wheel, rather than stopping more rapidly as would occur with a rigid column.

Padding on objects likely to be struck also increases the distance over which the occupant's speed changes.

Occupant protection devices

Devices designed for the specific purpose of reducing the occurrence and severity of injuries in crashes, as distinct from general improvements in the engineering of the vehicle, are referred to as *occupant protection devices*. These include safety belts, airbags, and helmets. Some devices are referred to as *passive,* meaning that they are supposed to provide protection without requiring any actions by road users, who need not be aware of their existence. *Active* devices provide protection only when their users do specific acts, such as fastening safety belts or wearing motorcycle helmets. The term *occupant restraint* is often used in place of *occupant protection device*, which is fine for belts but hardly includes helmets.

Occupant protection devices spread the change in speed of occupants over longer times. For example, in the example of a car crashing into a barrier, a safety belt (also called a seat belt) would have applied forces keeping the body more fixed to the seat. The belt helps the occupant "ride-down" the crash, so that impact with the steering wheel or instrument panel is less likely or less severe. Safety belts also prevent occupants from being ejected from vehicles during crashes. An ejected occupant might travel outside the vehicle at close to the vehicle's pre-crash speed, continuing at that speed until stopped by striking something in the roadway environment.

Airbags are restraint systems consisting of a bag that inflates rapidly when sensors detect an abrupt change in vehicle speed indicative of a crash. For a frontal airbag this is typically a delta-v in the range 10 to 20 km/h. Instead of striking the steering column or instrument panel, the occupant rides down the crash in contact with the airbag, which additionally spreads the impact forces over a larger area. A belted occupant can receive additional protection from an airbag because it may reduce loading forces on the belt. The airbag is a supplemental system – it is designed to be used in conjunction with the safety belt.

Effectiveness definitions

The effectiveness of an occupant protection device is defined in general terms as the percent reduction in some specified level of injury (such as fatality) that would result if a population of occupants changed from all not using the device to all using it, all other factors remaining unchanged. Equivalently, effectiveness is the percent reduction in risk an average occupant obtains when changing from non-use to use, without otherwise changing behavior. Three distinct effectiveness measures must be considered:

1. *Severity-specific effectiveness*, defined as the percent reduction in injuries (in crashes of a specified type) at a specific severity, or within a narrow range of severities.

2. *When-used effectiveness*, defined as the percent reduction in injuries that occurs when the device is used, taking into account the mix of severities in traffic.

3. *Field effectiveness*, defined as the percent reduction in injuries taking into account the use rate for the device and the mix of severities that occurs in traffic.

The severity-specific effectiveness depends only on the particular crash type, on the engineering of the device, and on the biomechanical properties of the human body. The when-used effectiveness depends on the types and severities of crashes that occur in actual traffic. The term effectiveness most often means when-used effectiveness. Field effectiveness is identical to when-used effectiveness only when the device is always used. When the device is not used at all times, field effectiveness is less than when-used effectiveness. When-used effectiveness applies in general, because even nominally passive devices are not always used. Airbags may be disconnected or not replaced after deployment, and automatic safety belts may still not be fastened. The collapsible steering column is a truly passive device – most drivers are so unaware of its existence that it is generally considered more part of the vehicle engineering than an occupant protection device.

Concepts central to all occupant protection devices

Figure 11-1 illustrates basic concepts that apply to occupant protection devices in general. Crash severity, S, is a variable that increases with impact speed and could be, for example, delta-v as introduced in Chapter 2. For expository convenience the formalism is discussed in terms of driver fatalities and safety belts, although the concepts are equally applicable to any occupant, any protection device, and any injury level.

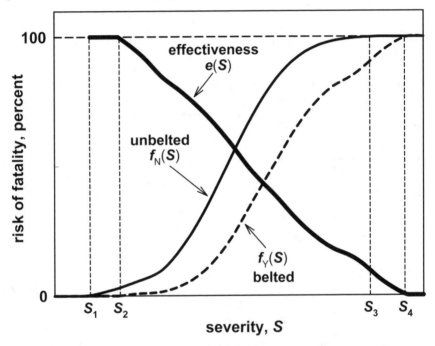

Figure 11-1. Schematic representation of how the risk of death might increase with crash severity for belted and unbelted occupants. The effectiveness is computed from the schematic risk curves using Eqn 11-2.

If $f_N(S)$ is the probability that an unbelted driver is killed in a crash of severity S, and $f_Y(S)$ is the probability that a belted driver is killed, the ratio

$$R(S) = \frac{f_Y(S)}{f_N(S)} \qquad 11\text{-}1$$

depends on the protection provided by the safety belt. (The subscripts indicate use, *Yes* or *No*). The variable R has many desirable mathematical properties, including always being greater than zero, and providing easily computed errors in terms of the errors in $f_N(S)$ and $f_Y(S)$. While calculations are in terms of R, there are advantages in presenting results in terms of the percent effectiveness, which, for the case of severity-specific effectiveness, is defined as

$$e(S) = 100[1 - R(S)] = 100[1 - f_Y(S)/f_N(S)] . \qquad 11\text{-}2$$

At very low severities, $S < S_1$, there is essentially no risk of a fatality to a driver, whether belted or unbelted. As the probability of death without the belt is zero, the belt cannot reduce this probability further. Because $f_N(S) = 0$ when $S < S_1$, effectiveness is not defined in this low severity region.

As severity increases, it reaches a value S_1 at which the probability that an unbelted driver is killed begins to exceed zero. Because the belt is designed to reduce risk, the probability that a belted driver is killed begins to exceed zero only at some higher severity S_2. In the region $S_1 < S < S_2$ effectiveness is 100% because $f_Y(S) = 0$ but $f_N(S) > 0$.

As severity increases further, it reaches a value S_3 at which the probability of death to the unbelted driver becomes 100%, but the belted driver's risk remains less than 100%, leading to an effectiveness of $100[1 - f_Y(S)]$. Eventually severity reaches a value S_4, at which even a belted driver's fatality risk becomes 100%, so that $f_N(S) = f_Y(S) = 100\%$, and effectiveness is zero. The bold curve showing the dependence of effectiveness on severity is mathematically derived from the assumed probabilities of death plotted for belted and unbelted drivers.

Laboratory evaluations of occupant protection devices tend to measure the severity-specific dependence at some chosen level of severity. As crash tests are difficult and expensive, the chosen level tends to be at a severity for which the device was primarily designed. Tests are less likely to be conducted at substantially higher or lower severities. Considerations such as these may have contributed to a history of disappointing field results relative to expectations based largely on laboratory tests, because in actual use there are likely to be many crashes at such extreme levels of severity that there is little opportunity for mitigation of injuries. In addition, a surprisingly large number of crashes are of a bizarre nature not readily encompassed in any laboratory-testing program.

When a crash is of such extreme severity that death cannot be prevented, then force reductions produced by occupant protection devices provide no benefits. In this regard, fatality is a unique level of injury, because for all other levels, reductions in forces lead to reductions in injuries. This general consideration suggests that the effectiveness of an occupant protection device is likely to be lower for fatalities than for injuries, though specific factors might lead to an opposite result.

An important inference from Fig. 11-1 is that the effectiveness of occupant protection devices decreases as severity increases. It is 100% at the lowest severities, and decreases monotonically to zero at the highest severities.

The above formalism does not apply in all respects to airbags. There is a designed threshold severity, S_A, below which the airbag does not deploy. At severities just above the threshold, some occupants, such as short females, will be at increased risk, so that effectiveness is negative for them. Apart from the discontinuity at $S = S_A$, airbags fit the pattern in Fig. 11-1.

Severity-specific effectiveness from data

The data used to produce Fig. 11-2 are the same NASS data used to produce Fig. 2-1 (p. 27). The belted drivers are wearing the integrated lap/shoulder belt system that became standard on all Model Year 1974 or later US cars. Some of the effectiveness values are negative because of noisy relationships resulting from small sample sizes (raw data from Ref. 5). However, the data show effectiveness of belts for drivers declining with increasing severity, as expected from the theoretical considerations above.

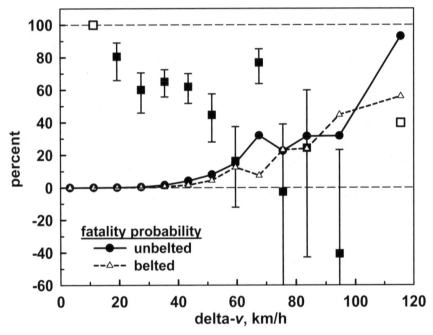

Figure 11-2. The probability of fatality to unbelted and belted drivers estimated from the same data used for Fig. 2-1 (p. 27). The square symbols represent the effectiveness computed using Eqn 11-2.[5] The open squares indicate insufficient data (less than 3 fatalities) to estimate an error in the effectiveness estimate.

Another example derived from data is given in Fig. 11-3 in which severity is measured using the *Collision Deformation Code*. This severity measure is based on a police officer identifying the best match between the appearance of the crashed car and a series of photographs of cars damaged in crashes of increasing severity. A declining effectiveness with increased severity is apparent. Effectiveness is determined with most precision at mid-range severities in Figs 11-2 and 11-3. At low severities there are few fatalities as risk is low, while at very high severities there are few fatalities because there are few crashes of very high severity (Fig. 2-1, p. 27).

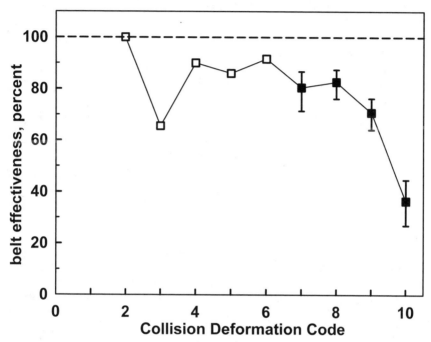

Figure 11-3. Safety-belt effectiveness computed using Eqn 11-2 versus severity estimated by *Collision Deformation Code*. The open symbols indicate insufficient data (less than 3 fatalities) to estimate an error.[5,6]

Difficulties in estimating safety belt effectiveness

The relationships in Figs 11-1 to 11-3 depend mainly on the engineering of the occupant protection device and the response of the human body to crash forces. They do not indicate the risk reduction the devices provide to populations that use them. If all traffic crashes were in the low severity region $S < S_2$, then the device would be 100% effective and the population using it would experience no fatalities. On the other hand, if all crashes were of severity $S > S_4$, then the device would have no effect on fatalities. The when-used effectiveness depends strongly on the distribution of actual severities that occur in traffic.

These distributions are known for the data used to produce Figs 11-2 and 11-3.[5] The when-used effectiveness is the weighted average of the severity-specific effectiveness, with weights equal to the number of unbelted fatalities at each severity. This does not produce the most precise estimates of when-used effectiveness because of the high uncertainty of severity-specific effectiveness estimates at high and low severities. More precise estimates can be derived from the much larger samples in FARS data. Because FARS does not have a useful measure of severity, the when-used effectiveness is estimated by other means. Whatever methods are used to estimate when-used effectiveness, there are intrinsic problems regardless of the quantity of data available.

Miscoding of belt use

In Chapters 6 and 10 we encountered problems from incomplete coding of alcohol measurements in FARS, leading to many missing values. For safety belts there is an even greater problem. Belt use is coded, but incorrectly. If miscoding were random, it would not bias effectiveness estimates. However, it departs systematically from randomness in a way that creates major problems. After the first US law requiring belt use was in effect in 1984, survivors of crashes became motivated to tell police officers that they were belted when they were not. Police officers are inclined to accept questionable survivor self-reports, as the alternative is to issue belt-law violations at fatal-crash scenes where officers have more pressing duties. When belt use is coded, it is therefore biased for survivors, but not for fatally injured occupants. The old rule that "Dead men don't tell lies" leads to at least some of the data being unbiased.

Effectiveness is estimated by comparing the percent of belted occupants who survive to the percent of unbelted occupants who survive. Coding an unbelted survivor as belted inflates the belted survivors total, while at the same time depletes the unbelted survivors total. Thus, miscoding one survivor generates two misclassifications, each of them biasing effectiveness estimates in the same upward direction. The result is that even a small percent of miscoding inflates effectiveness estimates by substantial amounts. The effect of this bias is apparent in many publications that accept post-law data as valid and report implausibly high effectiveness estimates.

Other clear evidence of miscoding is provided by estimating the effectiveness of the same belt system at different times.[7(p 13)] Effectiveness of belts in model year 1980-1985 cars was estimated at 47% using 1977-1985 FARS data, but at 63% using 1986-1999 data. As it is implausible for the same belt system to become more effective as it gets older, the large difference is likely due to data miscoding.

There are two approaches to the problem of miscoded data. First, use only pre-1984 data, as there was little reason to miscode in the pre-law era. While excluding post-law data leads to smaller samples, enough data remain for many evaluations. Second, attempt to correct for miscoding biases. An approach was developed in which a *universal exaggeration factor* was determined by examining how belt effectiveness estimates increased after belt laws were introduced.[7] Basically, using the example above, a measurement of 63% was interpreted to be really 47%, and other measured values were multiplied by a factor of 63/47. Applying this made it possible to use the large quantities of post-law data. The disadvantage is that estimates do not follow directly from the data, and involve a scaling factor known only approximately. This largely precludes quantitative estimates of errors. In what follows we show mainly results derived directly from pre-law data, but augmented by some additional results based on inferences from post-law data.

When-used effectiveness of safety belts

When-used effectiveness of safety belts in preventing fatalities to drivers and right-front passengers of cars was estimated using FARS data for the pre-law years 1975-1983.[8] Only cars of model year 1974 or later were included because all such cars came equipped with the integrated lap/shoulder system, also called a three-point belt system. Henceforth *safety belt* refers to this familiar system. Prior to model year 1974, lap and shoulder belts were generally separate, so that 'belted' could mean that one or the other, or both, were fastened.

The double pair comparison method was used.[9] Following the procedures described in Chapter 6, data for cars containing, say, belted drivers as subject occupants and unbelted right-front passengers as control occupants, were extracted from FARS data, and the ratio of belted drivers killed to unbelted passengers killed was computed. From a second set of crashes, the ratio of unbelted drivers to unbelted right-front passengers was computed. From the ratio of these two ratios, the when-used effectiveness, E, of the belts was estimated. Henceforth, effectiveness means when-used effectiveness. The study used 711 belted driver and 716 belted right-front passenger fatalities, together with over 30,000 fatally-injured unbelted occupants. In the pre-law period observed belt use was about 14%, with use in fatal crashes even less.

The subject and control data were disaggregated into three age categories, and occupants in all car seats (front and rear, and in center seats) were used as control occupants. In using this method to estimate belt effectiveness it is crucial that the control occupant be disaggregated by belt use. If this were not done, then the control occupant accompanying a restrained subject occupant would be more likely to survive a crash than a control occupant accompanying an unrestrained subject occupant, in violation of the assumptions of the method, because belt use by one occupant in a vehicle is highly correlated with use by other occupants.

The combination of control occupants used led to 46 estimates of E. Computing weighted averages provided the following estimates of fatality-reducing effectiveness:

$$E = (42.1 \pm 3.8)\% \text{ for drivers}$$

$$E = (39.2 \pm 4.3)\% \text{ for right-front passengers}$$

The slightly higher precision of the driver estimate is due to larger sample sizes. Vehicles with no right-front passenger, but with rear or center-front passengers still provided belt-effectiveness estimates for drivers.

Fatality reducing mechanisms

Safety belts protect vehicle occupants in two ways; they prevent ejection, and they reduce the frequency and severity of occupant contact with the vehicle interior. The when-used effectiveness, E (percent), can be written as the sum of two components,

$$E = J + I , \qquad\qquad 11\text{-}3$$

where J is the percent reduction in fatalities to an unbelted population if ejection were eliminated, assuming that those prevented from ejecting had the same fatality risk as those not ejected in similar crashes, and I represents the percent reduction in fatalities from preventing or reducing the severity of impact with the vehicle interior. The equation assumes that safety belts eliminate ejection, a more than adequately correct assumption for present purposes, even though the data in Fig. 3-13 (p. 51) show about 7% of fatally injured car drivers who were ejected were wearing belts.

The fraction of fatalities that would be eliminated if ejection were prevented was estimated by applying the double pair comparison method to 1975-1986 FARS data to estimate the ratio of the risk of death if ejected to the risk of death if not ejected.[10] For drivers, the risk of death if ejected is 3.82 times the risk of death in the same crash if not ejected. The data showed that 25.3% of unbelted drivers who were killed were ejected. If these drivers had not been ejected, then $J = (1 - 1/3.82) \times 25.3\% = 18.7\%$ of fatally injured drivers would not have been killed. Substituting this value into Eqn 11-3 gives that the interior impact reduction component of belt effectiveness is 23.4% (given that $E = 42.1\%$). These values and their associated errors, together with the corresponding information for right-front passengers, are presented in Table 11-1. Almost half of the effectiveness of the lap/shoulder belt in preventing fatalities comes from eliminating ejection.

The reduction due to eliminating ejection is in good agreement with the 19% value derived from post-law data.[7(p 32)] The same data show that eliminating ejection from light trucks would prevent 32% of fatalities, a major contribution to the 60% overall effectiveness reported.[7(p 28)]

Effectiveness by direction of impact

Table 11-2 shows belt effectiveness by direction of impact, and the contribution to that effectiveness from eliminating ejection.[11] Belts reduce fatalities for all principal impact points, much of the effectiveness being due to eliminating ejection. Much of the fatality reduction in rear impacts is from eliminating ejection. Similar effectiveness estimates are found in post-law data, where a 57% effectiveness is reported for rear impacts.[7(p 28)] The *universal exaggeration*

Table 11-1. Fatality reductions from lap/shoulder belt use and from eliminating ejection for outboard-front occupants.[11]

fatality reducing source	symbol	fatality reduction, percent	
		driver	right-front passenger
when-used effectiveness	E	42.1 ± 3.8	39.2 ± 4.3
ejection elimination	J	18.7 ± 0.5	16.9 ± 0.6
interior impact reduction	$I = E - J$	23.4 ± 3.8	22.3 ± 4.3

Table 11-2. Belt effectiveness (E) and the contribution from ejection elimination (J) according to principal impact point.[11]

principal impact points	description	fatality reduction,%	
		E	J
12	front	43 ± 8	9 ± 1
1, 2	front right	41 ± 18	21 ± 1
3	right	39 ± 15	17 ± 1
4, 5, 6, 7, 8	rear	49 ± 14	22 ± 1
9	left	27 ± 17	8 ± 1
10, 11	front left	38 ± 15	12 ± 1
13	top	59 ± 10	41 ± 1
0	non-collision	77 ± 6	63 ± 1
all combined		42 ± 4	19 ± 1

factor used to rescale estimates based on post-law data assumed an unbiased effectiveness of 45%, somewhat higher than the 42% value used here. As a consequence, inferences from the post law data will tend to be about $(45/42) = 1.07$ times higher than if a reference value of 42% had been selected.

Belts are (77 ± 6) % effective in preventing driver fatalities in *non-collisions*, of which 63% is due to ejection elimination, leaving $I = (14 + 6)$ %. Non-collisions normally imply rollover not initiated by striking a clearly identifiable object, such as a tree or other vehicle.

Table 11-3 uses 1978-1983 FARS data to estimate effectiveness in rollover crashes. Note the 82% effectiveness when rollover is the first event. The major portion of this, 64%, is from eliminating ejection. Belts reduce risk in all crashes involving rollover by 69%, with the major contribution from eliminating ejection. When no rollover is involved, 7% of belt effectiveness is due to ejection elimination.

Table 11-3.   Belt effectiveness, E, and the contribution from ejection elimination, J, according to rollover status.[11]

type of crash	percent of fatalities	fatality reduction, %	
		E	J
rollover is first event	8.5%	82 ± 5	64 ± 1
rollover is subsequent event	16.4%	55 ± 10	42 ± 1
any rollover	24.9%	69 ± 6	50 ± 1
no rollover	75.1%	31 ± 8	7 ± 1

Other factors

Because effectiveness depends on the mix of crashes it will be different for different sub-populations, depending on their use patterns. The dependence of effectiveness on a number of factors has been measured with the results summarized below.

Driver age. Effectiveness declines with increasing driver age, from about 50% in late teens to about half that value at age 80.[7(p 36),12,13(p 235)]   As shown in Fig. 7-18 (p. 164), the percent of fatalities that are rollovers declines steeply as drivers age. Since belts are most effective at preventing fatalities in rollovers and the fatal crashes of older drivers tend not be to rollovers, it is to be expected that belt effectiveness will decline with increasing driver age.

Single- versus multiple-vehicle crashes. $E = (62.2 \pm 5.2)$ % for single-vehicle crashes compared to $E = (29.5 \pm 8.4)$ % for two-vehicle crashes.[14] The post-law data gave 64% compared to 35%.[7(p 18)]   The higher effectiveness in single-vehicle crashes is due to the larger contribution of rollover to single-vehicle crashes.

Two-door versus four-door cars. The estimates are $E = (48.2 \pm 6.1)$ % for two-door cars compared to $E = (37.6 \pm 9.9)$ % for four-door cars.[14] This difference is consistent with the higher rollover rates of two-door cars (Fig. 4-2, p. 65).

Car mass. Two investigations using unrelated methods failed to show any clear relationship between belt effectiveness and car mass.[13(p 236),14,15] An analysis of post-law FARS data gives a weak indication that effectiveness was higher for the lightest vehicles,[7(p 18)] as did another study.[16] The larger role of rollover in light-car crashes would contribute to higher effectiveness. Any mass effect is small, so, to a reasonable approximation, it can be concluded that belts reduce risk in light and heavy cars by about the same 42%. The absolute risk reduction is, of course, greater in the lighter car because of its higher risk to occupants whether belted or not.

Car model year. There are no discernable effects in the 1975-1983 FARS data.[13(p 237)] The same model year cars show higher effectiveness in post-law FARS, a clear indication of miscoding effects.

Driver compared to right-front passenger effectiveness. The pre-law results nominally indicate higher effectiveness for drivers than for right-front passengers (42%, compared to 39%). A larger difference of 48% compared to 37% is found in post-law data,[7(p 34)] and another study reports higher effectiveness for drivers.[6] The evidence taken together supports that belt effectiveness is higher for drivers than for right-front passengers.

Other levels of injury. The above has focused exclusively on fatalities. All the technical problems that make it difficult to estimate fatality effectiveness apply also for injury effectiveness estimates. Injury data have additional limitations, making estimates additionally uncertain. There are many estimates of belt effectiveness for injuries, especially using post-law data. They vary from values much higher than for fatalities to values much lower than for fatalities. In the aggregate, estimates tend to be similar, but perhaps somewhat higher, than fatality estimates. Percent changes in injuries after passing belt laws are in some cases higher and in other cases lower than the percent changes observed for fatalities.

Effectiveness of other occupant protection devices

While the integrated lap/shoulder belt in front seats is the occupant protection system providing the most benefit to the most people, other occupant protection systems make important contributions to reducing fatalities.

Lap-only belts in rear seats

Prior to the mid 1980s the normal occupant protection system in the rear seats of cars in the US was a lap-only belt. A study[17] to estimate the fatality-reducing effectiveness of this system confronted sample sizes sharply reduced by lower occupancy rates, lower fatality risks,[18,19] and lower wearing rates. In order to obtain usable sample sizes, the 1975-1983 data used to estimate front-seat belt effectiveness was augmented by FARS data for 1984 and 1985. The inclusion of some immediate post-law data was considered a less serious problem than for front seats because rear-seat occupants were not covered by the early belt laws, and biasing effects are less important in the context of estimates with much lower precision. The study found that lap-only belts reduced fatality risk of passengers seated in rear outboard seats (left and right, but not center) by (18 ± 9) %.

A later study using post-law data to estimate effectiveness for lap-only and lap/shoulder belts in rear seats reported substantially higher effectiveness than (18 ± 9) % for lap only belts.[20] However, the results are likely biased substantially upwards by miscoding in post-law data.

Prior to the study that found (18 ± 9) % effectiveness,[17] the most widely accepted estimate was that lap-only belts reduced fatality risk by 30 to 40%.[21] The lower than expected effectiveness led General Motors to announce in June 1986 that it would install lap/shoulder belt systems in rear seats of all its passenger vehicles. Ford and Chrysler later announced similar policies. Later, lap/shoulder belts were required by NHTSA regulations. Prior to these changes there were some vehicles (mainly from Europe) on US roads with rear seat shoulder belts.

A further study examined the portion of the effectiveness that was due to ejection elimination, with the results[22]

$E = (18 \pm 9)$ %   (when-used effectiveness).

$J = (17 \pm 1)$ %   (contribution from eliminating ejection).

$I = (1 \pm 9)$ %   (contribution from reducing impact with interior).

The results indicate that the effectiveness of the lap-only belt derives almost entirely from eliminating ejection from the vehicle. A similar estimate of $E = (17 \pm 8)$ % was reported in another study using similar methods and data.[23]

Rear seat belts not only protect rear-seat passengers – they also protect front-seat occupants by reducing the risk of direct impacts from unrestrained rear passengers and by reducing the loading forces on the backs of front seats. The phenomenon has been called "the flying mother-in-law effect." Two studies found that the presence of an unrestrained rear occupant increases the risk to an unrestrained front-seat occupant by 4%.[24,25] When the front-seat occupant is restrained, the risk increase from the unrestrained rear occupant is 20%.[25] A published study contains the following: "The risk of death of belted front-seat occupants with unbelted rear-seat passengers was raised nearly five-fold."[26] This absurd result is another sad reflection of the way that traffic-safety research has not developed professional structures parallel to those in the traditional sciences to keep nonsense out of professional literature.

Motorcycle helmets

Helmet effectiveness in preventing fatalities to motorcycle drivers and passengers was estimated by applying the double pair comparison method to FARS data for 1975-1986.[27] Motorcycles with a driver and a passenger, at least one being killed, were used. In order to reduce as much as possible potentially confounding effects due to the dependence of survivability on gender and age, the analysis was confined to male drivers (there were insufficient female driver data), and to cases in which the driver and passenger age did not differ by more than three years. It was found that helmets are (28 ± 8) % effective in preventing fatalities to motorcycle riders, the effectiveness being similar for male and female passengers, and similar for drivers and passengers. By applying essentially the same method to 1982-1987 FARS data, another study obtained a near identical effectiveness estimate of 29%.[28]

A motorcyclist not wearing a helmet is 31 times as likely to be killed as a car occupant for the same distance of travel, based on 2001 data.[29] Because of the 28% effectiveness of the helmet, for the same distance of travel, a motorcyclist who wears a helmet is only 22 times as likely as a car occupant to be killed. A helmeted motorcyclist is more likely to be killed than an unbelted drunk driver traveling the same distance in a small car.

Motorcycles have traditionally been associated with young males, inspiring the quip, "Buy your son a motorcycle for his last birthday." Motorcycle fatalities in the US increased from 2,055 in 1997 to 3,126 in 2002, a more than 50 percent rise in five years. What is most remarkable about the increase is that the major component is from drivers older than 35, who registered a more than 100% increase from 738 deaths in 1997 to 1,491 deaths in 2002. In both periods 89% of all motorcyclists killed were male drivers, the remainder being passengers and female drivers. The reduction in helmet wearing rates, from 63% in 1994 to 58% in 2002,[37(p 9)] contributed, but only modestly, to the increased fatalities. The main factor was an increase in older motorcyclists. The 753 additional deaths of male motorcycle drivers over 35 years old in 2002 compared to 1997 exceed the total number of annual traffic fatalities in many countries. Sweden, for example, had a total of 554 traffic fatalities in 2001.[30]

Motorcycles in the US are used primarily for recreation rather than transportation, underlining the role of non-transportation motives in traffic safety discussed in Chapter 9. For all the vehicles on the roads of the US, the average crash risk is one crash per 12 years. Most of these involve just property damage or no more than minor injury. This is because of the inherent stability of vehicles with more than two wheels, and the protection provided by the safety cage and the vehicle structure. A helmeted motorcyclist is at high risk of serious injury when involved in any type of crash, and an unhelmeted motorcyclist is at even higher risk. The Highway Safety Act of 1966 prohibits the agency that is now NHTSA from recommending the banning of any category of vehicle on the grounds of safety. Although improvements in protection for motorcyclists in crashes are already incorporated in motorcycles, and additional improvements are always being sought, there seems no possibility that motorcycle riding can ever be other than an extremely high-risk activity relative to other risks in traffic.

Airbags

NHTSA has produced a series of estimates of the effectiveness of frontal airbags in reducing driver fatality risk using two methods of analysis.[31] The first considered crash-involved cars equipped with driver airbags but without passenger airbags. Although this combination was not generally produced after the mid 1990s, the cars with it remained in service and were available for analysis for many subsequent years. The ratio of driver fatalities to passenger fatalities was compared to the corresponding ratio for earlier similar cars with no driver airbags, thus providing a measure of the effect of the airbag. The second approach used the ratio of drivers killed in frontal crashes to drivers killed in non-frontal crashes for cars with and without airbags. As airbags are designed to deploy only in frontal crashes, this ratio estimates effectiveness. Both methods provided consistent estimates. The average values from both methods appear in the first row in Table 11-4. The same method produced the values published in 2001 shown in the second row.[32]

Table 11-4. Airbag effectiveness estimates.

source	effectiveness in reducing fatality risk		
	belted	unbelted	all
Kahane (1996)[31]	9%	13%	11%
NHTSA (2001)[32]	11%	14%	12%
Cummings et al.(2002)[33]	7%	9%	8%
average of above	**9%**	**12%**	**10%**

The third row shows results of a study published in 2002 that estimates the effectiveness of driver airbags by taking advantage of the increasing availability of passenger airbags.[33] Vehicles containing a driver and a right-front passenger, at least one being killed, were selected from FARS 1990-2000 data. Many of the model year 1987-2001 vehicles included in the study had a driver airbag but no passenger airbag. These cases provided the core information to estimate effectiveness of driver airbags. Vehicles, which had no airbags, or airbags for both the driver and passenger, provided data to control for other driver-passenger differences in risk, unrelated to risk changes associated with driver airbags. Because there are no vehicles with passenger airbags but without driver airbags, the method cannot estimate airbag effectiveness for passenger air bags. The results, shown in row 3 of Table 11-4, are consistent with the NHTSA estimates to within the published errors.

All the studies summarized in Table 11-4 estimate airbag effectiveness for belted and unbelted drivers. Miscoding of belt use has no more than a modest influence on the airbag effectiveness estimates. Indeed, the method which compares frontal to side fatalities uses only fatalities, for which belt use is considered to be correctly coded.

The combination of safety belt plus airbag cannot be estimated using pre-law data, as there were few airbags until the 1990s. However, it can be estimated by considering a population of cars without airbags driven by unbelted drivers. Assuming that this population experiences 100 driver fatalities, the number of deaths that would have occurred if all the cars had airbags, or if all the drivers were belted, can be estimated as shown in Fig. 11-4. The result is that the effectiveness of the belt plus airbag combination is 47%. At zero belt use, the airbag prevents 12 of the original 100 deaths, whereas at 100% belt use the airbag prevents 5 of the original 100 fatalities. The next chapter will be devoted to more on airbags because of the central role they have played in US safety policy.

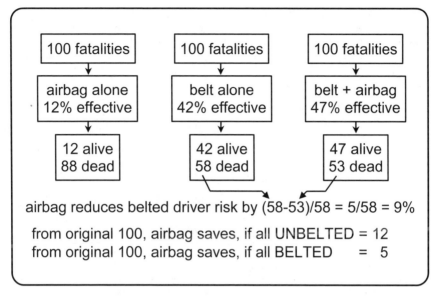

Figure 11-4. An initial population of drivers in cars without airbags sustains 100 driver fatalities. The figure shows the revised numbers of fatalities that would have occurred if different occupant protection scenarios had been in effect.

Summary of effectiveness estimates

The estimates derived here are summarized in Table 11-5. There are other occupant protection devices not listed, mainly because quantitative estimates parallel to those presented are not available, usually because evaluation is even more difficult than it was for the devices shown. There is copious evidence that bicycle helmets reduce risk, probably by an amount not substantially different from that shown for motorcycle helmets. Fatalities to bicyclists are included in FARS only if they occur in a crash involving a vehicle with an engine. FARS for 2002 records 662 bicycle fatalities compared to 3,126 motorcycle fatalities. There are many types of infant and baby seats with much evidence supporting that they provide major risk reductions in crashes. Effectiveness of airbags in light trucks is similar to that for cars.[32]

Estimating field effectiveness

If when-use effectiveness of a device is E, but no one uses it, then field effectiveness is zero. If everyone uses it, then field effectiveness is identical to when-used effectiveness E. For any active occupant protection device, the percent of users is always between these extremes, and estimating field effectiveness presents a number of problems.

Table 11-5. When-used effectiveness estimates for various occupant protection devices. Estimates derived by applying double pair comparison method to pre-law data, except as otherwise indicated.

vehicle	occupant	device	effectiveness
car	driver	lap/shoulder safety belt	$(42 \pm 4)\%$
	driver	belt plus frontal airbag	$(47 \pm 4)\%$
	driver	frontal airbag only*	$(12 \pm 3)\%$
	right-front passenger	lap/shoulder safety belt	$(39 \pm 4)\%$
	outboard-rear passenger	lap-only belt	$(18 \pm 9)\%$
light truck	driver	lap/shoulder safety belt	60%**
motorcycle	driver or passenger	helmet	$(28 \pm 8)\%$

*   from Table 11-4
** inferred from post-law data[7(p 28)]

Naive calculation

If a fraction, u_i, of random members of a population consisting exclusively of non-users were to convert to using a device, the fractional reduction in casualties, F, that would result is

$$F = Eu_i .$$
11-4

This will reduce an original N casualties to a new lower $N(1 - Eu_i)$ casualties. If at some later time the use rate increases to a new value, u_f, then the fractional reduction in casualties compared to the already lowered number is

$$F = \frac{E \Delta u}{1 - E u_i}$$
11-5

where Δu, the increase in use, is given by

$$\Delta u = u_f - u_i$$
11-6

These equations estimate far larger casualty reductions than are observed. The reason is that the assumption that users are random members of the population is grossly in error.

Selective recruitment

This term refers to the phenomenon that those who become users of an active occupant protection system are not recruited randomly from the population of non-users.[34] Instead, users differ from non-users in many ways that influence safety. Two effects are:

1. When non-wearers crash, they have more severe crashes.

2. Non-wearers are more likely to crash.

Crash severity and belt use

Figure 11-5 shows the percent of crash-involved drivers who were belted versus the severity of their crashes. The two graphs use the same measures of severity and data used to produce Figs 11-2 and 11-3. Both graphs, despite the different periods, driver populations, and severity measures show consistently that the more severe the crash, the less likely is the driver to be belted. The very drivers most in need of protection when crashes do occur are the very ones least likely to wear belts.

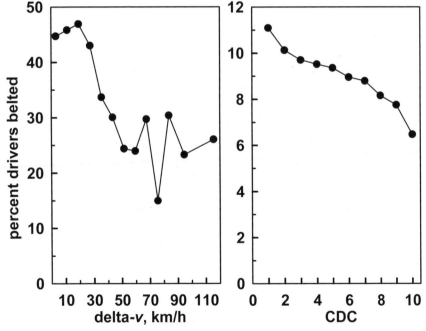

Figure 11-5. The more severe the crash, the less likely the driver is to be belted. The different absolute belt use rates reflect different periods when overall use rates were different (post-law on left plot, pre-law on right).[5,6]

Crash risk and belt use

If the effectiveness of belts in preventing fatalities is known, a number of inferences can be made from FARS data. Calculation details are given below because the approach has applications beyond the present case of inferring belt use in crashes. The inferences use only data for fatally injured occupants, for which belt-use coding is fairly reliable.

Inferring crash risks of unbelted relative to belted drivers from FARS data. Table 11-6 shows fatalities to drivers of cars (body type 1-10) killed in daytime crashes (6:00 am to 7:59 pm) from FARS 2002. Only drivers coded as either unbelted or using the lap and shoulder belt system are included.

It is helpful to introduce the notion of a set of *potentially lethal crashes*, defined as a set of crashes by unbelted drivers in which 100 unbelted drivers are killed. If all the drivers had instead been belted, then 100 (1 - *E*) belted driver fatalities would result. The number of potentially lethal crashes by unbelted drivers, C_N is proportional to the number of unbelted fatalities, K_N. For convenience, we take the constant of proportionality to be unity, so that $C_N = K_N$ for unbelted drivers. For belted drivers

$$C_Y = \frac{K_Y}{1-E} , \qquad\qquad 11\text{-}7$$

where K_Y is the observed number of belted fatalities, and C_Y is the inferred number of potentially lethal crashes by belted drivers. The total number of potentially lethal crashes, C_{TOTAL}, is given by

$$C_{TOTAL} = K_N + \frac{K_Y}{1-E} . \qquad\qquad 11\text{-}8$$

Dividing the number of crashes by belted drivers by the number of crashes by all drivers defines an inferred belt use rate in severe crashes, $u_{INFERRED}$, given by

$$u_{INFERRED} = C_Y / C_{TOTAL} . \qquad\qquad 11\text{-}9$$

A finding that $u_{INFERRED}$ is lower than the belt use rate estimated by roadside observations, $u_{OBSERVED}$, implies that unbelted drivers are crashing at greater rates than belted drivers. It can be shown[35] that

$$R = \frac{(1 - u_{INFERRED})}{u_{INFERRED}} \times \frac{u_{OBSERVED}}{(1 - u_{OBSERVED})} \qquad\qquad 11\text{-}10$$

where

$$R = \frac{\text{crash involvement rate for unbelted drivers}}{\text{crash involvement rate for belted drivers}} . \qquad\qquad 11\text{-}11$$

Table 11-6. Inferred belt use rates from observed belted and unbelted fatalities in FARS 2002.

	all crashes	single vehicle
effectiveness of belts, E	42%	62%
unbelted fatalities, K_N	3,128	1,347
potentially lethal crashes by unbelted drivers, $C_N = K_N$	3,128	1,347
belted fatalities, K_Y	3,777	850
potentially lethal crashes by belted drivers, $C_Y = K_Y/(1-E)$	6,512.1	2,236.8
total number of potentially lethal crashes, $C_{TOTAL} = C_N + C_Y$	9,640.1	3,583.8
inferred percent belted, $u_{INFERRED} = C_Y/C_{TOTAL}$	67.6%	62.4%
belt rate from roadside observations, $u_{OBSERVED}$	78%	78%
unbelted crash risk divided by belted crash risk, R	1.70	2.14

Substituting the observed daylight wearing rate for car drivers of 78% in 2002,[36,37(p 4)] and the inferred wearing rate of 67.6% into Eqn 11-11 gives that, for all crashes, unbelted drivers have crash risks 70% higher than those of belted drivers. For single-car crashes, for which the higher effectiveness $E = 62\%$ is used, the result is that unbelted drivers have single-car crash risks 114% higher than those of belted drivers. This fits the pattern discussed previously (p. 164-166 and in Chapter 10 on alcohol) that any driver risk-increasing factor will be more prevalent in single-vehicle than in multiple-vehicle crashes.

Empirical values of R. The two values of R derived in Table 11-6 appear in the first two rows of Table 11-7. The other rows show seven previously published R values.[35] Three use FARS 1975-1983 data. The driver fatality value was estimated using the calculation described above with $u_{OBSERVED} = 14\%$, a belt use rate that remained stable during the pre-law period covered by the data. Miscoding makes it impossible to use post-law FARS data to obtain estimates based on drivers involved in crashes killing pedestrians or motorcyclists. For example, FARS 2002 codes 1,672 belted and 238 unbelted drivers involved in crashes in which pedestrians were killed but the driver was uninjured. These data nominally imply an implausible 88% wearing rate, and therefore provide clear evidence that unbelted drivers are claiming to be belted.

The last four rows in Table 11-7 are from studies (described in Chapter 13) in which approaching cars were photographed on Michigan roads.[38-40] For all cases in Table 11-7 unbelted driver involvement rates are 28% to 114% higher than those for belted drivers. The tendency for the values relating more to single-vehicle crashes to be higher than the values relating to multiple-vehicle crashes is another illustration of risk-increasing behavior having a larger impact on single-vehicle crashes.

Table 11-7.   Unbelted driver risks relative to those of belted drivers.   All except the top two entries are from Ref. 35.

measure	R
driver fatalities, FARS 2002	1.70
driver fatalities, single-vehicle crashes, FARS 2002	2.14
driver fatalities, FARS 1975-1983	1.57
crashes in which pedestrians were killed, FARS 1975-1983	1.57
crashes in which motorcyclists were killed, FARS 1975-1983	1.37
police reported crashes (headway study)	1.32
police reported crashes (speed study)	1.28
traffic violations (headway study)	1.86
traffic violations (speed study)	1.73

Calculating fatality reductions from increased belt use

The higher crash risks of unbelted compared to belted drivers suggests a continuous relationship between propensity to not wear belts and crash risk. Consider all the drivers in a population rank ordered from the most to the least willing to wear a belt.   Conceptually, belt wearing might increase continuously from 0% to 100% in response to varying rewards and punishments. Increasing punishments for not wearing would result in belt-wearing by drivers with ever-increasing reluctance to wear – and correspondingly ever increasing risk of crashing.

Let us assume that a driver's crash risk can be represented by

$$c(\rho) \;=\; c_0(1 \;+\; \beta\rho^N) , \qquad\qquad 11\text{-}12$$

where ρ is a variable increasing from 0 to 1, reflecting the driver's rank ordered willingness to wear a belt and c_0 is the risk for the safest driver.   The safest driver is the most willing wearer with $\rho = 0$, and the least willing wearer has $\rho = 1$.   While a number of exponents were explored analytically,[41] the data presented below show that $N = 2$ is an appropriate choice.   To simplify subsequent equations we let $\beta = 3\lambda$, where λ is a parameter to be determined from data, so that Eqn 11-12 becomes

$$c(\rho) \;=\; c_0(1 \;+\; 3\lambda\rho^2) . \qquad\qquad 11\text{-}13$$

At a given population belt use rate, u, all the drivers with $\rho < u$ will be wearers, and all with $\rho > u$ non-wearers.   Integrating Eqn 11-13 gives

$$R = \frac{\text{average crash risk of belt non-wearer}}{\text{average crash risk of belt wearer}} = \frac{1 + \lambda(1+u+u^2)}{1 + \lambda u^2} . \qquad 11\text{-}14$$

The bottom 7 items in Table 11-7, which have an average value $R = 1.53$, were all for a belt use rate of 14%. Substituting $R = 1.53$ and $u = 0.14$ gives $\lambda = 0.47$. For $u = 0.78$, Eqn 11-14 gives $R = 1.65$, compared to 1.70 and 2.14 in Table 11-6. The value of R computed by Eqn 11-14 varies relatively little (from a minimum of 1.47 at $u = 0$ to a maximum 1.65 at $u = 0.77$) because with increasing belt use, numerator and denominator both increase. As u increases the average risk of the non-user population increases as it loses its safest drivers, while the average risk of the user population also increases as riskier drivers join it. Of course, the average risk of the entire population goes down as belt wearing increases.

The above equations allow us to express the percent reduction, F, in fatalities when belt use increases from u_i to u_f as

$$F = \frac{E\Delta u[1 + \lambda(u_i^2 + u_i u_f + u_f^2)]}{1 - Eu_i + \lambda(1 - Eu_i^3)} , \qquad 11\text{-}15$$

where $\Delta u = u_f - u_i$ is the increase in belt use rate. Substituting $\lambda = 0$ reproduces the naive Eqn 11-5. If belt use is initially zero and increases to 100%, substituting $u_i = 0$ and $u_f = 1$ gives $F = E$, the definition of when-used belt effectiveness. Below we always use $\lambda = 0.47$, and generally $E = 0.42$.

I have previously reported an equation producing results identical to those of Eqn 11-15. The earlier equation was derived by a similar approach to that used here, but the present derivation is more direct and simple leading to a simpler equation. [41,13(p 258)]

Selective recruitment is expected. Eqn 11-13 with $\lambda = 0.47$ (and $\rho = 1$) indicates that the crash risk of the most reluctant belt wearer is 2.41 times that of the most willing, a result to be interpreted in terms of populations rather than individuals. The individual highest risk driver has a crash risk above that of the safest driver by a much larger factor. Unwillingness to wear a belt is an unhealthy behavior, and individuals showing one unhealthy behavior are more likely to exhibit other unhealthy behaviors, leading one to expect non-wearers to have higher crash risks. When belt laws apply, non-wearers violate traffic law. Violators of one traffic law are more likely to violate other traffic laws, so it would be surprising if non-wearers did not have crash rates substantially higher than those of wearers. Selective recruitment is to be expected, and it would be remarkable if it did not occur.

Fatality changes compared to zero belt use

A simple case is estimating fatality reductions at a given belt use rate compared to zero wearing. This is obtained by substituting $u_i = 0$ so that Eqn 11-15 simplifies to

$$F = \frac{Eu_f[1 + \lambda u_f^2]}{1 + \lambda} , \qquad 11\text{-}16$$

which is plotted in Fig. 11-6. Also shown as a dashed line is the linear reduction in fatalities that would occur in the absence of selective recruiting. The data points are all inferred from FARS data using the approach in Table 11-6, except that data are not restricted to daytime hours. The bullet symbols are published estimates based on 1988 and earlier FARS data when belt wearing rates were lower.[42],[13(p 269)]

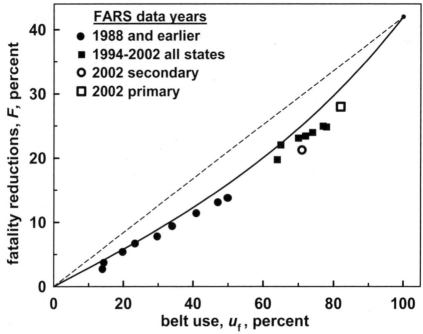

Figure 11-6. Calculated reductions in driver fatalities when belt use increases from 0 to u_i. The curve is Eqn 11-16 and the dashed straight line is the naive calculation ignoring selective recruitment. The points are calculated from FARS data for individual years for which the belt-use rate was measured.

It should be stressed that the data are not directly observed fatality reductions, but inferences from fatalities. The inferences use the same effectiveness as in the equation to plot the curve, so there is some circularity in the process. Also, points are plotted at the observed daytime belt use rate[37(p 4)] even though the rates averaged over the whole day are lower. Using only daytime fatalities runs into a problem because the when-used effectiveness is estimated using data for the entire day. Direct comparison with observed reductions is not possible because no jurisdiction has ever had a zero belt use in the "before" period of a before/after study, so that fatality reductions from an initial zero use cannot be measured directly. Changes in fatalities have been measured after belt wearing laws generated abrupt increases in wearing rates, thus providing actual fatality reductions that can be compared with the predictions from Eqn 11-15.

Belt wearing laws

Safety belts were first introduced into automobiles in the 1950s based on solid biomechanical understanding that they would reduce risk in crashes.[43]   Even though belts of some type were being installed in most of the world's new vehicles by the 1960s, wearing rates were low in all countries, and it seemed they would remain low unless wearing was required by law.

The first mandatory belt wearing law in a jurisdiction with a substantial driver population came into effect on 22 December 1970 in Victoria, a state in Australia.[44]   (Malawi and the Ivory Coast had formally included belt wearing in their legal statutes, but not otherwise acted.)[45]   In 1971 belt use increased in Victoria from about 15% to about 50%, and a reduction of about 12% in deaths to affected occupants (drivers and left-front passengers) was reported.[46] Substituting $u_i = 0.15$ and $u_f = 0.50$ into Eqn 11-15 gives $F = 12.2\%$, the first entry in Table 11-8.   The closeness of the agreement between the two is fortuitous given the uncertainties in the observed fatality change and belt use rates, and in the equation.

Table 11-8. Comparison of fatality reductions estimated by Eqn 11-15 with observed reductions from introducing mandatory belt wearing.

jurisdiction	belt use rates		fatality reductions	
	pre-law, u_i	post-law, u_f	Eqn 11-15	observed
Victoria, Australia	15%	50%	12.2%	12%
US secondary enforcement	14%	47%	11.2%	9%
UK	40%	90%	26.5%	20%

Influenced by reports of casualty reductions from the Victoria law, many jurisdictions eventually passed belt wearing laws.   Such laws are in place in all US states except New Hampshire, in all Canadian provinces, in all Australian states, and in nearly all of the world's countries.

Switzerland provides a particularly interesting case, because the law that became applicable in January 1976 was repealed by voter petition in July 1977 but became effective again after October 1977.[13(p 268)]   The following changes in fatalities were recorded:

- after law first passed   fatalities decreased
- after law was repealed   fatalities increased
- after law reinstated   fatalities decreased

A review of 33 US studies found that US belt laws in various US states reduced fatalities by a median 9%, and injuries by a median 2%.[47]   The laws were found to increase belt use by a median 33%.   If one assumes that the laws increased belt use from pre-law rates of 14% to post-law rates of 47% (a reasonable average for the extended period covered by the studies), substituting $u_i = 0.14$ and $u_f = 0.47$ into Eqn 11-15 gives $F = 11.2\%$.

The UK's belt wearing law

The belt wearing law that came into effect on 31 January 1983 in the UK has three factors favoring effective evaluation that are not available for any other jurisdiction.   First, belt use was closely monitored at 55 traffic census sites operated by the Department of Transport, generally from 8:30 am to 4:30 pm, before and after the law came into effect.   Second, a large increase in belt use occurred in a few months, from about 40% to about 90%.   Third, the UK, with over 16 million cars in 1983, provides one of the largest populations of occupants affected by a single law.

Despite uniquely favorable conditions, evaluating the UK's law has not been without difficulties or controversy.   There were claims that the increased safety provided by belts encouraged drivers to take more risks, thereby reducing the safety benefits to the drivers while increasing risks to other road users.[48]   The simplest evaluation, a count of casualties in an 11-month period before the law to an 11-month period after the law showed a 23% reduction in fatalities and a 26% reduction in serious injuries to occupants covered by the law.   Because of claims that such reductions could be due to other concurrent changes, the Department of Transport invited two outside distinguished statisticians to examine the monthly time series of casualties to various road users.   They found an 18% fatality reduction for drivers and a 25% reduction for front-seat passengers, together with fatality increases to rear-seat passengers, pedestrians and bicyclists.[49]   In the much larger sample of injuries they found larger injury reductions to occupants covered by the law without systematic increases to those not covered.   The extensive well-documented discussion (printed after their paper) is uninhibited by the politeness that often does such disservice to the search for truth in the US.[50]

Additional evidence of the efficacy of the law was provided by a 15% reduction in traffic crash patients brought to hospitals, a 25% reduction in those requiring admission to wards, and a similar fall in bed-occupancy.   Larger reductions are found for front-seat passengers than for drivers.[51]   I suspect that some front-seat passengers migrated to rear seats rather than wear belts, which explains reduced front-seat casualties and increased rear-seat casualties.

There were additional evaluations,[13(p 262-265)] justifying a consensus view that the law reduced fatalities to covered occupants by about 20%, and that the increases in pedestrian and bicycle fatalities with no corresponding increase in injuries were probably spurious effects in small samples (see also p. 301). Substituting $u_i = 0.40$ and $u_f = 0.90$ into Eqn 11-15 gives $F = 26.5\%$ (Table 11-8).   The lower observed than computed reduction likely reflects that nighttime wearing rates were lower than the observed daytime 90% rate, and that the crashes of unbelted drivers were of higher severity.

Primary and secondary laws

Laws requiring belt use are of two types. Primary laws allow police officers to stop drivers based solely on an observed safety belt violation. Secondary laws allow officers to enforce the belt law only if the driver is first stopped for some other violation. In 2002, eighteen states in the US had primary laws. An analysis of direct observations of belt use in 2002 and inferences from fatalities as described above finds that the change from secondary to primary enforcement increased daytime belt use rates from 70% to 83%.[52] Substituting $u_i = 0.70$ and $u_f = 0.83$ into Eqn 11-15 gives $F = 9\%$.

Calculating fatality reductions from increased belt use

The complexity of evaluating even the UK law shows how much more difficult it is to measure casualty reductions reliably in other jurisdictions which have fewer vehicles and do not experience large rapid changes in belt use when laws are passed (or strengthened). A real fatality reduction of, say 4%, represents an important safety benefit, but is essentially impossible to measure directly in the face of total fatalities changing for so many other reasons.

I believe the best approach available to estimate fatality changes that cannot be observed directly is to use Eqn 11-15. This equation incorporates a coherent interpretation of many of the key effects relevant to how changes in belt use rates affect casualties, and it fits reasonably well available observed changes in casualties from large changes in belt use.

One of the many derivations that can be made from Eqn 11-15 is shown in Fig. 11-7, which shows the percent reduction in fatalities that would result if belt use rate increased by 5%. The relationship computed from the naive Eqn 11-5 is also shown. It is not a straight line because even when selective recruitment is ignored and the same percent increase in belt use always produces the same absolute reduction in fatalities, the initial number of fatalities becomes less with increasing belt use.

If belt use is zero, increasing it by 5% reduces fatalities by only 1.4% because the first 5% of drivers to use belts will be the safest drivers. However, if belt use is 95%, increasing it by 5% reduces fatalities by 5.5%. The higher the belt use rate, the greater is the benefit of increasing it further by the same amount. One might refer to the effect as the *law of increasing returns*.

Benefits of belt laws

Many decades of experience with belt-use laws shows that after they are passed, use increases, but then generally declines from its immediate post-law peak. The pattern typical of US states was an increase from under 20% in the pre-law period to about 50% immediately after passage, but then dropping to about 40%. Rates increase in response to increased enforcement and additional law changes, especially the change from secondary to primary enforcement. Rates also increase in response to persuasion in media messages, and a general

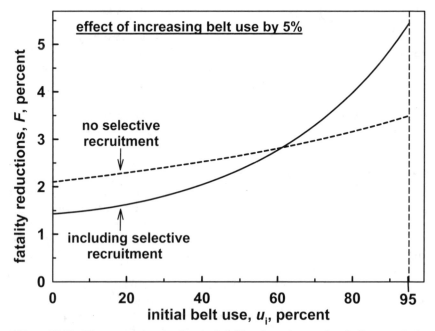

Figure 11-7. The percent reduction in fatalities from increasing belt use rate by five percentage points from the initial belt use rate indicated. Computed using Eqn 11-15.

incorporation of belt use into the social norm. In Canadian provinces, use rates were typically 50% some time after laws were passed in the mid 1970s, but have increased in response to various measures to around 90%.[53]

While Eqn 11-15 estimates different fatality reductions dependent on initial belt use rates, a fatality reduction is always estimated to result from an increase in belt use. Any measure that increases belt use is expected to reduce fatalities. When use rates are already high it becomes more difficult to increase them further, but the benefits of doing so also increase. Adopting primary laws and enforcing them vigorously will prevent many deaths.

Repeal of mandatory motorcycle helmet wearing laws

Following the Highway Safety Act of 1966, the US Federal Government made passage of mandatory helmet wearing laws for motorcycle drivers and passengers a precondition for the states to receive highway construction funds. All but three states passed such laws. In 1976, in response to pressures from many states, the US Congress revoked the financial penalties for non-enactment of helmet wearing laws. In the next few years, just over half of the states repealed their laws; half repealing and half not provides the optimum "natural experiment" to compare repeal and non-repeal states.

Each point plotted in Fig. 11-8 estimates the increase in motorcyclist fatalities in an individual state. This was computed by comparing the number of fatalities after repeal to the number before repeal to this same ratio for all the states that left their wearing laws in place.[54] The numbers along the horizontal axis give the states ordered by date of repeal, from 21 May 1976 for Rhode Island to 1 January 1982 for Louisiana. There are 27 data points for 26 states because Louisiana repealed its law, then passed another, which was subsequently also repealed. Nominally, 24 of the points indicate that fatalities increased after repeal, compared to 3 indicating a decrease, so the data provide extremely strong evidence that repeal led to a substantial increase in fatalities. The weighted average of all 27 values is (25 ± 4) %.

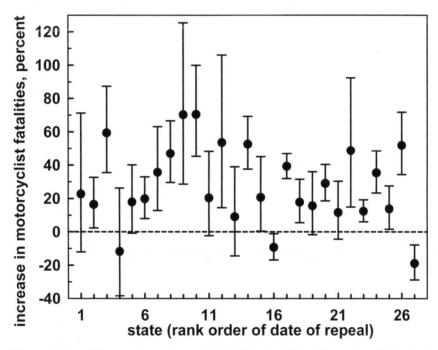

Figure 11-8. Change in motorcyclist fatalities in US states after 27 helmet wearing laws were repealed. Plotted from data in Ref. 54, which names the states.

Wearing rates (night and day) were estimated for drivers at 88% in states with laws compared to 42% for states without laws.[13(p 272)] Substituting $E = 28$, $u_i = 0.88$ and $u_f = .42$ into Eqn 11-15 gives $F = -18\%$. The corresponding calculation for passengers, with use rates of 80% in law states compared to 23% in no-law states, gives $F = -19\%$. The predicted increases of 18% and 19% are somewhat lower than the observed increase of 25%. It has been speculated that wearing laws discouraged some motorcycle travel, an effect which would amplify fatality changes when laws were passed or repealed. Eqn 11-15 was of course derived for safety belts, and is applied to motorcycle helmets because there is little possibility of deriving a corresponding equation based on motorcycle data.

Occupant-protection issues

The history of occupant-protection devices and laws requiring their use has included technical errors and much controversy. There were many early estimates of belt effectiveness based on comparing the percent of driver fatalities who were belted to the percent of drivers who were unbelted. Such calculations led to published effectiveness estimates as high as 90%, which in turn generated predictions of large reductions in casualties from increases in belt use. The failure to observe such reductions gave rise to much speculation, including the claim that drivers were negating the benefits of belts by increased risk taking.

Do drivers using occupant protection devices change their behavior?

This question has a very easy and certain answer, namely *yes*. However, neither this question nor its answer is of much importance. The two important questions are

    1. In what direction – more risk or less risk?

    2. By how much?

The answer to the first question is not known. Note that this question refers to changes in behavior when an individual driver fastens a belt, and should not be confused with the unrelated finding that non-users have higher crash risks than users, because that comparison is between different drivers.

One can provide a more substantive answer to the second question, namely, *not much*. The reason is that the agreement of so much data with Eqn 11-15 is sufficiently good to preclude the possibility of any additional <u>large</u> effect. The possibility that drivers might drive substantially more carelessly because of the additional protection a belt provides cannot be dismissed as unreasonable, but it is rejected by data.

It is of course certain that the act of wearing a belt does influence driver behavior to some degree because of the universal principle that anything of which we are aware affects our behavior. The act of fastening might reduce crash risk by reminding drivers that there are risks associated with driving, or increase risk because of reduced harm expected if a crash were to occur. Data collected in a test-track experiment suggested that the same drivers increased speed by about 1% when belted compared to when unbelted.[55] Any actual small speed increase would reduce the effectiveness of belt wearing laws, and could contribute to the general tendency for observed reductions to be somewhat less than predicted.

It was claimed that the UK belt wearing law led drivers to take increased risks in traffic, which killed more pedestrians and other road users.[48] The small samples of fatality data did indeed indicate increases. However, no other reports have associated increased pedestrian or other road user casualties with increased belt wearing. FARS data would be suitable for such investigations. Belt use rates can be inferred as in Table 11-6 for 50 states each year since 1975, so an enormous data pool is available to examine pedestrian fatalities relative to changes in belt use rates. While I would not attach high priority to such a study, it has more value than many studies that are performed.

Are there cases in which occupant protection devices kill?

This is another question with an easy and certain answer, namely *yes*. It requires no data to prove it – logic suffices as the following analogy establishes. Every year a number of pedestrians walking on the sidewalk are killed by out-of-control vehicles. These are cases in which walking on the sidewalk led to death, while walking in the center of the fastest traffic lane would have been safer (well, certainly not less safe). We choose the sidewalk not because it is always, under all circumstances, safer, but because it is, on average, safer. The same reasoning applies to all measures that reduce risk, including use of safety belts.

In many cases those killed do indeed receive their injuries from safety belts. A naive interpretation might be that the belt therefore killed the occupant. The more likely situation can be explained in terms of many people falling from different heights onto a concrete surface, resulting in many deaths. If a mattress were placed on top of the concrete, fewer deaths would occur. However, an examination of the fatalities and injuries would find that 100% of them had been caused by severe contact with a mattress.

While the above general principles apply, the specific situation remains that in a severe crash a belted occupant may receive injuries of a different type, and in different parts of the body, than would have occurred without the belt. In some cases the injuries might be more severe than without the belt. When a belt injury occurs it is generally difficult to estimate what the outcome would have been, absent the belt. Fractures of the sternum and sprained necks appear to have increased following the British belt wearing law.[51] Tharaco-lumbar spine injuries and serious cervical spine injuries increased following the French belt law.[56] The injuries that increased in frequency might be substitutes for more serious injuries if no belt had been worn. Part of the effectiveness of airbags is through reducing injuries from safety belts.

The effectiveness of a device being say, 12%, means that a population of non users that sustained 100 deaths would have sustained 12 fewer deaths if all members of the population had been users. It does not mean that 12 of the original 100 people killed would have survived, while 88 of the original 100 killed would still have died. In principle, the device could save every one of the original 100, but kill a different 88 who would have survived without it, still giving 12% effectiveness. Effectiveness measures the difference between deaths with and without the device, but does not convey information about deaths that could have been caused by the device.

There are occasional claims that unbelted occupants landed uninjured in haystacks after being ejected from vehicles in which they would otherwise have perished. Some non-wearers state such anecdotes to justify not wearing. Ejection increases the probability of being killed by a factor of 3.8. Occasional good outcomes from ejection are as inevitable as occasional good outcomes from walking in the middle of the road. It is imprudent to let either influence behavior.

There is one occupant protection device that is of a different nature from the others. Airbags inject additional energy into the crash event that may cause harm that would not otherwise occur. NHTSA reports that, as of July 2003, there were 231 confirmed deaths caused by airbag deployments in crashes that would otherwise not have been life threatening.[57]

Objections to occupant protection laws

Laws requiring the use of safety belts and helmets differ in a fundamental way from those against speeding and drunk driving. There is near universal agreement that governments have a high priority duty to protect citizens from being harmed by the actions of others. However, people not using occupant protection devices increase risk to nobody but themselves (except for the possibility of the small effects discussed above). Claims that wearing a belt helps a driver better control a vehicle in an emergency are not supported by any evidence, and seem to be grasping at straws to avoid the problem addressed in this section. The claim that motorcycle helmets increase crash risk by restricting peripheral vision is more plausible, but still unconvincing.

The fact that non-wearing hurts no one except the non-wearer has inspired objections to wearing laws, especially of motorcycle helmets, on the grounds that government has no right to restrict a citizen's right to do things that do not harm others. However, non-wearing does impose costs on others. All motorized societies have medical systems that treat those injured regardless of how they got injured. Non-participation is not an option. One cannot conceive of a contract in which a person would accept personal responsibility for not wearing a belt or helmet by agreeing to forgo medical attention if involved in a crash. Not only would this be ethically difficult, but it would also be impossible to administer. Non-wearers consume additional medical and rescue resources, making such resources possibly unavailable to others needing help. The belt-wearers who pay part of the many additional costs imposed on them by non-wearers are being merely prudent in using the legal system to coerce non-wearers into wearing. This is a question legitimately decided by the political process, and can be addressed without bringing up any issue of government paternalism. If the voters are willing to subsidize skiers and rock climbers, but not non-wearers, this is their legitimate choice. They are under no obligation to avoid sensible policies just to fit some critic's notion of consistency. Quantitatively, the costs imposed by belt and helmet non-wearers are enormous compared to those imposed by all the other subsidized risk takers.

Advances in safety belt technology

There have been ongoing efforts to improve the performance of the lap/shoulder belts installed in all 1974 and later model year vehicles. The two most specific advances are pretensioning devices, which pull belts snug as a crash begins, and load limiters, which allow belts to yield slightly during a crash to reduce the risk of injuries from the belt. Approximately 63 percent of model year 2002 cars and light trucks had pretensioners, and 84 percent had load limiters. These are shown to reduce forces on anthropometric dummies in laboratory tests in which vehicles crash into barriers.[58]

While such changes are expected to provide reduced risk in actual crashes, it is not possible to measure the differences from field data. This should be clear in the light of the problems of determining effectiveness for the entire vehicle population. Statistical uncertainty is not the only problem, but it presents a major hurdle. The overall belt effectiveness is $(42 \pm 4)\%$, so that if the population were divided into two equal subpopulations, the uncertainty in the estimate for each would be about 6%. Thus it would be difficult to observe any difference between the populations unless it exceeded 10%, an unrealistic expectation. Similar comments apply to attempts to address differences in the effectiveness of the belts in vehicles from different manufacturers. The best one can do is to rely on engineering inference and judgment. However, the earlier comments about how laboratory tests tend to overestimate field effects should be kept in mind.

Are more accurate and more precise estimates of belt use possible?

The $(42 \pm 4)\%$ estimate for the effectiveness of belts in reducing car driver fatality risk is based on pre-1984 FARS data, and therefore on cars of model year 1984 or earlier. In the time that has elapsed since then, does additional information suggest a higher or lower value? There are two reasons to suspect that the true effectiveness might have been a little lower. First, even after taking into account selective recruitment, reductions in fatalities have still tended to fall short of predictions based on 42% effectiveness. Second, before belt wearing laws, belt wearing was considered socially desirable. Many surveys found that the percent of respondents who claimed to always wear belts far exceeded the percent observed actually wearing them. A small tendency for unbelted survivors to indicate that they were belted even before non-wearing was illegal seems probable. The technical improvements in belts have likely increased effectiveness, perhaps to close to the 42%. NHTSA uses a slightly higher effectiveness of 45%. Although the difference between the two is smaller than anything that can be measured, I consider the lower estimate provides a marginally better general fit to what is known.

The introduction of *Event Data Recorders* offers the possibility of more accurate and more precise estimates of belt effectiveness.[59] Because of the need to determine whether or not to deploy an airbag, tens of millions of vehicles on the roads by 2003 already had such devices. They record many variables including the pre-crash speed and whether a belt was worn. Belt wearing is based on sensors in the belt system, so that there is the potential to provide, for the first time, substantial quantities of objective data on belt use by surviving occupants. Questions of privacy and ownership of data have precluded (at time of writing) the use of the data for research purposes.

Theoretical limits of crash protection

Before 1905 the question: "What is the theoretical fastest speed an object can travel?" would have produced a different answer than would be given today. In the earlier period the answer would likely start by stressing that while there is no theoretical limit, all sorts of engineering and other constraints place practical limits on attainable speeds. Today the answer would likely start by stating that no matter what is done, it is not possible to travel faster than the speed of light.

There is a somewhat analogous theoretical barrier which occupant protection cannot penetrate. The limit flows from the fact that the forces on occupants in vehicles that crash cannot be made less than limits dictated by physical laws. Consider a driver sitting 2.5 meters from the front bumper of a car that crashes head-on into an immovable hard barrier. The theoretical safest situation would be for the driver to decelerate at a constant rate over the entire 2.5 meters, arriving in contact with the barrier at zero speed. If the car's speed is v km/h, then the value of the constant deceleration is $v^2/635\ G$, where G is the deceleration due to gravity. For $v = 252$ km/h the result is 100 G, a value which some literature indicates is the limit the human body can withstand.[3] While 252 km/h is not of much relevance in normal traffic safety, there are nonetheless 19 car models available in the US claiming higher top speeds.[60] The assumption that the driver arrives at the barrier rests on the quite implausible assumption that the engine and other components in front of the driver compress to zero thickness. Any more realistic assumption will indicate a much lower maximum survivable speed. There are indications that some individuals can withstand forces well in excess of 100 G, leading to higher estimated maximum survivable impact speeds.

The example is given to show that there is a theoretical limit, even if it cannot be reliably estimated. Crashes can be of such high severity that it is impossible to make them survivable, even in principle. A main reason why many spectacular high-speed crashes by racing cars are survived is because the vehicles come to rest over very long distances and extended times. It is the reduction in speed over long distances that provides the spectacular pictures. Unsurvivable crashes are not spectacular. From the beginning to the end of the crash the vehicle travels a meter or so. The crash lasts about one tenth of a second, which to the unaided eye appears instantaneous.

Summary and conclusions

When a vehicle crashes, it undergoes a rapid reduction in speed. Occupants continue to move at the vehicle's prior speed until stopped, either by impact with objects external to the vehicle if ejected, or by impact with the interior of the vehicle. Occupant protection devices are designed to reduce the severity of impact, and to prevent ejection. The device that provides the most benefit to the largest number of occupants is the integrated lap/shoulder safety belt, or simply safety belt. It reduces car driver fatality risk in a crash by 42%. This effectiveness is increased to 47% by frontal airbags. Airbags are supplemental devices designed to increase the effectiveness of the primary occupant protection device, the safety belt. When used by unbelted drivers, airbags reduce fatality risk by 12%. Helmets reduce motorcyclist fatality risk by 28%. Compared to traveling the same distance by car, a motorcyclist not wearing a helmet is 31 times as likely to be killed, but only 22 times as likely if a helmet is worn.

Estimating fatality reductions when some percent of drivers fasten belts is complicated by *selective recruitment*, a term indicating that drivers who wear belts are not recruited at random from those who do not. Much empirical evidence shows that, compared to belted drivers, unbelted drivers have higher crash rates, and higher severity crashes. An equation estimating fatality reductions for arbitrary changes in belt use was developed incorporating selective recruitment. Observed changes in fatalities associated with large changes in belt use fit this equation sufficiently well to justify its use to calculate fatality changes for arbitrary changes in belt use. Increasing belt use by 5% from an initial zero use reduces fatalities by 1.4%, while increasing use by 5% from an initial 95% use reduces fatalities by 5.5%. This *law of increasing returns* provides increased motivation to pass stronger belt wearing laws and enforce them vigorously.

References for Chapter 11

1 Naahum AM, Melvin JW, editors. *Accidental Injury: Biomechanics and Prevention*. New York, NY: Springer-Verlag; 1993.

2 Mackay GM. A review of the biomechanics of impacts in road accidents. In: Amrosio JAC et al., editors. *Crashworthiness of Transportation Systems: Structural Impact and Occupant Protection*. Netherlands: Kluwer Academic Publishers; 1997, p. 115-138.

3 Crawford H. Survivable impact forces on human body constrained by full body harness. Report prepared for UK Health and Safety Executive. Report HSL/2003/09; September 2003. http://www.hse.gov.uk/research/hsl_pdf/2003/hsl03-09.pdf

4 Kahane CJ. Evaluation of current energy-absorbing steering assemblies. SAE paper 820473. Warrendale, PA: Society of Automotive Engineers; 1982. (Also included in *Occupant Crash Interaction with the Steering System.* SAE special publication SP-507; 1982, p. 45-49).

5 Evans L. Safety-belt effectiveness: The influence of crash severity and selective recruitment. *Accid Anal Prev.* 1996; 28: 423-433.

6 Campbell BJ. Safety belt injury reduction related to crash severity and front seated position. *J Trauma.* 1987; 27: 733-739.

7 Kahane CJ. Fatality reduction by safety belts for front-seat occupants of cars and light trucks: Updated and expanded estimates based on 1986-99 FARS data. Report DOT HS 809 199. Washington, DC: US Department of Transportation, National Highway Traffic Safety Administration; Dec. 2000. http://www.nhtsa.dot.gov/cars/rules/regrev/evaluate/pdf/809199.pdf

8 Evans L. The effectiveness of safety belts in preventing fatalities. *Accid Anal Prev.* 1986; 18: 229-241.

9 Evans L. Double pair comparison – a new method to determine how occupant characteristics affect fatality risk in traffic crashes. *Accid Anal Prev.* 1986; 18: 217-227.

10 Evans L, Frick MC. Potential fatality reductions through eliminating occupant ejection from cars. *Accid Anal Prev.* 1989; 21: 169-182.

11 Evans L. Restraint effectiveness, occupant ejection from cars and fatality reductions. *Accid Anal Prev.* 1990; 22: 167-175.

12 Evans L. Airbag effectiveness in preventing fatalities predicted according to type of crash, driver age, and blood alcohol concentration. *Accid Anal Prev.* 1991; 23: 531-541.

13 Evans L. *Traffic Safety and the Driver.* New York, NY: Van Nostrand Reinhold; 1991.

14 Evans L, Frick MC. Safety belt effectiveness in preventing driver fatalities versus a number of vehicular, accident, roadway and environmental factors. *J Safety Res.* 1986; 17: 143-154.

15 Evans L. Fatality risk for belted drivers versus car mass. *Accid Anal Prev.* 1985; 17: 251-271.

16 Partyka SC. Belt effectiveness in passenger cars by weight class. In: *Papers on Car Size – Safety and Trends.* Report DOT HS 807 444. Washington, DC: National Highway Traffic Safety Administration; June 1989, p. 1-35.

17 Evans L. Rear seat restraint system effectiveness in preventing fatalities. *Accid Anal Prev.* 1988; 20: 129-136. (Also see Evans, L. Rear compared to front seat restraint system effectiveness in preventing fatalities. SAE paper 870485. Warrendale, PA: Society of Automotive Engineers. (Also included in *Restraint Technologies – Rear Seat Occupant Protection.* SAE special publication SP-691; 1987, p. 39-43).

18 Evans L, Frick MC. Seating position in cars and fatality risk. *Am J Pub Health.* 1988; 78: 1456-1458.

19 Smith KM, Cummings P. Passenger seating position and the risk of passenger death or injury in traffic crashes. *Accid Anal Prev.* 2004; 36: 257–260.

20 Morgan C. Effectiveness of lap/shoulder belts in the back outboard seating positions. Report DOT HS 809 945. Washington, DC: US Department of Transportation, National Highway Traffic Safety Administration; June 1999.

21 National Highway Traffic Safety Administration. Final regulatory impact analysis, Amendment of FMVSS 208, passenger car front seat occupant protection. Washington, DC; 11 July 1984.

22 Evans L. Restraint effectiveness, occupant ejection from cars, and fatality reductions. *Accid Anal Prev.* 1990; 22: 167-175.

23 Kahane CJ. Fatality and injury reducing effectiveness of lap belts for back seat occupants. SAE paper 870486. Warrendale, PA: Society of Automotive Engineers; 1987. (Also included in *Restraint Technologies: Rear Seat Occupant Protection.* SAE special publication SP-691; 1987, p. 45-63).

24 Park S. The influence of rear-seat occupants on front-seat occupant fatalities: The unbelted case. General Motors Research Laboratories, Research Publication GMR-5664; 8 January 1987.

25 Cummings P, Rivara FP. Car occupant death according to the restraint use of other occupants: A matched cohort study. *J Am Medical Assoc.* 2004; 291: 343-349.

26 Ichikawa M, Nakahara S, Wakai S. Mortality of front-seat occupants attributable to unbelted rear-seat passengers in car crashes. *Lancet.* 2002; 359: 43-44.

27 Evans L, Frick MC. Helmet effectiveness in preventing motorcycle driver and passenger fatalities. *Accid Anal Prev.* 1988 ;20: 447-458.

28 Wilson DC. The effectiveness of motorcycle helmets in preventing fatalities. Report DOT HS 807 416. Washington, DC: National Highway Traffic Safety Administration; March 1989.

29 National Highway Traffic Safety Administration. *Traffic Safety Facts 2001.* Report DOT HS 809 484. Washington, DC: US Department of Transportation; December 2002. http://www-nrd.nhtsa.dot.gov/pdf/nrd-30/NCSA/TSFAnn/TSF2001.pdf

30 International Road Traffic and Accident Database (OECD) (2001). http://www.bast.de/htdocs/fachthemen/irtad/english/englisch.html

31 Kahane CJ. Fatality reduction by air bags: Analysis of accident data through early 1966. Report DOT HS 808 470. Washington, DC: National Highway Traffic Safety Administration; 1996.

32 National Highway Traffic Safety Administration. Fifth/Sixth Report to Congress: Effectiveness of occupant protection systems and their use. Report DOT HS 809 442. Washington, DC: US Department of Transportation; November 2001.

33 Cummings P, McKnight B, Rivara FP, Grossman DC. Association of driver air bags with driver fatality: A matched cohort study. *Brit Med J.* 2002; 324: 1119-1122.

34 Evans L. Human behavior feedback and traffic safety. *Hum Factors.* 1985; 27: 555-576.

35 Evans L. Belted and unbelted driver accident involvement rates compared. *J Safety Res.* 1987; 18: 57-64.

36 Glassbrenner D. Safety belt use in 2003. Report DOT HS 809 646. Washington, DC: US Department of Transportation, National Highway Traffic Safety Administration; Sept. 2003. http://www-nrd.nhtsa.dot.gov/pdf/nrd-30/NCSA/Rpts/2003/809646.pdf

37 Glassbrenner D. Safety belt and helmet use in 2002 – Overall results. Report DOT HS 809 500. Washington, DC: US Department of Transportation, National Highway Traffic Safety Administration, September 2002. http://www-nrd.nhtsa.dot.gov/pdf/nrd-30/NCSA/Rpts/2002/809-500.pdf

38 Von Buseck CR, Evans L, Schmidt DE, Wasielewski P. Seat belt usage and risk taking in driving behavior. SAE paper 800388. Warrendale, PA: Society of Automotive Engineers; 1980. (Also included in *Accident Causation.* SAE special publication SP-461; 1980, p. 45-49).

39 Evans L, Wasielewski P. Risky driving related to driver and vehicle characteristics. *Accid Anal Prev.* 1983; 15: 121-136.

40 Wasielewski P. Speed as a measure of driver risk: Observed speeds versus driver and vehicle characteristics. *Accid Anal Prev.* 1984; 16: 89-103.

41 Evans L. Estimating fatality reductions from increased safety belt use. *Risk Analysis.* 1987; 7: 49-57.

42 Partyka SC, Womble KB. Projected lives savings from greater belt use. Washington, DC: National Highway Traffic Administration Research Notes; June 1989.

43 Andréasson R. *The Seat Belt: Swedish Research and Development for Global Automotive Safety.* Sweden, Uppsala: Claes-Göran Bäckström; 2000.

44 Trinca GW. Thirteen years of seat belt usage – how great the benefits. SAE paper 840192. Warrendale, PA: Society of Automotive Engineers; 1984. (Also included in *Restraint Technologies: Front Seat Occupant Protection.* SAE special publication P-141; 1984, p. 1-5).

45 Grimm AC. International restraint use laws. Ann Arbor, MI: University of Michigan Transportation Research Institute. *UMTRI Research Review.* 1988; 18: 1-9.

46 Andreassend DC. Victoria and the seat belt law, 1971 on. *Hum Factors*. 1976; 18: 563-600.

47 Guide to community preventive services: System reviews and evidence based recommendations. Effectiveness of safety belt use laws. December 2002. http://www.thecommunityguide.org/mvoi/mvoi-safety-belt-law.pdf

48 Adams JGU. Smeed's law, seat belts and the emperor's new clothes. In: Evans L, Schwing RC, editors. *Human Behavior and Traffic Safety*. New York, NY: Plenum Press; 1985, p. 193-248.

49 Harvey AC, Durbin J. The effects of seat belt legislation on British road casualties: A case study in structural time series modeling. *J Royal Statistical Soc.* 1986; A149: 187-210.

50 Discussion of the paper by Professors Harvey and Durbin. *J Royal Statistical Soc.* 1986; A149: 211-227.

51 Rutherford WH, Greenfield T, Hayes HRM, Nelson JK. The medical effects of seat belt legislation in the United Kingdom. Research Report number 13. London, UK: Her Majesty's Stationery Office, Department of Health and Social Security, Office of the Chief Scientist; 1985.

52 Chaudhary NK, Preusser DF. Lives lost by states' failure to implement primary safety belt laws. Report prepared for the National Safety Council's Air Bag & Seat Belt Safety Campaign; November 2003. http://www.nsc.org/public/Preusser_Study.pdf

53 Transport Canada. Results of Transport Canada's July 2001 *Survey of Seat Belt Use in Canada*. Fact Sheet # RS 2001–07; October 2001. http://www.tc.gc.ca/roadsafety/tp2436/rs200107/en/menu.htm

54 Chenier TC, Evans L. Motorcyclist fatalities and the repeal of mandatory helmet wearing laws. *Accid Anal Prev.* 1987; 19: 133-139.

55 Janssen W. Seat-belt wearing and driver behavior: An instrumented-vehicle study. *Accid Anal Prev.* 1994; 26: 249-261.

56 Salmi LR, Thomas H, Fabry JJ, Girard, R. The effect of the 1979 French seat-belt law on the nature and severity of injuries to front-seat occupants. *Accid Anal Prev.* 1989; 21: 589-594.

57 Counts for air bag related fatalities and seriously injured persons. http://www-nrd.nhtsa.dot.gov/pdf/nrd-30/NCSA/SCI/2Q_2003/HTML/QtrRpt/ABFSISR.htm

58 Waltz MC. NCAP Test improvements with pretensioners and load limiters. *Traf Inj Prev.* 2004; 5: 18-25. (Also available as Report DOT HS 809 562. National Highway Traffic Safety Administration; March 2003. http://www.nhtsa.dot.gov/cars/rules/regrev/evaluate/pdf/809562.pdf)

59 National Highway Traffic Safety Administration. Event data recorders, summary of findings by the NHTSA EDR working group, final report; August 2001. http://www-nrd.nhtsa.dot.gov/edr-site/uploads/edrs-summary%5Fof%5Ffindings.pdf

60 All cars – cars are our life. http://www.allcars.org/top_lists_topspeed.html

12 Airbag benefits, airbag costs

Introduction

No safety device has consumed more attention and resources than the airbag. The *airbag mandate*, the requirement that vehicles be equipped with airbags, has been at the center of US safety policy since the 1970s. The cost and complexity of airbags, and the controversy surrounding them, calls for more detailed analyses than was devoted to any of the other occupant protection devices covered in Chapter 11. Chapter 15 discusses the profound impact airbags and the airbag mandate have had on overall US safety policy since the 1970s. This chapter discusses airbags as devices, with particular emphasis on their costs and benefits.

While airbags were originally intended to be primary occupant protection devices, all vehicle manufacturers now explicitly state that they are supplemental devices aimed at enhancing the effectiveness of the primary occupant protection device, the lap-shoulder belt. Here the term *airbag* refers only to frontal airbags.

The main component of the airbag system is a strong fabric bag folded and stored in a module on the steering column for the driver, and in the dashboard for the passenger. When onboard sensors detect a frontal crash of severity exceeding a set threshold, equivalent to a delta-*v* of about 10 mph, detonators deploy the airbag. High pressure chemically-produced gasses force the bag out of the module and inflate it sufficiently rapidly that it is in place in front of the occupant before the occupant has had time to move forward appreciably in response to the crash forces.

A plethora of technical and policy subjects relating to airbags is covered in a massive and rapidly expanding literature (see, for example, the summary in Ref. 1). Despite so much literature, many of the most basic questions still lack confident answers. The question of whether the benefits of airbags are commensurate with their considerable costs has received scant attention. This question constitutes a major portion of the present chapter. Even after over ten million airbag deployments, it is still not known with confidence whether airbags provide a net decrease or net increase in risk of different severity injuries. However, it is well established that when a crash occurs, airbags reduce fatality risks to belted or unbelted drivers, as summarized in Table 11-4 (p. 286).

Overview of frontal airbags

Before estimating airbag benefits and costs, some overview information on airbags in the US is presented. Because many key quantities are changing, the benefit-cost comparison must be locked to some specific time. July 2003 is selected. In situations in which data are not available for July 2003, projections will be made from available data.

Number of airbags on US roads in July 2003

Data on the growth of airbags in the US vehicle fleet provide the following estimates for July 2003: [2,3]

Driver airbags	139 million.
Passenger airbags	118 million.
Total number of airbags	257 million.

Number of airbag deployments

NHTSA estimates that 520,300 airbags deployed in 1996.[4] In July 1996 there were an estimated 74.6 million airbags on US roads,[2] leading to a deployment rate of 6.97 deployments per 1,000 airbags per year.

Elsewhere NHTSA estimates 3.8 million deployments from the 1980s to 1 October 1999.[5] From the data in Ref. 2, we estimate exposure as 606.9 million airbag-years. This implies 6.26 deployments per 1,000 airbags per year.

Let us take the average of these as the best estimate, leading to an airbag deployment rate of 6.6 deployments per 1,000 airbags per year. Applying this rate to the number of airbags leads to the following estimates for the number of airbag deployments in 2003:

Driver airbag deployments	917,000.
Passenger airbag deployments	778,000.
Total airbag deployments	1,695,000.

Airbag deployment and non-deployment in fatal crashes. Figure 12-1 shows the growth of deployments in fatal crashes as recorded in FARS data. Deployments in fatal crashes are closely proportional to the growth of airbags in the fleet – indeed for the nine years plotted, the probability that a crash was fatal given that the airbag deployed varied only between 1.06% and 1.19%, with an average of 1.12%. For 2002, the latest year plotted, 16,682 of the 1.54 million deployments occurred in fatal crashes. (The estimate for 2003, which we require later, is that about 19,000 of the 1.70 million deployments are expected to occur in fatal crashes).

Similarly stable was the probability of death, given that the airbag deployed in a fatal crash. Over the nine years plotted this probability varied only between

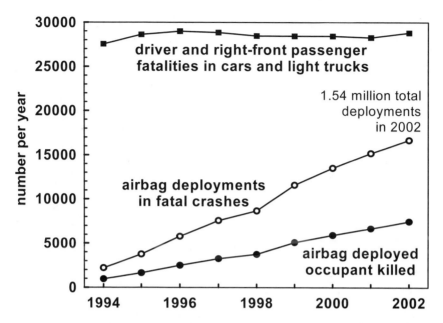

Figure 12-1. Changes concurrent with the rapid growth of airbags in cars and light trucks. The center curve shows airbag deployments in any fatal crash. The bottom graph shows occupants killed in seats at which airbags deployed. The top graph shows the number of occupants killed in all cars and light trucks (with and without airbags). All plotted data from FARS.

42.9% and 44.8%, with an average of 43.6%. The highest value of 44.8% was for the most recent year, 2002, in which 7,467 occupants were killed in 16,682 deployments. An increasing trend in this probability would follow if *second generation* airbags either reduced the number of life-saving deployments because of higher thresholds, or reduced the effectiveness when they did deploy because of the reduced power. Preliminary data indeed suggest lower effectiveness for second generation airbags.[6]

For 2003, about 8,300 occupants are expected to be killed in crashes in which their airbags deploy. The data in Fig. 12-1 include 37,223 occupants killed in seats at which airbags deployed, so by mid 2003 well over 40,000 occupants had died in seats protected by airbags.

The total number of driver and right-front passenger fatalities in cars and light trucks remained relatively unchanged from 1994 through 2002 even as the percent of drivers with airbags increased from 13% to 60% and the percent of passengers with airbags increased from 3% to 50%.[2] This finding alone is sufficient to reject the claim that airbags would prevent 12,100 fatalities, as promised in the documentation used to justify the airbag mandate.[7 (p 34298)]

Deaths caused by deploying airbags. In order to provide protection the airbag must inflate in the short time between the detection of the crash and the occupant beginning to move forward appreciably in response to crash forces. The only way things can happen in a short time is for them to happen quickly. The limited time available makes it necessary for the surface of the airbag to move rapidly towards the occupant, reaching speeds of around 150 mph. The goal is that when the occupant first contacts the airbag it should already be inflated. However, if the occupant is in the space into which the airbag inflates, he or she will be struck at up to 150 mph rather than striking the vehicle interior at a speed that could be as low as 10 mph. The impact from an inflating airbag poses a major risk of death or serious injury. People of any size are at risk if any part of their body is in the space into which an airbag deploys, as might happen if they were reaching to retrieve a dropped object. This risk was understood and named *out of position* since the 1970s.[8] Drivers of short stature sitting at their most comfortable distance from the steering wheel are *out of position*. Concerns about the injuries that inflating airbags might cause children appeared in the technical literature from the 1970s.[8,9]

NHTSA reports that, as of July 2003, there were 231 confirmed deaths caused by airbag deployments in crashes that would otherwise not have been life threatening.[10] Most of those killed were children. However, 77 drivers were killed, 58 of them female,[11] and 28 of these of height 62 inches or less.[10]

Beyond these specifically identified cases, about 40,000 occupants have been killed in crashes in which their airbags deployed. While it is not known how many of these were killed by deploying airbags, it is absurd to think that the number is zero. Some unknown number of occupants (say, N_1) die in crashes that they would have survived if no airbag had been present. The number (say, N_2) who survive because of the airbag is likewise unknown. Effectiveness estimates address only the difference $N_2 - N_1$, but provide no information on the values of either N_1 or N_2. If credence is given to the large numbers of *saved by the airbag* anecdotal claims, then there must be a correspondingly large number of *killed by the airbag* cases to balance most of these, otherwise net effectiveness would be far higher than the values found in large-scale epidemiologic studies (Table 11-4, p. 286. See also p. 327).

Direction of impact. While airbags are designed to deploy only in frontal crashes, deployments in fact occur for impacts in many directions. Fig. 12-2 presents driver fatalities in FARS 2002 for drivers of cars and light trucks according to the principal impact point, the point associated with most harm. The logarithmic scale is used because of the wide variation, from 3,154 driver deaths at 12 o'clock to 36 at 5 o'clock. For all 16,682 airbag deployments in FARS 2002 (driver or passenger, any injury outcome):

> 62% are for principal impact point 12 o'clock.
>
> 70% are for principal impact points 11, 12 or 1 o'clock.
>
> 75% are for principal impact points 10, 11, 12, 1, or 2 o'clock.

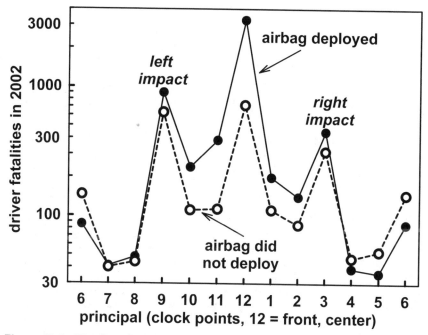

Figure 12-2. The number of driver fatalities in cars and light trucks according to principal impact point. FARS 2002.

Thus, 25% of deployments occur in crashes in which the principal impact is not by any criterion even approximately frontal. These include the side and rear crashes shown in Fig. 12-2 plus a number of categories not shown, including principal impact at top or undercarriage, and non-collisions.

The principal impact and initial impact variables in FARS relate to the region of damage on the vehicle (Fig. 3-16, p. 55). The direction of force is not normally known, as it would require a detailed post-crash investigation to determine it. The data above are not materially different if the initial impact point is used instead of the principal impact point. These variables have identical values for over 90% of the vehicles in FARS 2002.

Fatalities when airbags do not deploy

FARS 2002 codes 4,770 drivers of cars or light trucks killed in seats for which airbags were available and which had principal impact point at 12 o'clock. The FARS coding for these 4,770 fatalities is:

Deployed	3,274 fatalities.
Available, no deployment	719 fatalities.
Available, unknown if deployed	777 fatalities.

Thus the airbag did not deploy for 719/4,770 = 15% of drivers killed in frontal crashes in seats with airbags. This is a lower bound, because unknown deployment cases will include many non-deployments. Over the wider definition of frontal, clock points 10, 11, 12, 1 and 2, there were 6,357 drivers killed, 4,235 with deployments and 1,139 with non-deployments. A central problem for airbag system design is setting deployment thresholds. Lower thresholds lead to more deployments with the potential that the airbag might produce serious or fatal injuries in minor crashes. As the threshold is increased the airbag becomes unavailable for more crashes in which it has the potential to reduce injury severity. Regardless of what threshold is chosen, it is inevitable that there will be crashes that would have had better outcomes if the threshold had been different.

Airbag benefits, airbag costs

Estimating the benefits and costs of airbags involves many factors and much complexity. A 1984 NHTSA benefit-cost analysis,[12] which was reevaluated in 2002,[13] included over 50 inputs. More information could invite yet more complexity making it even more difficult to identify the factors of primary importance. For example, a major cost of airbags is the cost of replacing them after deployment. There is a specific estimated parts replacement cost for vehicles of every make and model year. The labor-cost component for replacement varies throughout the US and between one type of repair business and another. Whether a vehicle is repaired or scrapped depends on these same factors. It is, for example, estimated that nearly all vehicles more than seven years old are scrapped if they are involved in a crash in which their airbag deploys.[14]

The benefit-cost comparison presented here is based on my paper that avoided excessive detail by focusing on average values and ignoring minor factors.[15] For example, based on material in the literature,[14,16] it was assumed that half of the airbags that deploy are replaced, and that the same replacement cost applied to all.

Another reason for avoiding detail is that the values of so many key quantities, particularly the effect of airbags on injury risk, are highly uncertain. It serves little purpose to embark on a detailed calculation requiring a complex chain of assumptions to estimate less central quantities that are determined with adequate precision by simple approximate estimates. In the same spirit, we assume that cost estimates published for 2000 apply to July 2003 without fine-tuning to account for inflation. All monetary values are expressed in dollars without regard to whether they are for 2000 or 2003. This makes it easier to retain a clear connection with the original sources, and the cost values given in Chapter 2.

Benefits and costs expressed in dollars

Airbags are installed for one purpose – injury reduction. (The term *injury* includes *fatal injury* unless the context implies otherwise.) Only monetary costs are included in the quantitative comparison of benefits and costs, although there are additional non-monetary costs that will be discussed later. In comparing benefits and costs it is necessary to use a common metric. This is facilitated by the NHTSA study (discussed in Chapter 2) that finds that traffic crashes cost the US $231 billion in 2000.[17] Table 12-1 shows the injury portion of the total costs listed in Table 2-4 (p. 25). Fatal crashes always involve property damage, and crashes without injuries can incur injury costs in connection with, for example, ambulances driving to the crash site and diagnostic tests confirming no injury. All injury harm is converted to a dollar cost. For example, the lifetime economic cost to society for each fatality is estimated at just under a million dollars, over 80 percent of which is attributable to lost workplace and household productivity. As the original authors present reasoned discussion for the difficult decisions that are necessary for such conversions,[17] their results are accepted as the basis for estimating benefits of airbags.

Table 12-1. Estimates of the injury component of the total economic costs of motor vehicle crashes in 2000.[17]

source	cost, billions of dollars		
	injury component	non-injury	total
fatal	40.1	0.8	40.9
MAIS 5	10.2	0.2	10.4
MAIS 4	12.3	0.4	12.7
MAIS 3	22.5	1.0	23.4
MAIS 2	27.0	2.1	29.1
MAIS 1	27.7	21.5	49.2
MAIS 0	0.4	4.6	5.0
property damage only	5.8 ·	54.0	59.8
total	146.0	84.6	230.6

Injury-risk changes due to airbags

The effectiveness of airbags in reducing fatal injury risk was addressed in Chapter 11. Here we use the average value of 10% for drivers, whether belted or unbelted, given in Table 11-4, p. 286. We assume that driver effectiveness estimates apply also to right-front passenger. The literature indicates lower effectiveness for passengers, but this is one of the many details that are not included in the present calculations.

While fatal injuries conceptually involve only a yes or no determination, non-fatal injuries lie along a severity continuum. Accordingly, effectiveness must relate to some range of injuries, such as is categorized by the Abbreviated Injury Scale (AIS).[18] Effectiveness estimates are sought for specific AIS levels, whereas the cost estimates are given according to MAIS (p. 22). The uncertainty in the effectiveness estimates is sufficiently great that ignoring the distinction between AIS and MAIS will not introduce material additional uncertainty.

Another difference between injuries and fatalities is that no data file comparable to FARS exists for injuries. This makes determining effectiveness for injuries even more difficult than for fatalities. The best estimates rely on the National Automotive Sampling System Crashworthiness Data System, NASS (Chapter 2).

A 2000 study using 1993–1996 NASS data found that airbag deployment reduced driver fatality risk and risk of the most severe injuries (AIS$\geq$4).[19] However, airbag deployment was found to increase the probability that a driver (particularly a woman) sustained AIS 1 to AIS 3 injuries. The results were presented in terms of the delta-v at which airbag deployment produced a net increase or decrease in risk for female and male drivers rather than an effectiveness for different AIS levels. A 2002 study using 1995-2000 NASS data found that front-seat occupants whose air bags deployed had increased risk of AIS>2 injury.[20] These studies were based on cases in which airbags deployed, which may tend to bias effectiveness estimates downward. We therefore rely on the results of a later study[21] using the same 1995-2000 NASS data to compare outcomes for occupants in vehicles with and without airbags. The results of this study for belted and unbelted occupants are presented in the top plot in Fig. 12-3 in the format of Ref. 15. Even after 10 million deployments, estimates of airbag effectiveness for injuries remain highly uncertain.

Benefits of airbags

In order to estimate the benefits of airbags we use the effectiveness values in Table 12-2. For AIS = 5 (or MAIS = 5) or we use the same 10% value found for fatalities (typically, about half of AIS = 5 injuries prove fatal). For AIS = 4 we select a value half that for fatalities – somewhat more than midway between the values for AIS = 3 and AIS = 5. The values for AIS 1 toAIS 3 injuries are from Fig. 12-3, and discussed in more detail in Ref. 15.

To complete the estimates of effectiveness we need to estimate the percent of all road users protected by airbags. Of all 2001 traffic fatalities, 61% were drivers and 15% right-front passengers, percents that remain relatively unchanged from year to year. The previously used data[2,3] estimate 64% of all driver seats and 55% of all passenger seats were protected by airbags in July 2003. Thus the driver airbag is protecting 0.61 × 0.64 = 39% of all road users and the right-front passenger airbag 0.15 × 0.55 = 8% of all road users.

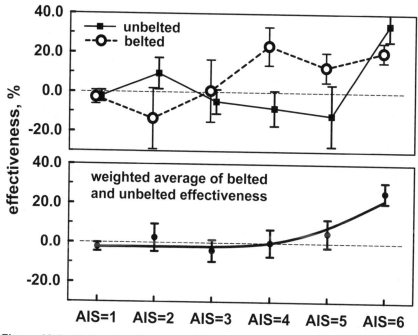

Figure 12-3. Estimates of the effectiveness of airbags in reducing injury risk,[21] as presented in Ref. 15.

Table 12-2. Fatality and injury reducing benefits of airbags for 2003 converted into dollar cost reductions.

injury level	injury-reducing effectiveness (%)	billions of dollars		
		total injury cost	risk-reduction benefits to drivers	passengers
fatal	10	40.1	1.57[a]	0.33[b]
MAIS 5	10	10.2	0.40	0.08
MAIS 4	5	12.3	0.24	0.05
MAIS 3	-2	22.5	-0.18	-0.04
MAIS 2	-2	27.0	-0.21	-0.04
MAIS 1	-2	27.7	-0.22	-0.05
	total	139.8	1.60	0.34

[a] computed as $0.10 \times 40.1 \times 0.61 \times 0.64$

[b] computed as $0.10 \times 40.1 \times 0.15 \times 0.55$

The conclusion is that the benefits of airbags in calendar year 2003 are:

for drivers	$1.60 billion
for right-front passengers	$0.34 billion
total 2003 benefits	$1.94 billion

Airbags reduce the total number of US fatalities by $0.10 \times (39\% + 8\%) = 4.7\%$. The total annual $1.94 billion benefits of airbags reduce the annual $231 billion cost of traffic crashes by about 1%.

Costs of airbags

There are a number of costs of airbags in addition to the original purchase cost of the devices. First we address a major annual cost associated with a fleet of vehicles equipped with airbags.

Cost of replacing airbags after deployment. Airbag systems differ from most safety equipment in that after they do what they are supposed to do, the complete system must be replaced. In 1998 NHTSA published the following estimates of the costs of replacing airbags:

Driver $400 to $550.

Passenger $480 to $1,300 without windshield replacement
            $1,130 to $3,350 with windshield replacement.

There are many changes since these estimates, especially increases in labor costs, and the increase in dual compared to driver-only systems. In July 2003, I telephoned a number of automobile repair businesses in four states to obtain estimates for replacing airbags in the four highest volume cars sold in the US. The responses varied in precision – in some cases to the nearest cent, while in others nothing more precise than "$2,400-$3,000, depending on the vehicle". Based on the responses, I concluded that a typical cost of replacing a dual system was $2,000 without windshield replacement. Estimates for driver-only replacement did not materially differ from half of the cost for the dual system. Therefore, I will assume a replacement cost of $1000 for any driver airbag, and the same amount for replacing a passenger airbag without windshield replacement. I assume that the windshield is replaced for half of passenger airbag replacements at a cost of $400, so that the following values will be used:

replacing driver airbag	$1,000
replacing passenger airbag	$1,200

These estimates are based on information for the four highest selling cars, with selling prices less than the average car (or light truck). Replacement parts generally cost more for more expensive vehicles. Airbag replacement costs for luxury cars can be up to $6,000 for dual systems – so actual average replacement costs are likely to be higher than the assumed values.

We assume that after an airbag deploys either it is replaced, or the vehicle is scrapped. In many cases the additional cost of replacing the airbag will lead to the decision to scrap rather than repair. This additional cost due to the presence of the deployed airbag will be ignored. These assumptions lead to the replacement cost estimates in Table 12-3.

Table 12-3. Estimates of airbag replacement costs for 2003.

seat protected	millions of airbags	number deployed[a]	number replaced[b]	unit cost	total cost
driver	139	917,400	459,000	$1,000	$0.46 billion
passenger	118	778,800	389,000	$1,200	$0.47 billion
totals	257	1,696,200	848,000		$0.93 billion

[a] assuming 6.6 deployments per 1,000 airbags per year
[b] assuming half are replaced

These replacement costs are compared in Table 12-4 to the benefits listed in Table 12-2. For passenger airbags, just one cost, replacement after deployment, exceeds benefits.

Table 12-4. Comparison of benefits and replacement costs of airbags for 2003.

seat protected	benefits	replacement costs
driver	$1.60 billion	$0.46 billion
passenger	$0.34 billion	$0.47 billion
totals	$1.94 billion	$0.93 billion

Cost of installing airbags. We assume the same cost estimates as used in an earlier study,[16] although these were criticized as being too low.[22] These were that the driver-only system cost $278 and the dual system $410. I could find no more specific or current estimates of cost. This amount represents about 2% of the cost of the typical $20,000 vehicle. A breakdown of all costs summing to the purchase cost of the vehicle could be informative. Using the assumed costs (and splitting the dual system cost equally between driver and passenger) leads to the estimates in Table 12-5. Driver airbags cost consumers $30 billion. The total cost to consumers of the airbags on the roads of the US in July 2003 is $54 billion. This exceeds the current Gross Domestic Product of more than half of the member countries of the United Nations (estimated by converting data in Ref. 23 to 2003 dollars).

Table 12-5. Estimates of the purchase cost to consumers of the 257 million airbags on US roads in July 2003.

occupant and system	millions of installations	unit cost	purchase cost to consumers
driver only	21	$278	$5.8 billion
driver (portion of dual system)	118	$205	$24.2 billion
driver total	**139**		**$30.0 billion**
passenger (portion of dual system)	118	$205	$24.2 billion
driver plus passenger total	**257**		**$54.2 billion**

Total costs of airbags. In order to express the total costs of airbags on an annualized basis, it is necessary to amortize the one-time purchase cost over the expected life of the vehicle. There are complex procedures to do this that involve assumptions about discount rates, etc. In keeping with the simpler structure of the present calculation, we assume that the initial purchase cost converts to an annual cost of 10% of the purchase cost over an assumed ten-year life span of the vehicle. This simple procedure provides a lower annual cost than a more detailed computation. We thus assume that the $30 billion spent to purchase the driver airbags on the roads in July 2003 is equivalent to an annual expenditure of $3 billion. Table 12-6 shows the total annual costs of keeping the airbags on the roads in 2003.

Table 12-6. Estimates of the total costs _per year_ for the airbags on the roads of the US in July 2003.

occupant	amortized annual consumer purchase cost	replacement costs	total cost
driver	$3.00 billion	$0.46 billion	$3.46 billion
passenger	$2.42 billion	$0.47 billion	$2.89 billion
totals	$5.42 billion	$0.93 billion	$6.35 billion

Benefit-cost comparison

Table 12-7 compares the annual costs and annual benefits of airbags on the roads in July 2003. The cost of the driver airbag exceeds the benefit by a factor of two. For the passenger airbag, the cost exceeds the benefit by more than a factor of 8.

Table 12-7. Comparison of estimates of annual costs (Table 12-6) to estimates of annual benefits (Table 12-2).

occupant	annual costs	annual benefits
driver	$3.46 billion	$1.60 billion
passenger	$2.89 billion	$0.34 billion
totals	$6.35 billion	$1.94 billion

Comparison with prior estimates. The 1997 study found that airbags were clearly not cost effective for passengers, but might be for drivers.[16] The major difference between that study and the one presented here is that the effectiveness estimates used here were not available then. The earlier study used an effectiveness of 11% for fatalities,[24] the best estimate available at the time, and not materially different from the 10% used here. Given that there were no estimates of effectiveness in injury reduction, the earlier authors made the then plausible assumption that effectiveness for injuries was the same as the 11% value for fatalities. Later research (discussed above) shows that airbag effectiveness in reducing injuries is not nearly so high.

The reason for such instability in benefit versus costs analyses is because effectiveness is so close to zero. Consider the contrast with safety belts. An error of 10 percentage points in the 42% estimated effectiveness would change estimated benefits, but not enough to affect policy materially. However, if an effectiveness close to zero can be determined only to an uncertainty of 10 percentage points, the difference between a +10% effectiveness and a -10% effectiveness has dramatic consequences. An AIS = 1 effectiveness of +8% rather than the -2% used here would have had a massive influence on the calculations, as would an equally likely -12% effectiveness.

Second generation airbags. In response to the many deaths and injuries caused by airbags, new design concepts keep being introduced. After 1998 so called *second generation* airbags appeared, so that some portion of the airbag fleet in 2003 consisted of such airbags. The effectiveness and cost estimates were all based on earlier first generation airbags.

Design changes include setting higher crash thresholds before deployment. This certainly reduces inflation-caused injuries in low severity crashes, and also reduces replacement costs. However, it also reduces the number of cases in which the airbag provides benefits, especially as airbags already do not deploy in over 15% of cases in which occupants are killed in frontal crashes.

Another change was reducing deployment forces – so called *depowering*. Lower power airbags reduce inflation injuries, but also provide less protection. In the limit one can depower an airbag so much that it hurts nobody, but also helps nobody. Depowering very likely reduces the net benefits.

The changes seem all in the direction of making the airbag less effective, thus decreasing its already low benefit to cost ratio. Preliminary data suggest lower fatality-risk reduction from second generation airbags.[6]

Replacement costs of passenger airbags can be reduced by suppressing deployment when no passenger is present. However, even perfect technology that suppressed all passenger airbag deployments when no passenger was present, while at the same time never suppressing deployment when one was present, would still leave the benefit to cost ratio for passenger airbags well below that for driver airbags. This is because passenger airbags inherently prevent fewer injuries because of lower passenger-seat occupancy, yet the passenger and driver airbags have similar purchase costs.

It will be many years before we have even the meager knowledge about effectiveness of second generation airbags that we now have for first generation airbags.

Other airbag costs

William Haddon, a giant in the history of US injury control, discusses the nature of injuries in the broadest terms as the transfer of energy in such ways and amounts and such rapid rates as to harm people.[25]   He lists 10 strategies to reduce risks. The first is to *prevent the marshalling of the form of energy in the first place.*   The airbag constitutes a topsy-turvy violation of this principle, by injecting yet more energy into an event in which energy is the source of harm. It is implausible to expect that 1.7 million annual airbag deployments, each an explosive event, will not cause human harm. The additional explosive energy released to inflate the airbag, in common with most sources of energy, produces its own set of injuries. For example, crashes generate much noise, but nothing approaching that produced by an airbag at the ears of an occupant.

Additional injuries caused by airbags

Beyond inflation-produced blunt trauma injuries, deploying airbags have been associated with many injuries that are unlikely to occur without airbags, including hearing loss,[26,27] eye injuries,[28] and asthmatic attacks.[29,30]   In one case a woman passenger in a vehicle with no passenger airbag suffered ear injuries that had a devastating effect on her quality of life. A driver-side airbag deploying in a low-severity crash caused her injury. She had no crash-related trauma – her only harm was from the airbag.[31]   These injuries are, in principle, included in the injury effectiveness estimates of airbags, but some are of a nature that might be missed in the usual processes of AIS coding.

Drivers sitting in ways they would not choose, or looking rearwards at children in rear seats, are actions likely to increase crash risk. Such actions will not change the effectiveness of airbags, as defined in Chapter 11, which is the risk reduction, given the crash, but they will increase harm by increasing the number of crashes. Behavior changes induced by airbags are discussed in more detail below.

Rescue crews must exercise additional care to protect trapped occupants and themselves against the risk that an undeployed airbag might deploy. NHTSA advises:

> *Although it is rare, an air bag can suddenly deploy during rescue operations, creating a hazardous operating condition, causing further injury, and delaying medical assistance to victims. While every crash poses unique conditions, there are some procedures that will help minimize risks.*[32]

Rescue workers are provided with over 1,500 words of instructions – an additional training cost, and further illustration of the non-passive nature of airbags.

Injuries caused by airbags at center of airbag design dilemmas. Efforts to reduce airbag injuries confront fundamental dilemmas. In order for the airbag to accomplish its primary mission it must deploy from its module at high speed, yet it is this speed that causes harm. Lowering the speed reduces the harm caused, but also the harm it is designed to prevent. Likewise, increasing the threshold crash speed reduces injuries caused, but also injuries prevented. Weight-measuring sensors in seats are under consideration to suppress deployment for at-risk short drivers. These may still allow the airbag to kill short overweight drivers, but suppress deployment for tall slim drivers. Each additional device adds cost, complexity, and requires selecting thresholds. Regardless of what threshold values are chosen, there will be many cases in which a higher value, and many in which a lower value, would have produced a better outcome.

Additional monetary costs

As airbags increase the purchase cost of vehicles, their owners face higher replacement costs if their vehicle is stolen or destroyed (without crashing). If the owner purchases comprehensive insurance, such potential losses translate into higher premiums. The insurance industry was an enthusiastic supporter of airbags, as might be expected because insuring more expensive items commands higher premiums. In pursuit of their support for airbags, the insurance industry promised that airbags would reduce premiums because of substantially reduced injury costs. The high annual cost of replacing deployed airbags overwhelms any such considerations, and must inevitably generate higher net premiums.

Additional disposal costs are associated with scrapping airbag-equipped vehicles because of the explosive nature of airbags. As with any complex system, there is likely to be some maintenance or inspection cost over the life of the vehicle, as acknowledged by NHTSA[4] and prior benefit-cost studies.[16] If permission to disconnect is obtained, then a cost to disconnect (in addition to the original purchase cost) is paid. The consumer is obliged to pay twice to get nothing.

Comfort and convenience

The need to avoid the dangers of deploying airbags has led motorists to do things contrary to their preferences.

Children in rear seats. Placing children in rear seats in situations in which they would otherwise be in front seats inhibits interactions between driver and child that have been traditionally pleasurable and beneficial to both. The child is denied the better view available from the front seat – and may consequently grow up knowing less about driving, with possibly adverse effects on safety. A parent driver with a busy schedule that permits limited time with his or her child is reducing the quality of in-vehicle time if the child is consigned to a rear seat. Absent the airbag, there is no differential safety advantage for a child compared to an adult sitting in a rear seat. Even the most caring individuals would hardly confine their adult companions to rear seats to enhance safety. Passengers travel in front because it is more pleasant, even though it is more dangerous in a crash. One study finds that an adult sitting in a front compared to in a rear seat has a 35% higher risk of being killed,[33] while another study finds the risk higher by 64%.[34] Note how enormous the difference is compared to any risk reductions associated with airbags. No campaigns have been mounted to get adult passengers out of front seats.

Short drivers and sitting comfort. Short individuals who adjust their seats to positions they would not otherwise choose in order to avoid airbag risks suffer a comfort cost. Pedal extenders or other ancillary devices to compensate for being unable to reach controls are sources of additional discomfort and inconvenience, and for multiple drivers, may need to be removed or installed for each change in driver.

Equity and ethics

While airbags are estimated to reduce fatality risk to the total population of front-seat car occupants, they do not provide equal protection for all. They provide negligible benefits for drivers age 70.[24] What raises larger issues is evidence that they increase risk to large identifiable sectors of the population, even beyond the risk increases they pose to children in front seats.

Gender differences. Taking into account injuries at all levels from fatal to minor, the effects of airbags on net harm to belted drivers were estimated as:[35]

> Male   11.6% decrease in net harm.
> Female   9.2% **increase** in net harm.

A major contributor to the difference was that females were substantially more likely to receive AIS ≥ 3 upper-extremity injuries. If one assumes that car driver crash rates for males are twice those for females, the effectiveness for the total population would be $(2 \times 11.6 - 1 \times 9.2)/3 = 4.7\%$. Thus, while the device provides an overall benefit, this benefit arises by reducing risks to males while increasing risks to females. The higher injury risk to females is found consistently in other studies,[19] while fatality studies report inconsistent effectiveness dependence on gender.[24,36]

Of the 77 drivers NHTSA identified as killed by airbags in low severity crashes, 75% were female. That is, for every male killed, three females were killed. For all drivers of cars and light trucks, FARS shows that for every male driver killed, 0.42 female drivers were killed. Thus females are over represented as fatalities caused by airbag inflation by a factor of $3.0/0.42 = 7.1$. Of the female drivers killed, 48% were 62 inches or less (about 20% of females are 62 inches or less). Short females are more than 15 times as likely to be killed by airbags as average drivers. It was unmistakably determined that the airbag was the source of the death because the crashes were of such low severity as to not pose serious injury risk. If these deaths had been caused in an identical manner, but the crashes had been of higher severity, the deaths would have entered FARS in the usual way, and would have been incorrectly attributed to crash trauma. The conclusion is inescapable that many of the fatalities that in fact occur at the lower end of normal fatal crash severities are caused by airbags and not by crash trauma, and that the victims are preferentially short females. The net effectiveness reflects the difference between lives saved, preferentially large males, and lives taken, preferentially small females. Small females are being knowingly killed in order to save large males, a situation that society would hardly tolerate in any context other than airbags.

Airbags fail medical ethical standards. At the core of medical ethics is the admonition, *First, do no harm.* The airbag clearly fails this standard. Airbags on the roads are known to place short females at increased risk, yet there is no high priority effort to deactivate them at public expense. Instead, the US government places hurdles in the way of owners who want to pay legitimate businesses to deactivate these devices that they were forced to buy. I believe it is unprecedented in any democracy for a citizen to have to petition government, and be required to make a convincing case, for permission to remove a device known to increase her risk of harm. Even if the petition is successful, which is not guaranteed, she is required to continue to be exposed to the risk of harm while administrative procedures are completed, and while she finds a business willing to disconnect the airbag.

A medication that kills some patients is likely to be quickly banned. The following three arguments would not be presented to defend it, and if they were, they would be rejected. 1. All the patients taking it are already sick. 2. It saves more patients than it kills. 3. If patients do not want it, they do not have to take it. The airbag exists in a different ethical universe without any convincing reasons why this should be so. It has already killed 231 people, nearly all of them young and healthy. Yet the US government compels the unwilling to purchase it, and keep it in their vehicles.

The airbag has no parallel with vaccinations that are known to cause a few deaths when administered to large populations. The crucial difference is that a vaccination would never be given to any individual if it was known that this would increase the risk of death to that particular individual. Patients are not given drugs if it is known that they will have an allergic reaction to them.

As for *second generation airbags*, we simply do not know. Finding out by compelling citizens to act as unwilling guinea pigs in a large scale experiment is outside the realm of anything that could be contemplated for a new untested drug, or modification to an unsuccessful (or even successful) drug.

Fundamental flaw in estimating benefits of airbags

The term effectiveness is often incorrectly interpreted to represent the change in casualties with and without the device. This is not so, because effectiveness measures the change in risk, <u>given</u> that a crash occurs. If the device affects crash risk, then the change in casualties will differ from the effectiveness. The change in casualties is identical to the effectiveness only under the assumption that the device does not affect driver behavior.

This assumption is demonstrably false for airbags. Airbags generate the clearest overt behavior change of placing children and infants in rear seats. A driver may crash because of distraction from a child in a rear seat. If the driver is injured but not killed, this non-fatality will likely be counted as a fatality prevented in the effectiveness estimates (see also Fig 15-8, p. 399).

Short drivers are advised to sit further from the steering wheel than they would otherwise choose. Sitting in a less comfortable, more tiring, and less natural driving position flies in the face of conventional advice for safe driving. Sitting further from the steering wheel makes it more difficult to steer and to brake, and likely increases total braking reaction time. When short drivers adjust their seats rearwards, their view of the road becomes more restricted. The combined effects of not sitting in the preferred location may increase crash risk.

When it became clear in 1997 that airbags were killing short ladies, a number of short ladies told me "When I discovered that my airbag could kill me, I started to drive more cautiously." If one accepts this statement, it is hard to dispute the corresponding conclusion that a belief that airbags dramatically reduce risk must lead to less cautious driving. For decades the public was exposed to images suggesting that airbags provided near total protection in crashes. Thousands of slow motion deployments were shown on television, conveying an impression that the occupant moved forward towards a gentle caress by a soft cushion. If knowledge of bullets came only through slow motion pictures, one might conclude that all one had to do to avoid being hit was to step leisurely away from the bullet's path when you observed it approaching you. In the bullet and airbag cases, the slow motion pictures conceal the near instantaneous nature, noise, and violence of the event.

If beliefs about airbags led to an undetectable 3% increase in average speed, an initial 100 potentially fatal crashes would increase to 113 (based on the 4th power relationship discussed in Chapter 9). The 10% effectiveness of the airbag would prevent 11 of these, leaving 102 fatalities, an increase of 2 over the original 100. Thus, instead of reducing fatalities by 10%, the airbag would increase fatalities by 2%. In Chapter 11 we addressed the possibility that belt-wearing could lead to behavior changes, and mentioned a test-track experiment suggesting that the same drivers increased speed by about 1% when belted compared to when unbelted.[37] Behavior changes associated with airbags are expected to be larger than those associated with belt-wearing, so a 3% effect is plausible. A 3% increase in speed would reduce the fatality reductions from universal belt wearing from 42% to 35%, an important reduction, but not one that would have crucial policy implications. Because of the lower effectiveness of the airbag, a 3% increase in speed turns a fatality decrease into a fatality increase.

All estimates of lives saved by airbags assume that there are no behavior changes associated with airbags. Logically, such an assumption cannot be exactly true. Empirically, there have been no measured speed increases associated with airbags, and given the difficulties of such measurements, there are unlikely to be. However, the information available makes it very likely that moderately higher risk-taking is associated with the mistaken belief that airbags provide far more protection than they do. Behavior changes smaller than can be observed can cause airbags to increase the number of casualties even though they reduce the risk of injury in a crash. Estimates of lives saved by airbags all assume no behavior changes, and accordingly are more in the nature of logical upper limits rather than best estimates. It seems to me just as likely that airbags have increased fatalities as that they have decreased fatalities.

"Saved by the airbag"

There are innumerable *saved by the airbag* reports. The *evidence* is in many cases simply that there was a severe crash, the airbag deployed, and the occupant survived. There are more than 8,000 cases per year in which there was a severe crash, the airbag deployed, and the occupant died. It is as unreasonable to claim that the dead were *killed by the airbag* as to claim that the survivors were *saved by the airbag*. Given the 10% effectiveness of the airbag in reducing fatality risk, it is only after a detailed post-crash examination that one can conclude whether an airbag prevented or caused a death.

What happens to airbag benefits if belt use increases?

The costs in Table 12-1 were based on what occurred in the US in 2000, a time when about half of fatally injured occupants were unbelted. If the half who were unbelted had been wearing belts, 42% of them would not have died. This is equivalent to a 21% reduction in total driver and front passenger fatalities. If all occupants were belted, then the 9% effectiveness for belted occupants rather than the 10% for all occupants (Table 11-4, p. 286) would apply. The benefit of airbags in reducing driver fatalities would therefore be multiplied by a factor $(1-0.21) \times (9/10) = 0.71$, so the estimated $1.57 billion benefit would decline to $1.12 billion. Additional reductions in benefits at other injury levels are likely to be approximately proportional, suggesting that universal belt use would reduce the benefits of airbags by about 30% of the values estimated.

Safety belts provide far greater benefits than airbags at minimal cost. A very approximate estimate of the benefits of moving from current to universal belt use can be obtained immediately from Table 12-2. Assume that belt effectiveness is 42% for all injury levels, and that half of all those injured were belted. The transition to universal use can be considered numerically equivalent to adding a new device with an effectiveness of 21% to all cars and light trucks. The result is that achieving 100% belt use would provide benefits of $17.9 billion for drivers of cars and light trucks and $4.4 billion for right-front passengers. The total benefit of moving to universal belt use, $22.3 billion, is more than 11 times the $1.9 billion benefit from airbags in 2003.

Studies from Transport Canada estimate that during the eleven-year period 1990-2000, belts prevented 11,690 deaths and airbags 313.[38,39] Over this period benefits were estimated (in Canadian dollars) at $17.5 billion for belts and less than $0.5 billion for airbags.

Other issues

While over $60 billion has been paid for airbags (those on the roads plus those already retired), only minuscule resources have been assigned to better determine the benefits and costs associated with them. Even after 10 million deployments, no reliable estimates of how the device affects different levels of injuries have been published in peer-reviewed literature. No ongoing benefit-cost studies are being performed. The simple analysis presented here was supported entirely out of my own pocket. Spending one hundredth of one percent of the cost of airbags on research evaluating their in-use performance could provide more confident answers to many key questions.

The airbag is not worth anything near what it costs. As belt use increases it becomes worth still less. If wiser safety policy leads to fewer crashes, the airbag becomes worth even less.

Even if airbags did not have innumerable problems, including killing occupants in minor crashes, it is still indefensible public policy to compel consumers to purchase items that provide less benefit than they cost. The present US airbag mandate requiring that vehicles be fitted with airbags should be rescinded. Vehicle manufacturers should be permitted to offer them as options, giving consumers freedom of choice. Government's role should be to generate and disseminate reliable information to help consumers make informed choices.

Summary and conclusions

In July 2003 there were 257 million frontal airbags on the roads of the US. These cost their (in many cases unwilling) purchasers $54 billion. Assuming that the purchase cost is amortized linearly over an assumed 10-year vehicle life-span, this is equivalent to $5.4 billion per year. An additional $0.9 billion per year is spent replacing deployed airbags for a total annual cost of $6.3 billion.

Benefits of airbags were estimated by converting injury reductions to monetary equivalents using a National Highway Traffic Safety Administration report. This produced the following comparison of costs and benefits:

	driver airbag	*passenger airbag*
costs	$3.46 billion	$2.89 billion
benefits	$1.60 billion	$0.34 billion

Costs exceed benefits by more than a factor of two for driver airbags, and by more than a factor of eight for passenger airbags.

Second generation airbags incorporating a series of changes and innovations are not expected to change these conclusions materially. They cause fewer injuries in low severity crashes, but likely provide lower average protection, leading to even lower benefits.

The benefit estimates ignore driver behavior changes stimulated by airbags that likely further reduce already low benefits. As belt wearing increases, the benefits of airbags decline. More effective safety policies leading to fewer crashes further reduce the benefits of airbags.

Airbags have many disadvantages in addition to cost. They have killed over 200 people in low severity crashes and caused other specific airbag injuries, including hearing loss. They introduce inconvenience, inequity in killing some classes of occupants (short females) to protect others (unbelted males), and violate medical ethical standards by forcing unacceptable risks on non-consenting, and often unwilling, subjects.

Even if airbags harmed no one, it is still indefensible public policy to compel consumers to purchase items that cost more than the benefits they provide. The present US airbag mandate that vehicles be fitted with airbags should be rescinded. Vehicle manufacturers should be permitted to offer airbags as options, giving consumers freedom of choice. Government's role should be to generate and disseminate reliable information to help consumers make informed choices.

References for Chapter 12

1 Kent RW, editor. *Air Bag Development and Performance – New Perspectives from Industry, Government, and Academia.* SAE Special Publication PT-88. Warrendale, PA: Society of Automotive Engineers; March 2003.

2 Ferguson SA. An update on the real-world experience of passenger airbags in the United States. Airbag 2000+. Fourth International Symposium and Exhibition on Sophisticated Car Occupant Safety Systems, 30 November - 2 December, 1998. Karlsruhe, Germany: Fraunhofer-Institut Fur Chemische Technologie (ICT); 1998.

3 Highway Loss Data Institute. Unpublished data. Estimated number and percent of vehicles in fleet with airbags. Arlington, VA; August 2003.

4 National Highway Traffic Safety Administration.   FMVSS No. 208, Advanced air bags, preliminary economic assessment, Chapter VI, *Technology, Costs, and Leadtime*. Washington, DC: Office of Regulatory Analysis & Evaluation, Plans and Policy; August 1998. http://www.nhtsa.dot.gov/airbag/PrelimEconAssess/chpt06.html

5 National Highway Traffic Safety Administration. *Safety Fact Sheet*, 11/02/99. http://www.nhtsa.gov/airbags/factsheets/numbers.html

6 Augenstein JS, Digges KH.   Using CIREN data to assess the performance of the second generation of air bags. SAE paper 2004-01-0842. Warrendale, PA: Society of Automotive Engineers; 2004. (Also included in: *Air Bags and Belt Restraints*. SAE special publication SP-1876; 2004).

7 Federal Register, Vol. 42, No 128, Part 571 – Federal Motor Vehicle Standards: Occupant protection systems, Docket No. 75-14, Notice 10, p. 34289-34305; 5 July 1977.

8 Patrick LM, Nyquist GW.   Airbag effects on the out-of-position child.   SAE paper 720442. Warrendale, PA: Society of Automotive Engineers; 1972.

9 Aldman B, Anderson A, Saxmark O. Possible effects of air bag inflation on a standing child. Proceedings of the 18th Annual Conference of the American Association for Automotive Medicine, Toronto, Canada; 12-14 September 1974.

10 Counts for air bag related fatalities and seriously injured persons. http://www-nrd.nhtsa.dot.gov/pdf/nrd-30/NCSA/SCI/2Q_2003/HTML/QtrRpt/ABFSISR.htm

11 Cases from National Center for Statistics and Analysis Special Crash Investigation Program. Drivers who sustained fatal or serious injuries in minor or moderate severity air bag deployment crashes. http://www-nrd.nhtsa.dot.gov/pdf/nrd-30/ NCSA/SCI/2Q_2003/HTML/SummTab/AdultD.htm

12 National Highway Traffic Safety Administration. Final regulatory impact analysis, Amendment of FMVSS 208, passenger car front seat occupant protection. Washington, DC; 11 July 1984.

13 Thompson KM, Segui-Gomez M, Weinstein MC, Graham JD. Validating benefit and cost estimates: The case of airbag regulation. *Risk Analysis*. 2002; 22: 803-811.

14 Werner J, Sorenson W. Survey of air bag involved accidents: An analysis of collision characteristics, system effectiveness and injuries. SAE Paper 940802. Warrendale, PA: Society of Automotive Engineers; 1994.

15 Evans L. Airbag benefits, airbag costs. SAE paper 2004-01-0840. Warrendale, PA: Society of Automotive Engineers; 2004. (Also included in *Air Bags and Belt Restraints*. SAE special publication SP-1876, 2004).

16 Graham JD, Thompson KM, Goldie SJ, Segui-Gomez M, Weinstein MC. The cost-effectiveness of airbags by seating position. *J Am Medical Assoc*. 1997; 278: 1418–1425.

17 Blincoe LJ, Seay AG, Zaloshnja E, Miller TR, Romano EO, Luchter S, Spicer RS. The economic impact of motor vehicle crashes, 2000.   Report DOT HS 809 446. Washington, DC: US Department of Transportation, National Highway Traffic Safety Administration,; May 2002. http://www.nhtsa.dot.gov/people/economic/EconImpact2000/

18 Association for the Advancement of Automotive Medicine.   The abbreviated injury scale. AAAM; 1990.

19 Segui-Gomez M. Driver air bag effectiveness by severity of the crash. *Am J Pub Health*. 2000; 90: 1575–1581.

20 McGwin G Jr, Metzger J, Jorge E, Alonso JE, Rue LW III. The association between occupant restraint systems and risk of injury in frontal motor vehicle collisions. *J Trauma.* 2003; 54: 1182–1187.

21 McGwin G Jr. Airbags and the risk of injury in frontal motor vehicle crashes. 2003. Submitted for publication.

22 Larkin GL, Weber JE. Cost effectiveness of air bags in motor vehicles (letter). *J Am Medical Assoc.* 1998; 279: 506.

23 United Nations, Department of Economic and Social Affairs, Statistics Division. GDP of 167 countries in current international dollars. http://unstats.un.org/unsd/cdbdemo/cdb_years_on_top.asp?srID=29923&crID=&yrID=1990

24 Kahane CJ. Fatality reduction by air bags: Analysis of accident data through early 1996. Report DOT HS 808 470. Washington, DC: National Highway Traffic Safety Administration; 1996.

25 Haddon W Jr. On the escape of tigers: An ecologic note. *Am J Public Health.* 1970; 60: 2229-2234. http://www.siu.edu/~ritzel/courses/313s/tiger/tigerarticle.htm

26 Yaremchuk K, Dobie R. The otologic effects of airbag deployment. *J Occupational Hearing Loss.* 1999; 2: 67-73.

27 Buckley G, Setchfield N, Framption R. Two case reports of possible noise trauma after inflation of air bags in low speed car crashes. *Brit Med J.* 1999;318, 499-500.

28 Duma SM, Kress TA, Porta DJ, Woods CD, Snider JN, Fuller PM, Simmons RJ. Air bag induced eye injuries: A report of 25 cases. *J Trauma.* 1996; 41: 114-119.

29 Gross KB, Kelly NA, Reddy S, Shah NJ, Grain TAK. Assessment of human responses to non-azide air bag effluents. Proceedings of the 43rd Stapp Car Crash Conference, SAE paper 99SC26. Warrendale, PA: Society of Automotive Engineers; 1999.

30 Gross KB, Haidar AH, Basha MA, Chan TL, Gwizdala CJ, Wooley RG, Popovich J. Acute pulmonary response of asthmatics to aerosols and gases generated by airbag deployment. *Am J Respir Crit Care Med.* 1994; 150: 408-414.

31 Saving lives, wrecking ears. U.S. News and World Report; 26April 1999, p.72.

32 National Highway Traffic Safety Administration. Rescue procedures for airbag-equipped vehicles. *Campaign Safe & Sober.* http://www.nhtsa.dot.gov/people/outreach/safesobr/16qp/procedures.html

33 Evans L, Frick MC. Seating position in cars and fatality risk. *Am J Pub Health.* 1988: 78; 1456-1458.

34 Smith KM, Cummings P. Passenger seating position and the risk of passenger death or injury in traffic crashes. *Accid Anal Prev.* 2004; 36: 257–260.

35 Dalmotas DJ, Hurley J, German A, Digges K. Air bag deployment crashes in Canada. Paper 96-S1O-05. 15th Enhanced Safety of Vehicles Conference, Melbourne, Australia; 13-17 May 1996.

36 Cummings P, McKnight B, Rivara FP, Grossman DC. Association of driver air bags with driver fatality: A matched cohort study. *Brit Med J.* 2002; 324: 1119–1122.

37 Janssen W. Seat-belt wearing and driver behavior: An instrumented-vehicle study. *Accid Anal Prev.* 1994; 26: 249-261.

38 Transport Canada. Estimates and lives saved among front seat occupants of light-duty vehicles involved in collisions attributable to the use of seat belts and air bags in Canada. Road Safety and Motor Vehicle Regulation, Fact Sheet RS 2001-03 E TP13187E; October 2001. http://www.tc.gc.ca/roadsafety/menu.htm

39 Stewart DE, Arora HR, Dalmotas D. An evaluation of the effectiveness of supplementary restraint systems ("air bags") and conventional seat belts: Estimates of the numbers of lives saved among front seat outboard occupants of light-duty vehicles involved in collisions attributable to the use of seat belts and the fitment of supplementary restraint systems ("air bags") in Canada, 1990-1997. Transport Canada Publication No. TP13187 E. Ottawa, Ontario; 1998.

13 Measures to improve traffic safety

Introduction

For over a century measures have been introduced in many countries aimed at reducing harm from traffic crashes. There is extensive world experience, many failures, and many successes. Some of these measures (or interventions, or countermeasures) have been discussed in detail in earlier chapters. In this chapter we address the relative contributions of different countermeasures.

Analogy with health

Traffic fatalities have sometimes been discussed as being comparable to some single disease. I consider such an analogy unhelpful because it tends to suggest that the problem might be solved by the type of elegant knockout blow that conquered smallpox or scurvy. Any such hope tends to divert attention and resources from potentially effective realistic approaches to unrealistic approaches. A more appropriate and fruitful analogy is to health in general, with traffic safety and public health having the same broad goal of reducing death and morbidity. One of the simplest measures of overall health in a nation is average longevity, which has been increasing in nearly all industrialized countries. Longevity is strongly related to national wealth, measured by variables such as gross domestic product per capita. However, people in richer countries live longer for reasons that are more complex than the mere ability to purchase better medical care, important though this is.[1] A country's traffic fatality rate (deaths per vehicle) is also strongly related to its wealth. However, some countries with similar wealth have important differences in longevity, and in traffic fatality rates. Those with the greatest longevity tend also to have the safest traffic.[2]

It is universally accepted that many factors have made major contributions to increasing longevity. Some are technological in nature – surgery, antibiotics, vaccines, organ transplants, and the like. Some involve improved physical and institutional infrastructure such as better housing, sewage, ambulance service, and refrigeration. Some are legislative, such as laws regulating food and air quality, building inspection, and worker safety. Some come from changes in collective human behavior in hygiene, diet, exercise, sexual behavior, and use of alcohol and tobacco. Traffic fatality rate declines reflect contributions from these same broad categories – technology, infrastructure, legislation, and behavior change.

Traffic fatality rates vary widely in time and between countries

Large changes in longevity in time and between countries have close parallels in traffic fatalities. Data in Fig. 3-5 (p. 40) showed that the number of traffic fatalities for the same distance of travel in the US declined by 94% from 1921 to 2002, and the number of traffic fatalities per thousand vehicles declined by 96% from 1900 to 2002. In both cases the comparison is between the earliest and latest data, and the declines were reasonably constant at about 3% per year over each entire period. The number of traffic fatalities per thousand vehicles in some countries is 99% lower than in others during the same year. Understanding the origins of such large variations in time, and between countries, would be a step towards identifying the factors that contribute most to traffic safety. I believe the degree of complexity inherently precludes quantitative analytical models that would effectively explain the factors that produce changes in traffic fatality rates or longevity. Models based on such techniques as multivariate analyses are often inadequate at addressing vastly simpler problems (p. 116). As progress using quantitative analytical methods seems unlikely, we instead combine and synthesize information developed in earlier chapters.

Factors influencing traffic safety

The large number of factors relevant to traffic safety can be conveniently placed into the broad categories shown in Fig. 13-1. Weather is not part of the main structure because there is not much that can be done to change it, and, unlike the other factors, it remains relatively constant over the decades. Improved medicine plays an important role in reducing harm from traffic crashes in all categories, but its more detailed role is outside the scope of this book. If a patient arrives alive at a modern trauma center, survival chances are high. One of the two occupants killed in the 1899 crash described on pages 36-37 would almost certainly have survived similar injuries today. However, FARS 2002 data show that 55% of those killed in traffic crashes died within an hour of their crashes. Recall that a typical fatality involves a single-vehicle crash at 2:00 am in a rural area, so that elapsed time from crash to arrival at a hospital is quite different than for daytime urban crashes.

The dominant role of driver behavior

The variation by a factor of more than a hundred in traffic fatalities per thousand vehicles between different countries (Table 3-1, Fig. 3-8, p. 43-44) cannot be due primarily to differences in vehicle engineering. While the mix of vehicles is certainly different in different countries, the vehicles in the high-rate (high values of fatalities per thousand vehicles) countries are essentially the same as in the low-rate countries, because the high-rate countries rarely manufacture vehicles, but instead import them from low-rate countries. In the high-rate countries the vehicles are older, but this is of little consequence

---

Factors influencing traffic safety

■ **engineering**
- ● **roadway and traffic engineering**
- ● **automotive engineering**

■ **road user**
- ● **driver behavior**
- ● **driver performance**

Figure 13-1. One way to characterize the main factors central to traffic safety. Weather and medicine are not included in the schematic.

because many analyses of data from low-rate countries find no large relationships between fatality rates and vehicle age. More recent vehicles may have stricter safety standards, but these could make no more than a modest difference, whereas the lowest rates are more than 99% below the highest rates. Roads, congestion, and other factors are also clearly different in the different countries. But these differences cannot come close to explaining the large variations observed. The only plausible explanation is that drivers are behaving sufficiently differently in the high-rate countries to generate a major portion of the observed difference.

The top photograph in Fig. 13-2 shows traffic in Cairo, Egypt, and the bottom photograph traffic in Adelaide, Australia. Table 3-1 (p. 43) provides the following values:

Australia	0.143	fatalities per thousand vehicles.
USA	0.190	fatalities per thousand vehicles.
Egypt	1.875	fatalities per thousand vehicles.

The Australian rate is 92% lower than the Egyptian rate. The vehicles in the upper photograph are somewhat different from those in the lower photograph, but not in any way that can explain much of the 92% difference. The Australian rate is 25% lower than the US rate. These differences in rates are consistent with observations of traffic in the three countries, which, while difficult to quantify, are nonetheless clear. I observed typical driving in Australia to be at somewhat lower risk than in the US, while driving in Egypt is at considerably higher risk than that in Australia or the US. The risk taking has many easily observable features, including less disciplined and less orderly traffic, as is clear in the photographs, and many more incidents of individual risk taking by drivers and pedestrians. The variations in rates among the countries in Table 3-1 and Fig. 3-8 (p. 44) fit a similar pattern. Low rates correspond to orderly, calm, and disciplined traffic, high rates to more disorganized competitive traffic.

Figure 13-2.   Top: Cairo, Egypt, September 2002.
Bottom: Adelaide, Australia, November 2002.

It has been suggested that the downward trend in fatality rates observed in all countries is due to road users learning safer behavior by observing traffic. The evidence that so many countermeasures do change safety is sufficient to refute the extreme claim that all that is occurring is spontaneous learning. However, it is essentially impossible to determine what would have occurred if there had been no interventions, as all societies have taken measures to improve safety. There is very likely a spontaneous learning effect, and if so, it is an example of a safety improvement due to a behavior change.

Some of the fatality rate decreases associated with behavior changes reported in earlier chapters are listed in Table 13-1. The magnitudes of these effects far exceed the types of risk reductions that are associated with other safety measures, justifying the conclusion that how drivers behave is overwhelmingly the most important factor determining overall safety.

Table 13-1. Risk reductions from changes in driver behavior.

behavior change	risk reduction	measure
drive 5 km/h slower on urban road (p. 209)	50%	crashes
drive 10 km/h slower than traffic on rural road (p. 211)	55%	crashes
decrease rural Interstate speed from 63.4 to 57.6 mph (p. 213)	34%	fatalities
drive at zero BAC compared to at 0.13% BAC (p. 247)	90%	crashes
not use a cell phone compared to using one (p. 196)	77%	crashes
wear a safety belt compared to not wearing one (p. 281)	42%	fatalities

Other factors

Driver performance, while much less important than driver behavior, still has many important impacts on traffic safety. The main reason why various crash rates increase as drivers age is because of deteriorating driver performance. One of the reasons why younger drivers have highly elevated crash risks is performance inadequacies due to inexperience.

The importance of roadway engineering is apparent in Table 5-5 (p. 103). For example, replacing a rural arterial road by an Interstate reduces fatality risk by 45%. This is much larger than the approximately 20% reduction estimated for the combined effect of all the FMVSS standards examined (p. 115), and larger still than the 10% reduction from frontal airbags (p. 286). The vehicle factor that produces a large change in risk is vehicle mass. However, this is more in the realm of a consumer choice than a vehicle factor, as such. The choice between a motorcycle and a large sedan is not generally considered a vehicle factor, although it is associated with a risk difference approaching a factor of 100. In the context of countermeasures, the term *vehicle factors* generally implies modifications and safety equipment for what is otherwise an equivalent vehicle.

Studies to identify factor contributions directly

In the 1970s two major studies, one in the US and one in GB, were performed to identify factors associated with crashes. Both studies were based on many thousands of crashes. The US study was performed by Indiana University, and is often referred to as the *Tri-level study* because crashes were examined in one of three levels of depth, depending mainly on their severity.[3] The British study was performed by the Transport and Road Research Laboratory.[4,5] In both studies a team of multi-disciplinary experts conducted a detailed post-crash examination of crashes satisfying specified selection criteria. The crash site was examined for physical evidence, the vehicles involved were examined by an engineer, and the participants in the crash were interviewed in depth. Based on such information, factors contributing to the crash were identified.

The results of both studies are summarized in Fig. 13-3. The interpretation is that, for example, in the US study, the vehicle is identified as the sole factor in 2% of crashes, the interaction between vehicle and road user in 6% of the crashes, the interaction between vehicle, road user, and road (including environmental factors such as weather or darkness) in 3% of crashes, and the interaction between vehicle and road in 1%; the corresponding values for the British study are 2%, 4%, 1%, and 1%. In most cases the vehicle factor was worn tires or brakes, so that it was really due to improper maintenance, a behavior factor.

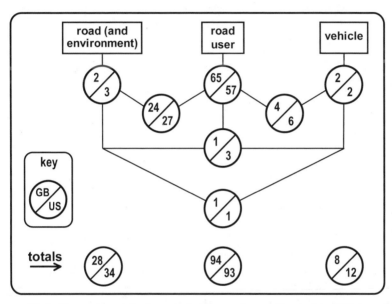

Figure 13-3 Percent contributions to traffic crashes estimated in British and US in-depth studies. Based on Ref. 6.

The studies were performed independently – indeed it appears that neither study group was aware of the activities of the other. The results are remarkably consistent. Each finds that the non-road-user factors of vehicle and road are rarely the sole factors associated with crashes – the British study finding 6% of crashes not linked to the road user, and the US study 7%. In both studies, when only one factor was identified, it was overwhelmingly the road user (65% in the British study, 57% in the US study). Road user factors were found to be the sole or contributory factors in 94% of crashes in the British study, and 93% in the US study.

A smaller scale study using exclusively urban injury crashes found that vehicle factors played an even smaller role of about 1%.[7] A study examining crashes in China attributes the following factors – human factors, 92.9%; motor vehicle, 4.5%; road 0.1%; and other 2.5%.[8] In China about 70% of crashes involve bicycles, but only about 1% involve alcohol.[9]

Studies such as the above should be interpreted with caution because identifying the mix of factors is not the same as identifying the most effective mix of countermeasures. An effective analogy points out that finding that mailed items are damaged by the human factor of careless handling does not mean improved handling is the most effective countermeasure. Better packaging is far more effective.[10] Similarly, the finding that human factors are overwhelmingly involved in traffic crashes does not logically imply that countermeasures should focus primarily on human factors. However, decades of research have shown that, unlike the packaging analogy, only modest additional improvements in acceptable packaging of humans in vehicles are now feasible. The most expensive and intrusive packaging intervention, the airbag, reduces driver fatality risk by 10%, a reduction not competitive with those listed in Table 13-1. It is changes in driver behavior that have the potential to make, by far, the largest improvements in traffic safety.

The dominant role of driver behavior

Figure 13-4 shows the relative importance of factors schematically. The figure is a non-quantitative judgmental estimate in which the areas indicate the importance I attach to the different factors. Given the enormity of the losses from traffic crashes, all factors are of immense importance, but some are more important than others. Road user (or human) factors are more important than engineering factors. Among engineering factors, the roadway produces larger changes in risk than are associated with engineering changes to given vehicles. The human factor that plays the largest role is driver behavior, and changes in driver behavior are the key to changes in traffic safety. Behavior-change theories may offer guidance that could contribute to harm reduction.[11]

In 1949 the comment *a man drives as he lives* entered the traffic safety literature (p. 220). The things that affect driving behavior are almost as diverse as those that affect life in general; they include family, personality, the era in which one lives, socio-economic status, religion, beliefs, traditions, etc. Below we address four areas of influence on driver behavior:

- Fear of adverse consequences.
- Social norms.
- Mass media.
- Legislative interventions.

These all interact with each other. What people fear is highly influenced by what their peers fear, and by what concerns the mass media stress, and so on.

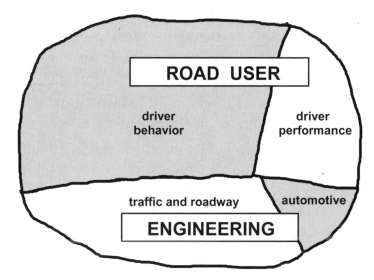

Figure 13-4. Sketch of non-quantitative judgmental estimates of relative importance of different factors.

Fear of adverse consequences

The most severe punishment for risky driving is not one issued by a court of law. It is a swiftly administered death penalty. While drivers are well aware that many people are killed in traffic, concern about joining their ranks is not normally present while driving. A subjective sense of control leads to a feeling that *it cannot happen to me.* Even if the occupant of a vehicle has no control over how it is driven, familiarity with road travel still generates a level of comfort higher than for far safer activities. Fear of terrorism and crime keeps many people from visiting certain cities and countries, yet the same people are happy to travel in a bus, taxi, or car driven by someone else, all far riskier activities. While driving is riskier than almost anything else a typical member of a motorized society is likely to do, there are reasons why it does not appear so to individual drivers.

The frequency of occurrence of a number of adverse events to drivers is listed in Table 13-2. More than 26,000 drivers were killed in the US in 2002. In the same year, US vehicles traveled over 4 billion km. Thus, on average, a driver is killed for every 172 million km of driving. A driver traveling 25,000 km per year would take 7,000 years to accumulate this total. From the perspective of the individual driver, a fatality can appear to be an event too improbable and remote to cause concern. This impression is further reinforced by driving day after day without any adverse consequences. The impression of safety does not appear to vary between countries with risks differing by a factor of more than one hundred. However, a passenger from a

Table 13-2. Approximate average frequencies with which various adverse consequences occur in the US, expressed relative to an individual driver.

event	number per year	average travel between events[a]	average time between events[b]
driver killed	26,549[c]	172 million km	7,300 years
driver involved in fatal crash	57,803 [c]	79 million km	3,400 years
MAIS 3 driver injury	78,000[d]	58 million km	2,500 years
MAIS 1 driver injury	3 million[d]	1.5 million km	65 years
involved in crash	16 million[e]	0.3 million km	12 years

[a] based on 4,554 billion km total travel by all vehicles in 2002 (p. 103).

[b] based on average annual travel distance of 23,400 km per driver per year (4,554 billion km traveled by 194,300,000 drivers).[1]

[c] 2002 FARS.

[d] values in Table 2-3 (p. 24) times the fraction (= 0.62) of all who are drivers.

[e] value on p. 12.

low-risk country does feel at risk in a taxi in a high-risk country, even though the driver does not.

Even when an adverse event does occur, it is rarely interpreted to be a natural consequence of normal driving behavior. Interpretations involving unpreventable bad luck are more prevalent. Notwithstanding the individual driver's perception of no risk, a by-product of current US average driving is over 40,000 traffic fatalities per year. In a paradoxical sense, individuals may not perceive there is a problem, although there clearly is.

While the rarity of the events in Table 13-2 may convey a personal sense of low risk, vastly rarer events, such as falling aircraft, shark attacks, tornadoes, and lightning cause greater concern.[12] This is in part due to a *media paradox*.[13] It is only rare events that make lots of news, and the more we hear about something, the more it enters our consciousness. Most people in the US know about an incident at the nuclear power plant at Three Mile Island in 1979.[14] No death has ever resulted from a mishap in a US nuclear power plant, yet since 1979 over a million people have died on US roads. It seems possible that if nuclear power had killed a few thousand people (like the production and delivery of conventional power has done) it would be feared less.

In traffic, non-fatal adverse events of course do influence behavior. After a major scare in traffic, drivers tend to slow down, but the effect is of short duration. More serious harm is likely to have a larger influence. As Shakespeare notes "The injuries that they themselves procure must be their schoolmasters." (*King Lear*: Act 2, Scene 4). Direct evidence of behavior change as a result of being injured is provided by interviews of former patients who had been treated in a trauma center for motor vehicle injuries. Self-reported belt wearing rates were 85% after their crashes, compared to 54% before.[15]   While some learning occurs in response to adverse outcomes, experiencing traffic crashes is an unsatisfactory way to learn how to avoid them.

Social norms

Individual behavior is enormously influenced by the behavior of the members of the society in which the individual is embedded. People are particularly inclined to behave in ways that they believe will win approval of those whose approval they value. In the case of teenagers such peer pressure is particularly strong.

Autonomous behavior, or habits. As a society becomes more motorized, institutional changes are initiated in response to increasing casualties, which in turn influence social norms relating to driving. Adherence to many traffic safety measures eventually evolves into habit, or autonomous behavior, without any conscious safety consideration.   Stopping at red lights is so ingrained that drivers rarely proceed after stopping at a red light until it turns green, even in the absence of crash risk, traffic, or police. There is a strong social norm against proceeding through a red light after stopping at it, even in conditions in which it would be no more dangerous to do so than proceeding after stopping at a stop sign. In Sweden and Switzerland pedestrians rarely cross roads against traffic signals, whereas in the US, Canada, and the UK they tend to cross when they judge it safe to do so without regard to traffic law or control devices.   In motorized countries even the most impatient risky drivers rarely consider driving on the sidewalk to save a few seconds, although the practice is quite common in many less motorized countries, though illegal.   In motorized countries driving even for short distances on the wrong side of the road attracts negative attention even if it poses little risk. When a social norm violation is unambiguous, condemnation is assured, and the practice tends to become rare.

However, the main behaviors that pose major risks involve continuous variables. Most motorists have on some occasions gone through traffic signals later than is prudent or legal, and have moderately exceeded speed limits. This clouds the intensity and clarity of their disapproval of other drivers who commit traffic light and speeding offenses that pose vastly greater risks than their own less frequent, less egregious violations.

Original motivations for improved personal hygiene were partially rooted in disease prevention. Such motivation rarely plays a role today. Rather, we find it difficult to conceive that prior highly civilized societies, such as Elizabethan England, did not share our fastidiousness. The cultivation of safe driving as habit seems a more productive approach than expecting drivers to be motivated by fear of consequences. A society that can evolve a social norm in which it is as unacceptable to speed or run red lights as it now is to proceed when facing a red light or drive on the sidewalk will enjoy an enormous safety improvement. There are precedents for large changes in social norms relating to safety behavior that would have seemed improbable before they actually occurred.

Changes in social norms relating to smoking. One of the most dramatic changes in social norms is in relation to smoking, an activity that caused more than 20 million Americans to die prematurely in the twentieth century.[16] From 1950 to 2000, the US adult smoking rate dropped from 44% to 23%.[17] Changes relating to smoking are obvious and dramatic. In the 1960s, when smoking in hospitals and doctors' offices (often by the doctor!) was common, few could have imagined a world in which smoking would be prohibited on airliners, and in airports, public buildings, restaurants, and even bars. No single event caused these changes – they were gradual and due to the cumulative effects from many inputs. The various Surgeon Generals' reports stressing the link between smoking and a host of illnesses stimulated increased discussion about the nature and origins of the habit, and its path to addiction. Health warnings on packages and the growth of smoking-cessation businesses and products resulted in reduced smoking. Various US commercial companies prohibited smoking in offices and cafeterias at a time when smoking was still allowed in the offices of the Environmental Protection Agency, an agency of the US Federal Government. Northwest Airlines prohibited smoking on all its North American flights long before any government-owned airline had adopted such a policy.

Speeding compared to drunk driving. While the social norm relating to drunk driving has changed, contributing to major reductions in drunk driving, the same cannot be said about harmful driving in general. Table 10-5 (p. 252) shows that 78% of traffic crash harm involves no alcohol. 87% of drivers in FARS 2002 do not have measured BAC > 0.08%. Even if all driving after consuming alcohol were eliminated, 62% of those killed in traffic would still be killed (Table 10-4, p. 251).

One of the largest reductions in traffic harm in the US can be attributed to Mothers Against Drunk Driving (MADD), which became influential under the leadership of a mother whose child, while walking, was killed by a drunk driver (p. 257). In the US, 367 child pedestrians (14 years or younger) were killed in 2002 in single-vehicle crashes. 28% of the involved drivers were administered alcohol tests, and of these, 81% had no detectable alcohol (measured BAC = 0). Recall that being intoxicated increases the risk of being tested, so the untested majority likely had lower BAC levels than the tested minority. It therefore is likely that well over 90% of the child pedestrians killed were killed in crashes with vehicles driven by sober drivers.

The behaviors associated with most of the harm in traffic do not attract the moral opprobrium focused on drunk driving. Driving 65 mph when the speed limit is 55 mph increases the risk of involvement in a fatal crash by a factor of two, similar to driving with BAC = 0.08% compared to driving at BAC = 0.

A prominent US politician (former Congressman and former Governor of South Dakota) boasted about his lead-foot driving, and received 12 speeding tickets from 1990 to 1994. In 2003, while speeding through a stop sign, he killed a motorcyclist, for which he received a 100-day sentence.[18] In the post-

MADD era nobody in US public life could have boasted about driving while drunk, nor retained a driving license after a long series of drunk driving convictions. If the social norm and legislative response to speeding had been more like that to drunk driving, the motorcyclist would not have died and the politician would not have had his own life devastated by the crash.

An activist movement to focus grief and anger on risk-taking sober drivers who harm others, especially children, has the potential to produce safety benefits like those produced by MADD.

Road rage. The claim that wildly aggressive driving has become more prevalent, as suggested by the term *road rage*, is not supported by any evidence.[19] Certainly, many drivers behave badly today, but so did many in the past. There are no reliable data on non-crash aggression in traffic. However, the downward trends in fatality rates are more consistent with the notion that, while risks are presently high in traffic, they were much higher in the past.

Education and persuasion. The normal role of education is to impart knowledge. As lack of knowledge is not at the core of traffic crashes, safety benefits from education are necessarily limited. This conclusion has tended to foster the incorrect notion that persuasion is similarly ineffective. One problem is that the word *persuasion* has negative connotations, so it is often instead called *education* (which is known to be relatively ineffective). At the other extreme, calling it *propaganda* would assure its instant dismissal. Efforts to persuade still generally include specific items of information. For example, attempts to persuade drivers to fasten safety belts should appropriately mention that belts reduce risk, and that wearing is required by law, even though these facts are already well known by nearly all of the intended audience of non-wearers.

The advertising industry is successful at persuading people to do all sorts of things that they would not otherwise do, yet it is often difficult to show specific behavior changes resulting from advertising campaigns. The assertion that driving cannot be changed by the same methods known to change other behaviors is unsupportable. The potentially large, but uncertain, gains from persuading drivers to behave differently seem a better investment than expensive minor vehicle engineering changes that do not produce benefits even large enough to be measured in field data.

Mass media

Of all the many factors that contributed to declines in smoking, the largest contribution was likely from prohibiting cigarette advertising on television (in 1965 in the UK, 1971 in the US). Once television advertising was banned, smoking largely disappeared from made-for-television programming. The situation was different in movies, where tobacco companies pay large placement fees to have their brands incorporated directly into the movie plot, resulting in smoking appearing in 2002 movies about as often as in 1950 movies, even though smoking was twice as prevalent in 1950.[17]

Changes by the media in response to legislation and business considerations, together with voluntary restraints, contributed to reductions in deaths from two major causes – smoking and drunk driving. No corresponding changes have occurred relative to the driving behaviors that are responsible for the majority of traffic deaths. As noted above, even if drunk driving were completely eliminated, most traffic deaths would still occur. Yet the media continue to portray positively the use of vehicles in ways that are known to cause harm. Vehicle manufacturers often advertise their products in ways that glorify irresponsible driving. Movies and television programs, especially those aimed at young people, often contain scenes depicting unrealistic occupant kinematics under crash conditions. For example, an unbelted driver, often the hero, may crash into a solid object at 60 km/h, jump out, and, uninjured and undaunted, pursue the chase by other means. In such fiction, car crashes are even presented as humorous events. The possibility that they can destroy lives is generally ignored.

There is unmistakable evidence that the massive portrayal of casual violence on television and movies leads to increased violent behavior.[20] It is hard to imagine how the massive portrayal of the irresponsible use of vehicles in programs and advertisements would not lead to increased driver risk taking. The claim by media executives that what viewers observe does not affect their behavior is absurd. Commercial television receives all of its revenues from clients who pay billions of dollars in the confident belief that what viewers see in their advertisements will indeed influence their behavior towards purchasing their offerings. Most television viewers seeing someone eat a cookie in an advertisement or program do not copy the portrayed behavior any more than most people who see reckless driving by unbelted drivers copy the behavior. But some do – otherwise there would be no advertising. While automobile manufacturers would likely oppose government advertising standards, those manufacturers that are currently already behaving as better public citizens would likely benefit from such restraints. It seems to me undeniable that the media causes a large number of traffic deaths by portraying risky, irresponsible, and illegal driving as an exciting, glamorous, heroic, or humorous activity without harmful consequences. The period known as *McCarthyism* ended in 1954 when Senator McCarthy was asked in front of a large live television audience "Have you no shame?" I believe media executives should be asked this same question, even if it is unlikely to be given much coverage in the media they control.

Legislative interventions

Traffic law has existed since the beginning of vehicular traffic. It has two goals – to insure efficient traffic, and to promote safety. One of the earliest laws adopted in all countries to further both goals was to require all traffic to travel on one side of the road. There are no known safety or efficiency advantages in choosing one side over the other. 166 countries, including all in North America and continental Europe, require traffic to drive on the right.   74 countries, including the UK, India, Japan, Australia, Ireland, and Malaysia, require traffic to drive on the left.[21]

Since the earliest days of motorization, it became clear that some drivers were behaving in ways that threatened public safety. Law contributes to safety by requiring drivers to behave in ways that professionals, based on analyses of data and collective expert judgment, have concluded are safer. Despite the subjective confidence of so many drivers, individual personal experience and common sense are inadequate guides to safe driving,[22] just as they are inadequate for identifying safe food or safe drinking water.

Because traffic law relating to speed, intoxication, signal devices, and the rules of the road has been evolving for so long it is not possible to estimate its total influence on safety today. The law has many effects, including education and influencing social norms. If all traffic law were to be suddenly abolished, traffic safety would change, but it would not revert to what it would have been if the laws had never existed. The case of belt wearing in the US will suffice to illustrate. Prior to belt laws, US wearing rates remained fairly constant for many years at about 14%. After the passage of belt laws, rates increased over many years to 75% by 2002. There is of course no way to know what would happen to wearing rates if all belt wearing laws were suddenly abolished. However, a sudden drop to 14% is implausible, whereas settling to a new level below 75% but far above 14% seems far more likely. Habits molded in part by prior law seem likely to persist for most drivers.

Although it is not possible to estimate the aggregate effect of law on safety, we can get a sense of how enormous it is by measuring the effects of adding a law, or strengthening or more strongly enforcing an existing law. Random breath testing in New South Wales, Australia, decreased total fatalities by 19% (p. 254). This large effect was relative to a prior period in which laws against drunk driving were already in place. Reductions in speeds on the US rural Interstate system in response to a change in the speed limit were largely responsible for a 34% reduction in the fatality rate (p. 213). Prior to the change, a speed limit was already in place, albeit a higher one.

Many studies have estimated the casualties that result from violating present law.[23] A review estimated that about 50% of traffic crashes in Europe could have been prevented if road users were completely dissuaded from committing traffic violations.[24] Considerably more than 50% of fatalities would be eliminated, because fatal crashes involve more egregious law violations than typical crashes. Eliminating the single violation of driving at illegal BAC limits would prevent about 34% of US traffic deaths (p. 251). The UK's belt wearing law decreased fatalities to affected occupants by 20% (p. 296). Repeal of US laws requiring motorcyclists to wear helmets increased motorcyclist deaths by 25% (p. 299).

These outcome changes produced by behavior changes resulting from changes in law overwhelm contributions from any of the other factors listed in Fig. 13-4. A road engineering safety improvement will apply to only a small fraction of all roads. A vehicle safety improvement takes years to design and manufacture, and much longer if it is part of a regulation. So a mandated device that reduces driver fatality risk by 10% will prevent no deaths for some years after it is proposed, and only about 1% of the driver deaths in the first year it is installed, because about 90% of the vehicles on the roads date from before the change. As about 60% of traffic fatalities are drivers, it will reduce traffic deaths by 0.6%. For a vehicle safety regulation, typically about 15 years elapses between proposal and essentially all vehicles on the road containing the regulated change. On the other hand, laws applying to all drivers can be passed quickly, and can immediately start generating large safety benefits for all road users.

Effect of enforcement of laws on casualties

The fact that a law is on the books will, by itself, change the behavior of some drivers who believe that obeying the law is a canon of good citizenship. Other drivers change their behavior to avoid the penalties specified in the law. The extent to which they do so depends on their perception of how well the law is enforced. This is related to how well it really is enforced. When new laws come into effect, compliance is often initially high, only to decline later as drivers discover by personal observation, or reports from acquaintances, that detection is unlikely. The goal of enforcing traffic law is, of course, not to achieve compliance with some set of rules for its own sake, but to reduce casualties. The effect of enforcement on casualties is therefore a central issue in traffic safety.

A direct relationship between a driver getting a traffic ticket and that same driver being subsequently involved in a fatal crash was established using data from Ontario, Canada.[25] The case-crossover method was applied to 8,975 licensed drivers involved in fatal crashes during an extended study period. The fatally injured drivers had received convictions at a rate of about one every 5 years before their fatal crash involvement. The risk of a fatal crash in the month after a conviction was found to be $(35 \pm 8)\%$ lower than in a comparable conviction-free month. The effect quickly dissipated, and had effectively disappeared after 3 months. However, it shows large reductions in the risk of fatal crash involvement as a direct result of law enforcement. The data suggest that about one death was prevented for every 80,000 tickets issued.

Other studies have associated enforcement with casualty reductions. Based on synthesizing the results from a large number of studies in many countries, a 14% reduction in fatal crashes was associated with manual enforcement.[23,26] Manual enforcement is the traditional arrangement of a police officer in a stationary or moving vehicle with speed-measuring equipment who stops and issues traffic citations to drivers violating speeding or other traffic law. While such enforcement is shown to make large differences, it is costly and resources permit its application to only a few locations at a given time.

Enforcement using newer technology. Vastly more effective enforcement is possible using the new technologies of photo radar and red-light cameras. These can enormously increase the probability of detecting law violations. I suggest in Chapter 16 that such technologies can form the core of a new approach that would produce huge reductions in traffic harm.

Interactive effects

Interactive effects can make it difficult to evaluate interventions, especially those that produce relatively small effects. The problem arises because the traffic in which crashes take place is a highly interactive system. Every component is connected to every other component to some extent. It is rarely possible to address the influence of one factor, all other factors remaining the same, because all other factors rarely remain the same.

There can be little doubt that driving on snow presents greater risks than driving on dry pavement, *all other factors being equal*. Yet Chapter 5 showed that fatality risks are systematically lower when it snows. Speed reductions in response to the perceived greater risk more than neutralize the increased risk from reduced roadway friction. Similarly, antilock brakes do not lead to harm reductions even though they improve braking. Less safe older drivers pose less threat to the safety of others because they drive less. Drivers react to changes in perceived safety, whether environmental, personal, or technological in origin.

Such interactive effects have generated much controversy and passion over the years, generally because the originators of devices with effective engineering performance or of seemingly effective policies are reluctant to accept evaluation results that show they did not work as planned. On the other hand, interactive effects have been blown out of proportion, and spawned much theoretical nonsense and needlessly complex explanations. Yet surely it has been obvious since antiquity that humans change their behavior in response to the perceived probability and severity of harm. We walk more carefully when the ground is icy than when it is not, and we walk more carefully on rough surfaces when barefoot than when wearing shoes. A warrior clad in armor may accept a greater risk of being struck by a weapon than one not so clad, and so on. In the 1988 movie *Dangerous Liaisons*, Valmont states, "But it is always the best swimmers who drown." (Data confirm this; if you want to reduce your children's chances of drowning, do not teach them to swim). Shakespeare writes, "Best safety lies in fear." (*Hamlet*, Act I, Scene 3).

Interactive effects in traffic have been recognized for a long time

In 1938 a paper titled, *A Theoretical Field-Analysis of Automobile Driving,* was published in the *American Journal of Psychology*, and contained the following:

> *More efficient brakes on an automobile will not in themselves make driving the automobile any safer. Better brakes will reduce the absolute size of the minimum stopping zone, it is true, but the driver soon learns*

this new zone and, since it is his field-zone ratio which remains constant, he allows only the same relative margin between field and zone as before.[27(p 458)]

In 1949 the following appeared in the *Journal of the Royal Statistical Society*:

It is frequently argued that it is a waste of energy to take many of these steps to reduce accidents. There is a body of opinion that holds that the provision of better roads, for example, or the increase in sight lines merely enables the motorist to drive faster, and the result is the same number of accidents as previously. I think there will nearly always be a tendency of this sort, but I see no reason why this regressive tendency should always result in exactly the same number of accidents as would have occurred in the absence of active measures for accident reduction. Some measures are likely to cause more accidents and others less, and we should always choose the measures that cause less.[28(p 13)]

Given how long interactive effects in traffic safety have been discussed in such reasonable terms in the technical literature, and recognized much earlier in other contexts, it is surprising how many later claims of discovery there have been, and more surprising still, how often the very existence of such effects has been hotly denied.

Human-behavior feedback – the technology/human interface

Various terms have been used to describe interactive effects in traffic, including *human-behavior feedback*[29,30(p 283)] and the *technology/human interface*.[31] Fig. 13-5 compares two models, labeled the *naive model* and the *realistic model*, of how technological changes affect safety. The names listed reflect historical usage, and do not imply that engineers deny interactive effects. Terms such as *risk compensation* and *danger compensation* have been used for the realistic model. I consider these inappropriate because mechanisms other than risk may be involved, and changes may not be only compensation.

Realistic model. Let us suppose that some change is introduced into a traffic system that is expected to change safety by some fraction, say ΔS_{eng}, assuming users continue to behave exactly as they did before the change. The subscript denotes that the change is of an engineering nature. For example, if design changes to a guardrail were estimated, by engineering methods, to reduce the probability of driver death on impact by 10%, then ΔS_{eng} would be 10% for drivers killed crashing into the guardrail. We use ΔS_{eng} more generally to indicate fractional reductions in some harm measure expected from changes to a system if users do not alter their behavior in response to these changes. The change might be modifying vehicles, reducing speed limits, etc. While safety interventions always aim at producing positive values of ΔS_{eng}, there are other changes motivated by different considerations, such as saving fuel in the case of smaller cars, for which the values of ΔS_{eng} are negative.

Two models of how people react to safety changes

1. naive model

also called

- *non-interactive*

- *zero feedback*

- *engineering*

assumes

users <u>do not</u> change their
  behavior in response to
  perceived changes in safety

validity

generally overestimates
  safety benefits (may predict
  wrong sign)

2. realistic model

also called

- *interactive*

- *behavior feedback*

- *behavior response*

- *behavior change*

assumes

users <u>do</u> change their
  behavior in response to
  perceived changes in safety

validity

provides correct estimates IF
  feedback parameter can
  be determined

Figure 13-5. Contrast between a *naive model* that ignores interactive effects and a *realistic model* that includes them.

Because road users may alter their behavior, the actual realized percent safety change that is observed, represented by ΔS_{act}, may differ from ΔS_{eng}. The quantities can be considered to be related in the following simple way:

$$\Delta S_{act} = (1 + f)\Delta S_{eng} \qquad\qquad 13\text{-}1$$

where f is a feedback parameter which characterizes the degree to which users respond to the safety change. In this context, feedback is synonymous with user reaction, behavior change, or interactive effects in the system. If users do not change behavior in response to the safety change, then $f = 0$, and the safety change is just as expected on engineering grounds. If the safety change is in the expected direction, but of lesser magnitude than expected, then $-1 < f < 0$, and the safety change is discounted compared to the expected amount. If the safety change has no effect, then $f = -1$.

The naive model assumes that $f = 0$, while the realistic model accepts that, in principle, f is not restricted to any range of values. It is a parameter that is determined by comparing observed outcomes with those expected if there were no interactive effects.

Rich variety of responses observed. An analysis of 24 studies provided examples in which interventions aimed at increasing safety produced the following observed outcomes:[29],[30(p 284-290)]

- Safety increased even more than expected ($f > 0$).

- Safety increased about as much as expected ($f = 0$).

- Safety increased, but less than expected (-1 $< f < 0$).

- Close to zero effect ($f = $ -1).

- Perverse effect – safety decreased ($f < $ -1).

Measures expected to reduce safety, but introduced for other reasons, had similarly varied outcomes.[29],[30(p 290-294)] For example, when Sweden changed from driving on the left to the right side of the road in 1967, and Iceland did the same in 1968, the naive expectation was that such a change would increase crashes. In fact, crashes declined in both countries.[32(p 139)],[33(p 215)]

Behavioral responses are likely for any intervention. Driver behavior changes are usually reliably observed in response to technologies that provide clear feedback to the driver. Antilock brakes provide such an example (Chapter 5). For technologies that affect only injury risk when crashes occur, behavior effects are expected to be smaller, and therefore more difficult to measure. Indeed, there is no definitive body of empirical evidence demonstrating such effects. This has given rise to some claims that devices that affect only the risk of being killed in a crash do not influence driving behavior. I believe that the following thought experiment establishes that they do.

Consider two hypothetical vehicles, identical in all respects except that one has the magical property that neither it nor its occupants can be hurt in any crash, while the other is wired with dynamite to explode on the slightest impact. Even in the unlikely event that a few drivers would ignore the difference, there can be no doubt that, on average, the vehicles would be driven differently. The same conclusion applies even if the vehicles were in fact identical, but falsely believed to possess the hypothesized properties.

Changes in perceived protection can be viewed as lying along a continuum bounded by these hypothetical extremes. It seems likely that any change in perceived outcome will have some effect on driving. In Chapters 11 and 12 we discussed the possibility of small increases in driver risk taking in response to the perceived increased protection from belts and airbags. It was suggested that a modest reduction in the benefits of belts is possible from such an effect. Because of the perception that airbags are much more effective than they are, it is possible that small behavior changes could be of sufficient size to even reverse the small effectiveness values (ΔS_{eng} in the present terminology) listed in Table 11-4, p. 286. Although it is not generally explicitly stated, such effectiveness estimates are all based on assuming the naive model.

To place the difficulties of measuring the behavioral parameter, f, in context, recall how difficult it was to obtain even the ΔS_{eng} values for occupant protection devices derived in Chapter 11. The effect that a device has on outcome when a crash occurs provides estimates only of ΔS_{eng}, which may not have even the same sign as ΔS_{act}, and it is ΔS_{act} that is crucial for safety.

Comment on "risk homeostasis theory"

This subject is included only because it keeps getting the occasional mention in the literature, and additional people encounter it for the first time and find it seductive. *Risk homeostasis theory* claims that drivers have a target level of risk per unit time, so that physical changes to the traffic system stimulate user reactions that reset safety to its prior level.[33,34] The finding that changes in safety systems generate outcomes all the way from effects greater than expected to opposite to expected is sufficient to dismiss this claim, which is categorically refuted by voluminous data. The distance fatality rate on local rural roads is over 400% higher than on urban Interstates (Table 5-5, p. 103). For the US, the rate was over 1,400% higher in 1921 than in 2002. Risks vary by more than a factor of 100 between countries (Table 3-1, p. 43). Such enormous variation in risk on different roads, in different countries, and at different times hardly invites an interpretation in terms of a target level of driver risk.

Risk changes by large amounts during an individual trip. Crash, injury, and fatality risks are enormously higher when driving through intersections than when driving between intersections. Although most drivers must surely be aware of this, they are in little better position to equalize these risks than is a pilot to equalize the risk per unit time at landing to that when cruising at 35,000 feet. Replacing roads containing intersections by limited-access freeways reduces crash risk as certainly as eliminating the take-off and landing risk would reduce air-travel risk.

When the homeostasis notion first appeared around 1970 it played a positive role in stimulating thinking about interactive effects, and highlighted the importance of motivational factors. The original specific claims were quickly demolished by data. The notion kept getting reformulated in one of two ways. In the first, revised specific claims were made which were quickly demolished by data. In the second, a more metaphysical formulation led to claims that could not, in principle, be falsified by data. So, one can regard this in either of two ways. First, either as theory in the usual way science uses the term, but one that has been convincingly refuted by data, and ought therefore to have quickly disappeared. Second, one can regard it as a collection of non-scientific metaphysical claims not addressable by data, in which case the term *theory* must not be used, and one must wonder why it is discussed at all. In my own view it has for far too long been *much ado about nothing*. Frank Haight comments:

> *There is some question as to whether the theory is meaningless (since incapable of testing) or simply false. Evans' conclusion[35] that "there*

is no convincing evidence supporting it and much evidence refuting it" is if anything generous. In my view, a sufficient argument against the validity of risk homeostasis is provided by the incoherence of its "theoretical" formulation.[36(p 364)]

Traffic safety and mobility

Traffic safety is all too often discussed as if the only goal in creating traffic systems were safety. On the contrary, the goal is mobility, and crashes are an unwanted by-product to be minimized while achieving, not abandoning, this primary goal. An important measure of mobility is trip time. While the goals of safety and mobility are often in conflict, this is not always the case.

Safety measures that increase mobility. Roadway engineering changes generally increase both safety and mobility. Replacing a rural arterial road by an Interstate reduces fatality risk by 45% while at the same time increasing travel speeds. Replacing signalized intersections with modern roundabouts increases safety and under most conditions also mobility. Replacing intersections with overpasses and providing elevated or underground pedestrian crossings increase safety and mobility. Vehicle technology improvements such as improved braking, tires, lighting, and navigation have the potential to improve both safety and mobility. Devices such as ABS designed with safety in mind can end up improving mobility more than safety. Night vision systems will certainly increase mobility even if their effect on safety is uncertain. Likewise, an effective drowsy driving detection device will likely increase mobility and safety.

Safety measures that have zero, or minimal, effect on mobility. Vehicle safety improvements and genuinely passive safety protection devices should increase safety at no mobility cost. Safer highway furniture (break-away signs, etc.) that reduce injury risk on impact improve safety without affecting mobility. The two seconds it takes a driver to fasten a safety belt increases the duration of a typical 15 minute trip by 0.2%, a mobility reduction, but one of inconsequential magnitude.

Safety measures that reduce mobility. Driver licensing reduces the mobility of those denied licenses. The main reasons for such denials are age (*per se*, before a specified age, but by less straightforward means for older drivers), performance impairment (medical, failure to pass test), or criminal sanction. Successfully prohibiting any fraction of the population from driving reduces crashes. The percent reduction in crashes exceeds the percent reduction in drivers if those prevented from driving have above average crash rates. However, an above average crash risk is not grounds to deny a license. If it were, the logical consequence would be to prohibit males from driving. If one had sufficiently detailed knowledge about all drivers, successive application of such a philosophy would eventually eliminate every driver except the one safest driver.

Speed control is the intervention with the greatest potential to reduce casualties, but it is also the one most in conflict with mobility. Reducing speed limits leads to real increases in trip time, which has economic consequences. In societies like the US in which most goods are transported by trucks, lower speed limits increase the cost of just about everything. As discussed in Chapter 9, such matters can be addressed in terms of socially optimum speeds that take into account safety and mobility costs. Stricter enforcement of existing speed limits likewise increases average trip times, and major reductions in casualties are obtainable through compliance with present speed limits. If tailgating were to be reduced, the maximum flow on freeways would drop producing increased delays at peak periods. Drivers who obey traffic lights have longer trip times than those who run red lights.

Interactive effects attenuate these mobility costs. Crashes produce long, but infrequent, delays to all motorists, made all the longer by gawkers who slow down even more than the altered traffic conditions require. Manual enforcement leads to substantial delays to those ticketed, but the ticketing process also slows other traffic (mostly by encouraging greater adherence to the speed limit). For many trips the expected variance is crucial. My average trip time to the airport is 45 minutes, but the standard deviation is 15 minutes. So I must allow 90 minutes to have a 99% chance of arriving in 45 minutes or less. If enforced safety measures increased my average trip time to 50 minutes but reduced the standard deviation to 10 minutes, then allowing 80 minutes would produce the same 99% probability of completing the trip in 50 minutes or less. The yellow phase in traffic signals is usually set with some allowance for vehicles running the red. If there were confidence that this would not occur, shorter yellow phases would lead to higher throughput and reduced delay. Increased enforcement generates more orderly traffic, which is often accompanied by travel efficiencies even beyond the avoidance of delay from crash incidents. Which traffic is more efficient – that in the upper or lower picture in Fig. 13-2? Also, it should not be forgotten that many of those injured in traffic lose much of their mobility, and those who die in traffic lose all of their mobility.

Contrast with airline safety

While traffic fatality rates have declined steeply in time, those for airline travel have declined far more steeply. On average, the risk of death for the same distance of travel on a scheduled US airline is about 99% less than in road travel. However, it should be kept in mind that the risk is the same to all on board an aircraft, whereas some road drivers have crash risks much lower than the average.[37] The main contributors to the road average are high-risk drivers. Intuitively, it would appear to be far more dangerous to fly 35,000 feet above the ground at a speed of 1,000 km/h in a vehicle designed with little safety margin due to overriding weight considerations than in a more robustly constructed road vehicle. The skies being empty while the roads are dense with threatening vehicles is not an explanation. Single-vehicle road crashes led to the deaths of 18,476 vehicle occupants in 2002 (see also Table 3-3, p. 48), whereas not even one occupant of a US scheduled airline was killed in 2002 in any type of crash.[38] It is therefore not surprising that one often hears the question, *Why does road traffic safety not make the dramatic progress of airline safety?* Table 13-3 presents a list of differences between the two modes.

Table 13-3.   Comparison of safety characteristics of US commercial air carriers and US road transportation.

	commercial airline	road traffic
deaths per billion km of occupant travel	0.07	4.9
countermeasures with most success and potential	crash prevention	crash prevention
main US policy emphasis	crash prevention	crashworthiness
impact of vehicle design or manufacturing flaws	vitally important	minimally important
driver selection	strict	essentially everyone
importance of driver skill and knowledge	high	may increase or decrease crash risk
main influence on driver behavior	following increasingly effective procedures	experience and personal judgment
violation of safety laws	rare	typically, many times per trip
use of alcohol/drugs	rare	alcohol in about 40% of fatal crashes
value of high technology driver training simulators	enormously high value	zero or minimal value
time to react to crash-threatening situations	often more than many seconds or minutes	usually less than a second
value of crash-avoidance advanced technology	enormously high value	minimal value
key to making largest improvements in safety	safer aircraft flown by better trained pilots adhering to better procedures	behavior changes resulting from changes in social norms, legislation, and enforcement

Deaths per billion km is not a good measure for airline safety because risk, being so concentrated at take-off and landing, is largely independent of trip distance.[37,39] The illustrative value, 0.07 deaths per billion km of occupant travel, is based on an airline trip of average distance, and fatalities averaged over a ten-year period.[39] The comparison, while approximate, leaves no doubt that average airline travel is dramatically safer than average road travel. The crucial difference is that pilots adhere to rules specified by combining the knowledge and experience of many experts. Pilots may not, for example, take off after another airline has taken off based on what their personal experience tells them is a safe following headway. In the airline case, learning to avoid crashes by experiencing them is unacceptable, yet it is a large component of the approach to road safety.

Much attention has been devoted to increasing cabin safety in the event of an airliner crash. There are standards for fire-retardant fabrics, seat strength, safety belts, emergency exits, emergency cabin illumination, and evacuation equipment and procedures. Important though such measures are, they are not the key to why airline travel is so safe. Improvements in crashworthiness never led to any ambiguity about what the main focus of aviation safety should be. The number one priority is to avoid the crash rather than marginally increase the probability of surviving it. When road safety transfers its main focus to the prevention, rather than the survival, of crashes, it can start moving in the direction of the extraordinary safety achieved in airline travel.

Relative importance of factors

The schematic in Fig. 13-1 summarizes what I consider to be the main components relevant to traffic safety, with my judgment of their relative importance indicated in Fig. 13-4 (p. 339). Safety has been conceptualized in other formalisms, including particularly the *Haddon Matrix*.[10] This is a 3×3 classification in which all factors are either human, vehicle, or environment, and either pre-crash, crash, or post-crash. While this has been helpful in the past, I believe it now places too much emphasis on the event – the crash. Pre-crash normally implies the few seconds prior to the crash, whereas I consider the really important pre-crash period to be the decade of socialization prior to the day of the crash. The focus needs to shift away from the details of the event, and more in the direction of eliminating it. The classification into nine cells may tend to place more emphasis on relatively less important factors at the expense of more important factors. Once occupants wear belts (a behavior and legislative matter), only modest further improvements in the crash phase features of vehicle design and occupant protection beyond those already in place are likely to occur. Likewise, improvements in rescue and medicine will save lives in the post-crash phase, but the potential from further improvements is limited by the already high level reached. In sharp contrast, no nation has more than touched the tip of the iceberg of harm reductions that can be achieved by behavior changes. Herein lies the opportunity for the breakthrough advance in traffic safety that is proposed in Chapter 16.

Summary and conclusions

The number of US traffic deaths per thousand vehicles declined by 96% from 1900 to 2002. Engineering improvements to roadways and vehicles contributed to this decline. However, engineering factors cannot account for more than a modest portion of it, or of the variation by more than a factor of a 400 between countries. This, and other information, identifies driver behavior as the dominant factor in traffic safety.

As countries motorize and casualties increase, inputs from education, law, and the mass media contribute to changing social norms relating to driving. Safer driver behavior is influenced more by these changing social norms than by personal experience, which is of limited value because useful feedback is too infrequent. The social norm encourages safety behaviors to evolve into habits lacking conscious safety motivation. Stopping at red lights is so ingrained that drivers rarely violate the rule even if it is safe to do so. By portraying risky, irresponsible, and illegal driving as glamorous, exciting, heroic, or humorous in advertisements and programs, the mass media play an important role in increasing the number of people killed in traffic.

The countermeasures that have produced the largest changes in behavior, and consequently largest reductions in traffic harm, are all legislative. Random breath testing in New South Wales, Australia decreased total fatalities by 19%. A speed limit change on the US rural Interstate system reduced the distance fatality rate by 34%. The UK belt wearing law reduced fatalities by 20%. Individual drivers who received a traffic ticket were found to be 35% less likely to be involved in a fatal crash in the month following their ticket. These reductions tower over any achievable by crashworthiness improvements. Even a vehicle change that reduced driver fatality risk by 10% would reduce fatalities by only about 0.6% in its first year, because most vehicles on the road date from before the change, and not all victims are drivers.

The largest reductions in harm in traffic are achievable from more effective enforcement of traffic law. The new technologies of photo radar and red light cameras provide the means to achieve this, as discussed in Chapter 16.

References for Chapter 13

1   Hertzman C. Health and human society. *Am Scientist*. 2001; 89: 538-545.

2   Evans L. Driving and human health (letter to the editor). *Am Scientist*. 2002; 90: 4-5.

3   Treat JR. A study of precrash factors involved in traffic accidents. *The HSRI Research Review*. Ann Arbor, MI; May-August 1980.

4   Sabey BE, Taylor H. The known risks we run: The highway. In: Schwing RC, Albers WA, editors. *Societal Risk Assessment – How Safe is Safe Enough?* New York, NY: Plenum Press; 1980, p. 43-63.

5 Sabey BE, Staughton GC. Interacting roles of road environment, vehicle and road user in accidents. Presented to the Fifth International Conference of the International Association for Accident and Traffic Medicine, London, UK; 1975.

6 Rumar K. The role of perceptual and cognitive filters in observed behavior. In: Evans L, Schwing RC, editors. *Human Behavior and Traffic Safety*. New York, NY: Plenum Press; 1985, p. 151-165.

7 Carsten OMJ, Tight MR, Southwell MT. Urban accidents: Why do they happen? Basingstoke, UK: AA Foundation for Road Safety Research; 1989.

8 Wang, Z. Road traffic accidents (RTA) in China – 1998 in retrospect. *J. Traf Med*. 2000; 28: 15.

9 Wang Z, Jiang J. An overview of research advances in road traffic trauma in China. *Traf Inj Prev*. 2003; 4: 9-16.

10 Haddon W Jr. A logical framework for categorizing highway safety phenomena and activity. *J Trauma*. 1972; 12: 193-207.

11 Gielen AC, Sleet D. Application of behavior-change theories and methods to injury prevention. *Epidemiologic Reviews*. 2003; 25: 65-76.

12 Slovic P, Fischhoff B, Lichtenstein S. Facts and fears: Understanding perceived risk. In: Schwing RC, Albers WA, editors. *Societal Risk Assessment – How Safe is Safe Enough?* New York, NY: Plenum Press; 1980, p. 181-214.

13 Ruscio J. Risky business. *Skeptical Inquirer*. 2000; 24: 22-26.

14 US Nuclear Regulatory Commission. Fact sheet on the accident at Three Mile Island (revised March 2004). http://www.nrc.gov/reading-rm/doc-collections/fact-sheets/3mile-isle.html

15 Passman C, McGwin GJ, Taylor AJ, Rue LW. Seat belt use before and after motor vehicle trauma. *J Trauma*. 2001; 51: 105-109.

16 Koop CE, Richmond J, Steinfeld J. America's choice: Reducing tobacco addiction and disease. *Am J Public Health*. 2004; 94: 174-176.

17 Glantz SA, Kacirk KW, McCulloch C. Back to the future: Smoking in movies in 2002 compared with 1950 levels. *Am J Public Health*. 2004; 94: 261-263.

18 CNN.com Law Center. Janklow sentenced to 100 days in jail. 22 January 2004. http://www.cnn.com/2004/LAW/01/22/janklow.sentencing

19 Fumento M. Road rage versus reality. *Atlantic Monthly Online*. August 1998. http://www.theatlantic.com/issues/98aug/roadrage.htm

20 Anderson CA, Bushman BJ. The effects of media violence on society. *Science*. 2002; 295: 2377-2378.

21 Lucas B. Which side of the road do they drive on? http://www.brianlucas.ca/roadside

22 Sivak M. How common sense fails us on the road: Contribution of bounded rationality to the annual worldwide toll of one million traffic fatalities. *Trans Res Part F: Psych Behav*. 2002; 5: 259–269.

23 Zaidel DM. The impact of enforcement on accidents. The "Escape" Project Contract No. RO-98-RS.3047; February 2002. http://www.vtt.fi/rte/projects/escape/escape_d3.pdf

24 European Transport Safety Council. Police enforcement strategies to reduce traffic casualties in Europe. ETSC report. Brussels; May 1999. http://www.etsc.be/strategies.pdf

25 Redelmeier DA, Tibshirani RJ, Evans L. Traffic-law enforcement and risk of death from motor-vehicle crashes: Case-crossover study. *The Lancet*. 2003; 36: 2177-2182.

26 Elvik R, Mysen AB, Vaa T. *Trafikksikkerhetshåndbok (Traffic Safety Handbook)*. Oslo, Norway: Institute of Transport Economics; 1997.

27 Gibson JJ, Crooks LE. A theoretical field-analysis of automobile driving. *Am J Psych*. 1938; 5l: 453-47l.

28 Smeed R. Some statistical aspects of road safety research. *J Roy Stat Soc, Series A*. 1949; 112: 1-34.

29 Evans L. Human behavior feedback and traffic safety. *Hum Factors*. 1985; 27: 555-576.

30 Evans L. *Traffic Safety and the Driver.* New York, NY: Van Nostrand Reinhold; 1991.

31 Evans L. Transportation Safety. In: Hall RW, editor. *Handbook of Transportation Science, Second Edition.* Norwell, MA: Kluwer Academic Publishers; 2002, p. 79-86.

32 Näätänen R, Summala H. *Road-User Behavior and Traffic Accidents.* Amsterdam, Netherlands: North Holland; 1976.

33 Wilde GJS. The theory of risk-homeostasis: Implications for safety and health. *Risk Analysis.* 1982; 2: 209-255.

34 Wilde GJS. Notes on the interpretation of traffic accident data and of risk homeostasis theory: A reply to L. Evans. *Risk Analysis.* 1986; 6: 95-101.

35 Evans L. Risk homeostasis theory and traffic accident data. *Risk Analysis.* 1986; 6: 81-94.

36 Haight FA. Risk, especially risk of a traffic accident. *Accid Anal Prev.* 1986; 18: 359-366.

37 Evans L, Frick MC, Schwing RC. Is it safer to fly or drive? – A problem in risk communication. *Risk Analysis.* 1990; 10: 239-246.

38 US Department of Transportation, Bureau of Statistics, Table 2-1 – Transportation fatalities by mode.
   http://www.bts.gov/publications/national_transportation_statistics/2003/html/table_02_01.html

39 Sivak M, Flannagan MJ. Flying and driving after the September 11 attacks. *Am Scientist.* 2003; 91: 6-8.

14 How you can reduce your risk

Introduction

I open this chapter with a confession. I am in the weak position of a male obstetrician. While I study traffic crashes, I have never had the ultimate experience of being involved in one myself. This fact alone does not provide sufficient information to determine whether I know how to avoid crashing, or have merely been lucky. However, Table 1-1 (p. 13) shows that the probability that a random driver will have at least one crash in 48 years of driving is 98.4%. Some researchers would almost certainly at this stage invoke the phrase *statistically significant.* This has not been used in this book for reasons I have explained elsewhere.[1(p 377)]

If merely lucky, perhaps I am foolishly tempting fate by my comments. At a White House news conference in 1960 a reporter asked President Eisenhower, "Sir, do you realize that on your upcoming birthday you will be the oldest President ever to serve?" Ike smiled and answered, "I believe it's a tradition in baseball that when a pitcher has a no-hitter going for him, nobody reminds him of it."[2(p 155)]

In previous chapters many results relating to aggregate effects were presented, and interpretations offered of factors that affect overall traffic safety. Here we address the more personal question of what steps you as an individual driver can take to reduce your personal crash risk. The generally sensible advice in so many "How to drive safely" guides will not be repeated here. Rather, we offer general approaches and principles that may be less familiar, illustrated in some cases with examples from my own personal experience.

Behavior, not knowledge, is crucial

An informal "show of hands" survey I conducted at an international traffic safety meeting provided unmistakable evidence that some safety professionals had well above average crash rates.

Objective data on the behavior of traffic-safety professionals were provided by the measured speeds of Finnish road-safety researchers as they approached the venue of a national road safety meeting.[3] Of the 13 researchers who could be tracked by radar in a 60 km/h speed-limit zone, nine exceeded 70 km/h, six of these exceeded 80 km/h, and three of those reached 90 km/h. The researchers' speeds were, on average, higher than those of the general public.

One of my highest risk trips was as a passenger in a vehicle transporting me between functions at a safety conference in a major US city. The vehicle was driven by a driving instructor!

I have not been much involved with the racing fraternity, and have chatted at length with only one racing driver – a great guy, as they tend to be. He had been involved in a fatal crash. Because there was no suggestion that he was legally at fault he was confident that there was nothing he could have done to prevent the death of the housewife who was killed in the crash.

Average behavior produces average crash risk

The low rates at which adverse events occur (Table 13-2, p. 340) repeatedly reinforce an impression that driving is extremely safe. Let us invoke the mental construct of a hypothetical *average driver*, who has the same 0.0858 probability of crashing per year as the US average, equivalent to one crash per 11.7 years (Table 1-1, p. 13). Such an individual has a slightly better than even chance of driving for 8 years without crashing (or 187,000 km, assuming 23,400 km per year). The copious feedback the average driver receives that average driving does not lead to unpleasant consequences cements the impression that average driving is safe driving.

However, in the same 8 years, this driver also has a more than 15% probability of being involved in two or more crashes (computed using Eqn 1-1, p. 12) with $\lambda = 0.0858$ and $N=8$). The average driver has no direct way of knowing that a natural and essentially inevitable consequence of average driving is involvement in one crash about every 12 years, or about 5 crashes in a driving career.

The probability that our hypothetical driver will experience at least one crash over a 55 year driving career exceeds 99%. Thus it is nearly certain that normal driving over a driving career will inexorably lead to a crash. A common reaction of drivers involved in crashes is to view them as rare unpredictable events outside reasonable human control, and of such a unique nature that nothing like them will ever recur. Yet, for our hypothetical driver, rather than being unpredictable, a crash is essentially inevitable. To realistically expect less than five crashes over a driving career, our hypothetical driver must adopt changed driving behavior that no longer matches the average behavior that copious direct feedback in the form of personal experience indicated was safe and appropriate.

For airline pilots it would be unthinkable to expect to crash about every 12 years, or for it to be inevitable to crash during a flying career. Yet flying is intrinsically more difficult and dangerous than ground travel. In my view, it is within the control of the ground-vehicle driver to approach the same low crash risks that commercial pilots achieve in flying. It seems pilots are fairly safe in road driving also, having the third lowest crash rate among 40 occupations examined.[4]

Most drivers think they are better than other drivers

While most drivers would likely choose to change their behavior rather than accept one crash per 12 years, they do not feel at risk because they think that it is only other drivers who crash. One reason is that the vast majority of drivers believe that they are safer than average. Many investigations have come to this conclusion, but the question tends to be ill defined because the concept of *average* is left vague. Does it refer to those who live in your city, nation, or the world?

Study showing that most drivers think they are better than others

The best-controlled study consisted of two experiments in which subjects ranked themselves relative to others in the same room at the same time.[5] One experiment had samples of drivers self-assess their safety compared to the safety of other drivers, while the other experiment applied the same approach to driving skill. The safety study used a group of 45 student subjects from a US state, Oregon, and another group of 35 students from Stockholm, Sweden. Each group was assembled in a room, so that every member was aware of the entire group. The participants were informed that, as there was bound to be a safest and a least safe driver in the room, all drivers could be rank ordered from the safest to the least safe. Each was then asked where they considered that they would be located in such a ranking.

The percentile at which each experimental point is plotted in Fig. 14-1 indicates the percent of the drivers who responded that they considered themselves to be safer than the drivers in lower percentile categories. For example, the values plotted at the median show that 88% of the US sample and 77% of the Swedish sample reported that they considered themselves to be safer than the drivers in the 0-50 percentile range. That is, they judged their safety to be superior to the median safety of the drivers sharing the room with them.

The *reality* data indicate what would be produced if every driver was given a list containing an objectively measured safety score for each group member, and had merely to report where his or her score ranked on the list. For experimental and *reality* data, the first point must be 100%, because all drivers must be as safe as, or safer than, the least safe driver. For the *reality* data each additional 10 percentile points along the x-axis must correspond to 10% of the population, leading to the linear decline shown.

By definition, 30% of drivers are actually as safe as or safer than the safest 70%, but 83% of the US sample and 51% of the Swedish sample considered themselves to be this safe. 60% of the US and 23% of the Swedish drivers considered themselves safer than 80% of drivers, whereas actually 20% are.

The skill experiment was conducted in the same way using different, but similarly recruited, students who were asked to rank their driving skills compared to the driving skills of the other drivers in the room. The safety and skill results show similar patterns of overestimation. Of the 36 experimental points in Fig. 14-1 all except three are above the *reality* line, indication that safety and skill were consistently overestimated. The three exceptions were all

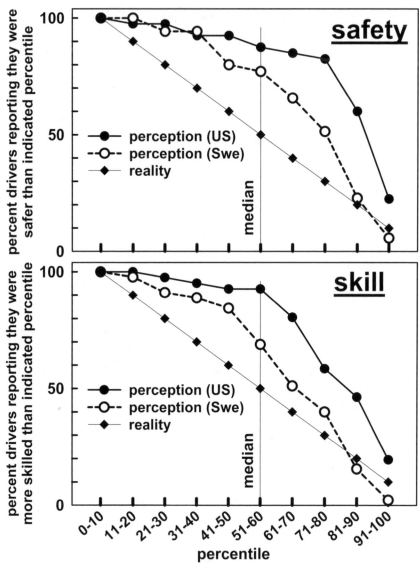

Figure 14-1. How drivers rated their own safety and driving skill relative to about 40 other drivers answering the same questions in the same room at the same time. All points above the *reality* relationship imply overestimation. Data from Ref. 5.

from the presumably more modest Swedish students not ranking themselves in the very highest categories; thus some necessarily ranked themselves lower than their true rank. Overestimation of safety and skill was far greater by the US than the Swedish students.

Other evidence of overconfidence

Australian drivers interviewed at home systematically rated their abilities as higher than average.[6] The overestimation was greater for males than for females of the same age, the differences being large and systematic.   The subjects similarly overrated their abilities, compared to the average, to drive safely after consuming alcohol. A study in New Zealand found that up to 80% of drivers rate themselves above average on a number of important characteristics, but also tended to rate themselves below 'a very good driver'.[7]   In a study of US students, 75% considered themselves to be safer than others, 89% thought they were more skillful, but only 54% thought they had lower crash likelihood.[8] Young and old Canadian drivers systematically rated their overall driving ability, and their abilities at specific driving tasks, as above average.[9] Another study further confirms that most US drivers rate their skills as better than average.[10]

These systematic misjudgments are not necessarily corrected by personal experience. Responses of 50 drivers seriously injured in crashes and of 50 matched crash-free drivers were compared.[11] When asked about how skillful they were, the two groups gave similar results, indicating that most of these early 1960s drivers, irrespective of crash records, considered themselves to be more skillful than most other drivers. On the other hand, another study finds that estimates of personal crash risk increase, and estimates of driving ability decline, with crash involvement.[9] Drivers self-reported greater willingness to wear belts after being seriously injured in crashes.[12]

Over 50% of all drivers do in fact have crash rates lower than the average. A parallel statement applies to many things, because real world distributions are more logarithmic than linear.   If 99 average people and one sports superstar were in a room, 99% of the people in the room would have below-average income. However, the sports superstar would not unduly influence the median income, the income that was greater than earned by half of the people but less than earned by the other half.   The distribution of crash rates cannot be symmetric, because no individual can have a rate lower than zero, or expressed differently, lower than the average value by more than the average value. However, a driver can have a crash rate higher than the average value by any amount. Thus the median crash rate (like the median salary) will always be less than the average. The focus of most of the studies reviewed is on medians. The public tends to think of average as meaning median, so the distinction is of little practical importance in the few studies that asked subjects to compare themselves to average drivers.

Why do most drivers think they are better than average?

Subjects asked to rate themselves on a collection of abilities or dispositions (gardening, clumsiness, house painting, intelligence, happiness, cooking, competitiveness, and musical ability), as well as safe and skillful driving, produced results generally similar to those for safe and skillful driving.[13] Thus the driving case is part of a more general pattern. There is a body of research showing that people have a systematic bias in favor of thinking that their personal risk is lower than that of others for a wide range of hazards.[14] While such optimism can contribute to an increased feeling of well-being, it encourages risky decision making in activities such as driving.

Because drivers think of themselves as safer than other drivers, according to the theory of cognitive dissonance, they are likely to interpret additional evidence as supporting this belief.[15] Reports of fatalities, rather than inducing fear, tend to confirm perceptions of driving superiority, in that it is other people who are being killed. Most drivers have not been injured, so reports of serious injuries similarly confirm perceptions of driving superiority.

While fear is present in learning to drive, the goal is to eliminate it. Good driving is relaxed and confident. The longer one drives, the greater is the accumulation of evidence that all the really bad things happen to others. When drivers perform actions in traffic (say, driving too fast for conditions), and no undesirable consequences follow, the belief that the action is safe receives reinforcement, and is more likely to be repeated in the future. Indeed if a speed is perceived to be safe, why should a marginally higher speed not also be safe? The process has a tendency to generate increasing speeds until some incident, such as near loss of control on a curve, or a speeding ticket provides corrective feedback.

We receive day-to-day feedback confirming our belief that we drive better than others. We notice when other drivers maintain poor lane position, or turn corners with inappropriate trajectories, or without signaling. We are unaware when others are making similar judgments about us. As Robert Burns laments, "O wad some Pow'r the giftie gie us -- To see oursels as others see us!" The systematic bias in our perception of our own driving is somewhat akin to people's perception that they find more coins than they lose. They are aware of finding, but generally unaware of losing. Experience can be a false teacher.[16]

Crashes and driver responsibility

Police procedures generally categorize drivers involved in crashes as being either *at fault* or *not at fault*. These designations are useful and necessary for administrative and legal purposes, and even on occasions for research. To assure completeness, I think it is helpful to place all the harm that can happen to drivers into one of three categories in order of increasing culpability:

1. Unavoidable.

2. Not at fault.

3. At fault.

Unavoidable harm in traffic

Terms like *unavoidable crash* occur with much greater frequency than events that are really unavoidable. The term occurs in innumerable formal documents and informal tales of woe. Some harm in traffic is genuinely unavoidable. There are cases of vehicles driving over bridges that collapse due to structural failure or earthquake, or vehicles being struck by falling parts from disintegrating aircraft. Drivers involved in such crashes are victims of random events over which they have essentially no control, given that they have decided to drive. There are no realistic changes they can make in their driving behavior to reduce such risks. In my view only a microscopic fraction of the risk a driver faces is due to events over which the driver has no control. Although the fraction is extremely small, the absolute number of drivers fatally injured in such events still far exceeds deaths from many other causes that command much more public attention and resources.

Not-at-fault crashes

The tendency to seek similarities between the not-at-fault legal designation and the random events portrayed above flows from a human tendency to blame bad luck rather than ourselves when things go wrong. While I cannot make a bridge fall down as I drive over it, nor cause an aircraft undercarriage to land on my roof, I could easily and quickly become the not-at-fault driver in a two-vehicle crash if I wanted to do so. All I would have to do is to drive in traffic until followed by a tailgater (usually not very long!) and then select an appropriate moment to brake briskly. It is, of course, not the purpose of this chapter to provide instruction in how to produce crashes, but how to avoid them. However, if the reader accepts that it is possible through purposeful actions to become the not-at-fault driver in a two-vehicle crash, then it follows that it must be possible through purposeful actions to avoid becoming a not-at-fault driver in some two-vehicle crashes.

Not-at-fault drivers who claim that there was nothing they could have done tend to view their crashes as inflicted upon them by a traffic system over which they have no control. After all, they cannot control the behavior of other drivers, so there is nothing more they can do beyond driving legally and carefully themselves. Rather than accepting this, I believe that the individual driver can reduce crash risk substantially by taking steps to avoid not-at-fault involvement. Indeed, I consider that a vast majority (but certainly not all) not-at-fault drivers involved in multiple-vehicle crashes could have avoided their crashes by changing their behavior.

At-fault crashes

The first priority in avoiding risk, the easy one, is never to be at fault. Obeying traffic law largely achieves this. However, there are other actions that are not specifically proscribed by law that should be avoided. Commercial drivers (of trucks and busses) are subject to much more specific rules regulating how long they can drive without a break, and how much alcohol may be in their blood. All drivers should be sensitive to the increased risk of driving while fatigued or after consuming legal amounts of alcohol.

Speed is central. One encounters often statements claiming that some percent of crashes involved speeding. Although the percent given is usually high, I believe it is an underestimation. Far fewer data document the role of speeding in crashes than that of alcohol. A post-crash alcohol measurement provides definitive evidence on alcohol in the blood just prior to the crash. However, after a crash a vehicle is stationary, and pre-crash travel speed is rarely available from objective measurements. Only a microscopic fraction of all crashes are shown by physical evidence to have occurred during travel at legal speeds. Although specific speed data are not available, I am convinced by the unstructured evidence that is available that the vast majority of crashes involve either violations of traffic law or clearly imprudent behavior.

Rear-impact crashes

The conceptual simplicity and frequent occurrence of rear-impact crashes makes them suitable to illustrate in detail the concepts introduced above. A rear-impact crash involves one at-fault driver, the follower, and one not-at-fault driver, the leader. This is legally how it is, and how it should be. It is the responsibility of following drivers to not crash into vehicles they are following, whereas lead drivers are entitled to slow down or stop, as the need arises, without incurring legal jeopardy. Close following, or tailgating, places a minimum of two vehicles at risk of crash involvement

The vehicle-following driver

It is the following driver's legal obligation to avoid rear-impact crashes by following in a legal, safe, and prudent manner. The extent to which this is generally not done is illustrated by the distribution of following headways on a US urban Interstate freeway in Michigan in 1978 (Fig. 14-2).[17] In this figure the headway of a following car is defined as the elapsed time between the front of the lead vehicle passing a point on the roadway and the front of the following vehicle passing the same point. The two groups of drivers are identified based on driving records from police files. One group had one or more police-reported crashes in a seven-year period, whereas the other group was crash free. 27.3% of the drivers with crashes had headways less than one second, compared to 23.3% of the crash-free drivers. While the crashes were not just rear impacts, tailgating correlates with other risk-taking in traffic. The drivers had their crashes before being photographed tailgating, again showing that crash experience did not teach them to behave even as safely as average drivers. Many of the same vehicles were photographed on multiple occasions. Those

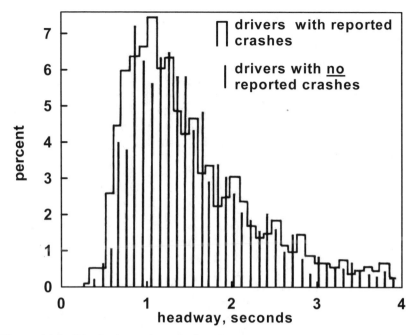

Figure 14-2. Distributions of headways of crash-involved and crash-free drivers on an urban Interstate freeway in Michigan in 1978.[17] Headway is defined as the elapsed time between the front of a lead vehicle passing a point in the road and a front of the following vehicle passing the same point. Driver manuals usually recommend headways of at least 2 seconds.

tailgating on one occasion were likely to tailgate on other occasions, underlying the habitual nature of the behavior.

Relative to the reaction times mentioned in Chapter 8, and to the advice in most driver manuals that headways should be at least two seconds, driving with a headway of less than one second must be viewed as risky. Most drivers choose following headways less than the recommended two seconds, one study finding an average headway of 1.36 seconds.[18]

Why do drivers choose to follow so closely? Tailgating becomes largely a driving habit, rather than reasoned conscious behavior. Drivers appear to do many things more for their own sake than for any utility benefit. Indeed, it is suggested that some criminal behavior is indulged in, not for the expected gain, but for the enjoyment of the activity.[19] We have all observed one vehicle dangerously tailgating another on a stretch of multi-lane freeway containing no vehicles other than our own and the tailgating pair. The tailgater could often reduce his or her personal risk by passing, thereby also saving time.

Unlike many other forms of driver risk-taking, such as speeding, overtaking, or running red lights, tailgating does not save much time. If you ignore the question of other vehicles cutting into the gap in front of you, then following at a headway of 2.0 seconds instead of 0.5 seconds means that you arrive 1.5 seconds later. If the 1.5 seconds is critical, it can all be recaptured by, say, closing up on the vehicle in front just prior to exiting from the freeway. In that way the risk of a closer following gap is incurred for just a few seconds. Larger gaps do increase the probability that another vehicle will cut in front, but probably at less than one per 10 km of freeway travel under the fairly uncommon traffic conditions in which this is most likely. Even if a few vehicles do cut into the gap in front, this adds only about 2 seconds per incident to the overall trip time.

Drivers probably object to other vehicles cutting in front of them not because it delays them a couple of seconds, but because it is interpreted as some sort of personal affront, an assault on their manhood or womanhood.

Why are drivers so relaxed when tailgating? There are two reasons why many drivers feel so comfortable following at headways that unreasonably increase their risk of at-fault involvement in rear-impact crashes. First, the dominant cue when following is the relative speed between your vehicle and the one in front. This is normally very close to zero. There is zero risk of a rear-impact collision if both vehicles maintain identical speeds, no matter how high that speed is. The largely static visual impression in vehicle-following tends to lower awareness and concern regarding speed. If the speed of the vehicle in front changes suddenly, then the ensuing dynamical behavior of both vehicles is strongly speed-dependent, with the amount of energy available to cause harm even more so. The second reason why drivers are comfortable tailgating, and being tailgated, is that experience, that false educator, has taught them that it is safe.

Tailgating and platoons of vehicles

Tailgating can produce particularly catastrophic results when a platoon of many consecutive tailgaters forms. This is because of intrinsic platoon dynamics that may amplify disturbances as they propagate down a line of vehicles. If the lead vehicle of a platoon slows down gently and then regains its prior speed, the second vehicle may respond by slowing down more rapidly (depending on reaction time and headway). The third vehicle will then be confronted with a more rapidly decelerating lead vehicle, so that as we progress down the platoon, each driver produces a larger deceleration, until eventually braking capability is exceeded. For a sufficiently long platoon of vehicles with identical following parameters, a multiple-vehicle pile-up becomes inevitable.

Fig. 14-3 shows results from a mathematical model of a situation in which a stream of identical cars follow each other, initially all traveling at the same speed and separated by 40 feet.[20] The position of each car is shown relative to the position of the first car (labeled 1), assuming that this first car continued at a constant speed. At time zero the first car reduces speed, but then returns to its initial speed. As we proceed down the platoon, each car approaches closer to the one in front, until car 8 crashes into car 7. One dear lady confessed that after seeing this result she always made sure she was never car number 7 in a platoon with more than 7 cars!

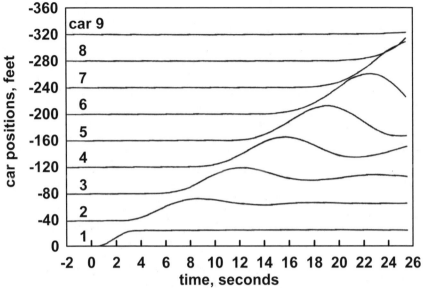

Figure 14-3. Mathematical representation of a stream of identical cars, initially all traveling at the same speed and separated by 40 feet.[20] The eighth car crashes into the seventh as a consequence of the lead car (number 1) reducing speed at time zero and then returning to its initial speed 3 seconds later.

Naturally, her concerns should not have been so specific, as Fig. 14-3 represents model output based on assumed parameters. Different choices would have predicted different specific outcomes. However, Fig. 14-3 does illustrate the intrinsic instability of rows of tailgaters, which manifests itself in the real world in the form of multiple-vehicle pile-ups, sometimes with multiple fatalities. Crashes involving the largest number of vehicles generally occur in fog. Fog may encourage closer following in order to maintain visual contact with lead vehicles, which will increase the risk of multiple-vehicle pile-ups. Different effects may also contribute, such as a lead vehicle suddenly appearing, rather than being followed.

An individual driver in a platoon following at a large headway may damp out the disturbance so that no collisions occur. If you find yourself following many consecutive tailgaters, and are yourself closely followed, then adopt a headway larger than the normally safe two seconds. Drivers choosing safer headways for themselves may thus make safety contributions to the system, and thereby prevent harm to drivers who will be entirely unaware that somebody else prevented them from being involved in a crash.

How to reduce your risk of at-fault involvement

An individual driver can dramatically reduce the risk of being involved in an at-fault rear-impact crash by following at recommended headways rather than the shorter ones that experience leads us to believe are safe. The experience that the vehicle in front does not suddenly slow down must be replaced by the intellectual understanding that for it to do so is not an event of cosmic rarity. Everyone knows that there is a small probability that a small animal unseen by a following driver will suddenly run across the road. Everyone also knows that some lead drivers will brake sharply to avoid striking the animal. There is a high price to be paid for driving in such a way that when rare but entirely normal events occur, you crash.

Adopting a recommended headway will increase the probability that drivers cut in front of you. The resulting delay to you is minor. Ignore any perceived affront. If detached rationality cannot dispel such feelings, seek comfort in the confident, if less noble, expectation that the offending driver is likely to have more than the average one crash per 12 years. Let such drivers save their few seconds and have their fun – you know, even if they don't, that they are paying a far higher price for it than they realize. Recapture your few seconds by walking faster to your vehicle, thus improving your cardiovascular health, which will enable you to outlive the scoundrel who cut in front of you!

A case when safer following saves time. When a lead vehicle signals an intention to turn, many following drivers maintain a near-constant headway. This locks the trajectory of their vehicle to that of the lead vehicle, even though the lead vehicle will normally reduce speed substantially to execute a turn. You can improve safety and efficiency if you gently reduce speed as soon as the lead driver indicates intention to turn. When the lead vehicle completes the turn, your vehicle, although traveling slower than prior to the initiation of the turn signal, is still traveling faster than the turning vehicle, thereby saving you time, fuel and brake linings. By being further from the lead vehicle during its main deceleration, you have reduced your risk of striking it, or being struck by the vehicle following you.

Can technology reduce rear-impact crashes? Subjective estimates of headways can be unreliable. They may be influenced by the type of vehicle we are driving, as demonstrated in Fig. 8-1, p. 180. However, headways are easy to estimate – simply judge when a lead vehicle passes a feature on the roadway surface (a sharp shadow is ideal), and count seconds. Saying "one thousand, two thousand" usually works, but calibrate with a stopwatch when you are not driving. Check your following headway periodically, because it may drift towards the shorter values that experience falsely indicates to be safe.

More sophisticated devices to warn drivers they are tailgating have limited utility, and for the same reasons that apply to devices to warn drivers they are speeding. Speeding and tailgating are problems of behavior, not inadequate knowledge. The speedometer, and the simple method of estimating headways, provide the necessary information.

More sophisticated devices which automatically apply braking have been developed. I never felt more at risk of being in a rear-impact crash than when I traveled as a passenger in a vehicle demonstrating one such device. Extreme tailgating was used to show the device's capability. Even if the technology were perfect, the risk would be high. If our vehicle were unable to match the braking of the lead vehicle, we would hit it. Yet we had no basis to be confident that the lead vehicle did not have better tires or brakes than our vehicle. We would be especially vulnerable if a slippery patch of roadway surface was encountered at the wrong time. The threat that we would be rear-impacted by another vehicle far exceeded that of the very short headway drivers represented in Fig. 14-2. What might Fig. 14-3 look like for a platoon of vehicles equipped with such devices?

How to reduce your risk of not-at-fault involvement

When another driver follows yours too closely, you bear the risk of being involved in a rear-impact crash without enjoying even the modest time savings of the tailgater. In many cases you can reduce or avoid this risk by using a variety of techniques to discourage other drivers from following you too closely. To do so involves frequent use of rear-view mirrors, which is in general a good driving practice. If a vehicle follows mine too closely on a non-crowded freeway, I simply speed up to get away from it, or slow down to encourage the close follower to overtake. Some drivers attempt to intimidate drivers of vehicles they are following to travel faster by tailgating them. Respond to this threat as one should respond to most threats in traffic – by slowing down. The tailgater will eventually pass you and go bother someone else.

If traffic is congested, increasing your own headway and level of attention is indicated. It is not safe to keep your concentration and attention at its peak level at all times. This will produce fatigue, as it quickly does in novice drivers who devote all of their attention to the driving task in the pre-autonomous phase.

One situation in which being tailgated is particularly unacceptable is merging onto a freeway. Here you may have to abruptly reduce your speed if an attempted merge must be aborted. The tailgater's need to share attention between the merging and following tasks places you at high risk. If I am tailgated on a freeway entrance ramp I monitor the tailgater, reduce my speed substantially well before the freeway, and when a potentially acceptable gap comes along, accelerate rapidly, observing the tailgater recede into the distance in my rear view mirror. The time lag before the tailgater responds to the acceleration is readily observed, and provides an interesting indication of his or her likely time lag if I had braked instead.

Another effective way to deter tailgaters is to flash your brake lights. This is most satisfying if the tailgater then brakes. When in a particularly feisty mood, I have occasionally applied the brakes mildly, followed by acceleration, with most pleasing results. This approach should not be used if the tailgater is also being tailgated, as you do not want to precipitate a rear-impact crash. Earlier I mentioned that it was easy to become the not-at-fault driver in a crash. It is likewise easy to cause a crash for which you bear no legal responsibility and in which you are not even involved (the lead driver in Fig. 14-3 did nothing improper or illegal). If your actions convince the following driver that you are too crazy to risk following, then you have achieved your goal of increased personal safety while at the same time reducing the tailgater's risk. However, you may increase risk to another driver. I invariably observe tailgaters select new targets after I make it clear I will not allow them to tailgate me.

When being tailgated while enjoying the scenery on quiet rural two-lane roads, I have pulled onto the shoulder forcing the tailgater to pass. It is not uncommon for the tailgater to then proceed at a slower speed than that used previously to tailgate me, providing additional indications that the source of the behavior is habit rather than time savings. In congested city traffic, slowing down and using a sweeping rearward hand gesture visible through the rear window to invite a tailgater to keep further away usually produces the intended result. You occasionally get satisfying indications that the offending driver receives additional helpful comments from a spouse sympathetic to your views on the subject.

Approaching traffic lights. Drivers of vehicles struck in the rear while stationary often seem to think that it is self-evident their crashes were unavoidable. While a few are indeed unpreventable, most can be prevented. The risk of being struck in the rear while approaching a red light, or the risk of being struck while stationary at the light, can be influenced by your behavior approaching the light. Rather than proceeding at prior cruising speed and braking strongly close to the stop line, you can reduce crash risk by gently coasting towards the stop line while maintaining just enough pressure on the brake pedal to activate the brake lights. A vehicle is more visible when moving than when stopped. Basically, the goal should be to arrive in front of the stop line just as the light turns green, having reduced your speed as little as possible. This strategy also reduces vehicle wear and fuel use. Delaying the decision to reduce speed or stop increases the risk of being rear impacted. Red light cameras encourage the decision to stop after such indecision, and lead to increased rear impacts.[21]

Sometimes you cannot avoid being so close to the light when it changes that moderate deceleration followed by a period of stationary waiting is unavoidable. For the period when your vehicle is the only one waiting, you are at some risk of being struck in the rear. Although there is not a great deal you can do, it is still worth keeping an eye on your rear view mirror. If any vehicle approaches in a threatening way, you will increase your conspicuity by flashing your brake lights off and on. This is because detection of dynamic cues is greater than the detection of the static cue of a constantly lit brake light, especially in peripheral vision.

System-wide effects. The system-wide effects of safe headways are not necessarily all positive. If all drivers were so selfish as to reduce their personal rear-impact crash risk by choosing two second headways, the capacity of freeways would decline. Indeed, freeway flow would have a theoretical upper limit of 1,800 vehicles per lane per hour. Incredibly, flows of 2,650 vehicles per lane per hour, which corresponds to an <u>average</u> headway of 1.36 seconds, have been recorded on a British motorway.[18] As this chapter is aimed at the individual driver, the wise individual decision is to protect yourself by choosing a safe following headway of about two seconds. Let other more altruistic drivers assure high flow by following at headways that place them at increased personal risk but provide them little personal benefit.

Other traffic situations

I treated rear-end crashes in detail to illustrate principles that apply also in other situations. I particularly stressed that we are not obliged to become a helpless not-at-fault partner for risky at-fault drivers. Similar notions apply to other traffic situations.

Intersections

Everyone knows that some drivers run red lights. If you are the first vehicle in line, it is prudent to glance left, and then right, before proceeding when the light turns green. The presence of stopped, or stopping, vehicles in each cross lane confirms that it is safe to proceed. Such increased caution is particularly important if you are able to approach the intersection without stopping just as the light turns green. In this case, by reaching the center of the roadway in less time than an initially stationary vehicle, you could surprise a driver running the red light.

In city streets do not place your faith in other drivers obeying stop signs, or adhering to right-of-way rules. Many drivers seem to attack stop signs at high speed, and brake at the last moment, even when they can clearly see traffic on the major road. This seems to be another driving behavior rooted in habit, rather than aimed at minimizing trip time. When I, and many other drivers, traveling on a major road see such a driver heading for our path, we slow down to see what develops. After the driver on the minor road makes the required legal stop, we regain our prior speed, and proceed normally. Thus aggressive drivers delay prudent drivers on the major road. But they also delay themselves, because they must wait until the delayed driver passes the minor road. It is another case in which more dangerous, aggressive driving is rewarded by increased crash risk, increased vehicle wear, increased fuel use, and increased delay. Pedestrians often similarly increase delays to themselves and others by standing so near the curbside that prudent approaching motorists slow down.

Overtaking

Many drivers tailgate a vehicle they desire to overtake. Assuming that the lead driver permits such behavior, it will generally increase overtaking risk. The maximum overtaking risk occurs when the overtaken and overtaking vehicle are adjacent, preventing the overtaking vehicle from quickly aborting and returning to its original lane. The time the vehicles are adjacent is reduced if the relative speed between the vehicles when they are level is increased. If the following vehicle starts very close to the lead vehicle, then the initial relative speed at the commencement of the overtaking maneuver is close to zero. If the following vehicle is further back, its speed can substantially exceed that of the overtaken vehicle by the time the vehicles draw level. Just prior to drawing level, the following vehicle can safely abort.

On relatively deserted freeways I often observe vehicles driving alongside each other on adjacent lanes. Such behavior increases crash risk for no apparent reason. If you find yourself alongside another vehicle, especially a long truck, then speed up or slow down. Be particularly wary of drivers who locate themselves behind your vehicle in positions in which they cannot be seen in your rear-view mirrors.

In general, keep as much space around you as possible. Major driving errors, skids, tire blow-outs, and such incidents are far less likely to lead to crashes if your vehicle is not close to other vehicles or objects. If a crash does occur, lots of empty space surrounding the vehicle is the safest occupant protection environment. In moments of lax concentration, drivers do drift out of lanes, change lanes without sufficient care, etc. Such threats cannot always be avoided in high flow traffic, but there is no point seeking them.

Speed

The above comments on methods for reducing risk all involved minimal, or no, delay. As speed involves a trade-off between safety and mobility, rational drivers might make different decisions on different occasions. Increased average speed can be obtained with the least increase in risk by focusing the speed increases preferentially on the least risky portions of the trip. Roadway portions with wide shoulders pose less risk than those with close guardrails, and guardrails pose less risk than solid structures such as walls, utility poles or trees. However, the basics should be kept firmly in mind. Increased speed increases crash risk, and, given that a crash occurs, injury severity increases steeply with speed (p. 209-217).

Consequences of rare events are highly speed dependent. The statement "There was nothing I could do – the child just ran onto the road" is rarely correct. Just because children are taught not to run onto the road without checking for traffic does not mean that the possibility that they will do so can be ignored. 295 child pedestrians under the age of 10 were killed in the US in 2002. Drivers should slow down substantially when driving close to parked vehicles or other objects from which pedestrians could appear suddenly.

Vehicle choice

Vehicle choice involves trade-offs between many factors, safety being just one. Few vehicles are purchased based on a single criterion, like the most comfortable, most fuel-economic, least expensive, most spacious, most fun to drive, best looking, or safest vehicle. Each individual will have a different solution to this complex problem.

I personally find it difficult to imagine benefits of motorcycling that are commensurate with the risk. But if people enjoy it so much, and do it knowingly, one must assume that they are making a choice that makes sense for them.

If you are in a crash, the vehicle attribute that most affects risk is mass. The heavier your vehicle, the more protected you will be. Although overall fatality rates are somewhat higher in SUVs than in cars of the same weight, the difference is due to rollover crashes. These are nearly all easily avoided *at-fault* crashes. The different fatality rates experienced by vehicles of the same type and mass manufactured by different companies are due mainly to the different types of drivers they attract, not the vehicles. Vehicles that acquire reputations for safety generally do so by attracting safe drivers. Crash ratings have no more than small effects on outcomes. The differences are minor compared to the effect of mass. A large, heavy vehicle may be the safest choice, but other vehicle attributes may be considered more important.

My own personal vehicle is a subcompact car with FARS weight 2,644 pounds (1,199 kg). With such a light weight, it is well represented in FARS! I like this car for easy parking and economy, and it is a pleasure to drive. Indeed, I am so delighted with it that it may be a long time before I replace it, which may be both good and bad news for GM. If I did replace it, it would be with a similar vehicle. I have little desire to own a Sports Utility Vehicle (SUV) or a large car.

Some people commend me for saving the planet by my vehicle choice. No such consideration influenced my decision, nor does the SUV have the enormous influence on national fuel use its critics claim. A year's driving of 12,000 miles in a SUV with fuel economy 21 miles per gallon consumes 143 gallons more fuel than a 28 mile-per-gallon car. One airline trip by a couple across the Atlantic or the North American continent causes substantially more fuel than this to be consumed.[22] Yet no one has accused me of destroying the planet because I fly a lot. It is only when the cost of running an SUV or flying is increased by additional taxes on fuel that such travel will decrease. A campaign led by anti-SUV clergy asked, "What vehicle would Jesus drive?"[23] This seems about as sensible as asking, "Where would Jesus vacation?" I would wager that those raising the question, joined by one mansion-dwelling broadcaster, were each responsible for consuming vastly more fossil fuel than those whose vehicle choice they deplored with such moral certainty.

Incentives to decrease or increase crash likelihood

The notion of incentives to decrease the likelihood of involvement in traffic crashes may seem unreasonable. After all, involvement in even the most minor crash is an extremely unpleasant experience, involving a ruined day, bureaucratic entanglements, and the loss of hundreds of dollars. A major crash may cause death. What penalties beyond these could possibly further motivate drivers to avoid crashes? Such an analysis fails to take into account the extent to which behavior is influenced by the perceived cost of crashing. Accepting that drivers would drive more carefully if their vehicles were wired to explode on minor impact implies that increasing the cost of a minor crash will reduce the probability of a minor crash (p. 350). My own risk-taking in traffic is reduced by the embarrassment cost I would suffer were I to lose the crash-free record that I was foolhardy enough to boast about at the beginning of this chapter.

Collision insurance increases collisions

If increasing the cost of crash involvement reduces the probability of crash involvement, then reducing the cost of involvement must increase the probability of crash involvement. Insurance sharply reduces the immediate cost of involvement in a specific crash by transferring most of the monetary cost away from those directly involved. The insurance industry uses the term *moral hazard* to describe insurance-induced changes in behavior, whether legal or illegal. It is clearly difficult to obtain empirical data on such matters, but there are compelling reasons to accept that they occur. I would certainly feel safer driving among drivers required to pay the full property damage cost of any crash in which they were involved rather than the actual situation in which almost all of the cost is borne by those not involved.

The non-purchase of collision insurance is a safety measure that slightly reduces mobility by encouraging more careful driving. But it saves a lot of money. Suppose you judge that your risk is average, and you possess resources that would allow you to pay for vehicle-repair or replacement costs without unbearable pain or financial ruin if a crash did occur. Under such circumstances I find it hard to think of any investment with an expected return approaching the investment decision of changing from purchasing to not purchasing collision insurance. Perhaps the decision to change from betting in casinos to not betting in casinos may have a better pay off.

If not purchasing insurance reduces your crash risk, the payoff is all the greater. If you are a safer than average driver, the payoff is dramatically greater still. My casual observation is that I and other motorists who carry no insurance beyond the legal minimum have crash involvement rates well below average, while motorists with abnormally high crash rates tend to shy away from even driving around the block without collision coverage. If you are a driver who does not crash and does not buy collision insurance, the insurance company will likely recoup your gratis premium by increasing deductibles and premium increases following crashes. So, not buying insurance yourself increases the cost of crashing to those who do buy insurance. This makes them less likely to crash into you, thus providing a small additional safety bonus from not buying insurance.

These remarks relate exclusively to the fiscal and safety benefits of not purchasing insurance to cover the repair or replacement of your own vehicle, provided you have the financial means to cover these costs yourself. Discharging obligations to others is a quite different matter, for which the law rightly requires every driver to carry insurance. Those driving illegally without insurance generally break other laws and are extremely high risk drivers, often at the fringes of society.

An experiment with a surprising result. While employed by General Motors I came up with what I thought was a neat way to investigate how risky everyday driving related to an individual driver's crash and violation record. My goal was to note cases of extreme risk taking (tailgating, speeding, weaving across lanes, unsafe overtaking, etc.) by drivers I observed during my commuting trip. I would use an on-board audio tape recorder to record the license plate of the offending vehicle together with my estimate of the gender and age of the driver, and record corresponding information for a nearby random driver judged to be of the same gender and similar age.

I was hoping to collect over a number of years a few hundred pairs of risky and control drivers, use the license plate numbers to identify the vehicle owners, and if there was no mismatch of gender or age, assume the owner was driving. The state files identify the driver license of the vehicle owner, so that the crash and violation records of the risky and control drivers could be compared. The aim was to apply the same procedure that led to Fig. 14-2 (p. 367), but for rare events that are much more extreme than occur within the time-frame of normal experimental observations. After collecting two dozen pairs I decided to check how things were proceeding by obtaining the vehicle and driver data from the state. This required a formal procedure to insure that no personal driver information beyond gender, age, and driving record was transmitted.

The data turned out to be useless for the purposes intended. Most of the vehicles with the high-risk drivers were owned by General Motors! They had accordingly no individual drivers associated with them. The drivers were participants in a program in which selected employees tested corporate products (at least, that is how the Internal Revenue Service interpreted it). If a participant crashed a vehicle, another vehicle was supplied, with the main costs being paperwork and embarrassment (unless there were police charges). The general demographics and other attributes of the drivers would suggest that they were likely to have otherwise been safer than average drivers.

An observational study in Britain found that people driving company cars traveled at a higher speed than those in their own vehicles.[24] Traffic in the US and UK seems to be providing additional support for the more universal principle annunciated by Nobel Laureate economist Milton Friedman:

Nobody spends somebody else's money as carefully as he spends his own.[25]

I believe that the original goal of my unsuccessful experiment is worth pursuing by a researcher not commuting to an automobile company facility. Collecting data is difficult and at times risky, as obtaining the license-plate numbers often required following a conspicuously high-risk driver, even a speeder, sufficiently closely to record the license plate number. I am not sure I would have done this in a vehicle that I owned!

Pleasure

Riskier driving is often indulged in simply because it is enjoyable. Driving is one of many activities in which pleasure and safety are in conflict. People in droves deny themselves the pleasures of ice cream, fried eggs, tobacco, and hard liquor in the expectation that it will keep them alive longer. Another approach to increasing longevity is to jog or lift weights, activities that would have astonished a laborer from an earlier age. Those taking such unappealing actions to extend their lives are never stigmatized as being more cowardly than others less afraid of dying. Important gains in life expectancy can be achieved by the rather modest behavior changes necessary to avoid participating in traffic crashes. Such behavior changes consume an infinitesimal fraction of the time required to jog, they are not all that unpleasant, and additionally extend the average life expectancy of other road users. Safe driving should, of course, be an addition to other healthy practices, not a substitution.

Altruism

One individual driving more safely benefits not just the safer individual, but the entire safety system. In the situation portrayed in Fig. 14-3 (p 369), if a driver of any one of the first seven cars had adopted a larger headway, car number 8 would not have hit car number 7. The drivers of cars numbers 7 and 8 would never be aware of the trouble the other driver had spared them. As it is, the drivers of cars number 2 through 6 all contributed to the crash but proceeded unaware that it even occurred. A driver avoiding involvement in a not-at-fault crash is sparing some anonymous driver from being involved in an at-fault crash. Drivers refusing to be tailgated provide useful feedback to tailgaters that may tend to discourage their behavior. A driver approaching a traffic signal in a safe manner often prevents another following driver from running the red.

In a more general sense, safe and courteous driving encourages similar behavior in others. Risky driving is deviant from average, or normal, driving. If average speeds decrease, the most extreme speeders also slow down, but remain about as deviant from the norm as before. They retain their deviance, but at less risk to themselves and others.

In the broader sense, a nation's total traffic fatality count is determined by the summation of the risks taken by all of its drivers. A driver reducing his or her personal risk is making an important contribution to reducing a major national problem.

Summary and conclusions

Your risk in traffic can be dramatically reduced, perhaps close to the levels that prevail in commercial aviation, by eight principles:

1. **Maintain space around your vehicle.** This simple rule pays the largest safety dividends. It applies when you are followed as well as when you follow. Take active steps to prevent other vehicles from tailgating yours. In freeway driving stay clear of other vehicles when conditions permit. Overtake quickly – do not drive alongside large trucks for longer than required to complete the overtaking.

2. **Do not be surprised by deplorable behavior of other drivers.** You drive in a system in which one percent of the drivers take greater risks than the other 99%. Deplorable behavior by some drivers should be regarded like the occasional very cold day in winter. Expect it, and treat it as a property of an external system in which it is your behavior that determines whether you crash (or get frostbitten). There is nothing to be gained by getting angry at such external conditions, and much to be lost if it increases your crash risk.

3. **Drive so that the consequences of rare events can be avoided.** On a typical trip, no extraordinary events occur. Likewise, even in a typical year. But in a driving career, a number of extremely rare events are bound to occur. Drive so that very rare events do not become *unavoidable* crashes.

4. **Don't let experience fool you into poor driving habits.** Experience is a poor teacher because it leads us to believe that our driving is safe because it has not led to bad consequences. Yet events we have never experienced do occur. Drive so that things you have not yet experienced will not harm you.

5. **Do not be an average driver.** If you are an average driver expect to crash about every 12 years. To avoid this you must drive more safely than an average driver.

6. **Don't overestimate your safety and driving skills.** Keep in mind that you are probably not as safe as you think you are. Additionally, keep in mind that other drivers think that they are safer and more skillful than you.

7. **Not buying collision insurance will probably make you a safer driver.** By reducing the cost of crashing, insurance increases the probability of crashing.

8. **Remember that your safer driving benefits others as well as yourself.** When you avoid not-at-fault involvement, you are doing an enormous anonymous favor to the driver who would have been at fault. Your safer behavior in approaching traffic signals or attenuating rather than amplifying disturbances in platoons of vehicles can prevent crashes involving vehicles far away from yours.

References for Chapter 14

1   Evans L. *Traffic Safety and the Driver.* New York, NY: Van Nostrand Reinhold; 1991.

2   Humes JC. *Podium Humor: A Raconteur's Treasury of Witty and Humorous Stories.* New York, NY: Harper and Row; 1975.

3   Summala H. Young driver accidents: Risk taking or failure of skills? *Alcohol Drugs and Driving.* 1987; 3: 79-91.

4   Quality Planning Corporation. More drivers are on the roads; Who are you most likely to run into? A student? A politician? A librarian? Press release; 30 October 2003. http://www.qualityplanning.com/news/031030%20-%20Occupations_2.pdf

5   Svenson O. Are we less risky and more skillful than our fellow drivers? *Acta Psychologica.* 1981; 47: 143-148.

6   Job RFS. The application of learning theory to driving confidence: The effect of age and the impact of random breath testing. *Accid Anal Prev.* 1990; 22: 97-107.

7   McCormick IA, Walkey FH, Green DE. Comparative perceptions of driver ability -- a confirmation and expansion. *Accid Anal Prev.* 1986; 18: 205-208.

8   DeJoy DM. The optimistic bias and traffic accident risk perception. *Accid Anal Prev.* 1989; 21: 333-340.

9   Matthews ML, Moran AR. Age differences in male drivers' perception of accident risk: The role of perceived driving ability. *Accid Anal Prev.* 1986; 18: 299-313.

10 Williams AF. Views of U.S. drivers about driving safety. *J Safety Res.* 2003; 34: 491-504.

11 Preston CE, Harris S. Psychology of drivers in traffic accidents. *J App Psych.* 1965; 49: 284-288.

12 Passman C, McGwin GJ, Taylor AJ, Rue LW. Seat belt use before and after motor vehicle trauma. *J Trauma.* 2001; 51: 105-109.

13 Groeger JA, Brown ID. Assessing one's own and others' driving ability: Influence of sex, age, and experience. *Accid Anal Prev.* 1989; 21: 155-168.

14 Weinstein ND. Optimistic biases about personal risks. *Science.* 1989; 246: 1232-1233.

15 Festinger LA. *A Theory of Cognitive Dissonance.* Palo Alto, CA: Stanford University Press; 1957.

16 Brehmer B. In one word: Not from experience. *Acta Psychologica.* 1980; 45: 223-241.

17 Evans L, Wasielewski P. Do accident involved drivers exhibit riskier everyday driving behavior? *Accid Anal Prev.* 1982; 14: 57-64.

18 Wasielewski P. Car following headways on freeways interpreted by the semi-Poisson headway distribution model. *Transportation Science.* 1979; 13: 36-55.

19 Katz J. *Seductions of Crime.* New York, NY: Basic Books; 1988.

20 Herman R, Montroll EW, Potts RB, Rothery RW. Traffic dynamics: Analysis of stability in car following. *Operations Res.* 1959; 7: 86-106.

21 Retting RA, Ferguson SA, Hakkert AS. Effects of red light cameras on violations and crashes: A review of the international literature. *Traf Inj Prev.* 2003; 4: 17-23.

22 Boeing – Green machines, clean machines. http://www.boeing.com/commercial/value/green.html

23 Evans L. We need higher taxes on gas (What would Jesus drive)? Editorial, San Francisco Examiner; 9 December 2002.   http://www.scienceservingsociety.com/p/148.htm

24 Maycock G, Brocklebank P, Hall R. Road layout design standards and driver behaviour. *Proc Inst Civil Engineers – Transport.* 1999; 135: 115-122.

25 Hoover Institute – Uncommon Knowledge. Milton's paradise gained: Milton Friedman's Advice for the Next President. Presentation; 10 March 2000. http://www.uncommonknowledge.org/winter00/421.html

15 The dramatic failure of US safety policy

Introduction

This chapter is intimately related to Chapter 12 on airbags. This is not because airbags, as devices, are central to traffic safety. In 2003 they reduced fatality risk by 10% for 47% of road users, thus reducing US total fatalities by almost 5%. Such a reduction, without affecting anything else, would be important, even if much less important than the driver factors discussed in Chapters 13 and 14.

The role of the airbag in US safety policy was not so much as a device, but as an icon for a safety philosophy that precipitated a national disaster. Below we use simple analyses of readily accessible public data to document the extent of the disaster, and then discuss the background that contributed to it.

The US compared to other countries

Prior to the mid 1960s the US had the safest traffic in the world, whether measured by deaths per registered vehicle, or deaths for the same distance of travel. A series of tabulated rates for the US and 11 other major industrialized countries for the years up to 1978 appeared under the headline *U.S. the Safest Place for Driving.*[1(p 52)] US rates were substantially lower than those in any of the other countries listed.

By 2002, in terms of deaths per registered vehicle, the US had dropped from first place into sixteenth place, behind Australia, Austria, Canada, Denmark, Finland, Germany, Great Britain, Iceland, Japan, Luxembourg, the Netherlands, New Zealand, Norway, Sweden, and Switzerland.[2]

Comparing rates in 2002 to rates in 1979

The decline in US safety relative to other countries is explored below by comparing changes in specific US fatality rates with the changes in the same rates in other countries. Three traffic fatality rates are examined:

1. Fatalities per year (the raw fatality rate).
2. Fatalities per thousand registered vehicles (the vehicle rate).
3. Fatalities per billion km of vehicle travel (the distance rate).

Three countries, Great Britain,[3] Canada,[4] and Australia,[5] are selected for the comparisons. These three countries are chosen because they have much in common with the US in terms of language, beliefs, and traditions. Performance is compared over the 23-year period from 1979 to 2002. It was in the late 1970s/early 1980s that the safety policies of the US and other countries began to diverge. The results are not all that different if the initial and final times were a few years earlier or later, or if some different comparison countries were chosen.

Fatalities per year comparisons. Figure 15-1 shows the change in the simplest measure of safety performance, total traffic deaths per year. While fatalities in the 23 year period declined in the US by 16.2%, declines of 46.0%, 49.9%, and 51.1% occurred in Britain, Canada, and Australia (Table 15-1). In the prior 1960-1978 period the comparison countries did not systematically outperform the US. On the contrary, fatalities in Canada and Australia increased by 65% and 50% (compared to a 38% increase in the US), but in GB decreased by 2%.

The number of traffic deaths that would have occurred in the US in 2002 if US fatalities had declined by the same percents as in the comparison countries from 1979-2002 are shown in Table 15-2. If the US total had declined by 46.0%, as it did in Great Britain, then US fatalities in 2002 would have been 27,598 instead of the 42,815 that occurred. (All derivations are based on calculations including more decimal places than shown in tables). By matching the British decline, 15,217 fewer Americans would have been killed in 2002. The corresponding fatality reductions for matching Canadian and Australian performance are 17,229 and 17,837.

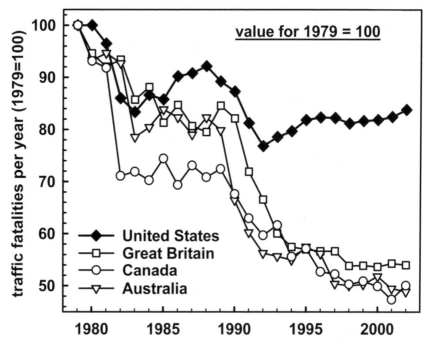

Figure 15-1. Traffic fatalities per year in the US and in three comparison countries. All values are rescaled by dividing the actual number for each year by the number in 1979, and multiplying by 100.

Table 15-1. The percent reduction in the number of fatalities per year between 1979 and 2002 in the US and in three comparison countries.

| country | fatalities | | percent change |
	1979	2002	1979 to 2002
United States	51,093	42,815	-16.2%
Great Britain	6,352	3,431	-46.0%
Canada	5,863	2,936	-49.9%
Australia	3,508	1,715	-51.1%

Table 15-2. Estimated number of fatalities that would have occurred in the US in 2002 if the US had achieved the same percent decline in fatalities per year between 1979 and 2002 as the comparison countries.

if US decline had matched	instead of –16.2%, 1979-2002 change would have been	instead of 42,815, fatalities in 2002 would have been	number of US lives saved in 2002
Great Britain	-46.0%	27,598	15,217
Canada	-49.9%	25,586	17,229
Australia	-51.1%	24,978	17,837

Fatalities per registered vehicle comparisons. Because of the disparate numbers of vehicles in different countries, raw fatalities can be compared effectively only by renormalizing in some way as in Fig. 15-1. However, rates such as fatalities per thousand registered vehicles (the vehicle rate) can be plotted without the need to select a reference year, as shown in Fig. 15-2. Prior to the late 1970s the comparison countries, in common with all countries, had rates higher than the US. The change in time from a higher to a lower rate than for the US is illustrated additionally for Sweden in Fig 3-6, p. 41. The US rate shows no indication of a drop in response to any major vehicle safety legislation, such as the National Traffic and Motor Vehicle Safety Act of 1966 that required all vehicles manufactured in 1968 or later to satisfy a number of Federal Motor Vehicle Safety Standards (FMVSS). The only notable downward spike, in 1974, is unrelated to vehicles, but reflects various changes stimulated by the 1973 oil embargo, including driver behavior changes, especially speed reductions in response to changes in speed limits (Fig. 9-3, p. 213).

Table 15-3 shows the changes in the vehicle rate from 1979 to 2002 for the US and the comparison countries. The US decline of 46.2% in a 23 year period might seem impressive, but it corresponds to a compound decline of only 2.7% per year. This is less than the average 3.1% from 1900-2002, and still less than the 3.2% from 1900-1978. Thus US safety policy in the 1979-2002 period did not lead to declines as large as occurred in earlier decades.

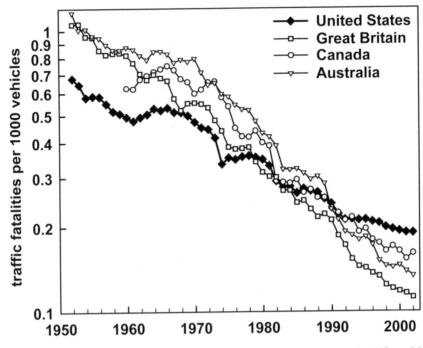

Figure 15-2. Traffic fatalities per thousand registered vehicles in the US and in the three comparison countries.

Table 15-3. The percent reduction in the vehicle rate (number of fatalities per thousand registered vehicles) between 1979 and 2002 in the US and in three comparison countries.

	US	GB	Canada	Australia
1979				
fatalities	51,093	6,352	5,863	3,508
vehicles (thousands)	144,317	18,616	13,329	7,358
fatalities/(thou veh)	0.354	0.341	0.440	0.477
2002				
fatalities	42,815	3,431	2,936	1,715
vehicles (thousands)	224,974	30,557	18,271	12,799
fatalities/(thou veh)	0.190	0.112	0.161	0.134
change in rate, 1979-2002	-46.2%	-67.1%	-63.5%	-71.9%

While the US vehicle rate declined by 46.2%, the rates in Britain, Canada, and Australia declined by 67.1%, 63.5%, and 71.9%. If the US rate had declined by the same 67.1% it did in Britain, then in 2002 the US rate would have been $0.354 \times (1-0.671) = 0.116$ fatalities per thousand vehicles, instead of the 0.190 rate observed. Applying the 0.116 rate to the 224,974 thousand vehicles in the US in 2002 would have led to 26,210 fatalities, 16,606 fewer than the 42,815 observed. The US fatality reductions from matching the declines in the Canadian and Australian vehicle rates are 13,718 and 20,429.

Fatalities for the same travel distance comparisons. The best estimates of distance of vehicle travel are for Great Britain, based on observations at fifty sites supported by the Department of Transport. Reliable estimates over a long period are not available for most countries, so the comparison will be confined to Great Britain. Because we compare how rates change in time, the fact that vehicles in the US travel greater distances per year than in other countries is not important provided trends in the distance of travel per vehicle are not markedly different between the countries compared, which they are not. Greater travel in the US leads to lower distance rates every year. While the US dropped from number one ranking to number 16 in deaths per vehicle, for deaths for the same travel distance it dropped from number one ranking to number 10, behind Australia, Canada, Denmark, Finland, Great Britain, the Netherlands, Norway, Sweden, and Switzerland.[2]

Figure 15-3 shows that while the distance rate in Britain was (as in all countries) previously higher than in the US, in 2002 it was lower. Table 15-4 shows the 1979 to 2002 comparison for the distance rate parallel to the Table 15-3 for the vehicle rate. If the US distance rate had declined by the same 71.3% that occurred in Britain, US fatalities in 2002 would have been $4,553.8 \times 20.8 \times (1-0.713) = 27,145$ instead of the 42,815 observed. By matching the British decline, 15,670 fewer Americans would have been killed in 2002.

Average comparisons 2002 versus 1979. I have presented results like the above in publications[6,7] and in many oral presentations, in most cases for just one of the rates due to limited space or time. One of the most common reactions from surprised readers and audiences is, "What would the result have been if instead of (say) the vehicle rate, you had used the distance rate?"[8] Anticipating such questions, all three rates are given, leading to the values summarized in Table 15-5.

Averaging over the rates available for the comparison countries gives the results that:

If US matched Great Britain	15,831 fewer US fatalities in 2002.
If US matched Canada	15,474 fewer US fatalities in 2002.
If US matched Australia	19,133 fewer US fatalities in 2002.

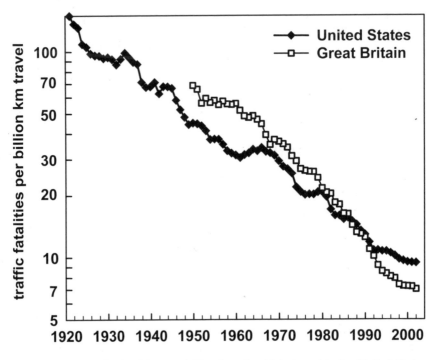

Figure 15-3. Traffic fatalities per billion km of vehicle travel in the United States and in Great Britain.

Table 15-4. The percent reduction in the number of fatalities per billion km of vehicle travel between 1979 and 2002 in the US and in GB.

		US	*GB*
<u>1979</u>			
	fatalities	51,093	6,352
	vehicle travel (billion km)	2,460.9	260.5
	fatalities/(billion km)	20.8	24.4
<u>2002</u>			
	fatalities	42,815	3,431
	vehicle travel (billion km)	4,553.8	490.0
	fatalities/(billion km)	9.4	7.0
	change in distance rate from 1979 to 2002	-54.7%	-71.3%

Table 15-5. Estimates of the reductions in US traffic deaths in 2002 if fatality rates had declined in the US by the same percents as they did in three comparison countries. The average of the seven values is 16,672 fewer US fatalities.

rate	reduction in 2002 traffic deaths if US had matched 1979-2002 percent changes in:		
	GB	Canada	Australia
per year	15,217	17,229	17,837
per thousand vehicles (vehicle rate)	16,605	13,718	20,429
per billion km (distance rate)	15,670	–	–

The average of all seven estimates in Table 15-5 is 16,672. This leads to the conclusion that if the US had matched the changes in safety achieved in the comparison countries from 1979-2002, instead of 42,815 fatalities in 2002, the US would have had 26,143.

Fatality differences accumulated over the 1979-2002 period

All the above has focused on comparing differences between 2002 and the reference year 1979. Table 15-6 shows the calculation of the vehicle rate for Great Britain for every year between 1979 and 2002. The 2002 data are the same as in Table 15-3. The conclusion from this table is that if the US vehicle fatality rate had declined each year since 1979 by the same percent as it did in Britain, 177,593 fewer Americans would have been killed in the 23-year period. Details of this and other calculations for the other values in Table 15-7 are in Excel files on the Internet.[9] The variation, from 163,007 to 266,686 is not surprising as the cumulative values reflect changes occurring at different times in the different comparison countries, as is apparent in Figs 15-1 and 15-2.

Averaging over the rates available for the comparison countries gives the results that:

If US matched Great Britain	163,007 fewer US fatalities 1979-2002.
If US matched Canada	247,972 fewer US fatalities 1979-2002.
If US matched Australia	207,854 fewer US fatalities 1979-2002.

The average of the 7 values in Table 15-6 is 214,286. The leads to the conclusion that because US safety performance failed to match that in the comparison countries in the 23-year period from 1979 to 2002, about 200,000 additional Americans died in traffic crashes.

Table 15-6. The change in the vehicle fatality rate (fatalities per thousand vehicles) in the US and GB from 1979 to 2002, and what US fatalities would have been if the US rate had matched changes in the British rate.

year	United States fatalities	vehicles (thou)	rate	Great Britain fatalities	vehicles (thou)	rate	change since 1979	A	B	C
1979	51,093	144,317	0.354	6,352	18,616	0.341	0.0%	0.354	51,093	0
1980	51,091	146,845	0.348	6,010	19,199	0.313	-8.3%	0.325	47,695	3,396
1981	49,301	149,330	0.330	5,846	19,347	0.302	-11.4%	0.314	46,819	2,482
1982	43,945	151,148	0.291	5,934	19,762	0.300	-12.0%	0.312	47,091	-3,146
1983	42,589	153,830	0.277	5,445	20,209	0.269	-21.0%	0.280	43,004	-415
1984	44,257	158,900	0.279	5,599	20,765	0.270	-21.0%	0.280	44,455	-198
1985	43,825	166,047	0.264	5,165	21,159	0.244	-28.5%	0.253	42,056	1,769
1986	46,087	168,545	0.273	5,382	21,699	0.248	-27.3%	0.257	43,375	2,712
1987	46,390	172,750	0.269	5,125	22,152	0.231	-32.2%	0.240	41,469	4,921
1988	47,087	177,455	0.265	5,052	23,302	0.217	-36.5%	0.225	39,919	7,168
1989	45,582	181,165	0.252	5,373	24,196	0.222	-34.9%	0.230	41,741	3,841
1990	44,599	184,275	0.242	5,217	24,673	0.211	-38.0%	0.219	40,428	4,171
1991	41,508	186,370	0.223	4,568	24,511	0.186	-45.4%	0.193	36,038	5,470
1992	39,250	184,938	0.212	4,229	24,577	0.172	-49.6%	0.179	33,018	6,232
1993	40,150	188,350	0.213	3,814	24,826	0.154	-55.0%	0.159	30,023	10,127
1994	40,716	192,497	0.212	3,650	25,231	0.145	-57.6%	0.150	28,894	11,822
1995	41,817	197,065	0.212	3,621	25,369	0.143	-58.2%	0.148	29,185	12,632
1996	42,065	201,631	0.209	3,598	26,302	0.137	-59.9%	0.142	28,619	13,446
1997	42,013	203,568	0.206	3,599	26,974	0.133	-60.9%	0.138	28,182	13,831
1998	41,501	208,076	0.199	3,421	27,538	0.124	-63.6%	0.129	26,820	14,681
1999	41,717	212,685	0.196	3,423	28,368	0.121	-64.6%	0.125	26,628	15,089
2000	41,945	217,028	0.193	3,409	28,898	0.118	-65.4%	0.122	26,564	15,381
2001	42,196	221,230	0.191	3,450	29,747	0.116	-66.0%	0.120	26,622	15,574
2002	42,815	224,974	0.190	3,431	30,557	0.112	-67.1%	0.117	26,210	16,605

total number of fewer US fatalities if US rate had declined in step with British rate   177,593

A: what US rate would have been if it had declined by same percent as British rate
B: what US fatalities would have been for US vehicle fleet if vehicle rate had been as in column A
C: the number of US fatalities prevented if US rate had declined in step with British rate

Table 15-7. Estimates of the number of fewer American deaths in the period 1979 to 2002 if changes in US rates had matched changes in rates of comparison countries. The average of the seven values is 214,286.

rate	reduction in 2002 traffic deaths if US had matched 1979-2002 percent changes in:		
	GB	Canada	Australia
per year	163,007	247,972	207,854
per thousand vehicles (vehicle rate)	177,593	221,413	266,686
per billion km (distance rate)	215,480	-	-

Search for an explanation

While 200,000 additional US fatalities were shown by straightforward analyses of publicly available data, it is not possible to explain why this occurred by a similarly simple analysis. Yet there must be an explanation, even if it cannot be formulated in simple multiplicative factors. The explanation below reflects my judgmental conclusions based on experience and involvement in many traffic safety issues in many countries spread over a number of decades. I believe that the interpretation owes much to my perspective from growing to adulthood outside the US before later becoming a US citizen.

As the difference between US performance and that in other countries is so great, it must flow from large basic differences between the US and other countries. I believe that the key is the uniquely powerful role litigation has come to play in the US, producing the following interlaced effects:

1. US safety policy priorities have been ordered almost perfectly opposite to where technical knowledge shows benefits are greatest (as represented in Fig. 13-4, p. 339).

2. This happened because US policy was defined and led by ideologically driven lawyers lacking knowledge or interest in technical matters.

3. Such leadership emerged because of the uniquely powerful influence of law on all aspects of US society, which is without parallel in any other country.

Comparison countries are normal

When I have mentioned safety differences between the US and comparison countries, the most common American response is to ask, "What do the comparison countries do that is so special?" It is natural to assume that you are normal, and all who differ from you are abnormal. Those asking the question are generally surprised by my answer that the comparison countries did nothing particularly special. They made mistakes, adopted flawed policies, etc. All their laws are passed by democratic legislative bodies answerable to electorates they must not displease. The performance of the selected countries is not particularly different from that of the Netherlands, Sweden, Finland, or Japan. The comparison countries do not, and nor should they, celebrate any traffic safety triumph. Over a thousand deaths per year to healthy young citizens in each country is no cause for celebration. Indeed, all the best performing countries acknowledge traffic crashes as a major public health problem requiring urgent attention to a much greater extent than occurs in the US.

It is the US that is aberrant

One of the most remarkable features of the extraordinary failure of US safety policy is that it is one of the nation's best-kept secrets. Those primarily responsible for so spectacular a failure receive only praise, and lots of it, from their long-time supporters and allies, the mass media. Even the US injury control establishment thinks all is well. Two injury-control academics (with law degrees) disagreed with my editorial in the *American Journal of Public Health*.[10] They wrote that the US "reduction in the risk of fatal motor vehicle crash is one of the major success stories of public health and injury prevention."[11] They supported this statement by noting a more than 70% decline in the distance rate in the 35 years from 1966 to 2001, and attributed the "success" to vehicle regulation and litigation. They were unaware that a larger decline occurred in the first 35 years (1921-1956) for which data were available, and in which the factors they claimed produced the declines were not present.[12]   More particularly, they were unaware that in the same 1966 to 2001 period they choose, the British rate declined by 84%, and that if US declines had matched those in Britain during this period, more than 300,000 fewer Americans would have been killed. The dramatic failure of US safety policy shows in any period after the mid 1960s.

Irrelevance of numbers and technical knowledge

A dramatic change in the US approach to safety occurred when activist lawyer Ralph Nader convinced the US media, government, and public that the problem was unsafe and defective vehicles. Even if claims in his 1965 book *Unsafe at Any Speed* had merit, their effect was to focus attention on a dozen or so deaths occurring over a number of years, while ignoring the 50,000 deaths occurring annually at that time.

A picture is worth a thousand words

The photograph in Fig. 15-4 shows Ralph Nader demonstrating an airbag simulator "safely" deploying into the face of an unbelted three-year-old girl. The photograph was taken on 5 July 1977 at a Washington, DC press conference convened to support airbags. By 1977 the technical community had been long aware that deploying airbags posed risks to occupants, particularly children. A study titled "Airbag effects on the out-of-position child" was presented at a Society of Automotive Engineers meeting in Detroit in May 1972, by which time the published paper was already available.[13] The study, performed in the US, used child dummies and baboons of size and weight similar to children to investigate if deploying airbags posed injury threats to children. It found that they did. A Swedish study titled "Possible effects of air bag inflation on a standing child" was presented at technical meetings in Canada and France in 1974, and documented in the proceedings of these meetings.[14,15] The study used pigs to simulate what would happen to an out-of-position child who leaned against the air bag as it deployed. In eight of the twenty-four trials the airbag deployment killed the pig.

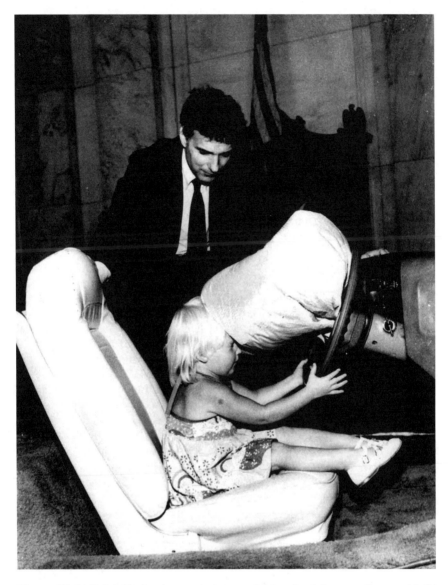

Figure 15-4. Ralph Nader demonstrates an air bag simulator on a 3-year-old girl .
at a press conference convened in Washington DC to support airbags. The
photograph was taken on 5 July 1977, long after the technical community had
documented concerns about risks to children from deploying airbags.
[credit: AP/Wide World Photos]

The individual exercising the greatest influence on US safety policy was untrained, uninformed, uninvolved, and uninterested in technical matters. Press conferences, not technical meetings, were his milieu. The individuals influencing safety policy in other countries were mostly technically trained, and attended technical meetings such as those at which the information on harm from airbags was communicated.

Quantitative information now augments the early 1970s qualitative understanding that airbags posed threats to children. Airbags increase fatality risk to unbelted children in front seats by 84%. Even if the child is belted, the airbag still increases risk by 31%.[16] NHTSA reports that (by July 2003) 144 children had been killed by airbag deployments in crashes that would not otherwise have caused major, or any, harm.[17] An important contributor to the failure of US safety policy is the advocacy role of the media. Reports of children killed by airbags rarely mentioned Ralph Nader or his disciples. Yet his name is mentioned often in the media to praise his role in making the US safer!

The airbag mandate

Nader's protégé, lawyer Joan Claybrook, had an even greater influence on US safety policy than her mentor. Claybrook became the senior safety official in the US when President Carter appointed her Administrator of the National Highway Traffic Safety Administration (NHTSA) in 1977. A NHTSA official is quoted as saying, "Joan came to NHTSA with a mission and that mission was air bags."[18(p 109)] More specifically, the mission was an airbag mandate, a government requirement that airbags be installed in vehicles. Technical information, such as the effectiveness of airbags, never impeded that goal.

Earliest quantitative estimate of airbag effectiveness

The earliest quantitative estimate of airbag effectiveness was reported in a study by General Motors published in 1973, before airbag field data were available.[19] A panel of four expert engineers examined details of fatal crashes in which 706 occupants died. Using crash reports, medical and/or autopsy reports, photographs, and other relevant information, the panel discussed the injury mechanisms for each fatally injured occupant, and arrived at a judgment about whether an airbag would have prevented the fatality. The study concluded that airbags would have prevented 18% of the fatalities to front-seat occupants.

The NHTSA effectiveness values used to justify the mandate

The airbag effectiveness numbers used to justify the mandate were published by NHTSA in 1977 in the Federal Register, the daily compilation of federal regulations, legal notices, etc. The relevant table is reproduced as Fig. 15-5.[20(Table I, p 34297)] Airbags were claimed to reduce AIS 4 to AIS 6 injuries by 40%. This injury range includes nearly all fatalities, so airbags are claimed to reduce fatality risk by 40%. The claims are for unbelted occupants.

Occupant Crash Protection System Effectiveness Estimates

AIS Injury Level	Lap Belt	Lap and Shoulder Belt	Air Cushion	Air Cushion and Lap Belt	Passive Belt and Knee Bolster	Knee Bolster
1	.15	.30	0	.15	.20	.06
2	.22	.57	.22	.33	.40	.10
3	.30	.59	.30	.45	.45	.15
4-6	.40	.60	.40	.66	.50	.15

Figure 15-5. NHTSA's 1977 estimates of effectiveness used to justify mandating airbags (called air cushions in the table). Reproduction of Table I on page 34297 of Ref. 20.

So great was the belief in airbags that part of the cost of installing them was to be offset by the cost savings due to not installing safety belts (Fig. 12-6).[20(Table III,p 34299)] Because US airbag standards are still defined for unbelted dummies, US airbags must inflate more rapidly than those of other countries, whose standards are for belted occupants. This contributes to the risk of airbag-caused injuries being so much greater in the US.

VARIOUS ESTIMATES OF THE COST OF FULL FRONT AIR BAGS

COST ITEM	GM 6-77	FORD 10-76	DELOREAN 10-76 4 Pass.	DELOREAN 10-76 6 Pass.	MINICARS 6-77 GM	MINICARS 6-77 Advanced	DOT 10-76	DOT 6-77
Purchase Cost								
Equipment	102	121	72	85	78	68	75	89
Manufacturing	66	68	9	12	44	39	28	28
Profit	45	56	35	42	122	107	12	13
– Removed Belts	-20	-10	-26	-27			-18	-18
Total	193	235	90	112	OTHER ELEMENTS		97	112
Operating Cost					NOT PROVIDED			
Deployment	9	9	NOT				2	5
Fuel	26	88	PROVIDED				30	23
Maintenance	18	63					-	-
Inspection	—	27	—	—			—	—
Total	53	187	18	27			32	28
Combined Total	246	422	108	139			129	141

Figure 15-6. In support of requiring airbags, NHTSA documents that the cost would be partially offset by savings from not having to install safety belts (4th row, negative costs labeled *Removed Belts*). Reproduction of Table III on page 34299 of Ref. 20, where it is cited as FR Doc.77-19137. Filed 6-30-77; 1:00 pm.

Key estimates of airbag effectiveness in reducing (mainly non-fatal) injury risks, in chronological order of their publication, are shown in Table 15-8 (more extensive lists for all injury levels are presented in Ref. 21). The second entry in Table 15-8 showing an approximate 9% effectiveness for AIS≥3 injury risk is based on a GM study of data from the fleet of 10,000 GM airbag-equipped cars sold in the mid 1970s.[22] While sample sizes were small, the evidence from this fleet (known well before the 1 February 1978 publication date of the paper[22]) was more than sufficient to reject as implausible the NHTSA estimates. The other values in Table 15-8 were discussed in Chapter 12.

Table 15-8. Key estimates of the effectiveness of airbags in reducing injury risk.

source	year	AIS injury level	effectiveness
NHTSA (Fig. 15-5)	1977	≥4	40%
		3	30%
		2	22%
Pursel et al. (GM)[22]	1978	≥3	9%
Segui-Gomez[23]	2000	≥4	>0
		1-3	<0
McGwin et al.[24]	2002	≥2	<0
McGwin[25]	2003	3	-2%*
		2	-2%*
		1	-2%*

* Values derived from original source for this table

Key estimates of the effectiveness of airbags in reducing fatality risk are listed in Table 15-9. As late as 1984, the 40% fatality reducing effectiveness figure had not been totally abandoned by NHTSA, but it was then included just as the upper limit of a wide (20-40)% range.[26] Although NHTSA has benefited from an entirely different type of leadership since 1981, it is always difficult for institutions to repudiate prior positions, no matter how indefensible. As distinct from the 1977 estimates published to support policy goals, NHTSA's technical staff applied technically sound methods to FARS data,[27] and estimated effectiveness to be substantially <u>lower</u> than the 18% estimate in the 1973 GM study. The method of the GM study systematically biases effectiveness estimates upwards. All the subjects were dead, so only factors that could have reduced the probability of death were considered. No information was considered about occupants who had not been killed. Yet if all of these had airbags, some would have been killed by airbags. Not estimating such effects would bias the estimate upwards, and contribute to the 18% estimate being higher than the current 12% estimate for unbelted occupants (Table 11-4, p. 286).

Table 15-9.   Key estimates of the effectiveness of airbags in reducing fatality risk.

source	year	effectiveness estimate
Wilson and Savage (GM)[19]	1973	18%
NHTSA (Fig. 15-5)	1977	40%
NHTSA[26]	1984	20-40%
Kahane (NHTSA)[27]	1996	11%
NHTSA[28]	2001	12%
Cummings et al.[29]	2002	8%

The triumph of ideological zeal

The 1977 NHTSA claim of a 40% fatality reduction effectiveness for airbags, and the 12,100 lives per year it was stated would be saved by driver and passenger airbags,[20(Table II,p 34298)] formed the basis for the airbag mandate pursued with such tenacity by Claybrook. As airbags deploy only in frontal crashes, which account for about half of deaths, an overall effectiveness of 40% would require about 80% effectiveness in frontal crashes. Such an expectation is in stark violation of the knowledge the science of biomechanics had established many decades earlier. The 40% figure, plucked out of thin air, is not just wrong; it is unrealistic, and arguably absurd. The 1973 GM study estimating 18% effectiveness was already available, augmented by actual deployment experience from the GM fleet of 10,000 airbag-equipped vehicles. The experience from this fleet was inconsistent with effectiveness approaching the NHTSA claims. NHTSA dismissed the GM findings, writing, "The Department finds the methods used in the General Motors study to be of doubtful value in arriving at an objective assessment of the experience of the air-bag-equipped vehicles. General Motors is a vastly interested party in these proceedings, and the positions that it adopts are necessarily those of an advocate for a particular result."[20(p 34292)] The document continues with a stream of baseless allegations and denies other claims supported by technical information, claims that subsequently turned out to be true. The case of an infant killed by a deploying airbag in a modest-sized fleet of 10,000 airbag-equipped cars[20(p 34294)] is dismissed as something anomalous that will never recur. The document states, "Considering all the arguments on both sides of the issues, the Department concludes that the observed experience of the vehicles on the road equipped with airbags does not cast doubt on the effectiveness estimates in the December 1976 decision."[20(p 34292)] The estimates referred to are those in Fig. 15-5.

When the auto industry wanted to delay or weaken the airbag mandate for reasons now established beyond doubt to be valid, Nader claimed (based on Claybrook's numbers) that each year of delay would mean 10,000 unnecessary deaths and 100,000 unnecessary disabling injuries.[18(p 113)]

While Claybrook's NHTSA made unsupportable claims about the benefits of airbags, the technical reports[13,14] identifying airbag threats to children were dismissed. A July 1980 NHTSA report states, "air bags will provide substantial crash protection to otherwise unrestrained small children in crashes."[30(p 71)] In the same document NHTSA cites, and dismisses, statements by General Motors, based on their own animal testing and other technical considerations, that a "child might be injured by an inflating bag." [30(p 70)]

Issues surrounding airbags and the mandate

A Claybrook aide is quoted as saying, "Joan didn't do much on mandatory belt use because her primary interests were in vehicle regulation. She was fond of saying 'it is easier to get twenty auto companies to do something than to get 200 million Americans to do something.' "[18(p 123)] The something she wanted the auto companies to do was to install airbags because they were claimed to be *passive* devices, while safety belts were *active* devices. Passive devices require no knowledge or actions on the part of the users, while active devices require users to do something, like fastening a belt.

A cornerstone of the support for the airbag mandate was the belief that attempts to influence the behavior of road users were futile. The nation's top traffic safety official believed that Americans could never be persuaded to wear belts. By contrast, the US surgeon general (not a lawyer) believed that Americans could be persuaded to stop smoking. He was right.

The support for airbags was based on philosophical and ideological advocacy unrelated to data-based performance measures. It was argued that it was self-evident that passive solutions were superior. The analogy that putting chlorine in the drinking water is a more effective cholera countermeasure than a campaign to get everyone to boil untreated water was considered persuasive. The fact that no passive device that could protect occupants in crashes existed, or was feasible, was denied. Affirming as a tenet of belief that such devices existed prevented the adoption of effective reality-based policies.

The airbag mandate prevented belt wearing laws

When other countries were following Australia's lead in passing belt wearing laws, the number one priority of safety leaders in the US was mandating airbags. Airbag-mandate enthusiasts saw belt laws as a threat to their campaign. The founder of an organization to advocate seat belt usage states, "Nader's organization went after me, saying that I was selling out the air-bag movement."[31(p 59)]

Not only did Claybrook not support mandatory wearing laws, she did not even accept that belts were effective when used. In a November 1983 television interview (transcribed below, and in Ref. 32), Joan Claybrook says of airbags:

"They're much better than seat belts, according to the government's most recent data,"

and continues to dismiss safety belts as

"the most rejected technology we have. So I believe that airbags would add a great dimension to cars and car safety, would protect all front seat occupants in those types of crashes where 55% of the public is now killed."

Claybrook continues,

"Airbags are really the best solution – they fit all different sizes and types of people, from little children up to 95th percentile males, very large males. ... So they really work beautifully and they work automatically and I think that that gives you more freedom and liberty than being either forced to wear a seat belt or having a car that's not designed with the safety engineering we know today."

Behavior <u>can</u> be changed – to save the airbag mandate

When it became clear in 1997 that deploying airbags were killing occupants in otherwise harmless crashes, pressure began to mount to rescind the airbag mandate. Airbag-caused injuries are the only traffic injuries for which there is a simple, feasible, enormously cost-effective countermeasure that is:

100% effective.

100% passive.

Simply removing the device is a perfect solution. If it is not installed in the first place, the safety benefits are accompanied by reduced vehicle cost.

The former enthusiasts for passive solutions vigorously rejected this simple, elegant, passive solution. In a strange irony, the supporters of the airbag mandate, who claimed that behavior could not be changed, provided one of the clearest illustrations of how behavior can be changed.

Those killed by airbags were mainly short female drivers, and children and infants in front seats with passenger airbags. A massive publicity campaign was mounted to persuade short drivers to sit further from the steering wheel, and to place children in rear seats. The success of this persuasion is apparent in the sharp decline in airbag inflation fatalities in Fig. 15-7.

The 90% decline in fatalities from 1997 to 2002 is mainly, but not exclusively, due to changes in behavior. From model year 1998 onwards there was a phase-in of second generation airbags that reduced the risk of inflation-produced injuries. However, as it takes many years for complete turnover of the fleet, much of the effect is from changed behavior by owners of earlier airbags.

Figure 15-7 provides clear evidence that road users were persuaded to change their behavior in order to save the lives of themselves and their families. If a similar effort had been applied to persuade people to avoid the crashes that kill over 40,000 annually rather than the airbags that were killing 50, dramatically more lives could have been saved. Even if the persuasion was focused only on occupant protection, persuading occupants to wear belts while getting rid of airbags would have had an enormously greater life-saving effect. More effort was directed at saving the airbag mandate than on saving lives.

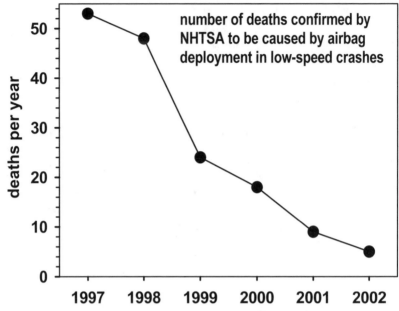

Figure 15-7. The effect of a change in behavior. The number of deaths caused by airbag-inflation declined after campaigns persuaded short women to sit further from the steering wheel and persuaded adults to place children in rear seats. The effect is largely due to behavior change, because the vehicles on the road remain largely the same vehicles in consecutive years. Data from Ref. 17.

On-off switches. Even for vehicles, such as pickup trucks, that do not have rear seats, the simple passive solution of not installing airbags was still rejected. Instead, off-on switches were installed which drivers were instructed to place in the off position when transporting children. As could have been predicted with certainty, children were transported with the switch on (and adults with it off).[33]

Children in rear seats – a source of driver distraction
One of the behavior changes successfully promoted to save the airbag mandate was to place children in rear seats to protect them from deploying airbags. It is natural for children to demand, and receive, parental attention. The study "The role of driver distraction in traffic crashes"[34] described in Chapter 8, found that children were about four times, and infants almost eight times, as likely as adult passengers to be a source of driver distraction. The cover of that report is reproduced in Fig. 15-8. The authors give more prominence to the picture of the mother looking rearwards at her infant than to the driver talking on a cell phone. In many jurisdictions talking on a cell phone while driving, which increases risk by more than a factor of four,[35] is banned. Yet placing children in rear seats is advocated as a safety measure.

DISTRACTIONS

IN EVERYDAY DRIVING

Prepared by

Jane Stutts   Kenneth Gish
John Feaganes   Michael Mercadante
Eric Rodgman   Loren Staplin
Charles Hamlett
Thomas Meadows   *TransAnalytics, LLC*
Donald Reinfurt

*University of North Carolina
at Chapel Hill
Highway Safety Research Center*

Prepared for

AAA Foundation for Traffic Safety
607 14th Street, NW, Suite 201
Washington, DC 20005
Tel: 202-638-5944
Fax: 202-638-5943
www.aaafoundation.org

June, 2003

Figure 15-8. Cover of report.[34] Reproduced with permission.

Summary of reasons for the airbag mandate

The mandate was enacted because advocates claimed that airbags:

1. Are passive (require no user knowledge or action).
2. Replace belts (permit vehicles to not have belts).
3. Reduce driver fatality and injury risk by 40%.
4. Reduce risk regardless of gender, age, etc.
5. Hurt nobody.

All 5 claims are false!

Particularly false is the claim that airbags are passive devices. Drivers, passengers, and parents must know a list of rules on how to avoid death and injury from deploying airbags. Arguably, airbags are the least passive safety devices ever installed on vehicles. Rather than being *passive* devices, they are *belligerent* devices. The collapsible steering column is a truly passive device – most of those benefiting from it do not know that it is there. The manual belt is a mixed passive/active device – the user has to know and do little – just follow one simple rule, "buckle up." The airbag is an active device which requires major actions on the part of occupants, including insuring that the distance from their chest to the module is at least 10 inches, and possibly adjusting the seat and fixing pedal extenders, and placing children and infants in rear seats. And of course, to avoid being killed by the airbag, the occupant must fasten the safety belt.

Why did the auto industry go along?

Although the auto industry opposed the airbag mandate prior to its enactment,[18] it later began to support and promote airbags. The auto industry had good reasons to accept defeat graciously once the mandate was in place, especially as continuing opposition would likely have been futile. More importantly, NHTSA also administered fuel economy standards which were more central to the industry's business, so it made good business sense to avoid ongoing friction on what became increasingly a settled historical matter.

The well-publicized claims of unrealistically high airbag benefits eventually generated consumer demand for airbags. The auto industry, in common with other businesses, was happy to sell in response to this demand, and also motivated to increase the demand by its own advertising. The auto industry installs, but does not generally manufacture, airbags. As airbags represent about 2% of the cost of a vehicle, the auto industry's earnings from them are a small fraction of total earnings.

The airbag manufacturing industry is totally committed to the mandate. What industry would not want a law compelling people to buy its products even if they did not want them? US consumers have paid over $60 billion for airbags. Most of this is in the pockets of airbag manufacturers, who naturally use a portion of it to lobby the political process to make sure that consumers continue to be compelled to purchase their products.

Other items

US lacks academic safety institutions. Countries like Sweden, Finland, the Netherlands, Australia, and New Zealand, with populations and resources far less than many US states, support important institutions devoted to performing traffic safety research. There are university departments, and scholars with titles like Professor of Traffic Psychology. The researchers from these institutions are invited to make technical inputs into policy-making. The university research that is supported in the US is nearly all in biomechanics and crashworthiness, reflecting the US priority of attempting to squeeze small increments of additional survivability in crashes rather than trying to reduce crashes. Reviewing the world's safety literature suggests that much of the best traffic safety research performed in the US is by the auto and insurance industries. The US would be well served if research addressing important safety issues was conducted in university departments receiving ongoing funding.

Blaming SUVs. The individuals who focused the nation's safety efforts so narrowly on vehicle factors are now blaming a vehicle, the SUV, for the nation's increasing fatalities. The SUV's popularity is partially due to the belief that vehicle factors offering crash protection are the most important safety factors. Another is due to the fuel economy standards administered by NHTSA, which treat SUVs as light trucks rather than cars (p. 88-91). While the shift to SUVs influences fatalities, it could not be by more than a few thousand per year up or down.

Regulating industry could save lives. If the lawyers spearheading US safety policy wanted to wage war on industry to improve safety, they would, if they had better understood safety, have chosen different industries and issues. The radar detector industry is not a major industry, but restricting its products and marketing would benefit safety. The industries that really impact safety are the alcoholic beverage industry and the mass media. Effective regulation of these would generate large safety benefits (Chapter 10). If the advocates felt they had to fight with the auto industry, there are two issues, which would really improve safety, that the industry would likely have resisted. First, regulating vehicle advertising to prohibit it from glorifying irresponsible driving. Second, requiring an inexpensive vehicle modification to prevent vehicles from exceeding a set speed (police and emergency vehicles exempted). Among the many lives that such a regulation would save would be those lost in present high-speed police chases, many involving stolen vehicles.

Where is US safety policy now?

The history of the airbag mandate contains lessons that may eventually benefit US safety policy. We must not forget George Santayana's celebrated aphorism, *Those who do not remember the past are condemned to relive it.*

However, it is not yet history. The most important elected official with safety responsibilities, Senator John McCain, has his door open to Claybrook,[36] but closed to science, thus keeping the same beliefs that led to the deaths of so many still at the heart of the US approach to safety. Now that NHTSA is acting more in the public interest, its Administrator is subject to more severe political oversight and criticism than occurred when it was making demonstrably absurd claims.

The most extraordinary aftermath of the debacle of the airbag mandate is that the architects of policies that led to the deaths of 200,000 additional Americans are routinely referred to in the mass media as *safety advocates*.

The importance of what the public believes

We have shown in earlier chapters that driver behavior factors have by far the largest effects on traffic safety. Driver behavior is largely determined by what people believe, and what they believe is enormously influenced by the mass media. The media do not merely report on safety, I believe they largely determine it. Attitudes to risk are based almost entirely on inputs from the media. People have no direct experience of dangers from things like cholesterol or radioactivity. Their concerns and protective responses are almost 100% due to inputs from the media.

There are no data on how safety is treated by US media compared to media in other countries today, or in the mid-1960s when the US had the best safety. Nor are there quantitative measures of safety attitudes in different countries. However, having visited 51 countries and spoken professionally about traffic safety in 25 of them, I have come to some fairly confident conclusions based on observing much media and interacting with large numbers of people in many countries.

I perceive a clear difference in attitudes between citizens of the US and citizens of countries with superior safety performance. When I mention traffic safety to an American, the response will likely bring up vehicle safety, product liability trials, vehicle defects, vehicle recalls, crash tests, specific vehicles that have been in the news, airbags, etc. That is, a collection of items focusing on the vehicle, all of which are relatively unimportant to safety. A citizen of a country with superior safety is far more likely to mention belt wearing, drunk driving, speeding, and risky driving, items that greatly influence safety. Of course the distributions have much overlap, but there is an unmistakably clear difference in the average answer of an American and a non-American.

Safety and US mass media

I believe that the reason why Americans think unimportant factors are important is due to massive media coverage of the unimportant and meager coverage of the important. Product liability trials seeking massive awards are unique to the US, and receive major coverage which does not include crucial information. A high profile trial may perhaps involve a driver who was severely injured (but not killed) after ejection in a rollover crash. The public is, perhaps, informed that a tire manufacturer was responsible, but not informed that the driver was speeding and illegally not wearing the safety belt that would have made ejection near impossible. In some states a jury must be kept ignorant of the fact that an injured plaintiff was not wearing a belt, even though such behavior is illegal.[37] Instead of providing evidence of consequences of disobeying traffic law, US media coverage fosters the belief that the problem is manufacturing and design decisions over which drivers have no control.

The media conveys no sense that during the period of a trial focusing on just one injury, thousands of Americans were killed in crashes in which no lawyer bonanza was identified. The US media is so supportive of the process that they never ask the most obvious questions. I have heard a television reporter ask a general for details of his battle plan, but I have never heard a reporter ask an attorney how much of the $5 million dollar settlement went into his or her pocket, how much went to the so called *expert* witnesses, how much went for lavish travel and other expenses, and how much (if any) went to the injured plaintiff.

In the course of a year, dozens of US national television and radio news bulletins start by reporting that a certain vehicle manufacturer has recalled so many vehicles for a defect in, say, the ignition system, and comment that there have been no injuries, or perhaps one minor injury. Why should anyone who does not own one of the vehicles be interested? The media claim that they are responding to public interest is unconvincing. The public would be far more interested in hearing the attorney explain why his or her fees and the plaintiff's compensation should be secret, especially if the explanations were followed by a few sharp follow-up questions regarding what public or safety interest is served by such secrecy. They would be much more interested in having the attorney explain (or refuse to explain) why the jury is prohibited from knowing if a belt wearing law was violated.

The net effect is that Americans are inundated with coverage of things that they are told are related to safety, when in fact they have negligible influence on safety. The view that safety is in the hands of a few institutions over which they have no control, except through litigation, is repeatedly reinforced. The reality that the most important element in their own safety is their own driver behavior is buried under a mountain of misinformation.

US law at the heart of the problem

The unifying factor at the heart of the failure of US safety policy is the uniquely powerful role of litigation in every aspect of US society. No other nation is burdened with anything resembling the US legal system. In other democracies elected legislators with varied backgrounds are influenced by inputs from diverse sources, including the technical community. In the US, legislators, who are overwhelmingly lawyers, get nearly all their inputs from other lawyers.

While it might not be a conscious goal, it is not too surprising that when lawyers are the main decision makers, measures that open deep pockets for legal assault are more appealing than measures that reduce harm. Since the period when the US was the world's safety leader, litigation in the US has exploded,[38] and has been spectacularly successful in directing focus away from countermeasures known to be successful in favor of vehicle factors that are of minor safety importance but are major sources of litigation wealth. No impartial observer can imagine that any net good emerges from the resulting system which lavishly supports a pestilence of avaricious lawyers, "expert" witnesses, consultants skilled at identifying jurors lowest in knowledge and reasoning skills, and a vast court superstructure. Even advocates of the US system rarely conclude that US cars must be much safer than Swedish cars because the US spends astronomically more per capita on litigation than does Sweden.

It is unfortunately difficult for anyone born in the US to be an impartial observer. Just as certain propositions are off limits for discussion in theocracies, in the US it is off limits to even discuss if the legal system now exists mainly to benefit its members, with everyone else compelled to pay an enormous law tax on everything they do in order to insure that right is not done. It is not uncommon for college educated Americans to recite to me, like a catechism, the statement "The US legal system is the best in the world". My response, "Can you identify six ways the US legal system is superior to that in Sweden?" generates a blank stare. I keep going until "Can you identify one way in which the US system is superior to that in any democracy?" produces the same non-response. It seems being better than the Soviet Union or the Third Reich is sufficient evidence to self-award the *best in the world* title. Americans are unlikely to demand changes to a system that is diminishing their freedom, stealing their wealth, making the products they purchase more expensive, less innovative,[39] and less safe, and killing them, if they really believe it is the best in the world. It is difficult to be optimistic about the future because the enormous wealth of the legal system allows it to be the major financial contributor to the US electoral process.

However, a cause for optimism is that once the US does recognize it has a problem, it moves with a speed and energy unequalled in other countries.

Specific differences

Ideally, one would like to account for the 200,000 additional Americans killed between 1979 and 2002 in a list quantifying contributions from specific factors. However, many of the likely contributions do not readily admit to quantification. For example, it is difficult to estimate the change in driver care caused by repetitive messages implying that vehicle factors are paramount.. There is, however, one factor for which a quantitative estimate can be made.

Deaths caused by not having belt wearing laws

Canada's first belt wearing law was in effect in January 1976 (in the Province of Ontario). The first belt law in the US was in effect in December 1984 (in New York State).[40] It took additional years before all Canadian provinces and nearly all US states had belt laws, so that most Americans were covered by belt wearing laws about a decade later than most Canadians. This delay had, and continues to have, a large impact on US safety.

Figure 15-9 shows that once belt laws were in effect in the US, belt wearing increased in a manner not dissimilar from the Canadian experience (pre-law Canadian rates were around 25%). This is convincing evidence of the absurdity of the claim by Claybrook's NHTSA that Americans would not wear belts. The evidence shows that drivers in the US were not all that different from those in Canada. The longer laws are in effect, the easier it is to strengthen them by, for example, moving from secondary to primary enforcement.[41]   Thus rates increase, but over long periods of time. The lower present rate in the US is due primarily to the US starting a decade later than Canada.

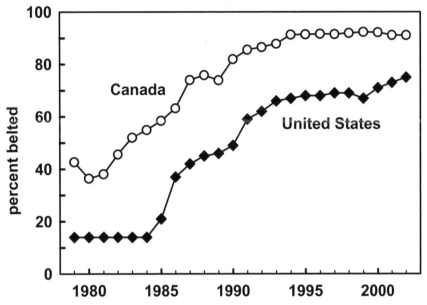

Figure 15-9. Increases in belt wearing rates in Canada (first belt law January 1976) and in the United States (first belt law December 1984).

The consequences of this late start, computed in Table 15-10, show that the late passage of mandatory belt wearing laws was responsible for an additional 96,000 American deaths from 1979 to 2002. The parallel comparison with Britain gives a larger difference, and with Australia, a much larger difference.

It could be argued that the 96,000 extra US deaths should be reduced by deaths prevented by mandated airbags. Extrapolating even the highest estimates to the 1979-2002 period produces a total that falls well short of 10,000,[28] leaving a net increase due to not having mandatory wearing laws in excess of 86,000. Studies from Transport Canada[42,43] estimate that, during the eleven-year period 1990-2000, belts prevented 11,690 Canadian deaths, and airbags 313.

The one specific policy of pursuing the airbag mandate and not working for mandatory belt laws accounts for about half of the additional 200,000 US fatalities.

Table 15-10. Reductions in US fatalities if belt use rates in the US had matched those in Canada.

	belt wearing rates (%)		observed US	F^{**}	US fatality reduction
	US	Canada	fatalities[*]		with Canadian belt use
1979	14	43	31,113	9.7	3,021
1980	14	36	31,068	7.2	2,226
1981	14	38	29,993	7.9	2,362
1982	14	46	26,402	10.9	2,865
1983	14	52	25,951	13.2	3,437
1984	14	55	26,782	14.5	3,883
1985	21	58	26,591	13.9	3,701
1986	37	63	28,690	11.4	3,267
1987	42	74	29,516	15.6	4,610
1988	45	76	30,338	15.7	4,777
1989	46	74	29,893	14.2	4,240
1990	49	82	29,074	18.1	5,253
1991	59	85	27,369	16.1	4,398
1992	62	86	26,221	15.4	4,044
1993	66	88	26,747	15.0	4,007
1994	67	91	27,540	16.8	4,638
1995	68	91	28,608	16.3	4,672
1996	68	92	28,980	17.1	4,969
1997	69	91	28,836	15.8	4,558
1998	69	92	28,463	16.6	4,733
1999	67	92	28,439	17.7	5,020
2000	71	92	28,440	15.6	4,423
2001	73	91	28,297	13.6	3,843
2002	75	91	28,837	12.5	3,594
				total	**96,541**

[*] fatalities to drivers and right-front-passengers of cars and light trucks.
[**] percent reduction in fatalities from increasing belt use from US to Canadian levels (computed by Eqn 11-15, p. 293).

Other specific differences

While other countries developed policies aimed at driver behavior, the US paid less attention to drivers, instead concentrating most effort on vehicle factors.

Drunk driving. The per se limit in the US during 1979-2002 was substantially higher than in any comparison country. For most states it was BAC > 0.1%. It was not until 2000 that the US Congress passed legislation providing financial incentives for states to have BAC > 0.08% laws in effect by 2004. During the time when the airbag mandate was being debated some even argued that the most effective approach to drunk driving was to have airbags in all vehicles. After all, this would reduce deaths to drunk drivers and most of their other victims by 40%, while policies aimed at changing such behaviors as drunk driving were doomed to failure. In Chapter 10 a number of measures that could substantially reduce annual deaths from drunk driving are described. The largest progress in reducing harm from drunk driving resulted not from government leadership, but from the creation in 1980 of Mothers Against Drunk Driving (MADD). As MADD helped change laws, government had a law-enforcement role in these harm reductions. Without MADD, US fatalities would exceed those in the comparison countries by even larger amounts.

Speed. Even though one of the largest reductions in US casualties was associated with reductions in the speed limit in response to the 1973 oil embargo, speed limits were later increased. How increasing speed affected safety was addressed in the normal US advocacy manner. Those who liked higher speed limits argued they would not affect safety, while their opponents argued that they would. There was little sense that this was a technical question that had a technical answer. This is where the US pays a safety price for not having research institutions that can provide technical results that the public finds credible. Even those who enjoy ice cream tend to accept that it is not a health food because they respect the qualifications and motivations of the experts providing them medical information.

Radar speed detectors. Devices to detect police radar are vigorously marketed in the US. These have only one purpose – to assist in violating traffic law. This is why they are prohibited in Canada. I believe the difference is another reflection of the US regarding safety more in terms of making vehicles safe to crash rather than in preventing crashes. It is not related to respect for personal liberty. The liberty of a short lady to purchase an airbag-free vehicle is denied by the US government. The US is far more ready than other countries to put people in prison for consuming specified drugs in the privacy of their homes. While consuming harmful drugs may be deplorable, it does not directly and immediately threaten other people's lives as does speeding. Not all of the countries with better performing safety records prohibit radar detectors. All countries have major inadequacies in their safety policy.

Epilogue

The anti-technical lawyer zealots who defined and led US policy precipitated a massive safety disaster that continues. If a fraction of the energy and tenacity devoted to counterproductive policies had been applied to promote effective policies, the US could have remained the world's traffic safety leader. Goethe (1749-1832) perhaps best summarizes what in fact happened:

There is nothing more fearful than ignorance in action.

Summary and conclusions

Prior to the mid 1960s the US had the world's safest traffic, whether measured by deaths per registered vehicle, or deaths for the same distance of travel. By 2002 the US had dropped from first to 16th place in deaths per registered vehicle, and from first to 10th place in deaths for the same distance of travel. From 1979 to 2002, over 200,000 more Americans were killed in traffic than would have been killed if the US had matched the safety progress of Britain, Canada, or Australia.

The critical change in the direction of US safety policy occurred when Ralph Nader convinced the US media, government, and public that deaths in traffic were mainly due to unsafe and defective vehicles. This began a process of ordering safety policy priorities almost perfectly opposite to where technical knowledge showed benefits to be greatest, and of ignoring and denying technical information.

In 1977 another activist lawyer, Nader protégé Joan Claybrook, assumed the most important US government safety position, Administrator of the National Highway Traffic Safety Administration. Her primary goal was an airbag mandate, the compulsory installation of airbags in vehicles. To pursue this she issued absurdly high claims of airbag effectiveness, ignored harm from airbags, denied the superior protection from safety belts, and did not support belt wearing laws for the US like those being passed in other countries.

The uniquely powerful role of the US legal system was central to the failure of US safety policy. Even if not at a conscious level, the lawyer-controlled process favored measures that opened deep pockets for legal assault over measures that saved lives. The public was inundated with information suggesting that product-liability trials, vehicle defect recalls, crash tests, and airbags were centrally important. As drivers have no control over such factors, the impression was conveyed that those whose lives were at risk in traffic were uninvolved hapless victims of large rich institutions. The media did not mention that these factors had little to do with the overwhelming majority of the 40,000 annual US deaths. The crucial factors over which drivers do have control, wearing belts, alcohol, speeding, and risky driving, were de-emphasized. Yet these are the factors that have massive effects on safety.

A major portion of the additional 200,000 American deaths is attributable to just one specific policy of NHTSA under Claybrook. Focusing on mandating airbags instead of placing the US on the same path as Canada in passing mandatory belt wearing laws led to the deaths of an additional 90,000 Americans from 1979 through 2002.

For US safety performance to improve, public understanding of what is important must be more related to what really is important.

References for Chapter 15

1 Motor Vehicle Manufacturers Association of the United States. *MVMA Facts and Figures 1981*. Detroit, MI; 1981.

2 International Road Traffic and Accident Database (OECD) (2002). March 2004. http://www.bast.de/htdocs/fachthemen/irtad/english/englisch.html

3 Department for Transport. Transport statistics, Table 9.10. Road accidents and casualties: 1950-2002. http://www.dft.gov.uk/stellent/groups/dft_transstats/documents/page/dft_transstats_506740.xls

4 Transport Canada. Canadian motor vehicle traffic collision statistics: 2002. http://www.tc.gc.ca/roadsafety/tp/tp3322/2002/menu.htm

5 Australian Transport Safety Bureau. http://www.atsb.gov.au/road/stats/current.cfm

6 Evans L. Transportation Safety. In: Hall RW, editor. *Handbook of Transportation Science, Second Edition*. Norwell, MA: Kluwer Academic Publishers; 2002, p. 67-112.

7 Evans L. Traffic crashes. *Am Scientist*. 2002; 90: 244-253.

8 Paulikas GA. Measuring risks (Letter to the editor responding to previous reference). *Am Scientist*. 2002; 90: 300. (Followed by Evans L. Dr. Evans replies – on same page).

9 Complete details of this and other calculations are available at http://www.ScienceServingSociety.com/data.htm

10 Evans L. A new traffic safety vision for the United States. *Am J Public Health*. 2003; 93: 1384-1386.

11 Vernick JS, Teret SP. Making vehicles safer. *Am J Public Health*. 2004; 94: 170.

12 Evans L. Evans responds (to previous reference). *Am J Public Health*. 2004; 94: 171-172.

13 Patrick LM, Nyquist GW. Airbag effects on the out-of-position child. SAE paper 720442. Warrendale, PA: Society of Automotive Engineers; 1972.

14 Aldman B, Anderson A, Saxmark O. Possible effects of air bag inflation on a standing child. Proceedings of the 18th Annual Conference of the American Association for Automotive Medicine, Toronto, Canada, 12-14 September, 1974.

15 Aldman B, Anderson A, Saxmark O. Possible effects of air bag inflation on a standing child. Proceedings of the International Research Council on the Biomechanics of Impact, Meeting on Biomechanics of Trauma in Children, Lyon, France; September 1974.

16 Glass RJ, Segui-Gomez M, Graham JD. Child passenger safety: Decisions about seating location, airbag exposure, and restraint use. *Risk Analysis*, 2000; 20: 521-527.

17 Counts for air bag related fatalities and seriously injured persons. http://www-nrd.nhtsa.dot.gov/pdf/nrd-30/NCSA/SCI/2Q_2003/HTML/QtrRpt/ABFSISR.htm

18 Graham JD. *Auto Safety: Assessing America's Performance*. Dover, MA: Auburn House Publishing Company; 1989.

19 Wilson RA, Savage CM. Restraint system effectiveness – a study of fatal accidents. Proceedings of Automotive Safety Engineering Seminar, sponsored by Automotive Safety Engineering, Environmental Activities Staff, General Motors Corporation; 20-21 June 1973, p. 27-38.

20 Federal Register, Vol. 42, No 128, Part 571 – Federal Motor Vehicle Standards: Occupant protection systems, Docket No. 75-14, Notice 10, pages 34289-34305; 5 July 1977.

21 Kent R, Viano D, Crandall J. The field performance of frontal air bags. In: Kent RW, editor. *Air Bag Development and Performance – New Perspectives from Industry, Government, and Academia*. SAE Special Publication PT-88. Table 14, Chapter 5. Warrendale, PA: Society of Automotive Engineers; March 2003.

22 Pursel HD, Bryant RW, Scheel JW, Yanik AJ.   Matched case methodology for measuring restraint effectiveness. SAE paper 780415. Warrendale, PA: Society of Automotive Engineers; 1978.

23 Segui-Gomez M.   Driver air bag effectiveness by severity of the crash. *Am J Pub Health*. 2000; 90: 1575–1581.

24 McGwin G Jr, Metzger J, Jorge E, Alonso JE, Rue LW III. The association between occupant restraint systems and risk of injury in frontal motor vehicle collisions. *J Trauma*. 2003; 54: 1182–1187.

25 McGwin G Jr. Airbags and the risk of injury in frontal motor vehicle crashes. 2003. Submitted for publication.

26 National Highway Traffic Safety Administration. Final regulatory impact analysis, Amendment of FMVSS 208, passenger car front seat occupant protection. Washington, DC; 11 July 1984.

27 Kahane CJ. Fatality reduction by air bags: Analysis of accident data through early 1996. Report DOT HS 808 470. Washington, DC: National Highway Traffic Safety Administration; 1996.

28 National Highway Traffic Safety Administration. Fifth/Sixth Report to Congress: Effectiveness of occupant protection systems and their use. Report DOT HS 809 442. Washington, DC: US Department of Transportation; November 2001.

29 Cummings P, McKnight B, Rivara FP, Grossman DC. Association of driver air bags with driver fatality: A matched cohort study. *Brit Med J*. 2002; 324: 1119–1122.

30 National Highway Traffic Safety Administration.   Automobile occupant crash protection, progress report no. 3. Report DOT HS 805 474.   Washington, DC: US Department of Transportation; July 1980.

31 Gladwell M. Wrong turn: How the fight to make America's highways safer went off course. *New Yorker*. 11 June 2001, p. 50-64.   http://www.gladwell.com/2001/2001_06_11_a_crash.htm

32 Hearing before the Subcommittee on Telecommunications, Trade and Consumer Protection of the Committee on Commerce, House of Representatives.   Reauthorization of the National Highway Traffic Safety Administration. Serial No. 105-30, Attachment D. Washington, DC: US Government Printing Office; 22 May 1997.

33 Morgan C. Results of the survey of the use of passenger air bag on-off switches. Report DOT HS 809 689. Washington, DC: US Department of Transportation, National Highway Traffic Safety Administration; November 2003.

34 Stutts J, Feaganes J, Rogman E, Hamlett C, Meadows T, Reinfurt D, Gish K, Mercadante M, Staplin L. The role of driver distraction in traffic crashes: Distractions in everyday driving. Washington, DC: AAA Foundation for Traffic Safety; July 2003.
http://www.aaafoundation.org/pdf/DistractionsInEverydayDriving.pdf

35 Redelmeier DA, Tibshirani RJ. Association between cellular-telephone calls and motor vehicle collisions. *New Eng J. Med*. 1997; 336: 453-458.

36 O'Donnell J. Republican senator, auto-safety advocate form unlikely alliance. *USA Today*. 28 July 2003. http://www.usatoday.com/money/autos/2003-07-28-cover_x.htm

37 Blair D. Seat belt defense deserves a fair hearing in Texas (editorial). *Houston Chronicle*. 17 February 2003.

38 Huber PW. *Liability: The Legal Revolution and its Consequences*. New York, NY: Basic Books; 1988.

39 National Academy of Engineering. *Product Liability and Innovation*. Washington, DC: National Academy Press; 1994.

40 Safety belt use laws. Insurance Institute for Highway Safety, Safety Facts.
http://www.highwaysafety.org/safety_facts/state_laws/restrain3.htm

41 Chaudhary NK, Preusser DF. Lives lost by states' failure to implement primary safety belt laws. Report prepared for the National Safety Council's Air Bag & Seat Belt Safety Campaign. November 2003.   http://www.nsc.org/public/Preusser_Study.pdf

42 Transport Canada. Estimates and lives saved among front seat occupants of light-duty vehicles involved in collisions attributable to the use of seat belts and air bags in Canada. Road Safety and Motor Vehicle Regulation, Fact Sheet RS 2001-03 E TP13187E; October 2001. http://www.tc.gc.ca/roadsafety/tp2436/rs200103/en/menu.htm

43 Stewart DE, Arora HR, Dalmotas D. An evaluation of the effectiveness of supplementary restraint systems ("air bags") and conventional seat belts: Estimates of the numbers of lives saved among front seat outboard occupants of light-duty vehicles involved in collisions attributable to the use of seat belts and the fitment of supplementary restraint systems ("air bags") in Canada, 1990-1997. Publication Number TP13187 E. Ottawa, Ontario: Transport Canada; 1998.

16 Vision for a safer tomorrow

Introduction

Traffic crashes have been harming enormous numbers of people for over a century. Much of this book is devoted to describing countermeasures that have helped prevent the harm from being even greater. Countermeasures in place today reflect ongoing evolution based mainly on building upon concepts originating in early decades of the twentieth century. This has resulted in what one might call a traditional approach, some variation of which is in place in all countries with vehicular traffic. Which components of this traditional approach are emphasized can make a dramatic difference to casualties (Chapter 15). The discussion below uses US experience and data, but the general themes are applicable to any jurisdictions.

The traditional approach has fostered attitudes that limit expectations. Despite the numbers of injuries and deaths, traffic safety is not generally viewed as a component of public health. Enormous casualties are largely accepted as normal, inevitable, and not particularly newsworthy. There is a public perception that crashes are due mainly to fate and bad luck, encouraging the notion that not all that much can really be done to prevent them. The still all too widely used word *accident* reflects and encourages such beliefs. Claims that something can be done often focus on factors, like vehicle design, which have little potential to make much additional difference.

Successes and failures are judged relative to well-established norms. There is acceptance that the best that can be done is slow ongoing progress. Risk reductions of a few percent are heralded as major achievements, which they indeed are. A measure that reduces risk in traffic by one percent prevents the deaths of more than 10,000 people in the world per year. It prevents the death of more than one person in the US per day. Any new product or process suspected of causing far less than one death per day in the US would generate massive headlines.

Efforts to reduce the toll from traffic crashes are conceived in terms of refinements and minor incremental improvements to present policies. However, even progress at a somewhat greater rate than has been achieved hitherto does not keep pace with the growth in vehicles. In the US the absolute number of people killed in traffic has actually increased from 39,250 in 1992 to 42,815 in 2002. Worldwide, deaths are increasing at a much greater rate than this.

I believe modest changes to a number of components of the traffic safety system currently in place can, in combination, lead to major reductions in harm. A breakthrough is achievable. It does not require major expenditures, although it does rely on new technology. Taken in its entirety, I believe the public would welcome the breakthrough I am recommending. Indeed, it can succeed only if the public does welcome it. The key to progress is a different relationship between those at risk and the institutions in place to protect them. Unlike other aspects of public health, those at risk in traffic are often hostile to the institutions aimed at protecting them.

Personal vehicles provide personal freedom, but harm many of those enjoying that freedom, and others besides. An effective approach to reducing this harm must start from the interests and perspectives of individual road users.

The two most important factors

The traffic safety research presented in the previous 15 chapters, and my more than 30 years of traffic-safety research, convince me that the two factors that overwhelmingly determine an individual's risk in traffic are:

1. The individual's behavior.

2. The behavior of other road users.

While an individual's behavior is 100% under his or her control, the behavior chosen is much influenced by social norms and public policy, especially traffic law. The role of traffic law is diminished because it attracts insufficient public support, and indeed is often the focus of public hostility. Public support for enforcing traffic law would increase if far more emphasis were placed on the second factor, the extent to which risk in traffic is due to other drivers.

If a driver is killed in a single-vehicle crash, that death involves only the driving of the deceased driver. The crashes killing all other road users involve actions of a driver other than the person killed. If a driver is killed in a two-vehicle crash, then this death involves the actions of the deceased driver and the actions of the other involved driver (who may also die). The deaths of all passengers and pedestrians involve the actions of some driver. Table 16-1 shows that in the US in 2002, only 31% of fatalities involved the driving of only the person killed. The vast majority of fatalities (69%) were in crashes in which a driver other than the person killed was involved. In countries other than the US the fraction of all road users killed that involve a driver other than the person killed is even larger. The fraction is especially large for less motorized countries.

Over 29,000 Americans were killed in 2002 in crashes involving actions of drivers other than the person killed. Of these, 1,769 were non-driving children under 14. An average of more than one child per day is killed while walking or riding a bicycle. Overwhelming, no alcohol is involved in such crashes. The risk families face from the actions of other drivers towers over any other risks they face. If this were better publicized, I believe the public would be more inclined to support effective measures to reduce risks from traffic.

Table 16-1. The 42,815 traffic fatalities in the US in 2002 separated according to whether or not a driver other than the person killed was involved.

persons killed	*deceased is only driver involved*	*driver other than deceased involved*
drivers in single-vehicle crashes	13,399	
drivers in multiple-vehicle crashes		13,150
passengers		10,571
pedestrians		4,875
bicyclists		662
others		158
total number of fatalities	13,399	29,416
percent of all fatalities	31.3%	68.7%

The issue of second-hand smoke played an important role in reducing smoking. The argument that smokers should not damage the health of their children, co-workers, or fellow diners proved persuasive. While there is uncertainty about the extent of harm from second-hand smoke, there is no question that 1,283 children under 14 died as passengers in vehicles in crashes involving the behavior of drivers. Furthermore, smokers themselves suffer the harm from smoking to a far greater degree than reckless drivers themselves suffer the harm from reckless driving.

Air travelers are willing to have their luggage searched even though they know it does not contain a bomb. They appreciate that the only way someone with a bomb can be stopped is if everyone is scrutinized, and they willingly subject themselves to intrusive and sometimes embarrassing searches. Yet other road drivers threaten their lives, and those of their children, far more than bombs on planes do. A major advance in safety will occur if the public realizes that more effective monitoring of other drivers provides them far more protection than searching luggage. If other drivers are to be monitored, then a policy of monitoring all drivers must be accepted. Later we address simple changes that can make drivers support such a policy.

The extraordinary safety of commercial aviation

In 2002, there were zero deaths on US scheduled airlines,[1] but 42,815 deaths on US roads. (Roads provide about 9 times as many passenger miles as airlines.)[2] Intuitively, flying is inherently much riskier than road travel. Many people are frightened of flying, but almost no one in a motorized society is frightened of being a passenger in a road vehicle. The dramatically greater safety of the riskier flying mode occurs for two reasons. First, the primary focus is on avoiding crashes, and second, pilots adhere strictly to established driving rules.

Avoiding crashes, rather than surviving them, is the primary goal

Weight is an overriding aircraft design consideration. Some airlines do not paint their aircraft to avoid carrying the additional weight of the paint, even though unpainted aluminum is more expensive to keep clean. Weight has a major impact on aircraft speed, range, and passenger-carrying capacity. As a result aircraft design adds little in the way of specific crash-management structure, and includes only modest structural safety margins.

Moving people through the air at high speeds in a flimsy vehicle precludes any debate about whether the primary safety goal should be to avoid crashing or to make it safe to crash. Airline safety focuses overwhelmingly on avoiding crashing. Crashworthiness is not ignored, and aircraft contain many features to increase safety during and after crashes. Research is always ongoing to increase survivability when airliners do crash. However, such efforts never divert attention from the paramount goal of avoiding crashes.

This is in sharp contrast to the automotive case in which crashes are often seen as inevitable, thereby assigning top priority to the quest for measures to reduce their consequences. Vehicle design changes introduced over the decades have reduced the risk of death in a crash by about 20%. Occupant protection from wearing a safety belt reduces fatality risk by 42% (safety belt plus airbag by 47%), so a belted driver in a modern car is less than half as likely to die as a driver in a 1950 car of similar mass in an identical crash. This is a major achievement that has saved many lives. Further modest reductions in the risk of death when a crash occurs are always possible from further refinements in vehicle crashworthiness and restraint design. However, it is now time to accept that this phase is largely complete. There do not appear to be any practical and acceptable means to reduce risk much further when a vehicle of given mass and size crashes at a given speed. It is counterproductive to keep devoting excessive attention to measures that have the potential to reduce the risk of death in a crash by no more than an additional few percent. This would still leave over 40,000 deaths per year in the US. In sharp contrast, crash reduction offers large benefits as long as crashes remain a problem.

There is, however, one area of survivability in which substantial gains are still possible, namely, increasing belt wearing rates. This is not a vehicle design factor, but a behavioral and law enforcement factor.

Air travelers rarely ask, "Which aircraft is safest?" yet I am often asked, "Which vehicle is safest?" When air crashes do occur, they are likely to be related to vehicle design or manufacturing problems. Such factors are of almost no consequence in road safety. It is important for road travelers to understand more clearly that it is the safety of the traffic system, and particularly the way the vehicles are driven, that is crucial, not how the vehicles perform when they crash.

Driving by obeying rules, not by experience

Commercial pilots adhere to rules that incorporate knowledge accumulated from many professional disciplines. They are guided by much more than their own personal experience. Pilots do not learn by going to the limit, and when something almost goes wrong, backing off a little. Road drivers use their personal experience to choose what they think is a safe speed or safe following distance. A large part of the basis for their decision is that prior similar behavior has not led to a crash. Their understanding may be augmented by experiencing crashes and near crashes. While currently normal for road travel, such processes are clearly unacceptable for flying.

Traffic law should reflect accumulated knowledge from many professional disciplines in a manner somewhat parallel to the rules for flying. However, unlike the air case, traffic law is routinely violated, perhaps many times per trip by most drivers. The social norm incorporates such violations as acceptable to a degree without parallel for other laws aimed at protecting the public.

Enforcement

There are two major problems that render traditional traffic law enforcement relatively ineffective. First, it provides a low, and capricious, probability of detection. Second, the public is justifiably suspicious about the motivations behind traffic law and its enforcement.

Low and capricious probability of detection

Traditional enforcement of traffic law involves police officers, usually in police vehicles, detecting the speeds of vehicles or observing the behavior of vehicles in traffic. Despite the considerable cost of traditional enforcement, it can monitor only a small fraction of traffic, so that the probability that any specific infraction is detected is exceedingly low. Receiving a traffic violation ticket depends far more on whether a police officer is present than on the behavior of the driver. Still, many tickets are given. Those who receive them generally consider themselves victims of being in the wrong place at the wrong time, rather than admitting to themselves that their behavior posed any safety threat. They are too often correct. This does not endear traffic law enforcement to the public.

Much of the harm in traffic is due to drivers who routinely and egregiously violate traffic law. Only a miniscule fraction of their violations are detected. A driver would almost certainly have to be a routine violator to receive, say, five citations in a two-year period. The capricious nature of the present system forges an inappropriate and harmful bond between average citizens and high-risk drivers. Average citizens often regard frequent violators to be just like themselves, but with worse luck, rather than the ongoing threats to them and their families that they in fact are.

Traffic law must not be used to raise revenue

Apart from its role in ensuring efficient traffic, the sole purpose of traffic law should be to prevent harm.   One of the most unfortunate developments worldwide is that traffic law is often used for a quite different purpose – to raise revenue.   Using it for such a purpose brings it into disrepute.   Instead of the public welcoming traffic law as protecting them, they consider it an illegitimate tax.   Those forced to contribute often feel that a process no more rational or fair than a lottery has selected them.   Some racial and ethnic groups view the selection process to be biased against them.   Everyone sees drivers commit extreme violations of traffic law with impunity, while others behaving little differently from the average are severely fined.   To make matters worse, there are cases of laws motivated for purposes other than traffic efficiency or safety, including *speed traps* (unreasonably low speed limits) enacted solely to raise revenue.   Traditional traffic law and traffic law enforcement practices have created a recipe for failure that I believe has rendered relatively ineffective the one remedy that has the potential to spearhead a safety breakthrough.

Enforcement using newer technology

New technology offers the way out from deficiencies of traditional enforcement. The technology can produce dramatic reductions in harm, but only if it is introduced in ways that the public welcomes. Below I first describe the technology, and then suggest how I believe it can be integrated into an overall policy package that would find public support.

   A number of automatic enforcement technologies have been developed, and are in use to some degree in many countries, including the US, UK, Canada, Australia, New Zealand, and a number of countries in continental Europe. Some of the technologies are completely automatic, while others enable police to perform enforcement work more productively than in manual enforcement. Technology to measure following headways and issue tickets for illegal tailgating has been developed and field-tested in Israel.[3] However, the main applications of new technology have been in detecting violations of speeding and traffic light laws.

Photo radar. This is a system designed to automatically detect vehicles violating speed limits. It includes a camera and attached radar speed measuring device. When a vehicle is measured violating the speed limit, the system photographs the driver and the license plate. The registered owner of the vehicle then receives a traffic ticket in the mail. Photo radar may be operated from marked or unmarked police vehicles. An evaluation of results from studies of various automatic speed detection systems found that they reduced crashes by 19%.[4] Another study found a photo radar program reduced highway mean speeds by 2.8 km/h.[5] Substituting $\delta v = -2.8$ km/h into Eqn 9-1 (p. 211) indicates that such a speed reduction would reduce fatality risk by 17%.

Red-light cameras. These are systems designed to automatically detect vehicles entering intersections after the traffic light has turned red. They have four advantages over photo radar. First, manual detection of red-light violations is less efficient because they are less frequent than speeding. Second, manual enforcement places police officers at greater risk than manual detection of speeding. Third, it already finds more public support.[6] Fourth, its technical implementation is facilitated because outputs from the traffic-light signal controller are available for input to the red-light camera system.

Cameras record images of an offending vehicle and the surrounding scene, together with vehicle speed, duration of the yellow signal, and how long after the red signal the vehicle began to enter the intersection. A second photograph may be taken to verify that the vehicle proceeded through the intersection on the red signal. A review of the literature found that most evaluations reported that red-light cameras led to an increase in rear-impact crashes.[7] It is possible that this might happen because lead drivers suddenly realized that a red-light camera is present, while the following driver did not. If so, the effect might disappear if cameras were generally expected (compare with Fig. 8-3, p. 186). What is crucial is that the review found that even with these extra rear impacts, injury crashes still declined by 25-30%.[7]

Advantages of automatic monitoring of driving

The new technologies are still in their infancy. They offer enormous advantages over manual monitoring. Assigning skilled police officers to monitor traffic is an ineffective use of valuable public resources. What humans do poorly, technology can do well at a tiny fraction of the cost. Automatic monitoring provides the following advantages.

High probability of detection. It is probability of detection, not severity of punishment, which is far more effective at changing behavior. Most would agree that a hypothetical on-board device that administered an instant and certain ten cent fine every time a speed limit was violated (and the same amount per additional second of violation) would have a vastly more dramatic effect on speeding than does the possibility that speeding might lead to death. New monitoring technologies do not provide such instantaneous feedback, but they provide the potential to move a long way in the direction of near-certain feedback a day or so after the offense.

Objectivity and completeness. Inanimate devices are immune from charges of caprice or bias. At a given site, all vehicles are monitored. Anyone receiving a citation will have little basis for thinking that others behaving in the same way did not also receive one. The photographs produced by automatic detection preclude most of the challenges to evidence provided by customary enforcement. Automatic detection is on duty 24 hours per day. Much of the most severe harm from crashes occurs at times when traffic volume is low, while traditional enforcement is more focused on times when traffic volume is high.

It is plausible that advances in mass production and information technology would eventually make it feasible to detect a large fraction of all the violations that currently occur. The *spillover effect* will lead to lower speeds on non-monitored roads adjacent to monitored roads, and, in general, more overall conformity with speed limits.

Drunk driving. Traditional enforcement detects about one drunk driver for every 2,000 trips driven by drunk drivers. Apart from sobriety checkpoints, a police officer must observe improper driving before testing for alcohol. Drunk drivers take higher driving risks than sober drivers – it is the behavior resulting from alcohol, not the alcohol itself, that causes crashes. Automatic detection is likely to record large numbers of speeding and traffic light violations by a drunk driver well before there is any realistic chance of a direct manual-enforcement citation for drunk driving. The most effective other countermeasure, the sobriety check lane, is expensive and inconveniences all drivers. Law-abiding drivers are stopped, and can be required to provide a breath sample, arguably a far greater privacy violation than being in the lens of a camera that records pictures only of lawbreakers. One of the strongest benefits of automatic monitoring of traffic (unlike airline security) is that it does not delay, inconvenience, or embarrass any driver who is not breaking the law.

A number of related policy changes are necessary to make automatic monitoring effective and acceptable. I believe that these changes, taken as a complete package, can attract popular support. Automatic monitoring can provide the catalyst for the other important changes.

Driving is a public, not a private, activity

An already implicitly accepted principle must be even more openly embraced. The principle is that driving is a public, not a private, activity. Privacy must be sacrosanct for private activities, but not for public activities. There is already universal support for massive government intrusion into matters relating to driving that would be intolerable for private activities. One may not drive at all without government permission in the form of a license. The permission can be revoked, even administratively without court process. It is none of the government's business if one is drunk in one's home, but few claim that it is nobody's business if you are drunk while driving. Police are permitted to monitor vehicles, and stop drivers suspected of violating traffic law. Traditional enforcement already uses technology, in the form of radar to measure vehicle speeds, and breathalyzers to measure alcohol. Traditional practices are rarely criticized as violations of privacy. Yet privacy arguments emerge to oppose using technology to better enforce existing traffic law.

Such opposition seems inconsistent with the widespread acceptance of invasive scrutiny of our persons and luggage by manual and electronic means before boarding an aircraft. Throughout the flight, the aircraft's controls are automatically monitored, as are its altitude, speed, and direction, yet no one claims that this should not be done because it violates the crew's privacy. It cannot be too strongly stressed that the behavior of other road drivers poses a far greater risk to law-abiding citizens than any risks they face when flying. Drivers running red lights kill about 850 people annually in the US.[7] The people killed are not usually occupants in the vehicle running the red light, which is frontally impacted, but those in the vehicle legally entering the intersection, which receives a far more lethal side impact.

Closed circuit television monitoring in stores is widespread. The public does not object even though the risk it reduces is the loss of someone else's property. It seems the public is happy to be photographed rather than pay modestly higher prices to cover increased shoplifting costs. Although government does not do the recording, crime-scene pictures that incidentally include innocent shoppers may be provided to police.

Automatic monitoring of traffic requires that only law violations be photographed. Safeguards could be in place to insure that data for vehicles driving legally would not be retained. Indeed, there may be no need for any human to see the photograph of the violation other than the recipient of the ticket.

Opposition to automatic monitoring of drivers on grounds of privacy should be rejected on three counts. First, driving has never been interpreted as a private activity. Second, video surveillance is routinely accepted to reduce far less harmful behavior. Third, the enormous harm drivers impose on other road users overwhelms claims of privacy while driving.

Policy and automatic monitoring

The benefits of automatic monitoring can be available to the public only if the public welcomes such monitoring as an effective approach to a massive problem. This is unlikely to happen if there is even a suspicion that it is just another revenue-raising scheme. Automatic monitoring in the US and the UK is already generating vociferous hostility on such grounds. Traffic safety must be conceived as a major public health problem which government has an obligation to address. Public health problems are not sources of revenue, but one of the most legitimate justifications for government expenditure.

The present system, which punishes the typical citizen, is never going to attract the level of public support that is crucial to dramatically enhance safety. The aim must be that a typical citizen should never have to pay a traffic fine. Infrequent violations should not be punished. Nearly all drivers occasionally exceed speed limits by modest amounts, or enter intersections somewhat late. An isolated violation should generate a gentle letter explaining that the purpose of traffic law is to prevent harm, and explain that stricter compliance in the future will help achieve that goal. A reminder of how much harm occurs in traffic might be included. A second offense within a short time period should generate a stronger letter. Information technology makes it easy to provide the individual's entire violation history with each letter. Only offenses exceeding some specified rate of occurrence, or extent of violation, would result in escalating fines and other criminal sanctions.

Automatic enforcement associates the traffic law violation with the vehicle through the vehicle license plate. Law changes would be required to make the vehicle owner more responsible for its use. The ticket is sent to the registered owner of the vehicle. Cases when the owner was not driving would likely lead to safety-enhancing discussions between owner and driver. More serious driving offenses would focus directly on the driver, and be handled by the criminal justice system in ways similar to the present.

Automatic enforcement can essentially eliminate habitual speeding. If frequent speeding occurs, it would soon lead to involvement with the criminal justice system. Under conventional enforcement, those punished generally continue with relatively unchanged driving behavior. With automatic enforcement, unchanged behavior will be quickly detected. Continued violations will lead to license revocation, and with automatic detection, unlicensed drivers are far more likely to be detected if they drive. The most likely effect is that formerly speeding drivers will become legal, safer drivers, the real goal.

To date the world has no experience of cases in which speed limits are rarely exceeded. As experience with automatic speed detection is accumulated, I believe we could set higher speed limits on certain roads and still end up with far greater safety than provided by the present lower speed limits and the patterns of violations that accompany them. So a possible outcome of automatic detection might be law-abiding drivers traveling safely at higher speeds.

What should be done with fines

In order to make it abundantly clear that the purpose of traffic law is to reduce harm, the money paid in fines should be kept in a separate account. At some date, perhaps just before the end of the calendar year, the total should be divided equally among all license holders, and distributed in the form of a check. The amount would be modest, likely around ten dollars. It would come with a letter from, say, the Secretary of State, stressing that the entire amount paid in fines by drivers was being returned to drivers. The letter would express the hope that we would all work together to insure that next year the amount would be even smaller, and that ideally the amount should approach zero as we progressed towards the goal of no driver committing offenses that exceeded the threshold leading to a fine. The goal of traffic law is not to apprehend and punish violators, but to reduce harm by preventing violations.

Costs and benefits of the new approach

The major government cost of the new approach is the loss of revenue from fines. Added to this is the capital cost of the automatic monitoring system, maintaining it, software development, and mailing and administrative costs, etc.

However, major benefits will flow from achieving the goal of reducing crashes, which cost the US \$231 billion per year. Any measure that reduces this amount by even a small percentage will pay handsome dividends. I believe the reductions would be not small, but substantial.

Raising the probability that a traffic-law violation will be detected to near certainty will reduce traffic law violations to near zero. Based on the material in Chapter 13, removing law violations would reduce the total number of crashes by about 50%, severe injury crashes by much more, and fatal crashes by yet more. I suspect that the estimates are in fact low. When a crash occurs there is often no evidence beyond the testimony of the driver who crashed, so that many law violations prior to crashes are likely to go unrecorded. The issuance of a traditional traffic citation reduces a driver's risk of involvement in a fatal crash by 35% in the month following the citation.[8] One can but speculate what the effect of an automatic citation for every infraction might be.

Other changes

While the most specific reductions in crashes are achievable from automated law enforcement, other changes that impact social norms can make important contributions. Driving is one of the most responsible human activities. Compared to any other activity of a typical citizen, driving is vastly more likely to cause death. The steps towards acquiring a full license should become important rites of passage to full citizenship and adulthood. Mass media glorification of the use of vehicles in ways that threaten life should generate the level of public outrage that has culminated in other self imposed and externally imposed restraints. The US Federal Communication Commission imposes large fines on radio and television stations for broadcasting material it considers indecent. Lives would be saved by similar policies prohibiting the positive portrayal of driving likely to kill. Such prohibitions should be applied also to vehicle advertising portraying irresponsible driving.

Suggestions of restraints on program content or advertising are often opposed as violations of First Amendment rights guaranteeing freedom of speech. As in the case of the privacy arguments against automatic enforcement, such claims ignore the innumerable voluntary and statutory restraints currently in place on what is broadcast in such areas as decency and cigarette advertising. As there are already constraints in place in response to many pressures, it is worth considering having some to prevent people from being killed in traffic.

There is unquestionably tension between human pleasures and safety. Fast driving, smoking, consuming large quantities of alcohol and other intoxicants, and eating cholesterol-rich high calorific food are activities enjoyed by many. However, they are pleasures that come with a cost. People have been intentionally forgoing many of them to reduce the risk of unwelcome consequences. One of the largest improvements in public health is due to reductions in smoking. It did not occur because smokers found smoking unpleasant. The hope is that parallel reductions in harm from traffic can arise because people forgo the pleasures of illegal fast driving.   As with smoking, people who do not themselves desist can be constrained from harming others by laws prohibiting their behavior in public.

A pedestrian-crash default

A default regarding responsibility when a vehicle strikes a pedestrian could generate reductions in harm well beyond the reductions in pedestrian casualties. There is already a well-established default for another crash type, the rear impact, for which the following driver is presumed to be legally *at fault*.   There are compelling reasons why this should be so.   Drivers should feel free to slow down or brake in response to traffic situations in front of them without having an additional burden of worrying about the vehicle following theirs.   The obligation of the following driver is clear.   Essentially regardless of what the lead vehicle does, a following driver is not entitled to crash into its rear.

I believe establishing a default responsibility in pedestrian crashes could provide important safety benefits, although the basis for assigning the responsibility is quite different from the rear-end crash case.   Currently if a pedestrian steps or runs off the sidewalk into the path of a vehicle whose driver is driving within the speed limit and exercising typical care, the pedestrian will be judged to be at fault, and the driver will be judged to be not at fault.   This reflects the fact that pedestrians are required to obey the law and exercise good judgment, and not step in front of vehicles.   The pedestrian and driver are presumed to have comparable responsibility to obey the law, and if one does and the other does not, then the law-breaker is judged to be at fault and the law-obeyer to be not at fault.

This symmetric arrangement does not encompass a crucial asymmetry.   The driver is in control of a massive vehicle traveling at high speed that can cause great harm to pedestrians while providing enormous protection to the driver.   On the other hand, pedestrians have no such protection.   This huge asymmetry in risk should be balanced by a corresponding asymmetry in legal responsibility.   It should be specified that drivers must not crash into pedestrians, whatever the pedestrians do, just as they are not allowed to crash into vehicles they are following.   The explanation that it was not the driver's fault but the fault of the five-year-old child, the elderly pedestrian, or the blind pedestrian, would become vastly less acceptable than it is today.

In proposing that the driver be presumed to be at fault, I am not suggesting that drivers currently are casual about hitting law-breaking pedestrians. Currently drivers normally exercise increased care when pedestrians are near. The goal is to further increase this care and sensitivity.   The law is a potent educator.   Formally defining pedestrian safety to be the overriding responsibility of the driver has the potential to generate greater driving care, and driver responsibility in general.

Summary and conclusions

A breakthrough in road traffic safety can be achieved by adopting the same two central principles that led to such outstanding safety in commercial air travel. First, the primary goal must be to prevent crashes, not to make it safer to crash. Second, drivers must follow rules based on inputs from many professional disciplines, rather than relying mainly on what they have learned from their personal experience.

Over 29,000 Americans, including 1,769 children under 14, were killed in 2002 in crashes involving actions of drivers other than the person killed. The risks families face from the actions of other drivers tower over any of the other risks that concern them. If this were better publicized, the public would be more inclined to support effective measures to reduce traffic crashes.

The key to reducing crashes is obeying traffic law. Two deficiencies of traditional traffic-law enforcement have crippled its effectiveness. First, it is seen as capricious and unfair, fining many average citizens for minor offenses while other drivers committing egregious offenses go undetected. Second, fines are seen as revenue-raising schemes rather than good-faith efforts to enhance public safety. For traffic safety policy to be successful it must have only one goal – protecting the public. The public must recognize and support this goal.

New automatic detection technology, if introduced as a component of changed safety policy, can dramatically reduce harm in traffic. The new technologies include photo radar and red-light cameras, which provide objective evidence, including photographs, of vehicles violating speed limits or running red lights. The registered owners of vehicles photographed violating traffic law receive automatically generated traffic tickets in the mail.

I believe that the public would welcome the widespread use of such technology to effectively enforce traffic law if it were the centerpiece of new policy containing all of the following four components:

1. Traffic law would have only one purpose – to prevent crashes and the injuries and deaths they produce. This must be the policy, and the public must
   know and accept that this is the policy.

2. Automatically-detected minor violations would receive no punishments for
   first, or infrequent, offenses. More frequent, and more severe, violations
   would be subject to escalating fines, and increasing criminal sanctions.

3. All traffic fines would be kept in a separate account, and distributed equally
   to all license holders as an annual bonus. This would come with an upbeat
   letter, expressing the hope that the small bonus would be even smaller next
   year as we all worked together to reduce the number of drivers exceeding
   the fine threshold to near zero.

4. Law changes would make the registered owner of the vehicle responsible
   for responding to traffic tickets.

These proposals would cut traffic harm in half. They would involve public expenditure, mainly through loss of revenue from fines, and the purchase and operation of technical equipment. Given that traffic crashes cost the US $231 billion per year, public expenditures that reduce crashes pay handsome dividends. While the cost of automatically detecting violations is minuscule compared with manual detection by police officers, the goal is not to increase the number of traffic tickets issued, but to dramatically reduce the number. It is probability of detection, not severity of punishment, that affects behavior. As automatic detection can make the probability of detection approach certainty, the number of violations can approach zero. The goal of traffic law is not to apprehend and punish violators, but to reduce harm by preventing violations.

Unlike airport security, which the public already accepts, the proposals above would save tens of thousands of US lives annually and not inconvenience, delay, embarrass, or disadvantage any law-abiding citizen.

References for Chapter 16

1   US Department of Transportation, Bureau of Statistics. Table 2-1. Transportation fatalities by mode.
http://www.bts.gov/publications/national_transportation_statistics/2003/html/table_02_01.html

2   US Department of Transportation, Bureau of Statistics. Table 1-34. U.S. passenger-miles.
http://www.bts.gov/publications/national_transportation_statistics/2003/html/table_01_34.html

3   Richter ED, Ben-David G, Ortiz R, Cortes J. A traffic monitoring and driver behavior modification system. USAID CDR Project C8-043; 1995.
http://www.ukspeedtraps.co.uk/speed01.htm

4   Elvik R, Mysen AB, Vaa T. Trafikksikkerhetshåndbok (Traffic Safety Handbook). Oslo, Norway: Institute of Transport Economics; 1997.

5   Chen G, Meckle W, Wilson J. Speed and safety effect of photo radar enforcement on a highway corridor in British Columbia. Accid Anal Prev. 2002; 34: 129-138.

6   Insurance Institute for Highway Safety. Officials nationwide give a green light to automated traffic enforcement. Status Report. Volume 35 (3); 11 March 2000.
http://www.highwaysafety.org/srpdfs/sr3503.pdf

7   Retting RA, Ferguson SA, Hakkert AS. Effects of red light cameras on violations and crashes: A review of the international literature. Traf Inj Prev. 2003; 4: 17-23.

8   Redelmeier DA, Tibshirani RJ, Evans L. Traffic-law enforcement and risk of death from motor-vehicle crashes: Case-crossover study. The Lancet. 2003; 36: 2177-2182.

Index

About the author

Leonard Evans, an internationally renowned expert on traffic safety, is president of *Science Serving Society*, Bloomfield Hills, Michigan. This is an organization he formed to continue research and other professional activities after completing a 33-year research career with General Motors Corporation in June 2000. Dr. Evans has a bachelors degree in physics from the Queen's University of Belfast, Northern Ireland, and a doctorate in physics from Oxford University, England. While most of his more than 150 publications document traffic safety research, he has also covered such diverse subjects as physics, mathematics, traffic engineering, transportation energy, human factors, and trauma analysis (complete list of publications at **http://www.ScienceServingSociety.com**). His research has appeared in 41 different technical journals. Since its publication in 1991, his widely acclaimed and much cited book *Traffic Safety And The Driver* has had a major influence on the study of traffic safety.

Dr. Evans' contributions to traffic safety have received many recognitions, including major awards from the *National Highway Traffic Safety Administration*, the *International Association for Accident and Traffic Medicine*, the *Association for the Advancement of Automotive Medicine*, the *Human Factors and Ergonomics Society*, and *General Motors*. He has been president of the *International Traffic Medicine Association* and the *Association for the Advancement of Automotive Medicine*, as well as a *Sigma Xi Distinguished Lecturer*. He is a fellow of the *Human Factors and Ergonomics Society*, a fellow of the *Society of Automotive Engineers*, a fellow of the *Association for the Advancement of Automotive Medicine*, and a member of the *National Academy of Engineering*.